ART

A History of Painting · Sculpture · Architecture

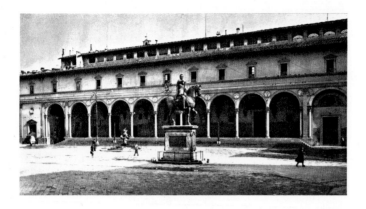

FREDERICK HARTT

Paul Goodloe McIntire Professor of the History of Art · University of Virginia

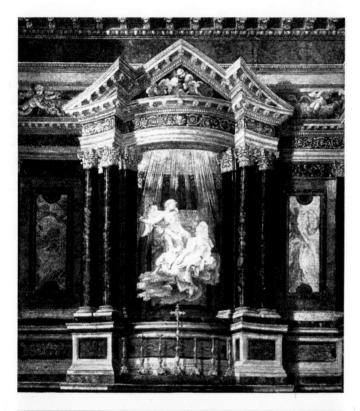

A History of

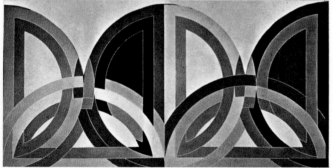

Volume II

ART

Painting · Sculpture · Architecture

RENAISSANCE · BAROQUE · MODERN WORLD

Prentice-Hall, Inc., Englewood Cliffs, N. J. and

Harry N. Abrams, Inc., New York

John P. O'Neill. *Editor*

Library of Congress Cataloging in Publication Data

Hartt, Frederick.
   Art: a history of painting, sculpture, and architecture

   Includes bibliographies and indexes.
   CONTENTS: v. 1. Prehistory, the ancient world, the Middle Ages. v. 2. The
Renaissance, the Baroque, the modern world.
   1. Art—History. I. Title.
N5300.H283 1976b   709   75-37738
ISBN 0-13-046961-0 (v. 2)

Library of Congress Catalogue Card Number: 75-37738
Published in 1976 by Harry N. Abrams, Incorporated, New York.

TO

MEYER SCHAPIRO

Scholar, teacher, counselor, friend

Contents

PART SIX

The Modern World

PAGE 299

PROLOGUE

Gothic Sculpture and Painting in Italy

During the late thirteenth and the fourteenth centuries, while the great period of building and decorating the Gothic cathedrals was coming to its close in Northern Europe, a new style of painting and sculpture arose in Italy, based on a revolutionary understanding of human values. Sometimes this style is referred to as Proto-

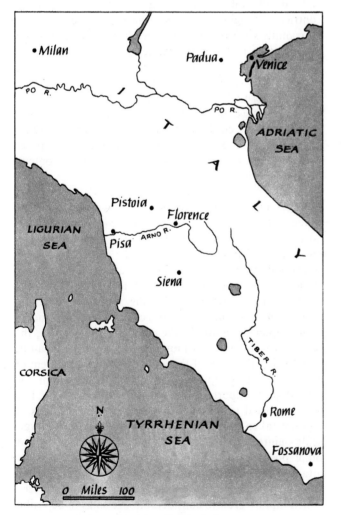

MAP 1. *Gothic Italy*

Renaissance, which is correct in the sense that the true Renaissance of the fifteenth century could not have taken place had it not been for the exploratory work of the great masters of the fourteenth. The society for which these Italian artists worked was strikingly different from any other in Europe and offered certain parallels to the city-states of ancient Greece. Remarkably few new artistic developments occurred in southern Italy, which, during this period, was under foreign sway. The shifting and sometimes divided region known as the Kingdom of Naples or the Kingdom of the Two Sicilies was governed at first by German, then by French, and finally by Spanish rulers. Much of Central Italy around Rome, including other important cities, was ruled by the popes as temporal monarchs.

But in the rest of Central Italy, particularly the region known as Tuscany (because in pre-Roman times it had been inhabited and ruled by the Etruscans), and in Northern Italy from the Apennines to the Alps and from the French border to the Adriatic, there was no central political power. Scores of republics, large and small, consisting of flourishing commercial cities and the surrounding towns, villages, and countrysides, were the scene for the new art. In Tuscany Florence was the most creative center, but lively artistic movements also took place in the rival Tuscan republics, especially Pisa and Siena. In all these Tuscan centers the demands of the dominant merchant and banking classes tended to produce an art based on calculated and rational proportion, a new interest in the human body set in real space, and a dramatic confrontation of human wills and emotions as manifested daily in the Tuscan marketplace, the center of political and economic life. Such humanistic values rendered the artists especially sensitive to suggestions from the surviving or newly unearthed fragments of the art of the ancient world.

NICOLA AND GIOVANNI PISANO. Two extremely original sculptors, Nicola Pisano (active 1258–78) and his son Giovanni (c. 1250–c. 1314), embody sharply

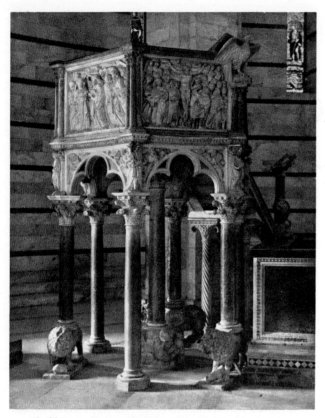

1. NICOLA PISANO. Pulpit. 1259–60. Marble, height
c. 15′. Baptistery, Pisa

different phases of the rather tardy change from Romanesque to Gothic style in Italian sculpture. Although Nicola's name indicates his Pisan citizenship, he came to Tuscany from southern Italy, where since the days of Frederick II (reigned 1215–50), more Italian king than German emperor, there had flourished a strong current of interest in ancient art. Nicola's first great work was the hexagonal marble pulpit in the Baptistery at Pisa (fig. 1), signed with a long, self-laudatory inscription in 1260. Sculptured pulpits were traditional in Italy; that one could be needed in a baptistery may indicate the special importance of the sacrament of Baptism in the Italian republics as the moment in which a child took his place in the Christian community. Nicola's handsome creation combines elements already familiar from central Italian medieval art, such as columns of red porphyry, red and gray granite, and richly veined brown marble with Gothic trefoil arches. The capitals, partly Corinthian, partly Gothic, seem to partake of both styles. Like his earlier namesake Nicholas of Verdun and like the Visitation Master at Reims, Nicola had a strong interest in ancient art. Luckily, he had no dearth of models in Pisa. The close packing of forms filling the entire frame of the *Adoration of the Magi* (fig. 2) recalls the density of Roman sarcophagus relief, and in fact Nicola repeated almost exactly the pose of a seated figure in a sarcophagus still in the Campo Santo in Pisa for his

Virgin, who has become a Roman Juno, impassive and grand. The carving of the beards of the Magi and the parallel drapery folds of all the figures also recall Roman examples, but the angular breaking of the folds betrays Nicola's familiarity with Byzantine mosaic art.

Giovanni, who claims in inscriptions to have outdone his father, was responsible for a sharply different octagonal pulpit at Pistoia (fig. 3), dated 1298–1301, distinguished by its greater Gothicism in the sharp pointing of the arches as well as in the freer shapes of the foliate capitals, which only here and there disclose Classical derivations. As we would expect from his unconventional shapes and animated statuary for the Siena façade, Giovanni's sculptural style is far more dramatic than his father's serene manner, and shows almost no interest in Classical art. Instead, the relaxed poses and free, full drapery folds of the corner statues suggest a familiarity with the portal sculptures of Amiens and Reims; Giovanni's inscriptions proclaim him as a traveler, and in all probability he visited the great French cathedrals. In the *Slaughter of the Innocents* (fig. 4), a panel of the Pistoia pulpit, he shows himself the master of a free narrative style, depending for its effect on rapid, even violent movement of ferocious soldiers and screaming mothers, and considerable undercutting, which produces sharp contrasts of light and dark. The expressive power of Giovanni's style is brought under firm control, possibly in emulation of the great painter Giotto, in the marble statue of the *Virgin and Child* (fig. 5), which Giovanni carved about 1305 for the altar of the Arena Chapel in Padua, whose walls and ceiling were being frescoed by Giotto (see figs. 8, 9, and colorplate 2). The boldness of the masses, the clarity of the contours, and the firmness of the pose of Giovanni's *Madonna* should be compared with the elegance and lassitude of the almost contemporary *Virgin of Paris*.

Changes in thirteenth-century religious ritual gave rise to the demand for a new kind of image—of immense importance for the development of art, especially painting—the altarpiece. Until now the Mass had been celebrated, as again in the Roman Catholic Church since Vatican II, behind the altar, with the priest facing the congregation, which precluded the placing of anything more than the required crucifix, candlesticks, and sacred vessels upon the altar. In the course of the century, the celebrant's position was moved to the front of the altar, thus freeing the back of the altar for the development of imagery, both sculptural and pictorial. Although the icon, that all-important focus of Byzantine devotion, had been imported to the West in the early Middle Ages, it had not taken root. But in the thirteenth century, large-scale painted crucifixes, which had already been used in other positions in Italian churches, began to appear on altars. Soon the Madonna and Child competed for this prominent place, and eventually won. The altarpieces, which rapidly grew to considerable size so as to be visible to the congregation, were painted in a technique known

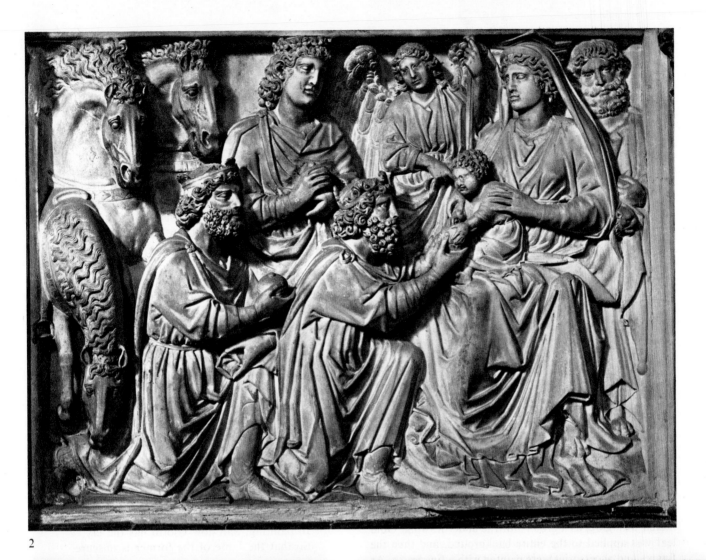

2

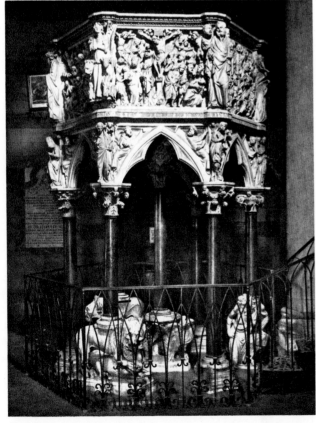

3

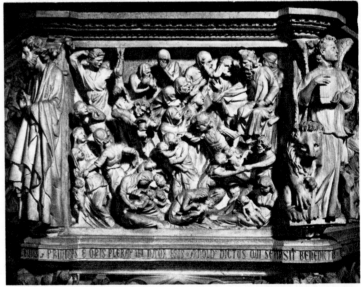

4

2. NICOLA PISANO. *Adoration of the Magi* (detail of
the pulpit at Pisa). Marble relief

3. GIOVANNI PISANO. Pulpit. 1298–1301. Marble.
Sant'Andrea, Pistoia, Italy

4. GIOVANNI PISANO. *Slaughter of the Innocents*
(detail of the pulpit at Pistoia). Marble relief,
33 x 40″

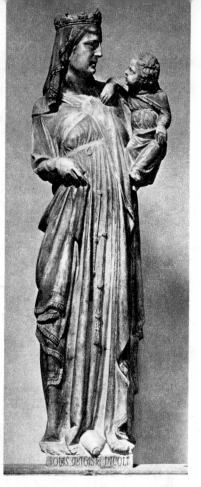

5. GIOVANNI PISANO.
Virgin and Child.
c. 1305. Marble.
Altar, Arena
Chapel, Padua

as tempera, with egg yolk used as the vehicle. The procedure was slow and exacting. A wooden panel had to be carefully prepared and coated with gesso (fine plaster mixed with glue) as a ground for the underdrawing. Gold leaf was applied to the entire background, and then the figures and accessories were painted with a fine brush. As egg dries fast and does not permit corrections, the painter's craft called for accurate and final decisions at every stage. Under the impulse of this new demand, and spurred by the intense political and economic life of the Tuscan republics, painting rapidly developed in a direction that had no Northern counterparts until the *Wilton Diptych.*

CIMABUE. Although at least two generations of Tuscan painters had preceded him in the thirteenth century, the first Italian painter known to Vasari was the Florentine Cenni di Pepi, called Cimabue (active c. 1272–1302). About 1280 Cimabue painted the *Madonna Enthroned* (fig. 6), an altarpiece more than eleven feet high, which in Vasari's day stood on the altar of Santa Trinità in Florence. The derivation of Cimabue's style from that of the Greek painters with whom Vasari said he worked is clear enough in the poses of the Virgin and the Child and also in the gold-striated patterns of their drapery folds, which resemble those of the *Pantocrator* at Cefalù. But in the delicate modeling of the faces and drapery of the angels, Cimabue also shows his familiarity with the refined Constantinopolitan style of his own time. Clearly, Cimabue was trying to rival in paint the monumental

effects of Byzantine mosaics, but the gabled shape of his huge altarpiece is unknown in the East, as is the complex construction of the carved and inlaid throne; the effect is that of strong verticality, increased by the constant flicker of color in the angels' rainbow wings.

CAVALLINI. A Roman contemporary of Cimabue, Pietro Cavallini (active 1273–after 1308), was certainly familiar with such advanced Byzantine works as the frescoes at Sopoćani, which show an extraordinary advance in the interrelationship of light and form. Cavallini's fragmentary fresco of the *Last Judgment* of about 1290 in Santa Cecilia in Trastevere in Rome (colorplate 1), impossible to photograph as a whole because of a gallery later built in front of it, carries the knowledge of the effects of light to a point inaccessible to Cimabue. Light and light alone brings out the fullness and sweep of the mantles that envelop these majestic figures. Their heads, however, especially those of the beardless Apostle in the center and the bearded James (?) on the right, show a familiarity with French Gothic sculpture, such as the *Saint Theodore* at Chartres and the *Beau Dieu* at Amiens.

GIOTTO. The final break with Byzantine tradition was accomplished by Giotto di Bondone (c. 1267–1337), the first giant in the long history of Italian painting. Even in his own day Giotto's greatness was recognized by his contemporaries. Dante puts in the mouth of a painter in *Purgatory* (XI, 94–96) his famous remark:

> Cimabue believed that he held the field
> In painting, and now Giotto has the cry,
> So that the fame of the former is obscure.

The *Chronicles* of the historian Giovanni Villani (d. 1348) list Giotto as one of the great men of the Florentine Republic, a position such as had been accorded to no other artist since the days of ancient Greece. The sources also indicate wherein Giotto's greatness was thought to lie. Vasari summed up Italian estimates when he said that Giotto revived the art of painting, which had declined in Italy because of many invasions, and that since Giotto continued to "derive from Nature, he deserves to be called the pupil of Nature and no other." Cennino Cennini, a third-generation follower of Giotto, wrote in his *Book on Art*, a manual on technical methods, that Giotto had translated painting from Greek into Latin.

A comparison of Giotto's *Madonna and Child Enthroned* (fig. 7) of about 1310 with its counterpart by Cimabue will test these traditional observations. Nature, in the modern sense of the word, would hardly enter our minds in connection with Giotto's picture any more than with Cimabue's. Both are ceremonial representations of the Virgin as Queen of Heaven, remote from ordinary experience, and both rule out distant space by the use of a traditional gold background. But in contemporary Italian eyes the step from Cimabue to Giotto was im-

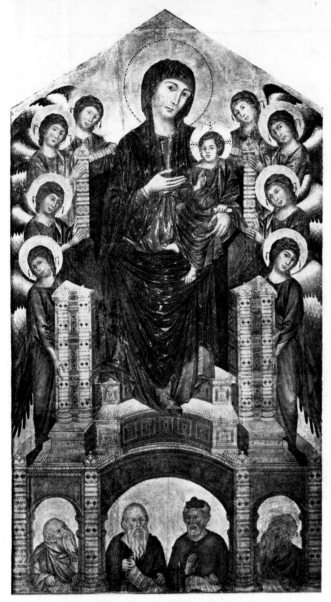

6. CIMABUE. *Madonna Enthroned*, from Sta. Trinita, Florence. c. 1280. Tempera on panel, 12'7½" x 7'4". Galleria degli Uffizi, Florence

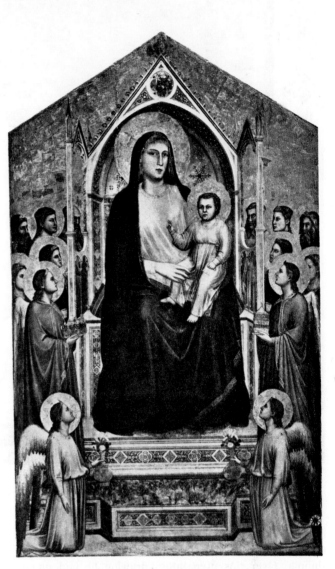

7. GIOTTO. *Madonna and Child Enthroned*, from the Church of the Ognissanti, Florence. c. 1310. Tempera on panel, 10'8" x 6'8¼". Galleria degli Uffizi, Florence

mense in that weight and mass, light and inward extension were suddenly introduced in a direct and convincing manner. In contrast to Cimabue's fantastic throne, which needs a steadying hand from the attendant angels, Giotto's structure is firmly placed above a marble step, which can be climbed, and the Virgin sits firmly within it. The poses of the angels kneeling in the foreground are so solid, in comparison to the uncertain placing of Cimabue's angels, that we are willing to believe that the angels and saints behind them, on either side of the throne, stand just as securely. Light, still diffused and without indication of source, models the forms so strongly that they resemble sculptural masses. By translating painting from Greek into Latin, Cennini meant that Giotto had abandoned Byzantine models in favor of Western ones, and in the early fourteenth century those could only have been French cathedral statues. Not only do Giotto's facial types and drapery motives recall the sculptures at Chartres, Reims, and Amiens, but also the

Virgin's throne is set in an aedicula whose pointed central arch, trefoil side arches, and culminating pinnacles are taken directly from the French architectural repertory. Giotto's miracle lay in being able to produce for the first time on a flat surface three-dimensional forms, which the French could achieve only in sculpture. Effects of shoulders and knees showing through drapery masses, of the Child's body and legs, and of the Virgin's hand holding his thigh are at every point convincing. For the first time since antiquity a painter has truly conquered solid form. Giotto did not, however, adopt as yet a naturalistic scale. The Virgin and Child are represented as almost twice the size of the attendant figures.

Cennini tells us that the painting of frescoes was the most agreeable of all pictorial activities. The technique he describes was probably based on that of Roman painting as handed down through the ages. The painter first prepared the wall with a layer of rough plaster, on which he proceeded to draw with the brush (probably on the

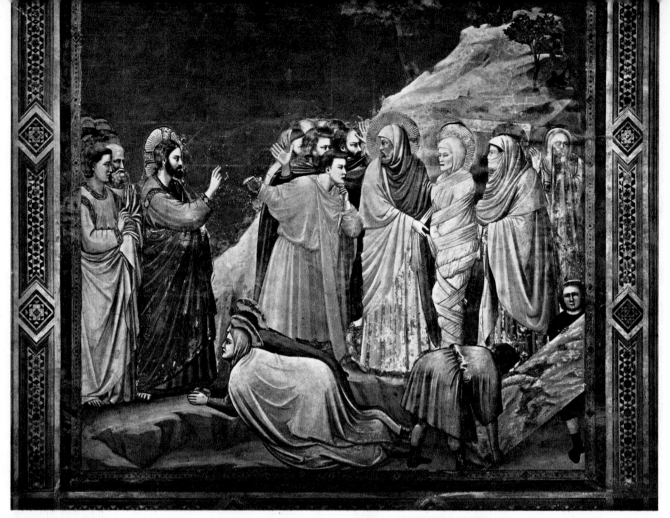

8. Giotto. *Raising of Lazarus.* Fresco. 1305–6. Arena Chapel, Padua

basis of preliminary sketches) the figures and background in a mixture of red earth and water known as sinopia. Over this preparatory drawing he laid on as much smooth plaster as he could paint in a day, and painted it while wet so that the color in its water vehicle would amalgamate with the plaster. The following day he added another section, covering up the sinopia as he went. This procedure meant that the fresco was literally built section by section, and acquired a solidity of composition and surface handling that would preclude such spontaneous painting techniques as those of Castelseprio or Nerezi or even the broad, fluid manner of the Kariye Djami.

Giotto's masterpiece is the cycle of frescoes illustrating the life of the Virgin and the life of Christ, dating from 1305–6, which lines the entire interior of the Arena Chapel in Padua in Northern Italy, not far from Venice. Here he shows the full range of his naturalism in a new kind of pictorial drama for which nothing we have seen in the history of art could prepare us. In one of the early scenes, Joachim, father of the Virgin, takes refuge with shepherds in the wilderness after his expulsion from the Temple because of his childlessness (colorplate 2). Humiliated, his head bowed, he stands before two shepherds, one of whom scans his companion's face to

see whether they dare receive the outcast. The subtlety of the psychological interplay is enriched by Giotto's delicate observation of the sheep crowding out of the sheepfold and of the dog, symbol of fidelity in the Middle Ages as today, who leaps in joyful greeting.

As in the *Madonna,* Giotto recognizes one scale for the figures, another for the surroundings, including the animals and the sheepfold. Cennini recounts that to paint a mountainous landscape one need only bring a rock into the studio, and that a branch could do duty for a tree. The results of this principle show that Giotto, for all his ability to project three-dimensional form, is far from accepting the notion of visual unity. His landscape, however, has an expressive purpose; the rock behind Joachim bends along with his head, and the jagged edges toward the center underscore the division between him and the shepherds. The cubic rocks form a definite stage in space, limited by the blue background, which, like that at the Kariye Djami, does not represent the sky—there are no clouds—but is an ideal, heavenly color continuing behind all the scenes and covering the barrel vault above. In order to emphasize the three-dimensionality of the columnar figure of Joachim, Giotto has designed his halo foreshortened in perspective.

In the *Raising of Lazarus* (fig. 8) the composition

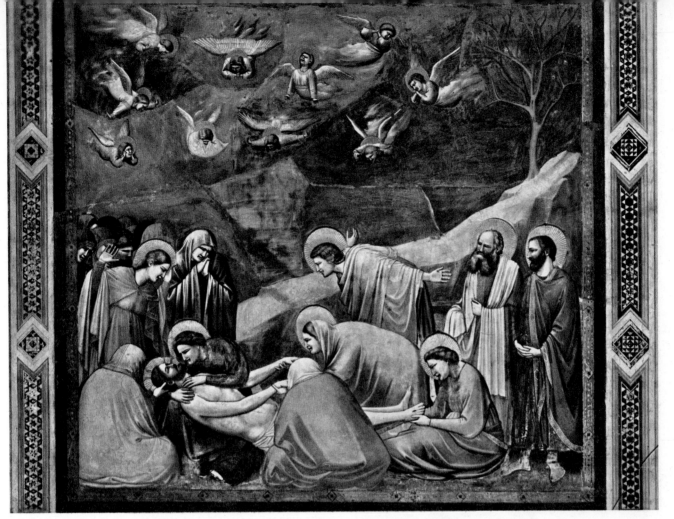

9. GIOTTO. *Lamentation*. Fresco. 1305–6. Arena Chapel, Padua

divides into two groups: one centered around Lazarus, who has just risen from the tomb, still wrapped in graveclothes, is read together with the rock; the other, beginning with the prostrate Mary and Martha, culminates in Christ, who calls the dead man forth by a single gesture of his right hand against the blue. Giotto's Christ strongly resembles the *Beau Dieu* of Amiens even to the pose and the gesture. His calm authority is contrasted with the astonishment of the surrounding figures. But the Byzantine tradition is by no means forgotten; the arrangement of figures in the *Lamentation* (fig. 9) owes a debt to the tradition exemplified at Nerezi. But Giotto has enriched the dialogue between life and death with all the subtlety of his psychological observation. Instead of an explosion of grief, he has staged a flawlessly organized tragedy, the equal of Sophocles or Shakespeare in its many-faceted analysis of a human situation. Each figure grieves in the manner possible to his individual personality—John, the beloved disciple, most deeply of all. Giotto has added to the scene anonymous mourners who turn their eloquent backs to us; one upholds Christ's head, the other his right hand. Instead of pressing her face impulsively to that of her son as at Nerezi, Mary, with one arm around Christ's shoulder, searches his countenance, conscious of the widening gulf of death.

Only the angels are released to cry in pure grief, each half-hidden in the clouds—the only ones that appear in the Chapel—to show that they are supernatural.

Giotto's brushwork remains as calm in this scene as in any other. He achieved his effect not only by the grouping of the figures but also by the inexorable diagonal line of the rocks, descending toward the faces of Mary and Christ, its course weighted by the downward tug of the drapery folds. At the upper right, as if to typify the desolation of the scene, a leafless tree stands against the blue. Giotto surely expected his audience to remember that, according to medieval legend, the Tree of Knowledge was withered after the sin of Adam and Eve and made fruitful again after the sacrifice of Christ, and that Christ himself was believed to have alluded to this doctrine on his way to Calvary: "For if they do these things in a green tree, what shall be done in the dry?" (Luke 23:31).

GADDI. Giotto indeed had the cry; within a decade after his great works made their appearance, the style of Cimabue had been relegated to country churches, and Giotto, his many pupils, and still more numerous followers dominated the Florentine scene. One of the closest of his pupils, Taddeo Gaddi (active c. 1330–

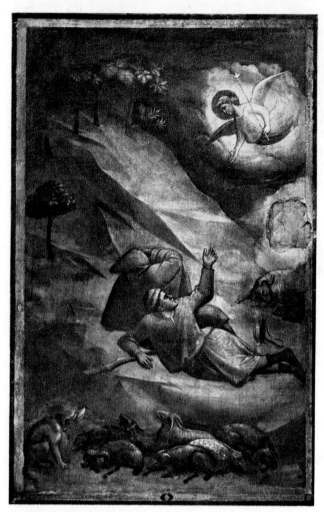

10. TADDEO GADDI. *Annunciation to the Shepherds.*
Fresco. c. 1332–38. Baroncelli Chapel, Sta.
Croce, Florence

upon the shepherds who have fallen to the ground in amazement and lights the whole dark landscape with its radiance. We are here experiencing the reversal of the process by which, at the beginning of the Middle Ages, the illusionistic art of the Helleno-Roman tradition was transformed into the otherworldly art of Byzantium. Techniques derived from naturalistic painting were used at Sinai to represent supernatural light. Now, at the end of the Middle Ages, that same spiritual light is used to aid the artist in the rediscovery of material reality.

DUCCIO. In Siena the Byzantine tradition continued into the fourteenth century and was refined to the ultimate in the work of Duccio di Buoninsegna (active 1278–1318). His great altarpiece, the *Maestà* (*Madonna in Majesty*), more than thirteen feet in length, was started in 1308 for the high altar of the Cathedral of Siena. It was considered such a triumph for the artist and such an important contribution to the welfare of the Sienese Republic (whose patron saint was the Virgin) that on its completion in 1311 it was carried at the head of a procession of dignitaries and townspeople from Duccio's studio to the Cathedral, to the ringing of church bells and the sound of trumpets. The high altar was freestanding, so that the back of the altarpiece and even its pinnacles were covered with a cycle of scenes from the life of Christ even more complete than that Giotto had just painted for the Arena Chapel. In the sixteenth century the altarpiece was taken down and partially dismembered; panels are scattered throughout the world, but most remain in Siena. The central panel shows the Virgin as Queen of Heaven (fig. 11), adored by her court of kneeling and standing saints and angels and half-length prophets in the arches above—a sort of cathedral façade in paint. And though the pose of the Virgin and Child shows that Duccio is still working in the Byzantine tradition, nonetheless, he has learned from the works of Giovanni Pisano new and Gothic ways to handle flowing masses of drapery and dense crowds of figures. While the oval shapes of the faces are Byzantine, their small almond eyes bear no relation to the lustrous orbs of the saints in most Byzantine mosaics, frescoes, and icons.

Although Duccio accepted neither Giotto's cubic rocks nor his columnar figures, and although he could not achieve Giotto's subtlety of psychological observation, he was an artist of great individuality, especially in the handling of landscape elements, as can be seen in the *Temptation of Christ* (fig. 12), once a part of the *Maestà.* The kingdoms of the world, shown to Christ by Satan, were depicted by Duccio, a good republican Sienese, as seven little city-states crowded into a panel not quite eighteen inches square. Obviously, they derive from the late Roman and Early Christian tradition of little nugget-cities, but each one is different, with its own houses, public buildings, city gates, and towers, all modeled in a consistent light. If we are willing to accept the medieval convention of the double scale for figures and setting, we must admit that within it Duccio was very successful in

c. 1366), although he could never approach the heights of Giotto's achievements, continued some aspects of his style, especially in the representation of light, perhaps under the master's personal direction, in his frescoes in the Baroncelli Chapel of Santa Croce in Florence, probably dating from 1332–38. In the fourteenth century natural light was always diffused and generalized, without indication of a specific source. But Taddeo has shown the traditional scene of the *Annunciation to the Shepherds* (fig. 10) as a revelation of light, which in a long Christian tradition symbolizes the second person of the Trinity. After all, every Catholic knew the sublime words of John 1: 4–5:

> In him was life; and the life was the light
> of men.
> And the light shineth in darkness; and the
> darkness comprehended it not.

As a devoted Giotto follower, Taddeo never represents natural light, but he presents the announcing angel in the midst of a wonderful display of light, which descends

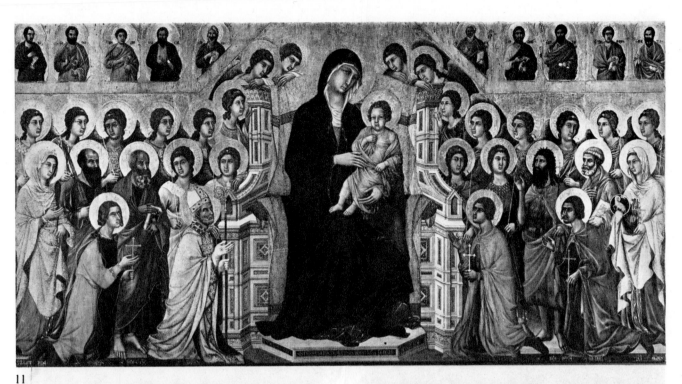

11

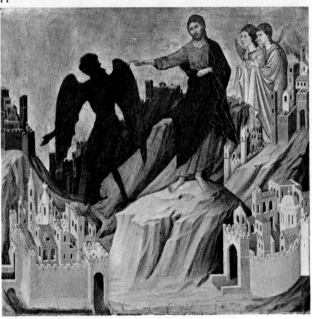

12

11. DUCCIO. *Virgin as Queen of Heaven,* center
panel of the *Maestà* altarpiece, from the
Cathedral of Siena. 1308–11. Panel painting,
7 x 13′. Museo dell'Opera del Duomo, Siena

12. DUCCIO. *Temptation of Christ* (detail of the
back predella of the *Maestà* altarpiece), from
the Cathedral of Siena. 1308–11. Panel painting,
17 x 18⅛″. ©The Frick Collection, New York

13. DUCCIO. *Entry into Jerusalem* (detail of the
back predella of the *Maestà* altarpiece), from
the Cathedral of Siena. 1308–11. Panel
painting, 40 x 21″. Museo dell'Opera del
Duomo, Siena

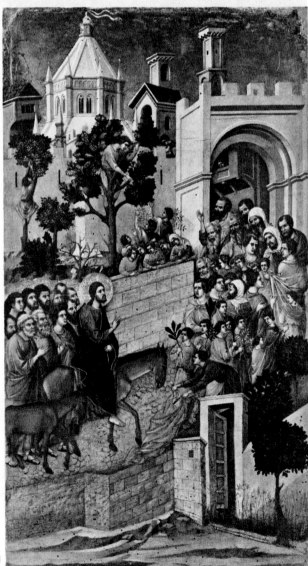

13

indicating the scope and sweep of landscape, which soon became Siena's great contribution to the history of art.

In one of the larger panels of the *Maestà*, Duccio set the stage, as it were, for the *Entry into Jerusalem* (fig. 13) in the suburban orchards outside the walls of Siena. We look over trees, garden walls, and a gate in the foreground to the road moving uphill, more garden walls on the other side, the city gates, and houses fronting a street. The towering octagonal building is the Temple, combining travelers' tales of the Dome of the Rock, built on the site of the Temple, with the familiar outlines of the Baptistery of Florence. This setting, of unexampled spatial complexity, Duccio filled with more than fifty people, all sharply individualized (within the range of Byzantine-Sienese facial types), from the solemn Christ mounted on an ass to the excited populace and children

climbing trees, including some inhabitants looking out of windows and over the city wall.

SIMONE MARTINI. Duccio's pupil, Simone Martini (active 1315–44), while fully abreast of all his master could achieve in the realm of landscape and urban settings, finally broke with the Byzantine tradition in favor of the more fashionable courtly French Gothic style of the early fourteenth century. He worked for the French king Robert of Anjou at Naples and brought back to Siena the latest French imports. Even more than the *Maestà* of Duccio, Simone's *Annunciation* (fig. 14) is a condensed cathedral façade, Gothic this time, with all the richness of Flamboyant double curvature, which had not as yet made its appearance in the architecture of Giovanni Pisano. The angel Gabriel is dressed magnificently in

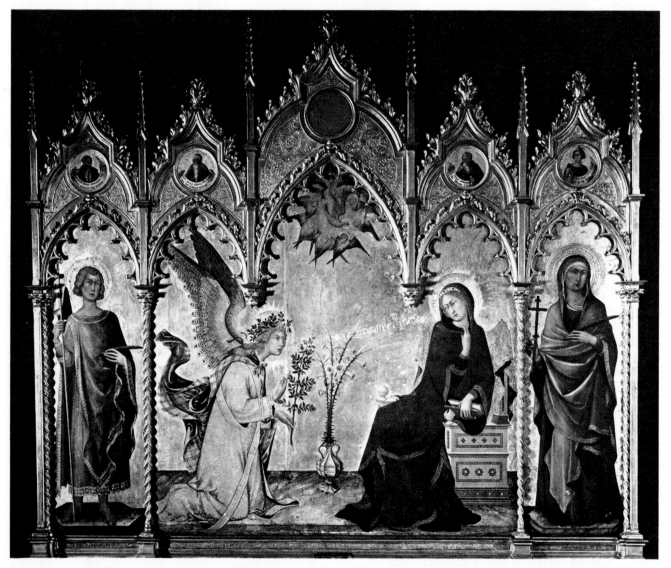

14. SIMONE MARTINI. *Annunciation.* 1333. Panel painting, 10′ x 8′9″. Galleria degli Uffizi, Florence

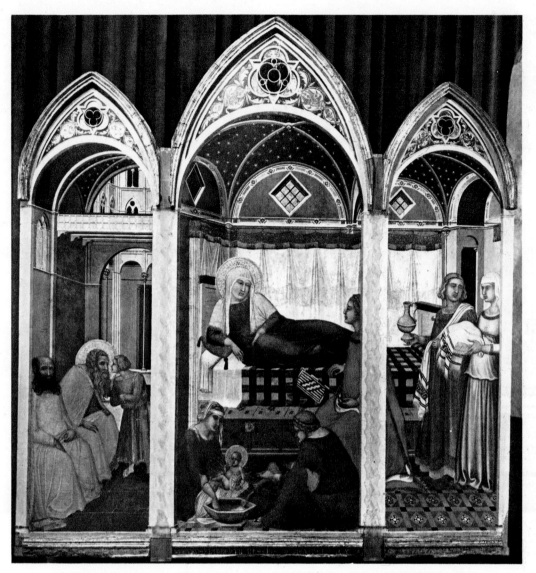

15. PIETRO LORENZETTI. *Birth of the Virgin*. 1342. Panel painting, 73½ x 72½". Museo dell'Opera del Duomo, Siena

white and gold brocade with a floating, plaid-lined mantle, and the Virgin's blue mantle is edged with a deep gold border. The swirling drapery rhythms recall the curvilinear exaggerations of the *Virgin of Paris* rather than the controlled shapes of cathedral statues. The angel's message, *Ave gratia plena dominus tecum* ("Hail, thou that art highly favored, the Lord is with thee"; Luke 1: 28), is embossed on the gold background. Mary, "troubled at his saying," recoils elegantly, her face clouded with apprehension. This is an extraordinary and unexpected style, but graceful in the extreme, with all the characteristic Sienese fluency of line translated from Byzantine Greek into Flamboyant French.

THE LORENZETTI. Giotto's new devices reached Sienese painting in the work of two brothers, Pietro (c.1280–1348?) and Ambrogio (c.1285–1348?) Lorenzetti, who, nonetheless, continued independently the Sienese

tradition of the exploration of landscape and architectural settings, and brought Sienese painting to a position of absolute leadership in Europe during the decade following Giotto's death. In Pietro's *Birth of the Virgin* (fig. 15), of 1342, for the Cathedral of Siena, we are aware of Giotto's cubic space and columnar figures, but Pietro has taken a significant step in the direction of illusionism. The gold background is eliminated save where it peeks through a tiny window at the left. The architectural setting has been identified with the actual carved shape of the frame, which it was customary for the artist himself to design and which was usually built and attached to the panel before the process of painting was begun. The picture thus becomes a little stage into which we can look, so that we cannot help wondering from the illustration what is carved and what is painted. Pietro's altarpiece is a pioneer attempt to build up the consistent interior space that never seems to have occurred to the

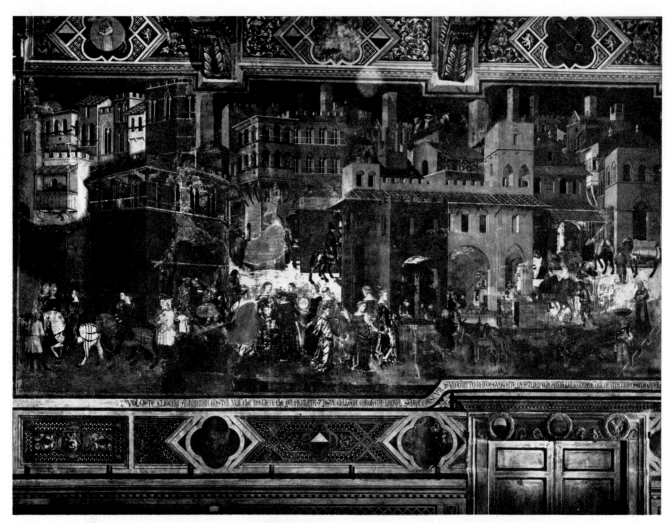

16. AMBROGIO LORENZETTI. *Allegory of Good Government: the Effects of Good Government in the City
and the Country* (portion of fresco). 1338–39. Salla della Pace, Palazzo Pubblico, Siena

Romans. His perspective is not entirely consistent, but the upper and lower portions of the interior are drawn so that the parallel lines in each converge to a single separate vanishing point. An enormous step has been taken in the direction of the unified perspective space of the Renaissance (see Masaccio, colorplate 6, and Donatello, fig. 42).

Not even Pietro's formulation of interior space is quite as startling as what Ambrogio had already achieved in the fresco representing the effects of Good Government in city and country (colorplate 3, fig. 16), a panorama that fills one entire wall of a council chamber in the Palazzo Pubblico (the Sienese counterpart of the Florentine Palazzo Vecchio), so extensive in fact that it cannot be shown in one photograph. Ambrogio has assumed the high point of view taken by Duccio for his exterior scenes, but he has immensely expanded it. On the right we look over the zigzag line of the city wall into open squares and streets lined with houses, palaces, and towers, some still under construction (note the masons at

work under the center beam). At the upper left can barely be made out the campanile and dome of the Cathedral. Richly dressed Sienese burghers and their wives ride by on horseback; one horse has already half-disappeared down a street in the center. The three arches of the building in the foreground contain (from left to right) a shoe shop, a school with a teacher at a desk on a platform and a row of pupils, and a wineshop with a little bar in front. Groups of happy citizens dance in the street.

To the right, under a friendly floating near-nude labeled *Securitas*, who brandishes a scroll with one hand and a loaded gallows with the other, the city people ride downhill into the country and the country people walk uphill into the city. The view of the countryside is amazing: roads, hills, farms and orchards with peasants hard at work, a lake, a country chapel, villas and castles, hills beyond hills, stretching to the horizon. But just where we would expect a blue sky with clouds, Ambrogio drops the Iron Curtain and reminds us that we are still in the Middle Ages. The background is a uniform gray

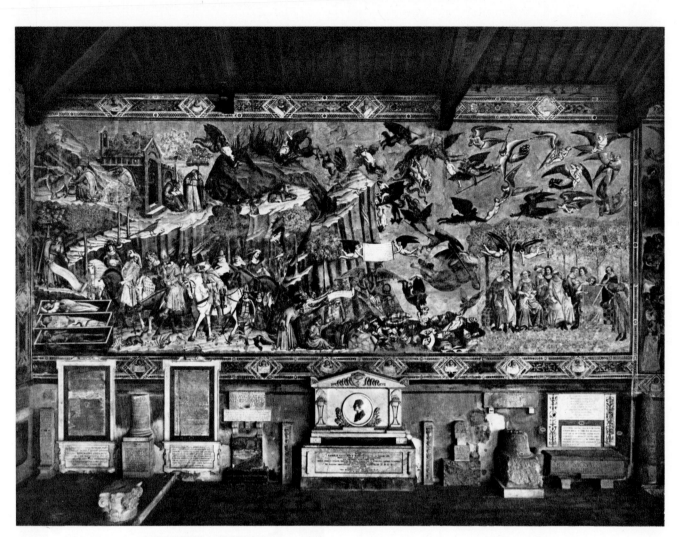

17. Francesco Traini. *Triumph of Death*. Fresco. Middle 14th century. Campo Santo, Pisa

black. This encyclopedic view of the Sienese world and everything in it is an exciting preview of the Renaissance, but there it stops. The Black Death, an epidemic of the bubonic plague that swept Europe in 1348, killed from half to two-thirds of the populations of Florence and Siena, probably including Ambrogio and Pietro Lorenzetti, and put an end to such explorations.

TRAINI. The frescoes representing the *Triumph of Death* (fig. 17) in the Campo Santo at Pisa, probably the work of a local master named Francesco Traini (active c. 1321–63), are doubtless a reflection of the universal gloom following the Black Death. In this panorama, very different from the carefree world of Ambrogio Lorenzetti, no one escapes. At the left three richly dressed couples on horseback, out a-hunting, come upon three open coffins containing corpses in varying stages of putrefaction, a common enough sight in 1348; they draw back in consternation, one rider holding his nose. At the right in a grove of orange trees sits a happy group of gentlemen and ladies, engaged in music and conversation, reminding us of Boccaccio's *Decameron*, written at the time of the Black Death. They seem not to see Death, a winged, white-haired hag, sweeping down on them with a scythe. In the air above angels and demons are in conflict over human souls, and the rocky path to the upper left leads to hermits' cells, as if to demonstrate that the only road to salvation is retreat from the world. The severe damage suffered by these frescoes in World War II necessitated the detachment from the wall of all those that still adhered; underneath was found the most extensive series of sinopias then known (fig. 18), which shows the boldness and freedom of brushwork, recalling Byzantine painting, that underly the meticulous finish of fourteenth-century frescoes.

GIOVANNI DA MILANO. In the wake of the Black Death, no new figures emerged of anything near the stature of the great masters of the early fourteenth century, but some painters showed new observations and insights.

18. FRANCESCO TRAINI. *Triumph of Death* (detail of sinopia)

19. GIOVANNI DA MILANO. *Pietà.* 1365. Panel painting, 48 x 22¾". Galleria dell'Accademia, Florence

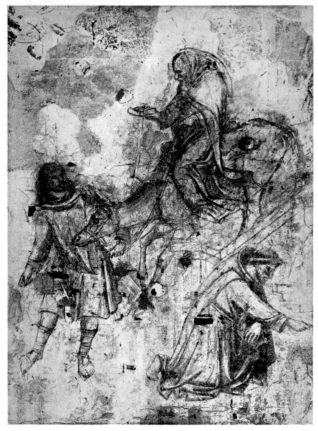

18

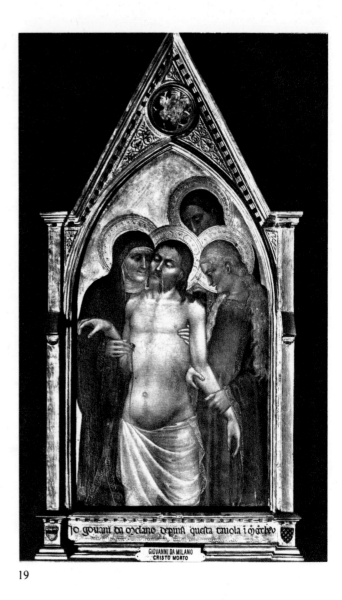

19

One of the most gifted was Giovanni da Milano (active 1346–66), a Lombard working in Florence, where he signed in 1365 a new kind of image, a *Pietà* (fig. 19), from the Italian word for both *pity* and *piety*, both of which it was intended to excite. The intensified religious life of Italy after the catastrophe required new images, which would draw from biblical sources figures, situations, and emotions rather than narrative incidents and recombine them in timeless configurations designed to strengthen the reciprocal emotional bond between sacred figures and the individual worshiper. In an attempt at once to arouse the sympathies of the observer and to demonstrate to him that Christ had shared the sufferings of all mankind, he is depicted after death in Giovanni's picture, lifted in the arms of Mary, Mary Magdalene, and John. The emotional intensity of the painting has reached fever pitch, but it is no longer expressed in outbursts; it is felt within, rather, like a self-inflicted wound. As impressive as the content of Giovanni's painting is his new attention to muscles, bones, and tendons not only where they affect the texture of an anatomical surface but also where they appear along the sensitive contour. His art illuminates to some degree the origin of the mysterious painter of the *Wilton Diptych* and also prepared the way for the great discoveries of the approaching Renaissance, in both Italy and the North.

PART FOUR
The Renaissance

Renaissance, the French word for *rebirth*, has generally been taken to signify the revival of the knowledge of Greek and Roman civilizations. Writers of the period believed that Classical literature, philosophy, science, and art had been lost in an age of darkness after the collapse of the Roman Empire under the onslaught of Germanic invaders and had awaited throughout the intervening centuries resurrection at the hands of the Italians, true heirs of their Roman ancestors. When the Tuscan poet and humanist scholar Petrarch (Francesco Petrarca), who seems to have been the first to proclaim the idea of barbarian decline and contemporary rebirth, was crowned with laurel on the Capitoline Hill in Rome in 1341, it was not in recognition of the beauty of his Italian sonnets, but rather in honor of the breadth of his knowledge of ancient history and of the purity of his Latin style.

Petrarch's literary classicism had little demonstrable effect on the art of his own time. Few fourteenth-century artists imitated Classical models; ironically, Petrarch's favorite painter was the Gothic master Simone Martini (see Prologue) and his favorite building the Gothic Cathedral of Cologne. Moreover, Petrarch could not have known that during the period he designated as "dark" repeated efforts had been made to revive one aspect or another of Classical art. We have already seen such attempts in Carolingian, Middle Byzantine, Romanesque, and Gothic art. When in the fifteenth century Italian artists adopted in earnest ideas and motives from the artistic vocabulary of ancient Rome (they did not know Greek buildings), they limited their efforts to architecture and decoration. Only for limited purposes were sculptors concerned with the imitation of specific models. There were almost no examples left for painters to follow, and it is sad to read the pages in which the sculptor Lorenzo Ghiberti, one of the founders of Renaissance art, wrote of the varying merits of Greek painters whose long-vanished works he knew only from literary descriptions.

But no one doubts that a tremendous change occurred in the visual arts in the fifteenth century, the consequences of which are with us yet, and the revival of Classical antiquity is not enough to explain it. The Swiss historian, Jakob Burckhardt, writing in 1860, used "The Discovery of the World and of Man" as the title for one major division of his great work, *The Civilization of the Renaissance in Italy*. In the formation of Renaissance art both in Italy and in Northern Europe, it is this discovery that distinguishes the artistic revolution of the fifteenth century from earlier Classical revivals and gives meaning to its borrowings from ancient art. The new vision of the Renaissance artist, whether in the generally Classical setting of Italy or in the still-Gothic enframement of Northern Europe, projects a believable picture of man and the world in which he lives. Not only is this the first such picture since ancient times, but also in many ways it goes further than ancient art in its inclusiveness and consistency.

At the height of the new movement, in 1451–52, the Florentine humanist Giannozzo Manetti wrote an influential work entitled *On the Dignity and Excellence of Man*, in which he refuted the claims of medieval theologians that man was worthless in the eyes of God. Manetti extols man as "lord and king and emperor in the whole orb of the world, and not unworthy to dominate and to reign and to rule." He finds not only man's soul but also his body beautiful, every part admirably adapted to its purpose, so perfect indeed that both pagans and Christians were justified in representing their gods in human form, and the Greeks in calling the human body a microcosm, since it mirrors in itself the harmony of the entire world. There is no miracle that the human intelligence cannot encompass, Manetti tells us, no mystery of the cosmos that it cannot fathom. But the highest peak of human genius is speculation about the divine. The world was created, not for God who had no need of it, but for man. Man is the most perfect work of God, containing in himself all the beauties scattered in various orders of the universe, and revealing them in his creative power, the true marvel of his genius. "Ours then," says Manetti, "are everything which you see, all the homes, the fortresses, the cities, all the buildings in the entire world which are so many and such that they seem the work of angels rather than of men .... Ours are the pictures, ours the sculptures, ours the arts, ours the sciences, ours the wisdom. Ours are all the regions of the earth, mountains, valleys, plants, animals, fountains, rivers, lakes and seas, and all the innumerable creatures." For Manetti man has his end, not in God, but in a knowledge of himself and his own creativity.

A similar pride in the autonomy of the Renaissance artist inspired the humanist and architect Leonbattista Alberti when he wrote in his treatise *On Painting* in 1435, "We have dug this art up from under the earth. If it was never written, we have drawn it from heaven." In the prologue he claimed "that it was less difficult for the ancients—because they had models to imitate and from which they could learn—to come to a knowledge of those supreme arts which today are most difficult for us. Our fame ought to be so much greater, then, if we discover unheard-of and never-before-seen arts and sciences without teachers or without any model whatsoever." This attitude culminates in Leonardo da Vinci's assertion that the painter is "Lord and God" to carry out whatever idea comes into his head, and Michelangelo's comparison of the sculptural process with that of divine salvation.

With few exceptions the humanists considered themselves Christians, and some were in religious orders, but it must be remembered that they represented an elite. Medieval piety still inspired the masses of the people, even in humanist Florence, and could occasionally resume control, as under the dominance of Saint Antonine, reactionary archbishop of Florence in the middle of the fifteenth century, and his fellow-Dominican Savonarola, effective ruler of the city just before the century's close. During the Counter-Reformation, in the middle of the sixteenth century, Manetti's work was put on the *Index Expurgatorius* (*List of Forbidden Works*) by the Council of Trent.

The Renaissance artist inherited from the Middle Ages such duties as the construction of churches and palaces, the painting of frescoes and altarpieces, the carving of pulpits and tombs. Interest in stained glass declined during the Renaissance, disappearing completely before its close, and the illuminated manuscript, still important in the early fifteenth century, was soon replaced by the printed book. The humanist attitude of the artist and his patron gave rise to three phenomena seldom seen since the eclipse of paganism—the nude human figure, the recognizable portrait, and the landscape, all in keeping with the above passages from Manetti. It is worth noting that, although Petrarch may have been the first person in history to climb a mountain on purpose (Mount Ventoux near Avignon), instead of observing the view from the top he read the *Confessions* of Saint Augustine. But in the fifteenth century descriptions of distant views parallel the splendid landscapes that appear in the works of the great painters—always as backgrounds for human activity.

Especially important is the versatility of the Renaissance artist. The same man can often excel at two of the three major arts, sometimes at all three. Alberti, Ghiberti, Piero della Francesca, Leonardo da Vinci, Albrecht Dürer, and Andrea Palladio also wrote extensive treatises on the principles of their arts. But the artist did not limit himself to the practice of what today we would call "Art." In the conquest of reality, he easily turned his attention to the sciences of perspective, anatomy, botany, geology, and geometry, basic contributions to all of which were made by Italian Renaissance artists. His genius could be placed at the service of the state in peace and war, for he was expected to plan cities, lay out canals and fortifications, and design bridges and arches, floats and pageants, and even weapons and engines of war. Perspective, the investigation of which was one of his great delights, was closely allied to the exploration of *actual* space, which culminated in the late fifteenth and the sixteenth centuries in the voyages of the great discoverers and the revolutionary theories of the astronomers and cosmographers. It was no accident that the map that led Columbus to resolve to set forth on his first journey to the New World was produced in Renaissance Florence.

The humanist concerns of the artist opened him to advice from the humanist leaders of the Renaissance state, particularly Florence; he was likewise involved perforce in the destinies of those very leaders. When the fifteenth century began, the artist was still a craftsman, firmly embedded in the system of merchant and artisan guilds that controlled the Florentine Republic. By midcentury he had become everywhere, except in Venice, an appanage of the princely society that was visibly or invisibly replacing the medieval republics. By the sixteenth century, when absolutism held sway throughout much of Italy, artists of the stature of Michelangelo, Raphael, and Titian had acquired aristocratic social status, wealth, and influence.

It is instructive that none of the artistically creative states of the Early Renaissance—the republics of Florence, Siena, and Venice, the Papal States, and the duchy of Burgundy—survive as political entities today. But with few exceptions it was in these relatively small, rich, disordered, and militarily insecure states, rather than in the kingdoms of Naples, France, England, and Spain, or the Holy Roman Empire, that the crucial developments of the Early Renaissance took place. It looks as though the turmoil that characterized the smaller states was more conducive to the development of artistic individuality than was the hierarchical structure of the monarchies. It is also important to note that, once the liberties of the Italian states had become extinguished in the sixteenth century, the Renaissance itself soon came to an end.

1

The Early Renaissance in Italy:
The Fifteenth Century

ARCHITECTURE IN FLORENCE AND NORTH ITALY

Architecture is the easiest of the arts in which to follow the rebirth of Classical motives in the Renaissance and their adaptation to contemporary needs. During a period notable for its political turbulence and almost continuous warfare, in which the very existence of the Florentine Republic was repeatedly threatened by outside enemies, the Italian city-states including Florence found the energy and the funds to adorn their still-medieval streets and squares with buildings in the new style. The harmony and

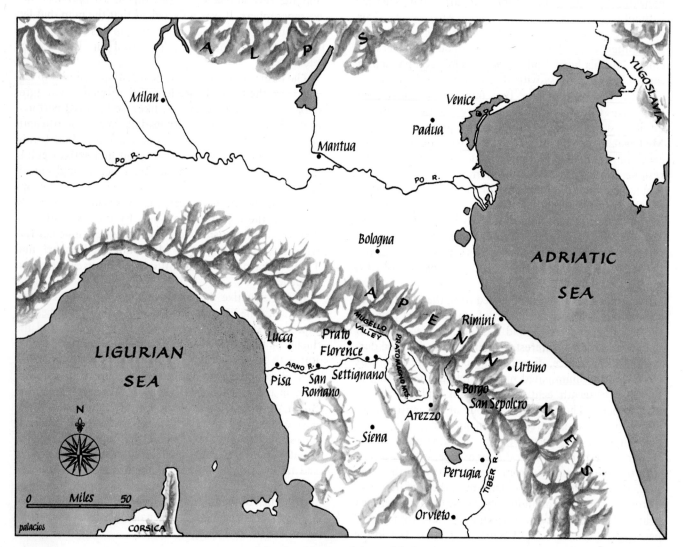

MAP 2. *North and Central Italy*

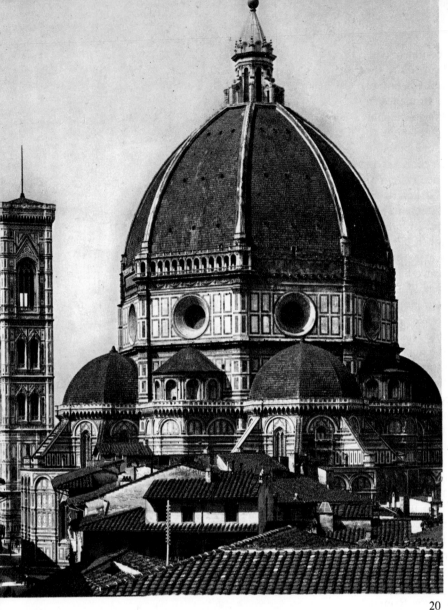

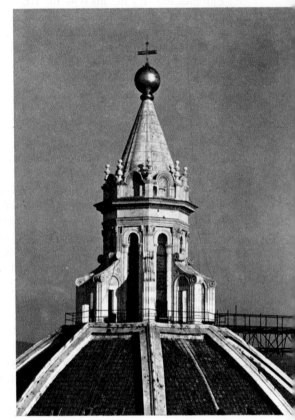

20. FILIPPO BRUNELLESCHI. Dome, Cathedral of Florence. 1420–36

21. FILIPPO BRUNELLESCHI. Lantern of the dome, Cathedral of Florence. After 1446

20   21

dignity of these structures made them examples for later architects for five centuries—and their influence continues.

BRUNELLESCHI. It is typical of the versatility of Renaissance artists and the interchangeability of the arts in the fifteenth and sixteenth centuries that Filippo Brunelleschi (1377–1446), the founder of the Renaissance style in architecture, was trained as a sculptor. After his defeat in 1402 at the hands of Lorenzo Ghiberti in the competition for the bronze doors of the Baptistery of Florence (see page 42, and figs. 45, 46), Brunelleschi made the first of several trips to Rome, where he spent many months, perhaps together with the somewhat younger sculptor Donatello, studying and measuring the buildings of ancient Rome, most of which were in a much better state of preservation in the fifteenth century than they are today. In 1417 Brunelleschi won the competition to crown the unfinished Gothic Cathedral of Florence with a colossal dome (fig. 20). Like many crucial works

of the Early Renaissance, Brunelleschi's dome still retains Gothic elements. The octagonal shape of the crossing of the Cathedral made it impossible to erect a circular drum like those on which Brunelleschi's later domes (such as that of the Pazzi Chapel, see fig. 25) are set. Brunelleschi therefore built an octagonal drum supporting a dome divided by eight massive ribs. Unlike the ribs used in Gothic vaulting, however, these do the actual work of upholding the dome and the lantern at its apex. An inner shell of masonry and an outer shell of tiles conceal between them a complex web of smaller ribs and connecting, horizontal flying buttresses that ties the principal ribs together. Brunelleschi's construction system and his device for hoisting the building materials to great heights were particularly attractive to the cathedral authorities because they made it possible to erect the unprecedented structure without the expensive forest of scaffolding that would otherwise have been necessary.

Only the lantern, built from Brunelleschi's still-extant model after his death, shows direct Classical borrowings,

The Early Renaissance in Italy / 27

in this case the Corinthian order (fig. 21), complete with pilasters and entablatures folded about the corners of the lantern and sustained by a highly original system of modified flying buttresses. From the start Brunelleschi based his masses, spaces, and enclosing surfaces on simple, proportional relationships of basic modules—one to two or two to three—utilizing the paneling of white and colored marbles characteristic of medieval churches in Florence to carry out his typically Renaissance system of rectangles and circles. The result is a structure of overwhelming mass, simplicity, clarity of statement, and intelligibility of design, rising (as Alberti put it) "above the skies, ample to cover with its shadow all the Tuscan people." In the early sixteenth century an attempt was made on one face to fill in the unfinished space between the drum and the dome with an ornamental gallery, whose trivial scale only emphasizes the grandeur of Brunelleschi's elemental shapes.

In the Ospedale degli Innocenti (Foundling Hospital), started in 1419 (fig. 22), Brunelleschi had a major opportunity to translate his knowledge of ancient architecture into fifteenth-century terms. The building faces the Piazza della Santissima Annunziata in Florence with a handsome arcade of eleven round arches supported on Composite columns, terminated at each side by Corinthian pilasters and surmounted by a second story of small, pedimented windows (the story above the roof is a later excrescence). Brunelleschi's proportion system can be easily followed; the height of each column equals the width of the bay between columns, and also its depth from column to wall. Each bay, therefore, becomes a cube of space, surmounted by a squared hemisphere in the shape of the pendentive vault (supported along the wall only by consoles). Both in general disposition and in the character of the capitals and entablatures, Brunelleschi has edited the splendor and richness of the Roman originals he studied in favor of an austere simplicity that emphasizes the clarity of his organization.

The great architect's mathematical turn of mind brought forth not only his system of basic geometrical shapes and simple proportions but also related invention of what appears to be the first consistent system of one-point perspective—that is, a perspective in which all parallel lines in a given visual field converge at a single vanishing point on the horizon. Brunelleschi's perspective was derived from the observation of actual buildings. In the interior of the Church of San Lorenzo in Florence (fig. 23), built at intervals from 1421 well into the fifteenth century under the patronage of the Medici family, circles, half circles, rectangles, and squares are kept as at the Innocenti within a clear-cut, all-embracing system of modules of surface and space, diminishing systematically as one looks down the nave.

At San Lorenzo Brunelleschi replaced the complexities of Gothic shapes and systems with the basic plan of an Early Christian basilica (fig. 24). The nave arcades, supported by unfluted Corinthian columns, sustain a flat wall without triforium, pierced by a clerestory of arched

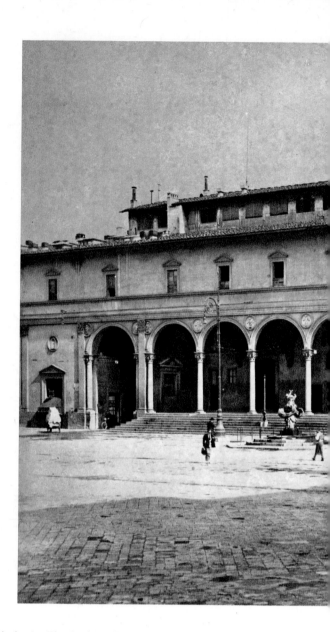

windows. Flanked by Corinthian pilasters, the side aisles are covered by pendentive vaults supported on transverse arches; the nave is roofed by a flat, coffered ceiling, whose squares provide a convenient graph with which to measure inward spatial recession. Even the floor is marked off into squares by stripes, thus measuring not only the perspective recession but also the proportions between the width of the bays, the height of the columns, and that of the arches. All is measure, reason, proportion, harmony, accentuated by Brunelleschi's choice of a gray Florentine stone known as *pietra serena* (*clear stone*) for the columns, entablatures, arches, window frames, and other trim to contrast with the white plaster covering the masonry walls. This austere two-tone color scheme was repeated in Florentine architecture well into the nineteenth century. Within Brunelleschi's crystalline, intellectual structure of harmonious spaces and surfaces, the lofty Corinthian columns stand with the cool perfection of statues.

The gem of Brunelleschi's later style is the chapel given

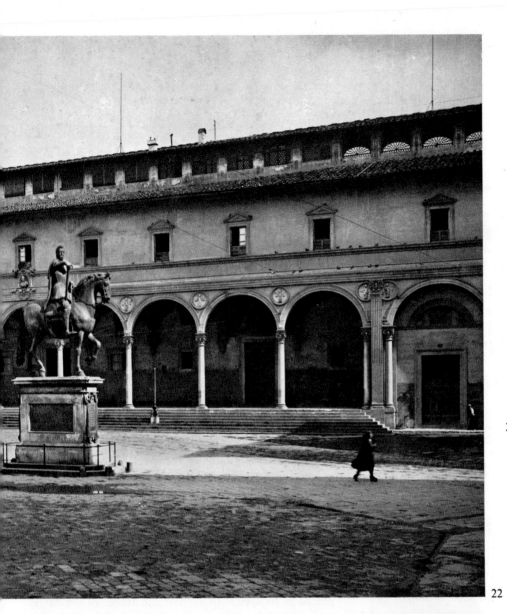

22. FILIPPO BRUNELLESCHI.
Ospedale degli Innocenti
(Foundling Hospital). Begun
1419. Piazza della SS.
Annunziata, Florence

22

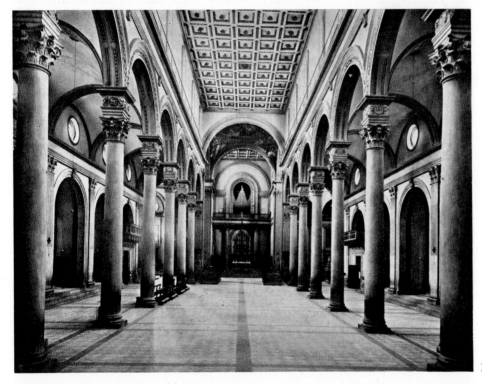

23

23. FILIPPO BRUNELLESCHI. Nave
and choir, S. Lorenzo.
1421–69. Florence

24. FILIPPO BRUNELLESCHI. Plan
of S. Lorenzo

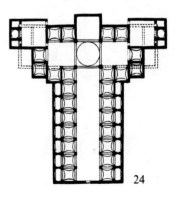

24

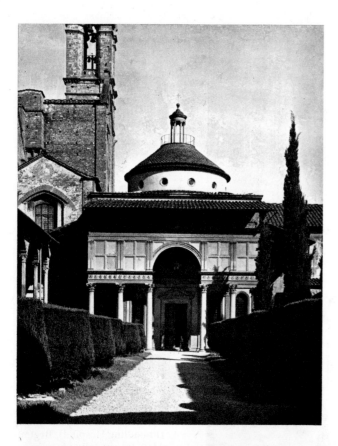

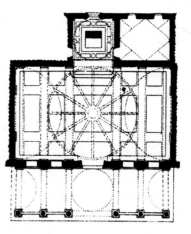

25. FILIPPO BRUNELLESCHI. Exterior, Pazzi Chapel, Sta. Croce. c. 1440–61. Florence

26. FILIPPO BRUNELLESCHI. Plan of the Pazzi Chapel

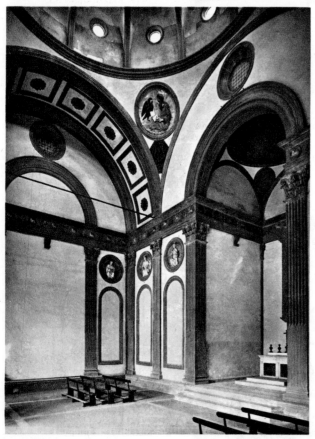

27. FILIPPO BRUNELLESCHI. Interior, Pazzi Chapel

to Santa Croce by the Pazzi family of Florence (figs. 25, 26) to be used not only for their services but also as the chapter house in which the monks of Santa Croce could meet; it was constructed from about 1440 to 1461. A central square surmounted by a round dome on pendentives is extended on either side by arms equal to half its width; their barrel vaults are divided into large panels of *pietra serena* moldings against plaster. The resultant rectangular hall (fig. 27) is lined with fluted Corinthian pilasters (again in *pietra serena*, like all the trim) so placed as to appear to support the arches of the barrel vault and of the altar space, and even the false arches inserted in the lunettes at either end of the chapel to complete the system. Smaller blind arches, reflecting the windows in the façade, appear in the spaces between the pilasters. These spaces furnish the basic module for the entire chapel. Over each of the twelve blind arches appears a small roundel, containing one of the Twelve Apostles in glazed terra-cotta, blue and white, by Luca della Robbia (see page 44). The pendentives display larger terra-cotta roundels of the Four Evangelists, probably by Brunelleschi himself. The dome with its twelve ribs and twelve oculi seems—like that of Hagia Sophia—to be floating, since the lower cornice of the drum does not touch the supporting arches. The portico was added after Brunelleschi's death, possibly by Giuliano da Maiano.

The Pazzi Chapel is one of the masterpieces of architectural history, harmonious and graceful in its proportions and spaces, luminous and simple in its color scheme of gray, white, and blue with occasional touches of green, yellow, and violet. Here we are very far from the Gothic cathedral, which sought at once to enfold and to dazzle us with the infinite complexity of the medieval universe. Yet Brunelleschi, like all great architects of the Renaissance, had foremost in his own mind the idea of the Divine Proportion. When we analyze his beautiful relationship of shape, space, line, and number, we would do well to remember Giannozzo Manetti's declaration that the truths of the Christian religion are as self-evident as the axioms of mathematics. Ironically, Brunelleschi was not destined to see any of his major structures completed. At his death the nave of San Lorenzo was barely begun, the dome of the Cathedral lacked its lantern, and the Pazzi Chapel its façade. Nonetheless, this inspired architect established, as if by fiat, a whole new order for the art of building, as valid in the century of Le Corbusier and Mies van der Rohe as in his own.

MICHELOZZO. We possess, unfortunately, no certain example of domestic architecture by Brunelleschi, but we do know that Cosimo de' Medici, uncrowned ruler of the still ostensibly republican Florence, first commissioned him to make a model for his new palace and then rejected it as too grandiose for the Medici's pretense of being private citizens. The building known today as the Palazzo Medici-Riccardi (fig. 28) was started in 1444 by the prolific architect and sculptor Michelozzo di Bartolommeo (1396–1472). In considering its present appearance, we have to make several mental adjustments. First, we must remember that the word *palazzo* means to Italians almost any fair-sized urban edifice, even a modern office building. Second, when the Medici Palace was bought by the Riccardi family at the end of the seventeenth century, it was extended on the right by one portal and seven bays of windows, which have to be thought away. Finally, the handsome, pedimented windows in the arches of the ground floor were added in the sixteenth century by Michelangelo, after the palace had ceased to be the seat of the Medici Bank. The arches originally gave direct access to the banking offices within, and were closed at night by giant oaken doors (fig. 29).

To modern eyes the building hardly looks palatial. Not only the fortress-like exterior, but also the lofty interiors, even when they were filled with the vanished collections of paintings (including battle scenes by Paolo Uccello, see fig. 61), sculpture, tapestries, and antiquities, must always have seemed austere. This was the taste of the time. Cosimo intended to impress the observer with the fortitude and dignity of his family, relative newcomers to the Florentine ruling class. The massive lower story, more than twenty feet high, is heavily rusticated, that is, built of roughhewn blocks in a manner somewhat resembling that of the Palazzo Vecchio, but actually imitated from such ancient Roman structures as the Porta Maggiore. The masonry of the second story, the family living quarters, is cut into flat blocks with strongly accented joints; that of the third is entirely smooth. The entire building is crowned by a massive cornice, towering

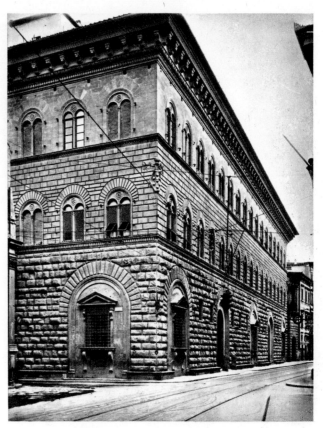

28. MICHELOZZO. Exterior, Palazzo Medici-Riccardi. Begun 1444. Florence

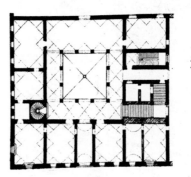

29. MICHELOZZO. Plan of the Palazzo Medici-Riccardi

some seventy feet above the street and imitated from those of Roman temples. But this is not the only Classical detail; the still faintly pointed arches of the windows on the second and third floors embrace two lights each, whose round arches rest on delicate colonnettes with modified Corinthian capitals.

The interior courtyard (fig. 30), in which much of the life of the palace went on, reminds one of the arcades of Brunelleschi's Innocenti, but the columns have squatter proportions in keeping with their function of upholding two stories instead of one. The second story is lighted by windows resembling those of the exterior, while the third (not shown in the illustration) was an open loggia, whose columns supported a beamed roof. Neither in propor-

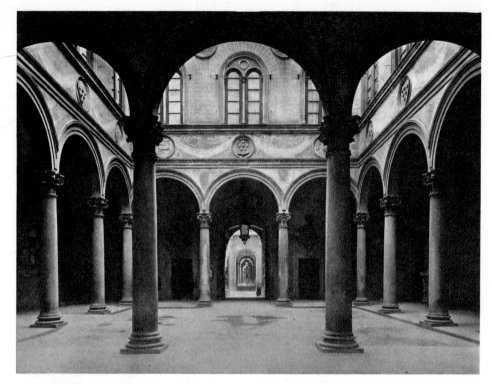

30. MICHELOZZO. Interior
courtyard, Palazzo
Medici-Riccardi

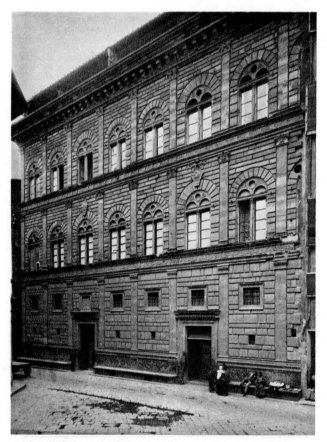

31. LEONBATTISTA ALBERTI. Façade, Palazzo Rucellai.
Begun 1461. Florence

tions nor in detail can Michelozzo's palace survive comparison with the masterpieces of Brunelleschi, but—perhaps because of the importance of the patron—it became the model for Florentine patrician town houses for the next two generations.

ALBERTI. From the middle of the 1430s, the Renaissance movement, not only in architecture but also in sculpture and painting, fell under the domination of a cultural colossus, Leonbattista Alberti (1404–72). This scion of one of the most powerful Florentine families of the Middle Ages was born in exile and revisited Florence briefly and infrequently, functioning by preference as a humanist adviser at the courts of popes and princes. The author of many learned works in classical Latin, Alberti wrote three treatises, *On Painting, On the Statue,* and *On the Art of Building,* that had an immense influence on his own and subsequent generations, and give us today a welcome insight into many aspects of Renaissance art. The wealthy Florentine merchant Giovanni Rucellai commissioned in 1461 the architect and sculptor Bernardo Rossellino (see page 57 and fig. 67) to build a palace from Alberti's designs. The façade (fig. 31), an obvious commentary on that of the Medici Palace, takes us, nonetheless, into a new era of Renaissance thought. In his writings and in his designs, Alberti adopted antiquity as a way of life. While he retains the three-story division, the doubled windows on the second and third stories, and the great cornice of Michelozzo's building, he rejects the heavy rustication of Michelozzo's ground floor as if unsuitable to the residence of a citizen of wealth and taste. Instead, he establishes a uniform system of simulated, beveled masonry joints, often not corresponding with the real ones, identical on all three stories. The windows of the ground floor, mere gaps in the masonry in the Medici Palace, are here given handsome, square frames. Then Alberti ornaments his façade by a superimposed three-story system of screen architecture—pilasters that do no work but only appear to uphold the entablatures above them. This device is derived from the superimposed orders of the Colosseum. It also corresponds to Alberti's doctrine that the basic proportions and divisions of the wall belong to beauty, defined as "the harmony and concord of all the parts, achieved in such a manner that nothing could be added, taken away, or altered," while the column and the pilaster belong to decoration. In contrast to Brunelleschi, Alberti's columns and pilasters almost never uphold arches. The arch, he tells us, is an opening in a wall and should remain as such. Today we see only a fragment of the building Alberti designed for Giovanni Rucellai; it would have been completed probably on the right by four more bays and one more portal. Alberti's complex and elegant design remained without following in Florence until very nearly the end of the fifteenth century, but its principles were of cardinal importance for the architecture of the High Renaissance.

About 1450 Alberti, although himself in Holy Orders, a doctor of canon law, and a secretary in the household of the pope, prepared for one of the most outrageous tyrants of the Renaissance a design for a building in which every tenet of Catholic Christianity was defied. Sigismondo Malatesta, lord of Rimini, was in the process of converting the Church of San Francesco at Rimini into a temple, honoring himself and his mistress Isotta degli Atti (for whose sake he had caused his wife to be suffocated). Their tombs were to appear on the façade, and those of the court humanists on the flanks of the nave, Greek scholars on one side, Latin on the other. At first Sigismondo seems to have desired only a remodeling of the existing Gothic church, but Alberti persuaded him to enclose it in a wholly new marble structure (fig. 32). Only the nave was completed before fortune ceased to smile on Sigismondo, but there is considerable evidence to show that Alberti intended it to terminate in a rotunda, with a hemispheric dome like that of the Pantheon. He considered the central plan ideal for a "temple" (the word *church* does not appear in Alberti's writings), not only on account of the Pantheon and certain Roman tombs he mistakenly believed to have been temples, but also because natural organisms are so often centralized, such as flowers, fruits, and cross sections of stems. A central-plan church had, in fact, already been designed in Florence by Brunelleschi, but left incomplete. The central plan, whether circular, square, polygonal, or cruciform, was to become the dominant ideal of church architecture in the High Renaissance, culminating in the design of various architects for Saint Peter's in Rome, because of the possibilities it offered for a harmonious composition of masses and spaces. Undoubtedly, the idea was strengthened by the knowledge of Byzantine architecture

brought to Italy by Greek scholars fleeing from Constantinople after its capture by the Turks in 1453. It must be admitted that the central plan presented obstacles for the Catholic liturgy, since an altar in its logical position under the dome would turn its back to half the congregation. Alberti's larger churches lead up to the domed space through a great nave, which he felt should be barrel-vaulted. At the Malatesta Temple, the vault would probably have been made of wood.

As a model for the façade, Alberti chose the Arch of Constantine, an appropriate symbol of triumph for Sigismondo. Many of the details, however, were patterned on a Roman single arch still standing in Rimini. The central arch contains the portal; the side arches were intended to hold the tombs of Sigismondo and Isotta, who in fact are interred in chapels in the nave. If the second story, whose single arch was to have been flanked by quarter circles terminating the side-aisle roofs, had ever been completed, the resemblance to a triumphal arch would have been less striking. As we would expect, the four massive engaged columns, with modified Corinthian capitals, uphold the entablature and embrace the arches. The arches continue on a somewhat smaller scale on the flanks of the church, each containing the sarcophagus of a humanist. In contrast to the lightness, linearity, and flat surfaces of Brunelleschi's architecture, the ponderous columns, piers, and arches of the Malatesta Temple produce an effect of imposing grandeur.

At Sant'Andrea, in the North Italian city of Mantua, designed in 1470 and almost entirely built after Alberti's death, his ideas come to fuller fruition (fig. 33). The plan

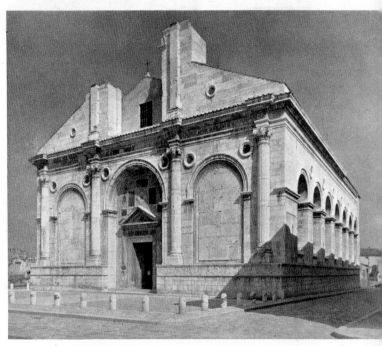

32. Leonbattista Alberti. Malatesta Temple (S. Francesco). c. 1450. Rimini, Italy

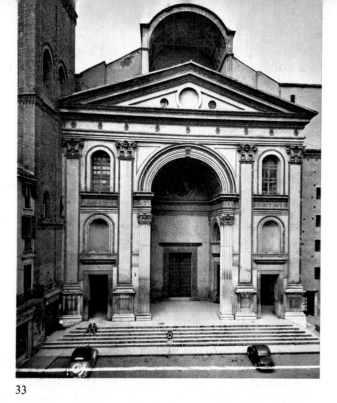

33

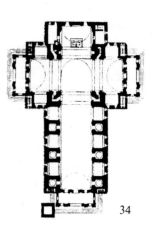

34

33. LEONBATTISTA
    ALBERTI.
    Sant'Andrea.
    Designed 1470.
    Mantua, Italy

34. LEONBATTISTA
    ALBERTI. Plan of
    Sant'Andrea

(fig. 34) is still a Latin cross, but different from any we
have seen so far. On the grounds that the ancient Romans
had invented the basilica plan for law courts, and that the
colonnades obstructed the view of the ceremony for those
standing in the side aisles, Alberti designed a single-aisle
interior, crowned by a huge barrel vault, whose inward
recession leads the eye to the apse and the altar (fig. 35).
The barrel vault is supported on massive piers, separating

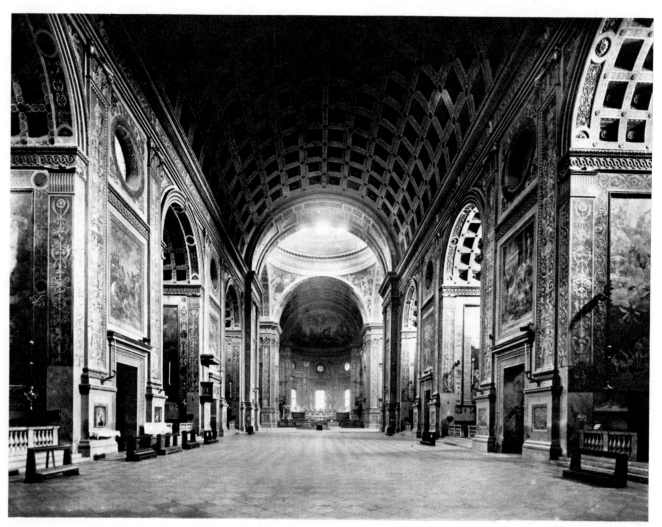

35. LEONBATTISTA ALBERTI. Interior, Sant'Andrea

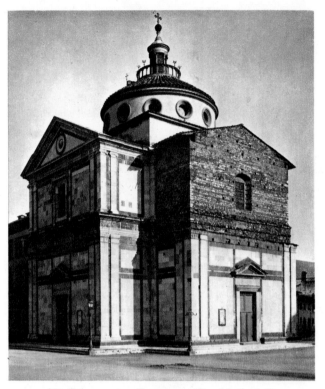

36. GIULIANO DA SANGALLO. Sta. Maria delle
Carceri. 1485–92. Prato, Italy

chapels covered by smaller barrel vaults running at right
angles to that of the nave. A single giant order of coupled
Corinthian pilasters ornaments the nave, embracing a
smaller order flanking the arches of the chapels. In all
probability a hemispheric dome would have completed
the crossing, but this was never built; the present dome
dates from the eighteenth century. The majestic and unified effect of the nave of Sant'Andrea was imitated by
Bramante later on, especially at Saint Peter's in Rome
(see fig. 235). Since the same plan was adopted by
Vignola for Il Gesù in Rome (see fig. 188) and subsequently followed in innumerable Baroque churches
throughout Europe, Alberti may be said to have dealt the
death blow to the basilica plan, which, with few exceptions, had dominated Christian church architecture for
eleven centuries.

In keeping with Alberti's belief that the illumination of
a temple should be high, so that one could see only the
heavens in order to inspire awe and reverence for the
mystery of the "gods," the interior of Sant'Andrea is
lighted only by oculi in the main and transept façades (invisible from the street) and by smaller oculi between the
piers and in the chapels. As in the Pantheon (and most
likely in the Malatesta Temple), light would probably
have come through an oculus in the center of the dome.

Since the preceding Gothic Church of Sant'Andrea
was completely surrounded by houses, Alberti had no
possibility of designing an exterior for his new building
beyond a façade that is a slightly enriched version of one
bay of the nave (see fig. 33), surmounted by a pediment.

Due to the lack of building stone in Mantua, the church is
constructed of brick faced with plaster, save for exposed
brickwork trimming the pilasters of the façade. Imported
marble, however, was used for the elegant pilasters of the
smaller order, including the central arch and entablature.
The façade is considerably lower than the church behind
it, but, given the angle from which it must be viewed in
the constricted piazza in front of it, this discrepancy is
not visible.

GIULIANO DA SANGALLO. A member of a remarkable
family of architects and sculptors, Giuliano da Sangallo
(1443?–1516) was a close student of Roman antiquity; in
fact, some of our knowledge of now-vanished Roman
buildings has been gained from his careful drawings.
Sangallo's Church of Santa Maria delle Carceri at Prato,
near Florence (fig. 36), built 1485–92 to enshrine a
miraculous image of the Virgin, owes debts to both
Brunelleschi and Alberti. The ribbed dome, with its circular drum pierced by oculi, is based on that of the Pazzi
Chapel (see fig. 25), as is the contrast between *pietra
serena* trim, glazed terra-cotta decoration, and white
stucco walls in the interior (fig. 37). But the exact cen-
trality of the Greek-cross plan is clearly Albertian, and so
is the beautiful exterior with its two stories of superimposed pilasters in white marble against white and green
marble paneling.

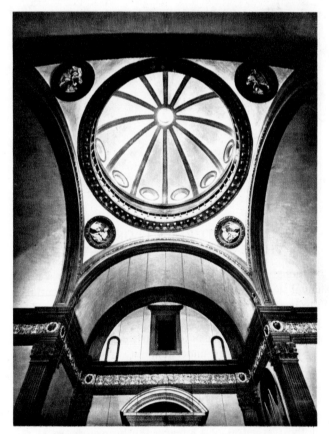

37. GIULIANO DA SANGALLO. Sta. Maria delle
Carceri

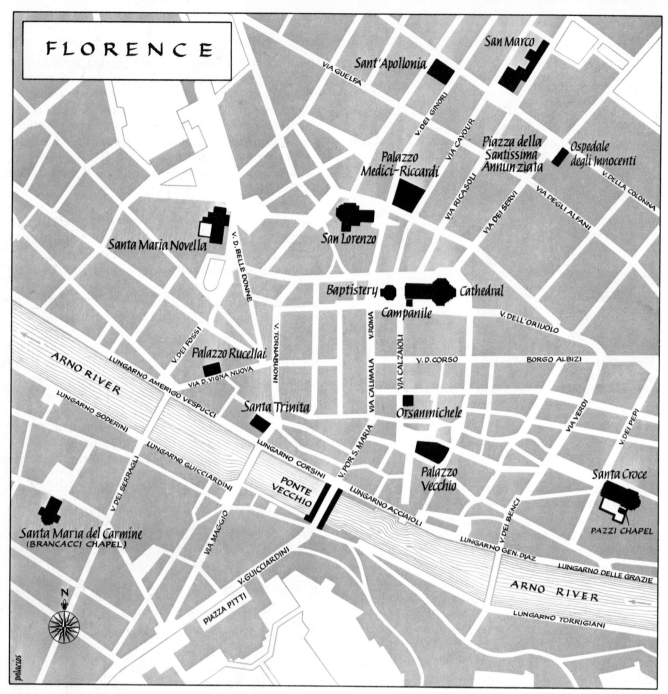

MAP 3. *Florence*

SCULPTURE IN FLORENCE:
THE EARLY FIFTEENTH CENTURY

Although the painters of the Early Renaissance were of equal stature with the sculptors, certain ideas essential to the new style appeared first in sculpture. This phenomenon was by no means accidental. The commissions offered to painters consisted of altarpieces and frescoes in churches; understandably, many painters continued to work in the Late Gothic tradition up to the middle of the fifteenth century. Sculpture, on the other hand, was generally intended for the exteriors of buildings with a strong civic purpose, such as the façade and Campanile of the Cathedral of Florence, the bronze doors of the Baptistery, or the niches of Orsanmichele, granary of the

republic, and appealed directly to the man in the street, sometimes from not far above eye level. The great sculptural works of the first third of the century were all done at a time when the Florentine republic was fighting for its life, first against the duke of Milan, then against the king of Naples, then against another duke of Milan. All three of these tyrants aspired to monarchic rule of the entire Italian peninsula, wishing to absorb Florence and her somewhat less energetic ally, Venice, into an imperial superstate to the extinction of republican liberties. The new human being who appears in the works of the great Florentine sculptors, then, is the first image of the man of the Renaissance, aware of danger from without, conscious of his dignity and of the meaning of freedom, self-analytical as never before in history. In a crucial moment, comparable in importance to the fifth century B.C. in Athens, or the mid-twelfth century in the Île-de-France, the stage was set for the crucial intellectual and spiritual drama, and the very nature of their art cast the sculptors in a leading role. It is worth noting that it took another generation before the Renaissance style could be established in either Naples or Milan, and then it was a diluted importation. It should also be noted that none of the thirty-two lifesize or over-lifesize statues that made their appearance in Florence in this astounding period has any back! All were intended to be seen only as integral parts of the buildings they brought to human focus and significance, and from which they presided over civic life.

DONATELLO. Donato di Niccolò Bardi (1386?–1466), to give the great sculptor his full name, scion of an impoverished branch of the Bardi banking family, appears to have been apprenticed to a stonecutter at an early age; in his twenties he was not only recognized as one of the two or three leading sculptors in Italy, but also had established himself as one of the founders of the new Renaissance style. His first work in which his style is clearly evident is the *Saint Mark*, executed from 1411–13, for Orsanmichele. Although each of the guilds of merchants and artisans who dominated the government of the republic of Florence had possessed since 1339 the responsibility of filling its niche at Orsanmichele with a statue, only two of these were completed before the opening of the fifteenth century. Donatello's *Saint Mark* (fig. 38) is one of a series of statues commissioned of him and of his rivals Lorenzo Ghiberti and Nanni di Banco in a sudden rush by the guilds to fulfill their obligations.

In contradistinction to all medieval statues, the position and function of each limb of the *Saint Mark* and its relation to the next and to the body as a whole are visible under the voluminous drapery. Vasari, the Late Renaissance painter, architect, and first art historian, to whom we have referred from time to time, described how a sculptor, in making a clothed statue, first models it in clay in the nude, then drapes about it actual cloth soaked in a thin slip of diluted clay, arranging the folds to cling or to fall as he wishes. There is evidence to show that Donatello was the first to use this method, so suggestive of the "wet drapery" of fifth-century Greek sculpture, and one must presuppose such a draped clay model for the marble *Saint Mark*. Appropriately enough, the statue was ordered by the guild of linen drapers. Donatello has represented not only a figure whose physical being is fully articulated, but also a complex personality summoning up all his psychological resources to confront an external situation. "The depth and passion of that earnest glance," to borrow a phrase from Robert Browning, the anxiety so brilliantly depicted in every detail of the lined face, the beauty of the free and sketchy treatment of the curling hair and beard place the statue in the forefront of the battle for the depiction of the whole human being.

Donatello's next commission for Orsanmichele, about

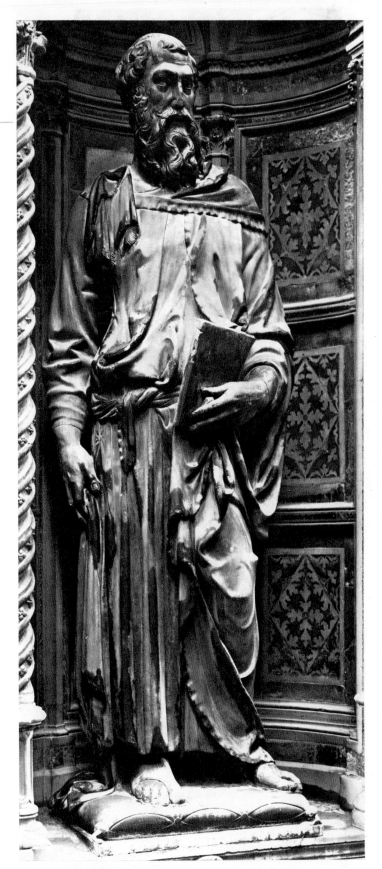

38. DONATELLO. *Saint Mark*. 1411–13. Marble, height 7'10". Orsanmichele, Florence

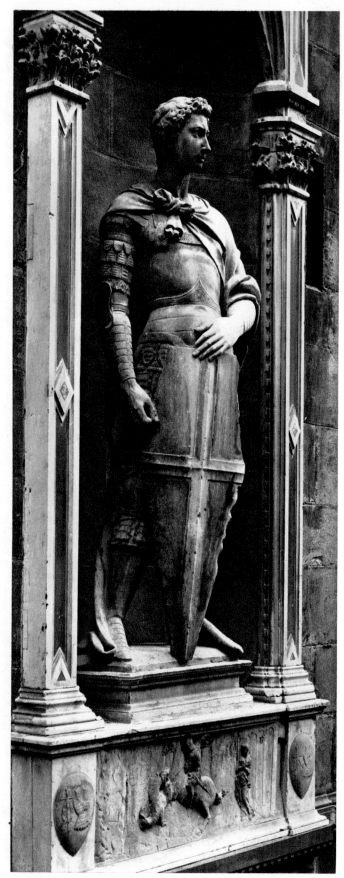

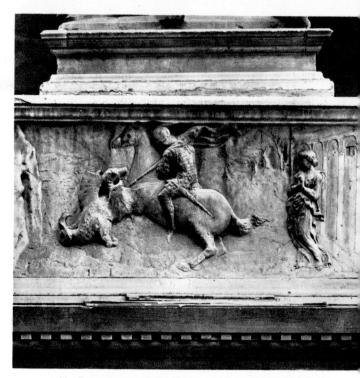

40. DONATELLO. *Saint George and the Dragon* (at base of niche that contained statue in fig. 39). Marble relief, 15¾ x 47¼". Orsanmichele, Florence

1415–16, the famous *Saint George* (fig. 39) carved for the guild of armorers and swordmakers, who must have been fairly prosperous in beleaguered Florence, gave him no such opportunity to display the movements of the body, thoroughly encased in his patrons' product. But the energetic stance of the young warrior saint, feet apart, both hands resting on the shield balanced on its point, show the tension characteristic of all the great sculptor's works, down to the tautness of the folds converging on the knot that fastens the cloak about Saint George's shoulders. The sensitively modeled face is hardly that of a conventional hero (compare it with the impassive, square-jawed face of the *Saint Theodore* at Chartres), but rather that of one who is no stranger to fear, yet can marshal the strength to overcome it. It should be remembered that (as can be demonstrated by drill holes still containing fragments of bronze) the head was once helmeted, and the right hand carried a sword, jutting out of the niche and into the street.

Perhaps more important historically than the statue itself, now removed to the shelter of a museum, is the relief representing *Saint George and the Dragon* (fig. 40) on the base of the niche in which the statue once stood. Here Donatello abandoned the concept of a relief sculpture that went back as far as ancient Egypt. The background of relief sculpture up to this time was a continuous flat surface, which the sculptor either carved down to as he cut away the original block, or built up from if he was working in clay, wax, or plaster.

39. DONATELLO. *Saint George*, from Orsanmichele, Florence (where it has been replaced by a bronze copy). c.1415–16. Marble, height 6'10". Museo Nazionale del Bargello, Florence

Donatello's innovation was to cut into the slab to any desired depth, counting on protrusions and depressions, as they reflect light or accumulate shadow, to produce on the eye the effect of nearness or distance. He has, so to speak, dissolved the slab, using it as a substance to paint or draw with, relying for his effects on what the eye *sees* to be there rather than what the mind *knows* to be there. He has, then, placed his sole emphasis on the autonomy of a single pair of eyes at a single position in time and space. This point marks, as sharply as any event can mark, the separation between ancient and medieval *ideal* art and Renaissance and modern *optical* art. From Donatello's discovery, adopted with varying rapidity by most sculptors and painters of his own day, spring all the other optical advances of later times, not excluding the Impressionism of the nineteenth century (see Part Six, Chapter 4). Given Donatello's optical method, it is no surprise to find that the little building (a premonition of Brunelleschi's Innocenti) behind the distressed princess is rendered in a remarkable approach to one-point perspective, or that between her and the rearing horse we can see in the distance low hills and a sky filled with clouds—perhaps the first in Italian art, preceded in Europe only by those of the Boucicaut Master and of the Limbourg brothers (see Chapter 2).

Donatello's series of prophet statues for the niches of the Campanile of the Cathedral of Florence are conceived in optical terms, cut in brutal masses with the features barely sketched in so that they could produce a powerful effect of light and shade from the street about thirty feet below. The most striking of these, possibly representing Habakkuk (fig. 41), was nicknamed *Lo Zuccone* (Big Squash, i.e., "Baldy") for obvious reasons in Donatello's own time. Fierce, like all of Donatello's prophets, he has little in common with the suave, beautifully draped and groomed prophetic figures, courtiers of the King of Heaven, on the portals of Gothic cathedrals. Swathed in a huge cloak that hangs in deliberately ugly folds, his eyes dilated, his mouth open, he denounces spiritual wickedness in high places.

In a gilded bronze relief (fig. 42) representing the *Feast of Herod*, done about 1425 for the baptismal font of the Cathedral of Siena, Donatello makes, as far as we know, the first complete visual statement of the new science of one-point perspective, controlling the inward recession and diminution of the masonry of Herod's palace—walls, arches, and columns, down to the very floor tiles—about ten years before Alberti wrote his difficult and confusing description of the method of one-point perspective in his treatise *On Painting* of 1435. But this epoch-making centripetal system is used by Donatello as a setting for an episode of passion, a composition organized only by its inherent centrifugal force. The presentation of the severed head of Saint John the Baptist at Herod's table has the effect of a bursting grenade, scattering the spectators to left and right in attitudes and expressions of horror.

In the early 1430s Donatello spent a prolonged period

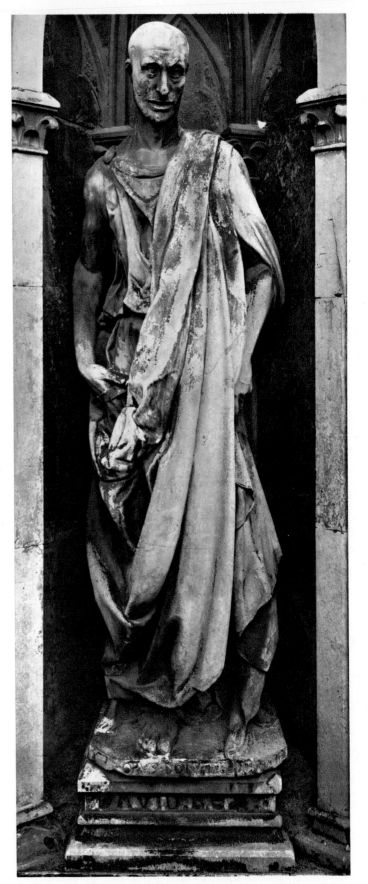

41. DONATELLO. *Habakkuk (Lo Zuccone)*, from the campanile of the Cathedral of Florence. 1423–25. Marble, 6'5". Museo dell'Opera del Duomo, Florence

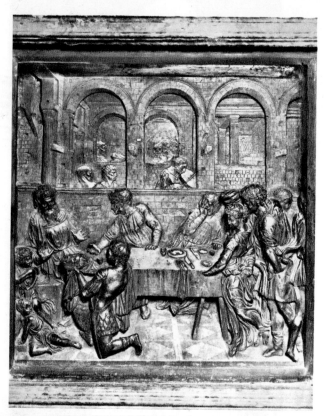

42. DONATELLO. *Feast of Herod.* c. 1425. Gilded bronze relief, 23⅝ x 23⅝". Baptismal font, Cathedral of Siena

Sant'Antonio. Donatello was doubtless impressed by the Roman statue of Marcus Aurelius, but the differences are instructive. The emperor appears unarmed, astride a horse reduced in scale as throughout ancient art. Donatello shows the general clad in a hybrid of Roman and contemporary armor, girded with a huge sword, wielding a baton as if marshaling his troops and guiding his gigantic charger by sheer force of will (the spurs do not touch the flanks and the bridle is slack). Throughout the statue the shapes are simplified to increase their apparent volume. A unifying diagonal axis runs from the lifted baton to the tip of the scabbard. Typical of Donatello's tension are the tail tied so as to describe an arc (repeating those of the buttocks and the neck) and the left forehoof toying with a cannonball, as David's left foot does with the head of Goliath. The general is a powerful portrait, but an ideal image of command rather

in Rome, which seems to have reinforced his interest in and knowledge of ancient art. Some time after his return he must have made for the Medici family his bronze *David* (fig. 43), which is not only the first nude David but also possibly the first freestanding nude statue since ancient times (but note in fig. 49 that Nanni di Banco shows a sculptor carving one). It is an astonishing work, whose beauty derives more from the sinuous grace of Donatello's line and surface than from the physical properties of the soft and unheroic youth. The sculptor has exploited the contrast between the detached, impassive stare of the victor and the tragic expression of the severed head, with which David's left foot lightly toys, and between the fluidity of the brilliant surfaces of bronze and the opaque roughness of the shaggy hair. In assessing the meaning of the statue, clothed only in open-toed leather boots and a laurel-crowned hat, it should be remembered that in the Middle Ages and in the Renaissance David's conquest of Goliath symbolized Christ's victory over sin and death, and that nudity still meant the nakedness of the soul before God. So despite its ambiguous appearance the statue may have had a moralistic content.

In 1443 Donatello was called to Padua to create a colossal equestrian statue in bronze (fig. 44), representing the Venetian general Erasmo da Narni, nicknamed for some unknown reason Gattamelata ("Calico Cat"), which still stands on its original pedestal before the Basilica of

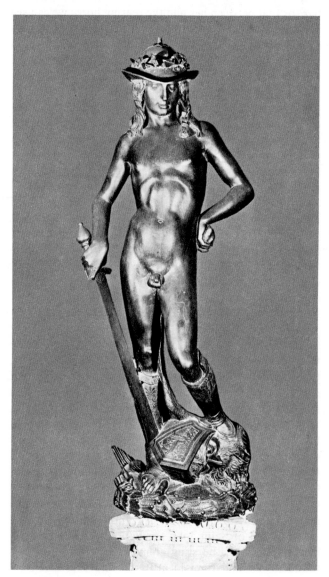

43. DONATELLO. *David.* c. 1430–32. Bronze, height 62¼". Museo Nazionale del Bargello, Florence

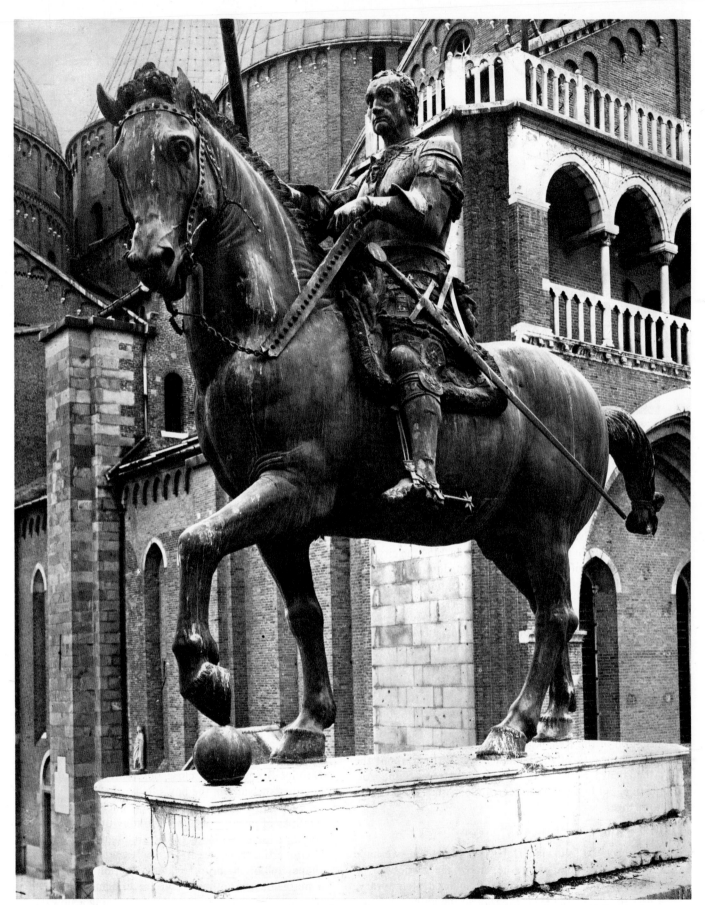

44. DONATELLO. *Equestrian Monument of Gattamelata.* 1443–53. Bronze, height 12'2". Piazza del Santo, Padua

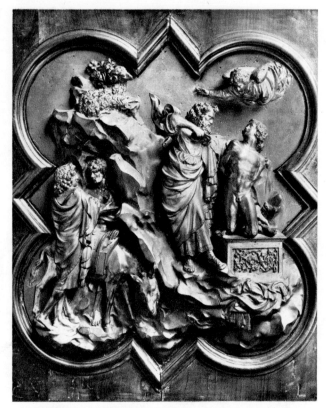

45. LORENZO GHIBERTI. *Sacrifice of Isaac*, from the
competition to design the North doors of the
Baptistery of S. Giovanni, Florence. 1401–2.
Gilded bronze relief, 21 x 17½″ (inside molding).
Museo Nazionale del Bargello, Florence

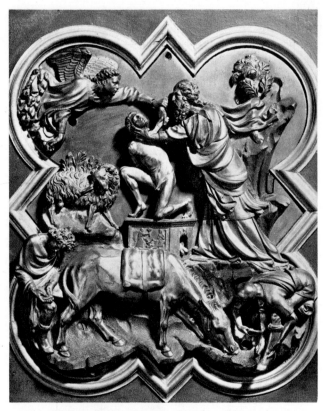

46. FILIPPO BRUNELLESCHI. *Sacrifice of Isaac,* from
the competition to design the North doors of
the Baptistery of S. Giovanni, Florence. 1401–2.
Gilded bronze relief, 21 x 17½″ (inside molding).
Museo Nazionale del Bargello, Florence

than a likeness; Donatello could never have seen Gattamelata, who died at an advanced age years before the
sculptor's arrival in Padua.

On Donatello's return to Florence in 1454 the city was
in the throes of a religious reaction dominated by its
archbishop, later canonized as Saint Antonine. Donatello
in his later years seems to have been swept along by this
antihumanist current, whose effects are evident in his
Mary Magdalene (colorplate 4), c. 1454–55. This
polychromed wooden statue shows the Magdalene in
penitent old age clothed only in her own matted hair,
which a recent cleaning has revealed to be lighted by
streaks of gold. Horrifying in its extreme emaciation, but
even more because of the air of spiritual desolation that
radiates from the ravaged features, this work seems the
negation of the Renaissance faith in the nobility of man
and the beauty of the human body. Writing about the
Magdalene, Saint Antonine quotes from Saint Augustine, "O body, mass of corruption, what have I to do
with thee?"

GHIBERTI. In following Donatello's long life, we have
gone past the point where he shared the glories of the
Early Renaissance with his slightly older contemporary,
Lorenzo Ghiberti (1381?–1455), also the author of three
statues at Orsanmichele, but important for this book on
account of his two sets of gilded bronze doors for the

Baptistery of Florence, especially the second, known as
the *Gates of Paradise*. Ghiberti won the commission in
competition with several other Tuscan sculptors, including Jacopo della Quercia, whose entries are lost. In
the finals, in 1401–2, he found himself competing only
with Brunelleschi, then still a sculptor, and their sample
reliefs in bronze (figs. 45, 46) with the figures and landscape elements gilded are splendid documents recording
the dawn of the Renaissance in the figurative arts. The
assigned subject was the Sacrifice of Isaac, and the required shape, the quatrefoil (four-leaf clover), was a
French Gothic form previously adopted by the sculptor
of the earliest set of doors for the Baptistery in the
fourteenth century. It is not hard today to determine who
won and why. Brunelleschi's relief shows the angel grab-
bing the hand of Abraham, who twists Isaac's screaming
head the better to thrust the sword into his throat.
Despite Brunelleschi's close observation of naturalistic
details, especially in the boy's body, the donkey, and the
crouching attendant, his relief is lacking in just the
qualities of linear grace and harmony of proportion that
we have found essential to his architecture.

Ghiberti's relief (see fig. 45) substitutes for the jagged
shapes and often abrupt and jerky motion of Brunelleschi
a marvelous smoothness and grace, achieved by curves
that move as if the figures were performing a slow dance,
following in their motions and in the flow of their drapery
the curves of the quatrefoil frame. This motion could be

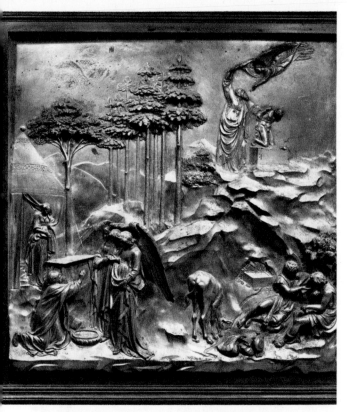

47. LORENZO GHIBERTI. *Story of Abraham*, from
the *Gates of Paradise.* 1425–50. Gilded bronze
relief, 31¼ x 31¼". Baptistery of S. Giovanni,
Florence

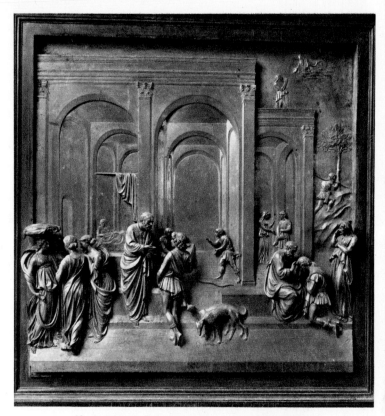

48. LORENZO GHIBERTI. *Story of Jacob and Esau*,
from the *Gates of Paradise.* 1425–50. Gilded
bronze relief, 31¼ x 31¼". Baptistery of S.
Giovanni, Florence

described as still Gothic were it not for an ease and
balance that make one wonder whether Ghiberti had not
seen Greek originals. His Isaac is surely the first nude
figure since ancient times to show real interest in the
beauty of the human body and knowledge of the interaction of its parts—a generation before Donatello's bronze
David.

In the doors themselves, whose execution took Ghiberti more than twenty years and whose subject was changed
to the Life of Christ, Renaissance elements enter
piecemeal. Only in the *Gates of Paradise,* 1425–50,
representing scenes from the Old Testament, did Ghiberti
assimilate the spatial devices of Donatello and the
architectural and perspective discoveries of Brunelleschi
and Alberti. His conception of the character of relief
sculpture changed, presumably after working with
Donatello on the font for Siena. Gone are the small
quatrefoils; instead Ghiberti has enclosed several
episodes from each Old Testament story in single, square
frames. Each entire relief is gilded, thus unifying figures
and background in a space suffused with golden light into
which we can look as into a picture. In comparing the
Story of Abraham as actually carried out (fig. 47) with
the competition relief, it is easy to see the depth and extent of this spatial revolution. As in Donatello's pictorial
reliefs, the flat background is dissolved, and the eye
carried by easy stages into great distances, past the scene
where Sarah prepares a table for the three angels, beyond

the rocky eminence where Abraham is about to sacrifice
Isaac, and between the trunks of lofty trees to the mountains on the far horizon.

Especially striking in all ten scenes on the *Gates of
Paradise* is the sense of space, not only *behind* the
figures—Donatello and, as we shall see, Masaccio (see
figs. 42, 55) had already achieved that—but *around* them.
This effect is managed by keeping the scale of the
foreground figures roughly the same as in the competition relief, within a frame whose area is quadrupled. Thus
at one blow Ghiberti has demolished the age-old convention of a double scale for figures and setting, and established a single, unified space in keeping with Alberti's
admonitions. This is evident in the *Story of Jacob and
Esau* (fig. 48). The open portico of Isaac's dwelling,
staunchly Albertian in the use of pilasters as decorations
and arches as supports, is Albertian also in the accuracy
of its perspective recession, taking the observer through
one arch after another into what appears to be great
depth, although the actual projections are never more
than an inch or so, and generally a mere fraction.
Renaissance art has here achieved a cubic graph of space,
in which the dimensions of every object and every person
are determined by the square on which he stands, and
therefore by his imagined distance from the spectator's
eye. The last traces of Gothicism in line and pose have
been transmuted into Hellenic grace and ease. Despite
their diminutive scale, such figures as the angry Esau

standing before his perplexed father or the three beautiful female figures at the left can be set against the masterpieces of Greek sculpture. Almost certainly this and the other reliefs from the *Gates of Paradise* provided inspiration for the youthful Raphael as he was working out the principles of High Renaissance style (see Chapter 3). All ten reliefs were modeled in wax by 1437, two years after the appearance of Alberti's *On Painting*. Well could Ghiberti boast that the new art of his time had achieved values unknown to the ancients. Like Alberti, Ghiberti was the author of a theoretical treatise, called in good Roman fashion *The Commentaries*, a remarkable amalgam of optical knowledge and Renaissance learning.

NANNI DI BANCO. A third sculptor highly influential in the development of the Early Renaissance was the short-lived Nanni di Banco (1385?–1421), the most openly classicistic of the entire group and, like Donatello and Ghiberti, entrusted with the sculptures for three niches at Orsanmichele. The most impressive is the group of *Four Crowned Martyrs* (fig. 49) for the guild of workers in stone and wood, commemorating four Christian sculptors who, according to legend, preferred death to betraying their faith by obeying an imperial command to carve a statue of the god Aesculapius. Their conspiratorial gathering is as clearly topical as Donatello's *Saint George*. Nanni intended the observer to draw the comparison between the martyrs and the contemporary Florentines united in defense of liberty. In spite of their still-Gothic niche, the figures are dressed in mantles that fall about them like Roman togas and impart a Roman gravity. Both the mantles and the forthright carving of the individualized faces were doubtless emulated from Roman originals in order to reinforce by the example of stoic dignity the resolve of the Florentine republic in adversity. The stoneworkers in the scene below, who are building a wall, carving a column, measuring a capital, and finishing a statue, are dressed in contemporary clothes. To the end of his brief career Nanni opposed the optical innovations of Donatello, never violating the flat background nor sketching a detail he could carve in the round.

LUCA DELLA ROBBIA. Nanni di Banco's classicism was continued in a gentler manner by Luca della Robbia (1400–82), whose name was included by Alberti with those of Brunelleschi, Donatello, Ghiberti, and Masaccio as founders of the new style. Alberti must have been thinking of Luca's *Cantoria* (musicians' gallery; 1431–38; fig. 50) for the Cathedral of Florence, in whose reliefs the sculptor combined a Classical harmony of fold structure with controlled diminutions of projection to indicate depth, emulated from such a monument as the Ara Pacis, with the warm, contemporary naturalness of Filippo Lippi (see colorplate 7). Alberti could not have foreseen that Luca would not progress beyond this point. Luca did invent a new technique of producing architectural sculpture

in terra-cotta, glazed white for the figures, sky-blue for the background, and relieved by occasional touches of color in the ornament. This terra-cotta sculpture was not only cheap and resistant but also extremely effective in the decoration of architecture in the Brunelleschian tradition (see figs. 22, 27). Luca's many works in this delightful manner conveyed the grace and charm of his personality, but the technique was obviously limited. In the hands of Luca's relatives and successors, who operated well into the sixteenth century, it eventually degenerated into manufacture.

JACOPO DELLA QUERCIA. Alberti's inclusion of Luca della Robbia in his list of the founders of Renaissance art is no more surprising than his omission of Nanni di Banco and a contemporary Sienese, Jacopo della Quercia (1374?–1438), the elemental power of whose style entitles him to be ranked above every Early Renaissance sculptor except Donatello and Ghiberti. Alberti's oversight is especially remarkable since Jacopo was one of the runners-

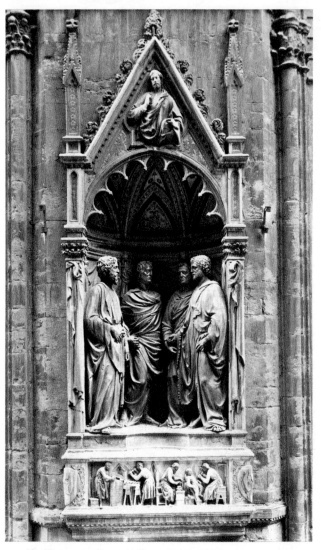

49. NANNI DI BANCO. *Four Crowned Martyrs.* c. 1413. Marble, life-size. Orsanmichele, Florence

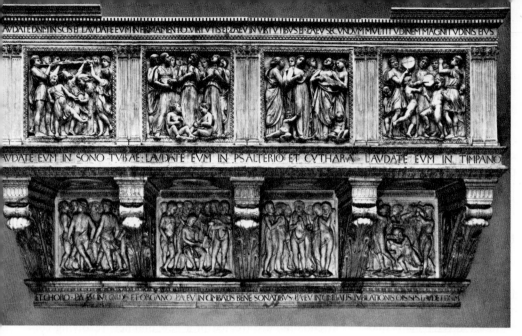

50. LUCA DELLA ROBBIA. *Cantoria,* from the Cathedral of Florence. 1431–38. Marble, length 17'. Museo dell'Opera del Duomo, Florence

up in the competition for the Baptistery doors, left important works in Siena and Lucca, and at the time Alberti wrote was engaged in carving the reliefs for the main portal of the Church of San Petronio in Bologna (figs. 51, 52). True, Jacopo's backgrounds were limited to the rock masses and miniature architecture familiar to us from fourteenth-century painting, but never since Hellenistic art had human figures been raised to such a plane of heroic action as in the San Petronio reliefs. In this respect Jacopo can be considered a real pioneer. His *Creation of Adam* and *Expulsion from Eden,* two of the San Petronio panels, were obvious sources for Michelangelo (see figs. 51, 52), and although the *Expulsion* was done after Masaccio had finished painting his version of the subject in the Brancacci Chapel (see fig. 55), it was derived not from Masaccio but from an almost identical composition in Siena by Jacopo himself, executed between 1414 and 1419 (too badly damaged to

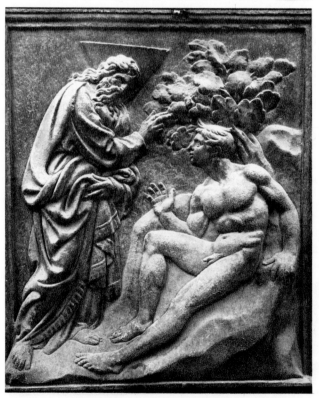

51. JACOPO DELLA QUERCIA. *Creation of Adam.* 1425–38. Marble relief, 33½ x 27¼". Main portal, S. Petronio, Bologna, Italy

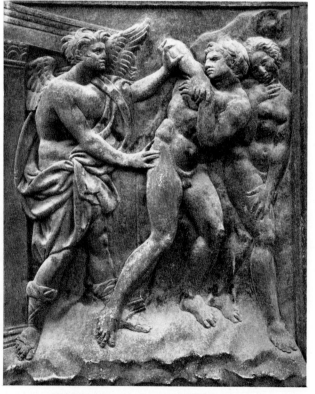

52. JACOPO DELLA QUERCIA. *Expulsion from Eden.* 1425–38. Marble relief, 33½ x 27¼". Main portal, S. Petronio, Bologna, Italy

reproduce here). In the first of these panels, the magnificent Adam, whose name in Hebrew means *Earth*, awakes from the ground at the Lord's command to a realization of his own power; in the second, in tragic contrast, Adam and Eve (the latter's pose surely derives from the Praxitelean Venus type) struggle helplessly against a powerful angel who lightly expels them from the gate of Eden.

PAINTING IN FLORENCE: THE EARLY FIFTEENTH CENTURY

GENTILE DA FABRIANO. The appearance in Florence in 1421 of Gentile da Fabriano (1380/5?–1427), a painter from the Marches on the Adriatic coast of Italy, marked the beginning of a revolution in the art of painting, which thus far had shown little interest in the developments that had just transformed architecture and sculpture. Gentile was probably in his middle or late thirties, and under strong influence from the art of the Burgundian region, where, as we shall see (Chapter 2), a vivid new naturalism paralleled in painting the discoveries of the Florentine sculptors. He had been highly successful in Venice at least as early as 1408, and later in other North Italian centers. If we judge by the completion date of May, 1423, inscribed along with his signature on his masterpiece, the elaborate altarpiece representing the *Adoration of the Magi* (colorplate 5), Gentile must have started it soon after his arrival in Florence. The altarpiece was painted for Palla Strozzi, the richest man in Florence, and he spared no expense. The Three Magi in the foreground stand or kneel before the cave of the Nativity and an adjacent ruin, inundating the desolate scene with the splendor of their richly colored and gilded robes, crowns, and spurs, and disturbing its silence with their restive horses and dog, and their chattering attendants, some of whom play with monkeys while others launch falcons upon their prey. In the distance the Magi and their train can be seen

journeying across sea and land, and winding up distant hills toward walled cities. Undoubtedly, Gentile had seen works, such as those of the Limbourg brothers (see colorplate 15), which this scene strongly recalls.

The Flamboyant frame, alive with prophet figures in the spandrels, the Annunciation in two roundels with a blessing God the Father in a third between them, and red-winged seraphim in the gables, and bursting with carved and gilded ornament, must have seemed both outlandish and outdated to Brunelleschi and Donatello. But the Gothicism of the frame should not blind us to the innovations of the painting itself. The horses are foreshortened in a manner unknown to Italian art before this time, and such figures as the groom in blue crouching toward us to remove the spurs of the gorgeously dressed youngest Magus, and the spherical heads of some of the attendants, are treated in a new manner, revolving convincingly in space. In the body of the altarpiece the landscape goes beyond Ambrogio Lorenzetti (see colorplate 3) in sheer extent, but shows no signs of assimilation of Florentine perspective innovations, and ends up with a gold background instead of a sky. Not so the predella scenes, set on little stages and betraying study of Donatello's *Saint George and the Dragon* relief (see fig. 40), and arcades looking a bit like those of Brunelleschi's Innocenti (see fig. 22).

Above all, the magical *Nativity* scene in the predella (fig. 53) shows a wholly new understanding of the nature of light. It is undoubtedly the first night scene we know in which all foreground illumination comes from a single source (in this case, the shining Child) within the picture. Clearly, Gentile must have experimented with an actual model of the ruined shed, the cave, and the figures, placing a candle in the foreground in order to study the way in which the light played upon the objects and the precise behavior of the shadows (the first cast shadows in Italian art). Nevertheless, the pool of spiritual light around the Child is still gold leaf. The scene, with the adoring Virgin,

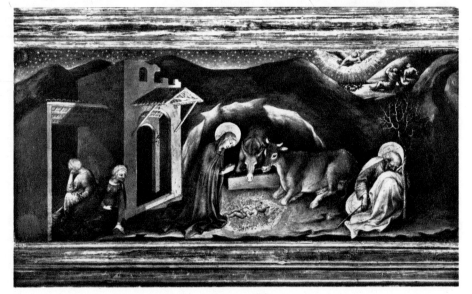

53. GENTILE DA FABRIANO. *Nativity,* from the predella of the *Adoration of the Magi* altarpiece. Completed 1423. Panel painting, 12¼ x 29½". Galleria degli Uffizi, Florence

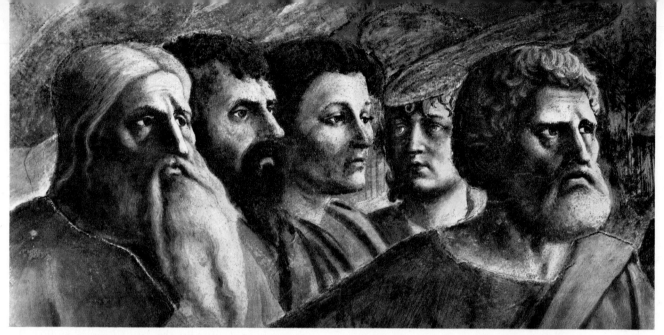

54. MASACCIO. *Heads of the Apostles* (detail of the *Tribute Money*). Fresco. c. 1425. Brancacci Chapel,
Sta. Maria del Carmine, Florence

the gentle animals, the sleeping Joseph, the curious
midwives, the secondary illumination from the angel
descending toward the shepherds on their dark hilltop under the stars, is intensely poetic. But its importance for
developing Renaissance painting is that here Gentile has
not only adopted but also extended the optical principles
first enunciated by Donatello in the preceding decade.
Gentile's altarpiece can fairly be called the most advanced painting in Europe in 1423. Such was the speed
with which Florentine painting was changing in the 1420s
that this claim was swept into the discard within two
years.

MASACCIO. An astonishing genius appeared upon the
scene to capture Gentile's title almost immediately; Tommaso di Ser Giovanni (1401–28?) was known to his contemporaries as Masaccio (untranslatable, but *Maso*
means *Tom*, and the suffix *accio* usually signifies *ugly*),
possibly because he was so completely devoted to his art
that he paid little attention to practical matters, including
his appearance. In his mid-twenties Masaccio
revolutionized the art of painting and, if the generally
accepted date of his death is correct, died just before his
twenty-seventh birthday. His innovations are visible in
the frescoes he painted about 1425 in the chapel of the
Brancacci family in the Church of Santa Maria del Carmine in Florence. A glance at the principal scene in this
series, the *Tribute Money* (colorplate 6), would seem to
place Gentile's *Adoration* two decades in the past instead
of only two years. The lessons of the new optical style,
which Gentile had learned piecemeal, were absorbed by
Masaccio at once and in their totality, and he created a
new and almost hallucinatory sense of actual masses existing in actual space.

The unusual subject, taken from the Gospel of
Matthew (17: 24–27), recounts how when Christ and the

Apostles arrived at Capernaum, the Roman tax-gatherer
came to collect the tribute; Christ told Peter he would
find the tribute money in the mouth of a fish in the nearby Sea of Galilee; Peter cast for the fish, found the coin,
and paid the tax-gatherer. The solemnity with which
Masaccio has endowed so apparently trivial an event
may well derive from its relevancy to a new form of taxa-
tion then being debated among the Florentines as a
measure for the support of their war of survival against
the duke of Milan. The artist has arranged the Apostle
figures in a semicircle in depth around Christ, with the
discovery of the money placed in the middle distance at
the left and the payoff at the right. The Apostles, as intense, as plebeian, as sharply individualized as
Donatello's contemporary prophets for the Campanile
(fig. 54), are enveloped in enormous cloaks that give
them not only the grandeur of sculpture but also a sense
of existence in space that recalls Giotto (see figs. 8, 9)
more than a century before.

But unlike Giotto, Masaccio has performed his
miracle almost entirely without the use of line, which for
him exists only when a mass of certain color and degree
of light overlaps a different mass. Form is achieved by
the impact of light on an object. Masaccio does not need
Gentile's candle in the darkness before a model; the actual light of the window of the Brancacci Chapel is
enough for him. The window, obviously to the right,
appears to throw light into the fresco as into a real space,
to send the towering figures into three-dimensional existence, and to cast their shadows upon the ground, just
as it affirms the cubic shapes of the simple building at the
right with actual light and cast shadow. In this picture
Masaccio proves the justice of a simple maxim in Ghiberti's *Commentaries*, "*Nessuna cosa si vede senza la luce*"
(Nothing is seen without light).

Giotto had attempted to take us only a few yards back
into the picture, where we immediately encountered the

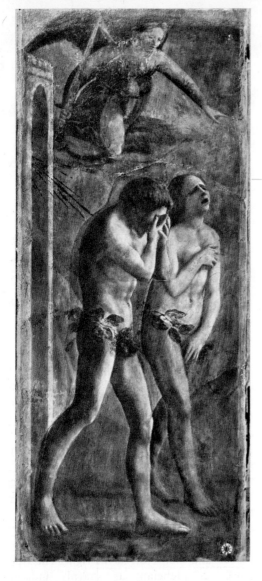

55. MASACCIO.
*Expulsion
from Eden.*
Fresco. c. 1425.
Brancacci Chapel,
Sta. Maria
del Carmine,
Florence

the doings of men. Here is a painting style to set beside the architecture of Brunelleschi and the sculpture of Donatello.

On the narrow entrance wall of the chapel, Masaccio painted his version of the *Expulsion from Eden* (fig. 55), obviously related to the composition of Jacopo della Quercia (see fig. 52), yet profoundly different. Quercia had characterized the scene as a losing battle between the resisting Adam and the expelling angel. In Masaccio the clothed angel floats lightly above, sword in one hand, the other pointing into a desolate and treeless world. Adam, his powerful body shaken with sobs, covers his face with his hands in a paroxysm of guilt and grief; Eve covers her nakedness with her hands as in Quercia, but lifts up her face in a scream of pain. Never before had nude figures been painted with such breadth and ease, their volume indicated almost solely by light and shade. Never before had man's separation from God been represented with such tragic intensity. By the late fifteenth century the Brancacci Chapel had become the place where young artists, including Michelangelo, went to learn—by draw-

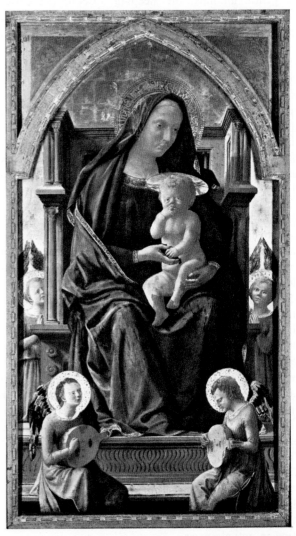

56. MASACCIO. *Enthroned Madonna and Child*, center panel of the polyptych from Sta. Maria del Carmine, Pisa. 1426. Panel painting, 53¼ x 28¾". National Gallery, London

flat, blue wall. Following Donatello and Gentile, but more convincingly than either, Masaccio leads the eye into the distance, over the shore of Galilee, past half-dead trees, apparently with new branches and foliage coming forth, to range on range of far-off mountains, and eventually to the sky with its floating clouds. The foliage, as indeed the faces of the Apostles, is painted in with quick, soft strokes of the brush, akin to Donatello's sketchy sculptural surface. The sense of real space is so compelling that we tend to forget the remnants of medievalism that remain (architecture and figures not yet represented according to the same scale). The setting is Florentine; the lakeshore resembles a curve in the Arno, and the mountains the familiar line of the Pratomagno, the range towering beyond Florence to the east. Even more, the simplicity and grandeur of the scene are intensely Florentine. Gone is the magnificence of Gentile's gold and of his splendid fabrics, along with the richness of his detail. Masaccio's style, characterized by Cristoforo Landino, the fifteenth-century commentator on Dante, as "*puro, senza ornato*" (pure, without ornament) deals in this sublime work with the essentials of man's relationship to the natural world and, even more, with God's mindfulness of

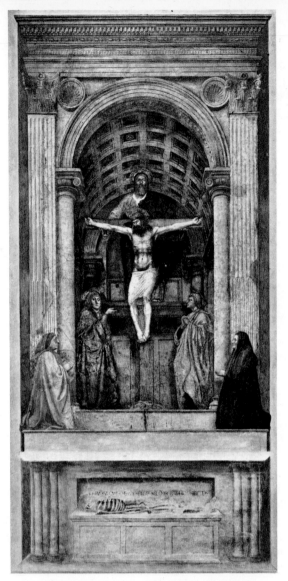

57. MASACCIO. *Trinity.* 1428. Fresco, 21'10½" x 10'5" (including base). Sta. Maria Novella, Florence

ing from Masaccio—the basic principles of form, space, light, and shade of the Renaissance style in painting.

Masaccio's *Madonna* (fig. 56), the central panel of a now widely scattered polyptych painted in 1426 for the Church of Santa Maria del Carmine in Pisa, is less than half the height of the *Madonna* by Giotto (see fig. 7), which it nonetheless rivals in majesty. In spite of the still-Gothic pointed arches used for the panels, and the gold background, possibly both demanded by the conservative Pisan patron, this is a fully Renaissance picture. Masaccio has set the Virgin so high that her feet are about at our eye level, and enthroned her upon a remarkable three-story construction with Corinthian columns, more or less in the Brunelleschian manner, whose suggestion of an actual building tends to increase the apparent bulk of the figure occupying all three stories. Masaccio's typical strong side light throws the figures, the drapery, the details of the architecture, even the angels' lutes into compelling relief against the shadows they cast on other masses. The Virgin, the Child, and the angels are homely

types, as if Masaccio were deliberately eschewing the tradition of physical beauty.

Probably the last work of Masaccio we possess before his departure for Rome and his untimely death is the fresco of the *Trinity* (fig. 57), whose painted architecture is so Brunelleschian that it seems impossible he could have painted it before the works we have just considered. The perspective view from below, which we have noticed in the *Madonna*, is employed systematically here to produce a striking illusion of three-dimensional reality; Vasari, indeed, speaks of the architecture as a painted chapel piercing the real wall. The Corinthian pilasters, similar to those that terminate the Innocenti (see fig. 22), flank a massive barrel vault, supported on Ionic columns two-thirds the height of the pilasters. Diagonals drawn from the Corinthian to the Ionic capitals would exactly parallel the orthogonals of the coffered vault. The viewpoint is precisely that of a person of average height standing on the floor before the fresco. Below the altar slab (now incorrectly restored), recent investigation has uncovered a painted skeleton, accompanied by an Italian inscription that reads in English: "I was once that which you are, and that which I am you also will be." On either side, on a step above the altar, outside the architecture and therefore in the space of the church, kneel two members of the Lenzi family praying for the soul of the departed, portraits of remarkable dignity and power. Within the painted chapel a solemn Mary and an adoring John flank the Cross of Christ, behind which, on a projecting pedestal, stands God the Father, his arms outstretched to the bars of the Cross, while the Holy Spirit in the form of a dove floats between the heads of Father and Son. The vertical pyramid of figures, from the praying donors through the interceding saints, intersects the descending pyramid of perspective in the body of the crucified Christ. Never have the essential mysteries of Catholicism—the sacrifice of Christ at the will of the Father to redeem man from sin and death, and the daily perpetuation of that sacrifice in the Mass—been presented in more compelling terms than in this painting, which sums up all that the Early Renaissance was trying to say.

FRA FILIPPO LIPPI. Masaccio left no gifted pupils; after his death the mantle of artistic leadership fell on the shoulders of two monks who could scarcely have been more different in their art and in their lives, Fra Angelico (see below), who was popularly believed to have been raised to the rank of *Beatus* (Blessed), just below sainthood, and Fra Filippo Lippi (c. 1406–69), who was eventually defrocked, and not a moment too soon. Placed in the Monastery of the Carmine at Florence by his father at an early age, Filippo was said by Vasari to have decided to become a painter when, at about nineteen years of age, he watched Masaccio at work in the Brancacci Chapel. A relatively early work, the *Annunciation* (fig. 58), beautifully placed in San Lorenzo, Florence, shows what this wayward master made of his artistic

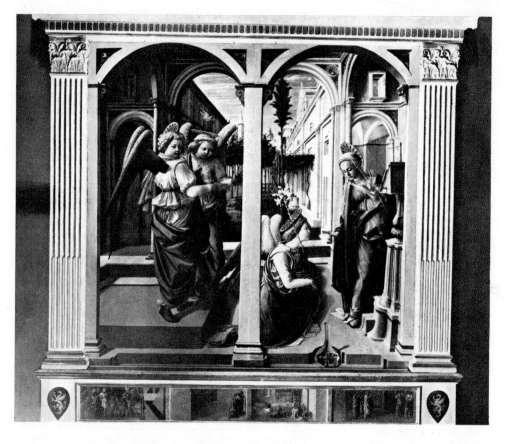

58. FRA FILIPPO LIPPI. *Annunciation.* c. 1440. Panel painting, 69 x 72″. S. Lorenzo, Florence

heritage. The cloister background starts as an inward extension of the vaguely Brunelleschian frame, but that great architect would have been less than pleased by the constantly shifting levels and odd architectural shapes and proportions. Nonetheless, the perspective view of the closed garden (age-old symbol of the virginity of Mary, drawn from the Song of Solomon) is delightful, with its trees and trellis and blue sky streaked with filmy clouds. Within the strongly Masaccesque light and shade of his deep space, Filippo has set not only the agitated Virgin drawn from her reading by the kneeling boy-angel, but also two supernumerary angels not mentioned in Scripture, one of whom looks out at the spectator while he points to the action, according to Alberti's directions for composing a picture. The chubby faces and blond curls, as well as the bright and sometimes arbitrary colors (one angel has bronze-green wings, another bright orange), have little to do with Masaccio's severity. The figures are powerfully modeled by direct light and deep shadow but, like all the elements in Filippo's paintings, are bounded by the neat, linear contours that Masaccio had rejected. An element of special beauty is the little crystal vase half full of shining water, in a niche cut out of the foreground step, from which the announcing angel seems to have plucked the lily.

Perhaps the finest example of Filippo's late, even more worldly style is the *tondo* (meaning *round*, a shape favored in the middle and late fifteenth century for pictures made to be hung in private homes) of 1452, representing the *Madonna and Child* (colorplate 7). The

wistful, delicate girl who posed for the Virgin is believed, following a tradition recorded by Vasari, to have been the runaway nun Lucrezia Buti, mother of the artist's son Filippino, and the principal reason for Filippo's expulsion. Painted with a grace that already points toward Filippo's great pupil Botticelli, the foreground figures introduce us to agreeable views into an upper-class Florentine home of the fifteenth century, with its cubic rooms and marble floors, as a setting for the Birth of the Virgin on the left and the Meeting of Joachim and Anna on the right. In this elegant world the severity of Masaccio has been all but forgotten.

FRA ANGELICO. Somewhat older than Masaccio but, if anything, more precocious, Fra Angelico (c. 1400–55) was still a layman named Guido di Pietro in 1417 and already a painter in the Late Gothic tradition. About 1423 he entered the Dominican Order, and eventually, succeeding Saint Antonine, became prior of the Monastery of San Marco in Florence. His unworldliness and his veneration for the tradition of Giotto (who came from the valley called the Mugello where Angelico was born) have perhaps been responsible for his incorrect classification as a "conservative" painter. Although he was closed—perhaps by choice—to the world of inner crisis so powerfully set forth by Donatello and Masaccio, Angelico was the greatest master of landscape and light of the 1430s. In 1438 he was mentioned by Domenico Veneziano (see page 52) as one of the two leading masters of Florence (the other was Fra Filippo Lippi) and in the 1440s was known at the papal court as "famous beyond all other Italian painters."

Well before 1434, when Palla Strozzi was exiled from Florence, he commissioned Angelico to paint a *Descent from the Cross* (colorplate 8) for the family chapel, the sacristy of the Church of Santa Trinita, where in 1423 he had placed the *Adoration of the Magi* by Gentile da Fabriano (see colorplate 5). The panel had been prepared and the Gothic frame carved and partly painted by an older master, Lorenzo Monaco, whose work was interrupted by death in 1425. Despite the initial handicap of the pointed arches, Angelico was able to create a composition of the greatest formal, spatial, and coloristic beauty, utilizing the central arch to hold the Cross and the ladders, and the side arches to embrace landscape views.

In keeping with its placement in a sacristy, where the clergy prepare to celebrate the Mass in which the sacrifice of Christ's body is perpetuated, the picture places less emphasis on dramatic elements of pain and grief than on the ritual presentation of the sacrificed Saviour. Bathed in strong sunlight, the scene sparkles with bright colors. The ground is a continuous lawn, receding into the middle distance, and dotted with wild flowers. A single rocky outcropping supports the Cross, and receives streams of the sacred blood from the footrest. The figures are scattered throughout the foreground and even into the middle distance, which is utilized more successfully than in any earlier Italian painting. At the left the Holy Women gather about the kneeling Mary, extending the shroud before her; Mary Magdalene kisses the feet of Christ. At the right a group of Florentines in contemporary dress, contemplating the Crown of Thorns and the nails, may include portraits of Palla Strozzi and his sons. The body of Christ, suffused with sunlight yet still showing the marks of the scourges, is reverently lowered, and at the same time displayed, by five men including John, Nicodemus, and Joseph of Arimathea. Although Angelico's reluctance to indicate the movements of the limbs within the tubular drapery masses makes his figures look at times Giottesque, he establishes them as freestanding volumes in space, modeled by light, in the manner of Masaccio. And in his delicate treatment of the body of Christ he shows an understanding of the nude worthy of the great contemporary sculptors.

The background landscapes are the most advanced in Italian art of the time, startling in the beauty of their space and light. On the left one looks over field and farm to the cubic, distinctly Florentine ramparts of Jerusalem, saturated by the late afternoon sun. A cloud mass has just rolled away from the city, as if in naturalistic explanation of the darkness that fell over the land while Christ hung upon the Cross. To the right, between the tall trunks of trees, the eye moves into an enchanting view of the landscape visible to the north of Florence, with rolling, olive-colored hills capped by villas and castle towers, receding range on range to the cloud-filled horizon. In

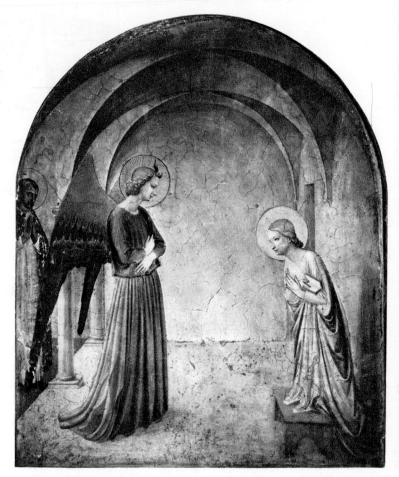

59. FRA ANGELICO. *Annunciation*. Fresco. 1438–45. Monastery of S. Marco, Florence

the poetry of this fully Renaissance picture, Christian mysticism is blended with a new joy in the loveliness of created things, transfigured by faith.

The mistaken notion of Angelico's conservatism, easily dispelled by the masterpieces of the 1430s, is doubtless based on his renunciation of natural beauties in order to enhance contemplation in the small frescoes he and his pupils painted during the early 1440s in each of the monks' cells in the Monastery of San Marco. In the *Annunciation*, for example (fig. 59), the background is reduced to two bays of a white-plastered, vaulted corridor. Mary kneels; the angel appears before her, along with the light. The rhythms of the architecture flow in harmony with the delicate, almost bodiless figures. Mary receives the Incarnate Word with quiet joy, as the monastic spectator, following the example of the adoring Dominican saint, was expected to do in solitary meditation. Superficially, the picture may seem archaistic, yet the knowledge of space and light proclaims it as a Renaissance work; so, in a deeper sense, does its appeal to the individual. This painting is the ancestor of some of the mystical pictures of the seventeenth century, above all those of Zurbarán (see fig. 315).

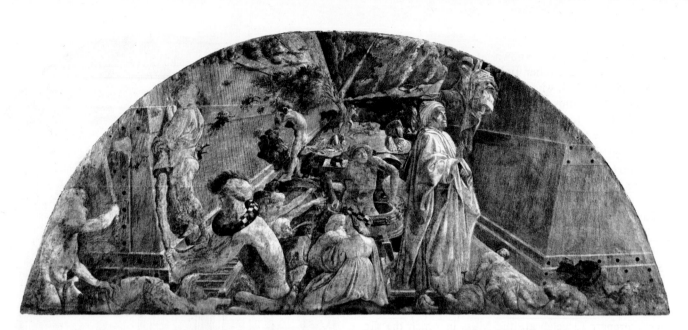

60. PAOLO UCCELLO. *Deluge.* Fresco. c. 1445–47. Chiostro Verde, Sta. Maria Novella, Florence

PAINTING IN FLORENCE AND
CENTRAL ITALY:
THE MID-FIFTEENTH CENTURY

UCCELLO. Albertian perspective is carried to extremes in the work of a beguiling master known even in the Renaissance as an eccentric. Paolo Uccello (1397–1475) is said to have burned the midnight oil over perspective constructions, including a seventy-two–sided polyhedron, from each facet of which projected a stick bearing a scroll, all projected in flawless perspective. His *Deluge* (fig. 60), one of a group of frescoes done largely in *terra verde* (*green earth*) in the Chiostro Verde of Santa Maria Novella in Florence, shows two episodes from the Flood within a single frame. On the left towers the Ark, its massive sides receding rapidly toward the vanishing point, just missed by a bolt of lightning, which illuminates the humans, clothed and nude, trying to keep afloat or clutching desperately at the planks of the Ark. Not only these but also a ladder with its rungs diminishing according to plan and even a *mazzocchio* (the wood-and-wicker construction that supported the turban-like headdress of the Florentine citizen), which has slipped down around the neck of a hapless youth, serve to exhibit Uccello's prowess in forcing unwilling objects to comply with the laws of one-point perspective. On the right the Ark has come to rest on a ground littered with corpses of humans and animals—seen in perspective, of course. Noah leans from a window of the Ark, in colloquy with a majestic, but still unidentified figure, reminiscent of the prophets and apostles of Donatello and Masaccio. Almost in spite of Uccello's obsession with perspective, the *Deluge* exerts great dramatic power.

This power is less evident in the three episodes from the *Battle of San Romano*, now split between three different museums, which once formed a continuous frieze in a principal bedroom of the Medici Palace. In one of them (fig. 61), showing the Florentine commander directing the counterattack against the Sienese forces, the hilly landscape near San Romano, in the Arno Valley near Pisa, appears only in the background. The foreground becomes a stage on which the artificial-looking horses with armored riders prance delightfully. Uccello seems less interested in the ferocity of battle than in the patterns that can be formed from armor and weapons. Broken lances have a tendency to fall according to the orthogonals of one-point perspective, and a fallen soldier even manages to die in perspective.

DOMENICO VENEZIANO. The new understanding of light and color brought to Florentine art by Fra Angelico was extended and enriched by an outsider, Domenico Veneziano (c. 1410–61) who, as his surname indicates, came from Venice. In a letter of 1438 written to Piero de' Medici, Domenico promised that he would show the Florentines marvelous things, never before seen. This he indeed did in his *Saint Lucy Altarpiece* (colorplate 9), depicting the Madonna and Child flanked by Saints Francis, John the Baptist, Zanobius, and Lucy, although it is clear that in turn he had learned much from the Florentines. The setting is partly Gothic, partly Renaissance courtyard of white, pink, and green marbles, whose pointed arches are supported on colonnettes resembling those by Michelozzo in the windows of the Medici Palace. Both the architecture and the intricate inlay patterns of the marble terrace are drawn in strict adherence to one-point perspective. The projection of figures and drapery and the close attention to anatomical construction, as well as the firm modeling of the features, betray careful study of the great sculptural and pictorial

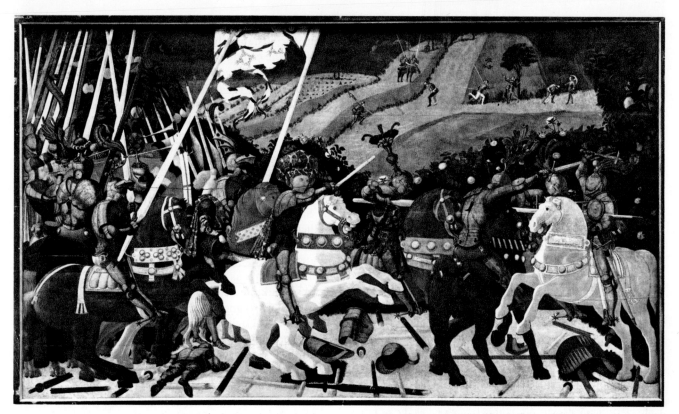

61. PAOLO UCCELLO. *Battle of San Romano.* c. 1445. Panel painting, 6' x 10'6". National Gallery, London

achievements of the founders of the Florentine Renaissance. But the chiaroscuro of the Masaccio-Filippo Lippi tradition and the brilliant coloring of Fra Angelico are alike muted by a new sensitivity to the effects of light. There are no dark shadows in Domenico's masterpiece. The figures and much of the architecture are saturated with sunlight, but so indeed are the shadows—with light reflected from the polished marble surfaces. Domenico takes a special delight in observing how the colors of the marble niche behind the Virgin are transformed as the eye moves from light to shadow, just as he sets intense greens against luminous blues in the Virgin's costume with an un-Florentine sense of the value of a momentary dissonance in the enrichment of an allover harmonic structure of color. Entirely his own, too, is the exquisite grace in his observation of faces, particularly that of Saint Lucy. The later work of Filippo Lippi, such as his tondo (see colorplate 7), was deeply influenced by the new poetry of light introduced into Florence by Domenico. The predella panels of the *Saint Lucy Altarpiece,* each a miracle of light and color, have been widely scattered; the most surprising is perhaps the tiny panel representing *Saint John the Baptist in the Desert* (fig. 62), in which Domenico was able to combine his native feeling for sunlight with a knowledge of the nude worthy of Ghiberti or Donatello. The youthful saint is shown wistfully shedding his garments in the wilderness in order to don a camel's skin. Domenico has turned the incident into an almost pagan enjoyment of the body; the boy seems to revel in the sunlight, which pours upon him from above and is reflected from the spiring rocks. The

brushwork with which the artist has depicted the scrubby vegetation is remarkable for its freedom from any Gothic linear convention, recalling the sketchy foliage in Masaccio's *Tribute Money* (see colorplate 6).

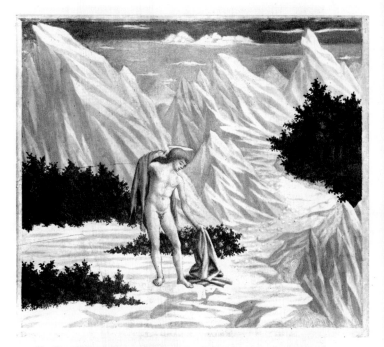

62. DOMENICO VENEZIANO. *Saint John the Baptist in the Desert,* from the predella of the *Saint Lucy Altarpiece.* c. 1445. Panel painting, 11 x 12¾". National Gallery of Art, Washington, D.C. Samuel H. Kress Collection

CASTAGNO. The third great Florentine master at midcentury was the short-lived Andrea del Castagno (1417/19–57), who for centuries was believed, following Vasari's account, to have murdered Domenico Veneziano out of jealousy of the latter's skill in the use of the oil medium, until it was discovered that Andrea died four years earlier than his supposed victim. Nonetheless, other stories of the artist's irascible temperament make it probable that they have some basis in fact. (Whether Domenico used oil or not is a matter yet to be determined by scientific analysis.)

Today Castagno's best-known work is the fresco of the *Last Supper*, which, situated in the refectory of the convent of Sant'Apollonia in Florence, then a convent of nuns *in clausura*, must have been impossible for an outsider to see in the Renaissance (fig. 63). Following a doctrine that the monastic life is a living death, Castagno paneled the room in which the Last Supper takes place (and which sanctifies the daily meals of the nuns) with a marble paneling strikingly similar to that used in contemporary Florentine tombs (see esp. fig. 67). Although the construction gives a convincing illusion that the spectator is looking into a stage lighted by actual windows from the right, this effect is achieved by the handling of light and dark on massive forms, reminding us of Masaccio and of the statues at Orsanmichele and on the Campanile—poles apart from the soft textures and glowing sunlight of Domenico Veneziano. An experiment with a straight edge will show the reader that the painter has ignored the laws of one-point perspective; there is no vanishing point governing the recession of the orthogonals,

and the distance between the transversals is uniform, both in the ceiling and the floor, instead of diminishing as it ought.

Castagno's mountaineer background seems to have affected his choice of rugged types for the Apostles, indeed even for Christ. He conceived the scene within a tradition of Last Suppers painted for refectories, in which Judas is easily distinguishable, given a chair by himself on the outside. The moment chosen for illustration is that in which Christ signifies who will betray him by saying (John 13: 26): "He it is, to whom I shall give a sop, when I have dipped it." Some Apostles converse with each other, but most are shown in intense meditation, each apparently foreseeing the moment of his own death. Bartholomew, for instance (the third to the left of Christ), who was later flayed alive, folds his hands and gazes at a knife held up to him by Andrew. In a startling new way Castagno has managed to suggest intense emotion by the activity of the veins within the marble paneling, especially in the expressionistic violence of the veining above the group of Christ, Judas, the grieving John, and the skeptical Peter.

Castagno's sculptural figures can sometimes move with unprecedented force, as in his *David* (fig. 64), whose odd shape is explained by the fact that it was painted on a leather ceremonial shield. Two moments are shown in one; David is striding forward, his left hand raised, about to cast the fatal stone from his sling, and the severed head of Goliath is shown already lying at his feet. Admittedly a bit stiff, this is a remarkable experiment in the depiction of motion, soon to be investigated much more fully

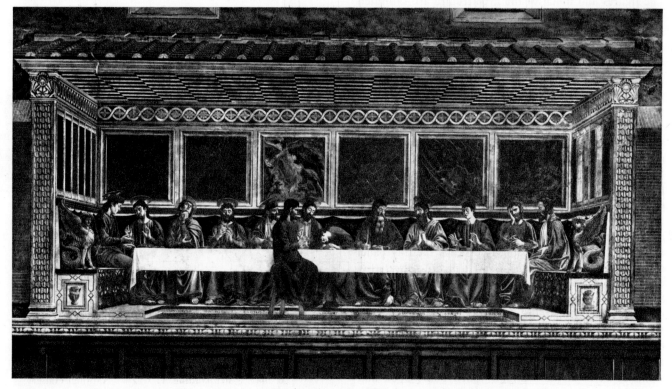

63. ANDREA DEL CASTAGNO. *Last Supper*. Fresco. c. 1445–50. Cenacolo di Sant'Apollonia, Florence

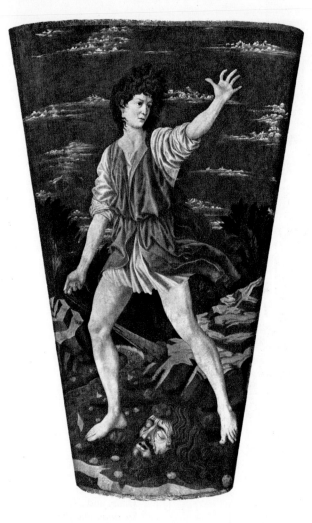

64. ANDREA DEL CASTAGNO. *David*. c. 1448. Paint on leather, height 45½″. National Gallery of Art, Washington, D.C. Widener Collection

by Antonio del Pollaiuolo (see pages 59, 60) and by the masters of the High Renaissance. Every element of the landscape background is painted with as much insistence on sculptural modeling and sharp contour line as the figures themselves.

PIERO DELLA FRANCESCA. For our own time the greatest Tuscan painter of the mid-fifteenth century is Piero della Francesca (c. 1420–92). He is, however, a relatively recent rediscovery, slighted in criticism before the beginning of the twentieth century. He seems hardly to have been appreciated in contemporary Florence, for that matter, for we know of only one sojourn there in 1439 as assistant of Domenico Veneziano. His work was largely done for provincial centers in southern Tuscany—Arezzo and his native Borgo San Sepolcro—and for the count, later duke, of the little mountain principality of Urbino. More than any contemporary Florentine, however, Piero managed to exemplify not only the knowledge of form that had been achieved by Masaccio and continued by Castagno, and of light and color in which Fra Angelico and Domenico Veneziano had pioneered, but

also the principles of space and perspective laid down by Alberti. In fact, in his later years, Piero wrote an elaborate treatise on perspective, postulating and proving propositions in the manner of Euclid's geometry.

Probably in the late 1450s Piero painted the majestic fresco of the *Resurrection* (fig. 65) for the town hall of Borgo San Sepolcro (now renamed Sansepolcro), on whose coat of arms the Holy Sepulcher appears. Piero has paid little attention to drama, but represented the event as a timeless truth. One foot still within the sarcophagus (whose paneling recalls that of the Bruni Tomb by Bernardo Rossellino and that of Castagno's *Last Supper*), the other planted on its edge, Christ stands as grandly as a Roman statue, gazing in utter calm toward us and beyond us. Below, the soldiers sleep in varied poses; above, we look into an almost barren landscape resembling the mountains above Sansepolcro. On the left the trees are leafless, on the right covered with foliage, doubtless a symbol of the rebirth of nature in Christ's Resurrection (see the discussion of the green and withered tree on page 15). The cool light of dawn has just touched the gray clouds in the sky, and bathes alike the marmoreal surfaces of Christ's body and the gently glowing colors of the soldiers' garments.

Every figural and architectural element in Piero's art was prepared for in perspective drawings, and simplified to bring out its essential geometrical character. Piero's severity, his concentration on geometrical forms, his stillness, and his cool luminosity of color often suggest the achievements of Cézanne in the nineteenth century. The grandeur and the mathematical basis of Piero's compositions are nowhere more impressive than in his great fresco series in the Church of San Francesco in Arezzo, dating probably from 1453–54. In the *Discovery of the Wood from Which the True Cross Was Made* and *Meeting of Solomon and the Queen of Sheba* (fig. 66), the queen kneels before a beam that, it has been revealed to her, will furnish the wood of the Cross, then is received by Solomon in the portico of his palace. The Albertian architecture, with its fluted Composite columns of white marble and its green marble panels, is no more strongly geometrical than the figures, especially the heads and robes of the attendants of the kneeling queen.

In Piero's later work he shows increasing evidence of having studied Netherlandish painting, and he used either an oil-and-tempera emulsion or perhaps oil alone to produce the effects of atmospheric perspective and of light on fabrics and jewels that characterize his profile portraits of *Federigo da Montefeltro* and *Battista Sforza*, count and countess of Urbino (colorplates 10, 11). There could be no more vivid illustration of the Early Renaissance belief in the inherent nobility of man and his domination over nature as expressed by Giannozzo Manetti (see pages 24, 25) than the ascendancy of these impassive profiles over the light-filled landscape. Doubtless at the direction of his noble patron, Piero has not concealed the deformity of Federigo's nose, mutilated in battle. His understanding of light enabled him to render the

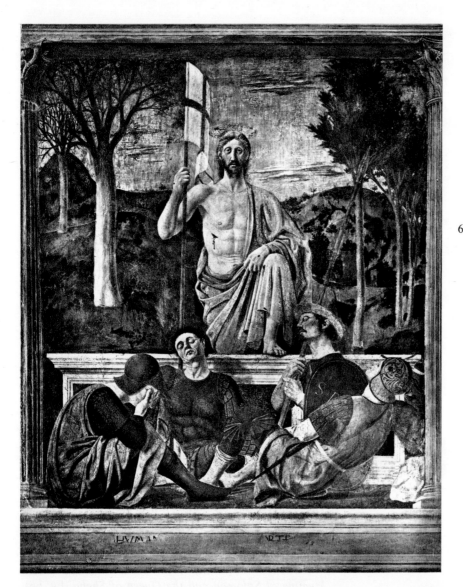

65. PIERO DELLA FRANCESCA.
Resurrection. Fresco. c. Late
1450s. Pinacoteca,
Sansepolcro, Italy

66. PIERO.DELLA FRANCESCA.
*Discovery of the Wood from
Which the True Cross Was
Made,* and *Meeting of
Solomon and the Queen of
Sheba,* from the *Legend of
the True Cross.* Fresco.
c. 1453–54. S. Francesco,
Arezzo, Italy

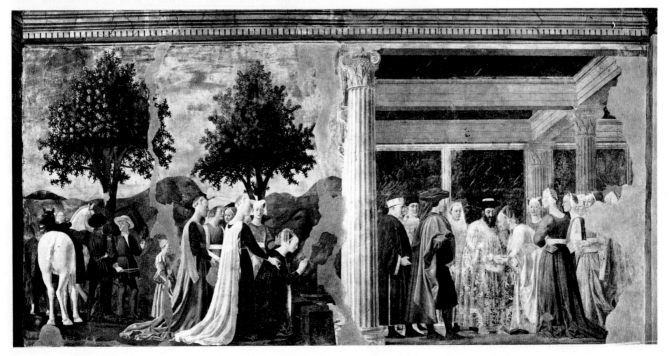

reflections of boats on a distant lake, the glow of sunlight from a chain of square towers as from a necklace of spherical pearls, and the softness of the haze that begins to dim the hills on the far horizon.

SCULPTURE IN FLORENCE AT MIDCENTURY

A number of gifted sculptors in marble carried well past the middle of the fifteenth century principles laid down by the innovators of the Early Renaissance. But aside from the last works of the aged Donatello few major monuments and no extensive statuary series were again attempted before the early sixteenth century. The role of the sculptor was reduced; he was called upon for funerary monuments, pulpits, altar furniture, reliefs that looked like paintings and were intended for private homes, and above all unsparing portrait busts of contemporary Florentines.

BERNARDO ROSSELLINO. The fourth of five brothers, all stonecutters from Settignano outside Florence, Bernardo Rossellino (1409–64) was an architect as well as a sculptor, and carried out the building of the Palazzo Rucellai (see fig. 31) from Alberti's designs. The architecture of the *Tomb of Lionardo Bruni*, erected for the historian, humanist, and statesman (fig. 67), is so far superior to anything we know Bernardo to have done by himself that it is probable that Alberti provided the inspiration and the design. After his death in 1444, Bruni was given a state funeral by the republic in "ancient style"; at its close the orator Giannozzo Manetti (see pages 24,25) put a laurel wreath on the dead man's brow. This event is immortalized in the monument, which shows Bruni recumbent on a bier, crowned with laurel, his hands folded upon a book, presumably one of his own.

Wall tombs such as this one were common in Florence in the Late Middle Ages and the Early Renaissance, but this is the first to be enclosed in a round arch, supported on Corinthian pilasters of great elegance. The tomb is colorful with three red porphyry panels set in white marble frames, but originally it was even more so; many of the details, especially the sculptured damask covering the bier, were painted and gilded. On the sarcophagus a tablet bears a Latin inscription recording how the Muses mourned at the death of Bruni. Angels (or are they Victories?) in low relief, resembling the style of Ghiberti, uphold the tablet. Roman eagles support the bier. Nude boy angels (or are they genii?) steady an oak garland surrounding the rampant lion of the Florentine republic. In the lunette a roundel flanked by praying angels holds a relief representing the Virgin with the blessing Child. This mixture of Classical and Christian is typical of the ambiguous position of humanism in the fifteenth century. The face of the deceased was probably carved after a death mask, a universal custom at the time. Grand though it is, the *Bruni Tomb* tells us less about Bernardo's style as a sculptor than about the society the monu-

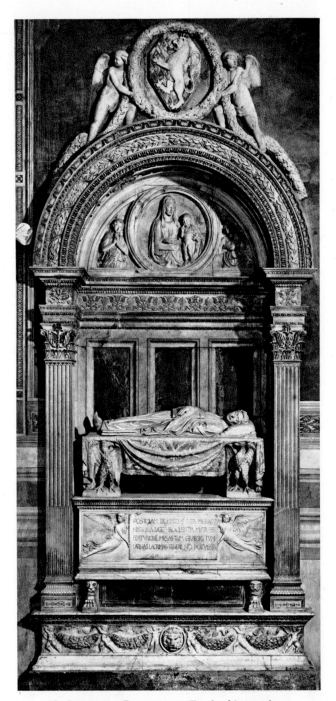

67. BERNARDO ROSSELLINO. *Tomb of Lionardo Bruni.* c. 1445. White and colored marbles. Sta. Croce, Florence

ment was intended to address. It became the standard for Florentine wall tombs for a generation.

ANTONIO ROSSELLINO. A far more sensitive and individual sculptor than his older brother Bernardo, Antonio Rossellino (1427–79) transformed the wall-tomb type established by the *Bruni Tomb* in his monument for the cardinal of Portugal (fig. 68), a prelate of royal blood who died in Florence at the age of only twenty-five years. The wall niche is retained, but the arch is partly masked by curtains carved in marble, drawn aside as if to show a vision. The youthful cardinal lies upon a bier above a sarcophagus copied from a Roman original. Winged angels kneel on either side of a cornice above him, as if they had just alighted; other angels, still flying, silhouetted in white against a solid porphyry background, carry a garland containing the Virgin and her smiling Child; against a blue disk dotted with gold stars the sacred figures look gently down toward the dead prelate. Forms and ideas that were static in the *Bruni Tomb* become dynamic in that of the cardinal of Portugal, which leads the way to the new sculptural action style of the late fifteenth century, especially that of Antonio del Pollaiuolo and Verrocchio (see pages 59–61, and figs. 73, 74).

Antonio's portrait of the aged physician, Giovanni Chellini (fig. 69), is one of the finest examples of the new type of portrait bust—head and shoulders, without ornamental pedestal—which made its appearance in Florence at midcentury. The glance is always directed straight forward, and the head never turned, raised, or lowered. Yet in spite of the rigid requirements of the mode, Antonio shows extraordinary sensitivity in the modeling of the wrinkled skin, which betrays the position of the underlying bony structure and yet is so smoothly polished as to reflect the gradations of light over the almost translucent surface. Above all, he communicates to us a convincing characterization of the old gentleman, learned, shrewd, yet kindly.

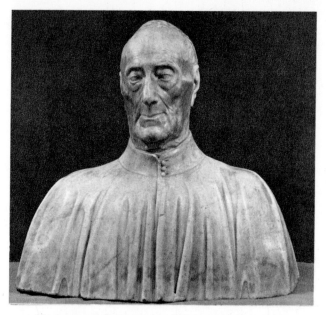

69. ANTONIO ROSSELLINO. *Giovanni Chellini.* 1456. Marble, height 20″. Victoria and Albert Museum, London

DESIDERIO DA SETTIGNANO. From a technical point of view the most remarkable of the marble sculptors is Desiderio da Settignano (c. 1430–64), who carried Donatello's relief style to a new pitch of delicacy, and was probably the finest sculptor of children the world has ever known. In a small marble tondo Desiderio shows *Christ and Saint John the Baptist* (fig. 70) as boys of about seven or eight, although no scriptural evidence indicates their meeting at that time; but, nonetheless, this was a favorite subject for painting and sculpture at midcentury. Saint John opens his mouth in speech, and places his hand on the wrist of the Christ Child, who gently touches John's camel's-hair garment. Clouds are shown in the background, and a soft breeze agitates the saint's curly locks. The gradations of marble have been so delicately handled that changes of a millimeter in projection alter the effects of light and shadow. Often details are blurred by filing so as to create soft, atmospheric effects as in painting.

PAINTING AND SCULPTURE IN FLORENCE AND CENTRAL ITALY: THE LATER FIFTEENTH CENTURY

In the last third of the century, few of the founders of the Renaissance remained alive; with the exception of Alberti, none were still influential. Florence itself had changed; under Medici domination, culminating in the rule of Lorenzo the Magnificent, the republic withered; so did the banking and commercial activity on which its prosperity was founded. Patrician life in urban palaces and country villas acquired a new tone of ease and luxury. Humanism was concerned less with the moral virtues of the ancients than with an elaborate structure of speculation that under Marsilio Ficino sought to recon-

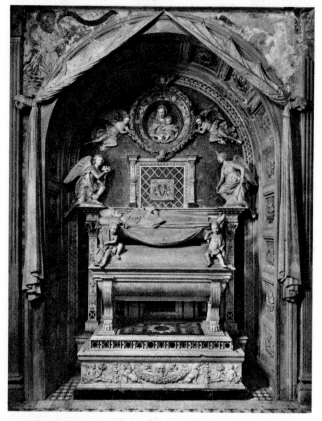

68. ANTONIO ROSSELLINO. *Tomb of the Cardinal of Portugal.* 1460–66. White and colored marbles. Chapel of the Cardinal of Portugal, S. Miniato al Monte, Florence

cile Neoplatonism with traditional Christianity. In the last decade of the century, Savonarola, one of the successors of Saint Antonine as prior of San Marco, sparked a religious reaction that united large sections of the populace against the Medici, who in 1494 were expelled for the second time from Florence.

During this period of deepening crisis, three major currents may be distinguished in Florentine art: a strongly scientific tendency on the part of painter-sculptors exploring the natural world and especially the structure and movements of the human body; a poetic tendency on the part of painters alone, inspired by Neoplatonism and characterized by withdrawal into a world of unreality; and a prosaic tendency on the part of both painters and sculptors, who sought to represent people as they were and upper-middle-class Florentine life under the guise of religious subject matter.

ANTONIO DEL POLLAIUOLO. The most inventive of the scientific artists, and incidentally the master preferred by Lorenzo the Magnificent, who spoke scathingly of Botticelli, was Antonio del Pollaiuolo (1431/2–98), tapestry designer, silversmith, sculptor, and painter. Antonio's major extant painting is a huge altarpiece representing the *Martyrdom of Saint Sebastian* (fig. 71), finished in 1475, for which three claims can be made: the background is the most extensive, comprehensive, and recognizable "portrait" of a landscape yet attempted in Italy; the figures are carried beyond anything achieved in the realm of action since ancient times; and most important, the composition itself is, for the first time in Renaissance art, built up from the *actions* of the figures rather than their *arrangement*.

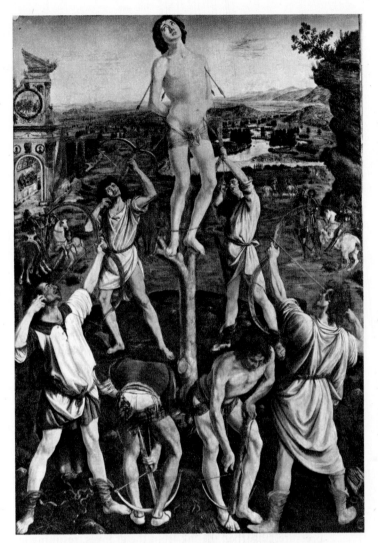

71. ANTONIO DEL POLLAIUOLO. *Martyrdom of Saint Sebastian.* Completed 1475. Tempera on panel, 9'7" x 6'8". National Gallery, London

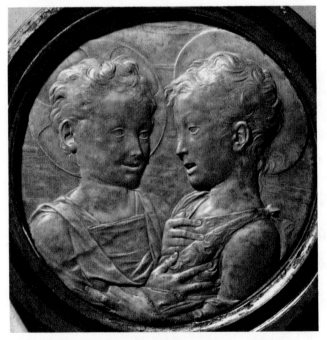

70. DESIDERIO DA SETTIGNANO. *Christ and Saint John the Baptist.* c. 1461. Marble. The Louvre, Paris

Let us take up these claims in order. Although the gap between the foreground and the middle distance, always the Achilles heel of a fifteenth-century painting, has yet to be bridged convincingly, the distant landscape is a view of the Arno Valley at the right and the telescopically remote city of Florence (difficult to make out in reproductions) at the left. The rich plain, the ranges and peaks of the Apennines at varying degrees of distance, the clusters of trees, the Arno rushing toward us—now dimly reflecting the trees along its banks in its troubled surface, now broken into turbulent rapids—have no parallel in the relatively schematic landscape backgrounds of Masaccio or of Piero della Francesca. For a competitor one has to look to the landscapes of Flemish masters, such as those of Jan van Eyck (see fig. 100), with some of which Pollaiuolo may well have been familiar.

The muscular figures, influenced by Castagno's

pioneer attempt at motion (see fig. 64), are shown under strain as they crank up their crossbows or pull taut their longbows to pierce the patient saint with their arrows. Pollaiuolo may even have made models from life, because the longbowmen at left and right seem to be the same figure painted from front and rear, as do the crossbowmen between them, differing only in their clothing (or lack of it). Finally, the figures form a pyramid not because of their placement but by virtue of their actions. The moment that the arrows are discharged the figures will assume other poses and the pyramid will dissolve. Whether or not Pollaiuolo could have foretold it, this kind of dynamic composition represented a long step in the direction of the pictorial and architectural principles of the High Renaissance.

Pollaiuolo seems to have placed mankind on a lower level than his Florentine contemporaries or forebears. In many of his works, humans are as cruel as wild beasts, for example, in his famous engraving entitled, for lack of any knowledge of its real subject, *The Battle of the Ten Nudes* (fig. 72). Before a background of dense vegetation ten men are slaughtering each other in a surprising variety of poses, unprecedented in their freedom of action, though as yet here and there uncertain in their precise anatomical construction. The medium of engraving, known earlier as a means of ornamenting suits of armor, was adopted at first by relatively few Italian artists, and this is an early example. The method consisted of incising lines on a plate of copper with a steel instrument called a burin, which dug up a continuous shaving of metal and left a groove. The plate was then inked, and the ink wiped off except that remaining in the grooves; a moistened piece of paper was placed over the plate and, under pressure, absorbed the ink from the grooves, resulting in a print or engraving.

Antonio's most brilliant piece of sculpture is a small bronze group representing *Hercules and Antaeus* (fig. 73). Antaeus was the son of the earth-goddess, invincible as long as he was in touch with her. Hercules broke this contact by lifting Antaeus off the ground, and then crushed him to death. Pollaiulo rendered fiercely the details of the struggle, and created thereby a new kind of sculptural group, as dynamic as his paintings and engravings. Head, arms, and legs fly off in all directions, against the embrace of Hercules, enlisting the space around and between the figures in the total composition. Pollaiuolo's invention of the action group was not taken up by his contemporaries; action groups were not seen again until the dynamic sculptures of the later Mannerists and the Baroque (see figs. 194, 237). It is worth mentioning that we know of nothing by Pollaiuolo in marble; only bronze, cast from a model in wax or clay, was suitable for compositions of this sort.

VERROCCHIO. Known to posterity principally as the teacher of Leonardo da Vinci, Andrea del Verrocchio (1435–88) tends to be overlooked. He was a good painter, but a superb sculptor, in fact the major monumental sculptor in Florence between the death of Donatello and the first large-scale statues of Michelangelo. His noblest work is the *Doubting of Thomas* (fig. 74), placed in a niche at Orsanmichele that had been carved by Donatello and Michelozzo for another statue in 1423. The loose grouping of figures—hardly more than high relief, for they have no backs—flows beyond the limits of the Early Renaissance frame. This composition is again dynamic, seizing the moment when Thomas is about to place his finger in the wound in the side of the risen Christ, who lifts his pierced hand above the Apostle and looks gently down at him, waiting for doubt to be dissolved by belief.

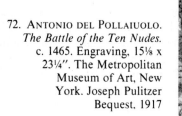

72. ANTONIO DEL POLLAIUOLO. *The Battle of the Ten Nudes.* c. 1465. Engraving, 15⅛ x 23¼". The Metropolitan Museum of Art, New York. Joseph Pulitzer Bequest, 1917

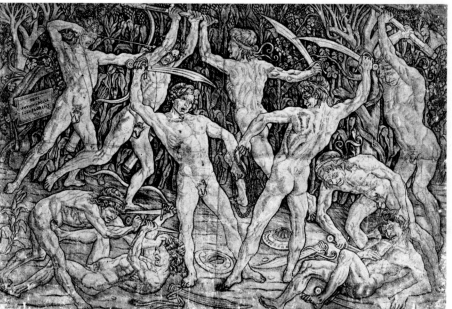

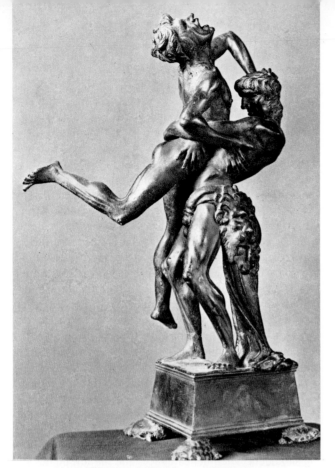

73. ANTONIO DEL POLLAIUOLO. *Hercules and Antaeus.* 1470s. Bronze, height 18″ (including base). Museo Nazionale del Bargello, Florence

The drama of the composition is enhanced by the vitality of the surfaces of hands, faces, and hair; the harsh realism of the open wounds; and the flickering lights and darks produced by the intricate succession of folds and pockets into which the drapery masses are shattered. Not a trace of the broad drapery construction of Donatello or Nanni di Banco remains.

Verrocchio's colossal equestrian statue of the Venetian general *Bartolommeo Colleoni* (fig. 75) invites comparison with Donatello's *Gattamelata* (see fig. 44). The Early Renaissance sculptor's conception of an ideal commander, wearing classicized armor, is replaced by a dynamic one of a helmeted warrior, armed with a mace, glaring fiercely as he leads his forces into battle. Placed before the Church of Santi Giovanni e Paolo in Venice, the composition builds up powerfully from every point of view, as the general twists in his saddle and the mighty charger strides forward. As in the *Doubting of Thomas*, the *Colleoni* is dependent for much of its effect upon the emotions of the moment and on the brilliant handling of surfaces, especially the tense muscles of the horse, his distended veins, and dilated nostrils.

BOTTICELLI. Among the painters of the poetic current in the late fifteenth century, Sandro Botticelli (1445–1510) stands alone in depth of feeling and delicacy of style. So intense is his concentration on line, so magical his research into the unreal, that it is hard to believe that he studied with Filippo Lippi, a follower of Masaccio. Although aloof from the scientific current, and criticized by the young Leonardo da Vinci, Botticelli was the leading painter resident in Florence in the 1480s and 1490s. He was profoundly affected by the preaching of Savonarola, turned to an intensely religious style in his later life, and after 1500 seems to have given up painting altogether. His most celebrated pictures, the *Primavera* (*Spring*; fig. 76) and the *Birth of Venus* (colorplate 12), were apparently painted at a slight distance from each other in time, the first on panel, the second on canvas (rarely used in the fifteenth century); Vasari saw them in the same room in the villa of Lorenzo di Pierfrancesco de' Medici, a second cousin of Lorenzo the Magnificent, and apparently the two paintings were then considered companion pieces.

Both have been interpreted in different ways, of late largely through the writings of Marsilio Ficino, leader of the Neoplatonic movement in Florence. While no interpretation of the *Primavera* is wholly successful, the most convincing is based on a letter from Ficino to his pupil

74. ANDREA DEL VERROCCHIO. *Doubting of Thomas.* 1465–83. Bronze, life-size. Orsanmichele, Florence

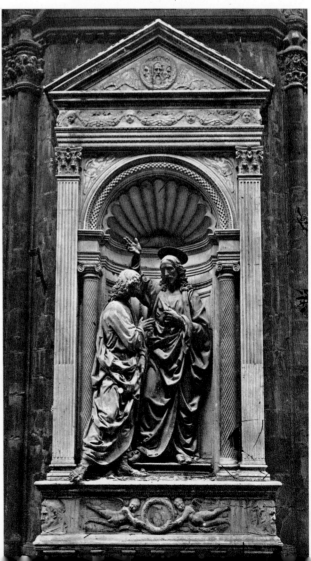

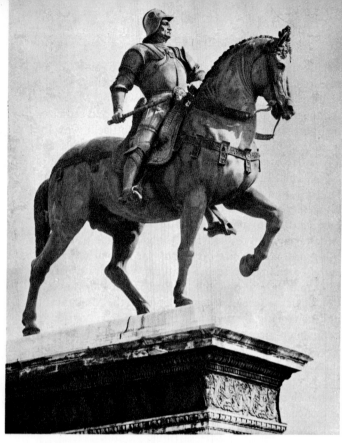

75. ANDREA DEL VERROCCHIO (completed by ALESSANDRO LEOPARDI). *Equestrian Monument of Bartolommeo Colleoni.* c. 1481–96. Bronze, height c. 13′. Campo SS. Giovanni e Paolo, Venice

Lorenzo, then a lad of fourteen or fifteen years, to whom the philosopher recommends Venus as his "bride" to make happy all his days. Lest such a recommendation to an Italian youth seem superfluous, it must be underscored that by Venus Ficino meant Humanitas, that is, the study of the Liberal Arts. What has been well described as a Christianized Venus, modestly clothed and strongly resembling Botticelli's Madonnas, presides in the midst of a dark grove of trees bearing golden fruit. At the right Zephyrus, the wind-god, pursues the nymph Chloris, from whose mouth issue flowers; she is transformed into the goddess Flora, clothed in a flower-covered gown, from whose folds she strews more blossoms upon the already flowering lawn. At the left stands Mercury, leader of souls to the other world, dispelling tiny clouds from the golden fruit. Between Mercury and Venus dance the Three Graces, emanations of Venus, as described in a passage from the Roman writer Apuleius and recommended by Alberti as a fit subject for painters, who were instructed to show these lovely creatures either nude or in transparent garments, dancing in a ring, their hands entwined. Botticelli has depicted this complex allegory in an image of utmost enchantment. As in all his mature works, the figures are extremely attenuated, with long necks, torsos, and arms and sloping shoulders. Their delicate faces and the soft bodies and limbs appearing through the diaphanous garments seem almost bloodless as well as weightless; their white feet touch the ground so lightly that not a flower or a leaf is

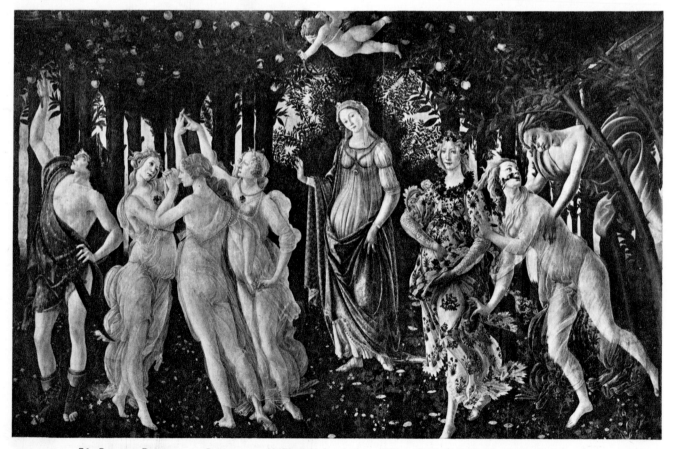

76. SANDRO BOTTICELLI. *Primavera.* c. 1478. Panel painting, 6′8″ x 10′4″. Galleria degli Uffizi, Florence

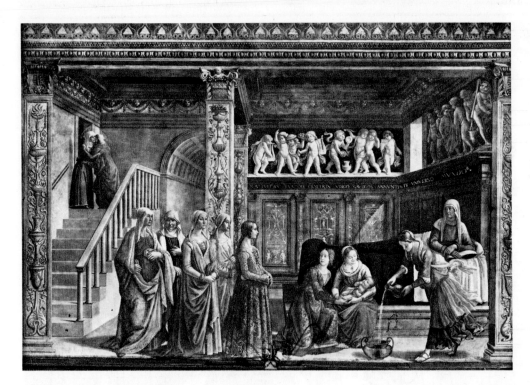

77. DOMENICO DEL GHIRLANDAIO.
Birth of the Virgin. Fresco.
1485–90. Cappella Maggiore,
Sta. Maria Novella, Florence

bent. Although individual forms are beautifully modeled, the composition is based on an interweaving of linear patterns, formed of drapery folds, streaming or braided hair, trunks, and leaves, like the many voices of a fugue. Such a picture, both in content and in style, represents a withdrawal from the naturalism of the Early Florentine Renaissance. Interestingly enough, Botticelli at this stage has renounced not only the mass and space of Masaccio and succeeding generations but also their strong coloring, preferring grayed tones of rose, green, and blue and pallid flesh colors.

The *Birth of Venus* (see colorplate 12), generally dated a few years later than the *Primavera*, is simpler in style, and may show the effects of Botticelli's residence in Rome in the early 1480s. Venus, according to an ancient myth, was born from the sea, fertilized by the severed genitals of the god Saturn; this cruel legend was interpreted by Ficino as an allegory of the birth of beauty in the mind of man through the fertilization by divinity. Upon a sea represented without concern for space, and dotted with little V-shaped marks for waves, Botticelli's Venus stands lightly upon—rather than in—a beautiful cockleshell, wafted by two embracing wind-gods toward a highly stylized shore. The *Venus pudica* (*modest Venus*) type, used by Quercia and Masaccio for Eve, now appears for the first time in her own right as Venus. But what a difference from the splendid Venuses of Classical antiquity! Botticelli's wistful lady, proportioned much like the Three Graces, uses the curving streams of her long hair, lightly touched with actual gold pigment, to conceal her nakedness, and seems hardly to be able to wait for the cloak that one of the Hours is about to spread around her. Again Botticelli's allegory is related

to the Christian tradition with which the Neoplatonists were trying to reconcile pagan legend; the composition has been compared to medieval and Renaissance representations of the Baptism of Christ.

While the unreality of Botticelli is a blind alley in the development of Renaissance painting, not to be explored again until the arrival of Mannerism, the brilliance and beauty of his line is not, and it may have influenced considerably the pictorial style of Michelangelo.

GHIRLANDAIO. While Pollaiuolo painted for Lorenzo the Magnificent and Botticelli for a learned elite, Domenico del Ghirlandaio (1449–94) pleased most of all the solid class of bankers and merchants who perpetuated some, at least, of the traditions of the earlier Renaissance. The host of frescoes and altarpieces produced by Domenico and his numerous assistants rendered his shop the most popular and prolific in Florence in the 1480s and 1490s. Not unconcerned with the rediscovered works of Classical antiquity, nonetheless Ghirlandaio had little interest in the mythological fantasies that charmed Botticelli and his followers. His solid paintings are conservative, still Albertian in their emphasis on one-point perspective and clear organization of masses, but matter-of-fact in their attitude toward subject matter. For example, when he filled the chancel of the Church of Santa Maria Novella in Florence with frescoes representing the lives of the Virgin Mary and of John the Baptist, he introduced contemporary Florentines in everyday dress as onlookers in the sacred scenes. He set the *Birth of the Virgin* (fig. 77), much as Filippo Lippi had (see colorplate 7), in a wealthy Florentine home, properly decorated with a sculptured frieze of

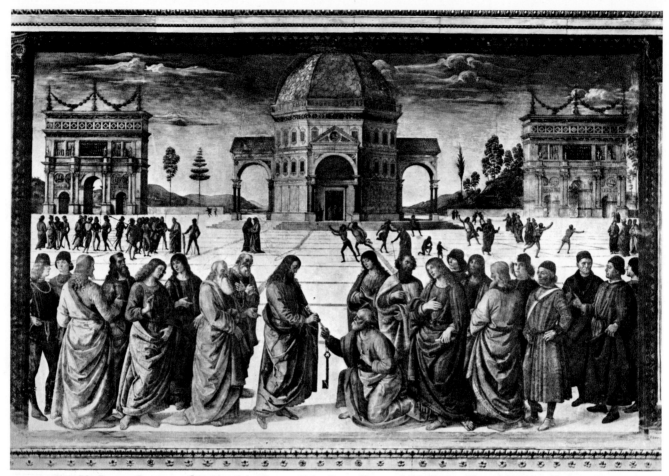

78. PIETRO PERUGINO. *Giving of the Keys to Saint Peter.* Fresco. 1481. Sistine Chapel, Vatican, Rome

music-making children above a wainscoting of inlaid wood. Ludovica, daughter of Giovanni Tornabuoni, the wealthy Florentine who commissioned the frescoes, appears, hands folded before her, accompanied by four ladies-in-waiting, all dressed as in real life, paying not the slightest attention to the event signalized in Latin capitals on the entablature. The workmanship is good, the drawing solid, the forms agreeable, the colors bright, and imagination is lacking.

Two outsiders complete the roll of major painters working on and off in Florence in the last decades of the century.

PERUGINO. A master from Perugia, the capital of the region known today as Umbria, Pietro Perugino (c. 1445–1523) was the leading painter of Central Italy outside of Florence in the 1480s and 1490s, with a flourishing school that included the young Raphael; Perugino enjoyed, in fact, considerable success in Florence as well. With Botticelli, Ghirlandaio, Luca Signorelli (see below), and a number of other painters, he was called to Rome in 1481 to decorate the walls of the chapel in the Vatican newly built by Pope Sixtus IV and known as the Sistine Chapel. One of Perugino's frescoes, the *Giving of the Keys to Saint Peter* (fig. 78), shows him at the height of

his powers. The figures are aligned much as in the paintings of Ghirlandaio along the foreground plane, and as in Ghirlandaio contemporary figures have intruded at right and left. But unlike Ghirlandaio, whose figures are often rigid, those of Perugino appear remarkably supple, in spite of their voluminous mantles. They unfold from the ground upward like growing plants, arms moving, heads turning, with a grace that is Perugino's own.

Characteristic of Perugino's art is his extraordinary sense of distance, partly achieved by means of Florentine one-point perspective, by which he constructs the vast piazza, with its scattering of tiny figures forming two more Gospel scenes. Entirely Perugino's own is the remote landscape, its hills sloping on either side to form a bowl of space and filled with soft atmosphere under a serene, blue sky. It is not hard to see where Raphael derived the grace of his early figures and the space of his landscape backgrounds.

The architecture in the middle distance, symbolic rather than real, places between two triumphal arches, modeled on that of Constantine, a central-plan structure suggesting the dome of the Cathedral of Florence, but adorned with four airy porticoes; this building probably signifies the Church that Christ is depicted founding on the rock of Peter, between relics of the power of imperial Rome.

SIGNORELLI. Since the lifetime of Luca Signorelli (1445/50–1523) spans the turn of the century (although slightly older than Leonardo da Vinci, he outlived both Leonardo and Raphael), it is hard to know whether to consider him an artist of the Quattrocento or the Cinquecento. For pure convenience he appears here in this book, although his major work, the series of frescoes in the Cathedral of the Umbrian town of Orvieto representing episodes from the Last Judgment, was influenced by the researches of Leonardo and the youthful works of Michelangelo. Some of the scenes, especially the *Damned Consigned to Hell* (fig. 79), represented the most daring venture into a composition made up of a great number of struggling nude figures. The whole scene looks like a colossal sculptured relief. At the upper right three archangels in shining armor exclude the damned from Heaven; they are carried off shrieking by demons into Hell, whose flaming mouth opens at the left. The foreground stage is populated with a struggling web of human and demonic bodies, the mortals colored white or tan, the demons parti-colored in shades of orange, lavender, and green. Fierce tortures are inflicted by the demons, who bite, twist, and tear at various portions of their victims' vividly projected anatomies. From such a work one would hardly realize that Signorelli had been a pupil of Piero della Francesca.

PAINTING IN NORTH ITALY AND VENICE

In the first half of the fifteenth century, Venice, the splendid city of the lagoons, empress of a chain of islands and ports protecting her rich commerce in the eastern Mediterranean, gradually extended her dominion over the North Italian mainland so that her frontiers reached within thirty miles of Milan. Becalmed in a local style

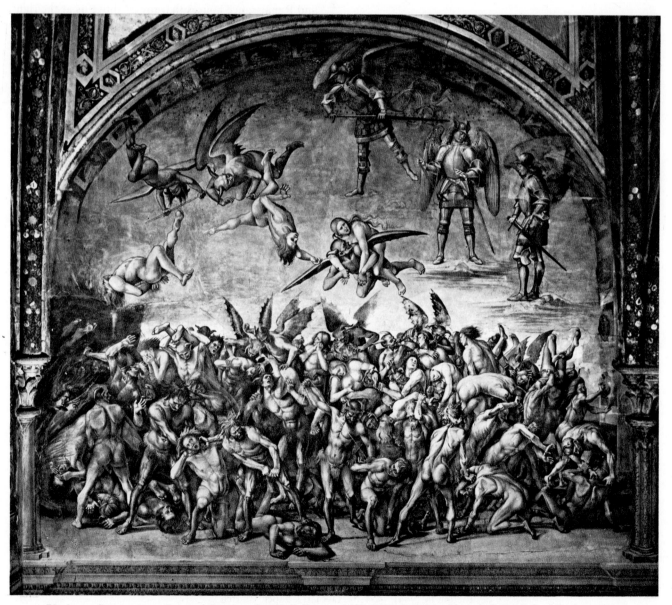

79. LUCA SIGNORELLI. *Damned Consigned to Hell.* Fresco. 1499–1504. S. Brixio Chapel, Cathedral of Orvieto, Italy

blended of Byzantine and Gothic elements, Venetian art was occasionally enlivened by visits of great masters from elsewhere. In their youth Gentile da Fabriano, Paolo Uccello, Filippo Lippi, and Andrea del Castagno had stayed for varying lengths of time and left traces on what remained a provincial art. But the eleven-year sojourn of Donatello, champion of the Renaissance, in the Venetian subject-city of Padua brought about a revolution in the art of the Venetian region. Florentine doctrines of form, perspective, and anatomy, not to speak of the Florentine ability to adapt Classical architectural elements to contemporary needs, took firm hold, and united with a Venetian predilection for richness of color and surface. Before long the last traces of medievalism disappeared from Venetian art, and a parade of great masters developed a new Renaissance style, which, in the sixteenth century, eventually/unseated Florence from her throne in painting and at least equaled her in architecture.

MANTEGNA. Already a full-fledged painter at seventeen, signing altarpieces on his own, Andrea Mantegna (1431–1506) was the first major North Italian artist to ex-

perience the full force of the Florentine Renaissance. In 1454, the year of Donatello's departure from Padua, Mantegna began, with several older artists, a series of frescoes in the chapel of the Ovetari family in the Church of the Eremitani in Padua. His competitors having been eliminated by death or discouragement, Mantegna finished the series himself in 1457, when he was twenty-six years old. *Saint James Led to Execution* (fig. 80) is a triumph of Renaissance spatial construction and Renaissance Classicism. The perspective is calculated for the eye level of a person of average height standing on the floor below, and the effect of figures moving in an actual space is even more startling than in Masaccio's *Trinity* (see fig. 57) because this fresco begins above eye level. Accordingly, the ground disappears, and as the figures recede and diminish, first their toes, then their feet, and then their ankles are cut off by the lower border. The vanishing point, below this border, controls the rapid recession of the Roman arch at the left and the medieval and Renaissance houses that tower above us at the right.

Mantegna's perspective, however, does not recognize a vertical vanishing point. In actuality, the vertical lines of the architecture should converge as we look up, but that

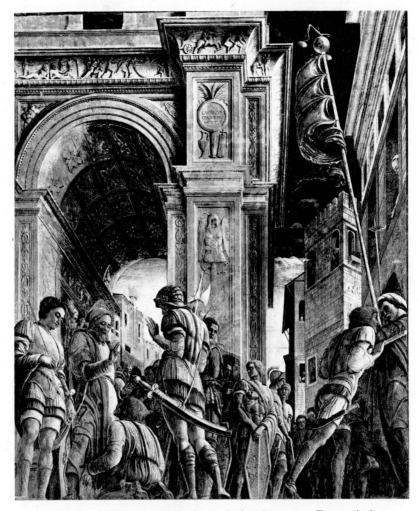

80. ANDREA MANTEGNA. *Saint James Led to Execution.* Fresco (before destruction in 1944). 1454–57. Ovetari Chapel, Church of the Eremitani, Padua

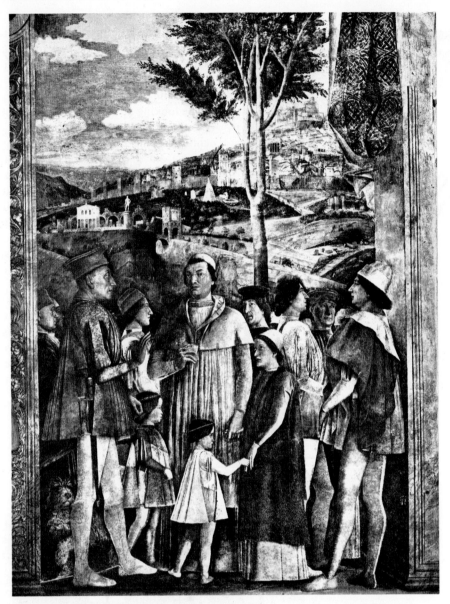

81. ANDREA MANTEGNA. *Arrival of Cardinal Francesco Gonzaga*. Fresco.
Completed 1474. Camera degli Sposi, Palazzo Ducale, Mantua, Italy

would have dissolved the unity of the wall surface with its superimposed rows of scenes and, consequently, was not attempted till the sixteenth century. Within Mantegna's carefully constructed space, the figures look like animated statues, carved rather than painted. But their marmoreal hardness only intensifies the drama. James, on his way to martyrdom, turns to bless a kneeling Christian who has broken through the Roman guards. The movements of the figures, the gentleness of the saint, and the emotion of the moment are as severely controlled as the perspective.

In Mantegna's maturity his austerity relaxed a bit, especially in the frescoes he finished in 1474 for the castle of the Gonzaga family, marquesses of the principality of Mantua, at whose court Mantegna remained as official painter until his death. Alberti, let us remember, had also been in Mantua more than once, and in 1470, when

Mantegna was already in residence, provided the designs for the epoch-making Church of Sant'Andrea (see fig. 34). The Gonzaga frescoes are continuous around two sides and over the vaulted ceiling of a square chamber, called the Camera degli Sposi, and represent scenes from contemporary court life. In one (fig. 81), the thirteen-year-old Francesco Gonzaga is greeted by his father, the marquess Ludovico, and by the bishop of Mantua, other dignitaries, and some charming children on his return from Rome, where he had just been made a cardinal. The background is not Mantua itself, perfectly flat, but an ideal Italian city on a conical hill; the circular walls are, of course, seen in perspective. Outside them can be distinguished assorted Roman ruins and statues. Mantegna still takes pleasure in geometrical forms and relationships, especially in the North Italian costumes. The coloring, vivid as it yet is, was undoubtedly more

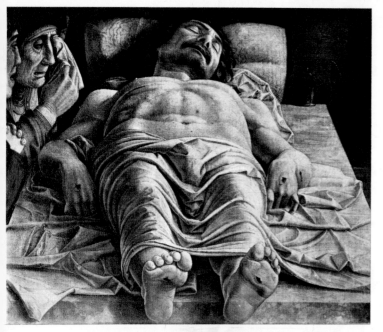

82. ANDREA MANTEGNA. *Dead Christ.*
After 1466. Tempera on canvas,
26¾ x 31⅞". Pinacoteca di Brera,
Milan

brilliant before certain portions, painted *a secco* (the hose of the marquess and the tunic of the central child, for instance), peeled off in the course of time.

The center of the ceiling is Mantegna's most astonishing perspective prank (colorplate 13). We seem to be looking up into a circular parapet as up through the mouth of a well, above which are sky and clouds. Winged children cling to the parapet, seen in sharp perspective from front and rear, and across one end runs a pole, which, if it rolled a bit, would allow a large tub of plants to fall on our heads. Ladies-in-waiting, including one black servant, peer over the edge, smiling at our discomfiture. With this odd beginning commences the long series of illusionistic ceiling and dome paintings that continued for three centuries and spread from Italy throughout Europe (see Correggio's dome fresco for the Cathedral of Parma, fig. 178).

Mantegna painted the *Dead Christ* (fig. 82) on canvas, probably late in life, and *in scurto* (extreme foreshortening), intended not as a trick in this case but as a device to bring home to the meditating observer with the greatest possible intensity the personal meaning for him of Christ's sacrificial death. The weeping Mary and John,

83. ANTONELLO DA MESSINA.
Saint Jerome in His Study.
c. 1450–55. Oil on panel, 18 x 14⅛".
National Gallery, London

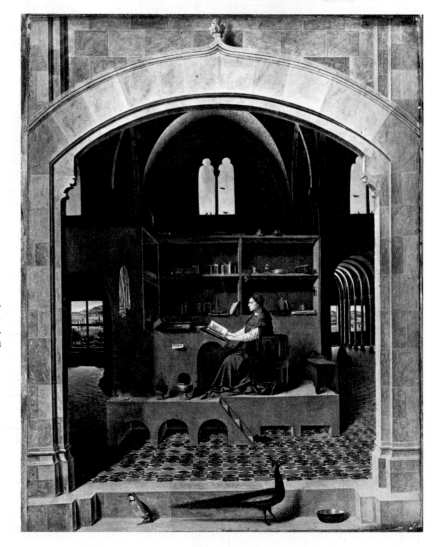

very likely later additions, jeopardize neither the picture's scientific exploitation of perspective nor its profoundly psychological effect.

ANTONELLO DA MESSINA. At this point an unexpected ingredient was added to the amalgam from which the great Venetian style of the Renaissance emerged, even more important, in fact, than all the science of the Florentine Renaissance. It is ironic that this essential element, the oil technique fully developed by the painters of the Netherlands, as we shall see in the following chapter, should have been brought to Venice by a painter from Sicily, which, since the days of its great Byzantine mosaics, had been something of an artistic backwater. As we know from the discussions of Domenico Veneziano, Castagno, and Piero della Francesca, oil painting, long known to the Italians in theory, was certainly practiced in Italy earlier in the fifteenth century, often in combination with tempera. But the little picture, *Saint Jerome in His Study* (fig. 83), painted in Sicily by Antonello da Messina (c. 1430–79) long before the artist's departure for Venice, was done in the oil technique, including glazes, as practiced by the Netherlandish masters, especially Jan van Eyck (see Chapter 2). No one has yet been able to determine where Antonello learned the Northern method, but his observation of almost microscopic detail and of minute gradations of light on reflecting or light-absorbent objects is so close to the great masters of the North that he must have had personal instruction from one of them. Antonello's eighteen-month stay in Venice, beginning in 1475, changed the whole course of Venetian painting.

BELLINI. Among the host of good painters who now appeared in Venice and its surrounding territory, the towering master in the last forty years of the fifteenth century, without competition until the appearance of Giorgione in the first decade of the sixteenth (see Chapter 5, and colorplate 26, fig. 160), was Giovanni Bellini (c. 1430–1516), who came from a family of excellent painters, and whose sister married Andrea Mantegna. The early phase of Bellini's incredibly long career shows, indeed, considerable relation to the austere style of his brother-in-law, but the arrival of Antonello put an end to all that. Without abandoning in any way the ideal breadth that is the essence of Italian art, Bellini was able to absorb rapidly all the wonders that the oil technique was to offer him. In his *Transfiguration of Christ* (colorplate 14), painted when the artist was perhaps almost sixty, he placed the scene in the midst of a subalpine landscape of a richness and depth that no Italian painter had been able previously to achieve.

A fence of saplings and the edge of a cliff separate us from the sacred figures. In traditional poses, Peter, James, and John crouch in terror, while on the knoll behind and slightly above them the Lord is revealed "in raiment . . . white and glistering" (Luke 9: 29) between Moses and Elijah in what appears to be merely the intensified light of the late afternoon; he stands calmly against the sky, apparently consubstantial with the white clouds above the distant mountains. Halos have disappeared as in Netherlandish painting; only a soft yellow glow surrounds the head of Christ. The long light models the Old Testament prophets and saturates the landscape and the distant towns at the right, while at the left a cowherd leads his cattle against the gathering shadows. In Bellini's art a new joy in nature is effortlessly blended with profound religious reverence into a landscape poetry the like of which had never been seen before.

When the great German painter Albrecht Dürer (see Chapter 7, and colorplate 31, fig. 195) visited Venice for the second time, in 1506, he found that Bellini, although very old, was still the leading Venetian painter. A work of this time, the *Madonna and Child Enthroned* (fig. 84) in San Zaccaria in Venice, proves Dürer's point. In a stately shrine, whose lateral arches open to sky and trees, the Virgin is seated on a marble throne. A soft light bathes her and the four meditating saints, and throws into shadow the gold and peacock-blue mosaic of the semidome above the Virgin's head. The solemnity of the composition, the perfect balance of the figures, and the breadth and freedom of the construction of the forms became the basis of the great Venetian style of the High Renaissance in the hands of Giorgione and Titian.

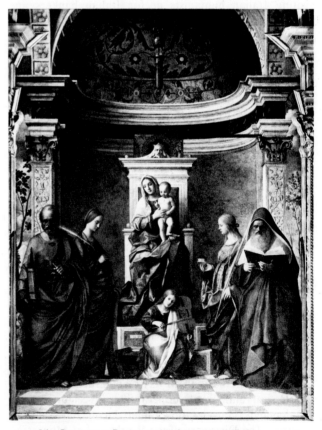

84. GIOVANNI BELLINI. *Madonna and Child Enthroned.* 1505. Oil on canvas (transferred from panel), 16'5½" x 7'9". S. Zaccaria, Venice

2

The Early Renaissance in Northern Europe

The developments we have just followed in Italy constitute only one aspect of a complex European situation, and cannot be entirely understood without a knowledge of the equally important events going on in Northern Europe, although not in architecture. France, the Netherlands, and Germany continued to build in the Flamboyant Gothic style, oblivious to the Classical revival in Italy. For that reason Northern fifteenth- and early sixteenth-century architecture is treated under the Middle Ages (see Vol. 1, Part Three, Chapter 9). For visiting Italian humanists or for Italian bankers and merchants looking out of the windows of their branch offices in Bruges, Ghent, or Paris, Flamboyant architecture can have held little interest; if we judge from written accounts, as we have seen, Italians considered it barbarous.

Painting was another story. The Italians looked on the achievements of the Northerners with openmouthed wonder. Here were kindred spirits! Even more—here were artists who had made visual conquests that to the Italians, notwithstanding their articulate theory, came as a total surprise. Cyriacus of Ancona, an Italian humanist who had been to Athens and looked at the Parthenon, recorded in 1449 his astonishment at beholding in a Northern triptych in the possession of Lionello d'Este, duke of Ferrara:

> . . . multicolored soldiers' cloaks, garments prodigiously enhanced by purple and gold, blooming meadows, flowers, trees, leafy and shady hills, ornate halls and porticoes, gold really resembling gold, pearls, precious stones, and everything else you would think to have been produced, not by the artifice of human hands but by all-bearing nature herself.

Even though the naturalistic achievements of the Northern masters can in no way be regarded as a rebirth of Classical antiquity, Northern fifteenth-century painting demands consideration under Jacob Burckhardt's heading "The Discovery of the World and of Man" (see above, page 24). In this sense Northern art is indeed a Renaissance.

The revolutionary developments of Northern art took place, for the most part, in the state of Burgundy. Through a series of gifts, marriages, inheritances, and treaties, the dukes of Burgundy in the later fourteenth and fifteenth centuries acquired piecemeal a region stretching from the Rhone Valley to the North Sea, including much of present-day eastern and northeastern France, all of Belgium and Luxembourg, most of Holland, and a strip of Germany. It all started when the duchy of Burgundy reverted to the French crown at the death of the last heir in 1363, and King John the Good took the ill-advised step of conferring the title and the lands upon his youngest son, Philip the Bold. Within decades Philip and his descendants had raised an eastern threat to their cousins, the kings of France, almost as dangerous as the English menace from the west.

Philip the Bold called numerous artists to his capital at Dijon, and another royal duke, John of Berry, Philip's older brother, brought equally gifted masters to his court in central France. The French artistic tradition seems, for the moment at least, to have played out; all the inventors of the new style in the North came from the Netherlands (modern Belgium and Holland), which, during the thirteenth and fourteenth centuries, had not contributed notably to the development of figurative art—save for the metalworkers of the Meuse Valley. In 1430 Duke Philip the Good (reigned 1419–67), grandson of Philip the Bold, transferred his capital to Brussels, where he held the most splendid court in Europe, profiting by the vast revenues from the prosperous Netherlandish commercial cities. In 1477 his son, Charles the Bold, lost his throne and his life in the Battle of Nancy against King Louis XI of France, and the rich Burgundian dominions reverted to other overlords (Burgundy itself to the French crown, the rest to the Habsburg Empire). But the Northern school of painting was by then firmly established, handing down its marvelous skill from one generation to another, and Bruges, Ghent, Tournai, Brussels, Louvain, and Haarlem became artistic centers to rival Florence, Siena, Perugia, Rome, and Venice.

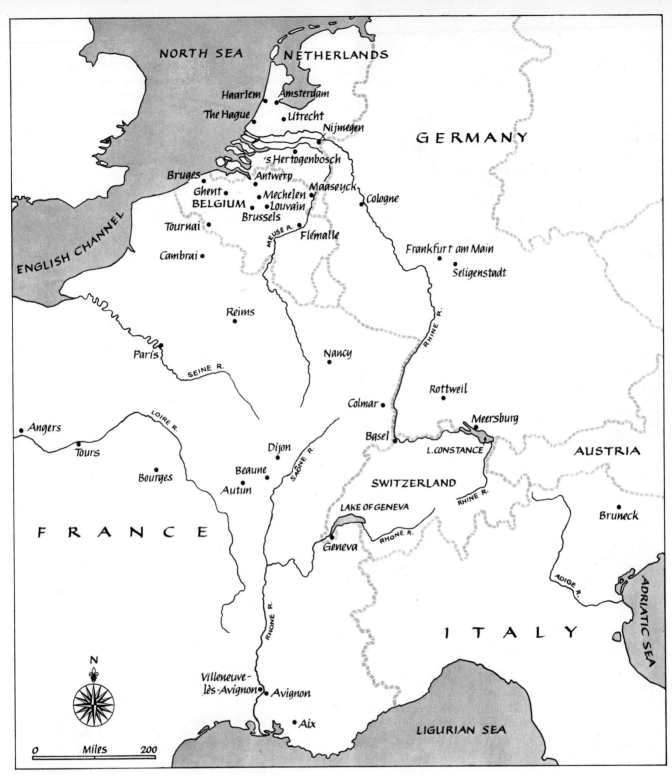

MAP 4. *North and Central Europe*

NETHERLANDISH ART IN FRANCE

We have already seen that Jean Pucelle was influenced by Italian fourteenth-century painting, and that at least one painter in his workshop may have been Italian. Other Italian artists came to France; the Italian masters at Milan Cathedral showed firsthand knowledge of Notre-Dame in Paris; Giovanni Pisano and Giotto probably experienced in person the majesty of French cathedral sculpture. Simone Martini we know worked at Avignon

from 1340 to 1344, and may have been to Paris. Doubtless, there were others. And whatever his country of origin, the painter of the *Wilton Diptych* must have passed through France on his way from Italy.

SLUTER. The first revolutionary developments in late fourteenth-century France, however, show no trace of this Italian heritage. The crucial figure is not a painter but a vigorous sculptor, Claus Sluter (active after 1379/80–1405/6) from Haarlem, near Amsterdam, who

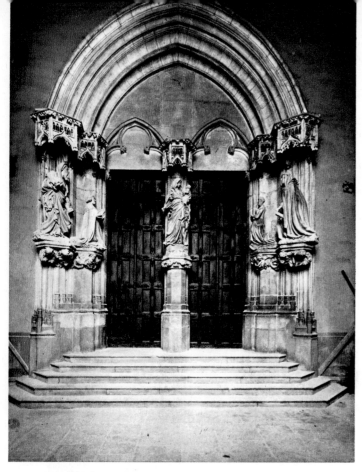

85. CLAUS SLUTER. Portal of the Chartreuse de Champmol. 1391–97. Dijon

arrived at Dijon in 1385 and was set to work as the assistant of the Netherlandish sculptor Jean de Marville, who had planned out the sculptures for the portal of the Chartreuse de Champmol, a Carthusian monastery built by Philip the Bold near Dijon. The Virgin and Child appear in their traditional place on the trumeau; the kneeling duke and his duchess, Margaret of Flanders, attended by their patron saints, on either side as in paintings (cf. the *Wilton Diptych*). At Jean de Marville's death, only the conventional Flamboyant canopies were ready. Sluter has imbued the portal sculptures with the sense of a dramatic event (fig. 85). Originally, the central canopy supported angels holding forth the symbols of the Passion (Cross, column, lance, crown of thorns, etc.), from which the Christ Child recoils in terror as his mother endeavors to comfort him. Passionate conviction radiates from these central figures as from the ducal couple and the saints; the billowing drapery movement that unites them has no more to do with the elegant excesses of the *Virgin of Paris* than the forthright portraits of the duke and duchess have with the saints of cathedral sculpture.

The only work that we know Sluter planned from the start is the *Well of Moses*, 1395–1403, in the cloister of the Chartreuse de Champmol; originally, the monument was a giant crucifix rising from the center of the fountain to symbolize the Fountain of Life in Christ. Only

fragments of the crucifix survive, but the pedestal with its six prophet statues and six grieving angels stands in its original position (figs. 86, 87). Sluter has dispensed with Flamboyant canopies; indeed, architecture of any sort is reduced to a secondary role, providing a perch for the angels whose powerful wings uphold the cornice below the original position of the Cross. From his projecting ledge each prophet juts forward, ignoring the architecture and holding a scroll bearing his prophecies of the sacrifice of Christ as he looks either upward toward the Cross, downward in meditation, or out into the future. The aged faces are carved with every facet of flesh, hair, wrinkles, and veins in a boldly naturalistic style that goes far beyond the impressive beginnings made by cathedral sculpture in the observation of reality.

Claus Sluter's revolution is immediate and far-reaching; in one thrust he has carried us from the delicacy of French court art to the humanism of the Renaissance. His fierce Moses, with his traditional horns (see Vol. I, page 335) and two-tailed beard, his body submerged by drapery folds as he holds with his almost veiled right hand the Tables of the Law, is a worthy precursor to the world-famous *Moses* of Michelangelo (see fig. 134). While we are admiring the powerful sculptural style of this majestic figure, the weary Daniel, and the tragic

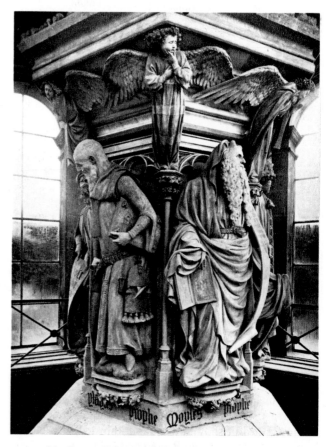

86. CLAUS SLUTER. *Well of Moses* (Isaiah and Moses). 1395–1403. Height of figures c. 6'. Chartreuse de Champmol. Dijon

Isaiah, we should recall that the naturalism of the moment required that these stone statues be completely covered with lifelike color applied by a professional painter; Jean Malouel, uncle of the Limbourg brothers (see below, page 74), finished the work on Sluter's statues, which had been started by a local painter. Considerable traces of color remain; one prophet was even supplied in 1402 with a pair of bronze spectacles.

BROEDERLAM. Sluter's exact contemporary was the Netherlandish painter Melchior Broederlam (active 1385–1409), who contributed the exterior painted wings for an elaborate carved and gilded altarpiece done in 1394–99 for the Chartreuse de Champmol. A delightful painter, if by no means a personality of the creative power of Sluter, Broederlam in his graceful style shows us the somewhat subservient role still occupied by painting—but not for long. His drapery motives are derived from those of Sluter, but treated more lightly and with great ornamental delicacy. The fantastic architectural interiors of the *Annunciation* (fig. 88) from the left wing recall remotely those of Pietro Lorenzetti, but diminish in perspective at a dizzying rate, just as the fanciful background landscape of the adjacent *Visitation*, which can trace its immediate ancestry to the rocky world of

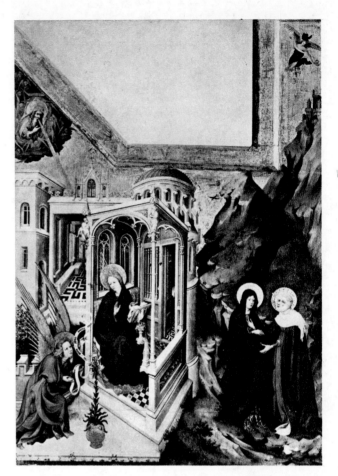

88. MELCHIOR BROEDERLAM. *Annunciation and Visitation*, exterior panel from the Chartreuse de Champmol altarpiece. 1394–99. Panel painting, 65¾ x 49¼". Musée des Beaux-Arts, Dijon

Duccio (see fig. 12), soars upward like flames. God the Father appears in the *Annunciation* waist-length in a circle of blue angels against the gold; from his mouth a flood of light pours through the tracery of Mary's window, which, as we have seen (see page 51), is a symbol of the Incarnation.

THE BOUCICAUT MASTER. Early in the fifteenth century a veritable genius, known as the Boucicaut Master after his principal work, the *Hours of the Maréchal de Boucicaut*, illuminated probably between 1405 and 1408, was at work in Paris. The patron who ordered the splendid book was a great soldier, whose military service took him to points as distant from France as Prussia and Mount Sinai. The artist may be identifiable with the painter Jacques Coene of Bruges, who was called to Milan in 1398 as an advisory architect for the Cathedral.

Since we will encounter other *Books of Hours*, an explanatory pause is in order. In contrast to breviaries, intended for the clergy, *Books of Hours* were written and illuminated for secular patrons. They contained, in addition to the prayers and readings for the seven canonical

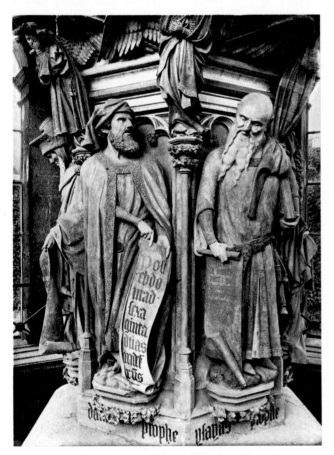

87. CLAUS SLUTER. *Well of Moses* (Daniel and Isaiah). 1395–1403. Height of figures c. 6'. Chartreuse de Champmol, Dijon

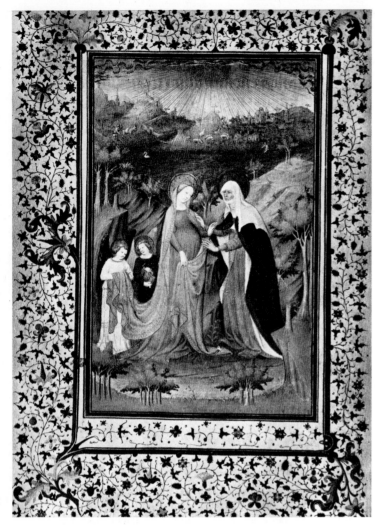

89. THE BOUCICAUT MASTER. *Visitation*, from the
Hours of the Maréchal de Boucicaut. c. 1405–8.
Illumination, 10⅞ x 7½″. Musée
Jacquemart-André, Paris

offices, an often varying selection of other services, including the Hours of the Cross, the Hours of the Holy Spirit, the Office of the Dead, various litanies, Masses for feast days, the penitential psalms, and a calendar of religious observances. They were illuminated as splendidly as the patron could afford with illustrations often not directly related to the text. The best of them were luxury objects in whose perusal our thoughts, like those of the patron, only now and then turn to pious matters; we are, as we were intended to be, lost in delight at the richness of the gold-studded borders and of the brilliant color, the delicacy of the style, and the manifold beauties of represented nature.

That the Boucicaut Master was an artist of unusual powers of discernment can be seen in the *Visitation* (fig. 89), a page from the *Boucicaut Hours*. The heritage of Classical landscape elements seen through Sienese eyes has been so thoroughly transformed that we hardly observe the traditional features. The Boucicaut Master has placed Broederlam's two figures in similar poses (but

how much more gentle and gracious!) in front of a distant scene in which we can distinguish a lake with rippling waves and a swan, a hillside with a farmer beating his donkey, grazing sheep (whose shepherd is down by the lake instead of looking after them), and a château with pointed towers, all indicated by delicate touches of the brush. This much we can parallel in Ambrogio Lorenzetti's *Good Government* fresco (see colorplate 3, fig. 16), but immediately above the hills and towers we notice what is the Boucicaut Master's historic breakthrough—just where Ambrogio stopped us at an inert background the Boucicaut Master carries the eye into the hazy horizon, floating clouds, and the bright blue zenith of an infinite sky. This is the first time, to our knowledge, since Roman painting that limitless natural extent has been recognized by an artist, some fifteen years earlier, in fact, than Gentile da Fabriano's Strozzi Altarpiece (see colorplate 5, fig. 53). The decisive step in the conquest of nature has been taken. But that it is still tentative, and that its consequences are as yet by no means thoroughly grasped is betrayed by the artist's retention of the traditional double scale for figures and setting, underscored by his introduction of tiny clumps of trees in the foreground less than a quarter the size of the figures. It should be noted that this enchanting painter has made a still further crucial distinction, that between real and spiritual light. In contrast to Giotto and Taddeo Gaddi (see Prologue, and figs. 9, 10), natural light in the Boucicaut Master is depicted as the eye sees it; spiritual light is rendered with rays of gold pigment ruled with the precision of an architectural draftsman. This distinction remained in Renaissance art with few exceptions until in his *Transfiguration* (see fig. 151) Raphael perfectly fused natural and spiritual light.

THE LIMBOURG BROTHERS. The next joyous assault on the real world was led by three young men, the brothers Paul, Herman, and Jean (also called Jeannequin or Hennequin) de Limbourg, from Nijmegen, now in Holland. They were nephews of Jean Malouel, who finished painting the statues of Claus Sluter. None of the three could have been born before 1385 and all were dead by 1416, possibly dying in the same epidemic that carried away their princely patron, the duke of Berry. He seems to have thought very highly of his three youthful artists, especially Paul, who by all accounts was the strongest personality and for whom the duke went to the unusual length of kidnapping a wife and settling the couple down in a lovely house in Bourges. When the duke's estate was inventoried, among the tapestries, jewels, gold and silver plate, splendid costumes of gold brocade and rich fur, and above all precious illuminated manuscripts (including some Italian examples) that this insatiable collector loved so dearly, and which filled his seventeen châteaux, were found the unfinished and unbound gatherings of a *Très Riches Heures* (*Very Rich Book of Hours*), which later, in the hands of another collector, were finished by a lesser master. The sections done by the

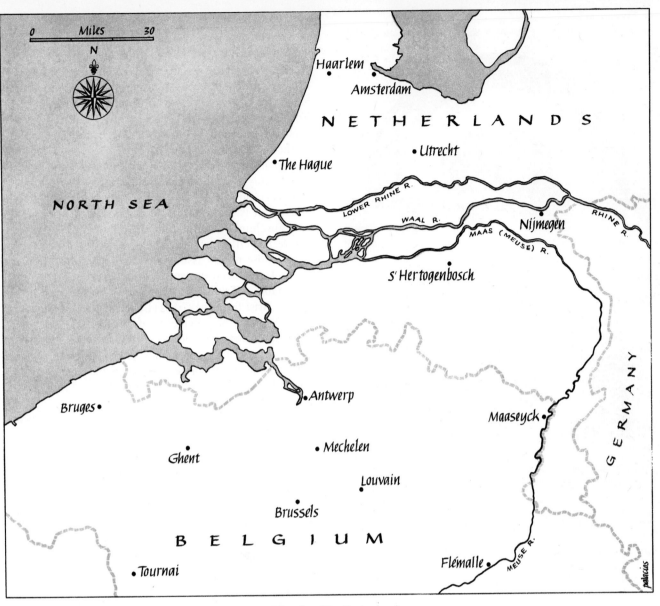

MAP 5. *The Netherlands*

Limbourgs between 1413 and their untimely deaths are among the loveliest creations of Northern painting. Beautiful as are the traditional illustrations from the Life of Christ and the Life of the Virgin, it is the calendar scenes that above all attract our attention.

These are, so to speak, dramatizations of the paired Signs of the Zodiac and Labors of the Months that appear on cathedral façades. Here, however, the appropriate signs appear in gold over the chariot of the sun in the blue dome of heaven, and the labors go on in the landscape below. In ten of the months these are contrasted with the delights of the aristocracy, but in such a way as to make the peasants appear carefree children of nature while the lords and ladies are prisoners of their own elegance. *August* (colorplate 15) is hot. A party of gentlemen and ladies, sumptuously dressed in the doubtless smothering fashion of the time (note the sleeves trailing below the horses' bodies) ride off a-hawking. The background has been brought forward as compared with

the Boucicaut Master, and is dominated by one of the duke's favorite residences, the Château d'Étampes, below which peasants reap wheat, bind it into sheaves, and pile them into a cart. In the middle distance men and women have cast off their clothes and swim delightedly in the River Juine. The artist has even studied the distortion caused by the refraction of light penetrating the water.

February (fig. 90) is bitterly cold, and the world is deep in snow, never convincingly represented before. Among white hills nestles a tiny village under a leaden sky. A peasant cuts branches for firewood, another guides his wood-laden donkey along the snowy road. In the foreground snow makes fluffy caps on a hayrick and a row of beehives, sheep huddle for warmth in their sheepfold (which has a hole in its roof), magpies peck at grain, and a shepherd stamps up and down and blows upon his freezing hands. The gentlemen and ladies are nowhere to be seen. Inside the farmhouse, with smoke curling from its chimney and the front wall removed for our con-

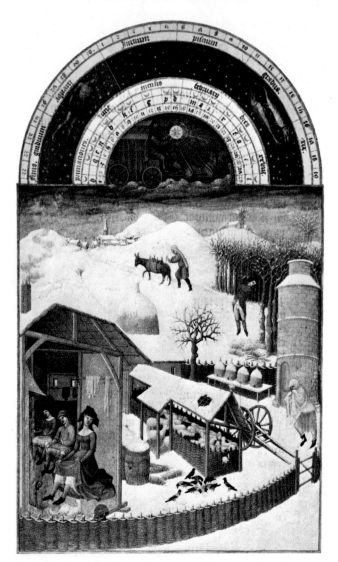

90. THE LIMBOURG BROTHERS. *February*, from the *Très Riches Heures du Duc de Berry*. 1413–16. Illumination. Musée Condé, Chantilly, France

THE ROHAN MASTER. After the delicacy of the *Très Riches Heures*, the macabre expressionism of the Rohan Master, so called because he and his assistants illuminated the *Grandes Heures de Rohan* (commissioned by Yolande of Aragon, wife of Louis II of Anjou), comes as a shock. His origin is unknown. He could have been a Netherlander, a German, or even a Spaniard; he may have painted at Angers, at Bourges, or at Paris, and at almost any date between the death of the Limbourg brothers and the early 1430s. The only thing certain about him is the devastating originality of his style. In one absolutely unique full-page illustration (fig. 92), before the Office of the Dead, he depicts a dying man from whose mouth issue the words, in Latin, "Into thy hands I commend my spirit; thou hast redeemed me, O Lord God of Truth." The first clause was uttered by the dying Christ from the Cross (Luke 23: 46), and the rest is a quotation from Verse 5 of Psalm 31. The man's emaciated body, rendered with gruesome fidelity to detail, is stretched upon a black silk shroud embroidered with gold and with a red cross; on the barren ground about him are strewn bones and skulls. From a blue heaven, made up entirely of tiny angels drawn in gold, Christ (so labeled in the halo) bends down, hair and beard

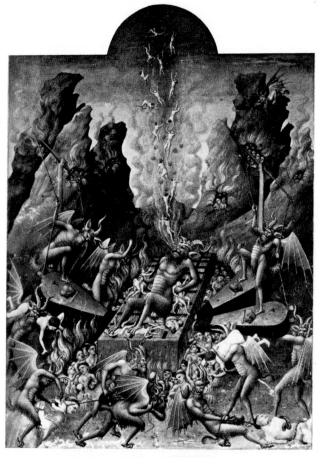

91. THE LIMBOURG BROTHERS. *Hell*, from the *Très Riches Heures du Duc de Berry*. 1413–16. Illumination. Musée Condé, Chantilly, France

venience, clothing and towels hang against the walls, and two peasants, conspicuously male and female, lift their garments somewhat too high to warm themselves before a (gilded) fire while the lady of the house turns disdainfully from such coarseness to warm considerably less of herself.

In contrast to the delights of earthly life, the Limbourg brothers let their imaginations produce a searing image of *Hell* (fig. 91), a gray immensity of spiring rocks on which there is, to quote John Milton, "no light but rather darkness visible." Crowned king of this desolate region, Satan extends himself on a giant grill, on which he roasts the helpless damned, while demons work the giant bellows on either side, whose mechanisms are meticulously represented. From the far dome of Heaven a torrent of souls pours down—into Satan's open mouth (for a Baroque transformation of this theme, see a painting by Rubens; fig. 286). To render the scene even more impressive all the demons and flames in this grim and otherwise colorless region are rendered in gold.

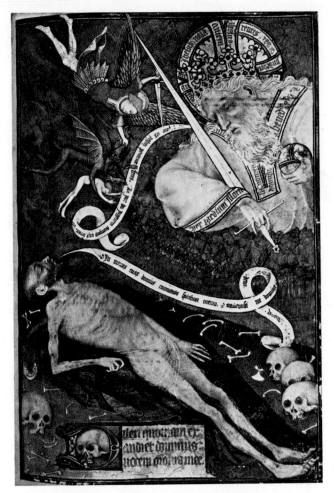

92. THE ROHAN MASTER. *The Dying Man Commending His Soul to God,* from the *Grandes Heures de Rohan.* c. 1418. Illumination, c. 10 x 7". Bibliothèque Nationale, Paris

as white as wool, and bearing a sword, as in Rev. 1: 14. He replies, in French, "For thy sins thou shalt do penance; on the day of judgment thou shalt be with me." An angel and a demon struggle over the dead man's soul. The strength of the drawing, the boldness of the composition, and the terrifying reality of the image show an artist of unusual stature, leading toward the majesty of Robert Campin (see fig. 93) and Rogier van der Weyden (see colorplates 18, 19), just as the Limbourg brothers point toward the serene perfection of Jan van Eyck.

NETHERLANDISH PANEL PAINTING

The glowing pages of the *Books of Hours* could be turned only by the rich and by their fortunate guests. The new style found its complete expression in altarpieces, which, whoever may have commissioned them, were visible to all in churches and addressed a public drawn from every class. Consequently, religious narratives were set in the context of daily life in Netherlandish towns and among the familiar activities of the merchants who dominated them. From a tentative beginning in such rare examples as Broederlam's pair of panels for the Chartreuse de

Champmol, these altarpieces were painted with increasing frequency in the 1420s and before the end of the century numbered in the thousands.

The oil technique invented by the Netherlanders was new. Not that oil was unknown—the Romans used it for painting leather or shields that were exposed to weather, and some aspects of oil technique are described in medieval treatises, culminating in Cennini (see pages 12–14). But it had never before been used for altarpieces. Apparently, the Netherlanders were dissatisfied with the appearance of a tempera surface, which, notwithstanding the varnish universally applied as protection, was dry, mat, and enamel-like, achieving its best effects with brilliant colors. Instead of egg yolk, then, the Northerners used a very refined oil vehicle, starting with linseed or walnut oil that had been fused when hot with hard resin, such as amber or copal, and then diluted with oil of rosemary or lavender. On the gesso panel, smoothed to porcelain finish, the painter drew his forms and light effects with a brush dipped in a single color, usually gray. On this base he applied his colors suspended in oil. The final layers were glazes, that is, solutions of oil and turpentine mixed with color to give a transparent or translucent effect. The final varnishes were also often mixed with color, so that the earlier layers were seen through them as through colored glass. The Netherlanders thus achieved a depth and resonance of color, and effects of shadow and half light, unobtainable in tempera. Given the optical interests of the fifteenth century, it was only a matter of time, as we have seen, before oil superseded tempera entirely, even in Italy.

CAMPIN. A tormenting aspect of early Netherlandish painting is the frequency with which the actual name of a master eludes us, however keen may be our feeling that we know his personality from his work. One of the leading pioneers of panel painting is a dramatic case in point. His work has been assembled (not without disagreement) on the basis of fragments of altarpieces thought to have come from the Abbey of Flémalle (see fig. 94), and it is clear from their style that the artist who painted them must have been the teacher of Rogier van der Weyden (see colorplates 18, 19). We have documentary accounts of a painter from Tournai called Robert Campin (c. 1378–1444), whose principal pupil was Roger de la Pasture. Since *Pasture* is French for *Weyden,* this would make Campin identical with the Master of Flémalle. Although many scholars accept the hypothesis, others maintain that all the paintings attributed to the Master of Flémalle are in reality early works of Rogier van der Weyden, and all must mournfully admit that the suggestion is, like the third verdict permissible under Scottish law, "not proven."

An early work by this brilliant master is the *Nativity* (colorplate 16), which is thought to have come from a monastery near Dijon, perhaps even the familiar Chartreuse de Champmol, and to have been painted about 1425. Campin (to use the name the majority want to use)

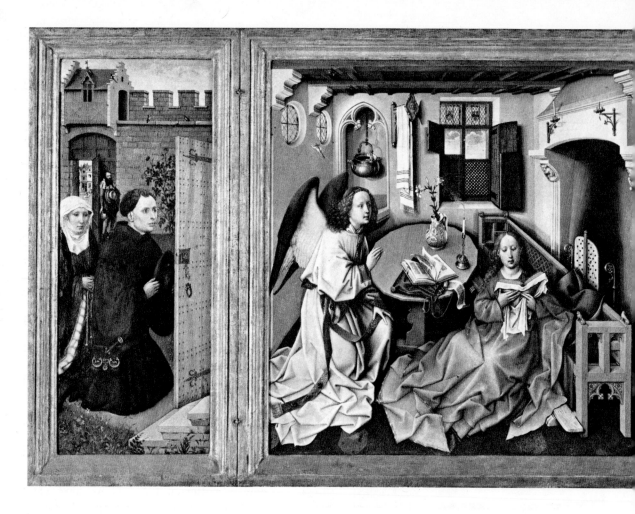

has shown the very moment of birth, according to the vision of Saint Bridget, a Swedish princess who in the late fourteenth century on a visit to Bethlehem saw the naked Christ Child appear miraculously on the ground before the kneeling Mary, while Joseph held a candle whose flame and even the light of the rising sun were set at nought by the light from the shining Child. Campin has grouped densely before a humble shed Mary, Joseph, and two midwives—one who believes in the miracle, the other incredulous—while angels float above. Their glad tidings and the dialogue of the midwives are represented, comic-strip style, on floating scrolls as in the Rohan *Hours* (see fig. 92). All the figures and their massive, broken drapery folds are projected with a sculptural power obviously under the influence of Sluter, whose sharp vision has also stimulated the care and subtlety with which the head of the aged Joseph, and the faces of the three shepherds who lean through the open window, are delineated, wrinkle by wrinkle.

The landscape is brought closer to the foreground even than in the *Très Riches Heures*, and the leafless trees, the rider who has just gone round the bend in the road, the wayside inn that had no room for the Holy Family, the distant (Gothic) Bethlehem, and the lake with its sailboat and rowboat are all shown with scrupulous care. However, in contrast to Masaccio in the almost contemporary *Tribute Money* (see colorplate 6), Campin has

adopted a high point of view, which we might call "rising perspective," so that the background can be seen over the heads of the figures. Although he has rendered beautifully the shadows of the banks and the bushes thrown by the rising sun on the road, he has attempted nothing like the light effects of Gentile da Fabriano's predella for the Strozzi Altarpiece (see fig. 53), possibly considering such darkness unsuitable to his larger panel. The sun, symbol of Christ, shines with gold rays as does the Child on the ground below. With the oil medium Campin is able to achieve a new softness and richness in the tones, from the russet colors of the landscape and the rich garments of the midwives to the muted gold of the rays and the delicate lavenders and blues in the shadow of Mary's white tunic. Like all Netherlanders henceforward, Campin omits the halos still customary in Italian painting.

A somewhat later work, called the Mérode Altarpiece because for generations it belonged to the Mérode family, painted about 1425–26, takes us into a contemporary Netherlandish interior as a setting for the *Annunciation* (fig. 93). Unlike the generally stationary altarpieces in Italy, Netherlandish equivalents were usually hinged, so that the side wings close over the central panel like doors; they were generally painted on the outside as well. The three panels of the Mérode Altarpiece, under the guise of descriptive realism, form a richly stocked triple showcase of symbols. In the central panel, the Virgin is seated,

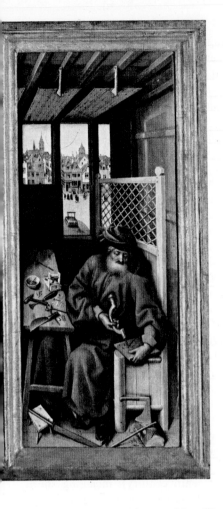

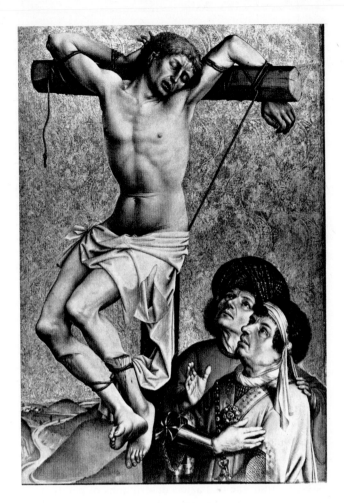

93. MASTER OF FLÉMALLE (Robert Campin?). *Annunciation,* center panel of the *Mérode Altarpiece.* c. 1425–26. Panel painting, 25¼ x 24⅞". The Metropolitan Museum of Art, New York. The Cloisters Collection. Purchase, 1957

94. MASTER OF FLÉMALLE (Robert Campin?). *Impenitent Thief Dead on His Cross* (fragment). c. 1428–30. Panel painting, 52⅜ x 36⅜". Städelsches Kunstinstitut, Frankfort

probably on a cushion, and is still reading (doubtless Isa. 7: 14, as often in representations of the Annunciation: "A virgin shall conceive, and bear a son") as she leans against a bench before a fire screen. On the polygonal table are another open book, a vase of lilies (symbol of the Virgin's purity), and a still-smoking candle, symbol of the Incarnation (Isa. 42: 3: "the smoking flax shall he not quench"); a copper ewer, hanging in a niche, and a towel on a rack have been claimed as an allusion to Christ washing the Apostles' feet, and to the washing of the world from sin, predicted for the morrow in the breviary prayers for Christmas Eve. The Christ Child can be seen, gliding down golden rays from the nearest round window, carrying the Cross over his shoulder, a representation frequent in Annunciations until now but soon to be forbidden as heretical. The closed garden in the left panel, in which the kneeling donor and his wife (a couple from Mechelen named Inghelbrechts) receive their view of the miracle through the door left open by the angel, is the closed garden of Mary's virginity (Song of Solomon 4:12: "A garden inclosed is my sister, my spouse"), and is filled with flowers symbolic of Mary.

The right wing, Joseph's carpentry shop, is packed with symbols. He is contriving a mousetrap, and according to Saint Augustine the Cross is the mousetrap and Christ the bait to catch the Devil. Not only are the ax, saw, and rod in the foreground all mentioned in Isa. 10:

15; but also the ax "laid unto the root of the trees" signifies the fate of sinners in Matt. 3: 10; the saw is the instrument of Isaiah's martyrdom; the rod is Joseph's rod, which bloomed miraculously to designate him as the Virgin's husband (see examples by Fouquet, fig. 118, and by Raphael, fig. 144). This listing by no means exhausts the symbols recently identified by scholars among the collection Campin exhibits so ostentatiously. Well may one ask who, in 1425, was supposed to know all these things, and how an artist, who presumably had no theological training, could find them out. These are unanswered questions, but one must suppose the existence of a learned adviser, consulted by both patron and painter.

The identification of the interior of the altarpiece as an inward extension of its frame obviously recalls Pietro Lorenzetti's invention (see fig. 15), and the drapery folds are clearly Sluteresque. Although the rising perspective is a bit dizzying, Campin's delight in rendering as accurately as possible not only the real objects in the interior but also the views out of Joseph's window and the garden gate into a little Netherlandish town is infectious.

Single-handedly, Campin took painting from miniature to lifesize, as is displayed dramatically by a fragment of the Flémalle altarpiece showing the *Impenitent Thief Dead on His Cross* (fig. 94). The entire altarpiece, a *Descent from the Cross,* is known only from a poor copy, but, if one judges from the scale of the fragment, the lost original must have been about twelve feet wide and about seven and a half feet high. Campin's combination of linear precision in the rendering of anatomy with strong shading makes this tormented figure seem prophetic of Michelangelo's struggling nudes (see figs. 136, 181), although there is slight possibility of direct influence. Especially impressive is Campin's ability to present as profoundly tragic such pieces of naturalistic observation as the dead man's agonized expression and the torn flesh of his broken legs, which in the work of the Rohan Master would have been merely frightening. Campin's ability to emulate in paint the monumentality and power of Sluter's sculpture is comparable to the relationship between Masaccio and his sculptural predecessors in contemporary Florence (see Chapter 1).

VAN EYCK. Among all the masters who outdid each other in efforts to enhance the new naturalism in the early fifteenth century, Jan van Eyck (c. 1385–1441) stood out in the eyes of his contemporaries; about 1456 the Italian humanist Bartolommeo Fazio called him the "prince of painters of our age." Without a doubt he was one of the greatest artists who ever lived, and to many he shares the summit among Northern painters only with Rembrandt in the seventeenth century. The absoluteness and self-sufficiency of van Eyck's work, which render all words about him superfluous, may be illustrated by a passage from one of Fazio's descriptions of paintings by him that have now disappeared. This passage describes a triptych painted for the Genoese Giovanni Battista Lomellino; he appears in one wing "lacking only a voice, and a woman whom he loved, of remarkable beauty, she too carefully represented just as she was; between them, as if peeping through a crack in the wall a ray of sun which you would take to be real sunlight." Other naturalistic artists *represent* nature; van Eyck seems to *present* it. Nor can his pictures be reproached with the

modern term "photographic," for no camera can approach the reality revealed by his pictures. One immediately accepts that what he shows really exists, down to the most minute detail, not separately catalogued as in the work of Campin but unobtrusively there. And nothing in his paintings is more convincingly real than the segment of atmospheric space his frame circumscribes, in which light, bright or dim, is dissolved, reflecting back to us from countless surfaces and textures. It is strange, therefore, that when the chips are down there should be any doubt as to which paintings are really by a master so universally acknowledged as great and which are not. Yet this is the case with this most enigmatic of artists, around whose work the arguments show no signs of subsiding.

We know little about Jan van Eyck's early life. A sixteenth-century tradition maintains that he came from Maaseyck in the northeast corner of present-day Belgium, across the Maas (Meuse) River from Holland. The first reference to him records his painting a Paschal candle at Cambrai in 1422; thereupon, he entered the service of John of Bavaria, count of Holland, and made decorations for his palace at The Hague. After John's death in 1425, van Eyck became *valet de chambre* (doubtless, an honorary title) to Philip the Good, duke of Burgundy, and retained the position until his own death. Philip not only considered him irreplaceable as a painter, but also sent him on diplomatic missions (as Rubens was employed in the seventeenth century), including short trips and "long and secret journeys" in 1426, as well as a trip to Portugal in 1428–29 to bring back Philip's bride, Princess Isabella. At least one of his journeys took him to Italy, where he must have seen the work of Masaccio and met Florentine artists. In 1430 he settled for good in Bruges, and then the signed and dated works begin, continuing until his death eleven years later.

Part of the controversy centers around the authorship of certain illuminations in the *Turin-Milan Hours*, begun

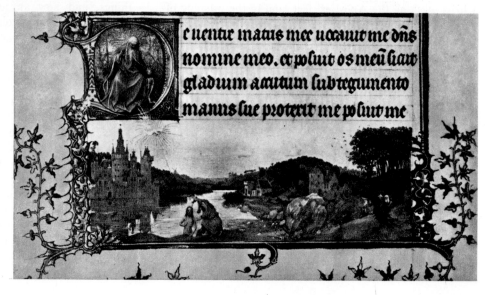

95. JAN VAN EYCK. *Baptism of Christ*, bas-de-page from the *Turin-Milan Hours*. c. 1422–24. Illumination, height c. 2″; entire page 11 x 7½″. Museo Civico, Turin, Italy

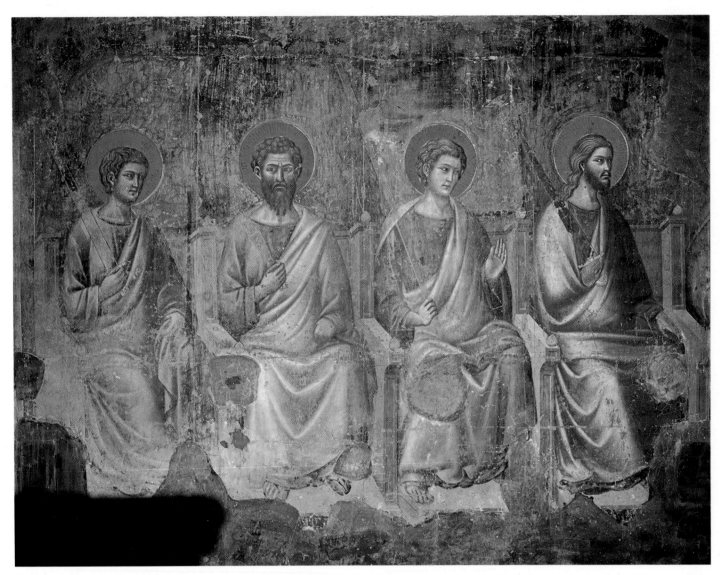

COLORPLATE 1.   Gothic. PIETRO CAVALLINI. *Last Judgment* (portion of fresco). c. 1290. Sta. Cecilia in Trastevere, Rome

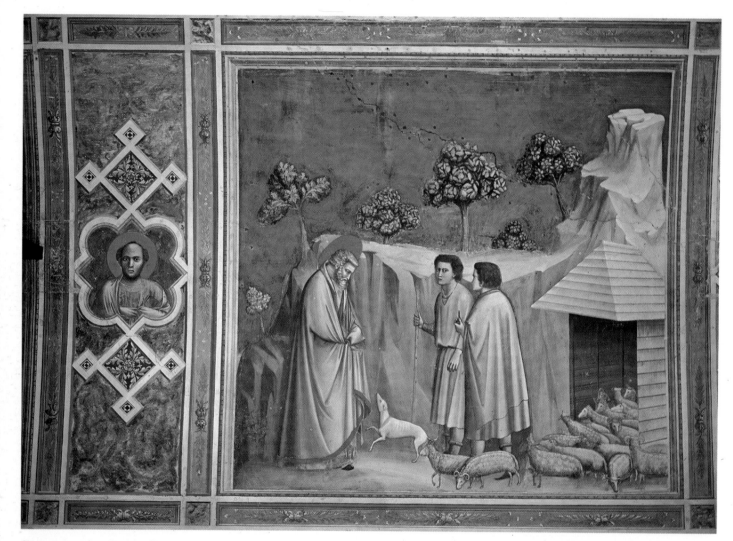

COLORPLATE 2.   Gothic. GIOTTO. *Joachim Takes Refuge in the Wilderness.* Fresco. 1305–6. Arena Chapel, Padua

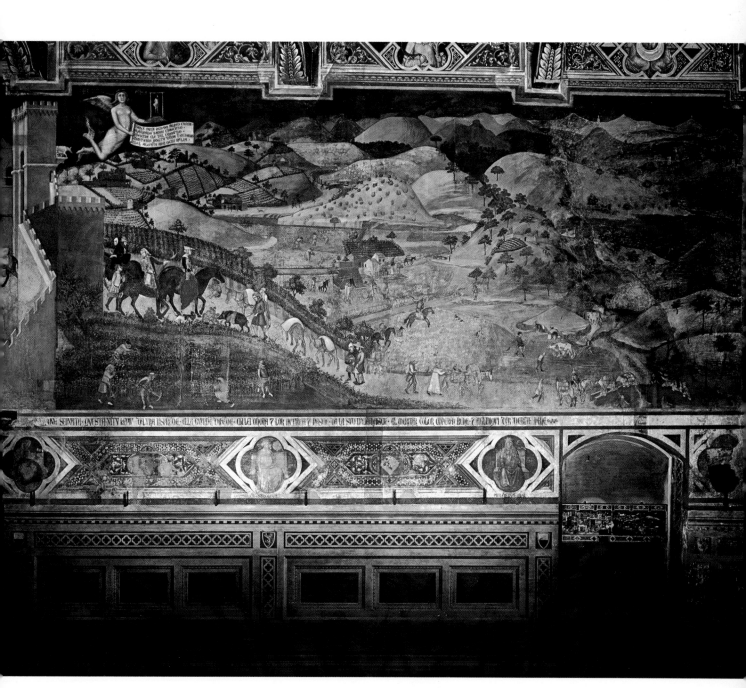

COLORPLATE 3.   Gothic. AMBROGIO LORENZETTI. *Allegory of Good Government: the Effects of Good Government in the City and the Country* (portion of fresco). 1338–39. Salla della Pace, Palazzo Pubblico, Siena

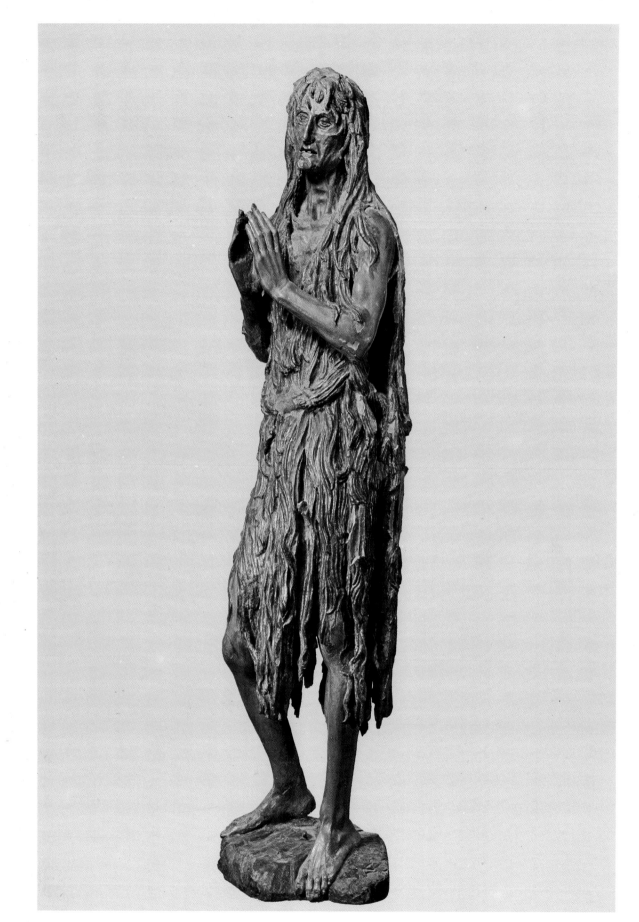

COLORPLATE 4.   Renaissance. DONATELLO. *Mary Magdalen.* 1454–55. Polychromed and gilded wood, height 74″. Baptistery of S. Giovanni, Florence

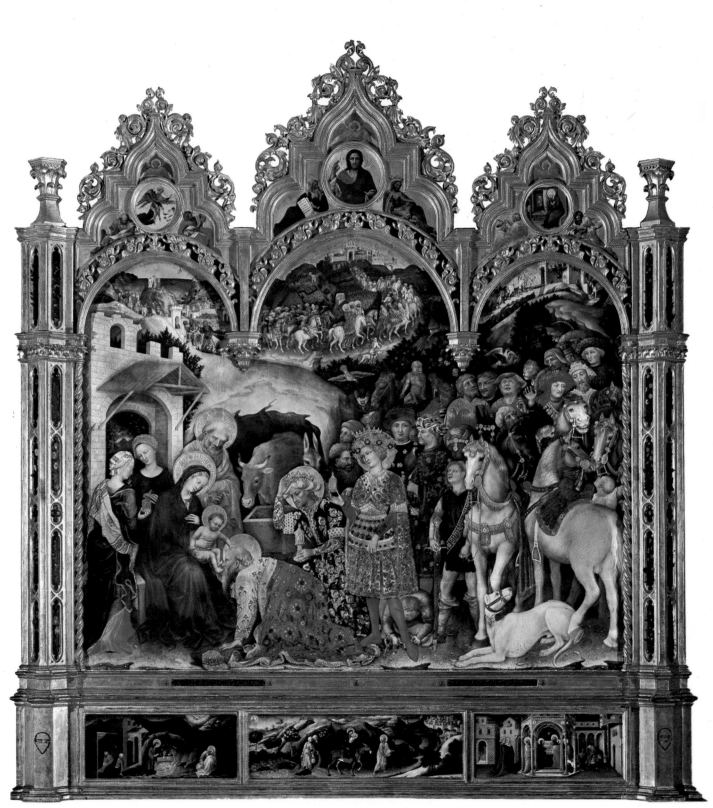

COLORPLATE 5.   Renaissance. GENTILE DA FABRIANO. *Adoration of the Magi*. Completed 1423. Panel painting, 9'10" x 9'3". Galleria degli Uffizi, Florence

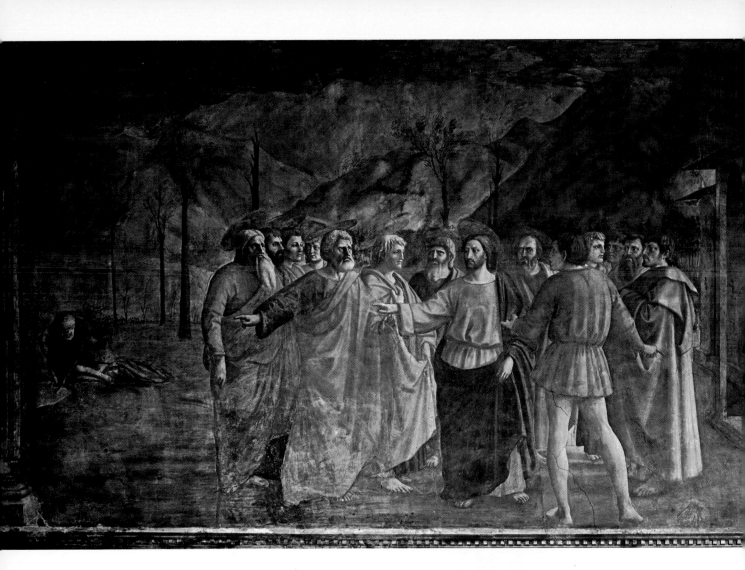

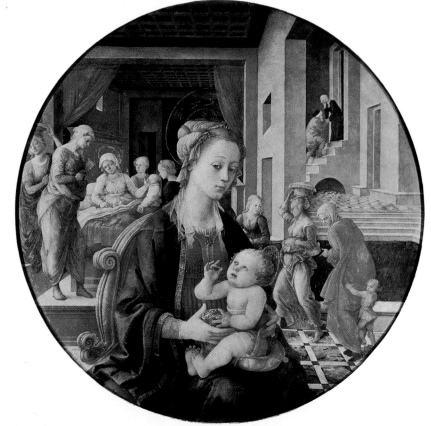

COLORPLATE 7.
Renaissance. FRA FILIPPO LIPPI.
Madonna and Child. c. 1452. Panel
painting, diameter 53″. Palazzo Pitti,
Florence

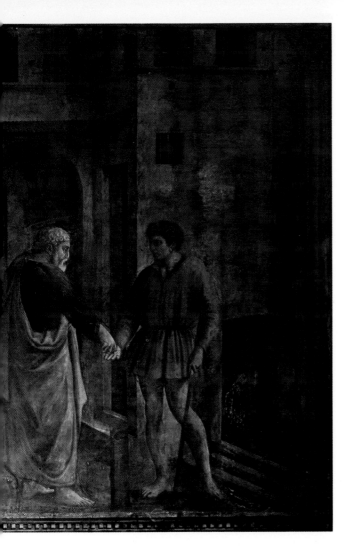

COLORPLATE 6.
Renaissance. MASACCIO. *Tribute Money*.
Fresco. c.1425. Brancacci Chapel,
Sta. Maria del Carmine, Florence

COLORPLATE 8.
Renaissance. FRA ANGELICO. *Descent
from the Cross* (frame and pinnacles by
Lorenzo Monaco). Completed
c. 1434. Panel painting, 69 x 72″. Museo
di S. Marco, Florence

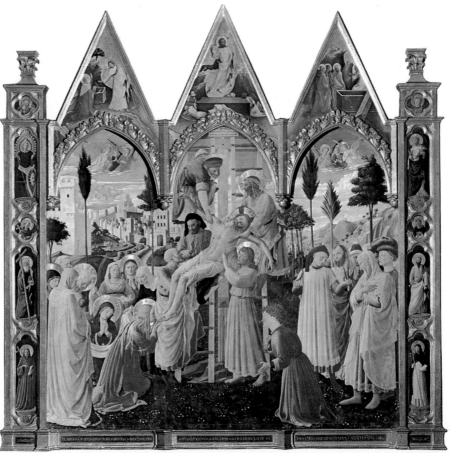

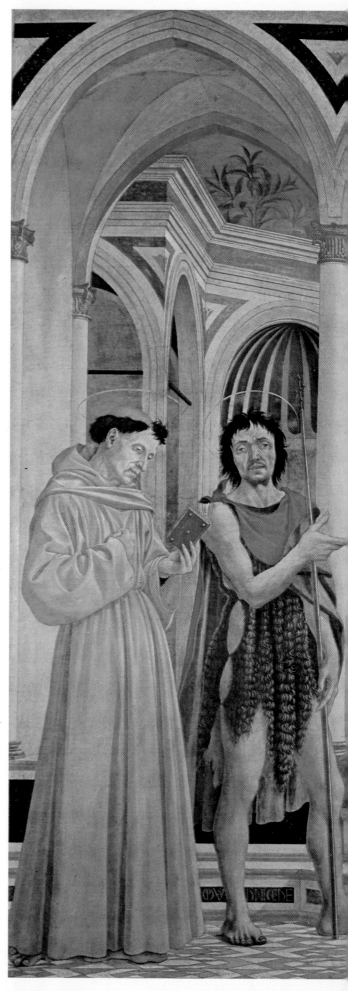

COLORPLATE 9.
Renaissance. DOMENICO VENEZIANO.
*Saint Lucy Altarpiece (Madonna and
Child with Saints).* c. 1445. Panel
painting, 82 x 84″. Galleria degli Uffizi,
Florence

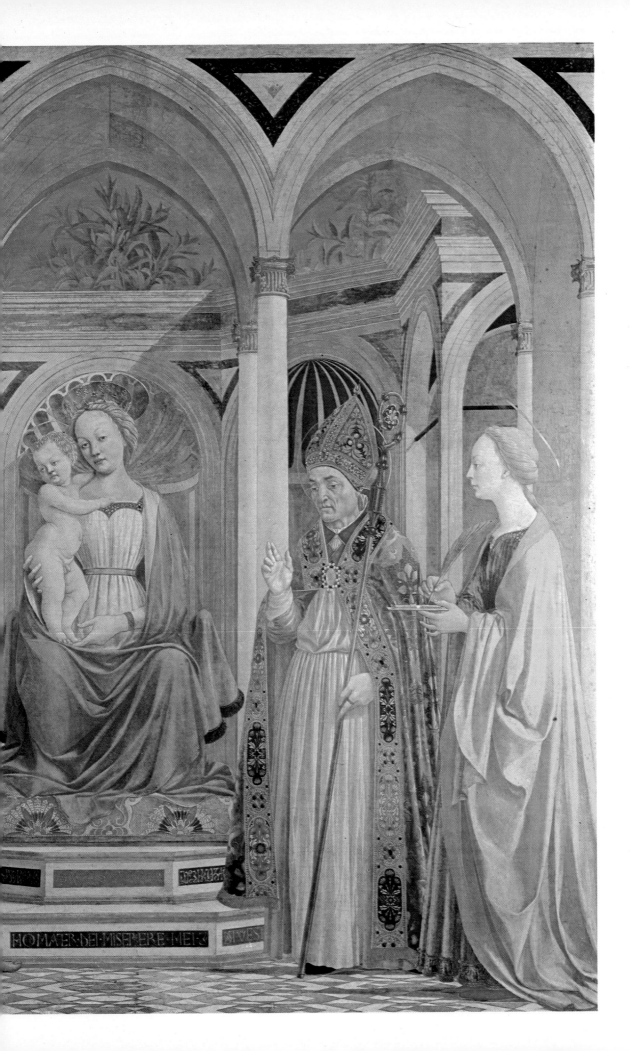

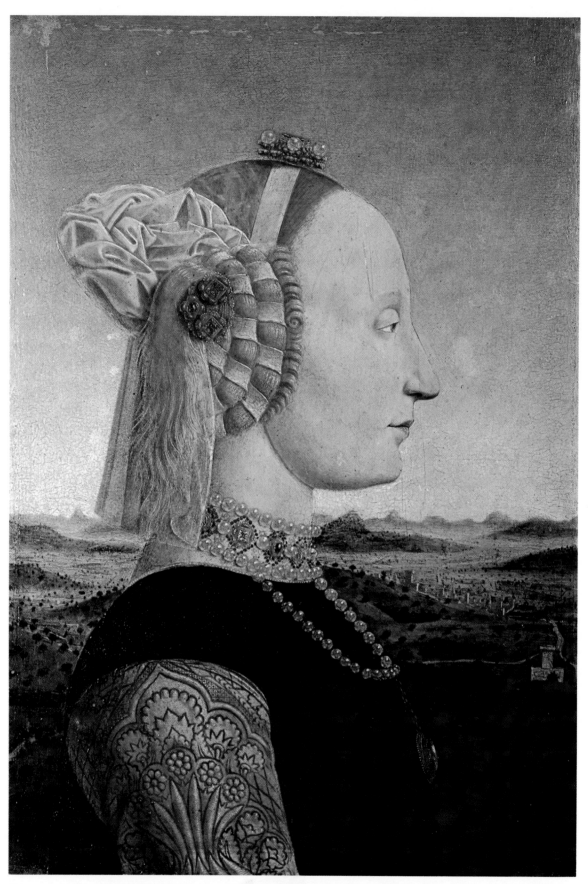

COLORPLATE 10.   Renaissance. PIERO DELLA FRANCESCA. *Battista Sforza*. 1465. Oil (and tempera?) on panel, 18½ x 13″. Galleria degli Uffizi, Florence

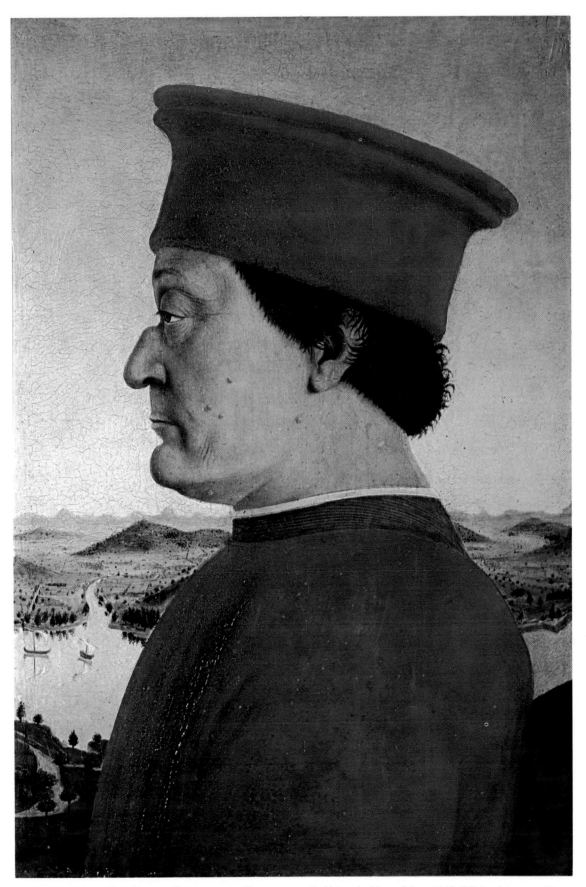

COLORPLATE 11.   Renaissance. PIERO DELLA FRANCESCA. *Federigo da Montefeltro*. 1465. Oil (and tempera?)
on panel, 18½ x 13″. Galleria degli Uffizi, Florence

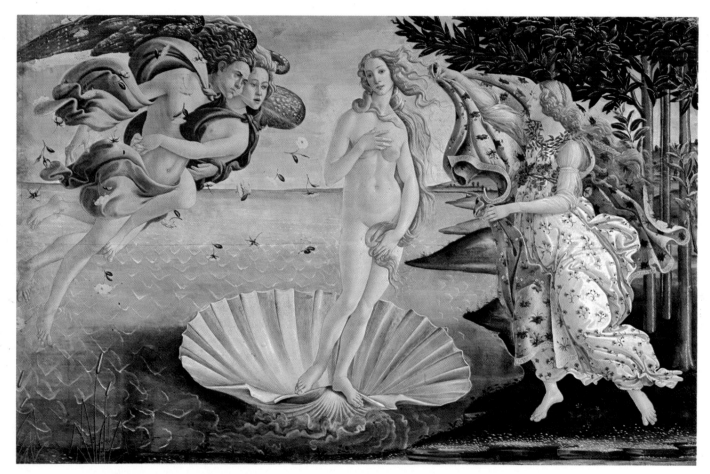

COLORPLATE 12.   Renaissance. SANDRO BOTTICELLI. *Birth of Venus.* After 1482. Paint on canvas, 5'9" x 9'2".
Galleria degli Uffizi, Florence

COLORPLATE 13. ▶
Renaissance. ANDREA MANTEGNA.
Ceiling fresco. Completed 1474.
Camera degli Sposi, Palazzo Ducale,
Mantua, Italy

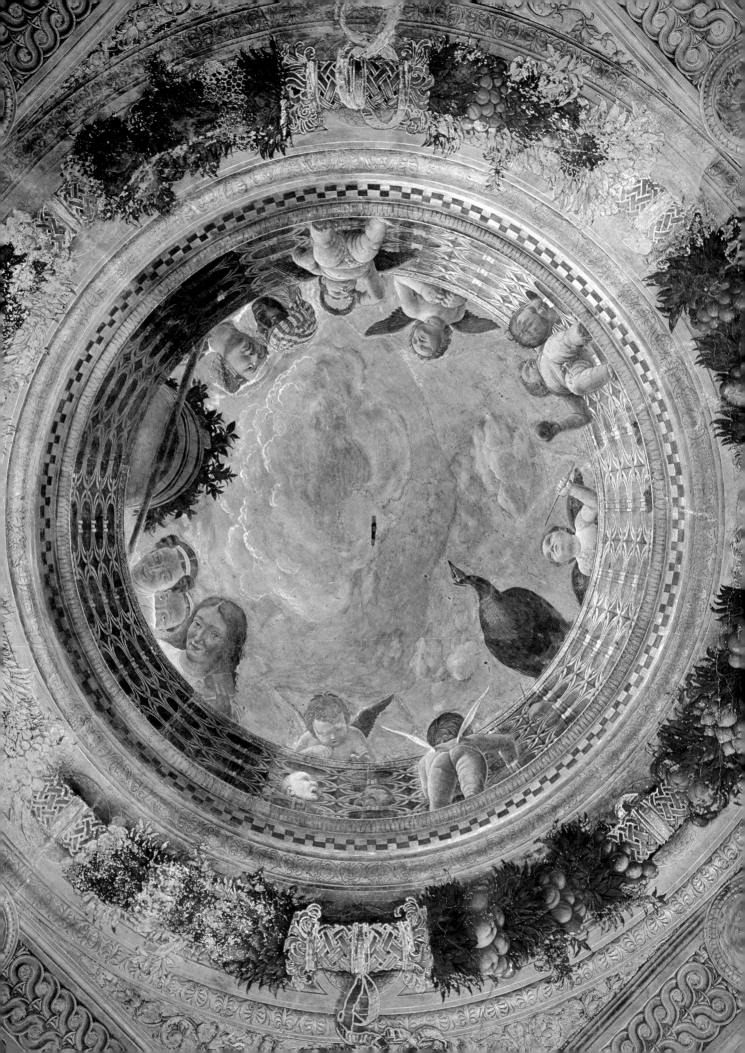

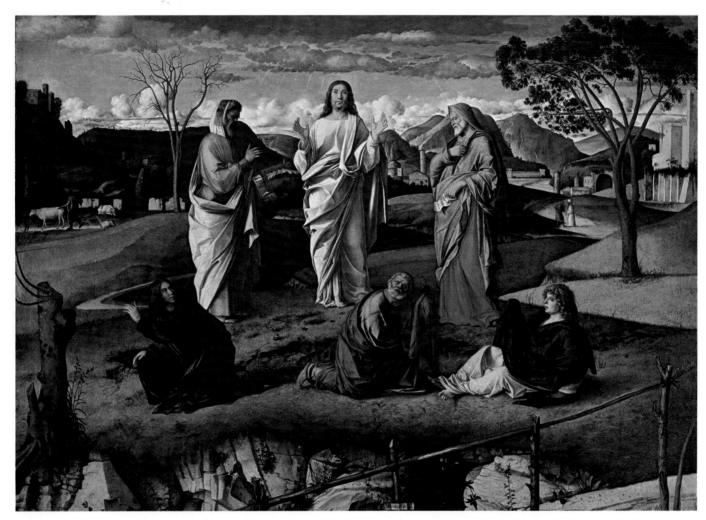

COLORPLATE 14.   Renaissance. GIOVANNI BELLINI. *Transfiguration of Christ.* Late 1480s. Oil on panel, 45¼ x 59″.
Museo di Capodimonte, Naples

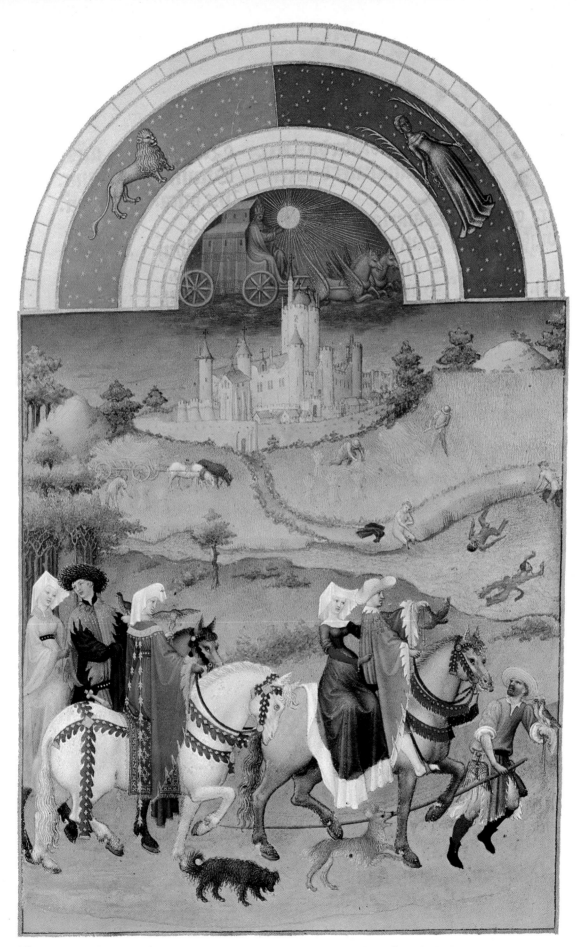

COLORPLATE 15.   Renaissance. THE LIMBOURG BROTHERS. *August*, from the *Très Riches Heures du Duc de Berry*. Illumination. 1413–16. Musée Condée, Chantilly, France

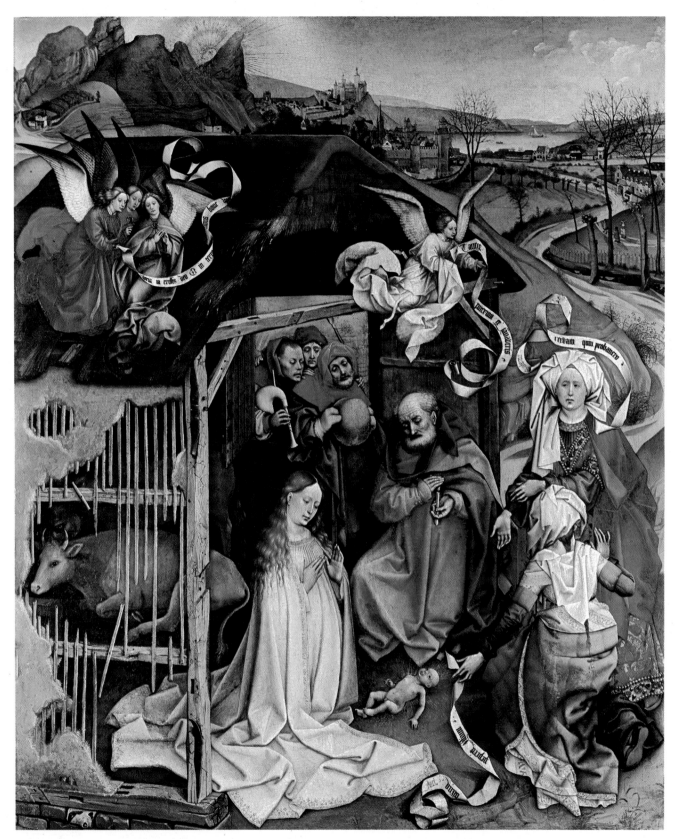

COLORPLATE 16.   Renaissance. MASTER OF FLÉMALLE (Robert Campin?). *Nativity.* c. 1425. Oil on panel, 34¼ x 28¾″. Musée des Beaux-Arts, Dijon

for the duke of Berry, left unfinished at his death, and worked upon thereafter by several painters at different dates. The group in question, done by an illuminator known as Hand G, contains at one point the arms of the house of Bavaria, and thus were presumably painted before the death of Count John in 1425 and perhaps before that of William IV in 1417. The author adheres to the view that Hand G was Jan van Eyck. One tiny miniature, scarcely two inches high, at the bottom of a page, shows the *Baptism of Christ* (fig. 95) as only a genius could have painted it, at this or any date. On a rocky ledge in the foreground crouches John the Baptist; he pours water from a pitcher over the head of Christ, who stands in the river. On the distant bank a castle rises from the water's edge; to our right other figures keep their distance, half-concealed by rocks. Upstream the eyes move off to mountain ranges, tiny in the distance, yet hardly above the heads of the figures—rising perspective is abandoned. For the most part the water is smooth, disturbed only by an occasional ripple; behind the Baptist, it breaks over the rocks.

Above this vividly real scene descends the dove of the Holy Spirit, sent by God the Father enthroned in the initial *D*, shedding rays of gold, or "spiritual" light. This illumination is contrasted with natural light as never before observed. The source is the sun, which has already set, leaving a pearly radiance in the sky; this afterglow is reflected by the water; the water in turn sends the light up to the castle from below; and finally the image of the castle, thus illumined, is mirrored in the stream. Within the microscopic limits of the painting, therefore, the light from the sun (which is no longer there) moves through the atmosphere in no less than four different directions, each serenely recorded. How far away and how naïve the Boucicaut Master seems.

The next controversial work, the altarpiece in twenty panels in Saint Bavo's, Ghent (figs. 96, 97, 98, 99), takes us from the microcosm to the macrocosm, encompassing as it does the entire range of Salvation. An inscription tells us that the work was begun by Hubert van Eyck and finished by Jan for the leading citizen and later mayor of Ghent, Jodocus Vyd, in May 1432. Here is another riddle. We know from an old copy of the epitaph that a now-vanished tombstone in Saint Bavo's recorded the burial of a painter Hubert (no surname) in 1426. The story that Hubert and Jan were brothers cannot be pushed farther back than the sixteenth century. It has recently been proposed (see Bibliography) that the Hubert of the inscription was not Jan's brother but merely came from the same village (Maaseyck means Eyck on the Maas), and that he was not a painter but the sculptor who carved an elaborate frame, destroyed in 1566 by Protestant iconoclasts from whose depredations the paintings of the altarpiece were hidden by the clergy. The proposal is attractive as no signature of Hubert van Eyck appears on a single painting, and as all attempts to distinguish different hands in the remarkably consistent altarpiece have met with defeat. This is, alas, another Scottish verdict, but a persuasive one. Jan would then have painted the entire altarpiece after his return from Portugal in 1429.

With the wings closed, the upper level shows the *Annunciation* (see fig. 97) taking place as in the Mérode Altarpiece in a Netherlandish interior, although more spacious and on an upper floor; from the windows one looks out at the gables of a town, with people in the streets and storks in the sky. The adjoining otherwise empty panel is devoted to an almost ceremonial representation of the familiar niche, towel, and gleaming ewer, with the addition of a basin and a trefoil window, which makes the Trinitarian symbolism explicit. Above the rafters, as in an attic, appear the prophets Zechariah and Micah and the Erythraean and Cumaean Sibyls, surmounted by scrolls that contain their prophecies of the coming of Christ. Below are four identical niches; in the central pair stand white simulated stone statues of Saint John the Baptist and John the Evangelist (amusing in that van Eyck was paid for painting the surfaces of actual stone statues in Bruges), and at left and right kneel unsparing portrait figures of Jodocus Vyd and his wife Isabel Borluut, recalling forcefully the patrons of Masaccio's *Trinity* (see fig. 57), which van Eyck might have seen in Florence only a year or two before, now freed from the foreground plane and turned in three-quarters view.

In order to maintain a sense of unity throughout the panels, Mary and Gabriel are robed in white, in keeping with the white statues below, and the four niches and the room are pervaded by a light from the front, clearly the actual light of the chapel because it has thrown the shadows of the vertical supports of the frame onto the floor of the room. This source conflicts with the sunlight from outside, which prints the shape of a double-arched window on the wall behind Mary—a light that could only come from the north, and is therefore a symbol of the miracle taking place. The stillness and perfection of the panels are so compelling that we realize almost with a shock that there is no room in their niches for the donors' lower legs, and that in the *Annunciation* figures and setting are still represented in different scales. The angel's greeting to Mary is beautifully lettered from left to right; her response (in Latin), "Behold the handmaiden of the Lord," is inscribed with equal care but, since it must run from right to left, is written upside down!

The wings open to reveal in the upper story the *Deësis*. The Lord appears in the guise of Christ (see fig. 98), crowned with a papal tiara, robed in scarlet with borders of gold and gleaming jewels, and holding a scepter whose component rods of shining crystal are joined by bands of gold ornament; at his feet rests a jeweled crown. On his right sits the Virgin in brilliant blue, wearing a jeweled crown from which spring roses and lilies, and over which hover twelve stars; on his left is John the Baptist, whose camel-skin garment is almost hidden by a cloak of emerald green. On either side are angels robed in gold and velvet brocade, singing and playing on musical in-

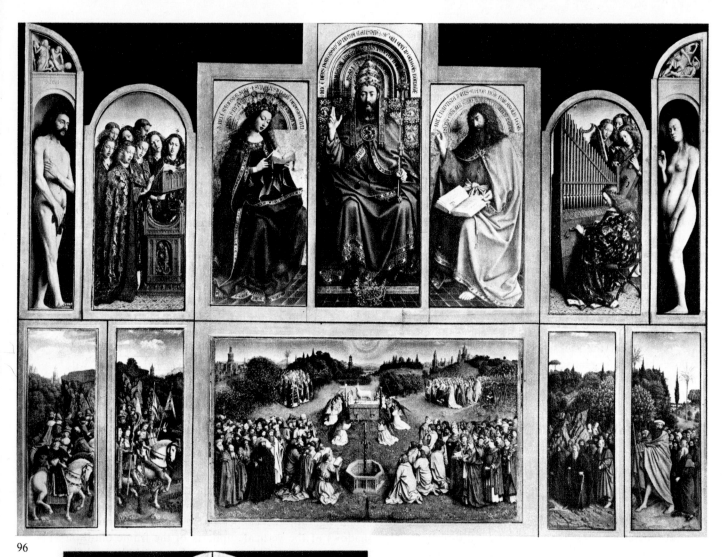

96

96. HUBERT and JAN VAN EYCK. *Ghent Altarpiece*
(open). Completed 1432. Oil on panel, 11'5¾" x
15'1½". Cathedral of St. Bavo, Ghent, Belgium

97. HUBERT and JAN VAN EYCK. *Ghent Altarpiece*
(closed)

struments; van Eyck has even defined the mechanism of
the carved wood and brass revolving music stand, and indicated a figure working the bellows of the organ. In the
dark niches at the extreme sides, and seen from below so
that they belong to our space, stand Adam and Eve (see
fig. 99), sullen with guilt and shame, Eve still holding the
long-withered forbidden fruit. In simulated relief sculptures in the half lunettes the *Sacrifice of Cain and Abel*
and *Cain Killing Abel* are represented with terrifying
power.

The five lower panels form a continuous view in rising
perspective (see fig. 96); in the emerald-green meadow of
Paradise, dotted with wild flowers, the Lamb of God
stands upon an altar, the blood from his breast pouring
into a chalice, surrounded by angels holding the Cross
and the column at which Christ was scourged. Below the
altar the Fountain of Life pours from golden spigots into
an octagonal basin, and thence around the fountain and

97

toward the observer "a pure river of water of life, clear as crystal, proceeding out of the throne of God and of the Lamb" (Rev. 22: 1). Through the water one can see that the stream bed is composed of rubies, pearls, and emeralds. On the left kneeling prophets holding their books precede standing patriarchs and kings from the Old Testament; on the right Apostles kneel in front of standing saints, many of whom wear papal tiaras or bishops' miters. From groves in the middle distance at the left advances a choir of confessors; at the right virgin martyrs bear palms. On the far horizon can be seen the Gothic domes, pinnacles, and spires of the heavenly Jerusalem. In the left-hand panels the just judges and knights approach on beautiful, placid horses through a rocky landscape; in those to the right hermits and pilgrims, led by the giant Saint Christopher, proceed on foot. Above the wonderfully real crowds, and the landscape represented down to the tiniest pebble and the last blade of grass, white clouds hang high up in a summer sky. In the center, above the Mystic Lamb, and below the throne of God, the dove of the Holy Spirit sheds golden rays, contrasted with the light reflected from armor, gold, and glossy leaves, glowing from grass, flowers, rich fabrics, and the depths of jewels, muted in the footprinted dust. No sun is represented, no source is shown for "the city had no need of the sun, neither of the moon, to shine in it: for the glory of God did lighten it, and the Lamb is the light thereof" (Rev. 21: 23). With

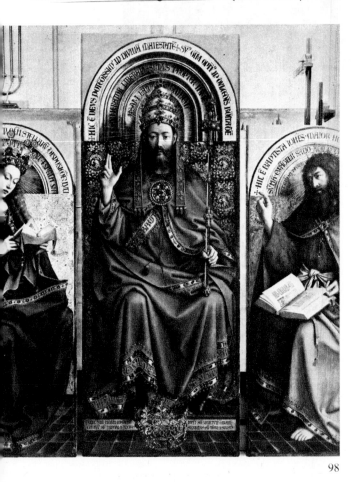

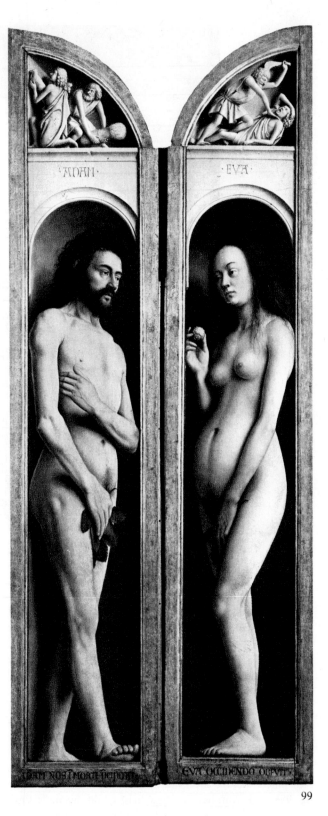

98. HUBERT and JAN VAN EYCK. *Deësis (The Virgin Mary, The Lord, and Saint John the Baptist).* Detail of the *Ghent Altarpiece* (open)

99. HUBERT and JAN VAN EYCK. *Adam and Eve,* upper wings of the *Ghent Altarpiece* (open)

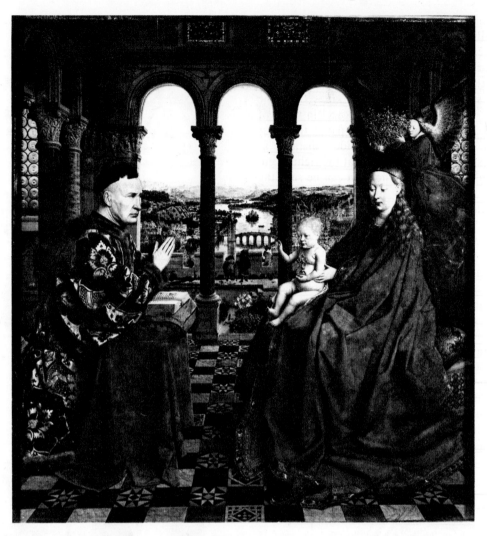

100. JAN VAN EYCK. *Madonna of Chancellor Rolin*. c. 1433–34. Oil on panel,
26 x 24⅜". The Louvre, Paris

total precision van Eyck has encompassed the drama of
Salvation in images of another world containing all the
beauties of this one, raised as it were to a higher power.

Probably in the year following the Ghent Altarpiece
van Eyck painted a work of lesser dimensions but equal
beauty, the *Madonna of Chancellor Rolin* (fig. 100,
colorplate 17), given by this high official of the duchy of
Burgundy to the Cathedral of Autun when his son was
made bishop in 1437. The chancellor, grimly calm, kneels
before the Virgin in her palace, while over her head an
angel floating on peacock wings holds a crown similar to
that placed before the Lord in the Ghent Altarpiece (see
fig. 98), and from her lap the Christ Child, his nude flesh
soft against her scarlet mantle, holds in his left hand a
crystal orb surmounted by a jeweled gold cross, while
blessing his brocade-clad worshiper with his right. The
palace is largely Romanesque, a style shown to be symbolic (in the fifteenth century) of things ancient and
venerated. Van Eyck has displayed his prowess in the
minute representation of sculptured scenes from the Old

Testament and in the interlace of the capitals, as well as
in the distinction between stained-glass and bottle-glass
windows, and in the softly diffused light over the inlaid
marble patterns of the floor. Through the three arches we
look into Mary's garden of roses and lilies and onto a
terrace on which peacocks stroll, and from whose
battlemented wall two men in fifteenth-century costume
look down to the river below. The city in the middle distance is complete; its cathedral, resembling that of
Utrecht, rises above a square scattered with strollers; on
the bridge move scores of people, to or from the suburb
whose pleasant houses are graced with trees. The river,
rich with reflections of banks and islands, flows toward
the distant mountains, some covered with snow, veiled in
the luminous haze.

One of van Eyck's most celebrated works is the *Arnolfini Wedding* (fig. 101), which it has been shown
represents the sacrament of Marriage (the only sacrament not necessarily dispensed by a priest) being contracted between Giovanni Arnolfini, a silk merchant

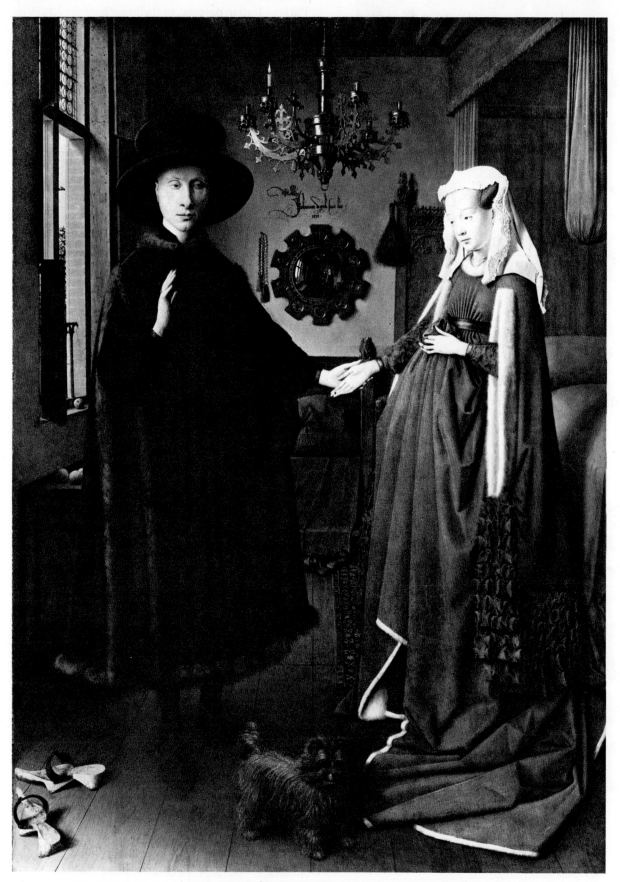

101. JAN VAN EYCK. *Arnolfini Wedding (Giovanni Arnolfini and His Bride)*. 1434. Oil on panel.
32¼ x 23½″. National Gallery, London

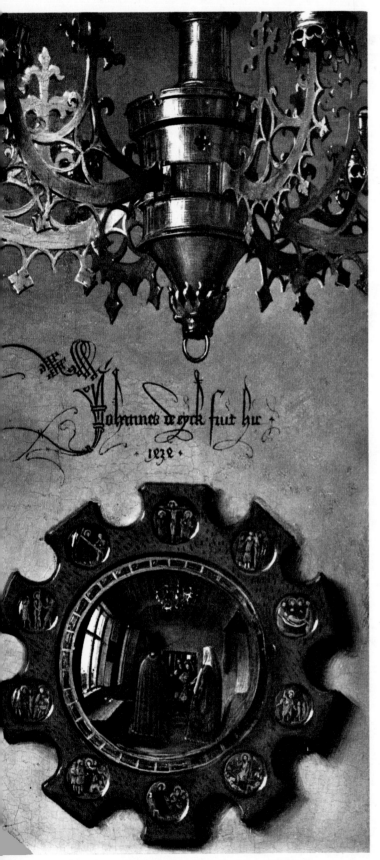

102. JAN VAN EYCK. *Arnolfini Wedding* (detail)

from Lucca resident in Bruges, and Jeanne Cenami, born in Paris of Italian parents. In their bedchamber Arnolfini takes his wife's hand and lifts his right in an oath of fidelity. All the objects in the room, represented with van Eyck's customary accuracy, are so arranged as to participate symbolically in the ritual. The little dog in the foreground is a traditional symbol of fidelity; the clogs, cast aside, show that this is holy ground; the peaches, ripening on the chest and on the windowsill, suggest fertility; the beautifully painted brass chandelier holds one lighted candle—the nuptial candle, according to Netherlandish custom the last to be extinguished on the wedding night. The post of a chair near the bed is surmounted by a carved Margaret, patron saint of childbirth. On the rear wall is the conspicuous signature, adorned by many flourishes, "Johannes de Eyck fuit hic 1434" ("Jan van Eyck was here 1434") (fig. 102); the artist thus takes part as witness in the solemn event. So, too, does the mirror, whose convex shape was essential for large reflections in an era when only small pieces of glass could be manufactured. Not only does the surface reflect the room and the couple from the back but also, barely visible between them, two figures, one possibly an assistant and the other—Jan van Eyck. The "mirror without spot" was a symbol of Mary, and its sanctity is reinforced by the garland of ten Gothic paintings of scenes from the Passion of Christ inserted in its frame, and by the rosary hanging beside it. In none of his paintings does van Eyck surpass this subtlety of interior illumination, bringing out the resonance of the red bedspread and hangings and the green costume of the bride, as well as the depth of the groom's purple velvet tunic edged with sable, and leaving on the window frame reflections of the peaches and on the wall light prints from the amber beads.

Jan van Eyck was at once one of the first and one of the greatest painters of independent portraits, a new art form for the fifteenth century. His painting of a *Man in a Red Turban* (fig. 103) shows the subject in middle life, illuminated so as to bring out every facet of the face and even the growth of stubble. The controlled expression and the calm, analytic gaze (this is the earliest known portrait whose sitter looks at the spectator) mask but do not conceal the possibility of deep emotion; it has been plausibly suggested that he may have been no less a person than Jan van Eyck, who signed the picture boldly on the frame, with the date October 21, 1433, and his motto, "Als ich chan" ("As I can"). In view of what we have seen he could do, such reticence is sobering.

VAN DER WEYDEN. Van Eyck had imitators but no followers approaching his stature; his style depended on his unique gifts of mind and vision. Rogier van der Weyden (1399/1400–64), the leading Northern painter of the middle of the fifteenth century, turned sharply away from van Eyck's quiet world of color and light toward monumental pictures, whose dramas are played in human terms on stages close to the observer. Both the linearity and the ability to characterize emotional expres-

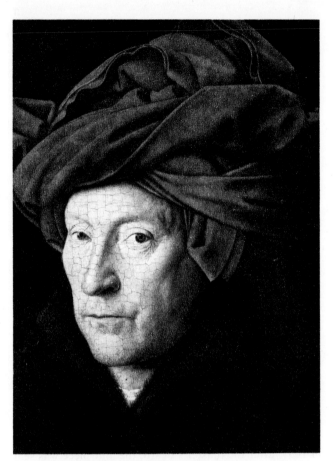

103. JAN VAN EYCK. *Man in a Red Turban
(Self-Portrait?).* 1433. Oil on panel. 10¼ x 7½".
National Gallery, London

sion, which he had possibly learned from Campin, aided him immeasurably in the establishment of his own loftier and more aristocratic style. The large *Descent from the Cross*, perhaps once the central panel of a triptych (colorplate 18), painted about 1435 for a church in Louvain, shows to the full the brilliance of van der Weyden's early period. The setting is entirely symbolic; the Cross is placed inside the sepulcher. Sacrificing entirely van Eyck's luminous shadows, the figures are revealed to us by a pitiless light that incises every wrinkle, every hair, every tear. The relentless pull toward death is emphasized by the way in which the pose of the swooning Virgin repeats the curve of the body of Christ lowered from the Cross, her hand almost touching Adam's skull. The Sluteresque folds that dominate the paintings of Campin, and even reappear in those of van Eyck, are swept away by a line or melody that is perhaps van der Weyden's most effective device for sustaining strong emotion on the plane of high tragedy. Such expressions as that of Joseph of Arimathea at the right, or such poses as the pain-wracked contortion of the Magdalene's shoulders, are never permitted to disturb the beauty of the whole conception.

In 1435 van der Weyden was made official painter to the city of Brussels, an office he held for nearly thirty

years. At the time of the papal Jubilee of 1450 he visited Italy, and not only influenced the Italians deeply but also returned with his vision enlarged by the monumentality of Italian painting. Probably in 1451 he finished his most ambitious work, a polyptych representing the *Last Judgment* (colorplate 19) for the Hôtel-Dieu, a splendid Gothic hospital founded by Chancellor Rolin, which still stands at Beaune in Burgundy. Van der Weyden has treated the nine panels as one, and minimized their frames, save for inscribing through the corners of the panels flanking the central section the slender rainbow of the Judge's throne. At either end of the rainbow Mary and John half-sit, half-kneel, and around it in two quarter circles Apostles and saints are seated on the clouds. Below the sphere that is Christ's footstool the drama centers on Gabriel, solemn and peacock-winged, weighing souls in the balance. Heaven and earth have passed away; the barren ground gives up its naked dead in an amazing variety of beautifully drawn poses. On Christ's right a gentle angel leads the naked blessed into the golden portal of a Gothic Heaven; on his left Hell opens before the damned, its horrors limited, in deference to the sick in the neighboring ward of the hospital, to the expressions on the faces of those about to fall into its depths.

BOUTS. Among the host of excellent painters working in the Netherlands later in the fifteenth century, Dirc Bouts (c. 1415–75) is impressive because of his striking combination of great technical accomplishments, in the tradition of van der Weyden, with touching naïveté of expression. Born probably in Haarlem, Bouts worked in later life in Louvain, where he painted in 1464–68 a major altarpiece whose central panel represents the *Last Supper* (fig. 104). The setting is the familiar Netherlandish interior—a room softly lighted from the side by windows through which the town can be seen, a view out the door into a garden, a patterned marble floor seen in rising perspective, a richly veined column with a carved capital. Although Bouts can control every resource of Netherlandish naturalism, the arrangement of the figures seems stiff until one realizes that the composition has been interpreted in the light of its destination for the Confraternity of the Holy Sacrament.

Two professors of theology at the University of Louvain are known to have dictated the theme. At the moment when Christ says, "This is my body which is given for you: this do in remembrance of me" (Luke 22: 19), he holds up not an ordinary piece of bread but the disk-shaped wafer of the Western Eucharist, and instead of a wineglass a chalice stands in front of him. Christ's head arrives exactly at the intersection of two mullions in the screen that closes off the fireplace when not in use to suggest a cross, and his face is exactly frontal. All the Apostles' faces are turned so that we can see them, and light falls on them to reveal their reverent expressions; even the two seen from the back are shown in profile, Judas instantly recognizable with his left hand (as in

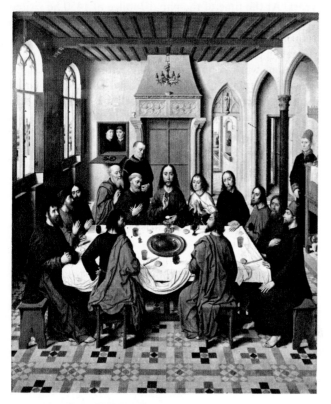

104. DIRC BOUTS. *Last Supper*, center panel of an altarpiece. 1464–68. Panel painting, c. 72 x 60⅛". Church of St. Peter, Louvain, Belgium

Castagno a symbol of treachery; see Chapter 1) hidden behind his back. The combination of symmetry, even lighting, and perspective lines concentrating directly above Christ's head gives the picture a meditative intensity appropriate to its liturgical theme.

VAN DER GOES. In the decades following the death of van der Weyden, the greatest Northern painter was Hugo van der Goes (c. 1440–82). Probably born in Antwerp, he moved to Ghent, joined the artists' guild in 1467, and in 1474 was made its dean. In the following year, notwithstanding his worldly success, van der Goes retired to a monastery near Brussels as a lay brother, but continued to paint. In 1481 he experienced a severe mental collapse, followed by fits of insanity, and the next year he died. His pictures are not numerous; all are marked by deep and, at times, disordered feeling and by sonority of color and sensitivity of drawing. His introspective personality stands at the antipodes from the carefree Limbourg brothers. Although he never emulated the jewel-like perfection of van Eyck, the richness of his color and the depth of his shadows owe much to the great master of Bruges. His debt to van der Weyden is somewhat less, residing largely in the beauty of his drapery rhythms.

Van der Goes' major work is the Portinari Altarpiece (figs. 105, 106), painted about 1476 for Tommaso Portinari, an agent for the Medici Bank in Bruges. Probably in 1483, after the master's death, the altarpiece was sent

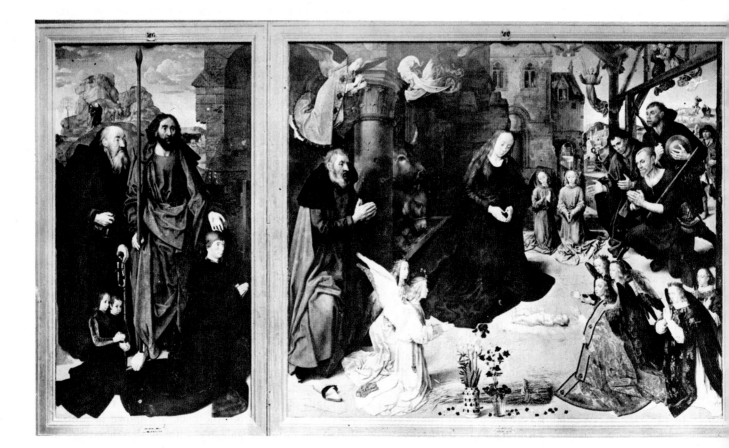

to Florence, where it made a sensation, and was set on the altar of the Chapel of Sant'Egidio, whose walls had been frescoed by Domenico Veneziano and Andrea del Castagno. Although the Florentines were familiar with the work of van Eyck and van der Weyden, they had never seen anything like the emotional power of van der Goes, nor the directness with which his new range of content was visually expressed.

The central panel of the Portinari Altarpiece shows the *Adoration of the Shepherds* in a new way. Mary has just given birth to the Child, miraculously while kneeling as in the vision of Saint Bridget, and he lies on the ground inside the half-ruined shed, shining with the gold rays of spiritual light. The brilliantly painted flowers in the majolica albarello (apothecary jar) and glass tumbler in the foreground are symbolic—the scarlet lily signifies the blood of the Passion, the columbine is a frequent symbol of sorrow, and the iris (in Latin, *gladiolus*: "little sword") refers to the prophecy made by Simeon to Mary in the Temple, "Yea, a sword shall pierce through thy own soul also" (Luke 2: 35). These allusions to the sacrifice of Christ are made explicit by the sheaf of wheat (the Eucharist) alongside the flowers, and the mood is established by the reverent poses and expressions and folded hands of Mary, Joseph, and the nearest shepherd, and even by the alert ox, who has stopped eating; the ass, who symbolizes the infidels, keeps on munching.

It has been shown that the angels who attend the scene are dressed as the assistant ministers (archpriest, deacon, subdeacons, and acolytes) would be at the first Solemn High Mass of a newly ordained priest, yet no one wears the chasuble, the garment of the celebrant. This is because the celebrant, the priest, is Christ himself (repeatedly extolled as priest in Hebrews). The deserted house in the background has been shown to symbolize the house of David, whose harp is sculptured over the door. It is noted here for the first time that this centrally placed door has other meanings: its role as the closed door of Mary's virginity is underscored by the fact that her face partly overlaps it, and the connection of the altarpiece with the Portinari family lies in their very name (i.e., "doorkeepers"). The atmosphere pervading the picture can best be described as that of solemn joy; the delight that a Child is born is tempered by foreknowledge of his sacrifice, and sadness is in turn transfigured by the revelation of the Eucharist. In the faces of the three shepherds (see fig. 106), one can discern three stages of understanding, in terms of nearness to the mystery. The furthest, almost bestial, has removed his hat in mere respect; the second, deeply human, opens his hands in wonder; the third, saintlike, joins his hands in prayer. The wealth of emotion in the central panel is shared by the adults and children of the Portinari family in the wings, and by their gigantic patron saints. Even the wintry landscapes participate in the story; in the distance, on the left, Joseph assists Mary, who can no longer stand the

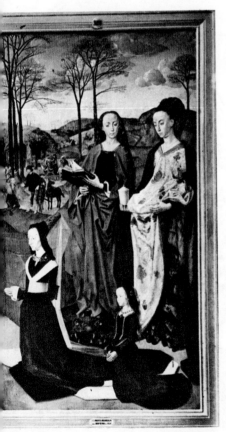

105

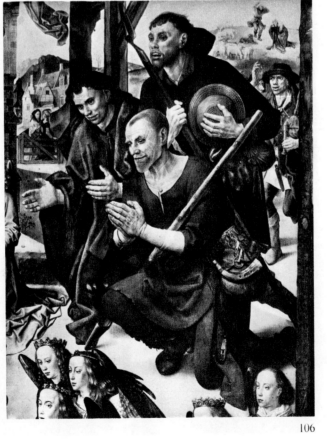

106

105. HUGO VAN DER GOES. *Portinari Altarpiece* (open). c. 1476. Panel painting, center 8'3⅝" x 9'10⅝"; each wing 8'3⅝" x 4'7½". Galleria degli Uffizi, Florence

106. HUGO VAN DER GOES. *Adoration of the Shepherds,* detail of center panel of the *Portinari Altarpiece*

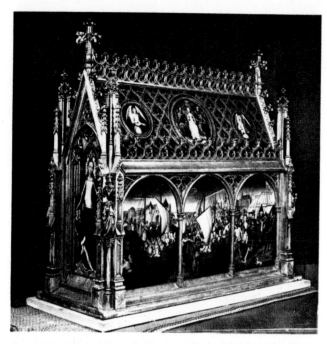

107. HANS MEMLINC. *Shrine of Saint Ursula.* 1489.
Gilded and painted wood, 34 x 36 x 13".
Memlinc Museum, St. John's Hospital, Bruges,
Belgium

pain of riding the donkey on the mountainous road to
Bethlehem; and among the leafless trees, on the right, an
outrider of the Three Magi asks a kneeling peasant the
way to the stable.

MEMLINC. Van der Goes' passionate and mystical style
is worlds apart from that of his pious and prolific contemporary in Bruges, Hans Memlinc (c. 1440–94). Born
at Seligenstadt, Germany, near Frankfurt am Main,
Memlinc was certainly trained in the Netherlands,
perhaps by van der Weyden, whose influence he shows.
He became a citizen of Bruges in 1465, and must have
studied the work of Jan van Eyck, his predecessor in that
city, with whom he was even confused in the eighteenth
century as "John of Bruges" (*Hans* and *Jan* both mean
John). His tranquil art represents a personal synthesis of
those tendencies in Netherlandish painting open to his
comprehension, and in that sense he may be considered a
parallel to his Florentine contemporary Ghirlandaio (see
Chapter 1). Among his numerous works one that shows
his technical ability and his narrative charm is the *Shrine
of Saint Ursula*, consecrated in 1489 (fig. 107), a carved
and gilded reliquary casket less than a yard high, built
like a little Gothic chapel with tracery and pinnacles and
painted on all four sides as well as on the gabled roof.
Memlinc's depiction of the Martyrdom of Saint Ursula

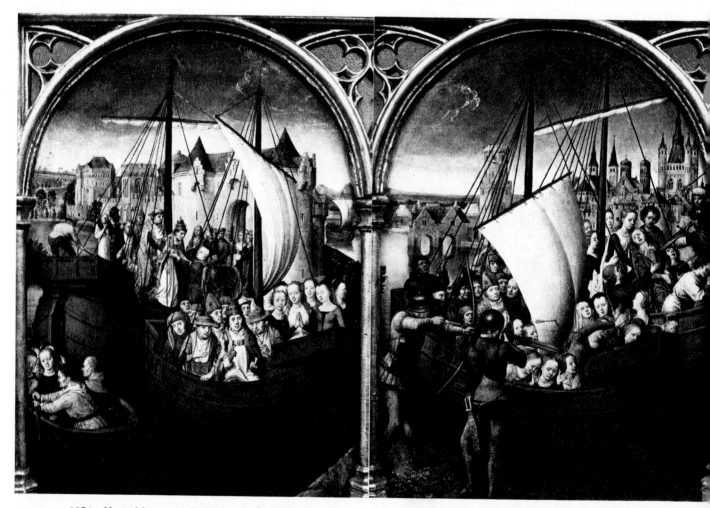

107A. HANS MEMLINC. *Embarkation from Rome,*
panel from the *Shrine of Saint Ursula*

107B. HANS MEMLINC. *The Martyrdom of Saint
Ursula's Companions,* panel from the *Shrine
of Saint Ursula*

would win him no drama prizes, but its naïveté is irresistible. In figure 107A, the saint, attended by pope and cardinals, leaves Rome in two ships, accompanied by as many of her eleven thousand virgins as Memlinc could crowd in. On their arrival at Cologne, in the central panel (fig. 107B), the waiting Huns slaughter both boatloads of virgins with crossbows, longbows, and swords, all explicitly and calmly represented. In the final scene (fig. 107C) Ursula, saved on account of her exceptional beauty, refuses an offer of marriage from Julian, prince of the Huns, who has her shot on the spot. With the boats, of course, Memlinc is merely following the age-old principle of double scale for people and settings; otherwise, he would not have been able to depict the martyrdoms in such detail. In the shining armor and in the beautiful landscape, which continues behind all three scenes with great understanding of light and color, Memlinc shows himself a superb technician in the tradition of van Eyck. His delineation of Saint Ursula's loveliness goes far to justify the prince's interest; German by origin, Memlinc has depicted faithfully the Romanesque churches of Cologne and its great, then-unfinished Cathedral (fig. 107C). Accepted on its own terms, this little reliquary is a work of magical beauty.

GEERTGEN TOT SINT JANS. The magic deepens in the art

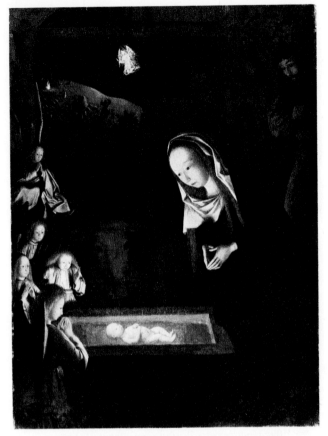

108. GEERTGEN TOT SINT JANS. *Nativity*. c. 1490. Oil on panel, 13⅜ x 9⅞″. National Gallery, London

of a painter called Geertgen tot Sint Jans (Little Gerard from Saint John's) because he was a lay brother at the Monastery of Saint John's in Haarlem. We know little else about him. At his death, which seems to have occurred about 1495, he was only twenty-eight years old, according to Carel van Mander, the Netherlandish Vasari. The brief list of his works includes one of the most enchanting pictures of the fifteenth century, a tiny panel of about 1490 that takes up the theme of the night Nativity where Gentile da Fabriano left off (fig. 108). Mary kneels before the manger at the right, angels at the left; in the shadows the ox and ass and Joseph are dimly discernible. The Child in the manger, although he sheds golden rays of spiritual light, is depicted as a real miracle, in that all the illumination in the foreground comes from his tiny incandescent body. In the background the announcing angel glows with real light high in the night. The poetry of the scene is the more intense in that Geertgen has reduced the faces to egg shapes, whose purity accentuates the calm with which these figures gently accept as fact the miracle of miracles, that a tiny Child can shine in a dark world.

BOSCH. The fifteenth century comes to an unbelievable close and the sixteenth to a fantastic beginning in the art of a lonely painter about whose external existence we know little, not even the date of a single picture, and

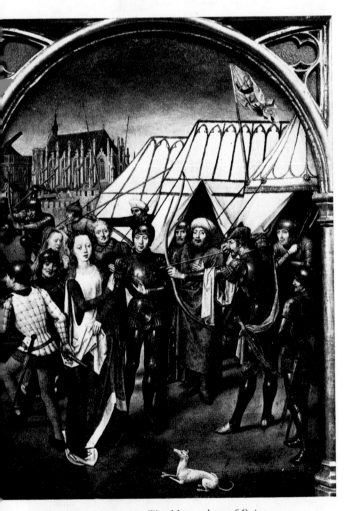

107C. HANS MEMLINC. *The Martyrdom of Saint Ursula*, panel from the *Shrine of Saint Ursula*

The inexhaustible wealth of Bosch's imagination fills the enormous triptych known as the *Garden of Delights* (colorplate 20, and figs. 110, 111, 112). The left panel, the *Creation of Eve* (see fig. 110), is easy enough to read. The Lord, strangely tiny and ineffectual, presents to Adam the already perfectly formed Eve, much to his apparent interest. Clearly, the trouble starts here. In the pool below and in the one around the fountain above move countless animals and birds, including a giraffe (the first

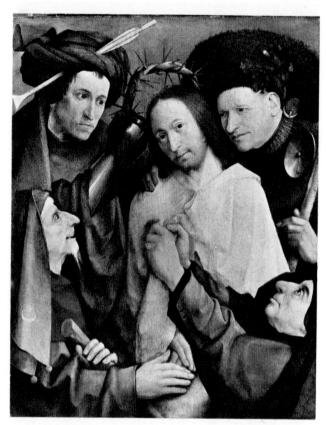

109. HIERONYMUS BOSCH. *Crowning with Thorns.*
After 1500. Panel painting, 29¼ x 23⅝".
National Gallery, London

whose inner life is revealed to us only in symbols of a defeating complexity. Hieronymus Bosch (c. 1450–1516) worked largely in the city of 's Hertogenbosch, in present-day southern Holland, where his father and grandfather executed wall paintings in the Cathedral, the most splendid Gothic church in Holland, under construction throughout Bosch's lifetime. His highly personal art is perhaps best accessible through what is generally considered a late work, that is, one after 1500, the *Crowning with Thorns* (fig. 109). With no setting whatever, and therefore in the space of our own minds, Christ stands, surrounded by four tormenters whose carefully delineated faces remind us of those daily seen in our own lives. An old gaffer, marked as a Muslim by the star and crescent on his headcloth (assumed as symbols by the Ottoman Turks after the capture of Constantinople in 1453), an archer with a crossbow bolt stuck in his turban, a soldier wearing a spiked dog collar, and an ordinary character with a downturned lower lip surround the surprisingly red-haired Christ, as the archer raises the crown of thorns to place it on Christ's head. Yet Christ shows no suffering—his bright blue eyes look out at *us* with searching yet calm accusation, as if we were the guilty ones. This look will not be easily forgotten, nor will the transparent delicacy of Bosch's light, nor the sensitive quality of his drawing, which in this picture at least owes little or nothing to Netherlandish tradition.

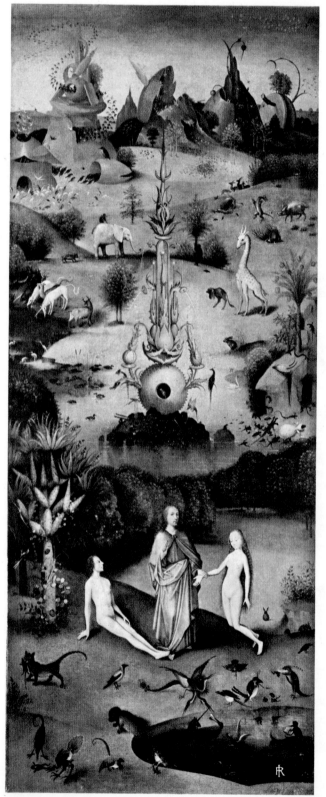

to reach Europe arrived in Florence in 1483), an elephant, and unicorns. All is not happy even here; at the lower left a cat stalks off with a mouse it has caught, and a serpent more than halfway up on the right slithers ominously around a tree—the palm tree, symbol of eternal life, endangered from this moment. Fantastic rocks rise in the background, from one of which emerges a dense spiral of birds.

The central panel shows a plain with rocky out-croppings punctuated by pools and leading toward a lake in whose center is a monstrous mechanism, a gigantic egg from which sprout pinnacles and fishlike forms; round it are four more fantastic combinations of rocks and living beings. In this landscape frolic hundreds of naked young men and women, emerging from or hidden in eggs, a colossal mussel shell, and spheres, domes, and cylinders of glass. All the figures are pale pink, youthful, un-muscular, and weak, and although many appear in

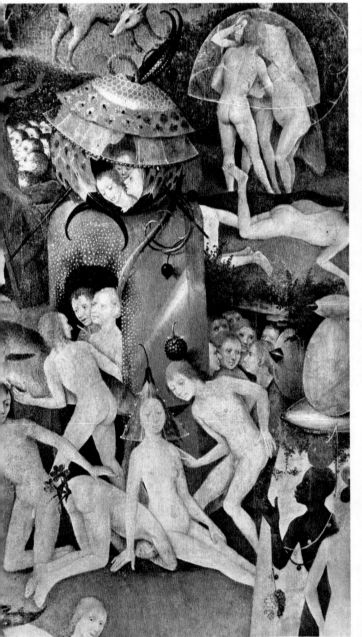

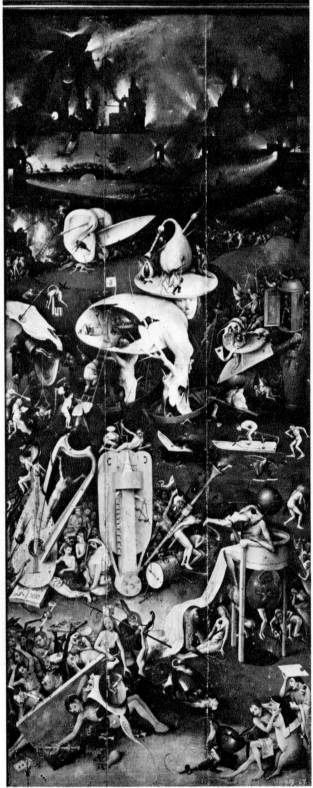

110. HIERONYMUS BOSCH. *Creation of Eve*, left panel of the *Garden of Delights* triptych. c. 1505–10. Panel painting, center panel 86⅝ x 76¾″; each wing 86⅝ x 38¼″. Museo del Prado, Madrid

111. HIERONYMUS BOSCH. Center panel of the *Garden of Delights* triptych (detail). See Colorplate 20

112. HIERONYMUS BOSCH. *Hell*, right panel of the *Garden of Delights* triptych

111

couples (or threes and fours), no explicit sexual activity is shown. But the erotic nature of the imagery is unmistakable; some figures caress or embrace gigantic strawberries or other fruit, as well as birds and fish, that have sexual significance in several languages. In the center the little people ride gaily not only horses but also animals legendary for their appetites, such as pigs and goats, in a circle around a little pool in which nude women bathe.

A full description would be endless. Obviously, Bosch is condemning all erotic activity and yet is irresistibly fascinated by it. His ambivalence is so strong that some writers have suggested that he belonged to a secret sect that looked forward to a Paradise not unlike the one in this picture. This idea has not won wide acceptance, especially since several of Bosch's major works, including this one, were later bought by the fanatically religious Philip II of Spain. Perhaps Bosch is saying that all people really want to do is to indulge their fleshly desires; in the words of Saint Paul (Rom. 3: 10), "There is none righteous, no, not one." The visual language Bosch uses for this message is in itself so fascinating that he has been claimed as one of theirs by the Surrealists in the twentieth century. But the vocabulary should not surprise us;

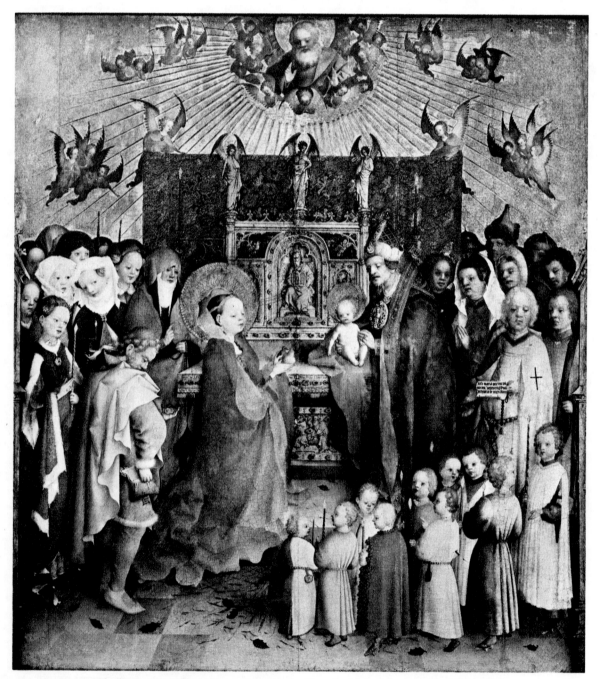

113. STEFAN LOCHNER. *Presentation in the Temple.* 1447. Oil on panel, 54¾ x 49⅝".
Hessisches Landesmuseum, Darmstadt, Germany

by and large, it is drawn from the pagan tradition of animal symbolism incorporated in the animal interlace of medieval art, reappearing in the Romanesque imagery that Saint Bernard recognized as evil, and again in the *drôleries* of fourteenth-century manuscript borders. What renders the central picture intoxicating is that this incredible repertory of symbols is brightly illuminated, daintily drawn, and suffused with high, pale color.

And yet Bosch is heretical; for such a world he can see no salvation. The common doom is Hell, a panorama of darkness illuminated by firelight, shown in the right panel (fig. 112). Instead of Satan this kingdom is presided over by a pathetic monster whose body is a broken egg, whose legs are tree trunks plunged through the bottoms of boats, whose head is crowned with a disk and bagpipe, and whose face turns toward us in despair as tiny people crawl in and out of him like vermin. Above him two immense ears impaled by an arrow and flanking an erect knife blade are pushed like an engine of war across the dark plain; below, the damned are impaled on the strings of musical instruments or eaten by a hawk-headed monster seated on a tall *chaise percée* and excreted in bubbles. At the top we look across the Styx to the burning city, lost in flame and smoke. Never before had an imagination that could conceive such things been coupled with the ability to paint them. Rather than backward toward the Middle Ages, the imagination of Bosch leads us in the direction of the Protestant doctrine of predestination, and eventually toward the inner world of dream symbols revealed by psychoanalysis.

FIFTEENTH-CENTURY PAINTING IN GERMANY AND CENTRAL EUROPE

The influence of Netherlandish art was immediate and far-reaching, more so in the fifteenth century than was that of the Italian Renaissance, which in the sixteenth broke like a flood over western Europe. Germany developed a host of competent masters, more or less formed by Netherlandish style, but only a few strong individualities.

LOCHNER. One delightful painter of the early fifteenth century stands out. Stefan Lochner (c. 1415–51/52), from Meersburg on Lake Constance, was trained in the studio of Campin and achieved great success in Cologne. A delightful late work is his *Presentation in the Temple*, of 1447 (fig. 113). Although he adopts the rising perspective of Netherlandish painting for the floor in the foreground, he never relinquishes the gold background of medieval art. In his figures he reveals all the delicacy of his famous "soft" style, dissolving the sculpturesque forms he inherited from Campin into a free movement of brilliant colors. Even when they are old, Lochner's people, with their round foreheads, chubby cheeks, and shy gazes, always resemble children. And such children! His procession of boy-choristers, placed according to size and led by the tiniest of tots, is disarming.

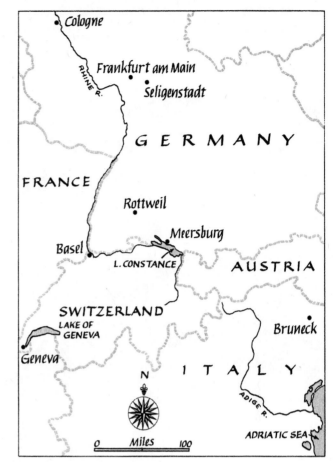

MAP 6.   *South Germany and Switzerland*

WITZ. A very different German master, Konrad Witz (c. 1400/10–45/46), was born at Rottweil in Württemburg, but moved to Basel in Switzerland, then the center of a church council that attracted princes and prelates from throughout Europe. Witz was accepted in the artists' guild in Basel in 1434, and bought a fine house. Much of his work fell a victim to Protestant iconoclasm during the Reformation, but what survives shows a vigorous and independent personality, with little patience for the niceties of perspective or anatomy, but acute powers of observation, particularly where nature is concerned. His *Miraculous Draft of Fish* (fig. 114), part of an altarpiece containing a cycle of scenes from the life of Peter installed in 1444 in the Cathedral of Geneva, displays all his best qualities. The background is the Lake of Geneva, a landscape "portrait" in the tradition already established by Masaccio and Fra Angelico, exactly painted, with farms and hills in the middle distance and a glittering array of snowcapped Alpine crags on the horizon. More surprising is Witz's observation of water, complete not only with reflections but also with refractions, distorting the stones on the bottom and the legs of Peter seen through its transparent surface; Witz even painted the bubbles thrown up, apparently, by passing fish.

PACHER. As a wood-carver Michael Pacher (c. 1435–98) exploited to the full the splendors of the fifteenth-century Austrian version of the Flamboyant style. But his

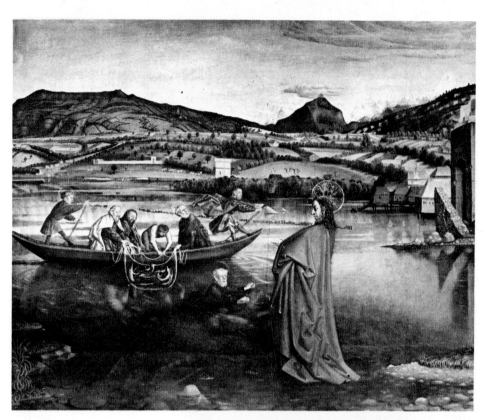

114. KONRAD WITZ.
Miraculous Draft of Fish,
from an altarpiece
depicting scenes from the
life of Saint Peter.
c. 1444. Panel painting.
52 x 60⅝". Musée d'Art
et d'Histoire, Geneva

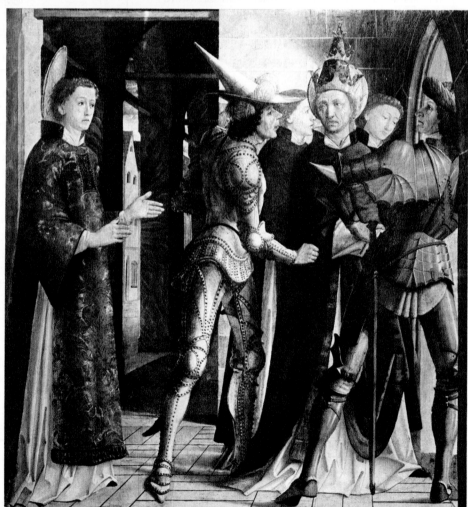

115. MICHAEL PACHER. *Pope
Sixtus II Taking Leave of
Saint Lawrence*, from an
altarpiece depicting scenes
from the life of Saint
Lawrence. c. 1462–70. Panel
painting, 41 x 39½".
Österreichische Galerie,
Museum Mittelalterlicher,
Österreichischer Kunst,
Vienna

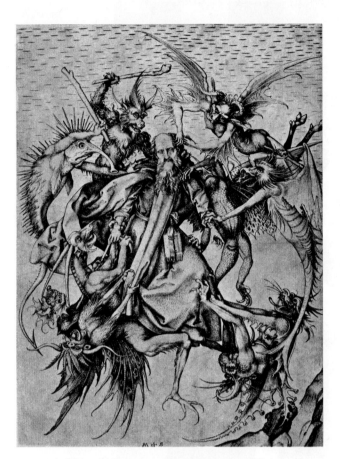

116. MARTIN SCHONGAUER. *Temptation of Saint Anthony.* c. 1470–75. Engraving, 12¼ x 9". The Metropolitan Museum of Art, New York. Rogers Fund, 1920

Tirolean home at Bruneck (modern Brunico; in Italy since 1919) was in the valley of the Adige, along the trade route descending from the Alps into northern Italy, and this location influenced his art profoundly. Such a painting as *Pope Sixtus II Taking Leave of Saint Lawrence* (fig. 115), from a cycle of scenes from the life of Saint Lawrence in an altarpiece painted about 1462–70, is strikingly Italianate. Pacher's strong interest in perspective recession, the solidity of his forms, and the construction of his drapery show so close a study of Mantegna's frescoes in Padua (see fig. 80) that the Northern gable seen through an arch at the left comes almost as a surprise. Yet in spite of these Italian elements, he handles light like a Northerner, especially in the exquisite play of tones across Saint Lawrence's brocade dalmatic.

SCHONGAUER. An important aspect of German art, and the means by which German influence spread throughout Europe, was engraving, whose most important practitioner and innovator was Martin Schongauer (c. 1450–91), from Colmar in Alsace. Schongauer was an excellent painter, in the tradition of Rogier van der Weyden, but was especially known for his copper engravings. As we have seen (Chaper 1), engraving was well known to the Italians, and was practiced with distinction by Pollaiuolo

(see fig. 72), Mantegna, and others. But Pollaiuolo's combination of contours and parallel hatching was simple compared to the elaborate refinements of Schongauer, who stippled and dotted the surface of the copper to produce a veil of shadow ranging from tones of filmy lightness to concentrated darks. His engraving of the *Temptation of Saint Anthony* (fig. 116) shows that the demons generated by Northern imagination were far from being the exclusive province of Bosch. The saint floats above the rocks, lifted, beaten, pulled at, mocked by hideous hybrid devils, their bodies prolonged and twisted into a dense foreground composition that recalls the persistent animal interlace of the migrations period and of Hiberno-Saxon manuscripts. Schongauer's engraving so impressed the boy Michelangelo that he copied it carefully in pen and watercolor in 1488 or 1489 when he was a fourteen-year-old assistant in Ghirlandaio's studio.

PAINTING IN FRANCE

The prolonged political and military chaos of the early fifteenth century, during which the Hundred Years' War with England drew to a close in France, was not conducive to the development of either bourgeois prosperity or local schools of painting patronized by the merchant class. Nonetheless, a few artists of great sensitivity were

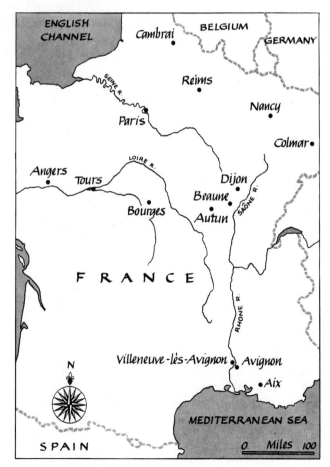

MAP 7. *France*

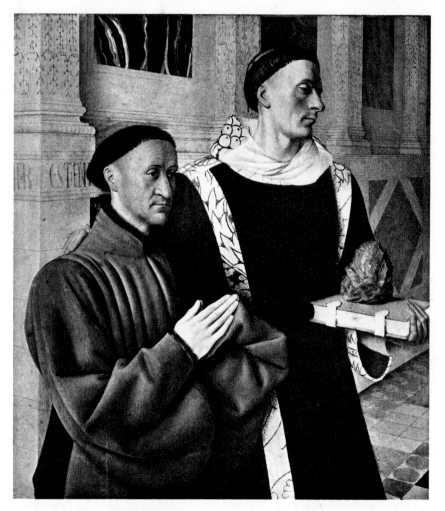

117. JEAN FOUQUET. *Portrait of Étienne Chevalier,* left wing of the
Melun Diptych (now divided). c. 1450. Panel painting, 36⅛ x 33½″.
Gemäldegalerie, Staatliche Museen, Berlin

active, largely in the entourage of royal courts, under combined influences from both Italy and the Netherlands, yet striking in their own individuality of feeling.

FOUQUET. The finest fifteenth-century artist connected with the court of the French kings was Jean Fouquet (c. 1420–before 1481), from the central French city of Tours, who worked for Charles VII, whose throne had been saved by Joan of Arc. Fouquet made a trip to Italy, and visited Rome certainly before 1447 and while Fra Angelico was working there. About 1450, probably in Paris, he painted the quiet and sensitive portrait of Étienne Chevalier, finance minister to Charles VII (fig. 117); this is the left wing of a diptych, whose other panel represents the Virgin and Child. The Renaissance architecture with its veined marble paneling is strongly Italianate, in fact Albertian, but the treatment of light and the detailed rendering of the surface, along with the deep inner glow of the coloring, reveal that Fouquet is still a Northern master, well aware of what was going on in Netherlandish art. His instinctive reticence masks great depth of feeling. Saint Stephen, dressed in a

deacon's dalmatic, holds in his left hand a book and the jagged stone of his martyrdom (a few drops of blood still cling to his scalp), while his right rests gently on the shoulder of his namesake.

Fouquet continued with great brillance the art of illumination, which was not renounced by the French in the fifteenth century, although in Italy and the Netherlands it became increasingly relegated to specialists rather than practiced by the leading masters. One of the about sixty miniatures that originally adorned the *Book of Hours* he illustrated for Étienne Chevalier in 1452–56 shows the *Marriage of the Virgin* (fig. 118) taking place before a triumphal arch that reminds us of that of Constantine, but which is labeled *Templum Salomonis* and decorated with two of the four spiral columns, apparently of Syrian origiṅ, that the artist must have seen in Saint Peter's, Rome, where they were believed to have come from Solomon's Temple. (For a later, monumental use of this motive, see Bernini's tabernacle; fig. 238.) In the brilliant coloring and the harmonious grouping of the figures, the dominant influence is that of Fra Angelico, although the portly character at the left is a meticulously rendered portrait type seldom found outside Northern art.

MASTER OF THE ANNUNCIATION OF AIX. Apart from the exceptional genius of Fouquet, the most striking developments of French fifteenth-century painting took place in the far-flung dominions of René I the Good, duke of Anjou and Lorraine, count of Provence, and briefly king of Naples (1435–42). René retired to Provence in 1442, and his court at Aix became a popular resort of poets and artists. An extraordinary painter is the unknown master who painted, probably about 1445, the *Annunciation of Aix* (fig. 119), which shows the event taking place in the interior of a south French hall church. The influence of Jan van Eyck is obvious and strong, especially in the pose of the angel and in the way in which the shadows are thrown across the church floor from the central column, which recall the Ghent Altarpiece (see fig. 97). God the Father appears in the heavens, and the light from him comes through a Gothic window, as often in Northern Annunciations, with the tiny Christ Child sliding headfirst down a beam as in the Mérode Altarpiece (see fig. 93). The drawing and modeling and the dark shadows are much coarser than in the work of Van Eyck or, in fact, of any major Netherlandish master, but the picture is appealing in its simplicity and directness. It has even been suggested that this anonymous master may

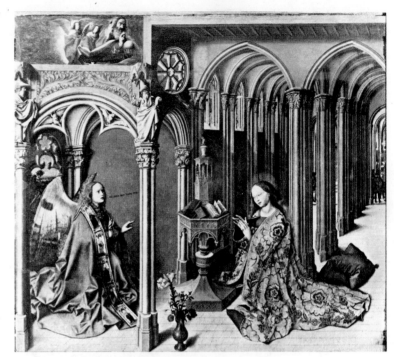

119. MASTER OF THE ANNUNCIATION OF AIX.
Annunciation of Aix. c. 1445. Panel painting, 61 x 69¼".
Ste.-Marie-Madeleine, Aix-en-Provence, France

have been the link between Antonello da Messina (see fig. 83) and Netherlandish art, although Antonello is far more subtle and expert both as draftsman and as colorist.

MASTER OF RENÉ OF ANJOU. Almost as interesting as the Master of the Annunciation of Aix, and more imaginative and poetic, is the also anonymous painter who illustrated an allegorical romance by King René, finished in 1457, *Le Livre du coeur d'amour épris* (*The Book of the Heart Taken by Love*). One painting (fig. 120), of inimitable mystery and grace, shows the love-sick monarch in his bed, while winged Love takes the heart from his body and gives it to Desire, a white-clad page whose garments are ornamented with flames. The night light, from a hidden candle, is one of the most magical attempts in this direction in the fifteenth century, and the whole picture is exquisite in its effects of color and surface. The bed is hung with purple, and the room with white and purple in a jagged pattern, and even the night sky outside the window is purple; against the purple are played brilliant tones of blue, red, and gold.

ENGUERRAND QUARTON. The leading panel painter of southern France at midcentury was Enguerrand Quarton (1410/15–after 1466), also known as Charonton. The celebrated *Avignon Pietà* (fig. 121) has now been successfully attributed to him. In the pose of the dead Christ over the Virgin's knees, as well as in the spareness and austerity of the forms, the picture looks very Italian, but the angular motions and haunting expressions are quintessentially French. Especially touching is the head of Christ, whose mouth hangs slightly open while his eyes

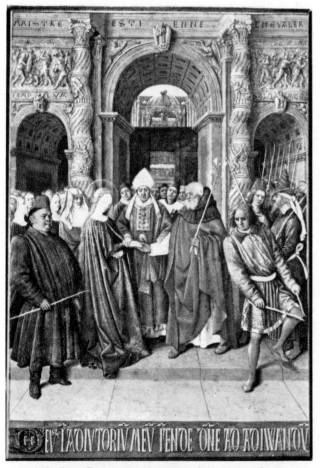

118. JEAN FOUQUET. *Marriage of the Virgin*, from the *Book of Hours of Étienne Chevalier*. 1452–56. Illumination, 6¼ x 4¾". Musée Condé, Chantilly, France

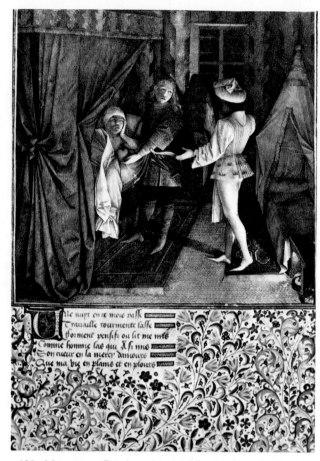

120. MASTER OF RENÉ OF ANJOU. *Amour Gives the King's Heart to Désir*, from *Le Livre du coeur d'amour épris.* Completed 1457. Illumination, 11⅜ x 8½".
Österreichische Nationalbibliothek, Vienna

are not entirely closed, and whose face is gently illuminated from below. The Pietà seems almost to be a vision of the kneeling priest at the left, whose face has been searchingly portrayed. After the muted color and quiet intensity of this panel, the splendor of the *Coronation of the Virgin* (colorplate 21), still in the hospital at Villeneuve-lès-Avignon, comes as a surprise. Painted in 1453–54, according to a minutely detailed contract with the prior Jean de Montagnac, which spelled out everything to be represented, the work shows the coronation taking place against a still-golden Heaven, with the Virgin and the Trinity depicted on a colossal scale compared to the medievally grouped ranks of saints on either side. Father and Son, exactly alike, wear mantles of royal crimson, dissonant against the sharp orange of the surrounding seraphim, and almost meeting before the kneeling, porcelain-faced Virgin. Her red and gold tunic is partly covered with a mantle of the same resounding blue as that of the sky below her, strewn with tiny clouds and tinier white angels bearing souls upward. The real world is reduced to a strip at the bottom of the panel, showing Rome on the left (a south French Gothic town) with the Mass of Saint Gregory taking place in Saint Peter's; Jerusalem on the right, with bulbous domes on its towers; and in the center the crucified Christ, before whom kneels the white-clad donor, Jean de Montagnac. At the lower left angels assist souls, naked save for their distinguishing headgear, out of Purgatory, while at the right the damned suffer the usual endless torments in Hell.

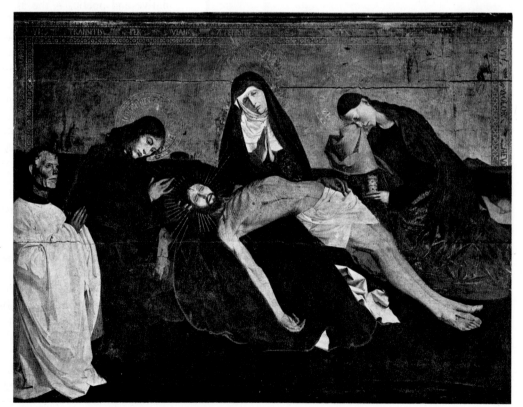

121. ENGUERRAND QUARTON. *Avignon Pietà.* c. 1460. Panel painting, 63¾ x 85⅞". The Louvre, Paris

3

The High Renaissance in Florence and Rome

The last decade of the fifteenth century was an ominous period for the Italians. The year 1492 was crucial not on account of Columbus' first voyage to the New World, which attracted little immediate attention, but because in that year the death of Lorenzo the Magnificent removed from the government of Florence, and from the turbulent Italian political scene, a firm and wise hand. The throne of Peter was occupied by the sinister Alexander VI, whose son, Cesare Borgia, was doing his best to turn the Papal States into a hereditary monarchy. In 1494 Pietro de' Medici and his brothers were expelled from Florence and the republic restored; that same year Charles VIII of France descended upon Italy to press his claims to the throne of Naples, thus commencing the cycle of foreign dominations that soon put a virtual end to Italian independence. The Italian response was mixed and confused, but the Florentines, at first under the leadership of Savonarola, rallied to the defense of their reestablished republic against the Borgia, and a coalition expelled the French in 1495; it was useless—in 1499 the French returned under Louis XII and occupied Milan. The death of Alexander VI in 1503 gave the new pontiff, Julius II, a free hand in the organization of papal military power in order to drive out the French and to reform internally the Church, grown corrupt under recent popes.

Nothing less than political unity, which was a practical impossibility, could have maintained Italian independence against the newly consolidated Western monarchies—France, Spain, and the Holy Roman Empire. Nonetheless, the resistance of the Florentines and the counterattack of Julius II created a heady atmosphere that did much to inspire a new style, the High Renaissance, which can be understood as an attempt to compensate on a symbolic plane for the actual powerlessness of the Italian states through a new vision of human grandeur and of heroic action and through a dynamic architecture to match. Like the images and norms created by Periclean Athens in a similarly precarious situation, those of High Renaissance Italy long outlived the collapse of the political entities that gave them birth. Despite the brevity of the High Renaissance—twenty-five years at the most—the principles established in Florence and Rome in the early sixteenth century provided a set of norms for much of European art for at least three centuries.

LEONARDO. High Renaissance style was founded upon the research and experiments of one of the most gifted individuals ever born. Leonardo da Vinci (1452–1519) was not only a great painter and sculptor but also an architect of genius, although he never erected a building. He was also the inventor of an incredible variety of machines for both peaceful and military purposes (some have recently been constructed from his drawings and actually work), an engineer, a musician, an investigator in the field of aerodynamics, and the leading physicist, botanist, anatomist, geologist, and geographer of his time. Much has been said about the ideal of the universal man in the Renaissance; in actuality, there are few examples. Leonardo is the one who most closely approaches the ideal, having left untouched only the fields of Classical scholarship, philosophy, and poetry. In a sense he began where Alberti left off; it is a remarkable coincidence that both were illegitimate, and perhaps thus freed from the trammels of convention. There is, however, a crucial difference between the two. In an era when the continuing power of the Church competed in men's minds with the revived authority of Classical antiquity, Alberti decided for the latter; Leonardo, a lifelong skeptic, accepted neither. Throughout the thousands of pages he covered with notes and ideas, God is seldom mentioned, but nature appears innumerable times. Classical authorities were never cited. For Leonardo there was no authority

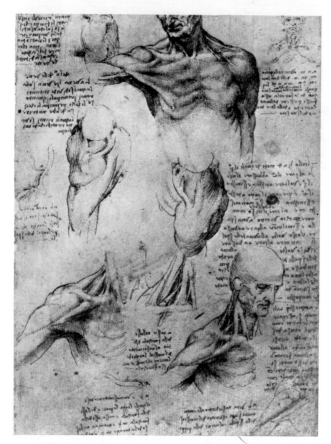

122. LEONARDO DA VINCI. *Anatomical Drawings of a Man's Head and Shoulders.* c. 1510. Pen and ink on white paper, 15 x 10″. Royal Library, Windsor, England

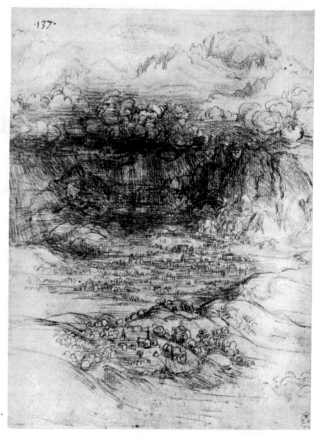

123. LEONARDO DA VINCI. *Storm Breaking over a Valley.* c. 1500. Red chalk on white paper, 8 x 6″. Royal Library, Windsor, England

higher than that of the eye, which he characterized as the "window of the soul." In many respects his pragmatic attitude was comparable to that of nineteenth-century scientists. Although he never focused his ideas concerning either science or art into an organized body of theory, Leonardo felt that the two were closely interrelated in that both were accessible to the eye.

Throughout Leonardo's writings we encounter the lament, "Who will tell me if anything was ever finished?" Little that he started was, least of all his lifelong pursuit of the elusive mysteries of nature. It is, therefore, to his drawings that we must look for the secrets of his art. In them, as in his notes, generally side by side on the same page, he analyzed the structure of rocks, the behavior of light, the movement of water, the growth of plants, the flight of birds, and the anatomy of insects, horses, and human beings. Although he derisively termed men "sacks for food," unworthy of the wonderful machine nature had contrived for them, he nonetheless wanted to see how that machine functioned, and did so by means of dissection. Possibly, Pollaiuolo's pioneer anatomical studies (see fig. 72) had been based on dissection, which was frowned on by the Church. Certainly in 1495 the young Michelangelo had dissected bodies, but for another purpose, as we shall see when we consider his profoundly different art.

Leonardo's dissections were scientific, and went as far as studying the process and the very moment of conception and the growth of the fetus in the womb; his studies of blood vessels enabled him to arrive at a preliminary statement of the circulation of the blood a century before William Harvey expounded his thesis. Hundreds of drawings of human anatomy remain. Fig. 122 shows the progressive dissection of the arm and shoulder of a cadaver in order to clarify the shapes of the muscles and tendons, their functions, and their insertion into the bones. In the upper right-hand corner Leonardo has substituted ropes for the muscles so as to clarify the mechanical principles involved. Since he was left-handed, he wrote his notes (but not his letters) from right to left, so that to read them requires not only a knowledge of fifteenth-century handwriting but also a mirror.

Nothing in Leonardo's scientific drawings is quite as exciting as his Olympian views of nature, which illustrate his standpoint in the Renaissance debate about the relative importance of the various arts. Leonardo maintained that painting deserved a position as one of the liberal arts, more so than music or poetry. Music, he noted, is dead as soon as the last sound has expired, but a work of painting is always there to be seen. Also, he pointed out, no one ever traveled to read a poem, but people journey hundreds of miles to see a painting. Ingenuous as these arguments may seem, in the Renaissance the issues they countered were burning

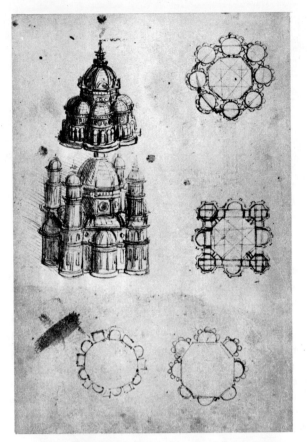

124. LEONARDO DA VINCI. *Plans and Perspective Views of Domed Churches*. c. 1490. Pen and ink. Institut de France, Paris

questions. But Leonardo was unwilling to admit sculpture to the liberal arts; the painter could work in quiet, sitting down, richly dressed, and listen to music while he worked, while the sculptor, poor man, was covered with sweat and dust, and his ears deafened by the noise of hammer and chisel on stone. It is by no means irrelevant that when Leonardo began his campaign to upgrade painting the artist was still a craftsman and a guild member; before the High Renaissance was over a great master could live like a prince, and in the late sixteenth century academies rendered the guilds obsolete.

Whatever the painter wants to do, said Leonardo, he is "Lord and God" to do it, an astonishing claim, the exact reverse of the medieval attempt to show that God is an architect. The painter's mind "is a copy of the divine mind, since it operates freely in creating the many kinds of animals, plants, fruits, landscapes, countrysides, ruins, and awe-inspiring places." The painter's genius can take us from the "high summits of mountains to uncover great countrysides," and whatever is in the universe "he has it first in his mind and then in his hands." This claim sounds like an extension, an almost blasphemous one, of Giannozzo Manetti's paean of praise for humanity (see pages 24, 25). In one of Leonardo's comprehensive landscape drawings (fig. 123), we look from a high place upon rolling hills bordering a rich plain in whose center rise the domes and towers of a city, then beyond to a

valley walled in by mountain crags and shadowed by rain clouds, and finally above the clouds to Alpine summits under eternal snow. Leonardo was an indefatigable mountain climber, and when he reached the top he had other things to occupy his mind than reading the *Confessions* of Saint Augustine (see page 25). Once his exhilaration at seeing the world at his feet subsided, he examined the rocks to discover how they were formed and deduced from fossilized sea animals that they were laid down under water. The world, therefore, could not have been created in 4004 B.C., although this biblical tradition was not again seriously doubted until the nineteenth century.

To Leonardo as to Alberti architecture was based on the twin principles of geometric relationships and natural growth, and, therefore, nothing was so important as the central-plan structure. Although we shall see this new organic architecture realized in Bramante's plans for Saint Peter's, Rome, the idea for it originated in the mind of Leonardo. He was reproached by Vasari for covering pages with geometric doodles, but these were of importance for his architecture since he was trying to elucidate the permutations and combinations that determine the forms of buildings. Leonardo abandoned both the planar architecture of Brunelleschi and the block architecture of Alberti, and began with plans and perspective drawings of the same structure (fig. 124), such as an octagon surrounded by eight circles, and a Greek cross whose arms, terminating in four semicircular apses, embrace four additional octagons on each of which a tower was to be erected (changed to cylinders in the perspective drawing).

Leonardo's knowledge of Albertian perspective was absolute, and was important for him as a mathematical structure for the understanding of space, but it is interesting that no sooner did he establish the linear structure than he began to dissolve it. For he was also acutely conscious of the forces of growth and decay, which provoke continuous change and renewal, and thus precluded his faith in the perfect, unshakable, and therefore somewhat artificial world of Piero della Francesca. This study (fig. 125) was made for the architectural setting of one of Leonardo's earliest paintings, an *Adoration of the Magi* commissioned in 1481 for a church outside Florence, but it was never carried any further than the monochrome underpaint. With a dark wash he began by brushing in the shadows and only gradually defined the forms in light on the assumption that darkness comes first in the world and light penetrates it. This is the exact opposite of the traditional method of drawing the outlines first and then bringing forms into relief by means of shadow (see the sinopia in fig. 18).

Leonardo's pyramidal composition (fig. 126) is constructed along principles already established by Pollaiuolo (see pages 59, 60; fig. 71) that groups are based on the actions of the component figures and will dissolve as soon as they move. Although Leonardo could not have

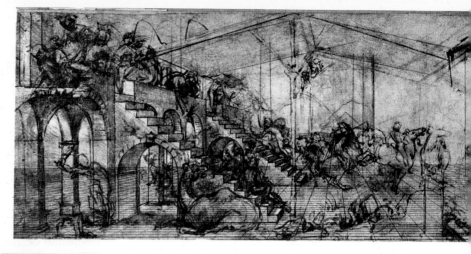

125. LEONARDO DA VINCI. *Architectural Perspective and Background Figures, for the "Adoration of the Magi."* c. 1481. Pen and ink, wash, and white, 6½ x 11½". Gabinetto dei Disegni e Stampe, Galleria degli Uffizi, Florence

126. LEONARDO DA VINCI. *Adoration of the Magi.* Begun 1481. Panel, 96 x 97". Galleria degli Uffizi, Florence

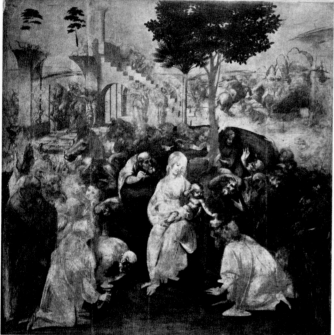

known it, this very discovery had been made in Greece in the fifth century B.C. (see Vol. 1, Part Two, Chapter 4). The enclosing shed that Leonardo had been at such pains to construct in the drawing is gone, leaving only the ruined arches and steps, and although these are projected in perspective, they no longer show any signs of the mathematical construction on which they are based. With the faces as with the composition, Leonardo starts with the moment of feeling and perception, defining expression first; form will follow. In the background at the right appears for the first time the composition of rearing horses that has little to do with the ostensible subject of the painting but that will turn up again in magnificent form in the *Battle of Anghiari* (see fig. 129).

Many of Leonardo's crucial works were executed away from Florence in traditionally inimical Milan at the court of Lodovico Sforza, who had seized the duchy of Milan from his nephew and ruled it with wisdom, foresight, and artistic taste. Lodovico was a perfect patron for so great an artist and Leonardo's almost exact contemporary (b. 1451; reigned 1481–99; d. 1508). When offering his serv-

ices to Lodovico, interestingly enough, Leonardo mentioned first his military inventions and his work as a hydraulic engineer, architect, and sculptor and only at the close his ability to paint. His first great work in Milan was the *Madonna of the Rocks* (fig. 127), begun in 1483 for the Oratory of the Immaculate Conception. The doctrine of the Immaculate Conception, unrelated to that of the Virgin Birth, means that at her own conception Mary was freed from the taint of Original Sin so that she could be a worthy vessel for the Incarnation of Christ. Leonardo has interpreted the doctrine dramatically by illuminating Mary in the midst of a dark world of towering rock forms and views into mysterious distances, which is mostly in shadow. She raises her hand in protection over the Christ Child, who blesses the kneeling infant John the Baptist, indicated by a pointing angel. The picture, almost certainly in oil, adopts many of the techniques invented by the Netherlanders, and in its concentration on the tiniest details of rocks and of plant life in the foreground, as on the glow of light from flesh, eyes, and hair, owes a debt to the encyclopedic naturalism of van Eyck; as in Netherlandish painting, traditional halos disappear. The wonderful sweetness and grace of faces and figures, treasured by Leonardo's patrons, are his own and inimitable.

Contrary to iconographic tradition, especially in Castagno and in Dirc Bouts (see figs. 63, 104), Leonardo's *Last Supper* (fig. 128), painted on the end wall of the refectory of the Monastery of Santa Maria delle Grazie in Milan in 1495–97/98, is not concerned with the institution of the Eucharist. Instead, Leonardo has based his composition on the passage that recurs in Matthew, Mark, and Luke, in which Christ says, "Verily, I say unto you that one of you shall betray me. And they were exceeding sorrowful, and began every one to say unto him, Lord is it I?" As in the *Adoration of the Magi*, the composition is a product of the moment of action and of meaning. Donatello had done something similar in the *Feast of Herod* (see fig. 42), but with a bombshell effect; Leonardo utilizes the revelation to throw the Apostles into four groups of three each, as if bringing out the inherent properties of the number twelve. Each of these numbers has many meanings—the multiplication of the Gospels by the Trinity is only one, and twelve itself is not merely the number of the Apostles but of the months of the year and of the hours of the day and of the night. Even the hangings on each of the side walls and the windows at the end number respectively four and three. The numerical division reveals the fundamental character of each of the Apostles (Leonardo even labeled them in his preparatory drawings), from the serene innocence of John on Christ's right to the horror of James on his left, who draws back, to the protestation of Philip, who places his hands upon his breast. Only Judas, also revealed by the moment of truth, has no doubt, for he already knows, and the light does not shine upon his face.

The *Last Supper* is really a humanistic and mechanistic interpretation of the narrative, yet in composing it the artist, almost without conscious intention, produced figures of superhuman scale and grandeur, operating within a perspective that, for the first time in any major work since Masaccio's *Trinity* (see fig. 57), is not related to the actual space of the room; there is no place in the refectory where one can stand to make the perspective "come right." It is as if Leonardo were painting for us a higher reality incommensurable with that in which we live, thus making a complete break with Early Renaissance tradition and establishing the ideal world in which both Michelangelo and Raphael later operated. Tragically enough, Leonardo's masterpiece could not be painted at a speed consistent either with true fresco in the Italian manner or with the Byzantine *secco su fresco*. In order to register all the shades of feeling and veils of tone

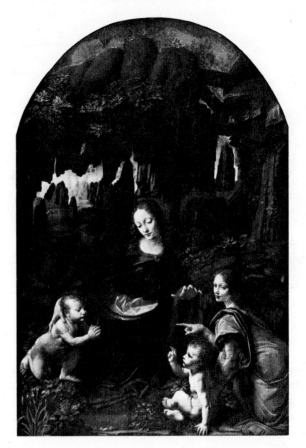

127. LEONARDO DA VINCI. *Madonna of the Rocks.* Begun 1483. Oil on panel (transferred to canvas), 78½ x 48". The Louvre, Paris

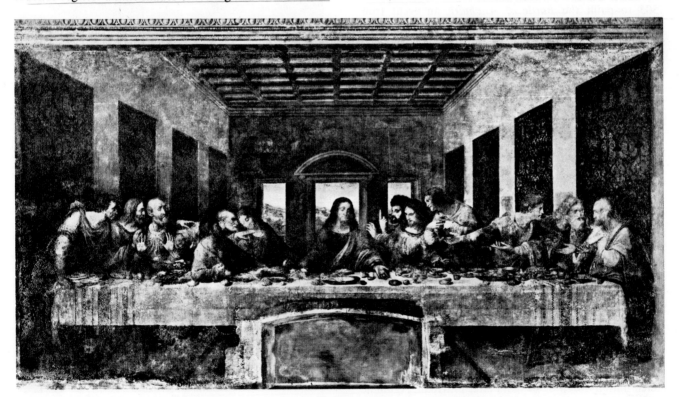

128. LEONARDO DA VINCI. *Last Supper.* Mural. 1495–97/98. Oil and tempera on plaster. Refectory, Sta. Maria delle Grazie, Milan

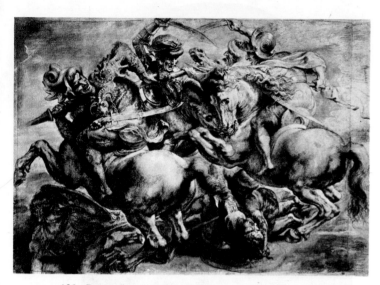

129. PETER PAUL RUBENS. Copy of Leonardo da Vinci's *Battle of Anghiari* (1503–6, destroyed). c. 1615. Pen and ink, and chalk, 17¾ x 25¼". The Louvre, Paris

necessary to his conception, he painted in what is apparently an oil-and-tempera emulsion on the dry plaster, and it began rapidly to peel off. In spite of all the efforts at restoration in recent years, the surface presents only a few intact passages. The rest is a ghost of Leonardo's intention.

For a year the great master worked for the infamous Cesare Borgia, designing battle engines and siege devices and making maps. The Florentines commissioned him in 1503 to paint the *Battle of Anghiari*, an event from fifteenth-century history, on a wall of the newly constructed Hall of the Five Hundred in the Palazzo Vecchio. The work was executed according to experimental and unsuccessful methods, and finally abandoned, but we have some knowledge of what the central section must have looked like through an imaginative recreation made in the seventeenth century by Peter Paul Rubens (fig. 129) on the basis of copies. Leonardo's own firsthand experience with battles is transmuted into what may be termed the first completely High Renaissance composition, produced by figures that are, so to speak, no longer added to each other but multiplied by each other. The nucleus, the battle around the standard, is formed of a pinwheel of violently struggling horses and riders, whose whirlwind ferocity makes fifteenth-century battle scenes, such as those by Uccello (see fig. 61), seem toylike by comparison. The beautiful fury of Leonardo's rearing horses was never forgotten; his lost composition became the model for scores of battle scenes throughout the late Renaissance, the Baroque period, and even the nineteenth century.

Leonardo's *Madonna and Saint Anne* (colorplate 22) was designed in Florence in 1501, but probably not completed until a dozen or so years later in Milan. Again he intertwined the figures to form a pyramidal composition. The Virgin, who in traditional representations sits on her mother's lap, is shown reaching for the Christ Child, who in turn attempts to mount a lamb, the symbol of his sacrificial death; Saint Anne, from the summit of the composition, smiles mysteriously at the drama being enacted. Even though the painting has been overcleaned in the past, and the surfaces have darkened under later varnish, the magic and beauty of the composition surpass any of Leonardo's other surviving works. The background, in fact, is one of the most impressive mountain pictures ever painted; it makes one believe Leonardo had seen and explored the Dolomites, those finger-like crags that tower above Belluno in northeastern Italy. Valleys, rocks, and peaks diminish progressively into the bluish haze of the distance until they can no longer be distinguished.

From 1503 until 1506, during the same period in which he was at work on the *Battle of Anghiari*, Leonardo was painting a portrait of the wife of a prominent Florentine citizen; this painting is known today as the *Mona Lisa* (fig. 130), and it is inseparable from the *Madonna and Saint Anne*, since it must have been done between the date of the cartoon for that work and the finished painting. As compared with the rigid profile portraits by Piero

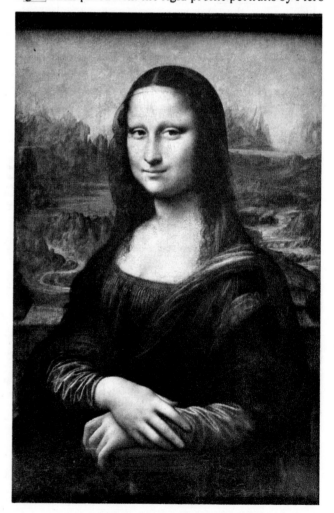

130. LEONARDO DA VINCI. *Mona Lisa.* 1503–6. Oil on panel, 30¼ x 21". The Louvre, Paris

della Francesca (see colorplates 10 and 11), the figure sits in a relaxed position, with hands quietly crossed, before one of Leonardo's richest and most mysterious landscape backgrounds, traversed by roads that lose themselves, bridges to nowhere, crags vanishing in the mists. This attitude of total calm became characteristic for High Renaissance portraits. The face, unfortunately, has suffered in the course of time—the eyebrows have disappeared—but nothing has spoiled the sad half smile that plays about the lips. Leonardo's later life was a succession of trips between Florence, Milan, and Rome, where he could see what his younger competitors, Michelangelo and Raphael, had accomplished with principles he had laid down. He painted little in his later years; in 1517 he accepted the invitation of King Francis I of France to retire to a small château on the Loire, where his sole duty was to converse with the king. The *Mona Lisa*, the *Madonna and Saint Anne*, and a *Saint John the Baptist*, the latter now in bad condition, went with him because they had absorbed so much of his inner life that he could no longer part with them. At his death, in 1519, Leonardo's artistic influence was immense, but much of his scientific work had to await later rediscovery.

MICHELANGELO. The sixteenth century in Central Italy was dominated by the colossal genius of Michelangelo Buonarroti (1475–1564), whose long life makes it necessary for us to consider him under three separate subperiods of the High and Late Renaissance. His personality could scarcely have been more different from that of Leonardo. In contrast to Leonardo's skepticism, we must set Michelangelo's ardent faith; against Leonardo's scientific concern with natural objects Michelangelo's disinterest in any subject save the human body; against Leonardo's fascination with the mysteries of nature Michelangelo's search for God, whose sublime purpose he saw revealed in the beauty of the human form, that "mortal veil," as he put it, of divine intention. Characteristically enough, poetry, the one art in which Leonardo did not excel, was a lifelong vehicle for Michelangelo's meditations.

When the long controversy as to the relative merits of painting and sculpture, sparked by Leonardo's claims for painting, was brought before Michelangelo in 1548, he claimed that sculpture was superior to painting as the sun is to the moon, which shines only with reflected light. By sculpture he meant that which is produced "by force of taking away" rather than "by process of putting on"; that is, he meant carving in stone instead of modeling in clay or wax. He began by drawing roughly on the faces of the block (in a manner that recalls that of the Egyptians; see Vol. 1, Part Two, Chapter 1) the contours of a figure, predetermined by preliminary sketches and perhaps models, and then proceeded to carve away the surplus stone. Contour line was, therefore, his dominant concept, and he pursued it passionately around the figure so as to free it from the block. From his many unfinished works

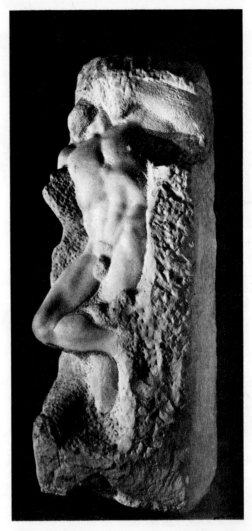

131. MICHELANGELO. *"Crossed-leg" Captive.* 1527-28, Marble, height 8'10" Galleria dell' Accademia, Florence

(fig. 131), one can watch the principles of Michelangelo's style in operation; the figure is almost finished, save for the final process of smoothing and polishing, as he goes; the rest is rough marble. Often the figure seems to struggle for liberation within the block, but sometimes, especially at the beginning and the end of Michelangelo's life, human forms are weightless and serene. There is a more than accidental correspondence between Michelangelo's method of liberating the figure from the block and the doctrine of the Neoplatonic philosophers (among whom Michelangelo was brought up as a boy at the court of Lorenzo the Magnificent) that man at death is freed from the "earthly prison" to return to his final home in God. To Michelangelo, as to Leonardo, artistic creation partakes of divinity, but in a diametrically different way; to Leonardo, the artist is himself a kind of deity, who can see with infinite range and precision and who can create objects and beings out of nothing; to Michelangelo, the artist's tools and his stone are instruments of the divine will, and the creative process an aspect of salvation.

Michelangelo learned the techniques of painting during a year of his boyhood spent in Ghirlandaio's studio; sculpture he studied with Bertoldo di Giovanni, a pupil of Donatello, and from works of ancient art in the Medici

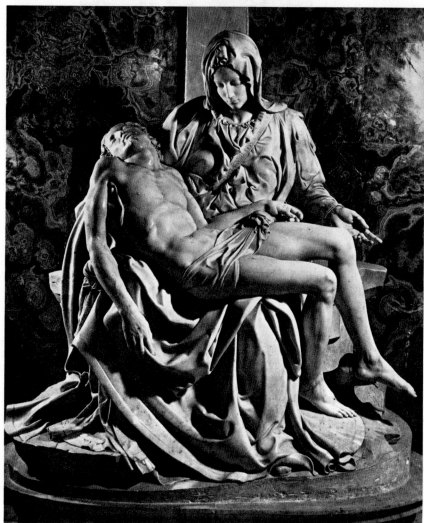

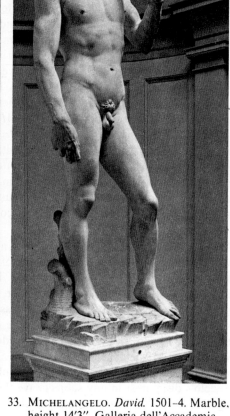

132. MICHELANGELO. *Pietà.* 1498–99/1500. Marble, height 68½″. St. Peter's, Vatican, Rome

33. MICHELANGELO. *David.* 1501–4. Marble, height 14′3″. Galleria dell'Accademia, Florence

collections. His earliest masterpiece, the *Pietà* (fig. 132), done in 1498–99/1500 during his first sojourn in Rome, is still a fifteenth-century work, almost Botticellian in its grace and delicacy. The perfect formation of the bones and muscles of the slender Christ, lying across the knees of his mother, excited the intense admiration of Michelangelo's contemporaries; this anatomical accuracy is undoubtedly the result of the dissections Michelangelo had been permitted to carry out in 1495 at the Hospital of Santo Spirito in Florence. The exquisite Virgin, whose left hand is extended less in grief than in exposition, looks as young as her son; contemporary queries were greeted by Michelangelo's rejoinder that unmarried women keep their youth longer. The explanation is more probably to be sought in a line from Dante, "Virgin Mother, daughter of thy son," which was elaborately paraphrased in a comment by Giovanni Strozzi, a contemporary of Michelangelo's. The Virgin is ageless, a symbol of the Church, who presents for our adoration the timeless reality of Christ's sacrifice. The

extreme delicacy in the handling of the marble and the contrast between the long lines of Christ's figure and the crumpled drapery folds produce passages of a beauty Michelangelo was never to surpass, despite the grandeur of his mature and late work.

The heroic style for which Michelangelo is generally known is seen in the *David* (fig. 133), more than fourteen feet in height, which Michelangelo carved in 1501–4 for a lofty position on one of the buttresses of the Cathedral of Florence. (Donatello had done a *Joshua* in terra-cotta, now lost, for an adjoining buttress, and Ghiberti had planned a *Hercules*.) When the work was completed, its beauty seemed to the Florentines too great to be sacrificed in such a position; after long deliberation the statue was placed in front of the Palazzo Vecchio, where it became a symbol of the republic ready for battle against its enemies, much like statues by Donatello, Nanni di Banco (see figs. 38, 39, 49), and Ghiberti at Orsanmichele nearly a century before. Almost by accident, therefore, the *David* became the first true colossus of the High

Renaissance. (For protection against the weather, it was moved indoors in the nineteenth century, and replaced by a copy.)

The block had been cut in the 1460s probably, as has been recently shown, for a David designed by the aged Donatello, after whose death the block remained unused. Michelangelo's conception is totally new; as compared with any earlier *David*, the bronze one by Donatello for instance (see fig. 43), Michelangelo's youth is no longer a child, but a heavily muscled lad of the people, still not fully grown, with large hands, feet, and head. As with all Michelangelo's figures, there is nothing anecdotal here; the sling goes over David's left shoulder, and the stone lies in the hollow of his right hand, but he is not about to launch it. He stands forever alert in body and spirit, every muscle vibrant with Michelangelo's newly gained anatomical knowledge and with his ability to communicate the life of the spirit through the beauty of the body. The strong undercutting of the hair and the features can be explained by the high position for which the statue was originally destined. Brought to near ground level, the figure towers above us as a revelation of a transfigured humanity; such a vision had inspired no one since the days of Phidias. It is characteristic of the High Renaissance that such a figure should appear dreamlike as compared to the everyday simplicity of Giotto, Masaccio, or even Donatello.

Mindful of his place in history, the warrior pope Julius II called Michelangelo to Rome in 1505 to design a tomb for him; it was projected as a freestanding monument with more than forty over-lifesize statues in marble and several bronze reliefs. It is typical of the unreality of the High Renaissance that it occurred to neither Michelangelo nor the pope that so ambitious a project would require a lifetime (we cannot account for forty over-lifesize statues from Michelangelo's entire career, including the lost works). The idea of the tomb was first abandoned by the pope in 1506, possibly because of his plans for rebuilding Saint Peter's, and revived after his death in 1513. After several successive reductions, the tomb was brought to completion only in 1545. Three statues remain from the 1505 version, the last of which was finished only after 1513.

This statue is the world-famous *Moses* (fig. 134), intended for a corner position on the second story of the monument so that it could be seen from below as a composition of powerful diagonals. Like all of Michelangelo's works, the *Moses* is symbolic and timeless, and the reader is cautioned to ignore fanciful explanations that suggest that Moses is about to rise and smash the Tables of the Law or that he is glaring out at the Israelites. Moses is conceived as an activist prophet, a counterpart to Saint Paul, who also would have appeared on the second story of the tomb. The bulk of the figure is almost crushing, as is the powerful musculature of the left arm, so unlike any statue created since Hellenistic times. Michelangelo knew the *Laocoön*, found in Rome in 1503, and studied it carefully. Moses' head, with its

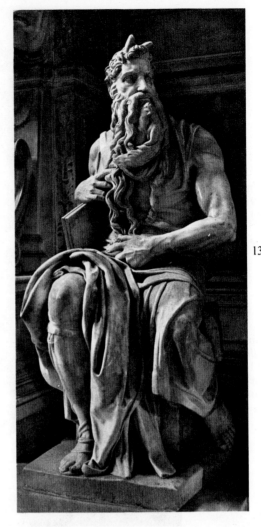

134. MICHELANGELO. *Moses.* c. 1515. Marble, height 92½". S. Pietro in Vincoli, Rome

two-tailed beard, is one of the artist's most formidable creations; the locks of the beard, lightly drawn aside by several fingers of the right hand, are a veritable Niagara of shapes. The drapery masses, instead of concealing the figure, as in the Virgin of the *Pietà*, are used to enhance its compactness.

The two *Slaves* for the 1505 and 1513 versions of the tomb were planned to flank niches around the lower story, in which were to stand Victories, an apparent contrast between the soul, held by the bonds of sin and death, and the Christian victory over both. The figure called the *Dying Slave* (fig. 135) is actually not dying, but turning his head languidly as if in sleep, one hand behind it, and the other plucking unconsciously at the narrow bond of cloth across his massive chest. The strikingly different companion figure (the two may have been intended for corner positions directly below the *Moses*), the *Rebellious Slave* (fig. 136), twisting in a powerful contrapposto pose, exerts all his gigantic strength in vain against the slender bond that ties his arms. The new figure type created by Michelangelo in the *David*, and for the first time here set in action, established a standard that it was impossible to ignore, and influenced even artists who were temperamentally incapable of experiencing the deep

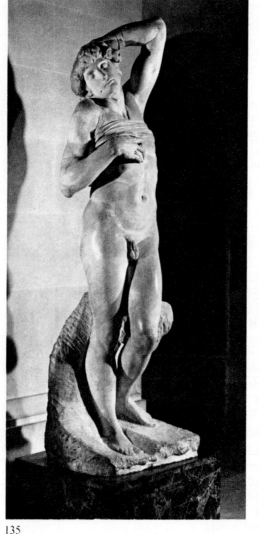

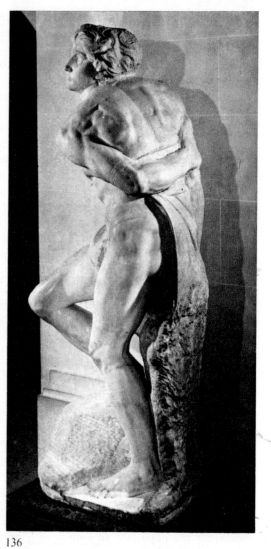

135. MICHELANGELO.
Dying Slave.
Before 1513. Marble,
height 90".
The Louvre, Paris

136. MICHELANGELO.
Rebellious Slave.
Before 1513. Marble,
height 84⅝".
The Louvre, Paris

135

136

spiritual conflict taking visible form in Michelangelo's heroic nudes. Nonetheless, throughout the late Renaissance and the Baroque period, it is the Michelangelesque heavily muscled figure that was almost universally imitated.

In 1508 Michelangelo was given his greatest commission, a work of painting rather than sculpture, the ceiling of the Sistine Chapel, the private chapel of the popes in the Vatican, used for important ceremonies and for conclaves of the College of Cardinals. As we have seen (Chapter 1), the upper walls had been frescoed by several of the leading Central Italian painters in the 1480s, including Botticelli, Ghirlandaio, Perugino (see fig. 78), and Signorelli, with scenes from the Life of Christ on one side and that of Moses on the other. The ceiling, a flattened barrel vault more than 130 feet long, was merely painted blue and dotted with gold stars, as was common in Italian interiors including that of the Arena Chapel. Well aware of the powers of Michelangelo's imagination, Julius II asked this sculptor—with the statues for the tomb temporarily in abeyance—to paint the ceiling, the most ambitious pictorial undertaking of the entire Renaissance. While Michelangelo did complain that painting was not his profession, there is no indication that (as he later claimed) he accepted the commission unwillingly.

Originally, the project was to consist of the Twelve Apostles seated on thrones in the spandrels between the arches round about the ceiling. In the minds of the pope and Michelangelo the program rapidly expanded to its final scope, representing the world before Moses, a synopsis of the drama of the Creation and Fall of Man reduced to nine scenes, four large and five small, beginning with the *Separation of Light from Darkness* and ending with the *Drunkenness of Noah.* These scenes are embedded in a structure of simulated architecture, whose transverse arches spring from twelve thrones, five along each side and one at either end, on which are seated the prophets and sibyls who foretold the coming of Christ. Above the thrones, at the corners of the scenes, sit twenty nude youths in poses of the greatest variety, clearly related to the *Slaves* of the tomb, but not bound; they hold bands that pass through medallions of simulated bronze. In the vault compartments above the windows, and in the lunettes around the windows, are represented the forty generations of the ancestry of Christ, and in the spandrels at the corners of the Chapel are pictured *David and Goliath, Judith and Holofernes*, the *Crucifixion of Haman*, and the *Brazen Serpent*.

In this intricate iconographic structure, resembling in its completeness the cycles of Gothic cathedrals and Byzantine churches, the coming of Christ is apparently foretold in the nine scenes from Genesis, according to the principle of correspondence between Old and New Testaments that, as we have seen (see Vol. 1, Part Three, Chapter 1), was announced by Christ himself and illustrated repeatedly throughout Christian art. An added element is the oak tree of the della Rovere (*oak*) family, to which Julius II and his uncle Sixtus IV belonged, a symbol repeated innumerable times in the decorations of the lower walls of the Chapel, as well as in the oak garlands, some wrapped and some open, held by many of the twenty nudes; it has been suggested that the della Rovere oak tree, even allowed to invade the scenes of Creation, was intended to allude poetically to the Tree of Life in the Garden of Eden, whose fruit in medieval theology was Christ.

The ceiling (colorplate 23) was frescoed by Michelangelo, with minimal mechanical help from assistants, in the short time of four years (1508–12); during this period he also produced the hundreds of preparatory drawings, and the cartoons (full-scale working drawings), which had by this time replaced the traditional sinopias. Michelangelo began painting in reverse chronological order, with the three scenes dealing with the Life of Noah and the adjoining prophets and sibyls; he soon realized that he had underrated the effect of the height of the ceiling, more than sixty feet above the floor, and that the figures looked crowded and small. In the other two early scenes, in the central section, painted in 1509–10, and in the final section, done entirely in 1511, the size of the figures was greatly increased and the compositions simplified. In the last campaign, 1511–12, he painted the lunettes above the windows (not shown in the reproduction).

When one stands in the Chapel, it is impossible to get a comprehensive view of the entire ceiling. When one looks upward and reads the scenes back toward the altar (see colorplate 23), the prophets and sibyls appear on their sides; if one turns the illustration so that those on one side are upright, those on the other are upside down. The contrary directions are bound together by the structure of simulated architecture, with its transverse arches and its diagonal bands separating the vault compartments. The placing of the twenty nudes at the intersections harmonizes the oppositions, since the nudes can be read together with the prophets and sibyls enthroned below them, or with the Genesis scenes at whose corners they are placed. Thus the basic High Renaissance principle of composition created by the interaction of the component elements is embodied in the very structure of the ceiling. The sober coloration is established by the large passages of simulated stone, and even the figures are clearly painted by an artist whose major interest is sculptural form.

The *Fall of Man* (fig. 137) combines the Temptation and the Expulsion in a single scene. Michelangelo was aware that his audience would recognize his allusion to the representations of the *Expulsion* by Jacopo della Quercia (see fig. 52) and Masaccio (see fig. 55), and for that very reason worked the two into a single scene, which in one motion leads the eye from the crime to the punishment, through the Tree of Knowledge, represented as a fig. It is noteworthy that the tree has only one branch; what appears to be a branch on the other side is the angel who expels the guilty pair from the Garden, and he is read together with the leaves of the della Rovere oak coming from the nude above the scene at the right. Never in history had nude figures been painted on such a colossal scale; the powerful masses, simple contours, and intense expressions of Michelangelo's figures operate with great success even at this size.

Michelangelo's vision of a new and grander humanity reaches its supreme embodiment in the *Creation of Adam* (fig. 138). Instead of standing on earth as in all earlier Creation scenes (see fig. 51), the Lord floats

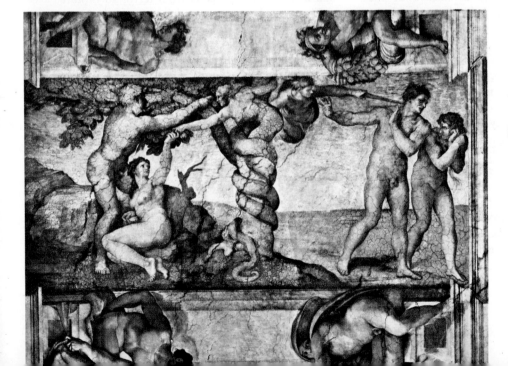

137. MICHELANGELO. *Fall of Man*. Ceiling fresco. 1509–10. Sistine Chapel, Vatican, Rome

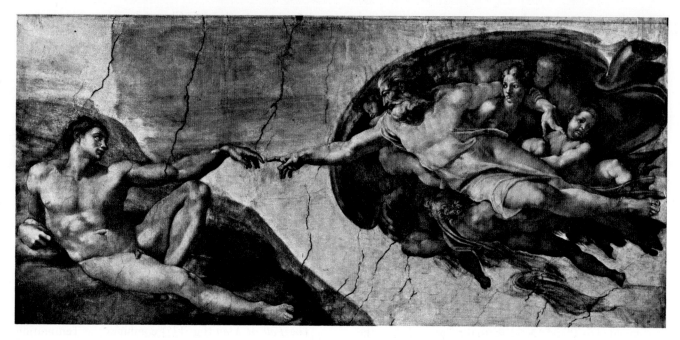

138. MICHELANGELO. *Creation of Adam.* Ceiling fresco. 1511. Sistine Chapel, Vatican, Rome

through the heavens, enveloped in the lavender-gray mantle he wears in all the scenes in which he appears, borne aloft by wingless angels (with only a single youthful exception, Michelangelo's angels are wingless, as if he could not tolerate violation of the beauty of the human body by an attachment from any other form of life). In comparison with the ceremonial, iconic Deity of Jan van Eyck, or in fact almost any earlier representation of God, Michelangelo's imagination for the first time makes believable the concept of omnipotence. A dynamo of creative energy, God stretches forth his hand, about to touch with his finger the extended finger of Adam, who reclines on the barren ground below. As we have seen in the discussion of Jacopo della Quercia (see Chapter 1, and fig. 51) *Adam* means *ground*, and the figure is shown not as in Jacopo's relief, merely astonished at the appearance of the Lord, but ready to be charged with the energy that will lift him from the dust and make of him "a living soul" (Gen. 2: 7).

Adam's body is probably the most nearly perfect Michelangelo ever created, a structure embodying all the beauty of Classical antiquity (this figure increases our amazement that he did not know the sculptures of the Parthenon) and all the spirituality of Christianity. As in all High Renaissance compositions, the action in this one, based on the mirroring of the convex curve of the fecundating Creator in the concave curve of the receptive creature, will vanish in seconds, and yet it is preserved forever. It should be noted that the oak garland is permitted to enter the scene directly below Adam's thigh, so that the Incarnation of Christ, the second Adam (I Cor. 15: 45), fruit of the Tree of Life, is foretold by the creation of the first Adam.

The final scenes as one moves toward the altar (see colorplate 23) were also the last in order of execution. The *Lord Congregating the Waters* was held to foreshadow the foundation of the Church; the *Creation of Sun, Moon, and Plants* shows the Lord twice, once creating sun and moon (which were darkened at the Crucifixion) with a cruciform gesture of his mighty arms, then seen from the rear creating plants, among which the della Rovere oak intrudes from under the neighboring nude. Just above the altar, the Lord separates the light from the darkness, which recalls the words of John 1:1: "In the beginning was the Word, and the Word was with God, and the Word was God." The figures have grown to such a scale that the frames will no longer contain them, and the athletic nudes exemplify every possibility of seated pose, and a range of expression from terror to rapture.

The seated prophets and sibyls show the majestic possibilities of the draped figure, related to the conception of the seated *Moses* (see fig. 134); Vasari wrote that even when Michelangelo's figures were clothed they looked nude, by which he meant that the powerful motions of his figures could only have been achieved by his total mastery of the nude. The Persian Sibyl is represented as immensely old, Jeremiah as grieving above the papal throne, Daniel aflame with prophecy as he writes in a small volume, the Libyan Sibyl no longer needing her book as she looks down upon the altar, the eternal Tree of Life. The final phase of the Sistine Ceiling is one of the supreme moments in the spiritual history of mankind. It is also significant that it was created during the years when Julius II, who commissioned and to a certain extent inspired the Sistine Ceiling, was fighting on the battlefield for the continued life of the Papal States against the armies of King Louis XII of France, and when the outcome of the struggle was in the balance.

BRAMANTE. For the moment we must leave Michelangelo to consider the work of the last two masters who assisted in creating the High Renaissance style. Julius II's favorite architect was Donato Bramante (1444–1514), from Urbino, a congenial spirit, almost exactly the pope's age, who used to read Dante to him in the evening. Bramante, also a painter, had enjoyed a long and distinguished architectural career in Milan, where he had worked in close touch with Leonardo da Vinci, many of whose ideas he reflects. In fact, the Tempietto (fig. 139), a small circular shrine built in 1502 in Rome on the spot where Peter was believed to have been crucified, is a concentration and simplification of Leonardo's central-plan schemes (see fig. 124). The cylindrical cella is surrounded by a circular peristyle, in the manner of an ancient tholos of Roman Doric columns, crowned by a balustrade. The cella rises one story above the peristyle, and culminates in a slightly more than hemispheric dome, ribbed on the outside. The proportions are simple, harmonious, and unified; in its smooth movement round the building, the peristyle has no equal in Renaissance architecture.

But the basic radial principle is derived from Leonardo, as can be seen in a sixteenth-century engraving showing the surrounding circular courtyard as it would have looked had Bramante's complete design been carried out (fig. 140). The reader should trace with a straight edge the relationship between the niches in the cella, the columns of the peristyle, the columns of the circular colonnade, and the niches alternating with chapels that ring the colonnade. The result is a radial relationship of all forms and spaces from the center outward, like the rays of a snow crystal, the petals of a flower, or the spokes in a Gothic rose window.

This radial principle determined Bramante's design for rebuilding Saint Peter's in Rome. In 1506 it occurred to Julius II to tear down the Constantinian Basilica of Saint Peter's, then more than eleven hundred years old, and to replace it with a Renaissance church; this new project may well have been the reason for the interruption of work on his tomb by Michelangelo. Several different possibilities for the church's plan may have been considered by Bramante, whom the pope entrusted with the commission, but the one he chose was strikingly Leonardesque (fig. 141). Basically, it was a Greek cross with four equal arms terminating in apses. Into each reentrant angle was set a smaller Greek cross, surmounted by a dome, two of whose apses merged in those of the central cross. Four lofty towers were to be erected in the angles of the smaller crosses and linked with the four major apses by triple-arched porticoes. The striking feature of the exterior was the culminating dome, which for the first time in the Renaissance entirely abandoned the vertical-ribbed form in the tradition of Brunelleschi (see fig. 20), still followed by Leonardo, and replaced it with an exact hemisphere modeled on that of the Pantheon. But Bramante did not wish to sacrifice the Renaissance notion of the drum, which gives a dome greater height; his drum is again a tholos, surrounded by a peristyle of Corinthian columns. How the whole structure would have looked from the exterior may be seen in the commemorative medal struck by Bramante's collaborator, the sculptor Caradosso, in 1506 (fig. 142).

At the time of the pope's death in 1513 and of Bramante's the following year, only the eastern half of the basilica had been demolished, but the four giant piers with their Corinthian pilasters upholding the four arches on which the dome was to rest had already been built. Although Bramante's dome remained a dream, his in-

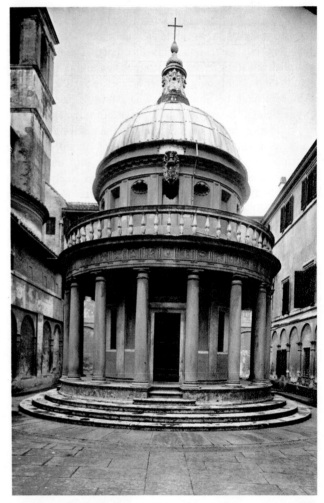

139. DONATO BRAMANTE. Tempietto. 1502. S. Pietro in Montorio, Rome

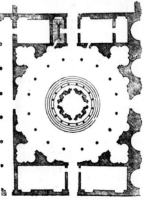

140. DONATO BRAMANTE. Plan of the Tempietto (from Sebastiano Serlio, *Il terzo libro d'architettura*, Venice, 1551)

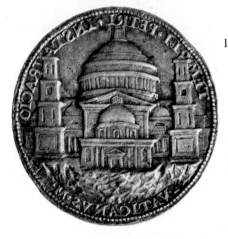

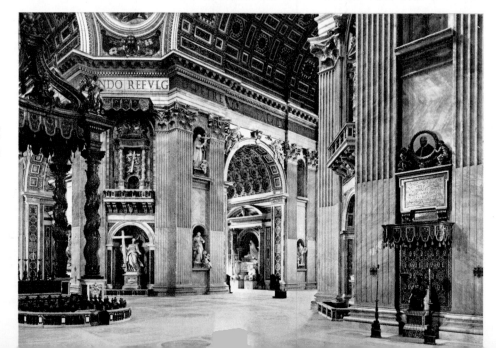

141. DONATO BRAMANTE. Original plan for St. Peter's, Vatican, Rome. 1506 (after Geymüller)

142. CRISTOFORO CARADOSSO. Bramante's design for the exterior of St. Peter's. Bronze commemorative medal. 1506. British Museum, London

terior plan was substantially realized (fig. 143), though the floor level was raised about three feet and the pilasters thus correspondingly shortened. The idea of the coupled pilasters in one giant story sustaining the barrel vaults and embracing smaller arches was drawn from Alberti's nave of Sant'Andrea in Mantua (see fig. 35). Nonetheless, the interior as Bramante originally planned it would have been very complex, as the reader can see by moving in imagination from one of the eight entrance porticoes into the adjoining apse, then into one of the smaller Greek crosses with its central dome, then through a barrel-vaulted arch into the greater barrel vault of one of the four transept arms, and finally into the central space to look up into the interior of the colossal dome. Although Bramante's plan was very different from that of Hagia Sophia, nonetheless, their effects must have been in some way related, as in the cumulative succession of movement from smaller into always larger spaces. Bramante's radial design was never carried out in its entirety, but his basic central structure was standing at his death; it was on such a scale that it could not be altered by any of the subsequent architects.

RAPHAEL. The fourth great master of the Florentine and Roman High Renaissance was Raffaello Sanzio (1483–

1520), known by the Anglicized form Raphael. It is in his art that the High Renaissance ideal of harmony comes to its most complete expression. First taught in Urbino by his father Giovanni Santi, a mediocre painter, Raphael worked for several years in the studio of Perugino, whose manner he approximated so exactly that it is often difficult to make sure whether certain works are by the master or his young pupil. In 1504 Raphael painted for a church in the little town of Città di Castello the *Marriage of the Virgin* (fig. 144), which at once recalls the *Giving of the Keys to Saint Peter* by Perugino (see fig. 78). Differences are instructive; what is diffuse in Perugino is brought to a focus in Raphael. His central group is unified around the motive of Joseph putting the ring on Mary's finger, and the lateral figures are made to join in this movement, including the disgruntled suitor breaking his rod over his knees. The architecture of the distant polygonal Temple grows out of the wide piazza, and is more carefully unified, in the spirit of the Tempietto, than the abrupt shapes of Perugino's octagonal building. Its dome is almost tangent to the arch of the panel, identifying the dome of the Temple (based on the Dome of the Rock) with that of Heaven. Moreover, the doors of the Temple are open so that the perspective of the squares in the piazza moves serenely through the building to the point of infinity. This combination of perfect unity

143. Interior view at crossing, St. Peter's (after plan by Bramante)

and airy lightness in Raphael's composition breathes through the figures as well. Perugino's characteristic S-curve is transformed by Raphael into an ascending spiral beginning at the tip of the toes and rising harmoniously and effortlessly to discharge in the glance.

About 1505 Raphael, twenty-two years old, arrived in Florence, and achieved immediate success. Leonardo and Michelangelo had established the High Renaissance style in Florence, but they were accessible to few private patrons. Raphael met the demand with ease and grace, and during his three-year stay painted a considerable number of portraits and Madonnas, one of the loveliest of which is the *Madonna of the Meadows*, dated 1505 (fig. 145). The pyramidal group established by the interaction of its members in Leonardo's design for the *Madonna and Saint Anne* (see colorplate 22), and certainly the pose of the Virgin with her foot extended, were strongly influenced by Leonardo's composition. But the Raphael picture is simpler; the gentle master from Urbino dissected no corpses, and was only slightly interested in anatomy. Harmony was to him the basic purpose of any composition, and the harmony is beautifully consistent throughout this work, from the balancing of ovoids and spheroids in the bodies and heads of the children to the encompassing shapes of the protective Virgin and finally to the background landscape, which is brought to a focus in her neckline and head, as is that of the *Marriage of the Virgin* in the dome of the Temple. The landscape bears the same relation to the figural composition as does the encircling courtyard to the Tempietto. Although Raphael reinstated the traditional halos in his Florentine Madonnas, perhaps at the insistence of his patrons, they appear as slender circles of gold, delicately poised in depth, and as an added element in his composition of circles and ovoids.

Julius II chose the twenty-six-year-old Raphael to supplement in the Stanze (chambers) of the Vatican the massive program of imagery being painted by Michelangelo in the locked Sistine Chapel across the narrow intervening court. Raphael maintained his position as court painter until his early death. His ideals of figural and compositional harmony, expanding and deepening from their relatively slight Florentine beginnings, came to be recognized as *the* High Renaissance principles, and it was to Raphael, therefore, rather than to Michelangelo, that classicistic artists of succeeding centuries, especially Poussin in the seventeenth century (see fig. 260) and Ingres in the nineteenth (see fig. 370), turned as the Messiah of their art and doctrine. The first room to be frescoed was the Stanza della Segnatura (1509–11), used for the papal tribunal whose documents demanded the personal signature of the pontiff. From the complex iconographic program we can single out the two dominant frescoes on opposite walls; they typify the Classical and Christian elements reconciled in the synthesis of the High Renaissance. The *Disputa* (*Disputation over the Sacrament*; fig. 146), the most complete exposition of the doctrine of the Eucharist in Christian art,

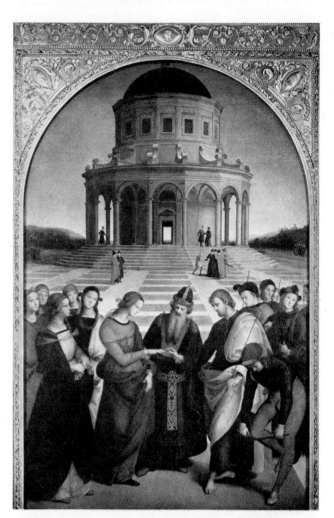

144. RAPHAEL. *Marriage of the Virgin.* 1504. Panel painting, 67 x 46½". Pinacoteca di Brera, Milan

faces the *School of Athens*, an equally encyclopedic presentation of the philosophers of pagan antiquity.

The *Disputa* begins in Heaven (still represented with gold, but for the last time in any major work of Christian art). God the Father presides over the familiar Deësis, with Christ enthroned, displaying his wounds, and on either side, in a floating semicircle of cloud recalling the arrangement in van der Weyden's *Last Judgment* (see colorplate 19), Apostles and saints from the New Testament alternate with prophets and patriarchs from the Old. Below the throne of Christ the Dove of the Holy Spirit, flanked by child angels bearing the four open gospels, flies downward toward the Host, displayed in a gold and crystal monstrance on the altar. On either side of the altar sit the Four Fathers of the Church, and farther out groups of theologians from all ages of Christianity engage in argumentation over the nature of the Eucharist, their vitality and agitation contrasting with the serenity of Heaven, where all questions are set to rest. Among the recognizable portraits are those of Dante, to the left of the door, and, in front of him, Sixtus IV. From the angels above the Deësis whose spiral forms

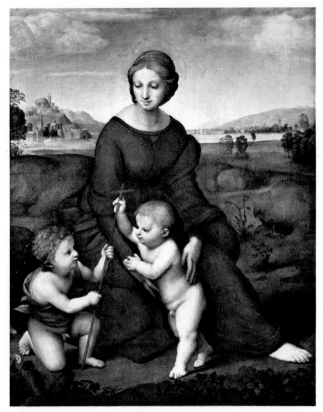

145. RAPHAEL. *Madonna of the Meadows.* 1505. Panel painting, 44½ x 34¼″. Kunsthistorisches Museum, Vienna

take on substance along the incised beams of golden spiritual light down to the statuesque groups of theologians on earth, every figure is based on Raphael's fundamental spiral principle.

More revolutionary in its composition, the *School of Athens* (colorplate 24; a misnomer applied in the eighteenth century) presents under an ideal architecture the chief philosophers from all periods of Greek antiquity engaged in learned argument. For the first time the medieval principle of double scale for figures and architecture is abandoned. The figures form a circle in depth within the lofty structure, culminating under the central arch, where against the distant sky Plato, holding the *Timaeus*, points toward Heaven as the source of the ideas from which all earthly forms originate, while Aristotle, holding the *Ethics*, indicates earth as the object of all observations. At the upper left Socrates may be discerned discussing philosophical principles with the youths of Athens; at the lower left Pythagoras delineates his proportion system on a slate before pupils; at the right Euclid (a portrait of Bramante) uses another slate to demonstrate a geometric theorem.

The embracing architecture, with its statues of Apollo and Minerva in niches (the legs of Apollo repeat those of Michelangelo's *Dying Slave*, but in reverse; see fig. 135), is strongly Bramantesque, and in its single giant story and coffered barrel vaults suggests how the spaces of Bramante's Saint Peter's would have looked. Nonethe-

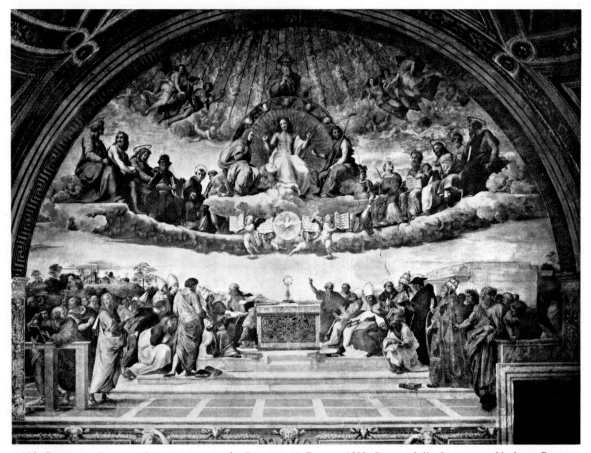

146. RAPHAEL. *Disputa (Disputation over the Sacrament).* Fresco. 1509. Stanza della Segnatura, Vatican, Rome

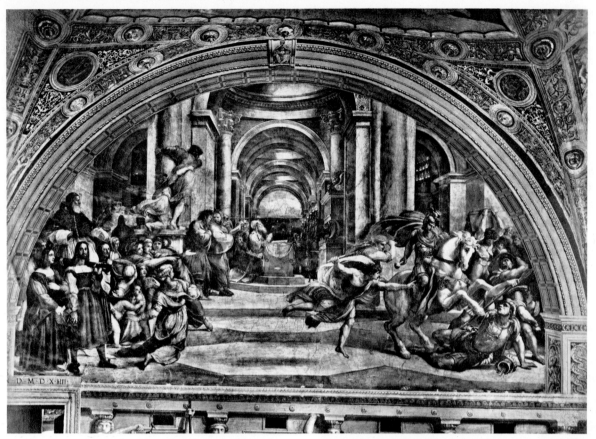

147. RAPHAEL. *Expulsion of Heliodorus.* Fresco. 1512. Stanza d'Eliodoro, Vatican, Rome

less, it is background architecture, essentially unbuildable; there are no arches to carry the outer borders of the central pendentives, which begin at the transverse arches and end in nothing. The isolated figure in the lower center, seated with one elbow on a block of stone in a pensive pose resembling that of Michelangelo's Jeremiah (see colorplate 23), has been identified as a portrait of the great sculptor himself, inserted by Raphael after he had seen Michelangelo's frescoes in the Sistine Chapel in 1511. Raphael was in one of the first groups admitted, and Michelangelo's style must have been a revelation.

In the Stanze painted afterward Raphael abandoned the perfect but static harmony of the Stanza della Segnatura in favor of always more dynamic compositions, which brought him to the threshold of the Baroque, under strong influence of the new style he had beheld in the Sistine Chapel. In the Stanza d'Eliodoro, 1512–14, the principal fresco (fig. 147) represents an incident from Macc. 3 (a book of the Apocrypha, not included in Protestant Bibles), which tells how the pagan general Heliodorus, at the behest of one of the Seleucid successors of Alexander the Great, attempted to pillage the Temple in Jerusalem, but was met by a heavenly warrior in armor of gold on a shining charger, and by two youths "notable in their strength and beautiful in their glory," who beat him to the ground with their scourges so that he fell blinded. For Julius II this was an omen of divine intervention on his side against the schismatic Council of Pisa, set up by the invading Louis XII to

depose him, and he had Raphael paint him, formidable with his newly grown beard, being carried into the fresco at the left; Raphael appears as one of the chairbearers, directly below the pope's left hand. Under the influence of the marvels Raphael had seen in the Sistine Chapel, the pace has quickened, the volume has increased, and the muscular figures have been set in violent motion. But Raphael does not abandon his spiral principle; energy courses through the action figures as through figure eights. The rearing charger recalls those Raphael had seen in Leonardo's unfinished *Battle of Anghiari* (see fig. 129); this kind of reference was not considered plagiarism in the Renaissance, but recognition of greatness, in the same sense as Michelangelo's bow to Masaccio and Jacopo della Quercia (see page 127). As the figures have been enlarged to Michelangelesque dimensions, the enclosing architecture has decreased in scale but gained in mass and power. Heavy columns and massive piers have replaced the slender pilasters of the *School of Athens.*

From this same period dates the *Sistine Madonna* (fig. 148), so called because Saint Sixtus II, patron of the della Rovere family, kneels at the Virgin's right. The picture was probably intended to commemorate the death of Julius II in 1513; the saint's cope is embroidered with the oak leaves of the della Rovere family, and the bearded face, a little older and less pugnacious than that in the *Expulsion of Heliodorus,* is a portrait of the aged pontiff. Saint Barbara, patron saint of the hour of death, looks down on his coffin, on which the papal tiara rests, and the Virgin, showing us the Child as if in response to the *Salve Regina*, walks toward us on luminous clouds in which more angelic presences can be dimly seen. In harmonizing form and movement this painting represents the pinnacle of Raphael's achievement; the dynamic composition should be compared with the static one of the *Madonna of the Meadows* (see fig. 145). The broad, spiral shapes rise from the tiara through the cope of the kneeling saint up to and around the bodies of the Virgin and the Child, and downward again through the glance of Saint Barbara. Even the curves of the curtains, drawn apart to display the vision, harmonize in alternating tautness and fullness with the lines of the entire composition. The motive of the Virgin and Child walking toward us on the clouds may have been suggested by the visionary Christ of the mosaic of Saints Cosmas and Damian in Rome. The two figures in their perfect beauty, warmer and more human than their counterparts in the *Madonna of the Meadows*, represent the ultimate in the High Renaissance vision of the nobility of the human countenance and form.

The death of the warrior pope was followed by the election of Giovanni de' Medici, younger brother of the exiled Pietro, a boyhood acquaintance of Michelangelo at the table of Lorenzo the Magnificent. The thirty-eight-year-old cardinal, still a layman at the time of his election as Pope Leo X, was unmoved by the ideals of church reform and political power that had driven Julius II to such extraordinary feats, but delighted with his new position, which gave him the opportunity to spend lavishly on worldly enjoyment the revenues accumulated by his predecessor to finance his conquests. In 1512, as Cardinal de' Medici, backed by Julius II, Giovanni had entered Florence, and governed it through his younger brother Giuliano, on whom King Francis I had conferred the duchy of Nemours. Raphael has shown Leo X as he was in an unsparing portrait (fig. 149)—corpulent, shrewd, pleasure-loving, engaged in the examination of an illuminated manuscript (the original still exists) with a gold and crystal magnifying glass; a gold and silver bell to summon servants is close to the pope's hand. On his left is Cardinal Luigi de' Rossi, on his right his cousin Cardinal Giulio de' Medici, later Pope Clement VII. The portrait was probably painted in 1517, the fateful year when Martin Luther, whom the pope excommunicated in 1520, nailed his ominous theses to the door of Wittenberg Cathedral. Raphael was able to endow his subjects with the new mass and volume he had learned from Michelangelo's seated figures, but his analysis of character is unexpected, and profound.

Among the offices to which the new pope appointed Raphael was that of inspector general of Roman antiquities, the first known attempt to place under legal authority all ancient objects excavated on purpose or by chance. The so-called Golden Age of Leo X produced as perhaps its most delightful monument the Villa Farnesina, then overhanging the Tiber, built to the order of the pope's banker Agostino Chigi, an important personage considering the astronomical financial demands of the Medici court. Raphael, his pupils, and other High Renaissance painters decorated room after room with frescoes entirely devoted to scenes from Classical antiquity, completely pagan in subject, without a hint of the Christian moralization that runs through the mythologies of Botticelli. In the *Galatea* (fig. 150), about 1513, he shows the sea nymph in triumph on a shell drawn by dolphins and attended by sea nymphs and Tritons. Above her three winged Loves draw their bows in a useless attempt to inflame her heart with passion for the Cyclops Polyphemus, who is pictured in a neighboring fresco by another painter. Raphael's figure-eight form underlies the entire composition. Galatea, in her physical abundance, little resembles the slender Venus of Botticelli. She stands in a Hellenistic contrapposto pose, in the plenitude of her powers, as do the other figures, male and female, whose white or tanned anatomies glisten against the green sea. Raphael has obviously adopted the Michelangelesque heroic muscular ideal, and the figures are convincing until one looks closely, when it becomes doubtful that he has based his drawing on anything approaching Michelangelo's anatomical knowledge.

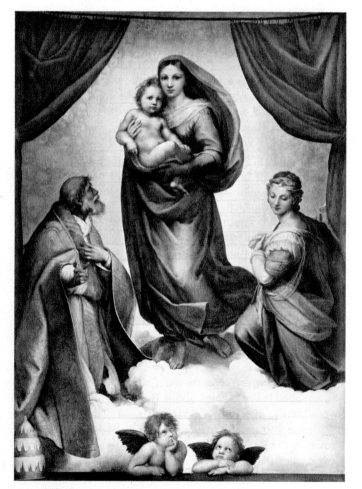

148. RAPHAEL. *Sistine Madonna.* 1513. Oil on canvas,
8′8½″ x 6′5″. Gemäldegalerie, Dresden, Germany

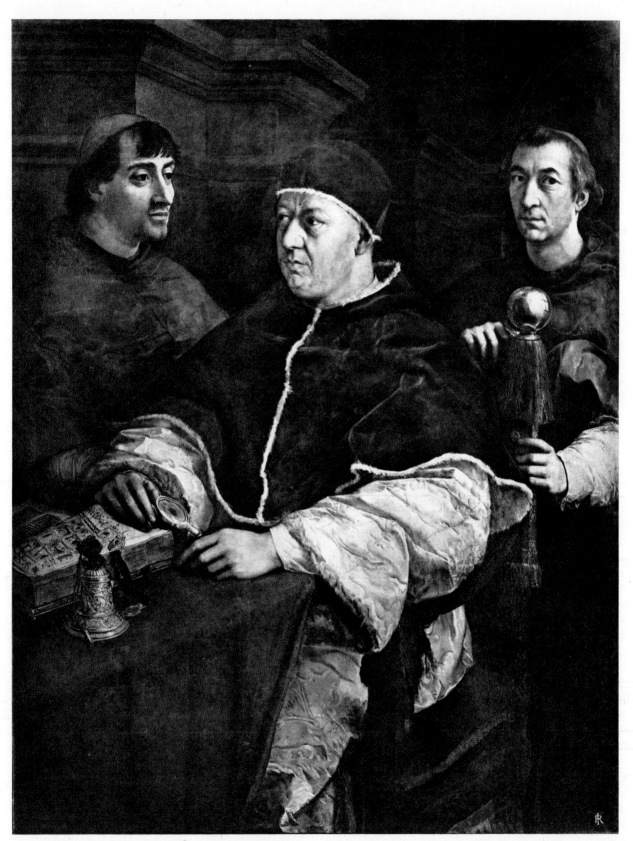

149. RAPHAEL. *Pope Leo X with Cardinals Giulio de' Medici and Luigi de' Rossi.* c. 1517. Panel painting. 60½ x 47″. Galleria degli Uffizi, Florence

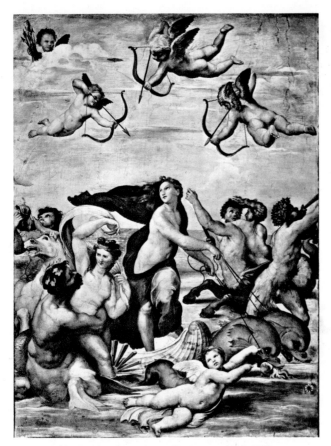

150. RAPHAEL. *Galatea*. Fresco. c. 1513. Villa Farnesina, Rome

The identical figure-eight composition was employed by Raphael for a diametrically opposed purpose in one of his last and greatest paintings, the *Transfiguration* (fig. 151), painted in 1517 for the Cathedral of Narbonne, of which Cardinal Giulio de' Medici was bishop. The completed painting was so powerful, however, that the cardinal kept it in Rome. In contrast to the traditional renderings of the subject (see that by Bellini, colorplate 14), Raphael painted an accompanying incident as well, told by Matthew and Luke. When Peter, James, and John had accompanied Christ to the top of a high mountain, the remaining Apostles were unable without his presence to cast out the demons from a possessed boy. The lower section of the figure eight is composed of the agitated and distraught figures of the Apostles and the youth (in part executed by Raphael's pupils) plunged into semidarkness, with shadows of fantastic blackness, lit only from above. The upper loop is composed of Christ, Moses, Elijah, and the three Apostles. Christ and the prophets soar in the air as if lifted up by the spiritual experience, their garments agitated as if from the center of brightness, which is Christ, came not only light but also the wind of the spirit, which has also cast the Apostles to the ground in terror. They, too, have fallen in Raphael's spiral poses.

Raphael, who at this point in the High Renaissance had at his fingertips the full resources of natural light, apparently no longer felt any need to distinguish it from spiritual light (gold rays are gone forever), and the long historical journey to a position analogous to that of Sinai in reverse is complete: revelation in spiritual light and the behavior of natural light are fused. Raphael may have been connected with a small group of priests and laymen called the Oratory of Divine Love, which, in the pagan magnificence of the Rome of Leo X, attempted to reform and rejuvenate the Church from within through Communion and prayer. In this vision of Christ, shining with delicate colors through his "white and glistering" garments, Raphael may well have embodied his beliefs. The great painter died on Good Friday, April 6, 1520, at the age of only thirty-seven. At his request his funeral was held in the Pantheon and the *Transfiguration* placed above his bier; his tomb is also there, lighted only by the sky through the great round opening in the dome. To his contemporaries Raphael's death seemed the end of an era, but a closer look shows that, in a way, the High Renaissance synthesis of Classical and Christian had already started to dissolve.

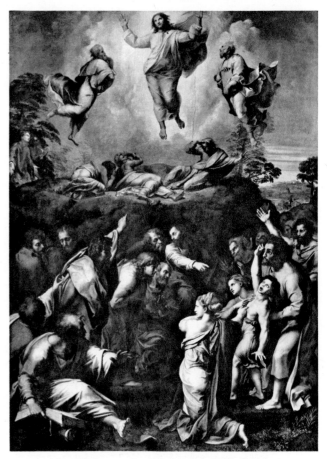

151. RAPHAEL. *Transfiguration*. 1517. Panel painting. 13'4" x 9'2". Pinacoteca, Vatican. Rome

4

The Mannerist Crisis

No less extraordinary than the unpredictability of the Florentine and Roman High Renaissance was its brevity—hardly more than twenty-five years from its tentative beginnings in Leonardo's *Last Supper* to the death of Raphael in 1520. A new style succeeded it or, to be more accurate, coexisted with its latest phase, a style which in the last two generations has come to assume the name of Mannerism. It is unfortunate that general agreement has not yet been reached on what it means or what it designates. The name comes from the Italian word *maniera* (*manner*), derived from *mano* (*hand*); it indicates a style founded upon repetition of learned manual techniques rather than on new observations. For example, present-day Italians would characterize the performance of the Mount Athos painter who could sketch out a complete fresco subject without a preliminary drawing or model or reference to nature (see Vol. 1, Part Three, Chapter 8) as *di maniera*.

Although in the later phases of sixteenth-century art in Central Italy there is indeed much rote repetition of types and devices invented earlier, especially those of Michelangelo, there is nothing mechanical about what went on in Florence and Siena just before and just after 1520. That moment has been justly recognized as a crisis. Two factors should be understood as formative. First, the Florentine republic, while it kept on electing its officials every two months according to the old system, had lost its independence to the Medici in 1512. On his election as pope in 1513, Leo X governed Florence through his brother Giuliano, and later replaced Giuliano with his nephew Lorenzo, who assumed absolute control of the supposed republic. In 1516 the pope expelled the Montefeltro family from Urbino and made Lorenzo duke. After the latter's death in 1519, the rule of Florence passed to Cardinal Giulio de' Medici, although the fiction of republican government was maintained. Conditions were dismal in Florence, and the population resented its subjection.

The second major factor was the presence of Michelangelo in Florence from 1516 to 1534, and it is on his turbulent and original art that much of the new style was based; in fact, the moment of crisis, in the late second decade of the sixteenth century, was seen largely through Michelangelo's eyes. When Giulio de' Medici became pope as Clement VII in 1523, after the brief pontificate of the unpopular Dutch Adrian VI (1522–23), his political machinations brought upon the papal city a scourge that had not been experienced since the days of the Huns—armies supposedly owing allegiance to Emperor Charles V, but actually out of control, sacking Rome in 1527; German Lutherans and Spanish Catholics outdoing each other in acts of cruelty and greed; and much of High Renaissance Rome reduced to a condition similar to that in which the Crusaders left Constantinople in 1204. The pope himself, a prisoner in Castel Sant' Angelo, escaped to Orvieto, where he lived under beggarly circumstances and from which he returned to an impoverished Rome.

MICHELANGELO TO 1534. Ironically enough, this was the very period when Michelangelo, despite his republican sympathies, found himself working for the Medici on a funerary chapel, begun in 1519 for the entombment of Lorenzo the Magnificent, his murdered brother Giuliano, and the two recently deceased dukes, also confusingly named Giuliano and Lorenzo, son and grandson respectively of Lorenzo the Magnificent. The Chapel was built as the right-hand sacristy of San Lorenzo, symmetrical in plan with the left sacristy by Brunelleschi (see fig. 24). Michelangelo's more or less Brunelleschian architecture of white walls and *pietra serena* supports and trim encloses the only tombs ever completed, those of the two dukes. Each tomb is a marble architectural composition, incommensurable with the enclosing architecture (figs. 152, 153). In simple rectangular niches sit the two dukes, dressed in Roman armor in their roles as captains of the Roman Catholic Church. The statues are idealized because Michelangelo said that a thousand years from now no one would know what the dukes had looked like and because he wanted to give them the dignity that belonged to their positions. The ornamental tabernacles on either side of each niche remain blank, although they may have been intended for statues.

The strangely shaped sarcophagi appear to have been

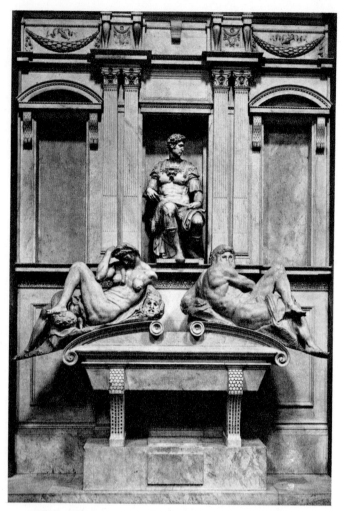

152. MICHELANGELO. *Tomb of Giuliano de' Medici.*
1519–34. Marble. Medici Chapel, S. Lorenzo,
Florence

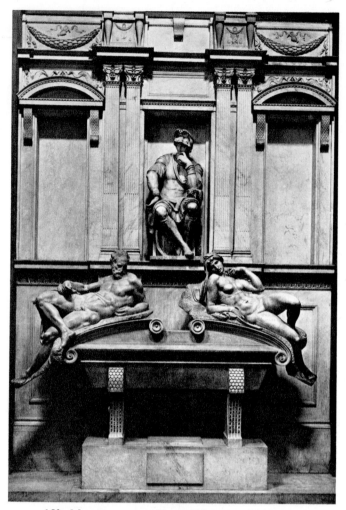

153. MICHELANGELO. *Tomb of Lorenzo de' Medici.*
1519–34. Marble. Medici Chapel, S. Lorenzo,
Florence

split in the center to allow the emergence of the ideal images of the dukes. On either side recline figures of the times of day, Night and Day under Giuliano (see fig. 152), Dawn and Twilight under Lorenzo (see fig. 153). An unaccountable theory to the effect that these statues were not made for their present positions has recently gained some support; Michelangelo's drawings for the tombs show how the tomb architecture and these very figures were developed together from early stages in his imagination. The compositions should, however, be completed by reclining figures of river gods, their feet pointing inward, in the empty spaces at right and left below the tombs. According to the sculptor's own explanation, written on a sheet of drawings for architectural details, Night and Day, who have brought the duke to his death, are subject to his revenge, for in death he has slain them. In other words the timeless symbol of princely power that the dukes represent has conquered the powers of time (the times of day) and of space (the four rivers). It is especially significant that when Michelangelo was engaged on this work glorifying Medici power, the Sack of Rome

destroyed temporarily the power of his Medici patron, the republic was revived for the third and last time, and Michelangelo was placed in charge of its defenses. The ambivalence of his position must have been painful to the artist, who escaped assassination when the Medici troops reentered the defeated city in 1530 only through the personal intervention of the pope.

In the languid figure of Giuliano the conviction and power of the Sistine Ceiling are absent. Muscular though the duke may be, he seems overcome by lassitude. Night, her body and breasts distorted through childbirth and lactation, a grinning mask (symbol of false dreams) below her shoulder, and an owl under her leg, is contrasted with the mighty Day (fig. 154), probably Michelangelo's most heavily muscled figure, turning in a gigantic motion as if to throw off his covers and arise to do battle. Yet each of these figures is trapped in a contrapposto pose that defeats the very meaning of contrapposto, originally an attempt to endow the figure with complete freedom of motion. For all their immense power, the statues of the Medici Chapel seem their own

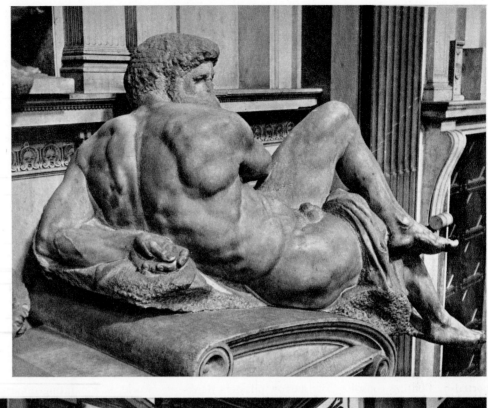

154. MICHELANGELO. *Day,*
from the *Tomb of
Giuliano de' Medici.*
Designed 1521; carved
1524–34. Marble, length
80¾". Medici Chapel,
S. Lorenzo, Florence

155. MICHELANGELO.
Entrance Hall, Biblioteca
Medicea Laurenziana.
1524–33; staircase
completed 1559.
S. Lorenzo, Florence

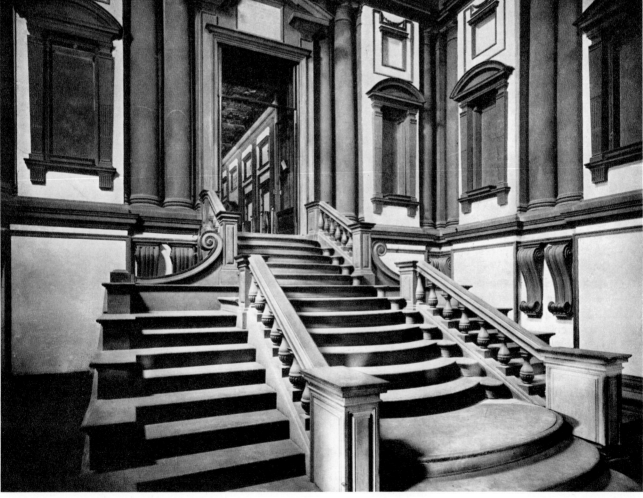

prisoners. A tragic view of human destiny has superseded the triumphant faith of the Sistine Chapel, and it is no wonder that the project, intended eventually for paintings as well, was never finished. Michelangelo continued work until Clement's death in 1534 and then departed for Rome never to return, leaving such a passage as the head of Day barely blocked out and the statues strewn about the Chapel.

At the same time as his work on the Chapel, however, and beginning in 1524, Michelangelo was designing for Clement VII a library (to be placed literally on top of the Monastery of San Lorenzo) to contain the Medici collection of books and manuscripts (including the *Rabula Gospels*). The reading room can be seen through the entrance door; it is divided into a succession of equal bays by continuous rows of pilasters, ceiling beams, and floor ornaments. The entrance hall (fig. 155), too high and narrow to be photographed in its entirety, is even more extraordinary, for the columns that should support the entablature are withdrawn into recesses in the wall, segments of which, bearing empty tabernacles, protrude between them. The effect is menacing, like the collapsing room in Poe's *The Pit and the Pendulum*. These columns that support nothing are themselves apparently supported by floating consoles. The narrow pilasters flanking the tabernacles are divided into three unequal segments, each differently fluted, and taper downward like Minoan columns (which Michelangelo never could have seen). Architecture as anticlassical as this must have brought Alberti, Brunelleschi, and Bramante out of their graves in horror, but Vasari delighted in it, since it showed that Michelangelo, so far from being bound by Classical rules, was superior to them.

The strangest of all the spaces of the Laurentian Library would have been the never-built rare book room at the far end of the reading room. The only remaining area was a triangle; nothing daunted, Michelangelo planned to turn it into a triangular room, perhaps the only one ever designed, with two triangular reading desks fitting one inside the other and encompassing a V-shaped one like a maze. For nearly a quarter of a century the Library was left with a temporary staircase; Michelangelo finally sent to Vasari in 1557 the design for a permanent version from Rome, which he said had occurred to him in a dream—hardly a pleasant one to judge from the result (see fig. 155). While the central staircase with its bow-shaped steps seems to pour downward, ascending lateral stairs besiege it from either side. Walking up or down this structure is an experience so disturbing as to leave little doubt that the harmonies of the High Renaissance have been left far behind. We shall return to Michelangelo and discuss his later work in Rome in Chapter 6.

ANDREA DEL SARTO. The Florentine painters of the second and third decades of the sixteenth century could hardly help but be influenced by the powerful presence of Michelangelo in Florence, but one of them, Andrea del

Sarto (1486–1530), remained faithful to the ideals of the High Renaissance. In his *Madonna of the Harpies* (fig. 156)—the harpies that adorn the Madonna's throne have given their name to the painting—the Virgin and Child, steadied on their pedestal by two child angels, communicate something of the harmony and grace of Raphael's *Sistine Madonna* (see fig. 148), and the figure of John reflects in reverse the pose of the writing philosopher just to the left of the portrait of Michelangelo in the *School of Athens* (see colorplate 24). However, some of the marmoreal quality of Michelangelo's figures is also suggested, and the folds break into cubic masses recalling those of Michelangelo's characteristic drapery forms in sculpture and in painting. The ideal facial types of Andrea del Sarto, calm, grand, and often very beautiful, show in their characteristic mood of reverie little of the torment that contorts the faces of his more overtly Mannerist contemporaries.

PONTORMO. A gifted pupil of Andrea del Sarto and friend of Michelangelo during this Florentine phase, Jacopo Carucci da Pontormo (1494–1557), responded very differently to the psychic pressures of the moment. One of his strangest and most outspokenly Mannerist works is a painting done in 1518, unbelievably enough while Raphael was still alive, as one of a series painted in collaboration with Andrea del Sarto and other eminent

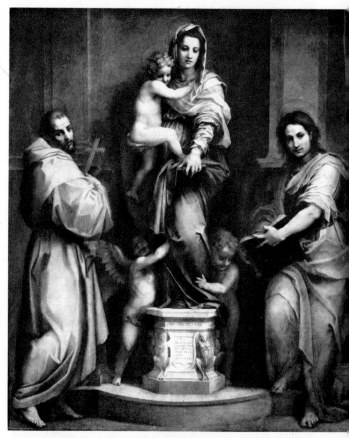

156. ANDREA DEL SARTO. *Madonna of the Harpies.* 1517. Oil on panel. 81½ x 70″. Galleria degli Uffizi. Florence

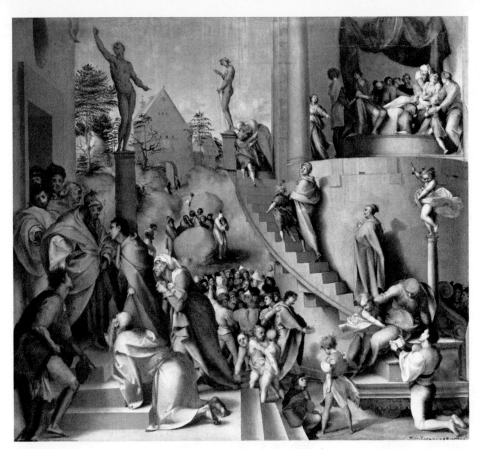

157. JACOPO PONTORMO.
Joseph in Egypt. 1518.
Oil on canvas, 38 x 43⅛".
National Gallery, London

Florentine masters for the bedroom of a Florentine palace. *Joseph in Egypt* (fig. 157) shows three successive scenes within the same frame. At the upper right is Pharaoh's dream, in the center the discovery of the cup in Benjamin's sack, and at the left Joseph's brethren are reconciled to him. But instead of the unified space of a High Renaissance picture, the work is split into compartments by such devices as a winding staircase to nowhere with no balustrade and few supports, and statues gesturing like living people on columns and pedestals; the chaotic groupings of excited people have been made even stranger by the flickering lights and darks playing over figures and drapery masses. Not only the compositional devices but also the very mood of the picture negate everything for which the High Renaissance stands.

Pontormo's *Entombment* (colorplate 25), of about 1525–28, hardly seems a Renaissance picture. Once it has been established at the bottom of the picture, the ground never reappears, and there is no setting whatsoever. The figures tiptoe as in Botticelli; the towering compositional structure rises parallel to the picture plane in a web of shapes recalling Cimabue's *Madonna Enthroned* (see fig. 6) of nearly two hundred and fifty years before rather than moving harmoniously into depth in the manner of a Renaissance composition. Christ is being carried toward the tomb, yet neither tomb nor crosses can be seen. It is not clear whether the Virgin is seated or standing, or on what. Figures float upward around her with the lightness of the cloud that hangs above, curving over at the top in conformity with the forces of the frame, so designed as to amplify the upward movement of the figures. These are

enormously attenuated; the bearer at the left is more than eight heads high. While the poses are in a way Michelangelesque, the figures are devoid both of strength and substance, and shorn of their natural coloring by the adhering garments some of them wear, which look as if strobe lights were playing on them. The expressions of paralyzed wonder, rather than sorrow, contribute to the dreamlike character of the painting, poignant and lyrical, floating between earth and sky.

ROSSO. Even stranger than Pontormo is his contemporary Rosso Fiorentino (1495–1540), who painted—only a year after Raphael's death—the profoundly disturbing *Descent from the Cross* (fig. 158). Instead of centralizing the composition as in a High Renaissance picture, Rosso has dispersed the elements toward the frame, so that they make a latticework of shapes, and instead of the harmonious, spirally moving figures of Raphael, he set stiff, angular beings in the spasmodic motion of automatons. The background landscape has shrunk almost to the bottom of the picture, so that the whole structure of figures, Cross, and ladders is erected against a sky like a slab of blue-gray stone. Expressions, when we are allowed to see them, range from a look of anguish on the face of one of the Holy Women to what can only be described as a leer on that of Joseph of Arimathea to a smile as of pleasure derived from pain on the face of the dead Christ. The nude figures look deliberately wooden, the draped ones mere bundles of cloth. John has collapsed into broken folds like the shards of a pot; strangest of all, the prostrate Magdalene, embracing the Virgin's knees, is turned into an almost cubist construction by a sharp crease that runs down her side from shoulder to waist, from waist to knee, and then into the shadows. Even the gold sash at her waist breaks as if her body were constructed like a box.

BECCAFUMI. Throughout the fifteenth century, memories of the great masters of the fourteenth persisted in Siena, blended with elements imported from Florence, but the perverse style of the Mannerist crisis affected Sienese as well as Florentine artists, especially Domenico Beccafumi (1485–1551); about 1524 he showed the *Fall of the Rebel Angels* (fig. 159; cf. an Early Renaissance treatment, as in the *Très Riches Heures*; see fig. 91) as a scene of nightmare intensity. The summit of the composition is largely occupied by the Archangel Michael, with wings spread and sword uplifted; on either side other angels wield swords against the rebels, and in the shadows below Michael's feet writhes a dragon-like Satan. Through these tangled figures one looks upward

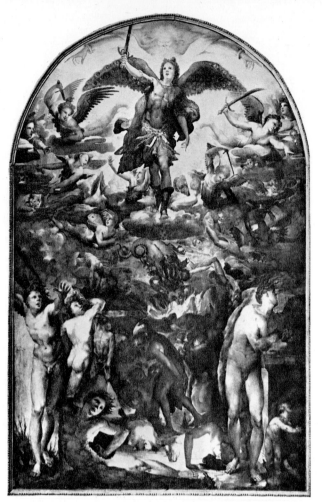

159. DOMENICO BECCAFUMI. *Fall of the Rebel Angels.* c. 1524. Panel painting, 11'4½" x 7'4". Pinacoteca Nazionale di Siena

toward the light as through the branches of a dark forest; in the lower two-thirds of the panel the only light is that coming in bursts of fire through the twisting bodies of the rebel angels. The top of the arch is occupied by God the Father, dim, remote, and seemingly powerless, his arms and fingers weakly extended along the frame. What shreds of High Renaissance beauty that still cling to the tormented nudes make the vision of a beneficent God and a noble humanity experienced in the Sistine Ceiling unrecapturable a mere dozen years later.

The High Renaissance had presented perfect solutions on a fantasy plane for problems that were in reality insoluble. Under the Mannerist reaction the ideal High Renaissance system fell apart. For centralization Mannerism substituted diffusion; for harmony, dissonance; for easy figural motion, tension and strain; for emotional balance, hysteria, paranoia, or withdrawal. These are by no means symptoms of inadequacy, for the Mannerist artists were capable of extreme refinement of observation and statement. It is their hypersensitivity to the collapsing structure of the traditional Italian world of artisan guilds, merchant republics, and unchallenged Catholicism that renders their works so moving. Perhaps for that very reason they are especially accessible to us today.

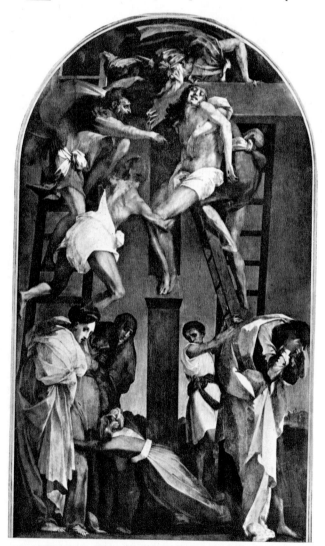

158. ROSSO FIORENTINO. *Descent from the Cross.* 1521. Panel painting, 11' x 6'6". Pinacoteca Communale, Volterra, Italy

5

High Renaissance
and Mannerism
in Venice and Northern Italy

With the exception of Michelangelo, who remained the dominant force in Central Italy, artistic preeminence in the sixteenth century passed gradually from Florentine to Venetian hands. After Raphael's death, Venice was unchallenged in Europe in the field of oil painting. Politically, the Republic of Saint Mark was in by no means so favorable a position. During the papacy of Julius II, she found herself isolated, with all of Europe united against her, and temporarily stripped of her mainland possessions. By the 1520s her fortunes, like those of the other Italian states, were compromised by the continuing warfare between France and the Empire (which, under

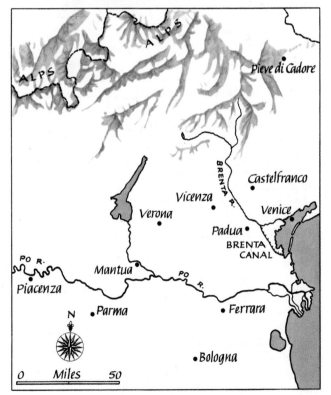

MAP 8. *North Italy*

Charles V, included Spain). Nonetheless, the Venetian School expanded in new aesthetic directions, aided by the adoption of flexible resins that made painting on canvas instead of on the traditional panels possible. Bellini survived until 1516 (see Chapter 1), still respected and productive. Under some Roman and Florentine influence, the High Renaissance style rapidly took root in Venice, even in Bellini's late works. But since Venice was the only major artistic center in Italy not to fall a prey to despotism, Tuscan Mannerism had slight influence. The Venetian style, however, fanning out over north Italy, encountered waves from Florence, and in such north Italian centers as Parma, High Renaissance and Mannerist tendencies coexisted side by side.

GIORGIONE. The founder of a new and at first exclusively Venetian tendency was Giorgione da Castelfranco (c.1475/77–1510), according to Vasari a happy and carefree personality given to a life of music and merrymaking. Among the small body of paintings attributed to Giorgione, none, unfortunately, are dated. Probably about 1505, the date of Bellini's *Madonna Enthroned* (see fig.84), Giorgione painted the same subject (fig. 160) for the cathedral of his native city of Castelfranco. At first sight the compositions are similar, but the differences are crucial. Giorgione's spacious picture is mysterious, in that the Virgin and Child are placed on a high throne without visible means of access, which renders the image incommensurable with the real world, like Leonardo's *Last Supper* (see fig. 128) or Raphael's *School of Athens* (see colorplate 24), in spite of Saint Francis' appeal to the observer. Also, through careful adjustments of directions, such as the parallelism between the lance of Saint Liberalis in his gleaming armor and the diagonals in the Virgin's robe, Giorgione unified his composition beyond the stage of Bellini. The landscape, seen over the low wall, dominates the picture, from the partially ruined castle at the left to the trees and port scene

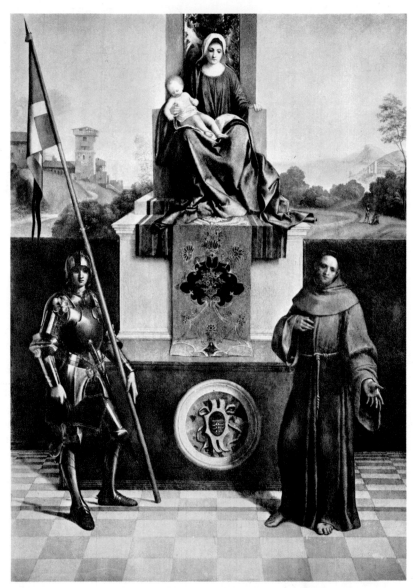

160. GIORGIONE. *Enthroned Madonna
with Saint Liberalis and Saint Francis.*
c. 1505. Panel painting, 78¾ x 60".
Cathedral of Castelfranco, Italy

at the right. The soft modeling of the gracious and simplified faces is even broader than that of the aged Bellini in its reliance on light and shadow rather than on definition of forms.

Giorgione's most influential picture, painted about 1505–10, is a small canvas called *The Tempest* (colorplate 26), showing a landscape in which a soldier, leaning on his lance, gazes quietly toward a young woman, insufficiently draped in a towel, who nurses her child as she looks out toward us. Scholars have ransacked literature in vain for the subject. The futility of further search was indicated by the X-ray discovery of a second nude woman underneath the soldier. Moreover, a Venetian diarist in 1530 recorded the picture as "the little landscape on canvas with the tempest, with the gypsy and the soldier." Clearly, Giorgione intended us to know no more than this about the subject; it is crucial that the diarist was prompted to mention the landscape first. Up to this moment we have encountered landscapes as backgrounds for figures; the roles are now reversed, and the figures are present here only to establish scale and

mood for the magical landscape. Nature, around the figures, is wild, weedy, and unpruned. The air is pregnant with storm. Ruins, a river crossed by a plank bridge, and the houses of a village are illuminated by a lightning flash, which casts the shadow of the bridge upon the water. The lightning is serpentine for the first time in any painting known to us, and it looks the way lightning really looks. In this little painting, exploiting to the full the luminary possibilities of the oil medium, Giorgione established a new and immensely influential theme, which might be described as the landscape-and-figure poem.

TITIAN. The monarch of the Venetian School in the sixteenth century, analogous to Michelangelo in Florence and Rome, was Tiziano Vecellio (c. 1490–1576), Anglicized to Titian. A robust mountaineer who came to Venice as a boy from the Alpine town of Cadore, Titian was long believed to have survived well into his nineties, but recent research has shortened his life-span somewhat. The young painter was trained in the studios of both Gentile Bellini and Giovanni Bellini, and then assisted

Giorgione with some of the lost frescoes that once decorated the exteriors of Venetian palaces. Once independent, Titian—on the basis of the new principles of form and color announced by the late Giovanni Bellini and by Giorgione—succeeded in establishing color alone as the major determinant. He did not visit Central Italy until 1545–46, when he was accorded Roman citizenship on the Capitoline Hill, but he was aware much earlier, probably by means of engravings, of what was going on in Florence and Rome, and rapidly assimilated High Renaissance innovations to his own stylistic aims. Titian generally began with a red ground, which communicated warmth to his coloring; over that he painted figures and background, often in brilliant hues. He is reported to have turned his half-finished pictures to the wall for months, then to have looked at them as if they were his worst enemies, and finally to have toned them down with glazes, as many as thirty or forty layers. Always imparting unity to the whole, these glazes became deeper and richer as Titian's long career drew toward its close.

It was a life marked by honors and material rewards. Titian's prices were high, his financial acumen the subject of caricature, and like Raphael and Michelangelo he made himself wealthy. His palace in Venice was the center of a near-princely court, fulfilling the worldly ideal of the painter's standing as formulated by Leonardo. In 1533 began his acquaintance with the emperor Charles V, whose rule comprised all of western Europe save France, Switzerland, Central Italy, and the Venetian republic. There is a legend to the effect that this potentate, on a visit to Titian's studio, stooped to pick up a brush the painter had dropped. Titian was called twice to the imperial court at Augsburg, and was ennobled by the emperor.

An early work, painted about 1515, is generally known as *Sacred and Profane Love* (colorplate 27), although its actual subject, in spite of much research, has not been satisfactorily determined. Two women who look like sisters sit on either side of an open sarcophagus, which is also a fountain, in the glow of late afternoon. One is clothed, belted, and gloved and holds a bowl toward her body with one hand and pink roses with the other, as she listens intently to the earnest discourse of her sister, nude save for a white scarf thrown lightly about her loins and a rose-colored mantle flowing over her left arm, uplifted to hold a burning lamp against the sky. The shadowed landscape behind the clothed sister culminates in a castle, toward which a horseman gallops, while two rabbits play in the dimness; behind the nude sister the landscape is filled with light, and huntsmen ride behind a hound about to catch a hare, while shepherds tend their flocks before a village with a church tower, touched with the evening light. Cupid stirs the waters in the sarcophagus-fountain, on which is represented, to the left, a figure leading a horse and followed by attendants, and, on the right, a nude man being beaten and a nude woman grasped by the hair. A golden bowl partly filled with water rests on the

edge of the sarcophagus, from which water pours through a golden spout to a plant bearing white roses. The roses and the sarcophagus filled with water are drawn from a passage in a widely read Renaissance romance, *The Strife of Love in Poliphilo's Dream*, which relates how white roses were tinted red by the blood of the dying Adonis.

What Titian's picture may refer to is the passage from virginity (symbolized by the clothed body and hands, the locked belt, the guarded bowl, the dark fortress, and the huntsman returning empty-handed) through the water of suffering, a kind of baptism through the death of the old self, to a new life in love, conceived as a sacred rite (the church spire, the lamp lifted heavenward). The picture then becomes an exaltation of the beauty and redeeming power of love in terms of the ample forms and perfect health characteristic of Titian's conception of womanhood. As compared with Giorgione's less attractive nude, Titian's glorious creation shares the Classical beauty of Raphael's *Galatea* (see fig. 150). Even the landscape, wild in Giorgione, is here subjected to discipline in the measurement of its elements. Just as characteristic of his art as the glowing colors of metal, heavy silks, white clouds, red-gold hair, and warm flesh is Titian's manner of composing the group in terms of triangles, a device that runs through his entire career.

Comparable to the pagan works that Raphael and others painted for the Farnesina in Rome is a series of mythological paintings made by Titian for a chamber in the palace of the duke of Ferrara. One of these, the *Bacchanal of the Andrians* (fig. 161), executed about 1520, is based on a description by the third-century Roman writer Philostratus of a picture he saw in a villa near Naples. The inhabitants of the island of Andros disport themselves in a shady grove in happy abandon to the effects of wine. The freedom of the poses (within Titian's triangular system) is completely new; the lovely sleeping nude at the lower right reclines in a pose later to be often imitated, notably by Goya (see colorplate 51). Titian has extracted the greatest visual delight from the contrast of warm flesh with shimmering drapery, and of light with unexpected dark, such as the shadowed crystal pitcher lifted against the shining cloud, and the golden light on the place deity on his hill against the dark blue sky.

Like his mythological pictures, Titian's early religious visions are warm affirmations of health and beauty. The *Assumption of the Virgin*, 1516–18 (fig. 162), is his sole venture into the realm of the colossal; it represents the moment (according to a belief not made dogma until 1950) when the soul of the Virgin was reunited with her dead body so that she might be lifted corporeally into Heaven. His dramatic composition is a Venetian counterpart to Raphael's *Sistine Madonna* (see fig. 148). Above the powerful, excited figures of the Apostles on earth, Mary—abundant and beautiful as the two sisters of the *Sacred and Profane Love*—is lifted on a glowing cloud by innumerable child angels, also rosy, robust, and

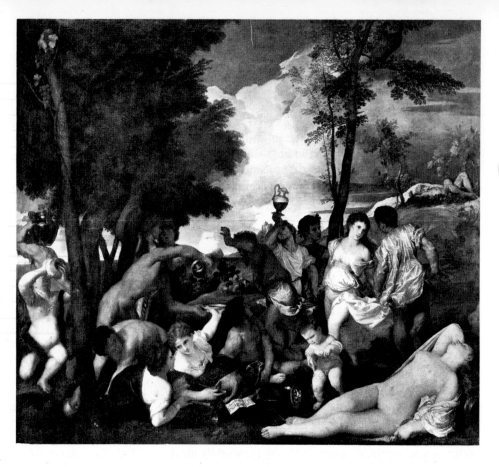

161. TITIAN.
Bacchanal of the Andrians. c. 1520.
Oil on canvas, 69 x 76".
Museo del Prado, Madrid

162. TITIAN. *Assumption of the
Virgin.* 1516–18. Panel
painting. 22'6" x 11'10".
Sta. Maria Gloriosa dei Frari.
Venice

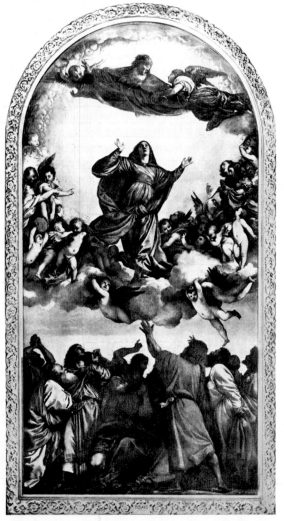

warm, into a golden Heaven, where she is awaited by God the Father, foreshortened like Michelangelo's Creator in the *Lord Congregating the Waters* on the Sistine Ceiling (see colorplate 23), of which the artist must surely have known. The glowing reds, blues, and whites of the drapery, the rich light of the picture, and the strong diagonals of the composition (in contrast to Raphael's spirals) carry Titian's triumphant message through the spacious interior of the Gothic Church of the Frari in Venice, upon whose high altar it still stands.

In his *Madonna of the House of Pesaro*, 1519–26 (fig. 163), Titian applied his triangular compositional principle to the traditional Venetian Madonna group (cf. figs. 84, 160), breaking up its symmetry by a radical view from one side. The scene is a portico of the Virgin's palace, the actors kneeling members of the Pesaro family, including Jacopo Pesaro, bishop of Paphos, and an armored figure who presents to the Virgin as a trophy a Turk captured in battle. The steps plunge diagonally into depth, and the columns are seen diagonally, their capitals outside the frame; reciprocal diagonals in one plane or in depth, in the pose of Peter, for example, or in the angle of the Pesaro flag, build up a rich fabric of forces and counterforces. At the top clouds float before the columns, on which stand nude child angels, one seen unceremoniously from the back, bearing the Cross. As compared with other paintings of the second decade of the century, the colors have become extremely rich and deep, veiled by glaze after glaze.

One would expect Titian's portraits to sparkle with color, but this does not often happen, partly because the male costume of the sixteenth century was characteristically black. In his *Man with the Glove* (fig. 164), possibly a portrait of Gerolamo Adorno (d. 1523), which Titian delivered to Federigo Gonzaga, duke of Mantua, in 1527, his triangular principle is embodied in the balanced relationship of the gloved and ungloved hands to the shoulders and the youthful face. The smooth and carefully modeled hands and features are characteristic of Titian's portraits, contrasting with the ideal simplification of the heads in his allegorical and religious paintings. Even in this picture, dominated by black and by the soft greenish-gray background, color is everywhere, dissolved in the glazes, which mute all sharp contrasts.

A subject that occupied Titian, and presumably delighted his patrons, in his mature and later years is the

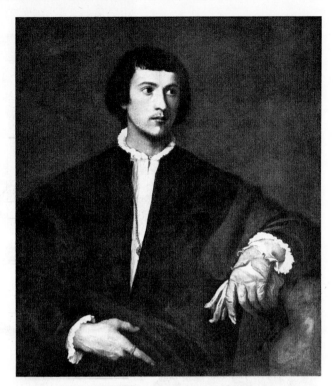

164. TITIAN. *Man with the Glove.* c. 1527. Oil on canvas, 39⅜ x 35″. The Louvre, Paris

nude recumbent Venus—a pose originally devised by Giorgione. In 1538 Titian painted the *Venus of Urbino* (fig. 165) for Guidobaldo della Rovere, then duke of Camerino, although it may be questioned whether this figure is really a Venus; the duke's eager letters refer to her only as a nude woman. Without any of the verve of Titian's earlier jubilant nudes, the opulent figure relaxes in pampered ease on a couch in a palace interior whose inlaid marble floor and sumptuous wall hangings make a golden, greenish, soft red-and-brown foil for the beauty of her abundant flesh and her floods of warm, light brown hair. Pure color, almost divorced from classical form, rules in the pictures of Titian's middle period.

In his later years form appealed to Titian even less; in fact, substance itself was almost dissolved in the movement of color. In the full-length *Portrait of Pope Paul III and His Grandsons,* painted in 1546 (fig. 166), the question even arises, as with many of Titian's later works, whether the picture is really finished. There can be no doubt that this painting was carried to a point that satisfied both artist and patron, but as compared with the consistent surfaces of the foreground figures in Titian's early works, it is far from finished. The brushstrokes are free and sweeping, especially in the drapery, in which Titian has revived Raphael's harmony of reds (see fig. 149). What the artist has done is to apply to the whole picture the sketchy technique characteristic of the backgrounds in his earlier works. Veils of pigment are so freely applied—with the fingers as much as with the brush, if we are to believe Titian's contemporaries—as to recall the Castelseprio frescoes and the *Joshua Roll.*

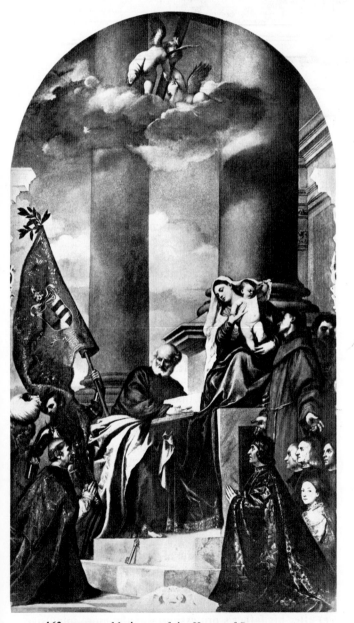

163. TITIAN. *Madonna of the House of Pesaro.* 1519–26. Oil on canvas, 16′ x 8′10″. Sta. Maria Gloriosa dei Frari, Venice

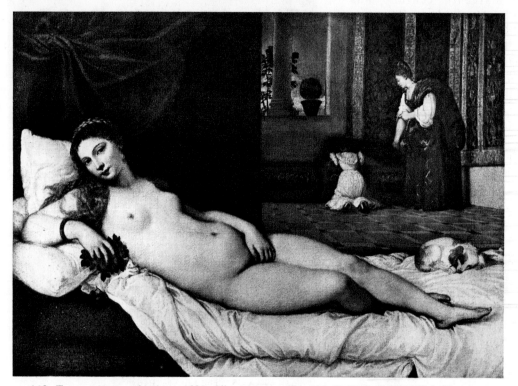

165. TITIAN. *Venus of Urbino*. 1538. Oil on canvas. 47 x 65". Galleria degli Uffizi, Florence

In his extreme old age form was to a certain extent revived and color grew more brilliant, but always looser and freer. The old man seems to have experienced a resurgence of passion, and his late paintings of pagan subjects are unrestrained in their power and beauty. Like so many of the artist's later works, the *Rape of Europa* (fig. 167) was probably painted off and on during several years, in this case about 1559–62. The white bull, one of the many disguises of Jupiter, whose amorous exploits fascinated Renaissance artists and patrons, carries the distraught yet yielding Europa in one of the most beautiful poses of Renaissance art, which combines surprise, abandon, and unconscious grace, over a glittering blue-green and foam-flecked sea. Cupid floats on a dolphin, and a glittering golden fish surfaces below. The nymphs left wailing on the shore are seen against a landscape that contains no solid forms or shapes—all is dissolved in veils of blue, gold, and violet. Nothing excelling this dematerialization of landscape forms was to be seen until the days of Watteau in the eighteenth century (see fig. 329).

The same devices of rapid movement and transcendent color, ignoring detail, were used to shattering emotional effect in the very late *Crowning with Thorns* (fig. 168), probably painted about 1570, six years before the artist's death. The hail of brushstrokes creates cloudy shapes; the agony of Christ and the fury of his tormentors are expressed in storms of color. The thick masses of impasto are contrasted with the encompassing glazes to create an effect as somber as if a cloud of smoke had come before

the brilliant coloring of the *Rape of Europa*. The last religious works of Titian reached a point beyond which only Rembrandt in the seventeenth century could proceed.

LOTTO. A conservative current in Venetian painting, interestingly enough one accepted less in Venice than on the mainland, is represented by Lorenzo Lotto (1480–1556). Like most Venetians, Lotto was above all a colorist, but without Titian's interest in conveying a pervasive glow to an entire composition. Lotto's *Madonna and Child with Saints*, of the 1520s (fig. 169), is sustained coloristically by the Virgin's voluminous tunic and mantle, more intensely blue than the sky. The figures are broadly grouped, with a clear-cut, linear movement running from element to element in a manner almost entirely absent from Titian's work, reflecting rather the brilliant art of Mantegna in the preceding century (see Chapter 1) and open to contacts with Florentine Mannerism. The extreme beauty of the Virgin's face and of that of the protecting angel was not surpassed by any other Venetian painter.

TINTORETTO. By the middle of the sixteenth century two great painters, sharply opposed in style, temperament, and methods, disputed the field with the aged Titian. Jacopo Robusti (1518–94), called Tintoretto (*Little Dyer*) after his father's profession, was the more impulsive of the two, in fact the most dramatic painter of the sixteenth century. Impatient with Titian's painstaking

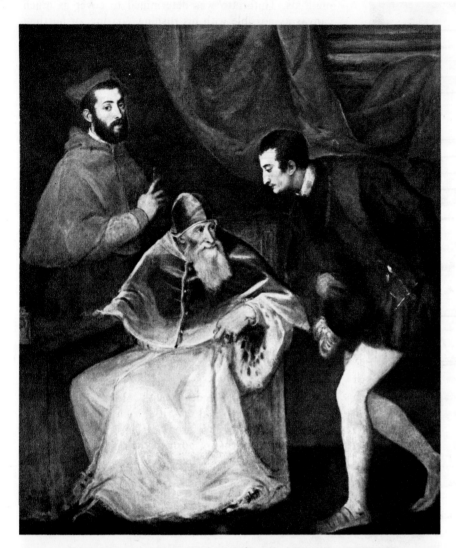

166. TITIAN. *Portrait of Pope Paul III and His Grandsons.* 1546. Oil on canvas, 78½ x 49". Museo di Capodimonte, Naples

167. TITIAN. *Rape of Europa.* 1559–62. Oil on canvas, 73 x 81". Isabella Stewart Gardner Museum, Boston

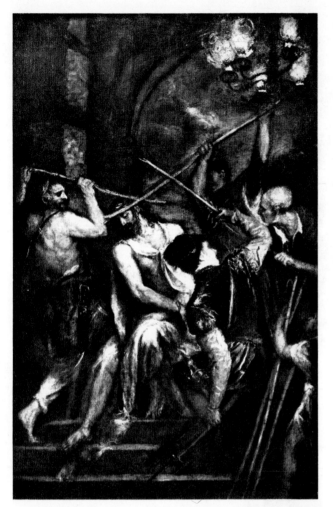

168. TITIAN. *Crowning with Thorns.* c. 1570. Oil on canvas. 9'2" x 5'1½". Alte Pinakothek, Munich

methods, Tintoretto was determined to cover as much canvas as possible with his rushing, soaring, or hurtling figures. His means could only have been successful in the hands of a painter of intense emotion and daring imagination. He began by arranging little modeled figures like puppets on small stages, or in the case of flying figures by hanging them from wires. He was thus enabled to draw the composition accurately, with the foreshortening predetermined. Then he enlarged the drawings to the enormous dimensions of his canvases by means of proportionate grids (fresco in the traditional Italian manner had been given up as hopeless in the damp atmosphere of Venice). He next primed the canvas with a dark tone, such as gray-green or deep brown, or divided it into areas of several dark hues. Once the preliminary sketch had been enlarged, he could paint in the light areas with great rapidity in bright colors, leaving the priming for the darks, and the painting would be finished save for contours and highlights. His paintings thus often look like night scenes illuminated by flashes of light.

Tintoretto advertised the drawing of Michelangelo and the coloring of Titian, but neither claim was strictly true. He has been called a Mannerist, but it is hard to find any common ground between his stormy creations and the calculated works of Pontormo, Rosso, or Beccafumi. For all the speed of execution with broad brushes (the nineteenth-century English critic John Ruskin accused him of painting with a broom), Tintoretto's paintings have an inner harmony born of their own momentum. His almost weightless figures swoop and swirl with unheard-of speed, but they never display the irresolutions and dissonances of Central Italian Mannerism.

169. LORENZO LOTTO. *Madonna and Child with Saints (Sacra Conversazione).* c. 1520s. Oil on canvas, 44¾ x 60". Kunsthistorisches Museum, Vienna

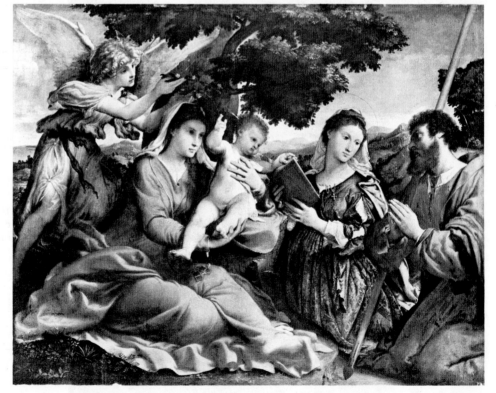

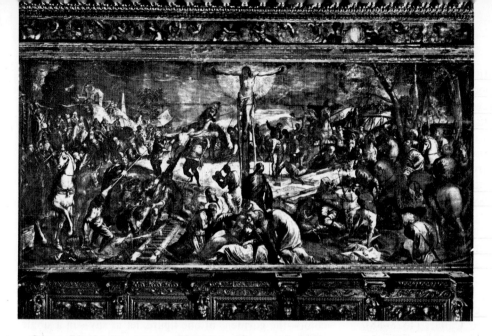

170. TINTORETTO. *Crucifixion.*
1565. Oil on canvas, 17'7" x 40'2".
End wall, Sala dell'Albergo.
Scuola di S. Rocco, Venice

Saint Mark Freeing a Christian Slave, of 1548 (colorplate 28), was Tintoretto's first brilliant success in his new style. The legend tells how a Christian slave left Provence, without his master's permission, to adore the relics of Saint Mark in Alexandria; on his return he was condemned to have his eyes gouged out and his legs broken with hammers, whereupon Saint Mark rushed down from Heaven, the ropes were snapped and the hammers shattered to the consternation of all, especially the master, ready to fall from his throne. Tintoretto's daring foreshortenings take up in an authoritative way what Mantegna had achieved with much labor in the *Dead Christ* (see fig. 82) and the ceiling of the Camera degli Sposi (see colorplate 13). The dazzling colors against the dark priming and the summary brushwork intensify the prearranged movement of the figures, always so constructed as to achieve a tension in depth between figures pouring out of the composition and those rushing into it; Saint Mark, for example, dives in upside down and feet toward us, his figure painted with only a few rapid strokes of lighter rose and orange against the dark red priming, his head merely suggested against a sunburst of rays.

Tintoretto's style was not a matter of mere virtuosity; it sprang spontaneously from the depths of a sincere and uncomplicated personality. He had no ambition to compete with Titian's life of ease; sometimes he painted only for the cost of the materials, and he left his widow in poverty. His personal style enabled him to communicate religious experience with the force of revelation. He was an ideal painter for the societies of laypersons, the so-called *scuole* (schools), which, under ecclesiastical supervision, carried out works of charity in Venice. The walls of the hall on the lower floor of the Scuola di San Rocco, and both walls and ceilings of the great hall and chapel on the upper floor, are covered with a continuous cycle comprising more than fifty canvases by Tintoretto, separated only by the width of their frames, executed throughout an almost twenty-five-year period (1564–87) for a small annual salary after 1577. These render the Scuola di San Rocco a monument to compete with the Arena Chapel, the Ghent Altarpiece, and the Sistine Chapel for sustained intensity of creative imagination.

The largest of the canvases is the *Crucifixion* (fig. 170), more than forty feet long, painted in 1565, a work of such power that no reproduction can do it justice. The reader should attempt to imagine the enveloping effect of the total image, stretching from wall to wall and wainscoting to ceiling, with foreground figures more-than-lifesize. The Cross appears to sustain the ceiling; at its base the swooning Mary, the comforting Holy Women, and John looking upward form a pyramid of interlocking figures, powerfully constructed in light and dark. The turbulent crowds of soldiers, executioners, and bystanders move about the Cross as if in the grip of forces beyond their understanding. Rays pouring from the head of the Crucified provide the light for the scene, the sun and moon having been darkened at Christ's death. The ropes, the ladders, and the cross of the penitent (but not that of the impenitent) thief move upward along these rays, as if in fulfillment of the passage (John 12: 32): "And I, if I be lifted up from the earth, will draw all men unto me." This is indeed the effect of the composition on all who enter the room.

Like those of Titian, Tintoretto's later works were inspired by the intense religiosity of the Counter-Reformation, and nowhere more than in the paintings he did in the last year of his life for San Giorgio Maggiore in Venice, a church whose luminous beauty (see below, page 155) seems unrelated to such outpourings. The *Last Supper* (fig. 171) breaks with the tradition of Castagno (see fig. 63), Bouts (see fig. 104), and Leonardo (see fig. 128). Judas is reduced to a subsidiary role on the outside of the table, which moves into the picture in a typical Tintoretto diagonal in depth; toward its center Christ rises in the act of distributing the bread, which is his body, to the Apostles, as in the Byzantine composition in Hagia Sophia in Kiev; it is possible that this idea came from Greek artists painting in Venice for the large Greek community. In the foreground, as if to contrast earthly with heavenly sustenance and greed with spiritual longing, the servants take away the uneaten food, a cat looks into the basket for tidbits, and a dog gnaws a bone. All except these foreground figures are insubstantial; the rays Tintoretto had used around the head of Saint Mark in the *Saint Mark Freeing a Christian Slave* now blaze around that of Christ; light starts like fire from the Apostles, blending with the rays from the hanging lamp. In Tintoretto's lightest of touches, angels are sketched in white strokes only, as if with chalk on a blackboard. All the substantiality and form of the Renaissance, hard-won in many an intellectual battle, are here renounced in favor of inner experience, which brings us to the threshold of a new era.

VERONESE. Tintoretto's chief competitor in late-sixteenth-century Venice was Paolo Caliari (1528–88), called Veronese because he came from Verona on the Venetian mainland. There is little spirituality in Veronese's works, concerned with the beauty of the material world—less landscape, which plays a minor role in his paintings, than marble, gold, and above all splendid fabrics. In contrast to Tintoretto's turbulent and dissolving world, everything in a Veronese picture appears under perfect control—solid, gorgeous, and very expensive. Venetian architecture, especially that of Sansovino and Palladio (see below), forms the setting for a succession of celebrations; in fact, Veronese is known above all for the pomp and splendor of his banqueting scenes. One of these paintings got him into trouble with the Inquisition as the third session of the Council of Trent, 1562–63, had promulgated a series of decrees governing religious imagery. Veronese's brush with the authorities was occasioned by a canvas more than forty feet long (colorplate 29) representing Christ at supper under a portico of veined marble Corinthian columns and bronze-relief sculptures intercepting a view of Renaissance (and Gothic) palaces and towers. The minutes of the trial make amusing reading. The artist was asked to justify the "buffoons, drunkards, dwarfs, Germans, and similar vulgarities" who crowded his supposedly sacred picture, and answered, tongue in cheek, that it was all a matter of the license enjoyed by artists, poets, and madmen.

The Inquisitors thought they were looking at a Last Supper, so to lay all doubts to rest Veronese painted on the balustrade the number of the chapter in Luke (5: 29–31) that narrates how Christ feasted in the house of Levi with "a great company of publicans and of others"—clearly casting the Inquisitors in the role of the Pharisees, who objected to his dining among publicans and sinners. Veronese was a colorist second in the sixteenth century only to Titian, although like Tintoretto he had worked out his own technical shortcuts for giant canvases. He adopted from fourteenth-century tempera technique the procedure of painting a whole area of color—the garment of one figure, let us say—in a single flat tone, then modeling highlights and shadows with lighter or darker mixtures of the same hue. His harmonies were obtained by a magical sensitivity to color relationships rather than by the overglazes that unify Titian's much smaller canvases.

Also like Tintoretto, Veronese was no stranger to the laws of perspective, which he utilized in a Mantegnesque manner. His oval ceiling decoration for the Hall of the Grand Council in the Doges' Palace, painted about 1585 with the help of his pupils (fig. 172), shows spiral columns seen from below, which carry the eye upward, and between them, above a balustrade crowded with richly dressed people, sits the allegorical figure of Venice, borne aloft on clouds, enthroned between the towers of her Arsenal, and surrounded by other allegorical figures as Fame holds a laurel wreath above her head. This work was the inspiration for many Baroque ceiling compositions (cf. figs. 230, 251).

SANSOVINO. Few of the churches and palaces that make Venice one of the most beautiful cities in the world were built by Venetian architects. Until the seventeenth cen-

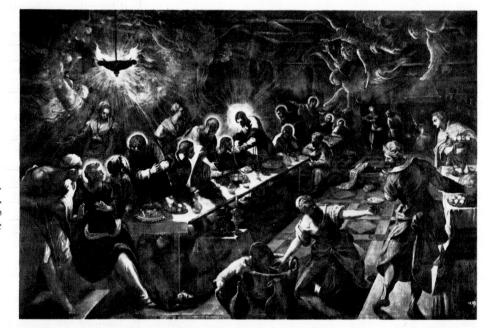

171. TINTORETTO. *Last Supper.*
1592–94. Oil on canvas,
12′ x 18′8″. Chancel, S. Giorgio
Maggiore, Venice

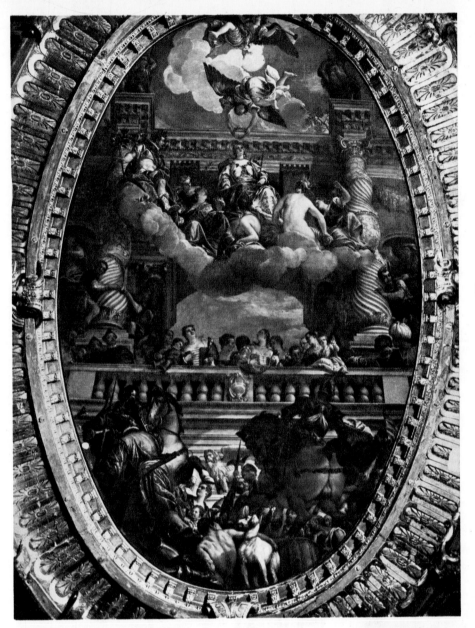

172. PAOLO VERONESE (and pupils).
Triumph of Venice.
Ceiling decoration. c. 1585.
Oil on canvas. Hall
of the Grand Council,
Palazzo Ducale, Venice

tury Venice drew on foreign masters, generally from Lombardy. The High Renaissance architectural style was brought to Venice by a Florentine refugee from the Sack of Rome in 1527, Jacopo Tatti (1486–1570), called Sansovino after his master, the sculptor Andrea Sansovino. But Sansovino erected buildings in Venice that would have been impossible to build in the narrow streets of turbulent Florence. His greatest achievement is the Library of San Marco (fig. 173), which he began in 1536; its construction, interrupted in 1554, was completed only in 1588, years after the architect's death. An even greater architectural genius, Palladio, who as we shall see continued the High Renaissance architecture of Sansovino on a somewhat more rarified intellectual plane, called this edifice the "richest ever built from the days of the ancients up to now."

In the two superimposed arcades that form the structure, Sansovino has translated into Renaissance terms the richness of forms and colors of such Venetian Gothic

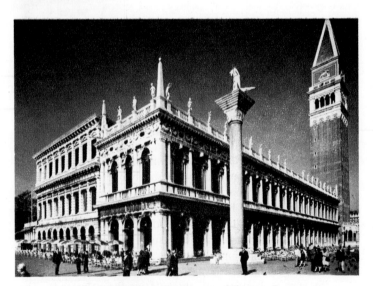

173. JACOPO SANSOVINO. Library of
S. Marco. 1536–88. Venice

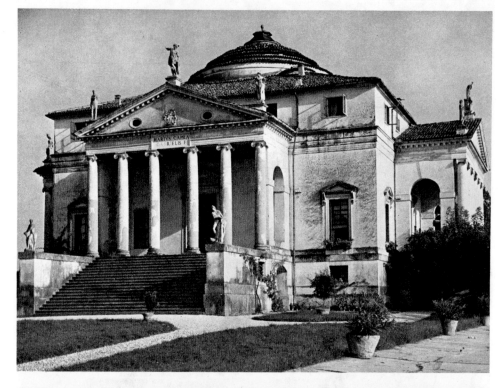

174. ANDREA PALLADIO (completed by VINCENZO SCAMOZZI). Villa Rotonda (Villa Capra). Begun 1550. Vicenza, Italy

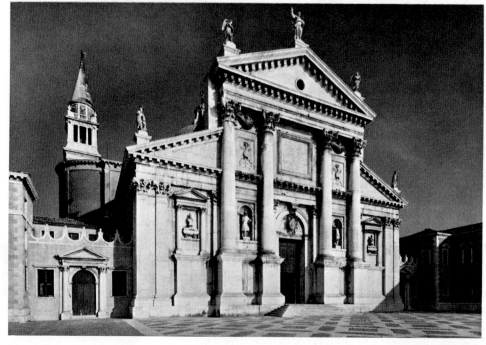

175. ANDREA PALLADIO. Façade, S. Giorgio Maggiore. Begun 1566. Venice

buildings as the Doges' Palace, which the Library faces, and the Ca' d'Oro. The Bramantesque Roman Doric order of the ground story is entirely open, embracing an arcade running around three sides of the building; the second story is Ionic, and embraces a smaller order of paired Ionic columns two-thirds the height of the principal ones, arranged in depth so as to flank the windows of the reading room. The vertical axes of the columns are prolonged against the sky by obelisks at the corners and by statues at every bay, interrupting the balustrade. The spandrels of the arches are sculptured with figures, and

the massive frieze of the second story, interrupted by the oval windows of a mezzanine, is also decorated with figures and garlands. The great sculptural and (given the Venetian light, colored by reflections from the water) pictorial richness would provide the perfect background for a Veronese feast.

PALLADIO. The greatest North Italian architect of the Renaissance, indeed the only sixteenth-century architect who ranks with Bramante and Michelangelo, was Andrea di Pietro (1508–80), known as Palladio, a nickname

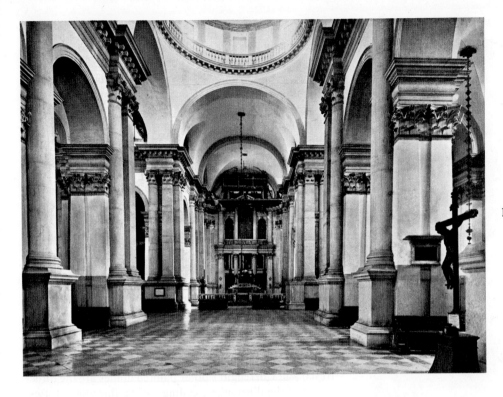

176. ANDREA PALLADIO. Interior, S. Giorgio Maggiore

derived from Pallas Athena and given him by his first patron, a humanist of Vicenza, a city between Verona and Padua, where Palladio was brought up. Insofar as a city can derive its character from the ideas of a single architect, Vicenza is Palladio's creation. Several of its palaces, its town hall, and its theater were built by him, and other buildings were erected by his pupils and followers. In 1570 Palladio published a beautifully illustrated work on architecture that became a kind of Bible for neo-Renaissance architects everywhere, particularly in England and the United States in the eighteenth century, culminating in the designs of Thomas Jefferson (see figs. 358, 359).

As beautiful as Palladio's palaces are his villas, erected near Vicenza and along the Brenta Canal, which connects Padua with the Venetian lagoon. The most influential example of Palladio's villa types is the Villa Capra, nicknamed Villa Rotonda (fig. 174), begun in 1550 on an eminence above Vicenza as a summer retreat and not meant for year-round habitation. Palladio revived the form of the Pantheon in the central hemispheric dome, but with significant changes. The villa is a square block, almost a cube, with an Ionic portico on each of its four sides affording different views over Vicenza and the surrounding subalpine hills. Each portico is protected against sun and wind by sidewalls pierced by arches, and the owners and their guests could therefore enjoy the views through Ionic columns according to the movement of the sun and the temperature of the day. As in the architecture of Sansovino, the axes of Palladio's buildings are prolonged by statues against the sky and, in this case, by long postaments that flank the stairs like those of a Roman temple. It has been demonstrated that Palladio's system for the proportions governing the

shapes and sizes of his spaces was based on mathematical ratios drawn from the harmonic relationships in Greek musical scales; in that sense his architecture really is "frozen music."

Like Sansovino, Palladio contributed to the incomparable picture of the canal in front of San Marco, Venice. In his Church of San Giorgio Maggiore (fig. 175), begun in 1566, he at last solved the problem that had plagued architects of basilicas ever since the days of Constantine—what to do with the awkward shape determined by the high central pediment and the lower sloping side-aisle roofs. Romanesque and Gothic architects had masked the juncture with screen façades, pinnacles, and towers; Alberti had used giant consoles (see fig. 33). Palladio conceived the notion of two interlocking Corinthian temple porticoes, one tall and slender with engaged columns, the other low and broad with pilasters. His solution worked so well and became so well-known that it could never be tried again without a charge of plagiarism. Visually, the relationships between the two dovetailing façades are a source of never-ending pleasure because of the alternation of low and high relief, flat and rounded forms. The interior (fig. 176) is a single giant story of Corinthian engaged columns, paired at the crossing with pilasters. Coupled Corinthian pilasters in depth sustain the nave arcade. With its contrast of stone and plaster, the interior is severely harmonious in its effect.

CORREGGIO. In Parma, a city in the Po Valley, a vigorous school of painting developed unexpectedly in the sixteenth century, led at first by Antonio Allegri (1494–1534), called Correggio after the small town of his birth, and later by his younger contemporary Parmigianino. Correggio, first influenced by Mantegna and then by

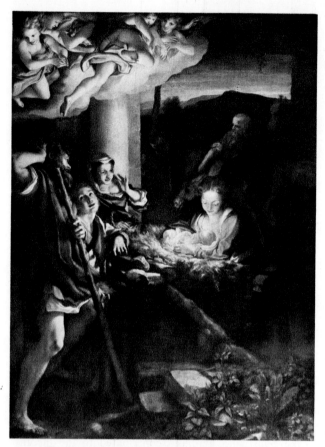

177. CORREGGIO. *Holy Night (Adoration of the Shepherds)*. 1522. Panel painting, 8'5" x 6'2". Gemäldegalerie, Dresden, Germany

Leonardo, never visited Rome, but he was profoundly affected by the Roman High Renaissance, probably through works by Raphael he had seen in Bologna and Piacenza (the *Sistine Madonna* was in Piacenza) and by engraved copies. After an uncertain start, he rapidly became a master of great importance, in fact one of the most independent and original painters in Northern Italy. Like Titian, Correggio tried to break up High Renaissance symmetrical arrangements, for example, in his *Holy Night* (fig. 177), painted in 1522. It is an Adoration of the Shepherds, the same theme as that depicted by van der Goes in fig. 105, but—for the first time—Correggio has treated the subject on a large scale with lifesize figures, entirely illuminated by the light from the Child as in Gentile da Fabriano (see colorplate 5) and Geertgen tot Sint Jans (see fig. 108). The glow illuminates the soft features of the happy and adoring mother, the shepherds, and the astonished midwife, but it barely touches Joseph, the ox, and the ass against the dark sky. Far off the first dawn appears above the hills. Most unconventional is the rush of adoring angels, seen from above and from below in amazing foreshortening and exhibiting the soft, voluptuous flesh that is Correggio's specialty. As in most of his pictures, a bond of warmth and tenderness is the motive force that draws all the figures together.

Correggio was given an opportunity to demonstrate his unconventional art on a colossal scale in the frescoes of the dome of Parma Cathedral; their effect is extremely difficult to communicate in reproductions. A section of the fresco of the *Assumption of the Virgin*, 1526–30 (fig. 178), suggests the extraordinary brilliance of the young painter, who followed Mantegna's lead in dissolving the interior of the vault, so that one seems to be looking directly upward into the clouds at the Virgin borne by angels toward Heaven. The reader should mentally complete the circle of real glass windows between which, in front of a painted balustrade, move the excited Apostles; through this rim one looks upward, never quite certain what is real and what is painted. Above the first circle moves a second, composed of angels uplifting clouds, past which we look into Heaven through ranks upon ranks of saints. The effect is of a colossal bouquet of beautiful legs, all seen from below in brilliant foreshortening. It is as if Correggio had turned Titian's *Assumption* into a cylindrical rather than a flat composition, and placed the observer below it, looking up. This fresco and Correggio's other painted domes are the direct origin of the illusionistic ceilings of the Baroque (cf. figs. 226, 251, 252, colorplate 36).

Almost contemporary with the *Assumption* is Correggio's series of the Loves of Jupiter, painted for Federigo Gonzaga, duke of Mantua, but never delivered. To elude the jealous Juno, Jupiter visited the maiden Io in the form of a cloud; Correggio has shown us the warm, yielding Io, her face lifted in rapture in the midst of a cloudy embrace (fig. 179). The delicate quality of Correggio's flesh has never been surpassed, and despite the strength of Venetian influence in north Italy, it retains a firm sculptural quality. The union of human and divine, frankly sensual in this uninhibited representation of physical climax, is a secular parallel to the sacred rapture of the *Assumption*.

PARMIGIANINO. If Correggio represents a late phase of north Italian High Renaissance, almost—like the mature Roman work of Raphael—on the edge of the Baroque, his slightly younger rival, Francesco Mazzola (1503–40), called Parmigianino, was much closer to the Mannerist currents then developing in Florence and Siena; the contrast between the two leaders of the Parmesan School can be compared with that between Andrea del Sarto and Pontormo. Unlike Correggio, Parmigianino went to Rome to absorb the principles of High Renaissance style, and in fact just escaped the Sack of 1527. In 1524 the painter, then twenty-one years old, executed one of the most original of all self-portraits (fig. 180), a paradigm of the Mannerist view of the world; he used the familiar convex mirror—in this case borrowed from a barber—to achieve his distorting effect, and even painted his picture on a section of a wooden sphere to complete the illusion. Jan van Eyck (and many Netherlandish imitators) had contrasted the distortions of a mirror with the correct

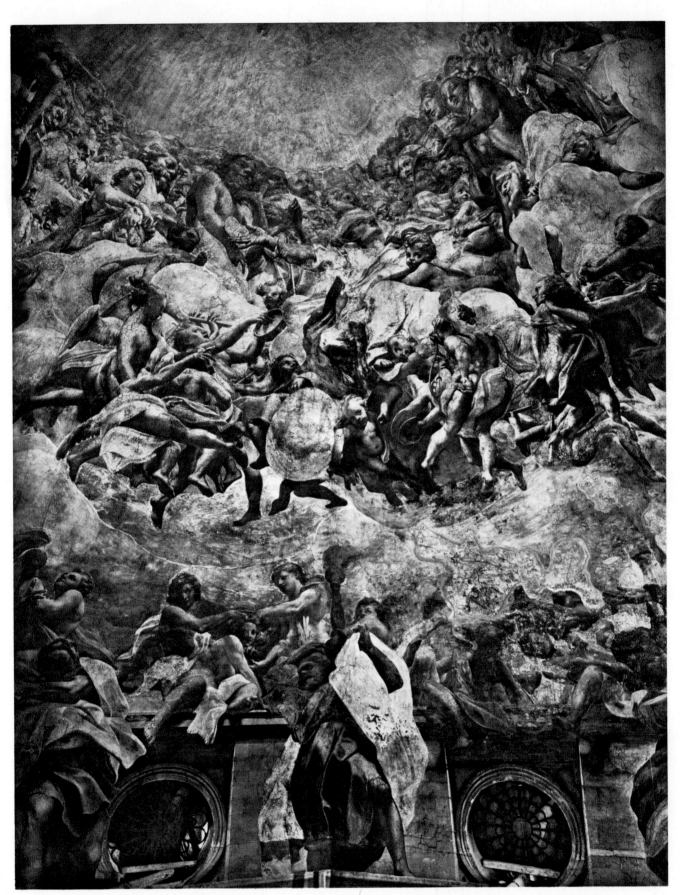

178. CORREGGIO. *Assumption of the Virgin* (portion). Dome fresco. 1526–30. Cathedral of Parma, Italy

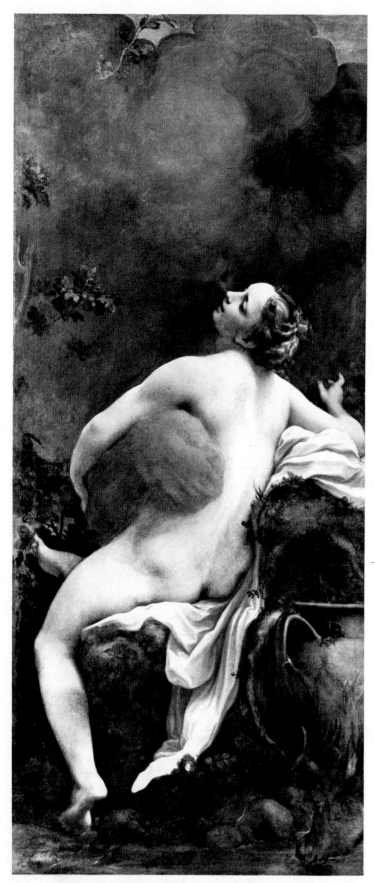

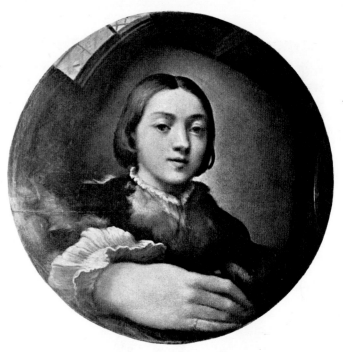

180. PARMIGIANINO. *Self-Portrait in a Convex Mirror.* 1524. Panel painting, diameter 9½". Kunsthistorisches Museum, Vienna

proportions in the real world surrounding it, and although Leonardo had recommended the use of a mirror, he warned against the false reflections given by a convex one. Parmigianino has identified the distortion with the entire pictorial space, curving the sloping skylights of his studio, and greatly enlarging what appears to be his right hand but is in reality his left so that it is larger than his face—which in the middle of this warped vision remains cool, serene, and detached.

In the *Madonna with the Long Neck* (colorplate 30), thus nicknamed for obvious reasons, painted between 1534 and 1540, he glories in distortion. The Virgin is impossibly but beautifully attenuated, even her fingers represented as long and as slender as those of the Madonnas by Cimabue and Duccio (see figs. 6, 11), while she looks downward with a chill prettiness—the very opposite of Correggio's warmth—at the Child, whose pose reminds one of a Pietà (cf. fig. 132). The surfaces resemble cold porcelain, even those of the exquisite leg of the figure at the left carrying an amphora (possibly John the Baptist). Additionally, the perspective is distorted; the figure unrolling a scroll in the middle distance, possibly the prophet Isaiah, seems a hundred yards away. In spite of the perfection to which all the surfaces of flesh, metal, stone, and drapery have been brought, the picture is unfinished. Parmigianino's drawing for the composition shows that he intended a complete Corinthian temple portico in the background, but he has painted only one of the columns, lovingly polished up to the necking band, but with blank underpainting left where capitals, entablature, and pediment should be. The enigma of the unfinished painting has never been solved; possibly Parmigianino, always perverse, did not want it to be.

179. CORREGGIO. *Jupiter and Io.* Early 1530s. Oil on canvas, 64½ x 28". Kunsthistorisches Museum, Vienna

6

Michelangelo
and Later Mannerism
in Central Italy

MICHELANGELO FROM 1534 TO HIS DEATH. The pover-ty-stricken Rome of the mid-sixteenth century was very different from the splendid capital of the High Renaissance. The golden age of the Medici popes had come to an inglorious close in the Sack of 1527. The building of Saint Peter's was at a standstill. In 1534 Clement VII asked Michelangelo to paint the Resurrection on the end wall of the Sistine Chapel to replace two frescoes and an altarpiece by Perugino from the cycle commissioned by Sixtus IV in 1481. After Clement's death later that year, the new pope Paul III ordered instead a gigantic *Last Judgment* (fig. 181); in order to paint it, Michelangelo had to utilize the whole end wall, thus mutilating his own masterpiece, the Sistine ceiling, by tearing down the two lunettes that contained the first seven generations of the ancestry of Christ. He conceived the fresco according to the account in Matt. 24: 30–31:

> And then shall appear the sign of the Son of man in heaven: and then shall all the tribes of the earth mourn, and they shall see the Son of man coming in the clouds of heaven with power and great glory.
>
> And he shall send his angels with a great sound of a trumpet, and they shall gather together his elect from the four winds, from one end of heaven to the other.

Michelangelo painted the gigantic fresco between 1536 and 1541. The earth below has been reduced to just enough ground to show the dead rising from their graves. A great circle of figures rises on the left toward Christ, following the commanding gesture of his left hand, and sinks on the right away from him in obedience to the gesture of damnation of his raised right arm. There are no thrones nor any of the other machinery of a traditional Last Judgment scene, and since, originally, all the male figures were entirely nude, the dominant color is that of human flesh against slate blue sky and gray clouds. To Michelangelo there was nothing improper about so much nudity in such a place, but given the prudery of the Counter-Reformation, he came under severe attack, and one of his pupils was eventually summoned to paint bits of drapery here and there.

The massive figures show little of the ideal beauty of those Michelangelo had painted on the ceiling more than twenty years before. Interestingly enough, the scale changes sharply with the rising levels; the lower figures, emerging from their graves at the left or pushed from the boat crossing the Styx at the right, are hardly more than half the size of the next rank of ascending or descending figures, which are about on a level with the wall frescoes; the group of saints and blessed surrounding Christ, on a level with the windows, are almost twice the size of the figures below them. Finally, the scale diminishes again for the mighty angels in the two lunettes, bearing aloft the Cross and the column.

In contrast to the delicate, slender Christ of the *Pietà*, the Heavenly Judge is a giant, immensely powerful, his raised right arm dominating the entire scene. The mood of awe and doom, and the artist's own sense of guilt, become clear in the figure of Bartholomew (fig. 182), who was martyred by being flayed alive. Michelangelo has turned him into a portrait of the poet Pietro Aretino, who, despite his own authorship of scandalous sonnets, was the artist's bitterest critic of the nudes in the *Last Judgment*. Even more unexpected, the face of the empty skin dangling from the Apostle's left hand is a self-portrait of the aging Michelangelo in a moment of torment. As a final reminder of the Last Judgment, Hell-mouth—a dark cavern in the rock—opens directly above the altar where the celebrant at Mass might be the pope himself. The *Last Judgment* set the pattern for many imitations, but none were so devastating because only Michelangelo could handle the human body with such authority, communicating to the tormented poses the inner tragedy of the spirit.

In 1546 the artist, then seventy-one years old and in poor health, accepted without salary the greatest of his architectural commissions, the continuation of the

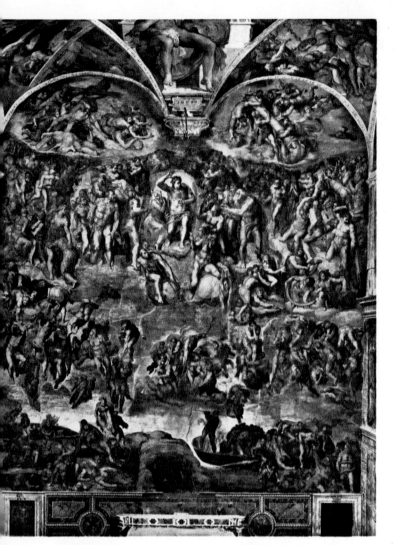

181. MICHELANGELO. *Last Judgment*. 1536–41.
Fresco, 48 x 44'. Sistine Chapel, Vatican, Rome

order of paired Corinthian pilasters, an attic story of paired pilaster strips, a drum with paired columns, a dome with paired ribs, and finally the paired columns of the lantern. The colossal cage of double verticals encloses firmly the stories of windows and niches, which no longer struggle against the supports as in the Laurentian Library (see fig. 155). Instead of the light, geometrical architecture of Bramante, the appearance of Michelangelo's Saint Peter's is that of a colossal work of sculpture, whose masses are determined by the paired verticals rather than by a radial plan. This impression would have been even more powerful had the dome been completed according to Michelangelo's designs with a hemispheric inner shell and an outer shell only slightly pointed (fig. 185). He died when only the drum was completed, and his pupil, Giacomo della Porta (see below), heightened the profile of the dome considerably. Michelangelo had also intended to set colossal statues on the projecting entablatures of the paired columns of the peristyle in order to bridge the gap between their cornices and the dome. In the early seventeenth century the nave was prolonged, so that from the front the effect of Michelangelo's dome is lost; only from the Vatican gardens can this noble building be seen as the artist intended.

Michelangelo's ideas are responsible for the present appearance of one of the first great civic centers of the Renaissance, the Campidoglio (Capitol) in Rome (fig.

building of Saint Peter's, which had been left untouched for so long that trees were growing out of the four great arches built by Bramante. Other architects had proposed extensive changes in the plan, but Michelangelo brought it back to the general dimensions laid down by Bramante at the same time simplifying it greatly. A comparison of his scheme (fig. 183) with Bramante's plan (see fig. 141) shows the differences. Michelangelo eliminated the corner towers and porticoes, doubled the thickness of the four central piers, reduced the four Greek crosses to squares, and preceded the whole by a portico of free-standing columns. From the exterior Michelangelo's transformation was well-nigh total (fig. 184). His dome is a fusion between Brunelleschi's dome for the Cathedral of Florence and Bramante's design, retaining the verticality and the ribs of the one and the peristyle of the other. The result is a peristyle broken into paired Corinthian columns between the windows. The motive of paired supports starts from the ground, with a giant

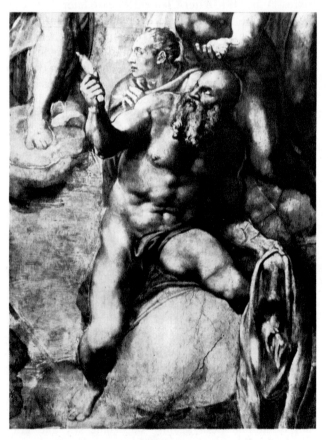

182. MICHELANGELO. *Saint Bartholomew* (detail of the *Last Judgment*)

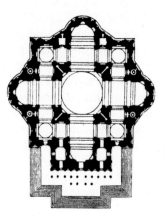

183. MICHELANGELO.
Plan of St. Peter's.
1546–64.
Vatican, Rome

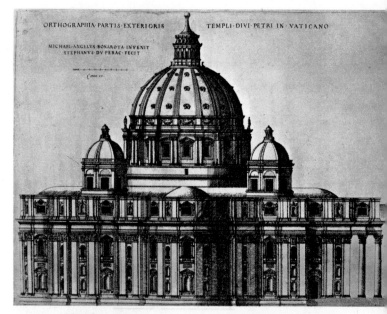

185. MICHELANGELO. Elevation of St. Peter's (engraving
by Étienne Dupérac). The Metropolitan Museum of
Art, New York. Harris Brisbane Dick Fund, 1941

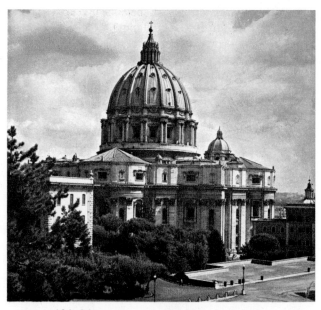

184. MICHELANGELO. Exterior, St. Peter's
(view from the southwest)

During his last years, occupied with architectural projects he was too unwell to supervise in person, Michelangelo in his thoughts, his poems, and his sculpture was
concerned almost exclusively with death and salvation.
Many drawings of the Crucifixion and two Pietàs date
from this final period; on one unfinished group he worked
until six days before his death (fig. 187). From an earlier
stage of about 1554 remain the beautifully carved slender
legs, close to those of the early *Pietà* (see fig. 132), and a
severed arm retained temporarily as a model for the new
arm being carved below it. Rather than across her lap, as

186). His first commission was merely to build a staircase
in front of the medieval Palazzo dei Senatori at the end of
the piazza in 1538 and to move—much against his
will—the Roman statue of Marcus Aurelius to a central
position in the piazza. The refacing of the Palazzo dei
Senatori and the construction of two confronting palaces
were begun only in the 1560s, a little before Michelangelo's death, and do not reflect his intentions in all details. Nonetheless, the general ideas are his, especially the
interlocking and radiating ovals of the pavement centering around the statue, and the giant order of Corinthian
pilasters binding in, as at Saint Peter's, the smaller elements of the building masses in contrast to Sansovino's
superimposed independent stories in the Library of San
Marco (see fig. 173). If Michelangelo's work can ever be
described as Mannerist—and art historians are by no
means agreed on this point—the powerful, positive
solutions of his late architectural style certainly cannot.

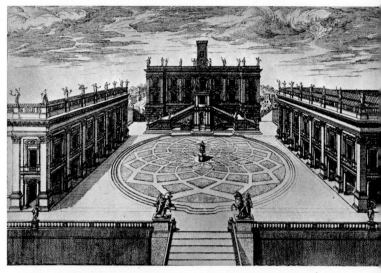

186. MICHELANGELO. Campidoglio. 1538–64. Rome
(engraving by Étienne Dupérac, 1569)

Michelangelo and Later Mannerism in Central Italy / 161

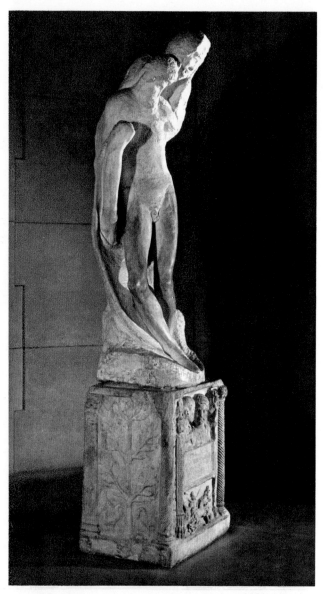

187. MICHELANGELO. *Rondanini Pietà*. c. 1554–64. Marble, height 63⅜″. Castello Sforzesco, Milan

VIGNOLA. A North Italian architect who worked mostly in Rome, Giacomo da Vignola (1507–73) designed the most influential church plan in Rome during the period of the Counter-Reformation. It was that of Il Gesù, the mother church of the powerful Jesuit Order, which spearheaded Catholic revival not only in Europe but also in missionary work from Latin America to India and China. As originally built beginning in 1568, the interior was extremely austere. Its single, overwhelming, barrel-vaulted space, with paired pilasters flanking side chapels rather than side aisles, is based on Alberti's Sant'Andrea in Mantua (see fig. 35), save only for the small clerestory let into the barrel vault (the painting in fig. 188 shows the appearance of the nave before its enrichment in the seventeenth century). The purpose of this plan, of course, was to concentrate all attention on the ceremony at the high altar. Unrelated to Michelangelo's architecture, Vignola's plan for Il Gesù cannot be called Mannerist—neo-Renaissance might be a better term if one is needed. The new solution—really the revival of one a hundred years old—was universally adopted in the seventeenth century not only in Italy but also throughout Europe, and it became *the* Baroque plan for larger

in the early *Pietà*, the Virgin holds the dead Christ up before us, as if, instead of grieving over him, she were prophesying his Resurrection. The line of the severed arm shows that the original head of Christ was hanging forward; in the last days of work Michelangelo cut it away, and began to carve a new head from what had been the Virgin's shoulder. Both figures are as slender as the early sculptures at Chartres and weightless, almost ghostly. The contrapposto, the violence, the contrasting movements have vanished; along with these vital elements mass and life itself have been dissolved. The eighty-nine-year-old artist asked the friends and pupils gathered round his deathbed to remember in his death the death of Christ, as if at the end, freed from guilt and pain, his mortality was fused in the love of the Creator.

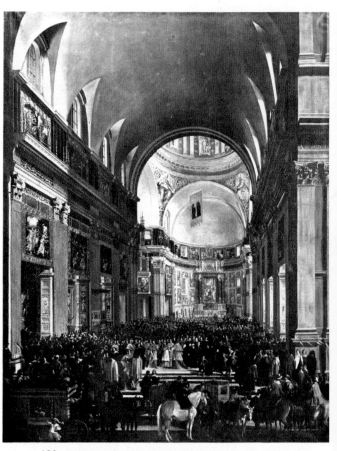

188. ANDREA SACCHI and JAN MIEL. *Urban VIII Visiting Il Gesù*. 1639–41. Oil on canvas. Galleria Nazionale d'Arte Antica, Rome

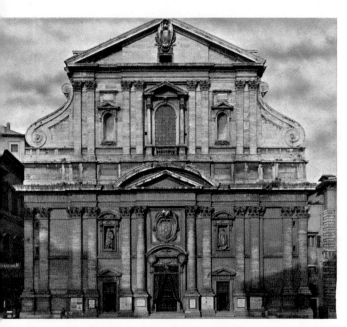

189. GIACOMO DELLA PORTA. Façade,
Il Gesù. c. 1575–84. Rome

churches. But the decision was made for religious rather than aesthetic reasons. Vignola's façade plan, essentially classicistic, was not, however, adopted.

DELLA PORTA. The pupil who completed Michelangelo's dome on Saint Peter's, Giacomo della Porta (1541–1604), received the commission to design the façade for Il Gesù. His design was a tentative but important step in the direction of Baroque architecture, within the artistic vocabulary of Michelangelo (fig. 189). The façade was built from about 1575 to 1584. Basically, the scheme consists of two superimposed orders as at San Miniato al Monte; although there are no side aisles, the lateral chapels posed a similar problem and were masked by giant consoles. Coupled Corinthian pilasters enclose an inner architecture of doors, windows, and niches, increasing in concentration and projection as they approach the center. On the lower story, for example, the outside pairs of pilasters support a continuous entablature; the next is enriched by an added half pilaster (related to a device Michelangelo had invented at Saint Peter's) and more strongly projected, breaking the entablature above; and at the center of the lower story the pilasters support an arched pediment enclosing a gabled one that projects beyond it and is supported by columns in the round. The progression in projection and vitality as the elements approach the center prepares the observer for the dramatic experience of the unified interior. Like the interior, the dynamic facade prepared the way for the more richly articulated and easily moving structures of the Baroque.

VASARI. Not so in Florence. The architecture of Giorgio

Vasari (1511–74), whose opinions on earlier masters have been so often quoted, is outspokenly Mannerist. His solution for the Uffizi (fig. 190), a collection of preexisting structures revamped between 1560 and 1580 to house the offices of the ducal government, bears no relationship to its counterpart in Michelangelo's designs for the Campidoglio. Still haunted by memories of the reading room at the Laurentian Library (see fig. 155), the seemingly endless porticoes are surmounted by a mezzanine, then by a second story, and finally by what was originally an open upper portico, now unfortunately glassed in. Conceivably, one could cut the building anywhere or extend it indefinitely without altering its effect; if, as Alberti says, beauty is that to which nothing can be added and from which nothing can be taken away without damage, then the beauty of Vasari's design lies in its very endlessness. When the structure does finally arrive at the Arno, it opens in a strangely slender arch, through which one looks out not to an open prospect but only across the narrow river to the buildings on the other side.

AMMANATI. A different kind of princely architecture is seen in the courtyard of the Pitti Palace (fig. 191), a fifteenth-century residence bought by Duke Cosimo I and enlarged from 1558–70 by the architect and sculptor Bartolommeo Ammanati (1511–92). The courtyard is spectacular; rather than Vasari's principle of endlessly repeated equal elements, Ammanati has adopted an all-over rustication of all the elements save only the entablatures, capitals, and bases—a kind of architectural overkill in which every drum is enlarged in the manner of the tires in a Michelin advertisement. In its own way the effect is quite as overpowering as that of the Uffizi. But while these two Mannerist architects were dominant in

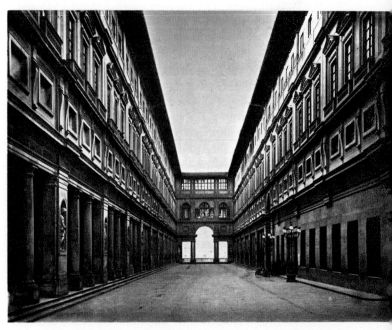

190. GIORGIO VASARI. Palazzo degli Uffizi. 1560–80. Florence

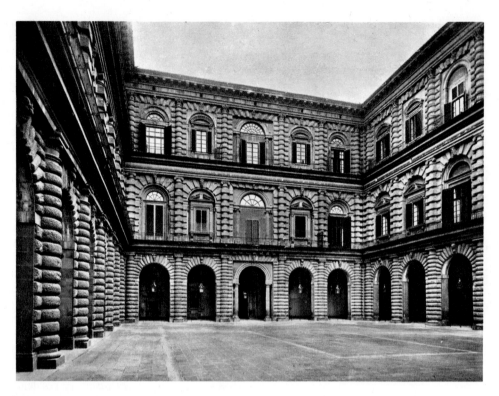

191. Bartolommeo Ammanati.
Courtyard, Palazzo Pitti.
1558-70. Florence

Florence, and their style was widely emulated throughout Tuscany and Northern Italy, their work was a blind alley. The Mannerist movement had come to the end of its course.

BRONZINO. Nor, in fact, did it have any clear issue in painting. Agnolo Tori, called Bronzino (1503–72), portrayed by his teacher Pontormo as the boy huddled on the steps in *Joseph in Egypt* (see fig. 157), developed his master's haunting style into formulas of exquisite and glacial refinement. His allegory painted about 1546 and formerly called *Venus, Cupid, Folly, and Time*, but more likely depicting the *Exposure of Luxury* (fig. 192), displays the ambivalence of the age in life and art. Bald, bearded Time at the upper right, assisted by Truth at the upper left, withdraws a curtain to display a scene of more than filial affection between Venus and the adolescent Cupid, pelted with roses by a laughing boy. At the lower left Venus' doves bill and coo, the old hag Envy tears her hair at center left, and at the right Fraud, a charming girl whose body ends in the legs of a lion and a scaly tail, extends a honeycomb with her left hand attached to her right arm; the message is characterized by masks, symbols of false dreams, as in Michelangelo's *Night* (see fig. 152). With magical brilliance Bronzino projects every surface, every fold, yet the substances of his nudes resemble marble more than flesh, and the hair seems composed of metal shavings. The Mannerist principle of interlaced figures seeking the frame rather than the center is brought to its highest pitch, as if to savor every lascivious complexity. Paradoxically, the very sixteenth century that repainted Michelangelo's heroic nudes (and at the

Council of Trent forbade all nudes in religious art) and condemned *Luxuria* (sensual indulgence) as the queen of vices could create and enjoy works such as this one, ordered by Cosimo de' Medici and presented by him to Francis I of France, both of them delighted by what their religion told them to condemn.

CELLINI. The engaging braggart Benvenuto Cellini (1500–71), whose *Autobiography* paints a vivid picture of sixteenth-century life, including the Sack of Rome in which the artist was trapped, was a skillful sculptor and metalworker. His *Perseus and Medusa*, 1545–54 (fig. 193), also commissioned by Duke Cosimo, shows a treatment of form that can be read as a sculptural counterpart to Bronzino's painting. Obviously influenced by the tradition of Michelangelo, the powerfully muscled figure and its elaborate pedestal are strongly ornamentalized. It is typical, perhaps, that the moment chosen—the decapitation of the dreaded Gorgon—is that when the blood gushing from her neck and severed head turns to precious coral, dripping in ornamental forms of great complexity.

GIOVANNI BOLOGNA. The most original sculptor working in Italy between Michelangelo and Bernini was a Netherlander, Jean Bologne (1529–1608), Italianized as Giovanni Bologna. Although the identity of the subject mattered little to him, he eventually decided on the *Rape of the Sabine Woman* as the title for his colossal marble group (fig. 194) set in 1583 in the Loggia dei Lanzi, near Cellini's *Perseus*. In contrast to all earlier statues, which concentrate on a principal view to which all others are subordinated, Bologna's composition sends us constantly

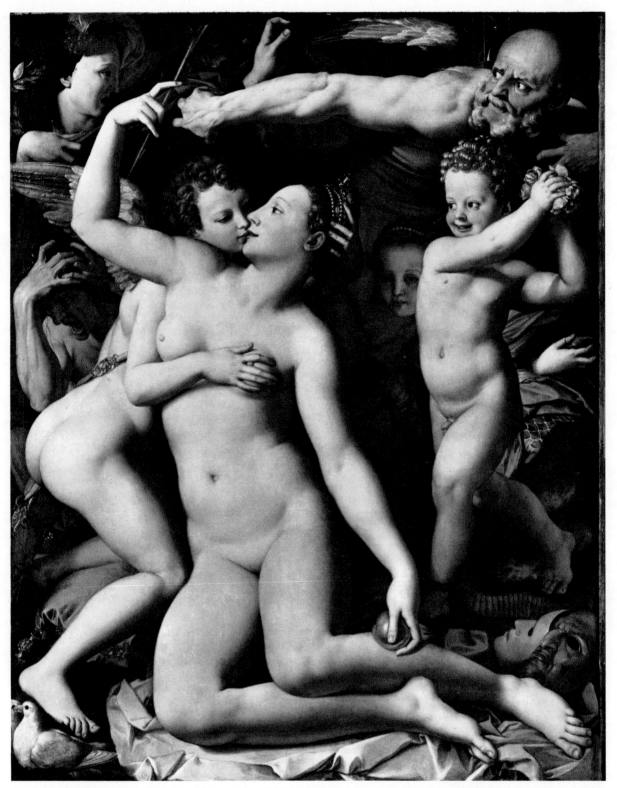

192. BRONZINO. *Exposure of Luxury.* c. 1546. Panel painting, 61 x 56¾". National Gallery, London

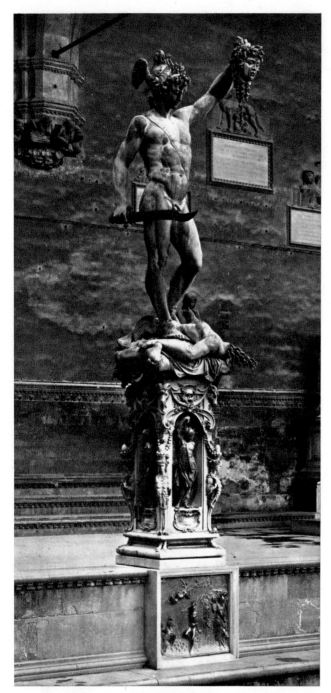

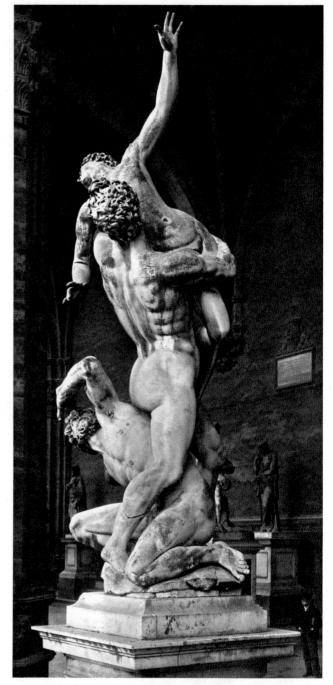

193. BENVENUTO CELLINI. *Perseus and Medusa.*
1545–54. Bronze, height 18′. Loggia dei Lanzi,
Piazza della Signoria, Florence

194. GIOVANNI BOLOGNA. *Rape of the Sabine
Woman.* 1583. Marble, height 13′6″. Loggia
dei Lanzi, Piazza della Signoria, Florence

around the group from one view to the next; as all the figures are engaged in the spiral movement, it is impossible to choose a principal view. The way arms and legs fly off into space was, of course, a violation of everything for which Michelangelo stood but also a dazzling display of

Bologna's skill in handling marble. As the forms and spaces of Vignola and della Porta at the Gesù lead us to the brink of Baroque architecture, so does the new diffuse sculptural composition of Giovanni Bologna point toward Bernini (see Part Five, Chapter 1).

7

High and Late Renaissance Outside Italy

GERMANY

In the artistic development of the fifteenth century, Germany followed at a certain distance the great innovations taking place in Italy and the Netherlands. But for reasons that cannot as yet be even partially explained, in the early sixteenth century German art moved to a commanding position, definitely surpassing that of the Netherlands in quality and inventiveness, competing with High Renaissance Italy, and at times influencing the greatest Italian masters. The sudden rise of the German School is no more surprising than its precipitate decline. All of the leading sixteenth-century German painters were contemporary with the Italian High Renaissance artists; by the second half of the century, no new artists appeared to replace them, and German art had passed its great moment.

Despite their mastery of the technique of oil painting, the Germans never understood the free Venetian interpretation of the medium or the Venetian range of coloring. Nor, try as they would, could they ever equal the Italians in their instinctive understanding of the beauty of the human body. The Classical tradition had to be imported, and was always ill at ease in a Northern environment. What the Germans did understand, and practiced with incomparable dexterity and expressive power, was line, which—as we have seen in our study of early medieval art—goes far back in the Germanic heritage, and which more immediately was exemplified in the tradition of Flamboyant Gothic architecture and in the art of engraving, at which Schongauer (see fig. 116) outshone his Italian contemporaries.

DÜRER. The founder of the German High Renaissance was Albrecht Dürer (1471–1528), who, on account of the breadth of his knowledge and the universality of his achievements, is often characterized as a German Leonardo da Vinci. Yet he was not a scientific investigator in the manner of Leonardo; his research into perspective and the theory of proportion was wholly dedicated to artistic purposes. Born in the city of Nuremberg, he was raised in a tradition of craftsmanship—both his father and his maternal grandfather were goldsmiths, and he was apprenticed to a wood engraver. He shared, however, Leonardo's belief in the inherent

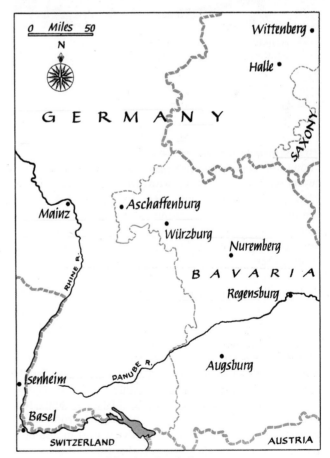

MAP 9. *South Germany*

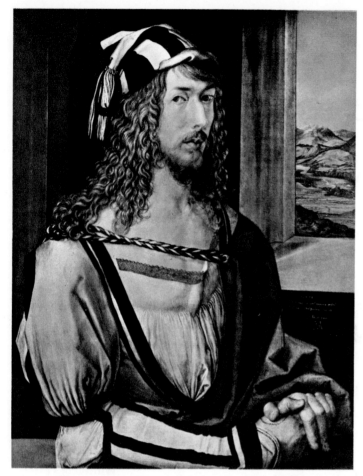

195. ALBRECHT DÜRER. *Self-Portrait.* 1498. Panel painting, 20½ x 16″. Museo del Prado, Madrid

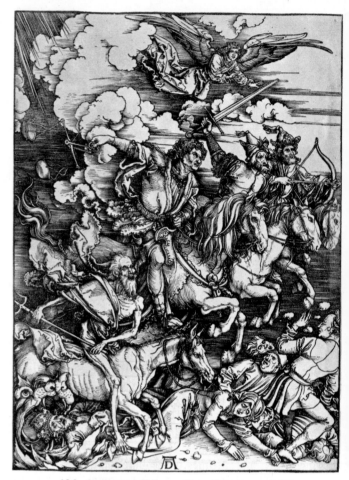

196. ALBRECHT DÜRER. *Four Horsemen of the Apocalypse,* from the *Apocalypse* series. c. 1497–98. Woodcut, 15½ x 11″. British Museum, London

nobility of art, which he endeavored to raise from its craftsman status in Germany to the almost princely level it had attained in High Renaissance Italy. He made two trips to Italy (1494–95 and 1505–7), visiting Mantua and Padua and staying for prolonged periods in Venice, but never reaching Florence, with whose intellectual activities his interests would seem to have had much in common. For a while, during his second Venetian sojourn, his style grew softer and his colors freer in emulation of the aged Bellini and the young Giorgione, but he never outgrew his German linear heritage and soon returned to it.

His brilliant *Self-Portrait* of 1498 (fig. 195) shows the artist at twenty-seven, three years after his return from his first Italian trip; it is one of the earliest known independent self-portraits, and one of the finest ever painted. The artist shows himself attired in the piebald costume fashionable in the late fifteenth century (soon replaced by the sober dress of the High Renaissance), his gloved hands folded in aristocratic ease, his handsome face gazing out with calm self-possession from what appears to be a tower room, with a view over mountains and valleys. Despite the obvious Italianism of the pose, it is surprising that Dürer had not caught the secret of

Italian form; we are everywhere conscious of lines and surfaces rather than of masses, even in the architecture. And what lines! Even Dürer's love for engraving is not enough to explain the intensity of the linear activity in the serpentine curls of the hair, or in the twisted cord of the mantle whose every nuance is accurately recorded. Bellini, who in his old age was the only Venetian painter who really admired Dürer, asked him to paint something, anything, as a favor to him, and wanted to see the special brush Dürer used to paint hair. It is a strange example of the fascination of a master who had freed himself from line for the style of one immersed in it.

But Dürer's greatest achievements were always in the realm of graphic art, which, in the manner of many ventures intended for the buyer of modest means, eventually made him rich. In the very year of this self-portrait he published his series of fifteen large woodcuts illustrating the *Apocalypse* (with accompanying texts in Latin and German), which brought the technique of the woodcut to an unforeseeable level of virtuosity and expressive power. Unlike copper engraving (see Chapter 2, page 113), in which the line is incised, woodcuts require the artist to draw his design in black on a block of wood, smoothed and painted white. All but the black lines are then cut

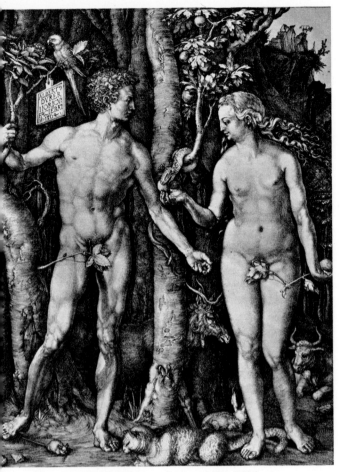

197. ALBRECHT DÜRER. *Adam and Eve*. 1504.
Engraving, 9⅞ x 7⅝". Museum of Fine Arts,
Boston

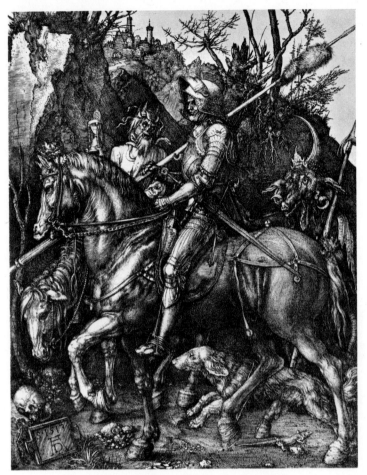

198. ALBRECHT DÜRER. *Knight, Death, and the Devil*. 1513. Engraving, c. 9¾ x 7½". Museum of Fine Arts, Boston

away, leaving the lines standing in relief. A slip of the knife or a gouge cannot be repaired, so the technique requires extreme accuracy. Since in Dürer's time the blocks were printed by the same method as pages of type, woodcuts could be reproduced at considerable speed, even as illustrations for printed books incorporated in a page of text. The accepted procedure utilized the relief lines as contours only; Dürer's refinement lay in his use of lines for shading, making them resemble the parallel hatching of copper engravings. Such a page as the *Four Horsemen of the Apocalypse* (fig. 196), one of the greatest prints ever made, shows the subtlety of shading Dürer was able to achieve in the changing tones of sky and cloud, and the different methods of rendering shadow on flesh, hair, and drapery. The work derives its power from the energy of Dürer's design; the four horsemen—war, conquest, famine, and death (Rev. 6: 2–8)—ride in a huge diagonal over helpless humanity, drawn with a breadth of vision and a linear intensity that recall Romanesque art, yet fortified with the Renaissance knowledge of anatomy and drawing. Ironically, though Dürer seldom achieved in painting the monumentality of Italian art, prints such as this could conceivably stand enlargement to mural proportions.

In the subtler medium of copper engraving, Dürer pushed the limits of the style even beyond those fixed by Schongauer. Dürer's *Adam and Eve* of 1504 (fig. 197) shows his application of straight and curved hatching, cross-hatching, and stippling to Italian ideals of sculptural form and physical beauty, as well as to the menacing shadows of the forest. His interest in the religious subject seems secondary to his fascination with physical perfection; the nude Classical figures were not drawn from life, but constructed after many preliminary proportion studies. They nonetheless exist in a world of dangers, by no means limited to the serpent who brings Eve the fig. The sleepy cat in the foreground has not forgotten the mouse; the distant chamois on a crag contemplates the gulf before him. Adam still holds to a bough of the mountain ash, probably signifying the Tree of Life, on which a wise parrot sits and to which Dürer has tied a tablet seen in perspective, bearing his Latinized signature.

The three so-called "master prints" of the years 1513 and 1514 show, as Dürer intended they should, that he could achieve with copper results comparable to what the Netherlanders could do with oil or the Italians with fresco or with bronze. The *Knight, Death, and the Devil,*

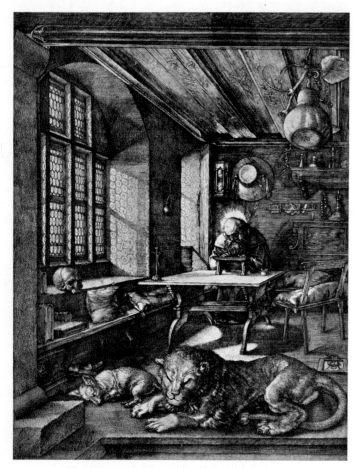

199. ALBRECHT DÜRER. *Saint Jerome.* 1514.
Engraving, 9¾ x 7⅜". The Metropolitan
Museum of Art, New York

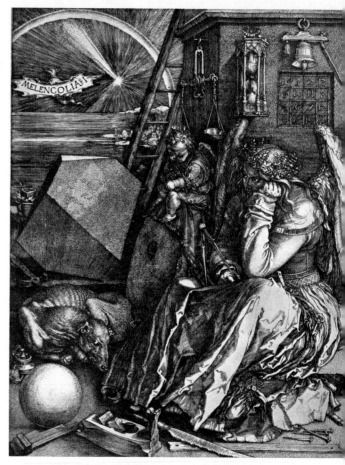

200. ALBRECHT DÜRER. *Melencolia I.* 1514.
Engraving, 9½ x 7⅞". The Metropolitan
Museum of Art, New York. Harris Brisbane
Dick Fund, 1943

of 1513 (fig. 198), recalls Verrocchio's *Colleoni* (see fig. 75), which was under completion when Dürer first arrived in Venice. Dürer's knight sits on a charger whose muscles ripple with all the anatomical knowledge of the Italians, but Dürer has reinterpreted the image in the light of the Christian warrior of Saint Paul's Epistle to the Ephesians, 6: 11: "Put on the whole armour of God, that ye may be able to stand against the wiles of the devil." Grimly, the knight rides through the Valley of the Shadow attended by his faithful dog, impervious alike to Death, who shakes his hourglass, and to the monstrous Devil, who follows.

In contrast to the *Knight, Death, and the Devil,* which symbolizes the life of the Christian militant, *Saint Jerome,* of 1514 (fig. 199), a combined tribute to Italian perspective and Netherlandish light, depicts the existence of the Christian scholar. The saint is shown in his study, deep in thought and in writing, with the instruments of knowledge, piety, and study arranged on the window ledge and table and hanging on the wall—a skull, books, a crucifix, a cardinal's hat, an hourglass, a rosary, scissors, letters, and a whisk broom—in an atmosphere so calm that both his tame lion and his dog are asleep. Reminiscent of the *Arnolfini Wedding* (see fig. 101) is the

light from the bottle glass window on the embrasure, and the shoes put aside, for this too is holy ground.

The *Melencolia I,* also of 1514 (fig. 200), deals instead with the inner problems of the artist. The seated winged genius, invested with all the grandeur of Michelangelo's sibyls although she is not drawn from any, symbolizes a special kind of Melancholy that afflicts creators; with burning eyes in a shadowed face, she sits among the useless tools of architecture, draftsmanship, and knowledge—plane and saw (used for another purpose in the Mérode Altarpiece; see fig. 93), a ruler, a hammer, compasses, a rhomboid, a book, a crucible, a ladder to nowhere, a tablet on which all the numbers add up to thirty-four whether one reads them vertically, horizontally, or diagonally, a chipped millstone, a silent bell, an empty purse, a sleeping dog, a child writing aimlessly, and the keys to nothing—all signifying the brooding sadness that overcomes the artist in the absence of inspiration. Her label is borne aloft by a bat below a comet and a lunar rainbow. It is by no means accidental that in all three of these autobiographical works Dürer—in middle life—has shown an hourglass half run out.

On occasion Dürer could lift painting to the level of his beloved engraving. A brilliant example is the *Adoration of the Trinity* (colorplate 31), completed in 1511 for a chapel dedicated to the Trinity and All Saints in a Nuremberg home for twelve aged and poor citizens (doubtless in commemoration of the Twelve Apostles). The lovely landscape at the bottom of the picture encloses a harbor, probably symbolic. Most of the picture is occupied by a heavenly vision: God the Father, enthroned upon a rainbow and robed and crowned as an emperor, upholds the crucified Christ against his blue tunic, while the green lining of his gold robe is displayed by angels; above, the Holy Spirit appears as a dove, and on either side angels with softly colored wings hold the symbols of the Passion. To the left kneeling and standing female martyrs, many recognizable through their symbols, are grouped behind the Virgin; to the right, Old Testament prophets flank John the Baptist. The lowest rank of floating figures includes, apparently, portraits of many still alive at the time Dürer painted the picture—popes, a cardinal, emperors, kings, and common folk; at the extreme left, bearded with long blond locks streaming over his shoulders, kneels Matthaeus Landauer, one of the two patrons of the chapel. On the ground below Dürer himself exhibits his usual tablet with its Latin inscription. It has been claimed that the picture is based on Saint Augustine's conception of the City of God, existing throughout all time, partly on earth and partly in Heaven. (The absence of the Twelve Apostles may be accounted for by their presence elsewhere in the decorations of the chapel.) In its spectacle of blazing reds, yellows, blues, and greens, the kind of brilliant coloring Titian would have been at pains to mute by glazes, the *Adoration of the Trinity* can stand as one of the most beautiful religious visions of the Renaissance.

Dürer's last major work is the diptych now known as the *Four Apostles* (fig. 201), a misnomer since it represents not only the Apostles John and Peter, to the left, but also Mark, who was not an Apostle, and Paul, who only became one after Christ's death and his own conver-

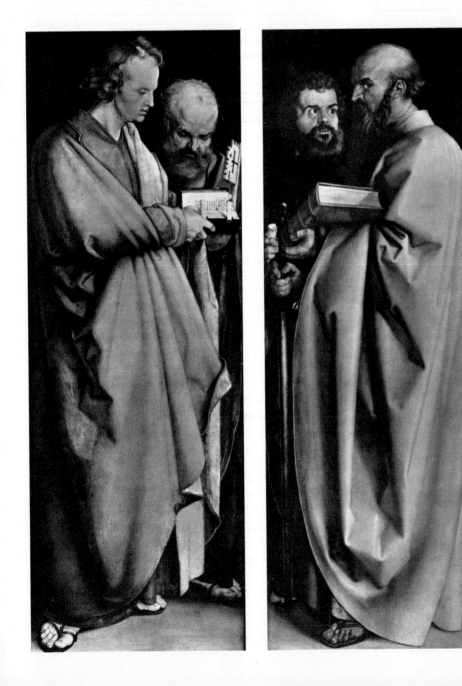

201. ALBRECHT DÜRER. *Four Apostles* (diptych). c. 1526. Panel painting, each wing 84½ x 30''. Alte Pinakothek, Munich

sion. These paintings were originally intended as wings for an altarpiece, whose central panel, a Madonna and Child with saints, was never painted because the rising tide of Protestantism, to which Dürer himself adhered, rendered such a picture impossible in Nuremberg in 1526, the year after the city "gave leave to the pope." Dürer presented his panels to the city, supplying them with inscriptions from Luther's translation of the New Testament that warn all who read them not to mistake human error for the will of God. Dürer had taken his position along with Luther, against papal supremacy on the one hand and on the other against Protestant extremists who advocated radical experiments ranging from polygamy to a kind of communism and who instigated the Peasants' War (1524–25). The professional calligrapher who wrote the inscriptions recalled later that Dürer intended his "Four Apostles" to typify the four bodily liquids or humors—sanguine, phlegmatic, choleric, and melancholic—believed to govern the four major psychological human types. When all is said and done on this complex subject, what remains are four forthright figures of extraordinary grandeur, summing up better than anything else Dürer achieved all he had learned from the tradition of Giotto, Masaccio, Michelangelo, and Raphael.

GRÜNEWALD. About Dürer's greatest German contemporary, we know far less—neither the date of his birth (he died in 1528, the same year as Dürer) nor, until the present century, his real name. He was unaccountably listed as Matthias Grünewald by the German writer Joachim von Sandrart in the seventeenth century, and the misnomer stands through long usage, like so many others. His actual surnames were Gothardt and Neithardt. He was by no means unknown in his own time; the leading humanist Melanchthon, three years after the artist's death, ranked him second only to Dürer among German masters. He may have been born in Würzburg, and worked for a while in Aschaffenburg. He was also an architect and hydraulic engineer, and remained for many years in the service of the prince-bishop of Mainz, one of seven electors of the Holy Roman Empire. He never went to Italy. Unlike the aristocratic Dürer, Grünewald was implicated in the Peasants' War, and had to flee to Halle in Saxony, where he died. Since few of the early documents, listing only a certain Master Mathis, can be securely connected with him, guesses concerning his birthdate range from 1455–83. But since the unquestioned dated pictures are all within the sixteenth century, the latter date is probably acceptable.

Grünewald's greatest work is the Isenheim Altarpiece, (colorplate 32), probably begun in 1512 and finished in 1515 for the church of the Hospital of Saint Anthony in the Alsatian hamlet of Isenheim near Colmar, where Schongauer had lived and worked. It is a creation of such shocking intensity that many are repelled by it, yet the central Crucifixion (fig. 202) is one of the most impressive and profound images of the culminating tragedy

in the life of Christ. The altarpiece was arranged originally in three layers, each containing pictures of sculptures (by another master) to be displayed at different seasons of the Christian year. The Crucifixion is on the outermost wings, visible when the altarpiece is closed. Few monumental representations of the subject make any real attempt to show the horror of the event, which is strange because devotional literature, particularly during the fifteenth and sixteenth centuries, was by no means so reticent.

Grünewald has shown the Cross as two roughhewn logs, still green, the crossbar drawn down by its dreadful weight. Christ has just expired in agony. Rigor mortis has set in; his fingers are frozen into a clutching position. The crown of thorns is a fearsome bunch of brambles, beneath which the face, contorted with pain, is greenish gray in death (fig. 203). The weight of the tormented body has drawn Christ's arms almost from their sockets. Arms, body, and legs are scarred and torn by the scourges and studded with thorns, as if Christ had been beaten by thorn switches. His feet are crushed together by a giant spike. Viscous, bright red blood drips from his wounds. Below the Cross on the right stands John the Baptist, a blood-red cloak thrown over his camel skin, and above his pointing arm his words (John 3: 30) appear: "He must increase, but I must decrease."

The Lamb of God stands below, a chalice to his wounded breast. On the left Mary Magdalene, in a transport of grief, has thrown herself at the foot of the Cross, and John the Evangelist, also in blood red, holds the swooning, death-pale Virgin. This is one of the earliest nocturnal Crucifixions; over distant hills the sky shows greenish black. While the horror of the scene can be traced to an expressionist current in German popular art and literature, indeed as far back as the violent expressionism of the Ebbo Gospels, the emphasis on the most physically repulsive details is traceable to the fact that this masterpiece was intended for a hospital church, where patients were brought before the altarpiece in order to realize that Christ understood their suffering because he had suffered as they did. Only thus can we explain that Christ's loincloth is made of the old torn linen used for bandages and that Mary Magdalene's jar of ointment appears in the painting, although it relates to a much earlier scene in Christ's life. The genius of Grünewald lies in his ability to raise mere horror to the level of high tragedy and so to unify deformed and broken shapes that the final composition is as beautiful as the greatest Italian work of the High Renaissance. The diagonals of the arms, for example, seem to erupt from the volcanic body as if in a gesture of self-immolation, linking the Cross to the inner angles of the T-shaped segments of the frame. These diagonals bind together all the other forces of the composition, sustaining by their positive strength the diagonals of the collapsing group at the left, of the gesture of John the Baptist, and of the distant hills. The final image is one of absolute unity and monumental grandeur.

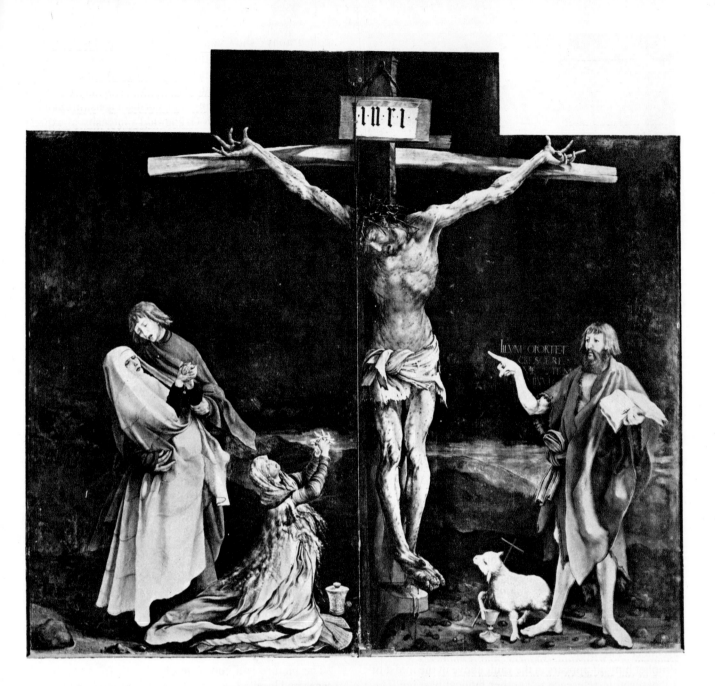

202. MATTHIAS GRÜNEWALD.
Crucifixion, from the
Isenheim Altarpiece (closed).
c. 1512–15. Panel (with
frame), 9′9½″ x 10′9″.
Musée Unterlinden,
Colmar, France

203. MATTHIAS GRÜNEWALD.
Christ (detail of the
Crucifixion), from the
Isenheim Altarpiece

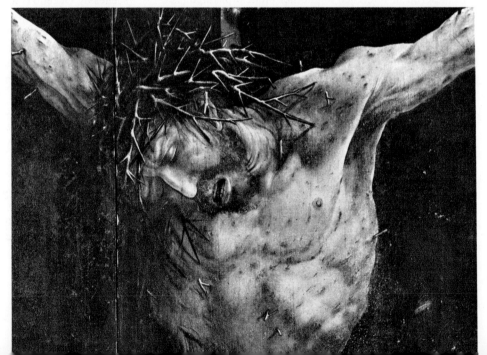

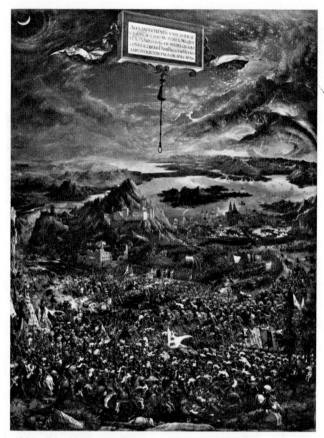

204. ALBRECHT ALTDORFER. *Battle of Alexander and Darius on the Issus.* 1529. Oil on panel, c. 63¼ x 48″. Alte Pinakothek, Munich

iconography) show again that Christ in his humanity took upon himself *all* the indignities of men. Yet in the heavens, far above a mass of glittering Alpine summits, the immaterial, ultimate Deity shines on his luminous throne, sending down tiny ministering angels through the blue clouds. Along with Grünewald's intensity of expression went a freedom of brushwork and color inaccessible to the tense and intellectual Dürer.

The cycle culminates in what is doubtless the most astonishing Resurrection in Christian art, shown in the right panel. A storm wind seems to have burst from Christ's tomb, blowing off the lid and bowling over the guards, and a flamelike apparition emerges, iridescent in blue, white, red, and gold—his graveclothes transfigured, as the patient's bandages will be, against the blue-green night dotted with stars. In the midst of an aurora borealis of red and gold rimmed with green soars the snow-white Christ, his body utterly pure, his hair and beard turned to gold, his wounds changed to rubies, surely in reference to the words of Saint Paul (Phil. 3: 21): "Who shall change our vile body, that it may be fashioned like unto his glorious body." The transformation is complete; agony and ugliness have been burned away in a vision of transcendent light.

ALTDORFER. A painter of great imaginative powers, closer to Grünewald than to Dürer, was Albrecht Altdorfer, probably born about 1480 in Regensburg, a Bavarian city on the Danube River, where he lived and worked until his death in 1538. His special gift was for landscape; his most celebrated painting is the *Battle of Alexander and Darius on the Issus*, of 1529 (fig. 204), in which the defeat of Darius III at the hands of Alexander the Great in 333 B.C. is seen in the guise of a contemporaneous "modern" battle, such as the Battle of Ravenna in 1512 or that of Pavia in 1525, the first mass conflicts since late antiquity. In a picture only a little more than five feet high Altdorfer has painted so many soldiers that it would be a hopeless task to count them—doubtless there are thousands.

The picture is a complete about-face from the battle scenes by Uccello (see fig. 61) and Leonardo (see fig. 129) in which a small group of warriors pitted against each other forms the nucleus of the battle and symbolizes the whole. Altdorfer, by means of a lofty point of view as if he were in flight, has spread out before us entire armies, tides of soldiers glittering in steel armor—bristling with spears and flags—yet painted down to the last tent and the last helmet. The eye roams freely over a landscape surpassing in extent even those of Leonardo. We look over a city, castles, Alpine lakes, islands, a river delta, range beyond range—with always another row of peaks when we think we have seen the last—and finally to the sun sinking in boiling clouds, which appear themselves to be in combat, and to the moon rising on the left. The plaque with its lengthy Latin inscription, streaming drapery, in perspective like Dürer's tablets, floats as if by miracle. The accuracy of Altdorfer's panoramic vision,

Once the doors are open (the joint runs next to Christ's right flank), the tones of greenish black and blood red are transformed to flame red, gold, and blue (see colorplate 32). The left panel is the *Annunciation*, with the angel appearing to Mary in a chapel whose Gothic vaults and tracery are drawn and painted with such understanding that it is not hard to believe Master Mathis was a trained architect. The Bible is open at Isaiah's prophecy and the Prophet himself appears in the vault above in the midst of a vinescroll in reference to another biblical passage (Isa. 11: 1): "And there shall come forth a rod out of the stem of Jesse, and a Branch shall grow out of his roots." Mary turns in terror, while the angel in his flame-colored cloak points to her with the same gesture used by John the Baptist toward the crucified Christ. Above Mary floats the dove of the Holy Spirit in a thin film of mist.

The central panel shows Mary caring for the Christ Child in the manner of a nurse for a patient before a richly carved and painted portico, symbolizing the Temple, in and before which several angels play on Renaissance viols and a viola da gamba as others sing, and a crowned saint (Catherine?) kneels in an aureole of flame. Mary holds her Child—in torn linen rags—whom she has taken from a cradle. A wooden tub covered by a towel, and a perfectly recognizable chamber pot (surely the only appearance of this humble object in Christian

which could only have been obtained from a mountain-top, can be verified by any air traveler who has flown over the Alps or, let us say, the Coast Ranges of California. The sparkling colors of the garments, caparisons, and flags give way before the green forests, the blue distance, and the blaze of orange and yellow in the stormy sunset.

CRANACH. A charming interlude in the study of the great German painters is offered by Lucas Cranach the Elder (1472–1553), a Protestant painter and friend of Luther, attached to the court of the elector of Saxony at Wittenberg. In collaboration with his sons and pupils, Cranach in a long and productive career turned out an astonishing number of agreeable paintings. Despite his high position and his acquaintance with the art of Altdorfer and Dürer, he remained a provincial; although he accepted the frank sensuality of much of Italian Renaissance art, he had no interest in such arcane matters as Classical literary texts or theories of harmonious proportion. His *Apollo and Diana* (fig. 205)—undatable like many of his pictures—should be compared with Dürer's elaborately constructed *Adam and Eve* (see fig. 197). Apollo is just a contemporary Saxon, beard and all but minus his clothes, while a slinky Diana, cuddling her right foot above her left knee, perches on a patient stag. The specialty of Cranach and his shop was the contrast of flesh, at once soft and enameled, with shaggy, wild landscape, and in this they had no peer.

HOLBEIN. The last great German painter of the High Renaissance was Hans Holbein the Younger (1497/98–1543); he was also one of the greatest portraitists who ever lived. He came from a family of Augsburg painters (his father, his uncle, and his brother), but excelled them all. His wide travels included journeys in both France and in North Italy, where he was deeply influenced by the works of Mantegna and Leonardo. Nonetheless, his artistic activity was almost entirely limited to the widely separated cities of Basel and London, the last mostly after 1532—Basel had become less and less profitable for a painter—until his untimely death. From 1536 onward Holbein was the favorite painter of Henry VIII, who fitted up for "Master Hans" a studio in Saint James' Palace. Although Holbein produced book illustrations by the hundreds, designs for stained glass, exterior frescoes (now lost) for houses in Basel, and a number of altarpieces, he is chiefly known for his portraits. At first he had difficulty reconciling a native interest in expressionistic wildness, in the tradition of Grünewald, with his careful study of Italian art, but by the mid-1520s the synthesis had been achieved, resulting in a style of cool reserve, total control of surface and design, and a neo-Eyckian concentration on the rendering of the most minute objects. The new style was stated in terms of enameled color and a linear accuracy in which he has

never been equaled. It can be counted as perhaps Holbein's greatest achievement that he transformed the Germanic linear tradition, still untamed in Dürer, into his major instrument for the conquest of visual and psychological reality.

The *Madonna of Burgomaster Meyer* (colorplate 33), painted in 1526, is an early triumph of Holbein's mature style. As originally set up on the altar of the chapel of the burgomaster's castle, Gundeldingen, near Basel, the painting lacked the most distant female figure in profile, a portrait of the donor's first wife, who had died in 1511, represented with her jaws bound in death. Neither this inconvenient insertion nor the still later addition of a third kneeling woman could disturb Holbein's sense of design; he was able to work both easily into the composition. The gracious Madonna and Child, the Italianate niche, and the charming portraits of Meyer's adolescent son and nude baby boy are more than faintly Leonardesque, but in the delineation of contour, so sensitive that it picks up the slightest nuance of form, Holbein displays the phenomenal accuracy of his vision. The flow of the Virgin's fingers, the rendering of the foreshortened left arm of the Child, and the searching definition of the burgomaster's features are the achievements of this linear analysis. Holbein went out of his way to exhibit his

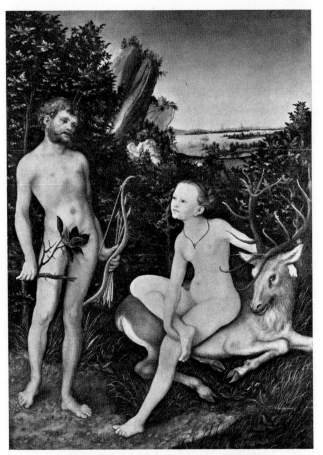

205. LUCAS CRANACH (the Elder). *Apollo and Diana*. Date unknown. Oil on panel, 18½ x 13¾". Gemäldegalerie, Staatliche Museen, Berlin

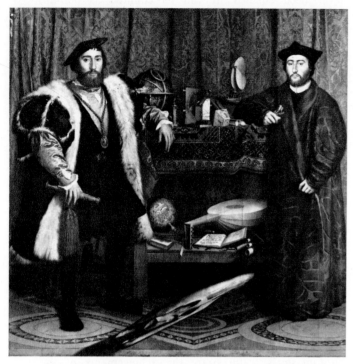

206. HANS HOLBEIN. *French Ambassadors.* 1533. Panel painting, 81⅛ x 82¼". National Gallery, London

we know the unpredictable monarch and his contemporaries. His Germanic feeling for linear pattern has adorned the ceremonial portrait of the king (fig. 207), dating from 1539–40, with an endless interlace of damask, embroidery, and goldsmith work, but this is only a frame for the royal face, drawn in all its puffy obesity, yet endowed with demonic intensity of will. We can only mourn the fact that "Master Hans" did not survive to leave us portraits of Queen Elizabeth I and her brilliant court.

FRANCE

In sixteenth-century France there were no artists of the stature of Fouquet or Quarton; nonetheless, the total picture of artistic activity at the courts of Francis I (reigned 1515–47) and Henry II (reigned 1547–59) offers a fascinating spectacle of artificial elegance. Francis, who greatly admired the achievements of the Italian Renaissance, tried to coax one Italian master after another to his court; as we have seen, Leonardo spent the last two years of his life in France, and at one time Michelangelo seriously considered accepting the king's

virtuosity in the rendering of the Oriental rug, rumpled so that every variation of its pattern had to be separately projected in perspective. By 1531, alas, the picture had become a funerary monument for both the burgomaster and his sons were dead.

Another tour de force is the splendid *French Ambassadors*, painted in London in 1533 (fig. 206), representing the emissaries Jean de Dinteville and Georges de Selve full-length and lifesize, flanking a stand on which, along with the indispensable Oriental rug, are exhibited geographical, astronomical, and mathematical instruments, an open book of music, and a lute with one of its strings broken, all seen in flawless perspective. Holbein's reserve is by no means passionless; he distills the quintessence of his subjects' characters all the more effectively in that no slightest change of expression is allowed to disturb the cool faces. The green damask curtain, the white fur, and the inlaid marble floor are all rendered with Holbein's characteristic steely control. The startling object in the foreground is a systematically distorted death's head, with which Holbein has toyed in fascination with the fact that his name means *skull*.

In England Holbein painted an extensive series of portraits of Henry VIII, four of his wives, scores of his courtiers, and many German merchants of the Steel Yard, a German enclave in London; we also know of a lifesize group portrait of the king surrounded by courtiers, now lost. In their quiet strength Holbein's English portraits are so compelling as to enhance our feeling that

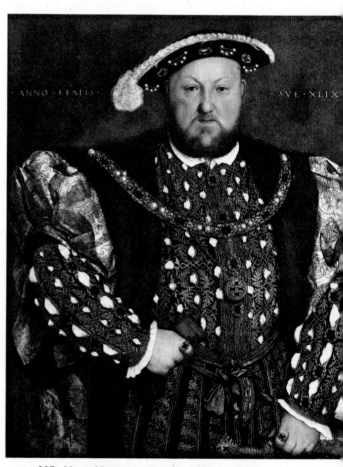

207. HANS HOLBEIN. *Portrait of Henry VIII.* 1539–40. Panel painting. 34¾ x 29½". Galleria Nazionale d'Arte Antica, Rome

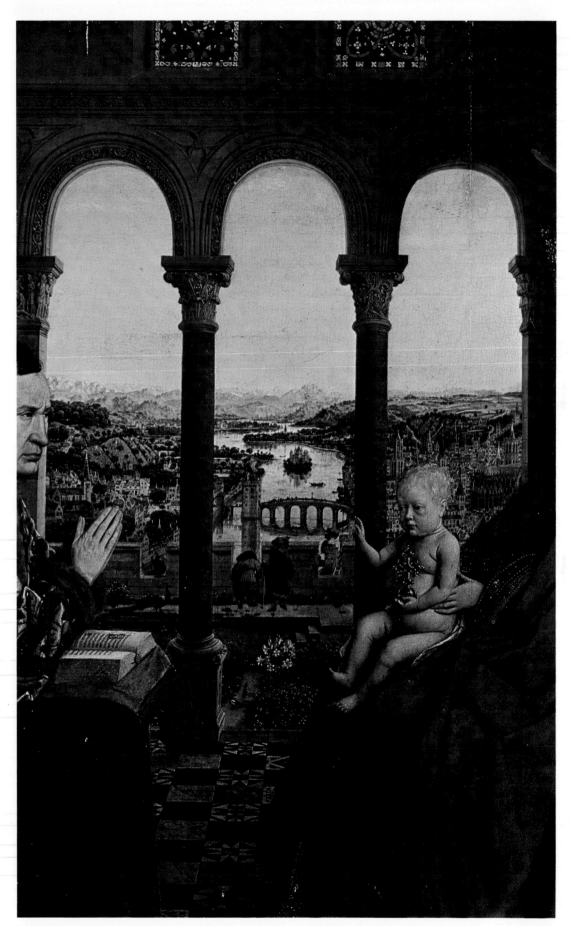

COLORPLATE 17.   Renaissance. JAN VAN EYCK. *Madonna of Chancellor Rolin* (detail). c. 1433.
Panel painting, 26 x 24⅜″. The Louvre, Paris

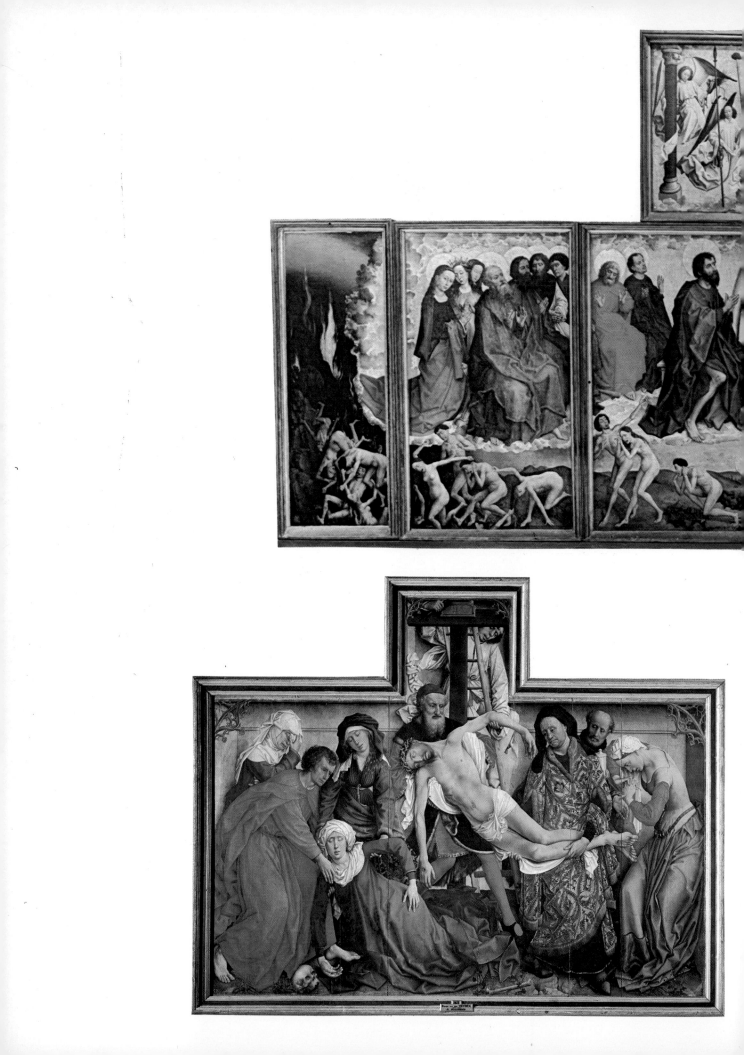

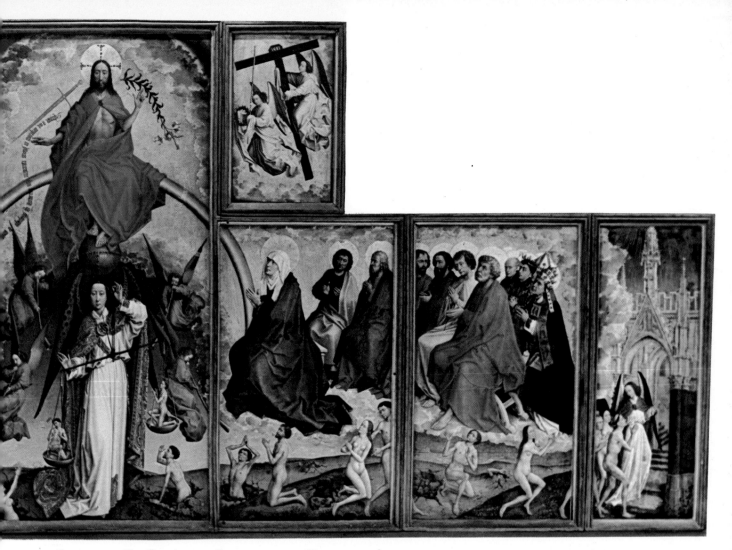

COLORPLATE 19.   Renaissance. ROGIER VAN DER WEYDEN. *Last Judgment Altarpiece* (open polyptych). c. 1444–48.
Panel painting, 7′4⅝″ x 17′11″. Musée de l'Hôtel-Dieu, Beaune, France

COLORPLATE 18.
Renaissance. ROGIER VAN DER
WEYDEN. *Descent from the Cross.*
c. 1435. Panel painting, 7′2⅝″ x 8′7⅛″.
Museo del Prado, Madrid

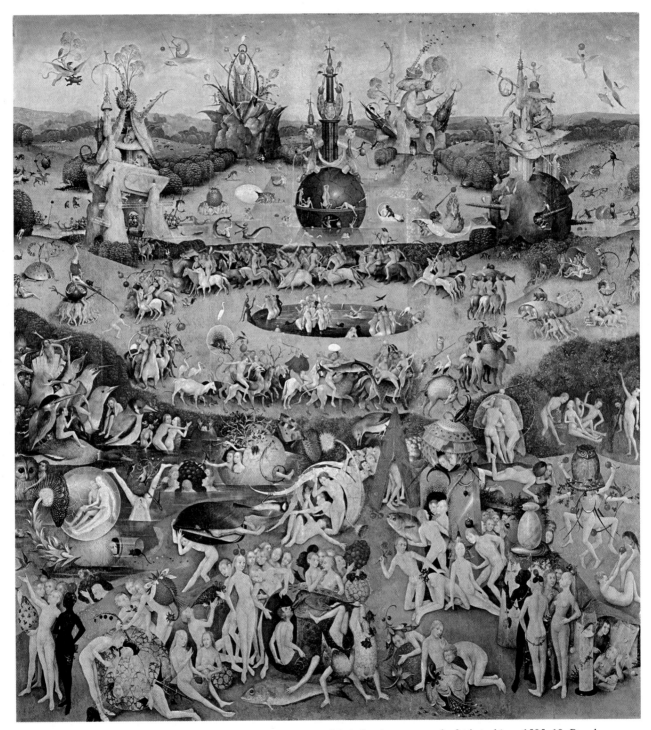

COLORPLATE 20.   Renaissance. HIERONYMUS BOSCH. *Garden of Delights* (center panel of triptych). c. 1505–10. Panel painting, 86⅝ x 76¾″. Museo del Prado, Madrid

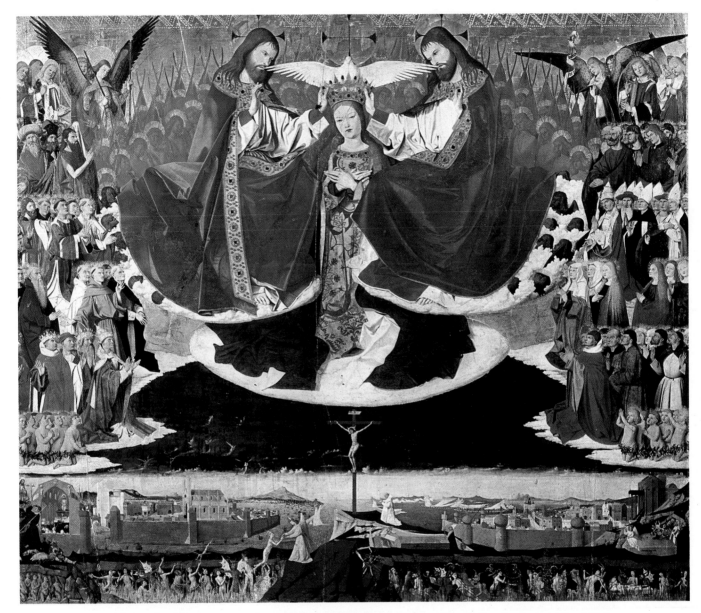

COLORPLATE 21.   Renaissance. ENGUERRAND QUARTON. *Coronation of the Virgin.* 1453–54. Panel painting, 72 x 86⅝″.
Musée de l'Hospice, Villeneuve-lès-Avignon, France

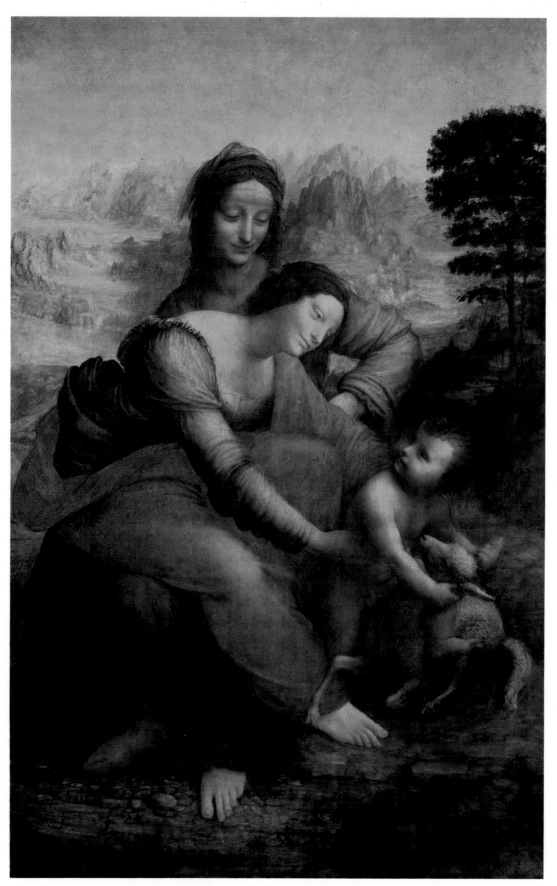

COLORPLATE 22.   Renaissance. LEONARDO DA VINCI. *Madonna and Saint Anne*. c. 1501–13(?).
Panel painting, 66¼ x 51¼". The Louvre, Paris

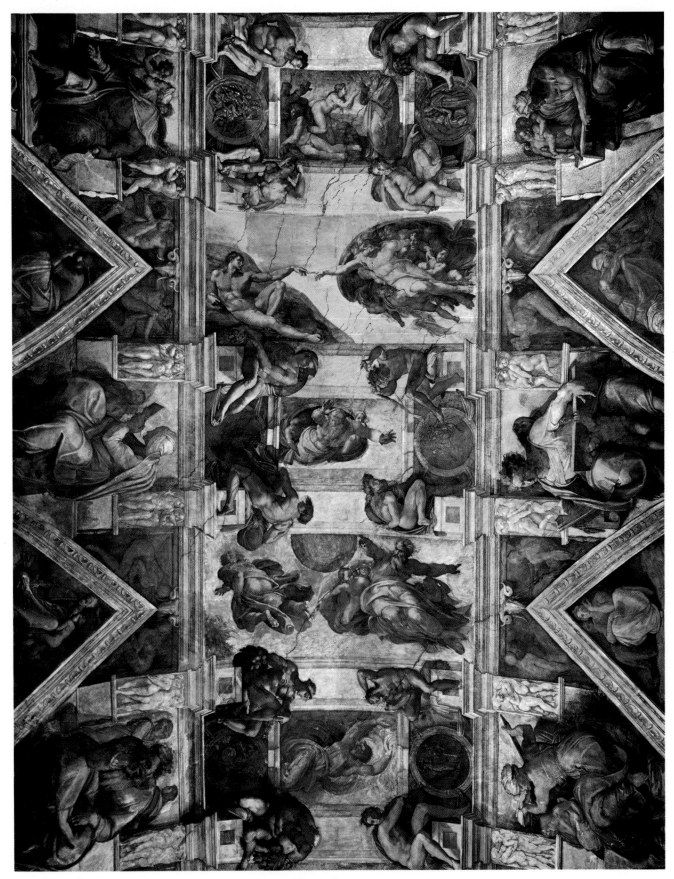

COLORPLATE 23.   Renaissance. MICHELANGELO. *Sistine Ceiling* (west section). Fresco. 1511. Sistine Chapel, Vatican, Rome

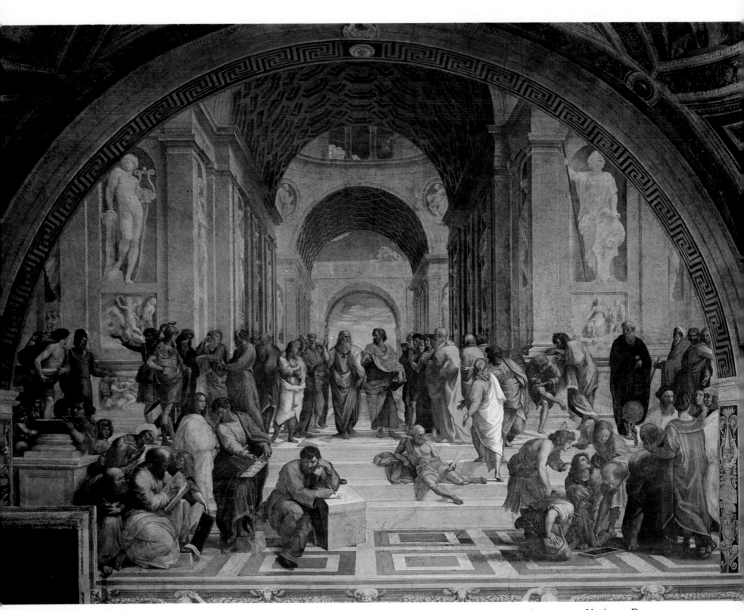

COLORPLATE 24.　　Renaissance. RAPHAEL. *School of Athens.* Fresco. 1510–11. Stanza della Segnatura, Vatican, Rome

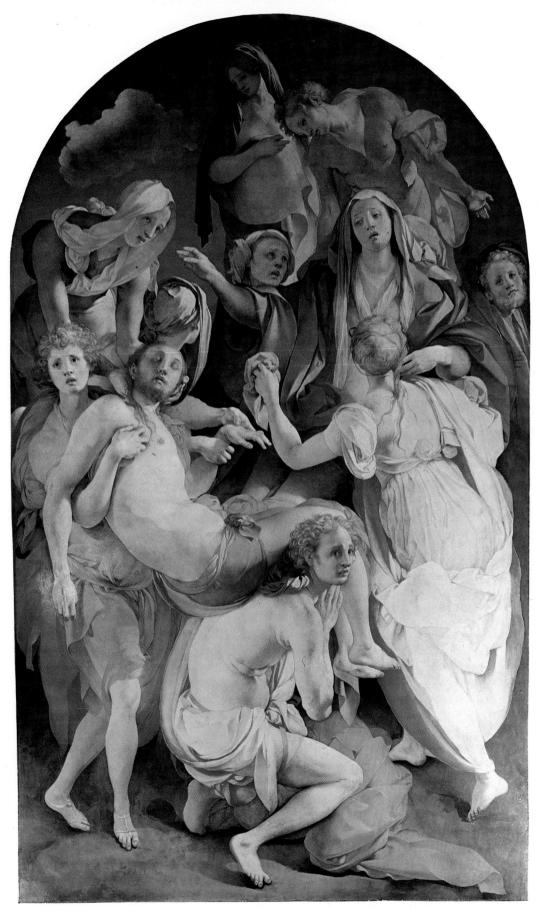

COLORPLATE 25.   Renaissance. PONTORMO. *Entombment.* c. 1525–28. Panel painting, 10'3" x 6'4".
Capponi Chapel, Sta. Felicità, Florence

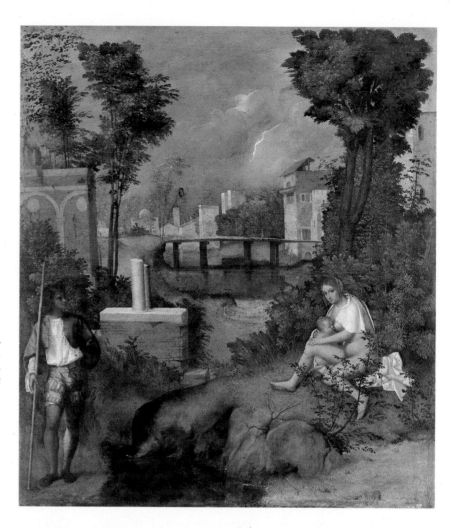

COLORPLATE 26.
Renaissance. GIORGIONE. *The Tempest.*
c. 1505–10. Oil on canvas, 30¼ x 28¾".
Galleria dell'Accademia, Venice

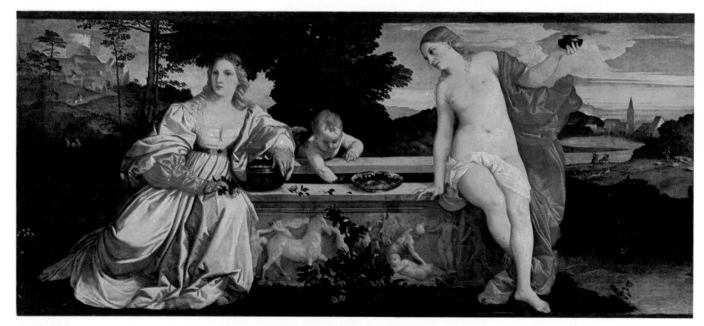

COLORPLATE 27.   Renaissance. TITIAN. *Sacred and Profane Love.* c. 1515. Oil on canvas, 3'11" x 9'2". Galleria
Borghese, Rome

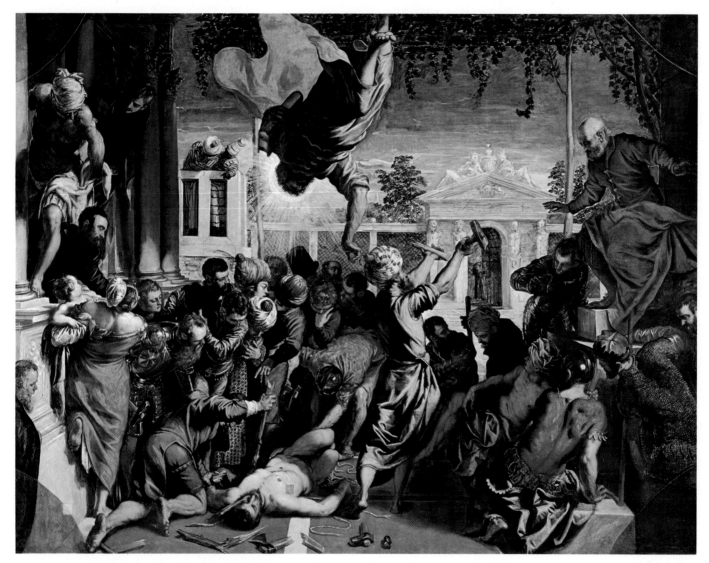

COLORPLATE 28.   Renaissance. TINTORETTO. *Saint Mark Freeing a Christian Slave.* 1548. Oil on canvas, 13′8″ x
11′7″. Galleria dell'Accademia, Venice

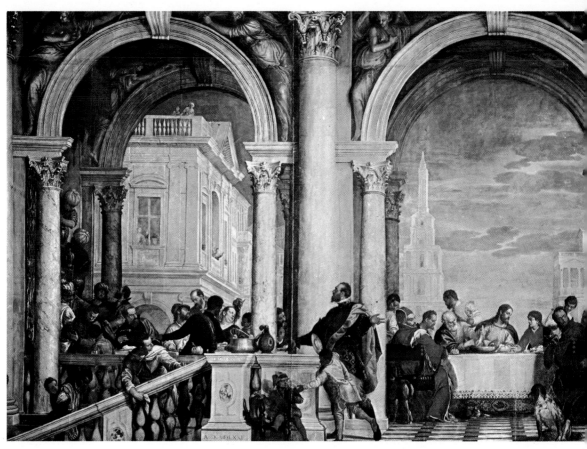

COLORPLATE 29.
Renaissance. PAOLO VERONESE. *Feast in the House of Levi.* 1573. Oil on canvas, 18′3″ x 42′. Galleria dell'Accademia, Venice

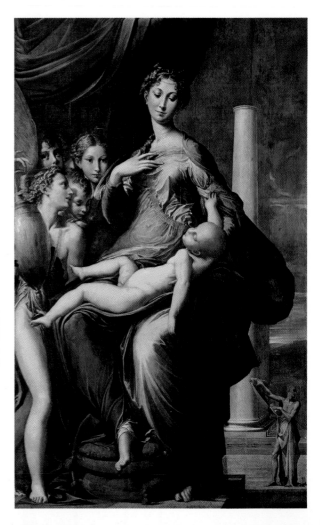

COLORPLATE 30.
Renaissance. PARMIGIANINO. *Madonna with the Long Neck.* 1534–40. Panel painting, 85 x 52″. Galleria degli Uffizi, Florence

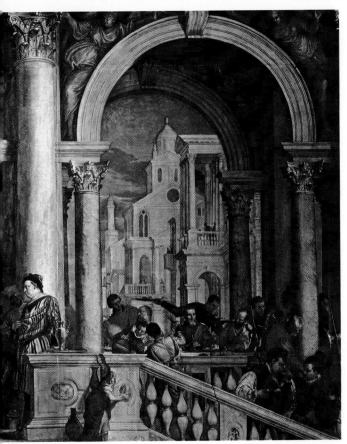

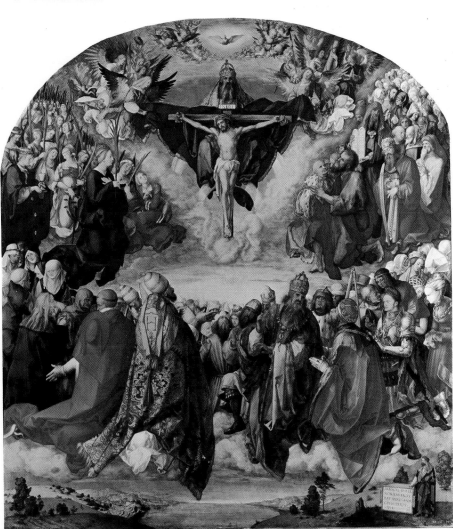

Colorplate 31.
Renaissance. Albrecht Dürer.
Adoration of the Trinity. 1508–11. Oil
on panel, 53⅛ x 48⅝".
Kunsthistorisches Museum, Vienna

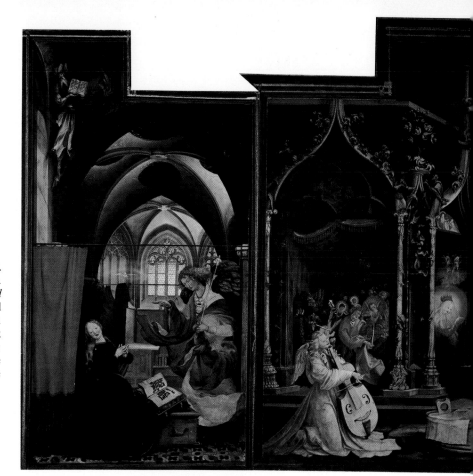

COLORPLATE 32.
Renaissance. MATTHIAS GRÜNEWALD.
*The Annunciation; Virgin and Child
with Angels; The Resurrection,* second
view of the *Isenheim Altarpiece.*
c. 1512–15. Oil on panel, left wing 8′10″ x
4′8″; central panel 8′10″ x 11′2½″;
right wing 8′10″ x 4′8¼″. Musée
Unterlinden, Colmar, France

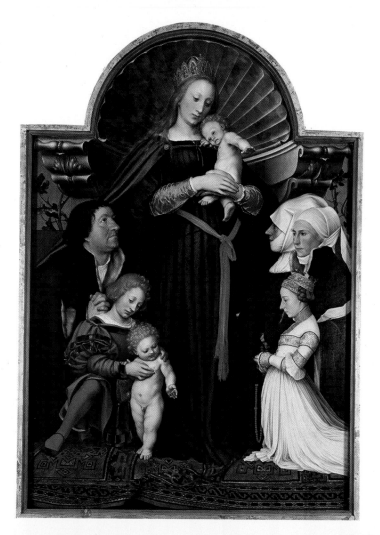

COLORPLATE 33.
Renaissance. HANS HOLBEIN (the
Younger). *Madonna of Burgomaster
Meyer.* 1526. Panel painting, 56¾ x
39¾″. Schlossmuseum,
Darmstadt, Germany

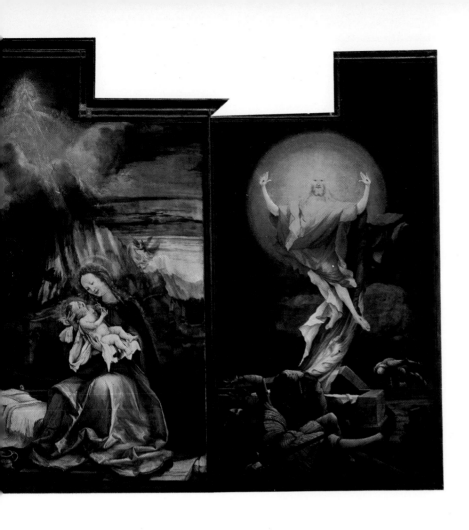

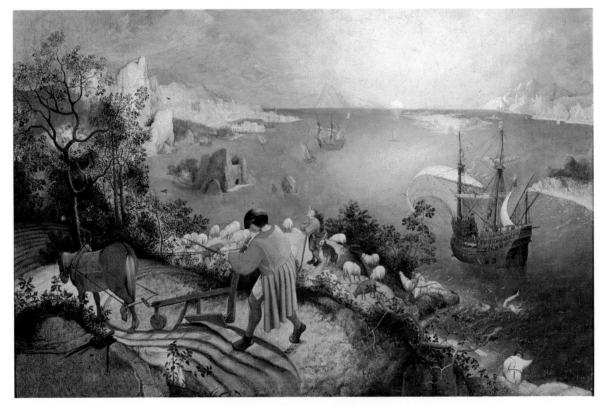

COLORPLATE 34.   Renaissance. PIETER BRUEGEL (the Elder). *Landscape with the Fall of Icarus.* c. 1554–55. Panel painting (transferred to canvas), 29 x 44⅛″. Musées Royaux des Beaux-Arts, Brussels

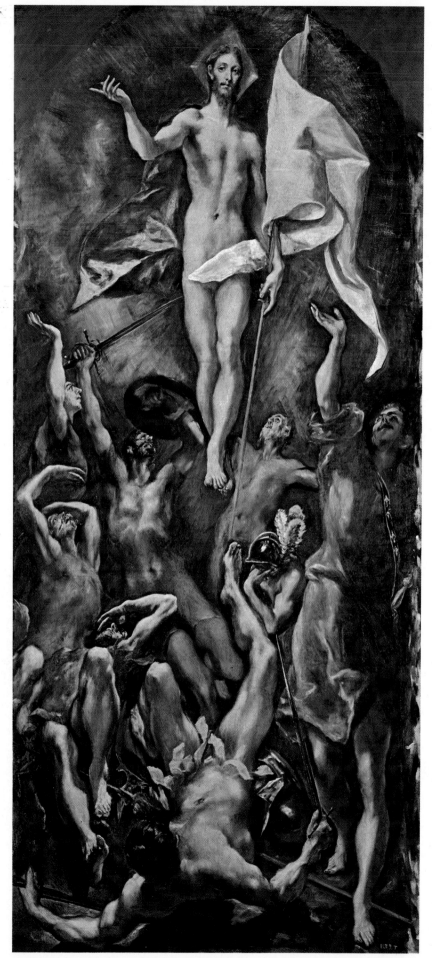

COLORPLATE 35.
Renaissance. EL GRECO. *Resurrection.*
c. 1597–1604. Oil on canvas, 9′1¼″ x
4′2″. Museo del Prado, Madrid

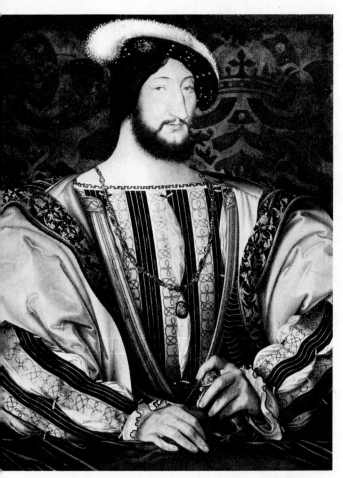

208. JEAN CLOUET. *Portrait of Francis I.* 1525–30. Panel,
37¾ x 29⅛″. The Louvre, Paris

by FRANCESCO PRIMATICCIO (1504–70) indicates the character and aesthetic level of this court style. It is as though something of the spirit of Flamboyant architecture and decoration still lingered on in France to transform, willy-nilly, the imported Italian style. The Mannerist figures, with their leg-crossed poses and sly concealment of some parts while exhibiting far more, form an endless pattern of modeled plaster decoration that eclipses the paintings. This one discloses Alexander the Great in amorous dalliance with the fair Campaspe, while Apelles stands at his easel, busily recording the scene for Francis and *his* mistress.

Despite Francis I's incessant wars with the emperor Charles V, and his disastrous attempts to claim the thrones of Naples and Milan and suzerainty over the Southern Netherlands, his reign was prosperous, and he and his court built a chain of opulent châteaux along the Loire River, in which were imaginatively combined the French Gothic heritage and Italian ideas. Chambord (fig. 210) is the most formidable example. Begun in 1519, the château has a central block with round corner towers clothed with a screen architecture of Renaissance pilasters in three stories; its plan is related to ideas developed by Leonardo for the dukes of Milan, and may have issued from the mind of the aged genius then still living at nearby Cloux, although a model was provided by Domenico da Cortona, a pupil of Giuliano da Sangallo. The central block of the château, far larger than one would suspect from a photograph, is divided into self-sufficient apartments, each concentrated on a corner tower and entered from a central double staircase, whose spirals are so intertwined that pedestrians going up

invitation. However strongly Francis may have thirsted for the Italian Renaissance, what he eventually got was Mannerism. Cellini spent several years in his service, and Rosso Fiorentino and a lesser, decorative artist, Francesco Primaticcio, carried out the king's ambitious projects. The best portraitists at Francis' court were, nonetheless, French, and the most important one was

JEAN CLOUET (c. 1485–1541), whose stiff and formal likenesses of the king may have influenced the visiting Holbein. Although Clouet cannot be ranked with the leading Italian or German masters, his characterization of the self-indulgent, calculating monarch, whose Don Juanism was notorious, in a portrait painted between 1525 and 1530 is keen and unsparing (fig. 208). Especially effective is the concentration of all the stripes and brocade patterns of the costume into a vortex, focused on the king's left hand, which nervously toys with his poniard.

The decorations in stucco and fresco for Francis I's palace at Fontainebleau, unfortunately much repainted, rank among the richest of Mannerist cycles. A detail from the room (fig. 209) of the king's mistress, the Duchesse d'Étampes, stuccoed and painted in the 1540s

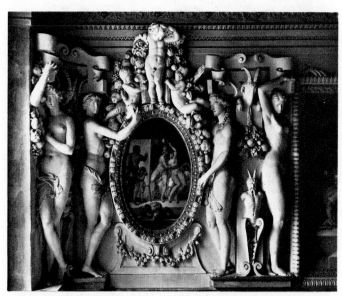

209. PRIMATICCIO. *Apelles with Alexander the Great and Campaspe.* Stucco and painting. c. 1540s (restored in 18th century). Chambre de la Duchesse d'Étampes, Château de Fontainebleau, France

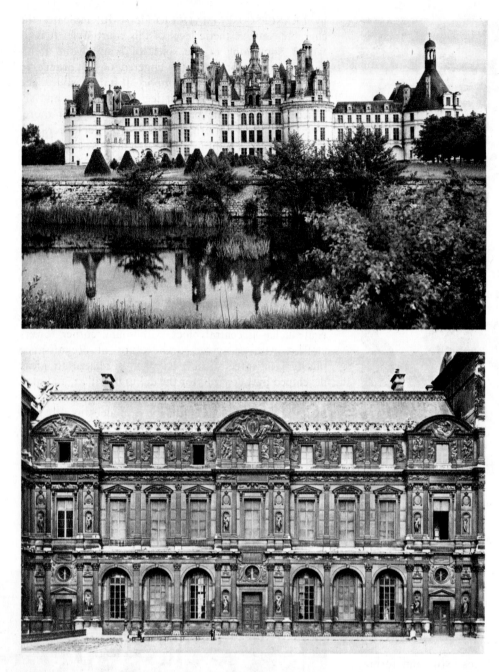

210. Château de Chambord. Begun 1519. France

211. Pierre Lescot and Jean Goujon. Square Court (Cour Carrée). Begun 1546. The Louvre, Paris

can only hear but not see those coming down. The southern outer walls and corner towers were not completed. The native French style conquered in Chambord in an eruption of dormers, ornamented chimneys, and openwork turrets stemming directly from the Gothic tradition; in the lovely light of the Loire Valley, the two opposites coexist harmoniously.

A style at once wholly French and wholly Renaissance did not develop in architecture and sculpture until midcentury in the Square Court of the Louvre, Paris (fig. 211), begun in 1546, the last year of Francis' reign, by the architect PIERRE LESCOT (1510–78) and the sculptor JEAN GOUJON (c. 1510–68). Given the Northern climate, steep roofs and large windows were necessities, but these are not the only French features; the façade is punctuated

by pavilions, recalling the towers of château architecture, which are crowned by arched pediments and linked by curtain walls, rather than being a block as in the Italian manner. The pavilions project only slightly, but their dominance is underscored by the pairing of engaged Corinthian columns in contrast to the single pilasters that emphasize the transitory character of the connecting walls. The sculptures in the niches and the rich reliefs of the attic story are of a type by no means unknown in Italy (see Sansovino's Library of San Marco, for example; fig. 173), but such decorative work on Italian palazzo exteriors was more commonly painted in fresco, and little has survived.

The style of Goujon is seen at its best in the turning and twisting figures from his now-dismantled *Fountain*

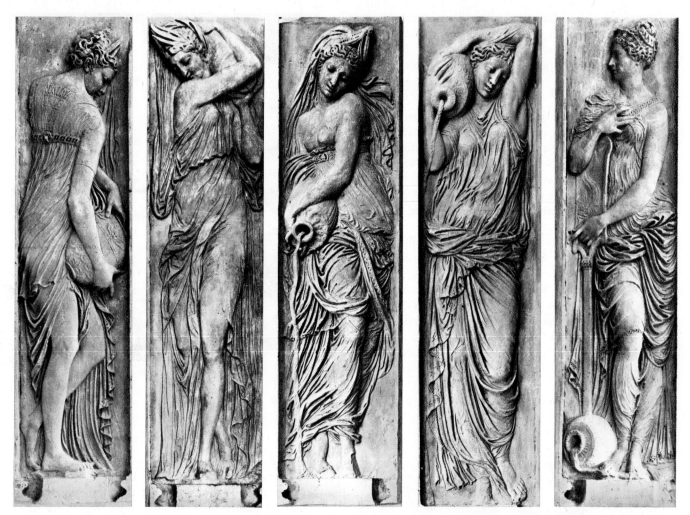

212-216. JEAN GOUJON. Nymphs, from the *Fountain of the Innocents* (dismantled). 1548-49. Five reliefs. The Louvre, Paris.

of the Innocents, of 1548–49 (figs. 212, 213, 214, 215, 216). Despite its uncanny resemblance to the *Victory Untying Her Sandal*, which Goujon could never have seen, the clinging drapery of these figures is probably derived from Roman models. But the figures, whose poses are certainly inspired by Italian Mannerism, are in the last analysis Goujon's own. Supple, graceful, moving with ease in nonexistent spaces, these lovely creatures are supremely French, foreshadowing in their diaphanous beauty the widely divergent arts of the Rococo and Neoclassicism (see Part Five, Chapter 7, and Part Six, Chapter 1).

The linearity of the French Renaissance takes on an unexpected expressive intensity in the sculpture of GERMAIN PILON (c. 1535–90), whose grim tombs at Saint-Denis are less interesting than some of his relief sculpture, such as the bronze *Deposition*, c. 1580–85 (fig. 217). Not the lines alone, as in the work of Goujon, but entire surfaces and underlying masses of figures and

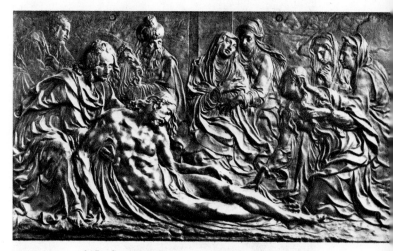

217. GERMAIN PILON. *Deposition*. Bronze relief.
c. 1580-85. The Louvre, Paris

drapery heave and flow as if molten. It is this inner movement, together with the striking freedom of the poses, rather than the somewhat standardized facial expressions, that acts as the true vehicle for emotion.

THE NETHERLANDS

The reversion of Burgundy to the French crown and the Netherlandish provinces to the Holy Roman Empire after the Battle of Nancy in 1477 had slight effect on the school of painting that had developed in the Netherlands under Burgundian sovereignty. Far more important were the tides of religious reform throughout the Netherlands in the sixteenth century, especially in the northern provinces. Before the abdication of the emperor Charles V in 1558, rule over the Netherlands, as well as Spain, had been given, in 1555 and 1556 respectively, to his fanatical son Philip II, and massive tyranny, including the Inquisition, had been imposed upon the Netherlands. The response of the Protestants, commendable enough insofar as it was directed toward political and religious freedoms, also took the less agreeable form of iconoclasm, and thousands of paintings and sculptured images were destroyed; in 1566 the Ghent Altarpiece had a narrow escape. The southern provinces, which today constitute Belgium, were pacified in 1576, but in 1579 the Union of Utrecht forged the northern provinces into the

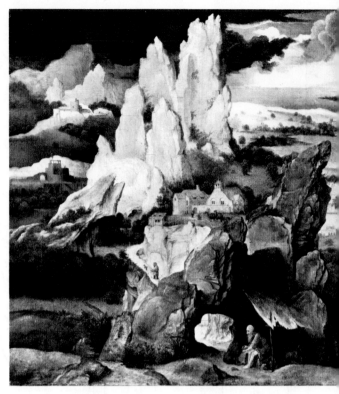

219. JOACHIM PATINIR. *Saint Jerome.* c. 1520. Panel painting, 14⅛ x 13⅜″. National Gallery, London

nucleus of present-day Holland, whose independence was assured early in the seventeenth century.

Little by little the novelty of the Netherlandish discovery of reality wore off. Although there were many competent painters in the opening decades of the sixteenth century, all were working more or less along lines laid down by van Eyck, van der Weyden, and van der Goes. Inevitably, Italian influence crept in, and just as inevitably it was misunderstood. No wonder that when Dürer—a German master—visited the Netherlands in 1520 he was hailed as a Messiah. Rather than discussing conservative or Italianate works, it seems preferable to underscore what was original and new in Netherlandish art in the early sixteenth century—an increased sensitivity to the moods of nature.

GOSSAERT. Jan Gossaert (c. 1478/88–1532), who eventually signed himself Mabuse after his native town of Maubeuge, visited Italy in 1508–1509, and later won Vasari's approval as the first Netherlander to compose with nude figures in the Italian manner. In 1517 his allegiance was still so uncertain, however, that he copied a famous early work by Jan van Eyck. Gossaert's special ability to render the effects of space and light is seen at its best in the *Agony in the Garden* (fig. 218), whose composition is indebted to a celebrated one by Mantegna, which Gossaert doubtless saw in Italy; he transformed it by his new and magical rendering of moonlight and clear night air. Christ kneels, as in Luke 22: 42–43:

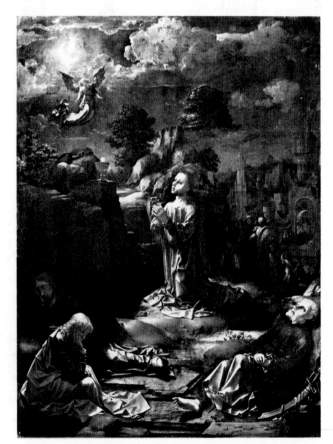

218. JAN GOSSAERT (MABUSE). *Agony in the Garden.* c. 1503–7. Panel painting, 33½ x 24¾″. Gemäldegalerie, Staatliche Museen, Berlin

Saying, Father, if thou be willing, remove this cup from me: nevertheless not my will, but thine, be done.

And there appeared an angel unto him from heaven, strengthening him.

The angel hovers in the moonlight, against the dark blue sky with its shining clouds; moonlight touches the edges of the rocks and the chalice (the "cup") and the host of the Eucharist, dwells on the lavender tunic of Christ, touches the face of Peter, shines on the armor of one of the soldiers, but leaves the ominous Judas among the soldiers on the right in shadow. Jerusalem looms in the distance, dim and foreboding.

PATINIR. A special kind of romantic landscape was invented by Joachim Patinir (active 1515–24); his *Saint Jerome* (fig. 219), of about 1520, shows the typical wild landscape forms in which he specialized. Saint Jerome in the Wilderness was a frequent subject in the second half of the fifteenth century in Italy, but Patinir's interpretation is his own. The figure of Saint Jerome merely establishes an ascetic mood for the wild landscape background, seen from a high vantage point. The towering, jagged rocks, introduced for expressive purposes, seem more invented than real. Invariably in Patinir's landscapes the foreground is dominated by brown, the middle distance by green; the rocks are blue gray; and a dark blue storm, generally raging in the distance, sends the crags into bright relief. The broad sweep of Patinir's landscapes emancipates them almost entirely from the ostensible subject; only after experiencing their immensity does one think to look for hermitages, travelers, and the meditating saint.

BRUEGEL. The one Netherlandish master of universal importance in the sixteenth century was Pieter Bruegel the Elder (c. 1525/30–69). He may have been born near 's Hertogenbosch, the home of Hieronymus Bosch; deeply influenced by both Bosch's pessimism and his fantasy, he turned out a number of designs for engravings on Boschlike themes. He spent the years between 1551 and 1555 in Italy, going as far south as Sicily, and brought back wonderful drawings of Alpine landscapes he had traversed on his journey. As for the lessons of Italian art, always dangerous for a Northerner, Bruegel mastered them in their essence. Rather than adopting Italian nude figures, which always seem to shiver in the cold North, he interpreted the message of Italy as a monumental harmony of form and space, and remained just as strongly Netherlandish in his outlook and subject matter as before his trip.

Bruegel's love for the beauty of South Italian landscape prompted the blue harbor and silvery cliffs of his *Landscape with the Fall of Icarus*, c. 1554–55 (colorplate 34). Icarus, who against the advice of his father Daedalus flew so high that the wax that held the wings to his body was melted by the sun, had appeared from time to time in Italian art not only as a symbol of overweening ambition but also because his depiction gave the artist an opportunity to display anatomical knowledge of a body in flight or falling. Bruegel instead concentrates our attention on the farmer plowing furrows behind his horse in a foreground field high above the sea, on a singing shepherd, and on a galleon with bellying mainsail and lateen buffeting the whitecaps in a stiff breeze. It takes a moment to find Icarus; only his waving legs are still out of water. No one pays his tragedy the faintest attention. An old Netherlandish and German proverb maintains that "when a man dies no plow stops." That brings us to the widely held belief that Bruegel belonged to a circle of Antwerp humanists who maintained that man is driven to sin by foolishness, and that he is bound to the inevitable cycle of nature, from which it is folly to attempt escape. With his vision liberated by the wide landscape prospects of Patinir, Bruegel was able to project the monumentality of Italian art in Netherlandish terms; the plowman's ancestry can be traced from Michelangelo, through Masaccio, back to Giotto; however, he remains Netherlandish all the while.

About 1561–62 Bruegel painted the devastating *Triumph of Death* (fig. 220), a barren landscape of dead trees, burning cities, and sinking ships in which no one will survive. An amorous couple make music, with Death looking over their shoulders; a feast is overturned by Death, who assails kings and cardinals; on a pale horse he mows down the living with his scythe. The chanting monks turn out to be skeletons; corpses hang from gallows, are stretched on wheels for the ravens to eat, and float bloated upon the sea. Those who remain alive are driven toward a gigantic coffin, whose end is lifted open like a trap; it is guarded by phalanxes of skeletons defending themselves with shields. Although the Dance of Death was a subject favored by sixteenth-century artists for woodcuts (Holbein, for example), never in a single painting had such a remorseless panorama of human mortality been attempted.

To Bruegel the peasant was an especially attractive subject because he typified the acceptance of man's bondage to the earth and to the cycle of the turning year. Five remaining paintings belong to a series that Bruegel made to illustrate the labors of the months, as in the calendar scenes of the *Très Riches Heures* (see colorplate 15, fig. 90). The picture signed and dated in 1565 called the *Harvesters* (fig. 221) represents July or August. A sky veiled in summer heat-haze extends over harvested fields and those still to be cut. The heads of plodding peasants are scarcely visible above the standing grain. Under what shade a tree can give on such a day, other peasants eat bread (made, doubtless, from the grain they raised last year), porridge, and fruit. One, his breeches loosened, his stomach distended, sleeps off the meal. A companion piece, the *Hunters in the Snow*, also from 1565 (fig. 222), represents January or February. The world is covered with snow, against which are silhouetted the weary

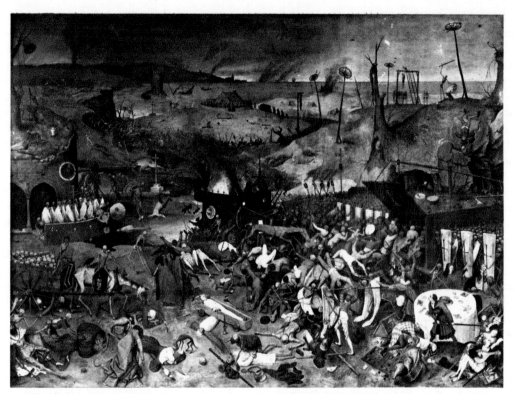

220. PIETER BRUEGEL (the Elder). *Triumph of Death*. c. 1561–62. Panel painting, 46 x 63¾″. Museo del Prado, Madrid

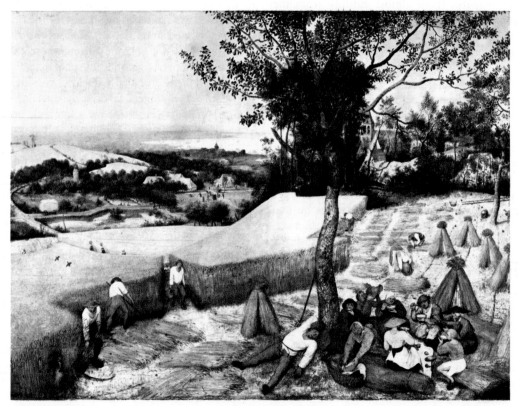

221. PIETER BRUEGEL (the Elder). *Harvesters*. 1565. Oil on panel, 46½ x 63¼″. The Metropolitan Museum of Art, New York. Rogers Fund, 1919

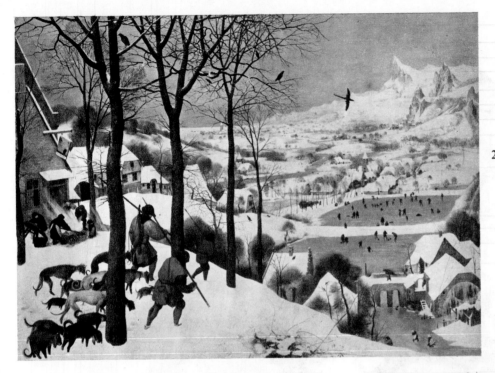

222. PIETER BRUEGEL (the Elder). *Hunters in the Snow.* 1565. Oil and tempera on panel, c. 46⅛ x 63¾". Kunsthistorisches Museum, Vienna

hunters returning to the village and their pack of dogs with drooping tails. Below the village skaters move over the frozen ponds. A crane flies above, lending greater distance to the Alpine peaks. Never again in Netherlandish art is there anything to equal the simple humanity of Bruegel's peasants or the breadth and dignity of his landscape. The fatality that binds man and nature is stoically accepted, and in this acceptance Bruegel is able to communicate an unexpected peace.

SPAIN

EL GRECO. In the late sixteenth century, Spain, in spite of its far-flung political and military power, its fervent support of the Counter-Reformation, and the rich art collections of King Philip II, was artistically provincial. By a curious coincidence of history it fell to a representative of another artistic tradition, which also had become provincial, to produce in Spain work of the highest quality. Domenikos Theotokopoulos (1541–1614), generally known as El Greco, was born in Crete, then a Venetian possession, and probably trained under icon painters still working in the Byzantine style. About 1560 he went to Venice, where a small group of Greek painters was active in translating compositions by Venetian masters from Bellini to Tintoretto into Byzantine style for the local Greek colony. Either El Greco was never caught in this backwater or extricated himself from it quickly, because during his stay in Venice he absorbed from the great Venetian masters their whole range of luminary and coloristic achievements and every nuance of their brushwork.

After a Roman sojourn during the 1570s, he arrived in Spain in 1576, and in the heady atmosphere of Counter-Reformation mysticism, led by such spirits as Saint Theresa and Saint John of the Cross, his work took fire. It was as if, under the new religious inspiration, he were suddenly able to recreate on a contemporary plane the splendors of Byzantine art. Undeniably, the Byzantine spirit remains in his work; in a sense he may be thought of as the last and one of the greatest of Greek painters, the heir of the pictorial tradition we have seen at Sinai, at Castelseprio, and at the Kariye Djami and as the close artistic relative of Theophanes the Greek, who had worked in Russia in the fourteenth century.

In *The Burial of the Count of Orgaz* (fig. 223), painted in 1586, El Greco's synthesis of Venetian color, Spanish mysticism, and the Byzantine tradition is complete. The subject is the interment in 1323 of a nobleman who had lived a life of such sanctity that after his death Saints Stephen and Augustine came down from Heaven to lay his body reverently in the tomb. El Greco has shown the burial in the lower half of the picture as if it were taking place in his own time; the priest on the far right reading the committal office and the solemn-faced Spaniards of all ages have for the most part accepted the miracle calmly. The black sixteenth-century costumes contrast with the splendor of the priest's cope, embroidered in gold, and with the sparkle of the white-and-gold damasks of the saints. These and the myriad reflections on the polished steel armor with its bands of gilded ornamentation are painted with a brushwork and quality of light that technically are the equal of the highest Venetian achievements. But the upward glance of the central mourner and the pose and gesture of the priest in a surplice at the right draw our attention upward to an even greater miracle: the clouds of Heaven have descended close above the heads of the living and have divided to allow an angel to

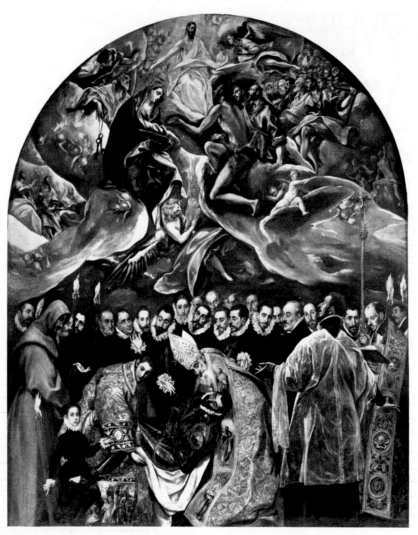

223. El Greco. *The Burial of Count Orgaz.* 1586. Oil on canvas,
16′ x 11′10″. S. Tomé, Toledo, Spain

transport the tiny cloudy soul of the count toward the Deësis above—Mary and Saint John the Baptist fairly near us, but Christ more remote, and robed in snowy white.

Here and there vortices filled with saints open in the clouds, and frosty cloud banks pile up, within which crowd angelic heads. The figures have already begun to assume the fantastically attenuated proportions of those in El Greco's later work, and light, from no visible or consistent source, seems to originate from within the figures. It makes no sense to talk of Mannerism in connection with El Greco; his inspired, profoundly spiritual art has nothing to do either with the first generation of Florentine and Sienese Mannerists or with the later art of Counter-Reformation Rome and grand ducal Florence. It is an anachronistic and highly personal amalgam, an art period in itself, and it hardly survived El Greco's death.

Every few years one or another oculist announces with an air of discovery that El Greco's astigmatism was responsible for his figural distortions. His malady must

have been widely shared, for his work was commissioned by every patron in central Spain who could afford it, and imitated, distortions and all, by a busy studio of pupils. His distortions were, moreover, abandoned at will when the subject required him to do so. His portrait of the *Grand Inquisitor Don Fernando Niño de Guevara* (fig. 224), painted about 1600, is naturalistically proportioned in the Venetian manner, The direct and piercing gaze, which makes one wonder how many heretics the inquisitor has committed to the flames, the dry features, the grizzled beard, and the glasses are all rendered with the same close observation that picks up the nervous clutch of the jeweled fingers of the left hand on the arm of the chair. In the crimson tunic, however, El Greco let himself go in an outburst of lightning brushstrokes in the tradition of Byzantine art at its most mystical.

An astonishing production of combined mysticism and virtuosity is El Greco's compressed view of one section of his adopted city, *Toledo*, painted about 1600–10 (fig. 225), all in greens, blue grays, black grays, and silver

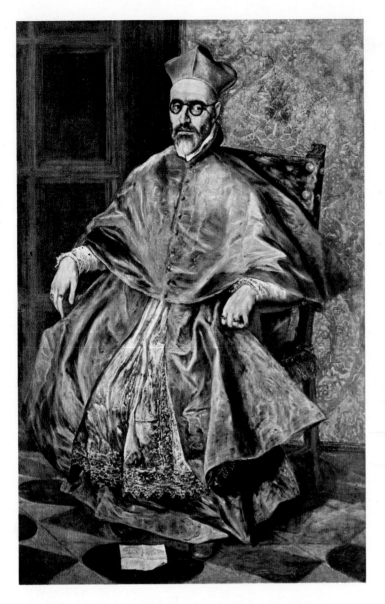

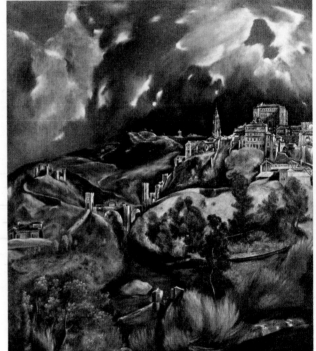

224. EL GRECO. *Grand Inquisitor Don Fernando Niño de Guevara.* c. 1600. Oil on canvas, 67½ x 42½". The Metropolitan Museum of Art, New York. Bequest of Mrs. H. O. Havemeyer, 1929. The H. O. Havemeyer Collection

225. EL GRECO. *Toledo.* c. 1600-10. Oil on canvas, 47¾ x 42¾". The Metropolitan Museum of Art, New York. Bequest of Mrs. H. O. Havemeyer, 1929. The H. O. Havemeyer Collection

grays, looking as if light were glowing from within the grassy slopes and witches were riding through the wild clouds. Tiny washerwomen in the river and travelers on the road are hardly more than touches of the brush.

El Greco's mystical late style is seen at its most exalted in his *Resurrection*, of about 1597–1604 (colorplate 35), in which Christ soars above us against a background of night, acting as a magnet that pulls upward the surrounding figures—drawn out to unbelievable lengths—of the Roman soldiers in an ecstasy of pain. In contrast to Christ's body in Grünewald's *Resurrection* (see colorplate 32), El Greco's Christ is more solid, white and glowing like the Eucharist in the light of an altar, his eyes looking calmly toward the observer. The Renaissance is now far behind us, but, as in the visionary late paintings of Tintoretto, El Greco does not lead toward the Baroque. The utter abandonment of physical reality in his personal and spontaneous surrender has nothing in common with the calculated art of the founders of the Baroque style in Italy.

TIME LINE

The numbers in italics refer to illustrations in the text.

	POLITICAL HISTORY	RELIGION, LITERATURE	SCIENCE, TECHNOLOGY
1200 1250	Conquest of Constantinople by Crusaders (1204) Siena defeats Florence at Montaperti (1260)	St. Francis of Assisi (d. 1226) *Golden Legend* by Jacobus de Voragine (1266–83)	
1300	Visconti rule in Milan (1312–1447) Black Death in Florence and Siena (1348)	Petrarch, first humanist (1304–74) Boccaccio (1313–75) Giovanni Villani writes *Chronicles* (1348)	Marco Polo returns from China (c. 1295)
1350		Lionardo Bruni (1369–1444)	
1375		Great Schism in Western Church (1378–1418)	
1400	Death of Giangaleazzo Visconti of Milan (1402) removes threat to political independence of Florence Joan of Arc (1412–31)	Council of Constance (1414–18) ends Great Schism	Prince Henry the Navigator of Portugal (1394–1460) promotes geographic exploration
1425	John Palaeologus (r. 1425–48) Battle of San Romano (1432) Cosimo Vecchio exiled from Florence (1433–34) Medici domination in Florence (1434–94) Florence and Venice defeat Filippo Maria Visconti at Anghiari (1440) Republic in Milan (1447–50)	Council of Basel (1431–49) François Villon (born c. 1431) Marsilio Ficino (1433–99) Leonbattista Alberti writes *De pictura* (1435; as *Della pittura*, 1436) Cennino Cennini writes *Il libro dell'arte* (1437) Council of Ferrara-Florence attempts to reunite Catholic and Eastern Orthodox faiths (1438–45) Lorenzo Ghiberti writes *Commentaries* (1447–55) Papacy of Nicholas V (1447–55)	Earliest record of suction pump (c. 1440)
1450	Sforza rule in Milan (1450–1500) Habsburg rule of Holy Roman Empire begins (1452) End of Hundred Years' War (1453) Fall of Constantinople to Turks (1453) Piero de' Medici (r. 1464–69) Giuliano de' Medici (r. 1469–78) Ferdinand and Isabella unite Spain (1469)	Leonbattista Alberti writes *De re aedificatoria* (c. 1450) Giannozzo Manetti (1396–1459) writes *On the Dignity and Excellence of Man* (1451–52) Papacy of Pius II (1458–64) Pico della Mirandola (1463–94) Plato's Works translated into Latin by Ficino (1463; published 1484) Niccolo Machiavelli (1469–1527) Papacy of Sixtus IV (1471–84)	
1475	Pazzi conspiracy in Florence: Giuliano de' Medici assassinated; Lorenzo the Magnificent escapes (1478) Lorenzo de' Medici, the Magnificent (r. 1478–92)	Giovanni de' Medici (1475–1521); Pope Leo X Giulio de' Medici (1478–1534); Pope Clement VII	

PAINTING	SCULPTURE	ARCHITECTURE	
			1200
			1250
Cimabue, *Madonna Enthroned (6)* Pietro Cavallini, *Last Judgment*, fresco, Sta. Cecilia in Trastevere, Rome *(colorplate 1)*	Nicola Pisano, pulpit, Baptistery, Pisa *(1, 2)*		
			1300
Giotto, *Madonna and Child Enthroned, Raising of Lazarus, Lamentation,* and *Joachim Takes Refuge in the Wilderness* from fresco cycle, Arena Chapel, Padua *(7-9, colorplate 2)* Duccio, *Maestà* altarpiece from Cathedral of Siena *(11-13)* Taddeo Gaddi, *Annunciation to the Shepherds,* fresco, Baroncelli Chapel, Sta. Croce, Florence *(10)* Simone Martini, *Annunciation (14)* Ambrogio Lorenzetti, *Allegory of Good Government,* fresco, Palazzo Pubblico, Siena *(16, colorplate 3)* Pietro Lorenzetti, *Birth of the Virgin (15)*	Giovanni Pisano, pulpit, Sant'Andrea, Pistoia *(3,4)* Giovanni Pisano, *Virgin and Child,* Arena Chapel, Padua *(5)*		
			1350
Traini, *Triumph of Death,* fresco, Campo Santo, Pisa *(17, 18)* Giovanni da Milano, *Pietà (19)*			
			1375
Broederlam, *Annunciation* and *Visitation.* Chartreuse de Champmol altarpiece, Dijon *(88)*	Claus Sluter, portal of the Chartreuse de Champmol, Dijon; *Well of Moses (85–87)*		
			1400
The Boucicaut Master, *Hours of the Maréchal de Boucicaut (89)* The Limbourg Brothers, *Très Riches Heures du Duc de Berry (90, 91, colorplate 15)* The Rohan Master, *Grandes Heures de Rohan (92)* Jan van Eyck, *Baptism of Christ* from the *Turin-Milan Hours (95)* Gentile da Fabriano, *Adoration of the Magi* altarpiece *(53, colorplate 5)*	Brunelleschi, *Sacrifice of Isaac,* competition panel for North doors, Baptistery of S. Giovanni, Florence *(46)* Ghiberti, *Sacrifice of Isaac,* competition panel for North doors, Baptistery of S. Giovanni, Florence *(45)* Nanni di Banco, *Four Crowned Martyrs (49)* Donatello, *Saint Mark; Saint George; Saint George and the Dragon; Habakkuk (Lo Zuccone) (38–41)*	Brunelleschi, Ospedale degli Innocenti; dome, Cathedral of Florence; S. Lorenzo, Florence *(20, 22–24)*	
			1425
Master of Flémalle (Robert Campin?), *Mérode Altarpiece; Impenitent Thief Dead on His Cross (93, 94, colorplate 6)* Masaccio, fresco cycle, Brancacci Chapel, Sta. Maria del Carmine, Florence. *Enthroned Madonna and Child (54–56, colorplate 6)* Masaccio, *Trinity,* Sta. Maria Novella, Florence *(57)* Fra Filippo Lippi, *Annunciation (58)* Hubert and Jan van Eyck, *Ghent Altarpiece (96–99)* Jan Van Eyck. *Man in a Red Turban; Madonna of Chancellor Rolin; Arnolfini Wedding (100–103, colorplate 17)* Fra Angelico, *Descent from the Cross (colorplate 8)* Rogier van der Weyden, *Descent from the Cross (colorplate 18)* Fra Angelico, *Annunciation.* Monastery of S. Marco, Florence *(59)* Witz, *Miraculous Draft of Fish (114)* Rogier van der Weyden, *Last Judgment* altarpiece *(colorplate 19)* Master of the Annunciation of Aix, *Annunciation of Aix (119)* Domenico Veneziano, *Saint Lucy Altarpiece (62, colorplate 9)* Uccello, *Deluge* from frescoes, Chiostro Verde, Sta. Maria Novella, Florence; *Battle of San Romano (60, 61)* Castagno, *Last Supper,* Cenacolo di Sant'Apollonia, Florence *(63)* Lochner, *Presentation in the Temple (113)* Castagno, *David (64)*	Ghiberti, *Gates of Paradise,* doors of the Baptistery of S. Giovanni, Florence *(47, 48)* Donatello, *Feast of Herod,* relief from baptismal font, Cathedral of Siena *(42)* Jacopo della Quercia, *Creation of Adam* and *Expulsion from Eden*, main portal, S. Petronio, Bologna *(51, 52)* Donatello, *David (43)* Luca della Robbia, *Cantoria (50)* Donatello, *Equestrian Monument of Gattamelata (44)* Bernardo Rossellino, *Tomb of Lionardo Bruni (67)*	Brunelleschi, Pazzi Chapel, Sta. Croce, Florence *(25–27)* Michelozzo, Palazzo Medici-Riccardi, Florence *(28–30)* Brunelleschi, lantern of the dome, Cathedral of Florence *(21)*	
			1450
Fouquet, *Melun Diptych (117)* Antonello da Messina, *Saint Jerome in His Study (83)* Fra Filippo Lippi, *Madonna and Child (colorplate 7)* Fouquet, *Book of Hours of Étienne Chevalier (118)* Piero della Francesca, *Discovery of the Wood from Which the True Cross Was Made* and *Meeting of Solomon and the Queen of Sheba* from fresco cycle, S. Francesco, Arezzo *(65, 66)* Quarton, *Coronation of the Virgin (colorplate 21)* Mantegna, *Saint James Led to Execution* from fresco cycle, Ovetari Chapel, Church of the Eremitani, Padua *(80)* Master of René of Anjou, *Le Livre du coeur d'amour épris (120)* Piero della Francesca, *Resurrection (65)* Quarton, *Avignon Pietà (121)* Pacher, *Pope Sixtus II Taking Leave of Saint Lawrence (115)* Bouts, *Last Supper (104)* Mantegna, *Dead Christ (82)* Piero della Francesca, *Battista Sforza* and *Federigo da Montefeltro (colorplates 10, 11)* Mantegna, fresco cycle, Camera degli Sposi, Palazzo Ducale, Mantua *(81, colorplate 13)*	Donatello, *Mary Magdalen (colorplate 4)* Antonio Rossellino, *Giovanni Chellini; Tomb of the Cardinal of Portugal (68, 69)* Desiderio da Settignano, *Christ and Saint John the Baptist (70)* Verrocchio, *Doubting of Thomas (74)*	Alberti, Malatesta Temple (S. Francesco), Rimini; Palazzo Rucellai, Florence *(31, 32)* Alberti, Sant'Andrea, Mantua *(33–35)*	
			1475
Pollaiuolo, *Martyrdom of Saint Sebastian (71)* Hugo van der Goes, *Portinari Altarpiece (105, 106)* Botticelli, *Primavera (76)* Leonardo da Vinci, *Adoration of the Magi (125, 126)* Perugino, *Giving of the Keys to Saint Peter,* Sistine Chapel, Vatican, Rome *(78)* Ghirlandaio, frescoes, Cappella Maggiore, Sta. Maria Novella, Florence *(77)* Botticelli, *Birth of Venus (colorplate 12)* Leonardo da Vinci, *Madonna of the Rocks (127)*	Pollaiuolo, *Hercules and Antaeus (73)* Verrocchio, *Equestrian Monument of Bartolommeo Colleoni (75)*		

TIME LINE

The numbers in italics refer to illustrations in the text.

	POLITICAL HISTORY	RELIGION, LITERATURE	SCIENCE, TECHNOLOGY
1485	Henry VII (r. 1485–1509), first Tudor king of England Granada, last Muslim holding in Spain, falls to Spanish (1492) Spain and Portugal divide New World (1492–93) Maximilian I, HRE (r. 1493–1519) Expulsion of Medici from Florence (1494) Charles VIII, Fr. king (r. 1483–98), invades Italy with help of the Sforza (1494) Cabot claims eastern North America for England (1497)	Pietro Aretino (1492–1556) Papacy of Alexander VI (1492–1503) François Rabelais (1494–c.1553) Sebastian Brant writes *Ship of Fools* (1494) Girolamo Savonarola (1452–98) burned at the stake for heresy in Florence	Diaz rounds Cape of Good Hope (1486) Columbus discovers America (1492)
1500	Spain rules Kingdom of Naples (after 1504) Restoration of Medici in Florence (1512) Charles V (1500–58) reigns as Holy Roman Emperor (1519–56) Cortes conquers Aztec empire in Mexico for Spain (1519) Suleiman I the Magnificent ascends Turkish throne (1520)	Papacy of Julius II (1503–13) St. Francis Xavier (1506–52) Erasmus of Rotterdam (1469–1536) writes *In Praise of Folly* (1511) Papacy of Leo X (1513–21) Baldassare Castiglione (1478–1529) writes *The Courtier* (1514; published 1528) St. Theresa of Avila (1515–82) St. Philip Neri (1515–95) Sir Thomas More (1478–1535) writes *Utopia* (1516) Lodovico Ariosto (1475–1533) writes *Orlando Furioso* (1516) Martin Luther (1483–1546) posts 95 theses at Wittenberg (1517); excommunicated and outlawed (1521) Felice Peretti (1521–90); Pope Sixtus V Papacy of Adrian VI (1522–23) Papacy of Clement VII (1523–34)	Paracelsus (1493–1541) opposes humoral theory of disease, crusades for use of chemicals in treatment of disease Balboa sights Pacific Ocean (1513) Portuguese reach China (1516); hold trade monopoly in Far East until 1602 First circumnavigation of the globe by Magellan and crew (1520–22)
1525	Peasants' Revolt in Germany (1524–25) Francis I, Fr. king (r. 1515–47), defeated by Charles V at Pavia (1525); taken prisoner to Madrid Sack of Rome by Spanish and German mercenaries of Charles V (1527) Expulsion of Medici and reestablishment of Florentine Republic (1527) Mogul dynasty founded in India (1527) Medici power reestablished in Florence (1530) Henry VIII, Eng. king (r. 1509–47) founds Anglican church (1534) Cosimo I de' Medici (r. 1537–74) Ivan the Terrible, Rus. czar (r. 1547–84)	Palestrina (c. 1525–94) Montaigne (1533–92) Papacy of Paul III (1534–49) John Calvin (1509–64) publishes *Institutes of the Christian Religion* (1536) First printed edition of Machiavelli's *The Prince* (1538; written 1513) St. Charles Borromeo (1538–84) Foundation of Society of Jesus in Rome by Ignatius Loyola (1540) Council of Trent (1545–63) undertakes reform of abuses and definition of doctrine in Roman Catholic Church Cervantes (1547–1616)	Copernicus refutes geocentric view of universe (1530–43) Principle of triangulation in surveying discovered by Gemma Frisius (1533) Leonhart Fuchs (1501–66) publishes herbal (1542) Vesalius (1514–64) writes *De Humani Corporis Fabrica* (1543)
1550	Wars of Lutheran vs. Catholic princes in Germany (1550); Peace of Augsburg (1555) allows each sovereign to decide religion of his subjects Charles V retires (1556) and divides empire; his brother Ferdinand I, HRE (r.1558–64), receives imperial office and Habsburg lands; his son Philip II (r. 1556–98) becomes king of Spain, the Netherlands, and the New World Elizabeth I, Eng. queen (r. 1558–1603) Lutheranism becomes state religion in Denmark (1560) Netherlands revolt against Spain (1568) Turkish sea power crushed at Battle of Lepanto (1571)	Giorgio Vasari publishes *Lives of the Most Eminent Painters, Sculptors, and Architects* (1550; second edition, 1568) Camillo Borghese (1552–1621); Pope Paul V Papacy of Paul IV (1555–59) Cellini writes *Autobiography* (1558) John Knox (1505–72) founds Presbyterian Church (1560) Francis Bacon (1561–1626) William Shakespeare (1564–1616) Palladio publishes *Quattro libri d'architettura* (1570) Giambattista Pamphili (1574–1655); Pope Innocent X	Agricola (1494–1555), *De re metallica* (1556) Mercator (1512–94) devises mercator chart (1569) Tycho Brahe (1546–1601) observes first supernova (1572); accumulates accurate data on planetary and lunar positions and produces the first modern star catalogue
1575 **1600**	Philip II seizes Portugal (1580) Northern provinces of the Netherlands declare independence (1581) Spanish Armada defeated by English (1588) Henry IV, Fr. king (r. 1589–1610) ends religious civil war; Edict of Nantes (1598) establishes religious toleration	Papacy of Sixtus V (1585–90) Lutheranism becomes state religion in Sweden (1593) France becomes Catholic power with the conversion of Henry IV (1593) Edict of Nantes (1598) Giordano Bruno (1548–1600) burned at the stake for heresy	Ramelli, *Diverse ed artificiose macchine* (1588)

PAINTING	SCULPTURE	ARCHITECTURE	
			1485
Memlinc, *Shrine of Saint Ursula (107, 107A, 107B, 107C)* Bellini, *Transfiguration of Christ (colorplate 14)* Geertgen tot Sint Jans, *Nativity (108)* Leonardo da Vinci, *Last Supper (128)* Dürer, *Self-Portrait (195)* Signorelli, *Damned Consigned to Hell* from frescoes, S. Brixio Chapel, Cathedral of Orvieto *(79)*	Michelangelo, *Pietà (132)*	Giuliano da Sangallo, Sta. Maria delle Carceri, Prato *(36, 37)*	
			1500
Leonardo da Vinci, *Madonna and Saint Anne (colorplate 22)* Leonardo da Vinci, *Battle of Anghiari; Mona Lisa (129, 130)* Bosch, *Crowning with Thorns; Garden of Delights (109–112, colorplate 20)* Gossaert (Mabuse), *Agony in the Garden (218)* Raphael, *Marriage of the Virgin; Madonna of the Meadows (144, 145)* Bellini, *Madonna and Child Enthroned (84)* Giorgione, *Enthroned Madonna with Saint Liberalis and Saint Francis; The Tempest (160, colorplate 26)* Dürer, *Adoration of the Trinity (colorplate 31)* Raphael, *Disputa* and *School of Athens*, Stanza della Segnatura, Vatican, Rome *(146, colorplate 24)* Michelangelo, ceiling frescoes, Sistine Chapel, Vatican, Rome *(137, 138, colorplate 23)* Raphael, *Expulsion of Heliodoro*, Stanza d'Eliodoro, Vatican, Rome; *Sistine Madonna*; frescoes, Villa Farnesina, Rome *(147, 148, 150)* Grünewald, *Isenheim Altarpiece (202, 203, colorplate 32)* Dürer, *Saint Jerome (199)* Titian, *Sacred and Profane Love (colorplate 27)* Andrea del Sarto, *Madonna of the Harpies (156)* Raphael, *Pope Leo X with Cardinals Giulio de' Medici and Luigi de' Rossi; Transfiguration (149, 151)* Titian, *Assumption of the Virgin (162)* Pontormo, *Joseph in Egypt (157)* Titian, *Bacchanal of the Andrians; Madonna of the House of Pesaro (161, 163)* Patinir, *Saint Jerome (219)* Rosso, *Descent from the Cross (158)* Correggio, *Holy Night (177)* Beccafumi, *Fall of the Rebel Angels (159)* Parmigianino, *Self-Portrait in a Convex Mirror (180)* Lotto, *Madonna and Child with Saints (Sacra Conversazione) (169)*	Michelangelo, *David; Dying Slave; Rebellious Slave; Moses (132–136)* Michelangelo, *Tomb of Giuliano de' Medici; Tomb of Lorenzo de' Medici*, Medici Chapel, S. Lorenzo, Florence *(152–154)*	Bramante, Tempietto, Rome; plan for St. Peter's, Vatican, Rome *(139–143)* Château de Chambord *(210)*	
			1525
Pontormo, *Entombment (colorplate 25)* Clouet, *Portrait of Francis I (208)* Holbein, *Madonna of Burgomaster Meyer (colorplate 33)* Dürer, *Four Apostles (201)* Correggio, *Assumption of the Virgin*, dome fresco, Cathedral of Parma *(178)* Titian, *Man with the Glove (164)* Altdorfer, *Battle of Alexander and Darius on the Issus (204)* Cranach, *Apollo and Diana (205)* Correggio, *Jupiter and Io (179)* Holbein, *French Ambassadors (206)* · Parmigianino, *Madonna with the Long Neck (colorplate 30)* Michelangelo, *Last Judgment*, wall fresco, Sistine Chapel, Vatican, Rome *(181, 182)* Titian, *Venus of Urbino (165)* Holbein, *Portrait of Henry VIII (207)* Titian, *Portrait of Pope Paul III and His Grandsons (166)* Bronzino, *Exposure of Luxury (192)* Tintoretto, *Saint Mark Freeing a Christian Slave (colorplate 28)*	Michelangelo, *"Crossed-Leg" Captive (131)* Primaticcio, stucco decoration, Chambre de la Duchesse d'Étampes, Château de Fontainebleau *(209)* Cellini, *Perseus and Medusa (193)* Goujon, *Fountain of the Innocents (211–216)*	Michelangelo, Biblioteca Medicea Laurenziana, S. Lorenzo, Florence *(155)* Sansovino, Library of S. Marco, Venice *(173)* Michelangelo, Palazzo dei Senatori and plan of Campidoglio, Rome; plan of St. Peter's, Vatican, Rome *(183–186)* Lescot, Square Court (Cour Carrée), The Louvre, Paris *(211)*	
			1550
Bruegel, *Landscape with the Fall of Icarus (colorplate 34)* Titian, *Rape of Europa (167)* Bruegel, *Triumph of Death (220)* Tintoretto, *Crucifixion*, Sala dell'Albergo, Scuola di S. Rocco, Venice *(170)* Bruegel, *Harvesters; Hunters in the Snow (221, 222)* Titian, *Crowning with Thorns (168)*	Michelangelo, *Rondanini Pietà (187)*	Palladio, Villa Rotonda (Villa Capra) *(174)* Ammanati, courtyard, Palazzo Pitti, Florence *(191)* Vasari, Palazzo degli Uffizi, Florence *(190)* Palladio, S. Giorgio Maggiore, Venice *(175, 176)* Giacomo da Vignola, Il Gesù, Rome *(188)*	
			1575
Veronese, ceiling decoration, Hall of the Grand Council, Palazzo Ducale, Venice *(172)* El Greco, *The Burial of Count Orgaz (223)* Tintoretto, *Last Supper (171)* El Greco, *Resurrection (colorplate 35)*	Pilon, *Deposition (217)* Giovanni Bologna, *Rape of the Sabine Woman (194)*	Giacomo della Porta, façade, Il Gesù, Rome *(189)*	
			1600
El Greco, *Grand Inquisitor Don Fernando Niño de Guevara; Toledo (224, 225)*			

PART FIVE

The Baroque

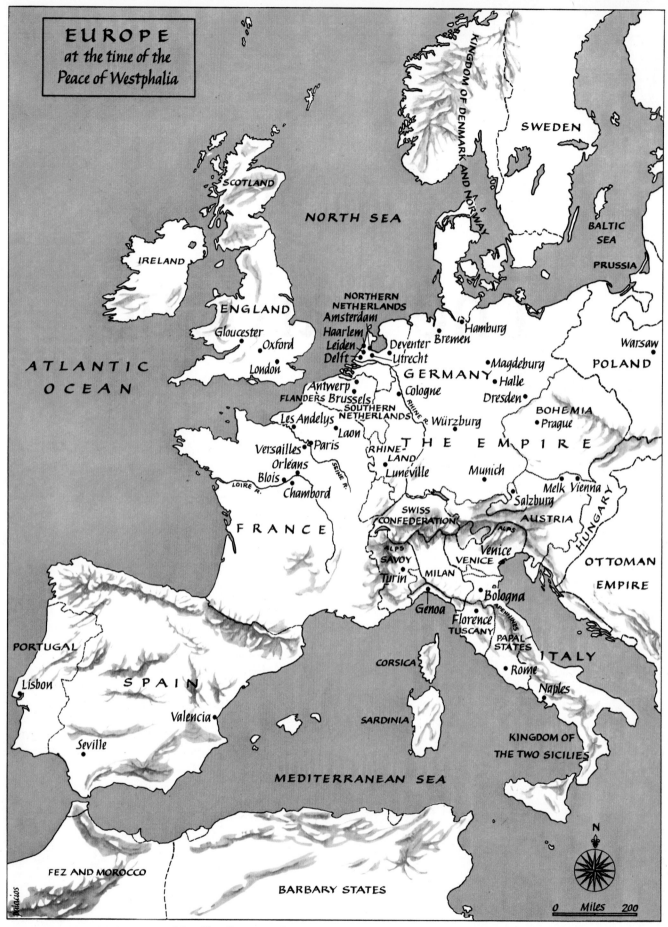

MAP 10. *Europe at the Time of the Peace of Westphalia*

The word *Baroque* is often claimed to derive from the Portuguese word *barocco*, of unknown origin, meaning *irregular* or *rough*, used specifically to describe pearls of distorted shape. As originally applied to art the term conveyed the contempt felt by Neoclassicists of the late eighteenth and early nineteenth centuries for what seemed to them exaggerated and perverse in the art of the preceding period. For about the last hundred years or so, the term, shorn like *Gothic* of any derogatory meaning, has been in general use to designate the architecture, painting, and sculpture of western Europe and the Americas from about 1600 to 1750 or so. It is arguable whether so brief a time span truly deserves to be considered an era in itself. In the sense that ancient art and medieval art constitute separate eras, each subsuming a wide variety of periods, the Baroque certainly does not. But then neither does the Renaissance. A completely consistent chronological division would place the Renaissance, the Baroque, and all periods since under the all-inclusive designation of *Modern*. On the other hand, the differences between the arts discussed in Part Four and those we are about to consider are so great that the term *Renaissance* cannot reasonably be stretched to cover them both. The Baroque period had its own problems and its own goals, and it makes sense, therefore, to preface our study of this age's arts with a consideration of the general situation in which European man found himself about the year 1600.

By the end of the sixteenth century, the "discovery of the world and of man" had wrought fundamental changes in man's views of himself, of society, and of the Christian religion. The frontiers of the world known to Europeans had been extended during the Renaissance voyages of discovery to include much of the Americas, Asia, and Africa. European authority held sway throughout many of the newly discovered regions. The Copernican view of the universe was empirically con-

firmed after Galileo's invention of the telescope in 1609, which extended man's intellectual frontiers into outer space. In spite of his trial by the Inquisition in 1633, it was only a matter of time before the Aristotelian system, which maintained that the earth was the center of the universe, would collapse.

The religious divisions of western Europe were wellnigh complete. After the religious persecutions, expulsions, and wars of the sixteenth century were over, Spain, Portugal, France, Italy, and the provinces that today form Belgium remained Roman Catholic. England, Scotland, Scandinavia, the Swiss Confederation, and most of the area comprising modern Holland were Protestant. In spite of continuing warfare between Holland and Spain, there was little serious possibility of change in either religious camp. In Central Europe wars, religious in origin but eventually political as well, raged until the Peace of Westphalia in 1648, which left, by and large, the Rhineland, Austria, Bohemia, Hungary, and Poland Catholic, and North Germany Protestant. Along with the victory of Catholicism in the Mediterranean and in Central Europe, and of Protestantism in the North, came the triumph of absolutism almost everywhere. With the exceptions of Holland, Venice, Genoa, and Switzerland, medieval and Renaissance republics were dead.

After the artistic experiments and achievements of the Renaissance, no problems of representation or composition offered any serious difficulties to a diligent and properly trained artist. Academies were established in major European centers, and instruction in them and in artists' studios was thorough. The wide differences in national styles can no longer be explained, therefore, in terms of stages in the conquest of reality or of changes in technical procedures, but in the light of the demands made by patrons, religious or secular, actual or potential, and local traditions. Architecture, sculpture, and painting of a dramatic nature were powerful tools in the hands of religious and secular absolutism, and flourished in the service of the Catholic Church and of Catholic monarchies. Protestant countries, on the other hand, had just completed an appalling destruction of religious images, and permitted no resurgence of them in their whitewashed church interiors. Even palace and villa architecture under Protestant monarchies was notably restrained, in England, for example, relying strongly on Italian Renaissance models, especially Palladio, and only occasionally accepting elements from contemporary Continental currents. With rare exceptions, in Protestant countries painters were thrown on the open market, and they competed for the attention of prosperous middle-class buyers with scenes drawn from daily life, history, or the Bible, intended for homes rather than churches.

It may well be asked what it is that draws together these widely varying styles and tendencies. The key word is probably allegiance. The religious division of Europe had placed a new emphasis on the inner life of the individual, for which both Catholicism and the various Protestant sects competed. The religious wars of the sixteenth century, still ablaze in Central Europe in the first half of the seventeenth, provided an object lesson in the dangers of dissent. In Catholic countries the punitive force of the Inquisition was supplemented by a more positive campaign to enlist and intensify conviction for which there had been less need in the Middle Ages, when occasional serious heresy could be rapidly extirpated and a general unity of Catholic faith in the West was more or less taken for granted. The decorations, the lighting, and even the shapes of Baroque churches and palaces were calculated for maximal emotional effect. Although religious outpourings on the order of those of the Counter-Reformation mystics were a thing of the past, artists in every sphere turned toward these great figures of the recent past and contrived, so to speak, rationally planned stage sets for the experience of the irrational, so that the worshiper could achieve at least the illusion of that union with the Divine that had been granted to Saint Theresa, Saint John of the Cross, and other Catholic and also Protestant mystics of the sixteenth century.

Rather than the miracles of saints (as in medieval and Renaissance art), their martyrdoms, transformed to heavenly bliss at the very moment of agonized death, and their ecstasies, interpreted as an earthly form of martyrdom, were the themes set before Baroque artists. The visual settings for divine-right monarchy in palaces, decorations, and festivals and in costumes, furniture, and carriages were conceived in the same climactic pattern. In Calvinist Holland, without either ecclesiastical or monarchical demand for art, the traditionally reverent Netherlandish approach to the most minute aspects of visual reality gave way to a climactic experience of natural forms, spaces, colors, and lights and the relationship between the observer and the literary or portrait subject in order to produce a strong, if muted, emotional experience. What unites the most disparate phases of the Baroque in European countries, therefore, is a common pattern of experience shared at all social levels by Catholic and Protestant alike.

1

The Seventeenth Century
in Italy

By common consent the transformation from late Mannerism to Baroque took place in Rome toward the end of the sixteenth century, where the ground had already been prepared by the late architecture of Michelangelo and his pupils, especially in the new spaces and forms of Saint Peter's and Il Gesù (see figs. 184, 189). In the last decade of the century the presence of an extraordinary group of North Italian painters in Rome heralded the beginning of the new era and its expression in two strongly divergent styles. Within twenty years forms and images established in Rome began to be diffused throughout western Europe, carrying the message of a humanity at ease with both its Christian religion and its Classical heritage and conscious of newly revealed depths of inner experience.

THE CARRACCI. The pioneers of Baroque monumental painting in Rome were the brothers Agostino and Annibale Carracci and their cousin Ludovico, all from Bologna, a city to the north of Florence across the Apennines with a long artistic tradition and a heritage of Renaissance masterpieces from other schools. Bologna was the northernmost city of the Papal States and had a direct cultural connection with the Eternal City. Annibale (1560–1609) was historically the most important artist of the Carracci family, and artistically the most gifted. In Bologna in the 1580s all three Carracci had been instrumental in the formation of a new kind of renaissance—not a revival of Classical antiquity nor a discovery of the world and of man (because the Renaissance had already achieved both), but a revival of the Renaissance itself after a long Mannerist interlude. The Carracci aimed at a synthesis of the vigor and majesty of Michelangelo, the harmony and grace of Raphael, and the color of Titian, less through direct imitation of these High Renaissance artists than through emulation of their method of idealizing nature. It will hardly be surprising to learn that this academic attempt at the revival

in the 1580s of the situation prevailing in 1510 was connected with the Academy of Bologna, in whose life the Carracci played an important part.

The first major undertaking of Baroque painting in Rome was the gallery (or formal reception hall) of the Palazzo Farnese, painted almost entirely by Annibale Carracci in 1597–1600 (the vault) and 1603–4 (the side walls). The frescoes were commissioned by Cardinal Odoardo Farnese, son of Alessandro Farnese, late duke of Parma, and great-great-grandson of Paul III, the Farnese pope painted by Titian (see fig. 166). The ceiling frescoes (colorplate 36) adopted from the Sistine Ceiling (see colorplate 23) such ideas as large scenes, small scenes, apparently real seated nudes, and simulated marble architecture and both marble and bronze sculpture. But these were organized according to a new principle in the illusionistic tradition of Mantegna (see colorplate 13) and Correggio (see fig. 178). The simulated architecture applied to the barrel vault (and at times piercing it) is "sustained" by the simulated sculptural caryatids that, along with the "real" youths, flank pictures incorporated into the structure. Four additional paintings with gilded frames, one at each end of the vault and one at each side, are made to look as if they had been applied later by their overlapping of the architecture and their covering up of parts of the medallions. The complex layer of forms and illusions comes to a climax in the central scene.

A recent study has shown that the subject matter, the Loves of the Gods, on the face of it incompatible with the ecclesiastical status of the patron, is by no means so frivolous as the decorations of the Palace of Fontainebleau (see fig. 209) and veils a deeper, Christian meaning that accounts for the complex organization and for the central climax. In summary, the four smaller lateral scenes represent incidents in which the loves of gods for mortals were accepted, the two horizontal framed pictures those in which mortals refused, the two end ones of the lunettes (of which only one may be seen in the

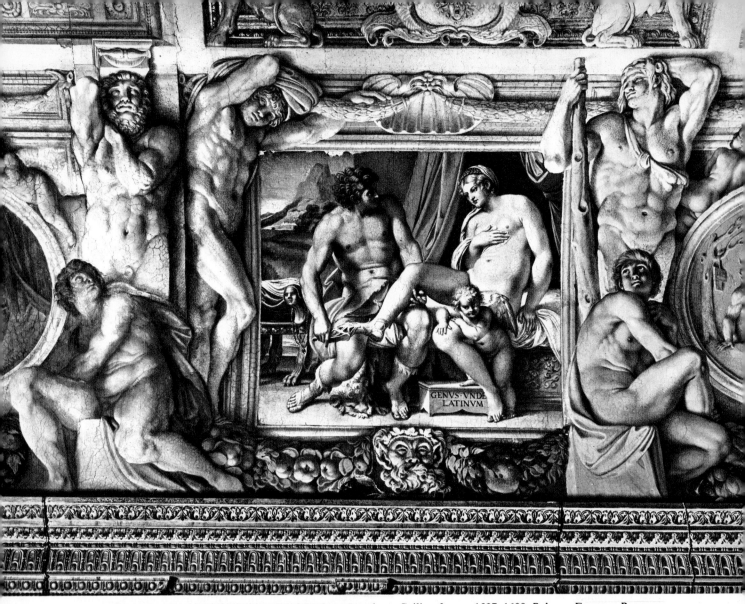

226. ANNIBALE CARRACCI. *Venus and Anchises* (portion). Ceiling fresco. 1597–1600. Palazzo Farnese, Rome

photograph) the disastrous love of the Cyclops Poly-phemus for the nymph Galatea, and the central panel the Triumph of Bacchus and Ariadne. This central scene is flanked by Mercury and Paris and by Pan and Selene. It, with its buoyant composition in which the chariots of the god and the mortal he redeemed from despair are borne along in splendid procession, accompanied by deities and Loves and victorious over all obstacles, explains the extraneous framed pictures and justifies the four unframed lateral scenes. The entire complex structure of eleven scenes thus symbolizes the Triumph of Divine Love, although in physical form. After the Mannerist interlude of prudery and prurience, it is typical of the new Baroque attitude that a cardinal could commission a Christian interpretation of ancient erotic myths. Even more, it is essential for our understanding of the Baroque that divine love, conceived as the principle at the heart of the universe, should be the motive power that draws together all the elements of the ceiling and resolves all conflicts in an unforeseeable act of redemption.

At the time it was painted, the Farnese Gallery was widely proclaimed as a worthy sequel to the Sistine Ceiling and the Stanze of Raphael. While present-day criticism would hardly place the work at that exalted level, it is a superb creation, whose full beauty of form and color can be experienced only by the observer in the actual room. Seventeenth-century viewers were delighted by the coloring of the shadows, which eliminated black, and they testified to their difficulty in distinguishing reality from representation. No wonder, because "real" and "sculptured" figures are expertly foreshortened, and the light, coming from windows along one side of the room, casts their shadows onto the surrounding elements. The love of Anchises for Venus, whom he is in the last stages of disrobing, is typical of the directness of the representations and the physical abundance of the figures (fig. 226). In the experience of the entire work the weight of the figures is carried easily along by the energy and gay coloring of the whole. Both the substance and the drive of the Farnese Gallery proved definitive for most other ceiling compositions of the seventeenth century, and for Baroque monumental painting in general, especially the work of Peter Paul Rubens (see Chapter 4), profoundly influenced by Annibale's style.

In addition to the principles of ceiling painting, Annibale established a new type of landscape with figures, in such works as his *Landscape with the Flight into Egypt*, of about 1603–4 (fig. 227). Although the tiny scale of the sacred figures in relation to the vastness of the landscape may recall Patinir (see fig. 219), there are two important differences. First, the high point of view has been abandoned so that the figures are on a level with the observer, and second, the landscape is no longer fantastic but based

on a real one, in this case the actual surroundings of Rome—the Tiber, a fortified village, and the distant Alban Hills. The landscape in this painting, as almost always in the seventeenth century, was derived from studies made outdoors, but constructed in the studio.

OTHER BOLOGNESE PAINTERS IN ROME. A conservative solution to the problem of ceiling painting was offered by GUIDO RENI (1575–1642), whose *Aurora* (fig. 228), painted in 1613 for the ceiling of a garden house behind the Palazzo Rospigliosi, could as easily have been

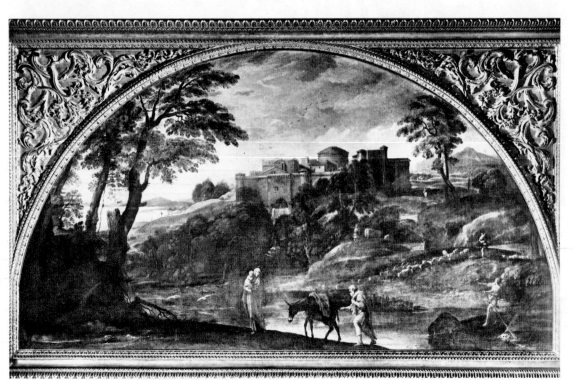

227. ANNIBALE CARRACCI. *Landscape with the Flight into Egypt.* c. 1603. Oil on canvas, 48¼ x 98½". Galleria Doria Pamphili, Rome

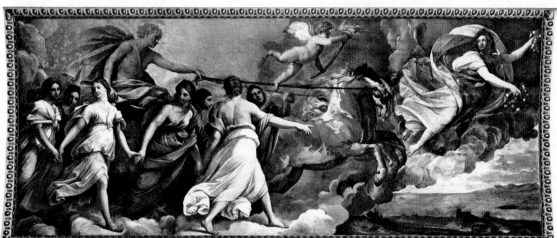

228. GUIDO RENI. *Aurora.* Ceiling fresco. 1613. Casino Rospigliosi, Rome

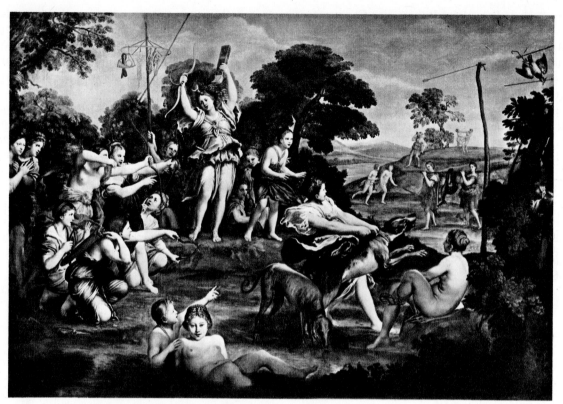

229. DOMENICHINO. *The Hunt of Diana.* c. 1615. Oil on canvas, 7′4⅝″ x 10′6″. Galleria Borghese, Rome

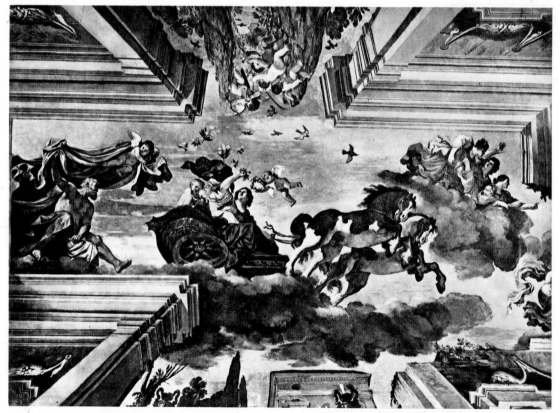

230. GUERCINO. *Aurora.* Ceiling fresco. 1621–23. Casino Ludovisi, Rome

designed for a wall. As the chariot of Apollo, radiant with light, surrounded by dancing Hours, preceded by Cupid with a torch and by Aurora, goddess of the dawn, rolls away the clouds of night over the distant landscape, one can hardly help thinking of Raphael. While in no sense a copy, the Cupid is based on the three winged Loves in the *Galatea* (see fig. 150), and Aurora herself is close to the angels at the upper left in the *Disputa* (see fig. 146); the spiral construction of all the figures is obviously Raphaelesque. But the freshness and luminosity of the picture are new, and so indeed is its subject. The swift pursuit of darkness, the moment of revelation in light, were vital for Baroque subjects and for Baroque style.

Equally conservative is the work of another Bolognese master in Rome, Domenico Zampieri (1581–1641), called DOMENICHINO. His delightful *The Hunt of Diana*, c. 1615 (fig. 229), with its parade of lovely figures, draped and nude, is a slightly unstable combination of Raphael and Titian, but the harmonious way in which the figures are grouped in a Carraccesque landscape leads the way to the Classical figural compositions of Poussin (see Chapter 2).

The final Bolognese painter of the Early Baroque, Giovanni Francesco Barbieri (1591–1666), called GUERCINO because of his squint, was the first to apply the lessons of Mantegna, Correggio, and Annibale Carracci to an illusionistic ceiling fresco seen from a single point of view. In his *Aurora* (fig. 230), painted in 1621 for the garden house of the Villa Ludovisi, Guercino carries the actual architecture of the modest-sized room upward into the vault so accurately that his prank of ruining it (at the lower right in the illustration) is alarmingly effective. The dark clouds still shadow the Villa Ludovisi and its gardens (which are right outside the actual room); above them rolls Aurora's chariot drawn by piebald horses seen from below. Birds soar beyond it, a Cupid holds a crown of roses over Aurora's head, and she drops blooming oleander twigs on the spectators below. Although the horses and chariot make a convincing impression as they thunder overhead, Guercino was obliged to place them at one side and to tilt them slightly so they would not seem grotesquely foreshortened. The opulence and grace of his style, the rich soft coloring, and the strong light-and-dark contrasts place him in a more naturalistic current than either the Carracci, Reni, or Domenichino.

CARAVAGGIO. The one real giant of seventeenth-century painting in Italy is Michelangelo Merisi (1573–1610), called Caravaggio after his native town in Lombardy. After studying with an obscure local master, he arrived in Rome as a boy of about seventeen; he lived on the fringe of respectable society, his life being marked by violence and disaster. A lifelong rebel against convention, Caravaggio is the first artist on record who went out of his way to shock conventional people, chiefly by representing religious scenes in terms of daily life, no matter how seamy. He was in chronic trouble with

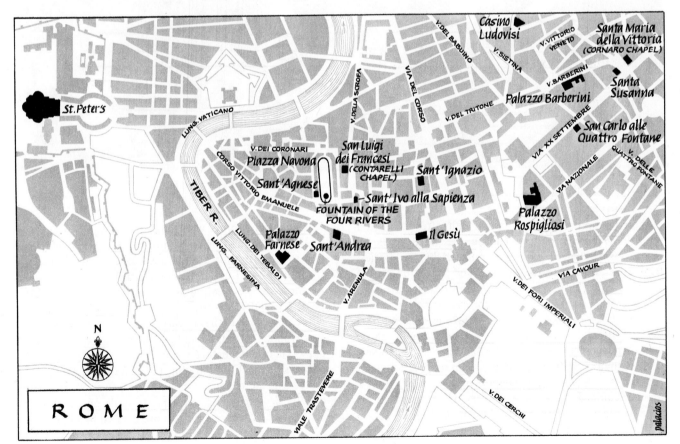

MAP 11. *Rome*

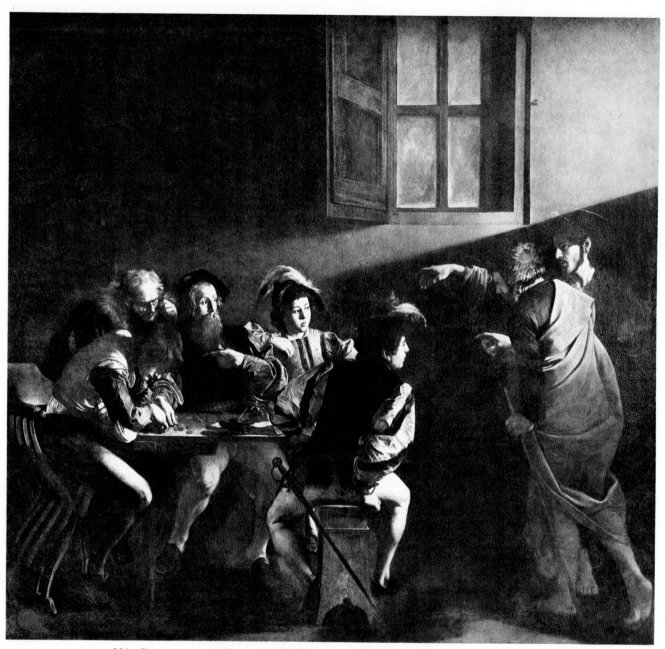

231. CARAVAGGIO. *Calling of Saint Matthew.* c. 1599–1600. Oil on canvas, 11'1" x 11'5"
Contarelli Chapel, S. Luigi dei Francesi, Rome

authority, and had to flee Rome in 1606 after he killed a man in a tennis match. During the next years he wandered around, like Orestes pursued by the Furies, from Naples to Palermo, Messina, and Malta; he died of malaria in his thirty-seventh year on his return journey to Rome, with a papal pardon in sight. Nevertheless, it is to this unruly genius that we must look for the style that was to revolutionize European art, less on account of its visual naturalism—the Netherlanders had already carried that as far as it could go—than its psychological realism, which plumbed the depths of human feeling in a manner comparable in some respects to the insights of his slightly older contemporary, William Shakespeare.

The young man came to the attention of the powerful Cardinal del Monte, who obtained for him, probably in 1597, the commission to paint three pictures of Matthew and scenes from his life for the Contarelli Chapel in the Church of San Luigi dei Francesi in Rome. The greatest of these is the *Calling of Saint Matthew* (fig. 231), painted about 1599–1600, an event often represented but never in this soul-stirring way. The background is a wall in a Roman tavern; a window, whose panes are the oiled paper customary before the universal use of glass, is the only visible background object. The publican Matthew is seated "at the receipt of custom" (Matt. 9: 9) with three gaudily dressed youths at a rough table on which coins are visible; figures and objects are painted in a hard, firm style that seems to deny the very existence of Venetian

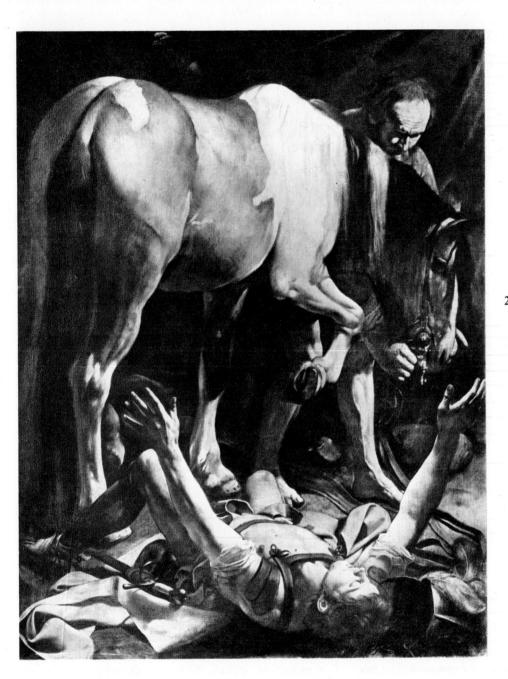

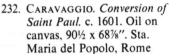
232. CARAVAGGIO. *Conversion of Saint Paul.* c. 1601. Oil on canvas, 90½ x 68⅞". Sta. Maria del Popolo, Rome

colorism. Suddenly, Christ appears at the right, saying, "Follow me." His figure almost hidden by that of Peter, Christ shows only his face and his right hand, illuminated by a strong light from an undefined source at the upper right.

Despite his oft-expressed contempt for Renaissance masters, Caravaggio never forgot that he shared a common Christian name with Michelangelo Buonarroti, from whom he often quoted—in a vernacular translation. Christ points along the beam of light with a strikingly real hand whose gesture repeats that of God the Father in the *Creation of Adam* (see fig. 138). Matthew points to his own breast as if to say, "Who, me?" What happens in this apparently realistic scene is the essence of the com-

plex contemporary allegory of the Farnese Gallery: the triumph of divine love. With the same gesture by which God made Adam "a living soul" Christ instills a new soul in Matthew.

An even more drastic breakthrough is the *Conversion of Saint Paul*, painted about 1601 (fig. 232); a favorite subject during the Catholic Reformation, this scene was usually shown with a vision of Christ descending from heaven, surrounded by clouds and angels. Caravaggio represented the miracle as an interior event. Against a background of nowhere, as in Jan van Eyck's portraits (see fig. 103), Saul has fallen from his horse toward us, drastically foreshortened like the Christian slave in Tintoretto's *Saint Mark Freeing a Christian Slave* (see colorplate 28), his arms rigidly outstretched as in a catatonic trance, his eyes closed. He hears the words, "Saul, Saul, why persecutest thou me?" (Acts 9: 4), but his servant hears nothing and looks down at his master, unable to account for the light that shines all around and has blinded Saul. Climax reaches in this picture the stage of cataclysm, the more intense for the hardness with which everything is represented, down to the horseshoe, the rivets in Saul's armor, and the varicose veins in the servant's leg. A remarkably similar appeal to violent inner conversion beyond reason can be seen in a sonnet by John Donne, written little more than a decade after this painting was done:

> Batter my heart, three person'd God; for, you
> As yet but knocke, breathe, shine, and seeke to mend;
> That I may rise, and stand, o'erthrow mee, 'and bend
> Your force, to breake, blowe, burn and make me new.
> I, like an usurpt towne, to'another due,
> Labour to'admit you, but Oh, to no end,
> Reason your viceroy in mee, mee should defend,
> But is captiv'd, and proves weake or untrue.
> Yet dearely'I love you, 'and would be loved faine,
> But am betroth'd unto your enemie:
> Divorce mee, 'untie, or breake that knot againe,
> Take mee to you, imprison mee, for I
> Except you'enthrall mee, never shall be free,
> Nor ever chast, except you ravish mee.

Caravaggio's hard, clear image, which presents inner reality less to our senses than to our minds, is almost contemporary with El Greco's diametrically opposite attempt to paint the unpaintable in the *Resurrection* (see colorplate 35).

One of the last works the artist painted before he left Rome for good is the despairing personal confession, *David with the Head of Goliath* (colorplate 37). Like Michelangelo Buonarroti again (see fig. 182), Michelangelo Merisi shows himself in a tragic light—as the head of Goliath in the left hand of the almost wistful boy David, who holds in his right the naked sword of decapitation. Caravaggio's paintings were understandably condemned by Bolognese artists and critics in Rome, and some were even refused by the clergy. Nonetheless, a decade after his tragic death Caravaggio's everyday naturalism, his hard pictorial style, his intense light-and-dark contrasts, and above all his way of using these as devices to open the inner recesses of the soul had inspired a host of imitators in Rome, Naples, Spain, France, and the Netherlands. His revolutionary art must be considered a major factor in the formation of two of the greatest painters of the seventeenth century, Rembrandt (see Chapter 5) and Velázquez (see Chapter 6).

MADERNO. The first definitive steps in Early Baroque architecture were taken by Carlo Maderno (1556–1629),

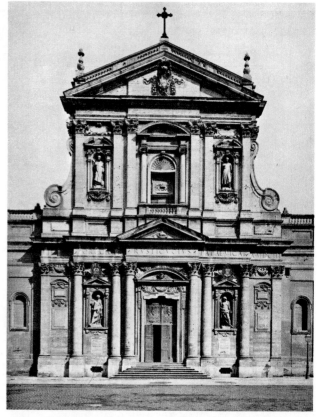

233. CARLO MADERNO. Façade, Sta. Susanna. 1597–1603. Rome

another Lombard working in Rome. His façade for the Church of Santa Susanna, 1597–1603 (fig. 233), must be considered the first true Baroque façade in Rome. Nonetheless, it recalls della Porta's façade for Il Gesù (see fig. 189) so insistently that for a moment we are hard put to define the differences. Both are two stories high, crowned by pediments; in both the lateral extension of the lower story forced by the side chapels is masked and joined to the central block by consoles; in both the movement of the orders toward the center is dramatized by an increase in projection. But the differences are crucial. The movement in Il Gesù seems tentative, halting, incomplete. At Santa Susanna it is definitive, rapid, and fulfilled. The lateral sections of the façade are set back slightly so that the entire central block emerges unified and dominant.

Columns are consistently restricted to the lower story of the central block and pilasters to the upper. Both columns and pilasters are single in the outer bays, double in the center. The clumsy device of a triangular pediment enclosed by an arched one is renounced in favor of a single gabled pediment so related to the crowning pediment of the façade that diagonals drawn through the outer corners of both converge on the worshiper about to cross the threshold. This, in turn, is approached by an easy flight of steps. The result is a steady crescendo of forms and spaces culminating in the central climax of the portal in the lower story and the window in the upper—the breakthrough into the building, which corresponds to the stylistic and ideological climax in the Farnese Gallery and the psychological rupture in Caravaggio. From this moment on the numerous architects building church façades in Rome—in the seventeenth century these architects transformed Rome into a predominantly Baroque city—outdid each other in always more dramatic effects, achieved by clustered columns, broken pediments, even pulsating wall surfaces (much in the manner of the architects of the French cathedrals competing for greater height in the late twelfth and early thirteenth centuries), but they concentrated all effects toward the central climax. Although we cannot here follow every stage of the competition, it will be instructive to look later at the culmination of this development in Borromini's quivering façade for San Carlo alle Quattro Fontane.

Maderno's work at Saint Peter's was not entirely fortunate. Pope Paul V (reigned 1605–21) commissioned him to extend the Greek-cross plan of Bramante and Michelangelo in order to cover all the consecrated ground once enclosed by the Constantinian basilica. From the exterior the effect is disastrous in that Michelangelo's dome is dwarfed by the nearer façade (fig. 234) and appears to descend behind it as one approaches; also the effect of a close-knit sculptural mass

he intended Saint Peter's to produce can now be experienced only from the Vatican Gardens. The width of Maderno's façade would have been acceptable enough if his projected campaniles over the lateral arches had ever been built. Unfortunately, a later pope commissioned Bernini to build higher towers, for which the foundations proved inadequate, and the one actually erected had to be torn down. Maderno was also trapped between his respect for Michelangelo and the ceremonial requirements imposed by the pope. He maintained the general lines of Michelangelo's façade but telescoped his projecting portico into mere engaged columns so as to provide the essential papal benediction loggia.

Although in the interior Maderno had to retain Bramante's giant order and barrel vault, he adapted these elements successfully to Baroque requirements, providing lateral views into side aisles, whose bays are divided by climactic broken arched pediments supported on richly veined columns. The splendid decoration of the gilded coffering in the vaults and arches is due to Maderno's Baroque taste (fig. 235), although the marble paneling and sculptures are the additions of Bernini (see below). Inevitably, the prolongation of the interior by a nave of three bays in a single giant order, on the models of Alberti's Sant'Andrea (see fig. 35) and Vignola's Il Gesù (see fig. 188), led to a curious falsification of scale.

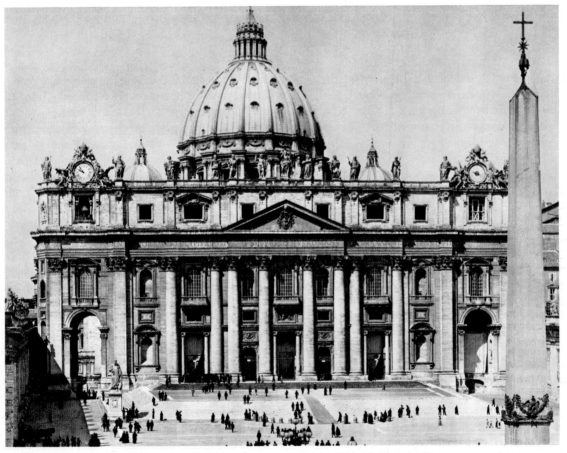

234. CARLO MADERNO. Façade. St. Peter's. 1606–12. Vatican, Rome

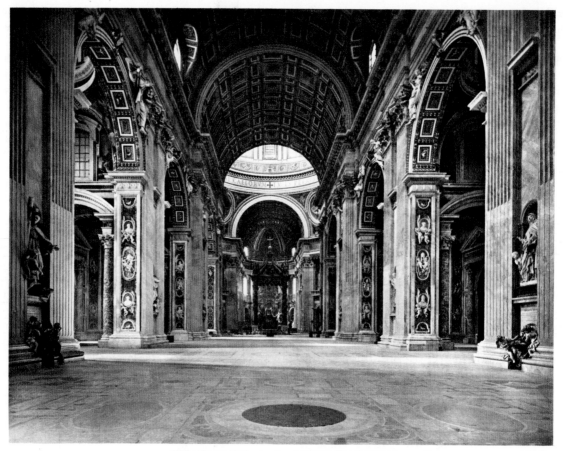

235. CARLO MADERNO. Interior, St. Peter's

One hardly notices the immense dimensions of the interior, which is vastly longer than any other Christian church, until one has been walking for a while in the direction of the papal altar without seeming to get much nearer.

BERNINI. The undisputed monarch of the Roman High Baroque, and one of the three or four most influential artists in Europe in the seventeenth century, was Gianlorenzo Bernini (1598–1680), architect and sculptor of genius, and also painter, dramatist, and composer. Born in Naples of a Florentine father and Neapolitan mother, he seems to have combined the intellectuality of the former with the passionate nature of the latter. Not only was he the first of the great Baroque sculptors, but also no sculptor until the early twentieth century was entirely able to escape his influence. A brilliant youthful work, the *David* of 1623 (fig. 236), done for Cardinal Scipione Borghese when the artist was twenty-five years old, shows the extraordinary transformation sculpture underwent at Bernini's hands in total opposition to the statues on the same subject by Donatello (see fig. 43) and Michelangelo (see fig. 133). Bernini has captured the precise moment in which the young prophet—now a full-grown youth of about seventeen or eighteen—is twisting vigorously, about to launch the stone. The pose is derived from Annibale Carracci's Polyphemus (see the lunette painting in colorplate 36), but carried out with complete devotion to physical and psychological reality. The left hand's tightening about the sling and stone produces sharp tensions in the muscles and veins of the arm, the toes of the right foot grip the rock for further purchase, and the expression, unprecedented even in Hellenistic sculpture, shows the boy biting his lips with the strain. A contemporary source tells how Bernini carved the face while studying his own in a mirror, sometimes held for him by Cardinal Maffeo Barberini, later Pope Urban VIII. The intensity of Bernini's personal identification with the subject can be felt in every detail of the vibrant body.

An even more transient moment of climactic action, perception, and feeling is represented by a companion work for Cardinal Borghese, the *Apollo and Daphne* (fig. 237), started the year before the *David* and finished two years after. Bernini has seized on the second in which the panting god, in hot pursuit of the chaste Daphne (Ovid, *Metamorphoses* I: 450–567), is foiled when she calls on her father, the river-god Peneus, for rescue and is transformed into a laurel tree. The toes of her left foot have already taken root, bark has shot up around her left leg and started to enclose her waist, her fingers and her hair are already turning into leaves and twigs, but the change is so sudden that the expression of terror has not yet left her face nor that of desire the Classical features of Apollo. The fidelity with which the softness of female flesh; the lithe body of Apollo; the textures of hair, bark, and leaves are rendered is no more dazzling than Bernini's craftsmanship in carving the scores of minute and slender projections from fragile marble. He has reached in his mid-twenties the height of his ability at pictorial sculpture—the negation of everything Michelangelo stood for, but the fulfillment of promises made by the daring Ghiberti in the *Gates of Paradise* (see figs. 47, 48)

and by Desiderio da Settignano in his marble reliefs (see fig. 70). Evanescent effects of melting texture, translucency, and sparkle so dissolve the group into the surrounding space that it is as if Bernini had been able to carve light and air as well as marble.

When his friend Cardinal Barberini ascended the Throne of Peter as Pope Urban VIII (reigned 1623–44), Bernini entered on the parade of commissions for Saint Peter's and its surroundings that was to occupy him on and off from youth to old age, and that was to determine more than any other single factor the relation of the immense structure to the individual pilgrim and tourist. His first undertaking was the baldachin or canopy of gilded

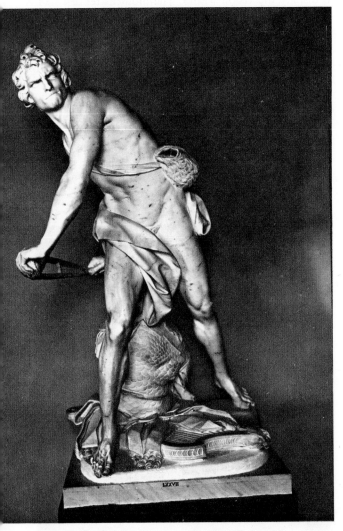

236. Gianlorenzo Bernini. *David.* 1623. Marble, height 67". Galleria Borghese, Rome

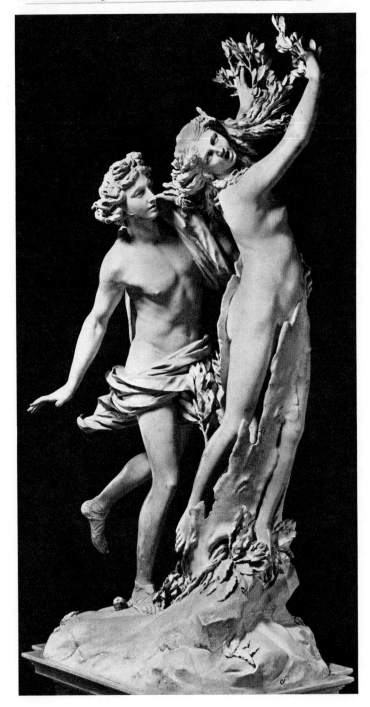

237. Gianlorenzo Bernini. *Apollo and Daphne.* 1622–24. Marble, height 96". Galleria Borghese, Rome

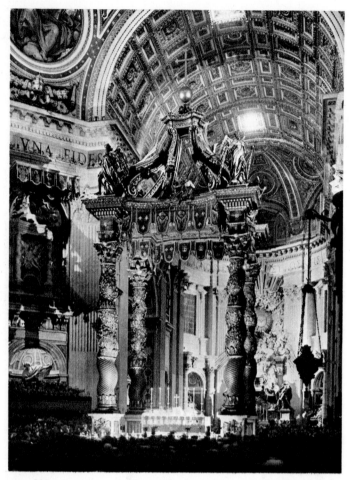

238. GIANLORENZO BERNINI. Baldachin. 1624–33. Gilded bronze, height c. 100'. St. Peter's, Vatican, Rome

tense religiosity and theatrical splendor that constitutes the Roman High Baroque is the Cornaro Chapel at Santa Maria della Vittoria, 1645–52, centered around the *Ecstasy of Saint Theresa* (fig. 239). The entire chapel was designed by Bernini as an "environment" (to use today's expression) for this sculptural group. The total effect eludes photography, and is best reproduced by an anonymous eighteenth-century painting (fig. 240). The barrel-vaulted ceiling is painted away in a burst of clouds and light, disclosing angels adoring the dove of the Holy Spirit, executed by a decorative painter from a sketch by Bernini. The altarpiece becomes an operatic stage, convex as if swelling toward us, the pediment breaking apart to display the vision within. The moment represented is the Transverberation of Saint Theresa, a vision in which she beheld a smiling youthful angel of surpassing beauty, who pierced her heart again and again with a golden arrow, producing a "pain so great that I screamed aloud; but simultaneously I felt such infinite sweetness that I wished the pain to last eternally." The saint hangs strengthless on marble clouds, her eyes closed, her mouth open, in an almost clinically accurate study of her rapture. (In this respect it should be remembered that Bernini not only attended Mass daily but also practiced

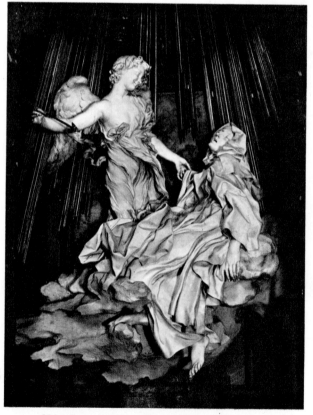

239. GIANLORENZO BERNINI. *Ecstasy of Saint Theresa.* 1645–52. Marble, height of group c. 11'6". Cornaro Chapel, Sta. Maria della Vittoria, Rome

bronze, nearly 100 feet high (fig. 238), erected between 1624 and 1633 over the high altar and just behind the opening in the floor above the tomb of Peter. Bernini took as his theme the eight spiral columns (probably Syrian but supposedly from Solomon's Temple), which Fouquet had seen in Old Saint Peter's (see fig. 118) and which Bernini later incorporated in the niches he carved from the four piers upholding Michelangelo's dome (see fig. 143). It was his brilliant idea to translate these small columns to gigantic scale and to set them in a kind of dance, still upholding their massive entablatures, as well as a simulated valance, angels, and the four consoles that form the open top, crowned by the orb and cross under the dome. The contrast of the columns with the piers of the dome, in fact, is the only element that helps the visitor grasp the true scale of Saint Peter's. Like their ancient prototypes, the columns are not only spiral but also divided into fluted segments and segments entwined by vinescrolls; golden bees, the Barberini emblem, displayed on the bronze valance, have alighted here and there among the leaves.

The culminating moment of that special blend of in-every day the *Spiritual Exercises* of Saint Ignatius of Loyola, intended to induce in the worshiper exact physical and visual counterparts of the experiences of Christ and the saints.)

There could hardly be a more compelling embodiment of the Baroque climactic experience of divine love than this group, in which Bernini has reinforced the concept with his usual virtuosity in the handling of textures of flesh, drapery, feathers, and hair. The background of richly veined marble is the same that clothes the actual interior of the chapel, thus placing the saint in our own space. The gilded bronze rays descending in clusters come apparently from a concealed window, identified with the breakthrough in the ceiling. The side walls are apparent theater boxes, in which kneel in marble relief members of the Cornaro family; unable because of the shallow space of the chapel to witness the Ecstasy, they nonetheless piously discuss its meaning.

Baroque Rome is a city of fountains, which were practical as well as ornamental, providing the water supply for the growing populace. Bernini's *Fountain of the Four Rivers* (fig. 241) was the most spectacular of its time. Pope Innocent X (reigned 1644–55) commissioned the

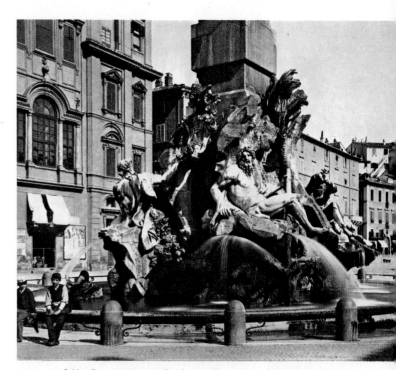

241. GIANLORENZO BERNINI. *Fountain of the Four Rivers.*
1648–51. Travertine and marble.
Piazza Navona, Rome

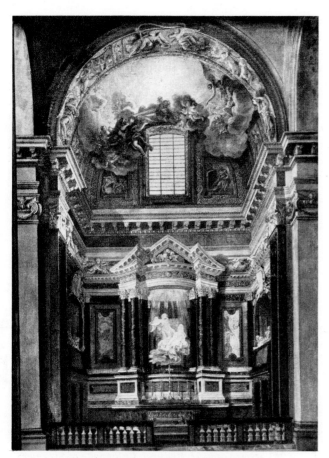

240. ANONYMOUS. *The Cornaro Chapel.*
Painting. 18th century. Staatliches
Museum, Schwerin, Germany

fountain in 1648 as part of the Baroque transformation of the Piazza Navona, once the site of the stadium of Domitian; his palace fronted the piazza, adjacent to the Church of Sant'Agnese (see fig. 249) by Bernini's rival, Borromini (see below). An actual Egyptian obelisk, one of several set up as focal points in the new city plan adopted in the late sixteenth century by Pope Sixtus V, stands on a mock mountain of rough travertine, made to look "natural" but carefully calculated for its effects of light and form by Bernini in preparatory drawings. The giant marble statues of Nile, Ganges (in the illustration), Danube, and Plate were designed by Bernini and carved by his pupils. The playful contrast of the muscular white figures with the rough gray rocks, vegetation, and animals is enriched by the water jets, all designed by Bernini to emerge in spouts, ribbons, or dribbles. If he could sculpture light, why not water?

Bernini's work for Saint Peter's included the complete sculptural program for the nave—the white marble cartouches and medallions against colored marble panels in the piers, and the figures dangling out of the spandrels (see fig. 235). The scale can be imagined by recalling that the child angels upholding the holy water stoups on either side are nine feet high. Designed in 1645–46, the work was carried out in the incredibly short period of 1647–48 by no fewer than thirty-nine sculptors and stonecutters under Bernini's supervision. Like all his work at Saint Peter's, these sculptures have the effect of enlivening what had become almost too large and impersonal a structure. His final creation in the interior was the colossal Cathedra Petri (fig. 242), of 1657–66, a reliquary

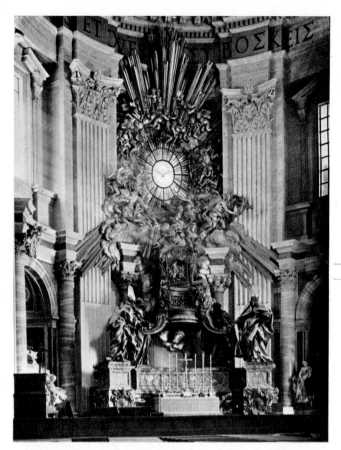

242. GIANLORENZO BERNINI. Cathedra Petri. 1657–66.
Marble, gilded bronze, stucco, and stained glass.
St. Peter's, Vatican, Rome

to enshrine what was believed to be the chair of Peter
(but has turned out on recent examination to be Carolingian!). The result is an incredible amalgam of marble,
bronze, gilded bronze, stucco, and stained glass between and overflowing Michelangelo's pilasters in the
apse. Again we have a rupture of the surrounding structure in that the vision of the dove of the Holy Spirit in
stained glass, with a real window behind it, surrounded
by clouds of gilded angels and golden rays, seems to have
burst the very architecture above the chair, carried on
clouds above four Fathers of the Church, two Latin
(Augustine, Ambrose) and two Greek (Athanasius and
John Chrysostom), who supported Roman Catholicism's
claim to universality.

In its climactic character, exuberance of forms, textures, colors, and materials, and theatrical brilliance of
effect, the Cathedra Petri would seem to have spelled the
ultimate in Bernini's long career. The final surprise,
therefore, is the austere simplicity of his designs of 1656,
carried out over many years, for the enclosure of the
whole piazza in front of Saint Peter's by means of two
facing exedrae of Tuscan columns, each four columns in
depth, supporting an unbroken entablature, surmounted
by a statue above each column of the inner row (fig. 243).
The oval form of the piazza is based on a central obelisk
as its focus; two magnificent fountains flank it left and

right. The dynamism of the design lies in the power of its
movement; it suggests two gigantic arms outstretched to
embrace the approaching pilgrim. The intended climactic
effect of this experience of space and light, intense when
one emerged into the piazza from the narrow dark adjacent streets, was unfortunately lost when the area
between the piazza and the Tiber was modernized in the
1930s. Nonetheless, as one moves through the tall colonnades, apparently in motion, the experience of form and
space, constantly changing as if in obedience to un-
alterable law, is one of the most compelling of any
Baroque design, surpassing even the effect of the imperial
Roman forums, which must have inspired Bernini.

Sculptors and architects trained by Bernini carried the
principles of his style throughout Italy and into Northern
Europe. In 1665 he was called to France by Louis XIV,
the most powerful European monarch of the age, for
whose ambitions his grandiose ideas would seem to have
been especially appropriate. That his projects for the
completion of the Louvre were not accepted, and that his
one statue of the king was altered to represent a figure
from Roman history and banished to a remote spot in the
park at Versailles, tell us much about the fundamental
differences between Italian and French attitudes toward
the Baroque style.

BORROMINI. A strong countercurrent to Bernini in High
Baroque Rome was offered by the at once capricious and
austere architecture of Francesco Borromini (1599–
1667), a solitary genius born at Bissone, on Lake

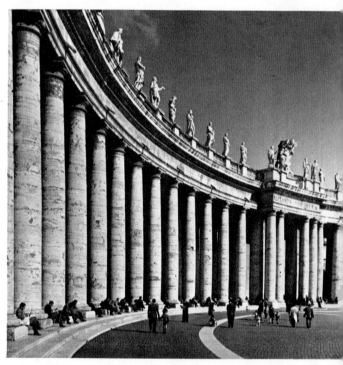

243. GIANLORENZO BERNINI. Colonnade of St. Peter's.
Begun 1656

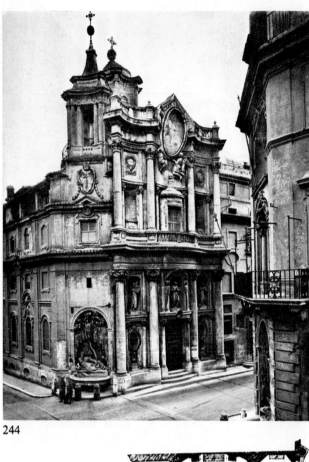

244

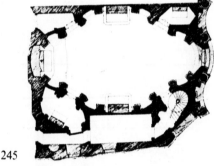

245

244. Francesco Borromini. Façade. S. Carlo alle Quattro Fontane. 1665–67. Rome

245. Francesco Borromini. Plan of S. Carlo alle Quattro Fontane. 1638–41

246. Francesco Borromini. Interior, S. Carlo alle Quattro Fontane

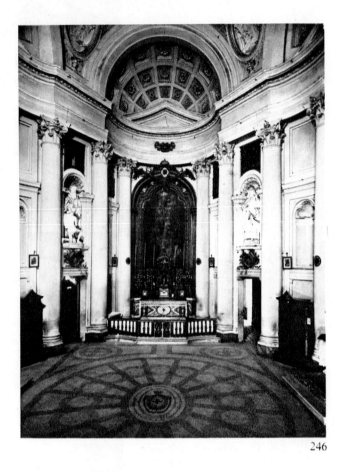

246

Lugano, whose brooding, introspective nature was the very opposite of that of the easygoing, expansive Bernini, and whose career ended in suicide. Rather than the splendid accompaniments of richly veined marbles and decorations in stucco and painting as often as not designed by others, in which Bernini reveled, the essentially linear and spatial interiors of Borromini resisted encroachments from sculpture or painting, and needed only occasional accents of gold against white plaster. Bernini sketched out his projects with sovereign ease, and left the details to an army of assistants; Borromini instead worked obsessively on the designs for the tiniest object or decorative motive, rejecting many before approving his final choice with the word *questo* ("this one") on his careful drawings, and supervised with a craftsman's care the execution of his designs.

The Baroque preoccupation with the organization of colossal spaces was matched by its concern for the very small, finding expression in the building of oratories; it is not beside the point that the seventeenth century saw the invention not only of the telescope but also of the microscope. Borromini's plan for the small monastic Church of San Carlo alle Quattro Fontane, 1638–41 (figs. 244, 245), was immediately and widely emulated throughout Catholic Europe, probably because it touched the very fountainhead of Baroque individual piety. The shape was based, after characteristically long geometrical experimentation, on intersecting ellipses dissolving into each other. Standing inside the church (fig. 246), however, one feels the effect is that of a central-plan structure, in Byzantine or Renaissance tradition, but one made of soft and elastic materials, in fact alive and pulsating; if it were compressed from side to side and lengthened along its axis, the viewer feels it could reverse itself in the next pulsation, on the principle of a beating heart. To emphasize the systolic and diastolic motion of

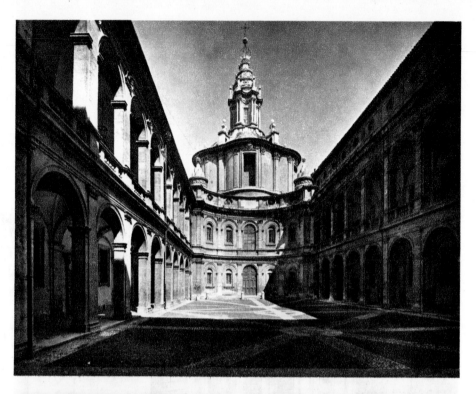

247. FRANCESCO BORROMINI.
Exterior, Sant'Ivo della
Sapienza. 1642–60. Rome

248. FRANCESCO BORROMINI.
Interior of dome, Sant'Ivo
della Sapienza

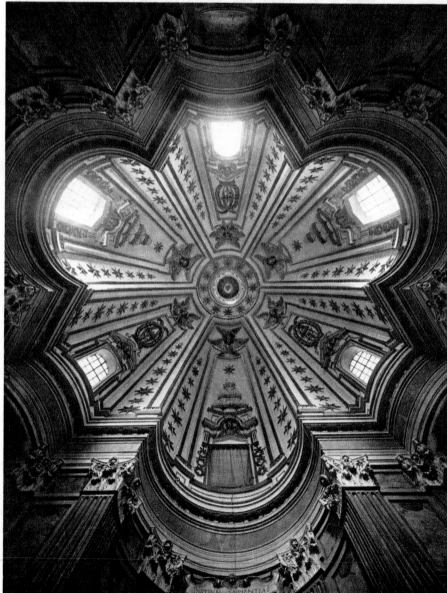

the components, even the Corinthian capitals were so designed that the volutes of one turn over and out, the next under and in. The dynamic plan was intended to arouse a state of instability preparing the worshiper for the Baroque goal of divine union in ecstatic meditation.

The brilliance of Borromini's imagination is manifest on a considerably larger scale in his spectacular Church of Sant'Ivo, erected between 1642–60 (fig. 247), set at the end of the courtyard of the Sapienza (later the University of Rome), which had been designed in the late sixteenth century by della Porta. The ornamentation of the exterior and interior of the church was carried out later during the pontificate of Alexander VII (reigned 1655–67), a member of the Chigi family, whose arms, an eight-pointed star shining from the top of a mountain, appear throughout. Borromini wisely continued della Porta's Late Renaissance arcades of superimposed Doric and Ionic orders, but made the court terminate in a shallow exedra, actually a concave façade, later surmounted at each end by the Chigi mountain and star. Above towers the six-lobed drum of a fantastic dome, surmounted by a step-pyramid whose lobes are separated by concave buttresses terminating in volutes and balls. The lantern obviously suggests in its concave faces the apse of the Temple of Venus at Baalbek, whose design had been known in Europe as early as the sixteenth century. Unconventional even in his choice of sources, Borromini may have derived his spiral spire from the great minaret at Samarra; it was to be repeated again and again throughout Europe as far north as Copenhagen. The work culminates in an open construction of forged iron, a dainty linear motive carrying aloft the orb of power and the Cross. The concave and convex movements work against one another like motives in the polyphony of Bach, with whose music Borromini's architecture has often been compared; the whole design has the effect of a great organ fugue.

Not even the complexity of the exterior quite prepares us for the exquisite mathematical logic of the interior. The plan is an equilateral triangle overlapping a trefoil so that the intersections establish the points of a regular hexagon. The points of the triangle, in turn, are cut into concave arcs, the radius of each of which is equal to that of the adjacent sides. This plan, perfectly preserved in the crowning cornice, governs the convexities and concavities of the pulsating walls and their giant Corinthian order like a perfectly executed rhythmic dance figure. The fantastic shapes blend smoothly together at the apex of the dome to meet in a circle (fig. 248). Originally, the only color on the white walls, dome, and pilasters (the imitation marble is nineteenth-century repaint) was the gold of the ornamentation, the eight Chigi stars on each rib and above the windows the Chigi mountain decorated with the three crowns of the papacy, alternating with Borromini's favorite motive of interlaced palms.

In one lordly work, the design for the Church of Sant'Agnese in Piazza Navona (figs. 249, 250), where Bernini's *Fountain of the Four Rivers* (see fig. 241) was nearing completion, Borromini was able to carry his

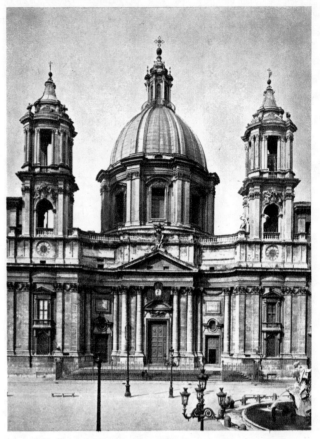

249. FRANCESCO BORROMINI. Façade, Sant'Agnese in Piazza Navona. 1653–66. Rome

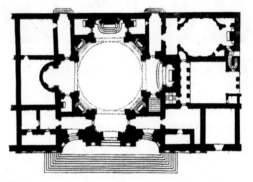

250. FRANCESCO BORROMINI. Plan of Sant'Agnese in Piazza Navona. Begun 1652

ideas into a major Roman square. His façade, on which he worked from 1653–66, was eventually completed by others. The heavy attic story and the conventional pediment are foreign to his artistic vocabulary, but the basic ideas and proportions are his. For the first time the relationship between central dome and flanking campaniles, which had been the dream of Maderno and Bernini at Saint Peter's, was actually realized. The concave façade working against the convex dome and the beautiful convex shape of the campaniles are typical of Borromini's thinking. The group was repeated innumerable times in Italy, in Central Europe (see fig. 336), in England (see fig. 282), and even in Mexico, finding

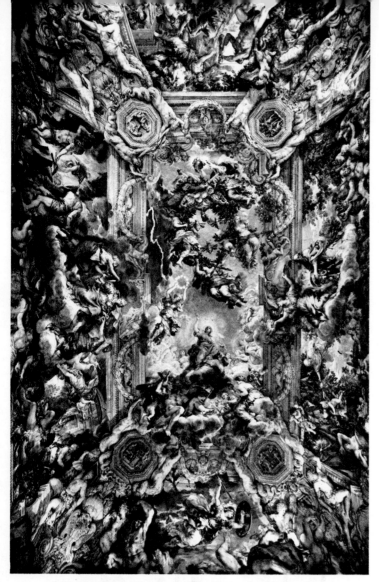

251. PIETRO DA CORTONA. *The Triumph of the Barberini.*
Ceiling fresco. 1633–39. Gran Salone, Palazzo
Barberini, Rome

universal acceptance possibly because in essence it is a
revival of the Gothic combination of two-tower façade
and crossing tower or lantern.

At his death Borromini was still at work on his most
subtle and complete expression, the façade added in
1665–67 to San Carlo alle Quattro Fontane, whose interior he had designed nearly twenty-five years before.
His favorite intertwined palms framing the windows on
either side of the portal may serve as symbols of the rich
interrelationships of concave and convex that continue
throughout the masses of the undulating structure and all
the minor elements. Had Bernini designed such a façade
he would have carried the image of San Carlo Borromeo
in the upper story effortlessly through the cornice—clouds, angels, and all; Borromini allows it merely
to lift the elastic balustrade and compress it, as if struggling for the release from this world that the architect
himself achieved, alas, only by his own hand.

ROMAN BAROQUE CEILING PAINTERS. In the wake of
Annibale Carracci and Guercino, many large Roman

Baroque palace and church interiors—with the notable
exception of Saint Peter's, too large for the purpose—were endowed with illusionistic ceiling paintings;
all of them take for granted what ordinary reason denies:
that with or without the support of an occasional cloud
human beings customarily fly through the air. Careful
study of perspective, and expert manipulation of
foreshortening, overlapping, and contrasts of light and
dark and color precalculate the effects so accurately as to
overwhelm both reason and experience, and turn the
most unrealistic of situations into believable reality. All
formalize the basic pattern of Baroque experience in the
establishment of a reasonably acceptable order, the violation of that order by forces also presented as real, and the
final deliverance in an upper luminary realm.

PIETRO BERRETTINI DA CORTONA (1596–1669), equally
gifted as architect and painter, was the first to carry
the idea beyond the point at which Guercino had left
it. In his ceiling for the Palazzo Barberini, 1633–39
(fig. 251), *The Triumph of the Barberini*, the vault is par-
titioned by an illusionistic structure of simulated architecture and sculpture, whose central panel is open to the
sky. In a mighty fountain figures from the side frescoes
rush over the border, thus seeming to move in the very
space of the room, and then ascend through the frame
into the heavens. The subject is an allegory of divine support for the papacy of Bernini's old friend Urban VIII.
At the apex of the ascending pyramid of cloud sits Divine
Providence, glowing with light, above Time, uselessly
brandishing his scythe, and the Three Fates. With a
generous gesture, Providence commands Immortality to
place a crown of twelve stars above the bees of the
Barberini arms, which fly by in heraldic formation, and
from other clouds allegorical figures weave a crown of
laurels (a reference to Urban's poetic accomplishments)
about the bees in space; still others uphold the papal keys
and tiara, into the latter of which the perspective permits
us to look. Like all Baroque effects, these must be experienced on the spot, but even in a reproduction the upward
rush toward, over, and past the architecture moves with
the force of a geyser.

An even more brilliant theatrical effect was achieved
by the Genoese painter Giovanni Battista Gaulli (1639–
1709), called BACICCIO. In collaboration with the sculptor ANTONIO RAGGI (1624–86), a pupil of Bernini, Vignola's severe barrel vault in Il Gesù was covered with rich
ornamentation in ribs and fields of gilded stucco between 1676 and 1679 (colorplate 38). Allegorical figures
modeled in white stucco, in violent motion, flank or sur-
mount the windows, and four white stucco angels uphold
the central frame. Into and through the frame float Jesuit
saints and angels on clouds painted on fields of plaster
laid on the vault outside the frame, so that we can follow
with precision their progress from the space of the church
across the frame and into Heaven above, drawn upward
by the dazzling brightness of the Sacred Name of Jesus,
made deliberately almost indistinguishable in white on

yellow as if we were looking into the sun. The same force throws downward with alarming speed evil spirits and vices, who pour pell-mell through the opening, and fall toward us as if to crash at any moment on the floor at our feet. To complete the illusion all the figures and clouds outside the frame cast shadows on the gilded ceiling.

The ne plus ultra of the illusionistic ceiling, reaching a phase properly termed Late Baroque, is represented by the allegory of the *Missionary Work of the Jesuits* (fig. 252), 1691–94, painted in the Church of Sant'Ignazio by a Jesuit lay brother, ANDREA POZZO (1642–1709) from Trent, author of an elaborate perspective treatise on how to design and execute complex ceiling projects. The entire barrel vault is painted away, and the architecture of the church carried up an additional story beyond the windows, in front of, through, and above which float allegorical figures. Between the windows appear the four continents, each labeled. America is at the upper left, wearing an Indian crown of red, white, and blue feathers, an unexpected feature in a seventeenth-century Roman painting. On clouds, leading Jesuit saints follow Christ, carrying the Cross over his shoulder, high in the heavens at the apex of the perspective. A moment's reflection will indicate that such perspective triumphs correspond to the actual perspective lines of the church only from a single

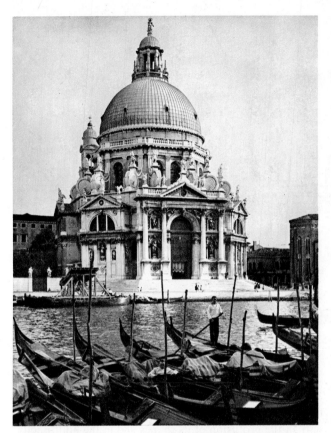

253. BALDASSARE LONGHENA. Exterior, Sta. Maria della Salute. 1631–87. Venice

254. BALDASSARE LONGHENA. Plan of Sta. Maria della Salute

point of view. Pozzo thought of that. In each of the churches in which he painted an illusionistic ceiling, he indicated with a square of white marble in the floor just where to stand to make the illusion "come right."

NORTH ITALIAN BAROQUE. Some strikingly independent Baroque developments occurred in Northern Italy. Although the Venetian school of painting was almost dormant in the seventeenth century, awaiting its triumphant reawakening in the eighteenth, Venice could boast one native architect of genius, BALDASSARE LONGHENA (1598–1682), whose masterpiece, Santa Maria della Salute (fig. 253), begun in 1631 and finished only in 1687 after the architect's death, is as inseparable a component of the central Venetian picture as San Marco, the Doges' Palace, the Library of San Marco, and San Giorgio Maggiore. The ideas we have followed throughout the Roman Baroque cannot help us here; Longhena makes no reference to them. His church was

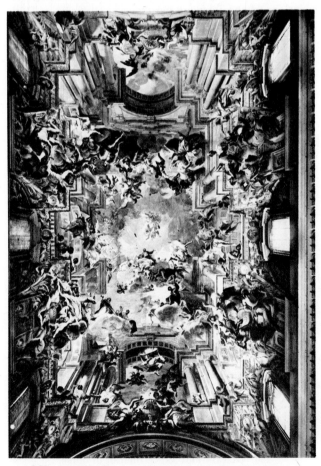

252. ANDREA POZZO. *Missionary Work of the Jesuits.* Ceiling fresco. 1691–94. Sant'Ignazio. Rome

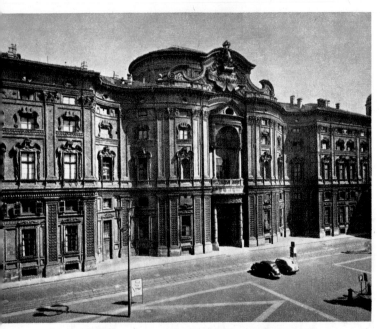

255. GUARINO GUARINI. Façade, Palazzo Carignano. 1679–92. Turin, Italy

based on local Byzantine and Renaissance traditions, and only in the profusion of its shapes and in the multiplicity of its inner views can it be said to be truly Baroque. The plan (fig. 254) is an octagon surrounded by an ambulatory, obviously related to the type that from San Vitale at Ravenna was carried into Germany in the Carolingian period. Each bay of the ambulatory frames a separate projecting rectangular chapel, illuminated by mullioned lunettes as in Roman baths. The main façade with its flight of steps spilling down to the Grand Canal is related to Roman triumphal-arch designs. The sixteen buttresses of the lofty dome rest on the outer walls of the chapels. All the basic elements, therefore, are structural, with a rational relationship between interior and exterior. But the buttresses are gratuitously prolonged into huge spirals, on which float rather than rest the podiums for sixteen statues. The relatively unobtrusive Doric pilasters of the drum recede behind these splendid ornaments. The almost white tone of the Istrian stone, used here as well as in so many Venetian buildings, and the pale gray of the lead covering of the dome make the structure appear to shimmer over the water like the large, irregular pearls that may have given the Baroque its name.

More startling buildings were erected in the western side of North Italy in Piedmont, where the Theatine priest GUARINO GUARINI (1624–83), from Modena, worked out a brilliant new architectural style under the influence of Borromini, whose early work he had seen in Rome, and of Islamic architecture, which he had studied in detail in Sicily and possibly in Spain, not to speak of Gothic, which he had encountered in France and praised glowingly in his treatise on architecture for its daring

lightness and fantasy (at almost the same moment as Molière's denunciation; see Vol. 1, page 368). He invented a new kind of brick architecture in the Palazzo Carignano at Turin, begun in 1679 (fig. 255); for all the Classical and Baroque derivations of its ornament (Borromini's palms flanking the windows) and its undulating façade, its linearity recalls Flamboyant architecture. Guarini's structural feeling for the material forbade him from masking it with stucco as was customary; every detail of the ornament, even the capitals, is of brick or terra-cotta.

His most amazing achievements were his domes. In the Chapel of the Holy Shroud, built between 1667 and 1694, which towers above the relatively modest Renaissance Cathedral of Turin, the interior is entirely paneled in a funereal dark-gray marble, almost black. The arches of the drum (fig. 256) support segmental arches bridging the intervening spaces, from keystone to keystone. The entire fabric of the dome, in fact, is made up of such arches superimposed in a staggered system to form an open web. Although the idea was derived from Islamic flying arches, such as those in the Great Mosque of Córdoba, the result is as light as any High Gothic structure; the top of the dome has been glazed to eliminate the outer surface entirely. The light filtering through the openings into the dark sanctuary communicates to it a mysterious effect beyond description, surely one of the most original inventions of the Baroque period.

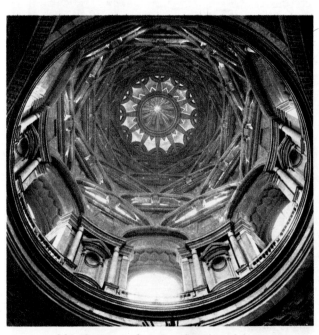

256. GUARINO GUARINI. Interior of dome, Chapel of the Holy Shroud. 1667–94. Turin, Italy

2

The Seventeenth Century in France

The religious wars of the sixteenth century left France in a prostrate economic and political condition, from which it was rescued by a succession of ambitious monarchs, each assisted by an able minister—Henry IV by Sully, Louis XIII by Richelieu, and Louis XIV by Colbert. The Baroque, in the rationalized version the French could accept, was first and foremost an emanation of growing absolutism. Deeply though the influence of Caravaggio and Bernini penetrated the French consciousness, in their age of power and glory the French rejected the excesses of Baroque enthusiasm and forged a temperate, elegant, classicizing style, which they are today reluctant to call Baroque. Its ties with Italy are so strong, however, that the term can hardly be avoided. Paradoxically enough, the most classicistic painter of the seventeenth century, indeed one of the most rational painters in history, Nicolas Poussin, preferred to live and work far from his native France, in Rome, the epicenter of the Baroque earthquake, to whose contemporary art he remained sublimely indifferent. During the seventy-two-year reign of Louis XIV in the second half of the seventeenth century and the early eighteenth, Paris began to replace Rome as the principal artistic center of Europe, a position it maintained almost unchallenged until World War II.

LA TOUR. Like most European countries, France experienced its wave of Caravaggio imitators, whom it would be useless to discuss here. The first important French painter of the seventeenth century, Georges de la Tour (1593–1652), highly regarded in his own time, soon slipped into oblivion, from which he has been rescued only in the present century. Born in Lorraine, then a duchy under the Empire, La Tour worked in Lunéville, the summer home of the dukes, and after the French conquest in 1638 continued to paint for the royal governors. He traveled in Italy and Holland, and although there is little direct influence of Caravaggio in his work, he was affected by the tide of psychological realism Caravaggio set in motion; in his hard and polished surfaces and in his strong light-and-dark contrasts, he even intensifies elements of Caravaggio's style. But his content could hardly be more different. While his works do indeed deal with religious subjects in terms of everyday life, La Tour's special quality is an intimate poetry engendered by night light. The *Newborn*, painted about 1630 (fig. 257), is in the tradition of Geertgen (see fig. 108) and of Correggio (see fig. 177), though the light comes from a candle held by the midwife rather than emanating from the Child. Yet La Tour allows us only to surmise that the picture represents Mary and Jesus. The quiet humanity breathing through all his paintings renders the question of identity almost irrelevant. The beginning of new life is a sacred moment; its mystery is silently shared by mother and midwife, and made manifest by the candle whose effect on the pure sculptural forms and surfaces, and on the glowing red garments, is exquisitely studied.

THE LE NAIN BROTHERS. Another recent rediscovery has been the art of the three Le Nain brothers—Antoine (1588–1648), Louis (1593–1648), and Mathieu (1607–77). Born in Laon, they lived and worked together in placid harmony in the Saint-Germain-des-Prés quarter of Paris, then a suburb and, as ever since, the home of artists. Louis seems to have been the most important artist of the three; as they never signed their first names to their pictures, the assignment of many works is still conjectural. All three were devoted to scenes of daily life, although Louis was apparently responsible for the most convincing of the peasant scenes. Nothing in his *The Cart* of 1641 (fig. 258) recalls the bumptiousness of Bruegel's peasantry; there could be nothing more ordinary than their activities, yet these people are treated as reverently as La Tour's religious subjects. They stand or sit calmly among the poultry and pigs of a farmyard, in groups composed with such dignity that the rough cart is endowed with monumental grandeur. The wheat, related to the

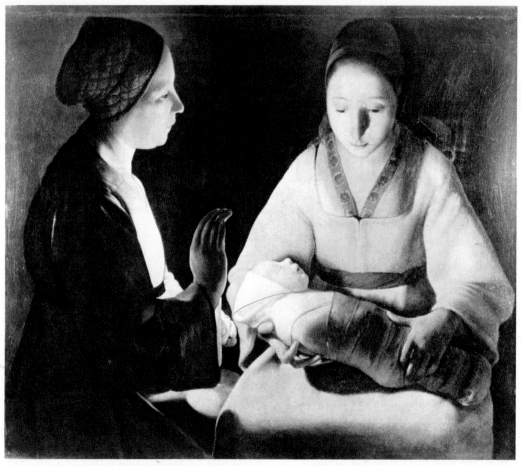

257. GEORGES DE LA TOUR. *Newborn.* c. 1630. Oil on canvas, 29⅞ x 35⅞″. Musée des Beaux-Arts, Rennes, France

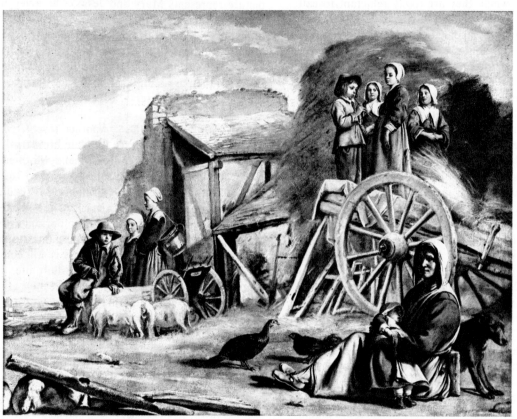

258. LOUIS LE NAIN. *The Cart.* 1641. Oil on canvas, 22 x 28¼″. The Louvre. Paris

Eucharist, and the brass pot to ritual cleansing as in Early Netherlandish paintings (see figs. 93, 97) may here retain a hint of their former symbolism. The richly painted colors—muted grays, tans, and browns in the clothing with an occasional touch of red, soft grays and blues in the pearly sky, grays and greens in the landscape—make this little masterpiece a worthy ancestor of Chardin in the eighteenth century (see fig. 332) and Corot in the nineteenth (see fig. 401).

POUSSIN. To his own period and to us today, Nicolas Poussin (1593/94–1665) is the very embodiment of the Classical spirit, not in the Renaissance sense of adapting ancient ideas to contemporary needs, but rather in an attempt to take contemporaries back to antiquity. His paintings are not only the product of great imagination and pictorial skill, but also of a discipline and control that grew firmer as the painter aged. Born near the small town of Les Andelys on the Seine in Normandy, Poussin went to Paris in late adolescence, and seems to have had access to the royal collection of paintings, where he was chiefly impressed by the works of Raphael and Titian, and to the royal library, where he studied engravings after Raphael. After two trips to Italy in attempts to reach Rome, he made it on his third try in 1624 and settled down for good, returning to France only for a single unsuccessful visit of eighteen months. Given his stubborn personality and his overriding Classical interests, it was unlikely that he would ever enjoy official success. The world of prelates, nobles, popes, and monarchs in which Bernini moved was not for him. Poussin made only one large altarpiece for Saint Peter's, and was dissatisfied with it.

An attempt by King Louis XIII to have Poussin work on ceiling paintings for the Long Gallery of the Louvre ran afoul of the artist's refusal to consider ceiling paintings different from those on walls, to adopt a low point of view (he maintained that people do not normally fly through the air), and to turn over the execution of vast projects to assistants. The latter objection effectively ruled out the customary colossal Baroque monumental commissions. In Rome he preferred the society of learned Parisian visitors, who bought (and sometimes ordered) his paintings, and the antiquarian Cassiano dal Pozzo, friend of artists and secretary to Cardinal Francesco Barberini, who commissioned artists to draw for him every work of ancient sculpture and architecture he could track down. Like his Dutch contemporaries (see Chapter 5), Poussin reflects to an extent the ideas and tastes of a class—in this case, one intensely interested in antiquity and in Stoic philosophy.

In such early works as the *Inspiration of the Poet*, painted about 1628–29 (fig. 259), with its Classical figures arranged before a landscape in low afternoon light, Poussin reveals his allegiance to the Bolognese tradition (see Chapter 1). Even more important, he attempted independently to recapture the magic of Titian through warm coloring unified by soft glazes, and through subtle and surprising passages of lights and darks, especially the way light touches the edge of Apollo's lyre and part of his cheek, leaving the rest in shadow. But a comparison with Titian's *Bacchanal of the Andrians* (see fig. 161), to which this picture is in some ways related, shows that Poussin had no intention of reviving the frank sensuality of the great Venetian. This is an allegorical scene in keeping with seventeenth-century ideas; the yearning poet (one could as easily view him as a painter) owes his gifts to divine inspiration. The works of ancient sculpture from which Poussin derived his poses are evoked as memories of a vanished past (existing largely in imagination) for which the artist's nostalgia makes these early paintings poignant in the extreme.

About 1630 Poussin's ideas underwent an essential change, possibly because a severe illness provided a break during which he could formulate the theoretical basis of his art. He abandoned his earlier lyric style and Venetian color, in favor of what in his notes and letters he called *la maniera magnifica* (*the grand manner*), which required first of all a lofty subject—drawn from religion, history, or mythology—that avoided anything "base" or "low." One wonders, parenthetically, what he must have thought of La Tour, of the Le Nain brothers, or for that matter of the whole Caravaggist movement. Poussin maintained that the subject must first be so clarified in the painter's mind that he will not clog the essence of the narrative with insignificant details. Then the painter must consider the conception, that is the couching of the story in an impressive way, such as Phidias' idea of the Olympian Zeus as a god who by a nod could move the universe. Then the artist must devise the composition, which must not be so carefully constructed that it looks labored, but should flow naturally. Last comes the style or manner of painting and drawing, which Poussin considered innate in the painter.

At another point Poussin expounded his theory of the modes of painting by analogy with the modes or scales in Greek music, and mentioned five, the Dorian, the Phrygian, the Lydian, the Hypolydian, and the Ionic. He really did carry his ideas of the modes systematically into execution. His *Rape of the Sabines* (colorplate 39), of about 1636–37, exemplifies the Phrygian mode adapted to "frightful wars"; nonetheless, its "modulations are more subtle than other modes," and Plato and Aristotle "held in high esteem this vehement, furious, and highly severe Mode, that astonishes the spectator." The picture also fulfills all Poussin's requirements for the *maniera magnifica*. The subject is lofty, for the abduction of the Sabine women by the bachelor Romans assured the perpetuation of the Roman race; the conception is powerful; the composition effortless and natural for all its references to ancient and Renaissance statuary figures and groups; and the style beyond all praise. In comparison with works of Poussin's early period, the picture seems drained of atmosphere; in this vacuum his colors ring brilliantly clear, dominated by the primary hues of

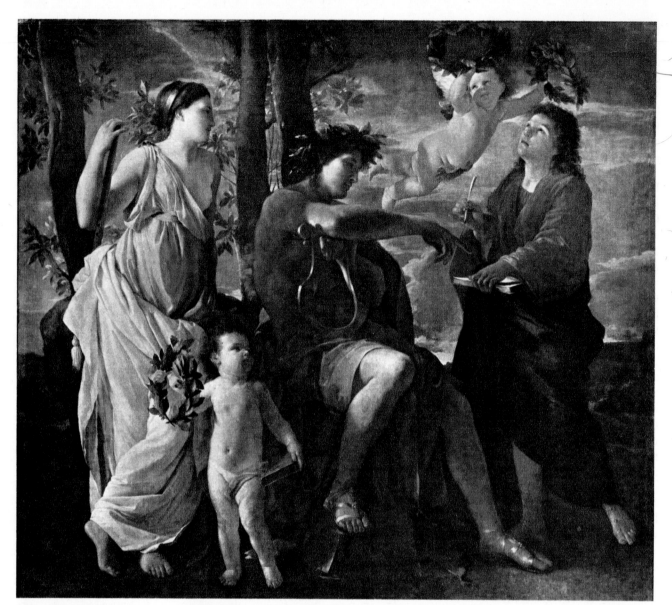

259. NICOLAS POUSSIN.
Inspiration of the Poet.
c. 1628–29. Oil on
canvas, 72½ x 84¼". The
Louvre, Paris

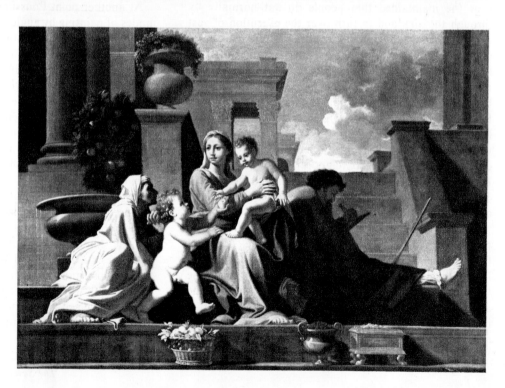

260. NICOLAS POUSSIN. *Holy
Family on the Steps.*
1648. Oil on canvas, 27 x
38½". National Gallery
of Art, Washington, D.C.
Samuel H. Kress
Collection

red, blue, and yellow, each self-contained without the tendency to melt into or to reflect one another (which forms one of the delights of much Baroque painting). The composition is staged in a limited space, flanked on one side by the temple portico in which Romulus stands and limited at the rear by a structure whose appearance is reconstructed from Vitruvius' description of a basilica. The building in the landscape in the background recalls the hill fortress of Annibale Carracci's *Landscape with the Flight into Egypt* (see fig. 227). The rhythm surges along with the driving energy of a fugue by Bach or Handel, every melody of torso or limb clearly distinguishable and perfectly modeled. Although the result may seem artificial, accepted on Poussin's own intellectual premises the painting is brilliantly effective. And, perhaps in spite of Poussin, the grand sweep of forms and colors has an undefinable something that we can call Baroque.

A later work, the *Holy Family on the Steps*, of 1648 (fig. 260), is probably in the Hypolydian mode, which "contains within itself a certain suavity and sweetness which fills the soul of the beholders with joy. It lends itself to divine matters, glory and Paradise." The pyramidal composition suggests the Madonna groups of Leonardo (see fig. 127) and Raphael (see fig. 145), which Poussin knew and studied. Like Tintoretto, but for different reasons, he arranged little draped wax figures on a stage, with the lighting carefully controlled and with a backdrop of landscape and architecture. He would experiment with figural relationships till he found the right grouping, then build a larger and definitive arrangement of modeled and draped figures, and paint from it, referring to reality only when necessary. This procedure is evident in the present picture. The grave, ideal quality of Poussin's art triumphs in such Classical compositions arranged before simple, cubic architecture that bypasses the Baroque, the Renaissance, and the Middle Ages, going straight back to Roman models. While the faces of his figures often appear standardized and almost expressionless, the grandeur of Poussin's art—always on an intimate scale—appears in the balance of forms, colors, and lights. Such compositions were to inspire Ingres in the early nineteenth century (see fig. 370) and to form the basis for the still life and figure paintings of Cézanne in the late nineteenth and early twentieth centuries (see figs. 434, 435).

CLAUDE LORRAIN. A diametrically different aspect of the relationship of figures and landscape forms the lifelong theme for the paintings of Poussin's fellow emigré, Claude Gellée (1600–82), called Claude Lorrain from his origin in Lorraine, who settled in Rome at an early age and never left. Lorrain had so little interest in narrative that he often commissioned others to paint the tiny figures in his pictures. Nonetheless, these figures form an indispensable element in the composition, less to suggest a mood as in Giorgione (see colorplate 26) and Patinir (see fig. 219), for historical, religious, and mythological subjects were interchangeable in his mind, than to establish scale—and scale is all-important. The tiny figures make Lorrain's landscapes at once habitable and immense. In the *Marriage of Isaac and Rebecca*, 1648 (fig. 261), the typical spacious background of the Roman Campagna appears. The Tiber, in the center, has been widened a bit for pictorial effect. Such landscapes, like those of Annibale Carracci and Domenichino, and the landscape backgrounds of Poussin, were constructed in the studio. The giant tree on the right is an obvious *repoussoir* (a device to suggest recession in space) from which the eye moves to the trees in the middle distance, then to the shape of Mount Soracte on the horizon. The mood is provided by Lorrain's soft light, usually the idyllic and dreamy light of late afternoon or sunset, and from visual memories of landscapes he knew.

Lorrain's connection with landscape was intimate and profound. He was almost uneducated, wrote in a mixture of French and Italian, and went off for long periods to live in communion with nature with shepherds in the Campagna. In the open air he produced rapid sketches in pen and ink, with shading in ink wash (fig. 262), which not only record in fluid masses of dark the play of light and shade on foliage but also convey a rhapsodical response to nature; such an attitude was the direct ancestor of that of the early nineteenth-century English Romantics, especially Constable (see Part Six, Chapter 2). These rapid notes were the foundation of Lorrain's studio pictures.

Strikingly original are Lorrain's port scenes, recalling his love for the Bay of Naples, which he saw as a youth, and pervaded by the light of gentle Italian sunsets, which last for hours. In the *Embarkation of Saint Ursula* of 1641 (colorplate 40)—which could just as well be the embarkation of almost any other group of ladies—the rippling surface of the water leads the eye effortlessly to the point where perception dissolves in the soft gold sunlight. The foreground figures serve as a foil, and the water is framed on one side by the meticulously rendered shipping, on the other by a fanciful architecture that transports Bramante's Tempietto (see fig. 139) to the seashore, along with a two-tower Roman Renaissance villa.

OTHER FRENCH PAINTERS. Among the many French painters who stayed at home the most gifted was PHILIPPE DE CHAMPAIGNE (1602–74). Born in Brussels, Champaigne was brought up in a strong Flemish Baroque tradition, but after 1643, the probable date of his conversion to the austere Catholic Jansenist movement, his work underwent a fundamental change. His most original paintings are his sober portraits, such as the *Unknown Man* (fig. 263) of 1650, which shows a man in a window. His calm face is illuminated in an almost Eyckian light that reveals every wrinkle and every vein. Yet the face, ravaged by time and emotion, shares the common Baroque experience of suffering undergone, assimilated, and controlled.

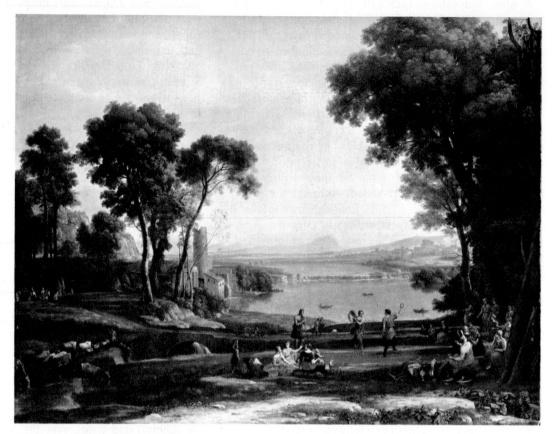

261. CLAUDE LORRAIN.
*Marriage of Isaac
and Rebecca.*
c. 1648. Oil on
canvas, 58¾ x
77½″. National
Gallery, London

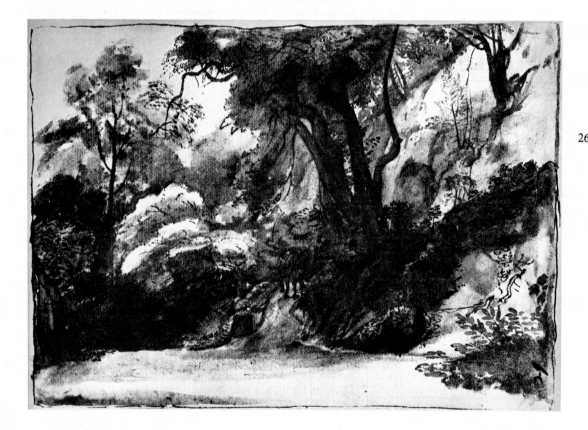

262. CLAUDE LORRAIN.
*On the Slopes of
the Janiculum.*
Date unknown.
Pen and ink, with
bister wash
shading, 8⅝ x
12½″. Accademia
Nazionale dei
Lincei, Rome; on
loan from the
Gabinetto
Nazionale delle
Stampe, Rome

Such simple and unsparing portraits contrast sharply with the official art that dominated the period of Louis XIV. Among the principal practitioners, HYACINTHE RIGAUD (1659–1743), more than any other, was responsible for determining the character of ceremonial Baroque portraiture throughout Europe. His *Portrait of Louis XIV* (fig. 264), painted in 1701 when the king was sixty-three years old, is the prime example of the type. The monarch is shown in ermine-lined coronation robes tossed jauntily over his shoulder to reveal his white-stockinged legs, the feet pirouetting in the high-heeled shoes the king invented. The Baroque magnificence of the pose and the dramatic array of gorgeous fabrics and bits of architecture are clearly intended to endow divine-right absolutism with some of the air of revelation derived from the images of ecstatic saints. Rigaud worked out a production system for such official portraits; he alone painted the subject's head from life on a small canvas, and designed the whole composition; then his assistants enlarged the design, gluing the part by Rigaud in the proper place. A team of specialists in painting armor, fur, fabrics, architecture, and at times landscapes and battle scenes then went to work. The theatrical quality of the result should not blind us to the fact that as a portraitist Rigaud was unexcelled anywhere at the turn of the century; his delineation of the face of the king in old age, who still acted the Grand Monarch in spite of severe military setbacks, is chilling in its directness.

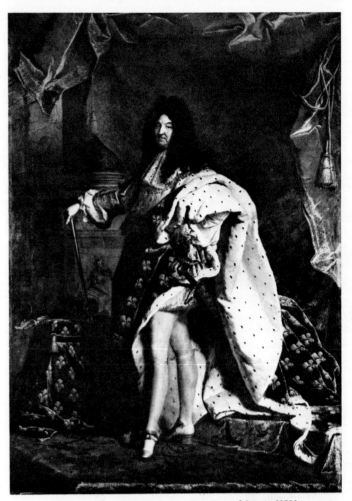

264. HYACINTHE RIGAUD. *Portrait of Louis XIV*. 1701. Oil on canvas, 9'2" x 7'10¾". The Louvre, Paris

ARCHITECTURE AND DECORATION: THE ROAD TO VERSAILLES

The truly original contributions of French seventeenth-century architecture lay in the secular sphere, especially the châteaus built for royalty, nobility, and wealthy officials, culminating in the Royal Palace at Versailles (see figs. 268, 269, 270, 271, 272). An early leader was FRANÇOIS MANSART (1598–1666), who built in 1635–38 a wing for the earlier Château of Blois (fig. 265) that takes its name (the Orléans Wing) from the patron, Gaston, duke of Orléans, brother of Louis XIII. The three-story façade with steep roofs and central pavilion derives from the tradition established by Lescot in the Square Court of the Louvre (see fig. 211). In its canonical superimposition of Doric, Ionic, and Corinthian orders, Mansart's façade is, if anything, more Classical than Lescot's. But the Mannerist linear web of architecture and sculptural decoration is here replaced by a new mastery of space and mass. The dominant central pavilion comes to a typically Baroque climax around and above the entrance in engaged columns, rather than the pilasters used elsewhere throughout the façade; the effect

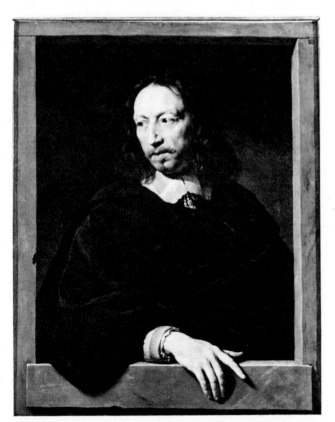

263. PHILIPPE DE CHAMPAIGNE. *Unknown Man*. 1650. Oil on canvas, 35¾ x 28¾". The Louvre, Paris

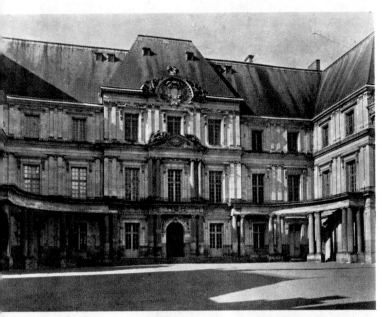

265. FRANÇOIS MANSART. Exterior, Orléans Wing, Château de Blois. 1635–38. France

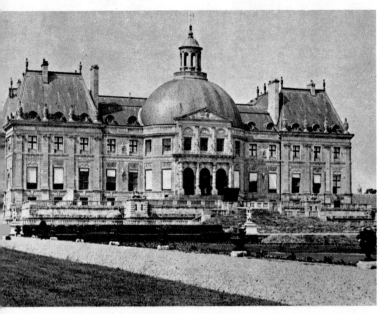

266. LOUIS LE VAU. Garden façade, Château of Vaux-le-Vicomte. 1657–61. France

is completed by a gabled pediment in the second story and an arched pediment in the third, which receive the only sculptural decoration on the otherwise austere exterior except for that around the portal. In a bold and novel invention, a quadrant of freestanding, paired Doric columns on each side leads up to the entrance, and bridges the gap between the central structure and the projecting wing. These dramatic effects, however, are moderated by a lightness, elegance, and precision remote from the dynamism of Italian Baroque designs.

Oddly enough, the first French Baroque venture into grandiosity, the Château of Vaux-le-Vicomte (fig. 266), was built in 1657–61 for a commoner, Nicolas Fouquet, finance minister of Louis XIV, who was determined to erect the most splendid château in France; his success also proved his undoing, because three weeks after his lavish housewarming, including fireworks and a specially commissioned comedy by Molière in the presence of the king and queen and the entire court, Fouquet was arrested on orders from Colbert for embezzlement, and all his property, including Vaux-le-Vicomte, was confiscated by the king. The architect, LOUIS LE VAU (1612–70), the landscape designer ANDRÉ LE NÔTRE (1613–1700), and the mural painter and interior designer CHARLES LE BRUN (1619–90), who had functioned so brilliantly as a team at Vaux-le-Vicomte, were absorbed into royal service, and within a few years achieved their triumph at Versailles.

The Garden Façade of Vaux-le-Vicomte, despite its adoption of such Italian elements as a central dome (over an oval grand salon) and a giant Ionic order for the side pavilions, would probably have impressed an Italian of the period as timid; nonetheless, the characteristic elegance and grace of the elements and their articulation are typical of French taste of the period, and were carried out in harmony with the broken silhouette and lofty lantern that recall Chambord (see fig. 210). The formal gardens, with their elaborate geometrical planting, urns, and statues, were the germ of ideas Le Nôtre later carried out on a colossal scale in the gardens and park at Versailles.

Louis XIV had summoned Bernini to France to complete the East Façade of the Louvre. Bernini, arrogantly critical of everything French, submitted designs that would have dwarfed the sixteenth-century sections of the palace and completely encased the court by Lescot. They were rejected as impractical and incompatible with French taste, and the great Italian master returned to Rome. The design finally accepted was so classicistic that it has little connection with anything in previous French (or for that matter Italian) architectural history (fig. 267). The authorship of the East Façade of the Louvre, 1667–70, is still a matter of dispute; apparently, both Le Vau and Le Brun helped with its design, but the decisive idea seems to have come from an amateur archaeologist and architect (and professional physician), CLAUDE PERRAULT (1613–88). All that remains of traditional French design is the idea of central and terminal pavilions and connecting walls, restated in terms of a stately peristyle of coupled Corinthian columns two stories high, with central pediment. Since the ground story is treated as a podium, for the first time a French building presents itself as a single giant story embracing the entire structure. Although both the rigorous classicism and the airy lightness of the peristyle are alien to Italian Baroque architecture, the giant order on a podium and the balustrade against the sky were taken

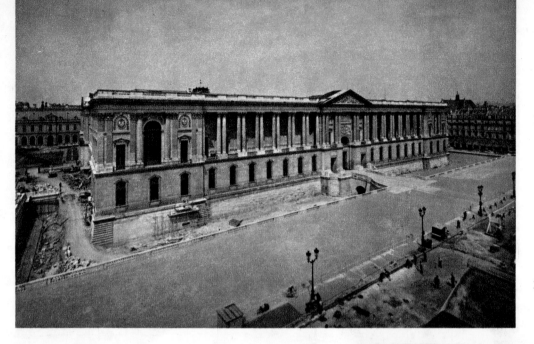

267. CLAUDE PERRAULT. East façade, The Louvre. 1667–70. Paris

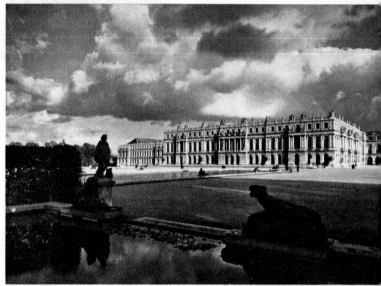

268. LOUIS LE VAU and JULES HARDOUIN-MANSART. Garden façade, Palace of Versailles. 1669–85. France

over from Bernini's designs. The new severe mass of the East Façade of the Louvre, with its hidden roof and unbroken architectural profile, proved definitive for French palace architecture for the next century.

Despite the pleas of Colbert, who wanted to keep the king in Paris, at the time the East Façade of the Louvre was still under construction Louis XIV decided to move the court to Versailles, a few miles outside the capital. Here he envisioned an ideal architecture and landscape, centering on the royal person and taking no note of the commonplaces of urban existence. The result was one of the most ambitious constructions ever conceived, on a scale with the imperial forums of Rome and the temple complex at Karnak, with which it has more in common than with the scattered arrangement of Hadrian's Villa. The nucleus, a hunting lodge built by Louis XIII, was enveloped in 1669–85 by a new structure, originally designed by Le Vau. His West or Garden Façade consisted of what is now the central block (fig. 268). A lightly rusticated podium supports the principal story, with arched windows and a modest Ionic order, and a massive attic story, whose balustrade is enriched by urns and trophies. Originally, the façade was U-shaped; the projecting wings were united, beginning in 1678, at the king's command, by the construction of the immense Hall of Mirrors, designed by JULES HARDOUIN-MANSART (1646–1708), grandnephew of François Mansart, thus creating a unified façade, for which some critics believe the Ionic order to be inadequate.

In order to keep the nobility where the king could control them, and to house royal offices and guards, a small city was built to the east of the palace, and the original block extended by enormous wings to a total length of six hundred yards, often criticized as out of scale with the proportions of the Ionic order used throughout. Judged by Italian standards, the final effect of the palace (fig. 269) is disappointing, but viewed with the gardens, with which it forms a whole, it looks unexpectedly fragile and very beautiful, especially on bright days when the warmth

of the creamy stone glows against the sky. On such a scale a giant order in the Italian manner might have proved crushing, and it might have spoiled the festive lightness of the exterior, intended as a backdrop for gorgeous festivities, often lasting for days, with comedies, balls, music, fireworks, and torchlight suppers in the open air. Even today the full effect of the architecture cannot be appreciated unless the fountains are functioning.

The central axis of the landscape design is the east-west path of the sun, which Louis XIV adopted as his symbol, traveling along the road from Paris, passing through the king's bedroom at the exact center of the palace, and out along the walks and canals that extend some three miles through the park to set over the low hills in the distance. It is no accident that the great event of each day at Versailles was the *levée* (*rising*), a term applied indiscriminately to the appearance of the sun over the horizon and the emergence of the Sun King from

269. LOUIS LE VAU and JULES
HARDOUIN-MANSART.
Palace of Versailles (aerial
view)

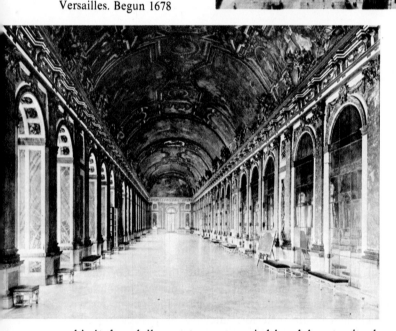

270. JULES HARDOUIN-MANSART
and CHARLES LEBRUN. Hall
of Mirrors, Palace of
Versailles. Begun 1678

his bed, a daily event accompanied by elaborate ritual, and awaited by courtiers in the Hall of Mirrors (fig. 270), whose central doorway was that of the royal bedchamber. No wonder that the principal theme of the Hall of Mirrors is light; the sunlight through the seventeen arched windows is reflected in seventeen mirrors, and illuminates a vaulted ceiling decorated by frescoes on mythological and historical subjects relating to royalty, framed by gilded stucco ornamentation on the model of the gallery of Palazzo Farnese (see colorplate 36), all designed by Charles Le Brun. Enhanced by acres of transparent or reflecting glass, the effect of the pink marble pilasters, the gilded Corinthian capitals and entablatures, and the colors and gold of the ceiling decorations yields in splendor to no Roman Baroque in-

terior in spite of the typical French primness of long straight lines. But the frescoes, rapidly executed by battalions of painters, scarcely hold up under inspection. Le Brun, whose administrative authority extended the absolute power of the monarchy even into the sphere of the arts, was an ingenious designer, and no detail of decoration, furnishings, or hardware was too small to escape his attention, but the monarchical system was unlikely to produce great art. It had, nonetheless, been codified regarding the arts since 1648 in the formidable institution of the Royal Academy. Under Le Brun, director from 1663 until his death, a program of instruction and a series of rules were devised to enforce conformity to official standards, exalting the ancients, Raphael, and Poussin; the consequences of the academic codes and norms were felt acutely into the late nineteenth century, and periodic revolts against them characterized the initial stages of most new movements in European art.

Perhaps the single best decorative work at Versailles is the brilliant stucco relief of *Louis XIV on Horseback* (fig. 271), in the Salon de la Guerre, by ANTOINE COYSEVOX (1640–1720). Garbed as a Roman imperator, the king tramples on enemies on whom he does not deign to bestow a glance, while Eternity embracing a pyramid extends the French royal crown over his bewigged head. She competes uselessly for his attention with marble Victories who lean into the frame, one blowing a trumpet, the other offering a laurel crown, while wretched prisoners are fettered to consoles below, and Fame in the lowest relief writes the king's immortal deeds upon a shield. Strongly influenced by Bernini, the style is nonetheless French in its measured pace, its linearity, and the careful control of all details.

Hardouin-Mansart's triumph at Versailles, freed from

any inheritance of Le Vau's proportions, is the Palace Chapel (fig. 272), 1689–1710, a work of extreme classicism yet brilliant lightness. The lower story, intended for courtiers, is formed by an arcade supported by piers, and serves as a support for the principal story, a widely spaced, archaeologically correct colonnade of fluted Corinthian columns running round the apse, which provides a deep gallery for the royal family. The frescoed, groin-vaulted ceiling, pierced by an arched clerestory, is subordinated to the grandeur of the columns, and the altar itself is hardly more than a necessary piece of furniture.

The formal gardens, with their geometrical flowerbeds, urns, statuary, trimmed hedges, grottoes, planted groves, lofty fountains, canals, and pools, are an extension of the palace itself over the landscape, and are the masterpiece of Le Nôtre, who also designed systems of avenues through the park, radiating from circles or ovals, as if to submit the last recesses of nature to the royal will. It is not surprising that from time to time the king found it necessary to escape from his mythological self and live the life of a human being. In consequence he set aside a section of the park for a one-story dream house, the Grand Trianon (fig. 273), designed by Hardouin-

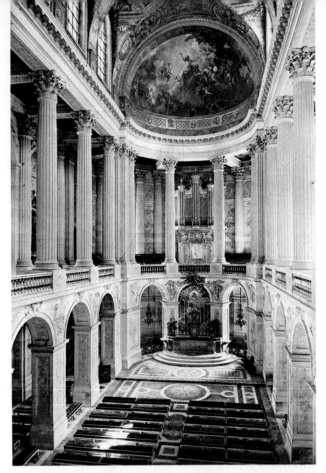

272. JULES HARDOUIN-MANSART. Royal Chapel, Palace of Versailles. 1689–1710

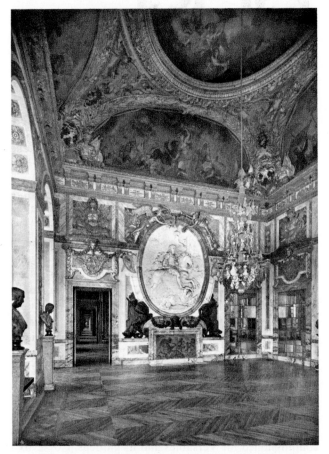

271. ANTOINE COYSEVOX. *Louis XIV on Horseback.* Stucco relief. 1683–85. Salon de la Guerre, Palace of Versailles

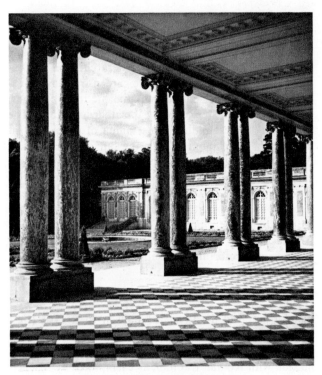

273. JULES HARDOUIN-MANSART. Grand Trianon. Begun 1687. Versailles

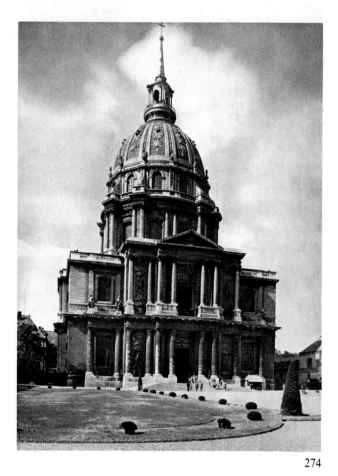

274

274. JULES HARDOUIN-MANSART. Façade, Church of the Invalides. 1676–1706. Paris

275. JULES HARDOUIN-MANSART. Plan of the Church of the Invalides

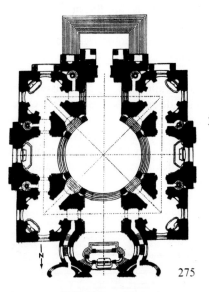

275

276. ANTOINE COYSEVOX. *Portrait Bust of Colbert.* 1677. Marble. Palace of Versailles

Mansart in 1687—the only architectural element in the entire seventeenth-century complex at Versailles to attain the high quality of the Royal Chapel. The two sections of the house are united by a peristyle, arched on the entrance side, but supported on the garden front by an exquisite colonnade of paired, pink marble Ionic columns, continuing as pilasters between the arched windows. The enchanting little building is a triumph of grace and intimacy, in perfect union with the out-of-doors, which flows through its very center. While the peristyle provided a cool place to sit or dine in summer, the interior spaces, of modest size and unceremonious arrangement, were grouped in apartments of four rooms, united at the corners by efficient porcelain stoves for winter comfort. All glass, white limestone, and pink marble, the Grand Trianon is as colorful and insubstantial as a soap bubble.

AWAY FROM VERSAILLES

In his Church of the Invalides, built in 1676–1706 (figs. 274, 275) as an addition to a home for disabled veterans, Hardouin-Mansart displayed an unexpectedly close connection with Roman tradition as exemplified by Michelangelo, della Porta, Maderno, and Bernini. The dome with its paired columns recalls Saint Peter's (see fig. 184); the two-story façade with its central crescendo of clustered columns derives from such models as Il Gesù

(see fig. 189) and Santa Susanna (see fig. 233). Yet the Baroque climax is attained by methods sedately French; there are no broken pediments, no floating sculpture, no concavities or convexities. Columns remain solid and classically correct. The structure is bound together by delicate adjustments of its components, which make it one of the most harmonious exteriors of the seventeenth century. For example, to establish the dominant role of the central pediment, Hardouin-Mansart suppressed the central pair of columns directly above it in the drum of the dome, and created a highly original rectangular lantern whose point, continued in the steeple, carries the angle of the pediment to the apex of the entire structure.

When not restrained by officialdom, Coysevox maintained a portrait style second only to that of Bernini in seventeenth-century sculpture. His bust of the king's great finance minister Colbert, of 1677 (fig. 276), while recalling the movement of line and surface of the great Italian sculptor who had so recently visited France, nonetheless preserves a sobriety not far from the honest pictorial style of Philippe de Champaigne (see fig. 263), and is far more impressive than the decorative works commissioned for Versailles and its gardens. Coysevox's contemporary, FRANÇOIS GIRARDON (1628–1715), author of an immense amount of decorative and official sculpture of high quality, was responsible for a new type of freestanding dramatic tomb, showing the deceased at

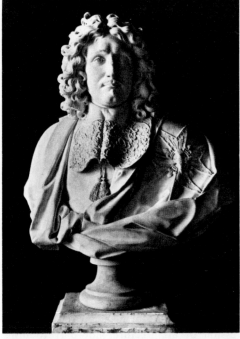

276

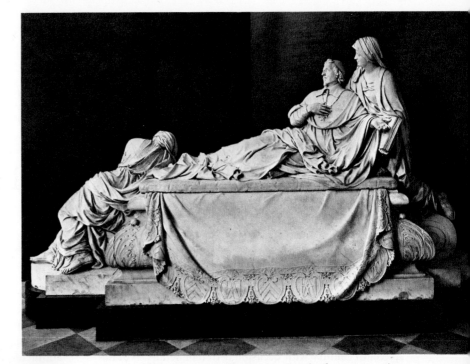

277. FRANÇOIS GIRARDON. *Tomb of Richelieu.* 1675–77. Marble. Church of the Sorbonne, Paris

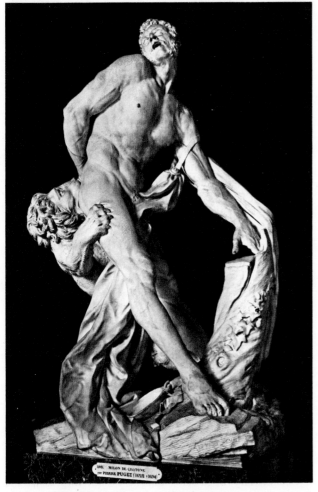

278. PIERRE PUGET. *Milo of Crotona.* 1671–83. Marble, height 8'10½". The Louvre, Paris

the moment of translation to a higher realm without any of the Italian machinery of angels, clouds, rays, and billowing curtains. His *Tomb of Richelieu*, 1675–77 (fig. 277), still in its original position in the Church of the Sorbonne in Paris, was intended to be seen from all sides. Its principal group, the dying cardinal upheld by Piety, facing the altar and looking toward Heaven, builds up with the dignity of a composition by Poussin, although the contrast between the crumpled masses of the cloak and the billowing pall was derived from a study of Bernini's technique. From the altar the composition, seen foreshortened in depth, is equally effective. The maverick among French Baroque sculptors was PIERRE PUGET (1620–94), whose independence of official taste cost him popularity at court. His *Milo of Crotona*, 1671–83 (fig. 278), shows with brutal realism the fate of a Greek athlete who, unable to extricate his hand from a split tree stump, was attacked by a lion. Obviously, Puget had studied Michelangelo's *Rebellious Slave* (see fig. 136) and Bernini's *David* (see fig. 236). The rendering of the abdominal muscles pulsating with pain and the convulsed facial expression shows that Puget had also learned a great deal from independent observation. The group is a work of tremendous emotional and compositional power. Tradition has it that the statue was uncrated at Versailles in the presence of the queen, who, when she came to a full realization of its subject, murmured, "*Ah, le pauvre homme!*" Puget's vivid Baroque realism was better appreciated in Italy, where he had considerable success.

3

The Seventeenth Century
in England

The Tudor monarchs and nobles built handsome palaces and country houses, for the most part along Perpendicular Gothic lines, studded here and there late in the sixteenth century with occasional Italian details. Not until the eighteenth century did English concern for the visual arts begin to rival the passions for poetry and music that won for England so high a place in the creative life of the Renaissance and Baroque periods. During the seventeenth century the best painters in England were Flemish visitors, notably Rubens and Van Dyck (see Chapter 4), who painted some of their finest works in England. But under the Stuart monarchs English architecture entered a new period of intense productivity.

INIGO JONES (1573–1652) visited Italy, but he seems to have been unimpressed by the beginnings of the Italian Baroque. The style he brought back was pure Palladianism, destined for a long and fruitful life in England and North America. The Banqueting House (fig. 279) that Jones built for King James I in 1619–22 as an addition to the now vanished palace of Whitehall in London does not reproduce any specific building by Palladio; in its cubic severity, in fact, it avoids any of the more pictorial aspects of Palladio's architecture. The façade is a firm restatement of basic Italian Renaissance principles; a lightly rusticated building block is articulated by a screen architecture of superimposed Ionic and Corinthian orders, pilasters in the two bays at either side, engaged columns in the three central bays, unrelieved by any ornamentation save for the sculptured masks and swags that unite the Corinthian capitals. It cannot by any stretch of the term be called Baroque; like all of Jones' structures, it is an elegant and purified revival of a style the Italians themselves had abandoned.

WREN. The great flowering of English architecture in the late seventeenth century was largely due to a single disaster and a single genius. The fire of 1666, which destroyed most of the City of London, gave an un-

paralleled opportunity to a youthful professor of astronomy at Oxford, Dr. Christopher Wren (1632–1723), subsequently knighted for his achievements in his adopted profession of architecture, not only to bring English buildings into line with Continental developments, but also to produce in the course of his immensely long life an array of handsome structures unequaled in number and variety by any other Baroque architect. The very year of the fire Wren had projected for the Gothic Cathedral of Saint Paul's a central dome with a Bramantesque peristyle (see fig. 142), a high profile like that of Saint Peter's (see fig. 184), and an openwork wire finial in emulation of Borromini's at Sant'Ivo (see fig. 247). After the fire King Charles II intended to rebuild the City on Wren's rational Baroque plan with broad avenues, squares, and vistas. For considerations of private property this proved impracticable. Wren was called upon first to redesign the choir of Saint Paul's and then to rebuild the entire cathedral; eventually, almost every church in the City was rebuilt on a Wren design, so that the present picture of bristling Baroque steeples (or those that survived the Blitz of World War II) is due to Wren. His first attempt at the total rebuilding of Saint Paul's, preserved in the so-called *Great Model* of 1672 (fig. 280), was more Renaissance than Baroque, and in most respects brilliantly original. His Greek-cross plan, with eight piers, was to connect the arms with four concave quadrants, articulated on the exterior by a single giant story of Corinthian pilasters, with intervals varying in accordance with the fenestration, surmounted by an attic story and a dome whose drum was enveloped not by a peristyle but by an arcade of Corinthian pilasters. A Baroque climax was to be achieved in the façade by a colossal arched portal, breaking the lower cornice of the central pediment.

The novelty of Wren's unique design impressed the king but not the clergy; liturgy and custom demanded a longitudinal axis. Regretfully, Wren abandoned this scheme, and worked out two others, one of which was

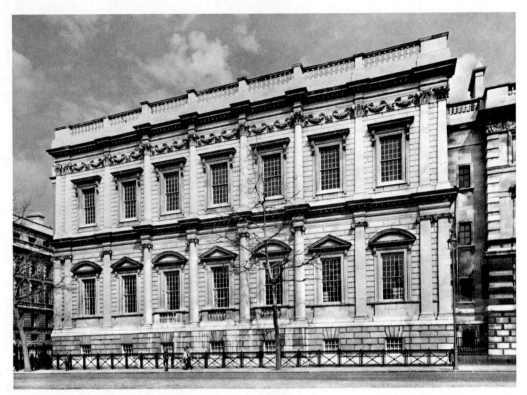

279. Inigo Jones. West façade, Banqueting House, Whitehall Palace. 1619–22.
London

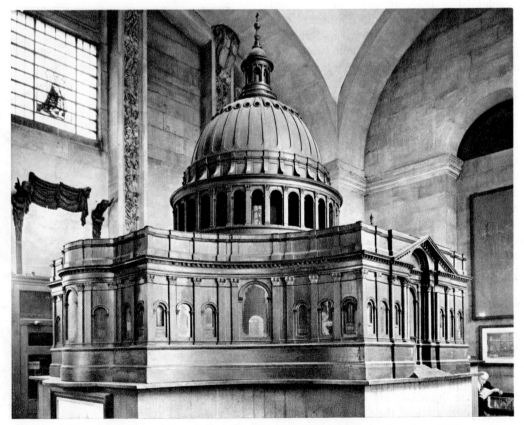

280. Christopher Wren. *Great Model* (of St. Paul's Cathedral, London). 1672.
Library, St. Paul's Cathedral

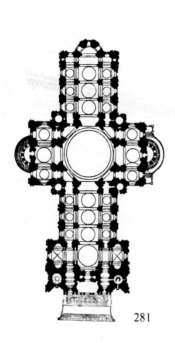

281

281. CHRISTOPHER WREN. Plan of St. Paul's Cathedral. 1675–1710

282. CHRISTOPHER WREN. West façade, St. Paul's Cathedral

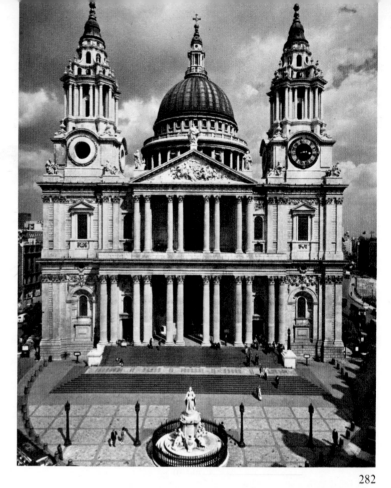

282

substantially adopted in 1675, although the dome and bell towers did not receive their final form for years. The essentially Gothic directional plan was reinstated (fig. 281); flying buttresses to support the vaults were concealed on the exterior by a second story that is merely a screen. The façade with its magnificent central climax (fig. 282) derives in part from the East Façade of the Louvre (see fig. 267), recapitulated in two stories of paired Corinthian columns, the lower story wider to accommodate the side portals. The flanking towers, reviving the Gothic tradition, are Baroque campaniles along lines established by Borromini in Sant'Agnese (see fig. 249). For all Wren's debt to Continental models, his cathedral, not completed until 1710, stands as one of the finest Baroque architectural compositions anywhere. The dome, combining a Bramantesque peristyle with a Michelangelesque verticality, punctuates the peristyle with a wall containing an arch after every fourth intercolumniation. The host of imitations of Wren's dome, in Europe and North America, attest to the finality of his solution. In comparison with Continental churches, the interior (fig. 283) strikes one as cold, perhaps inevitably in view of Anglican opposition to gilding and profuse ornamentation. The long Gothic space is divided by giant Corinthian pilasters supporting transverse arches on whose pendentives are floated saucer domes; a smaller order of paired pilasters sustains the nave arcade. As in all Wren's interiors, the emphasis is placed on the linear elements of arches, frames, and circles.

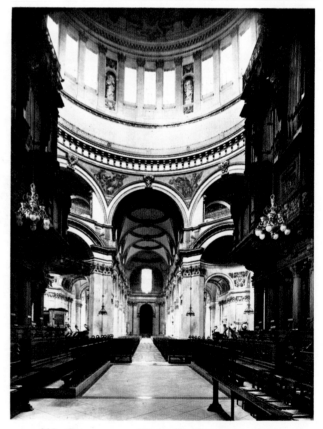

283. CHRISTOPHER WREN. Interior (view of nave from choir), St. Paul's Cathedral

4

Flemish Painting
in the Seventeenth Century

The separation of the Netherlandish provinces into what are today the independent kingdoms of Belgium and Holland was well-nigh complete by the opening of the seventeenth century. It was, first and foremost, a division along religious lines, but it had far-reaching political and economic consequences. The Calvinist northern provinces, democratic in outlook under their chosen governors, conducted a flourishing trade with most of the known world, and established a major empire in the East Indies and West Indies. The Catholic southern provinces remained under Habsburg control; the archduchess Isabella of Austria, daughter of Philip II of Spain, and her husband Albert, brother of the emperor, encouraged learning and the arts, but commerce stagnated; during its period of artistic preeminence in the first half of the seventeenth century, the southern Netherlands was in constant political and economic difficulties. Although *Flanders* and *Flemish* properly refer to only one of the ten southern Netherlandish provinces, they are the most convenient words with which to designate the entire region and its inhabitants during the period before the founding of the kingdom of Belgium in 1830. The early seventeenth century in Flanders was not a period conducive to large-scale building, with the exception of some impressive Jesuit churches, and none of the major European architects or sculptors of the age were Flemish; the glory of Flemish art during this brief period derives largely from the work of a single extraordinary painter.

RUBENS. Peter Paul Rubens (1577–1640) exercised in Flanders a stylistic authority at least as great as that of Michelangelo in Central Italy a century before, and surpassing that enjoyed by Bernini in contemporary Italy. Born near Cologne, the son of a Protestant emigré from Antwerp, he spent his childhood in Germany. He received a thorough grounding in Latin and in theology, spent a few months as page to a countess, and grew up as an unparalleled combination of scholar, diplomat, and painter. He spoke and wrote six modern languages—

Italian with special ease—read Latin, and was probably the most learned artist of all time. Through wide travels in diplomatic service, he established contacts with kings and princes throughout western Europe. His house in Antwerp, which still stands, well restored, was a factory from which massive works emerged in a never-ending stream. Two of its most impressive features are the balcony in the studio from which Rubens could survey the work of his assistants in the laying out of colossal altarpieces and display them to powerful patrons, and the door, only about three feet wide but at least twenty feet high, through which the monumental panels and canvases were carried sideways to be shipped to destinations near and far. He charged in proportion to his own participation in a given work, and although most paintings were designed by him in rapidly painted color sketches on wood, all the large ones were painted by pupils, and then retouched by the master, who provided his inimitable brushwork and glowing color in the final coat—or left the students' work untouched if the price was not high enough. To understand Rubens' production system, one has also to grasp his extraordinary character and intelligence; one visitor recounted how Rubens could listen to a reading of Roman history (in Latin, of course), carry on a learned conversation, paint a picture, and dictate a letter all at the same time. Seemingly, a single body and a single lifetime could not contain the activities of this astonishing man.

Rubens first emerged on the international scene during his visit to Italy in 1600, where, except for a diplomatic mission to Spain in the service of the duke of Mantua, he remained for eight years. If he had stayed there to exploit his initial successes, the history of the seventeenth century would have been very different. More than anything else, artistically at least, Rubens was an adopted Italian, with surprisingly little interest in the Early Netherlandish masters, whom he apparently regarded as too remote to be any longer relevant. With rigorous system and indefatigable energy, he set out to conquer the fortress of

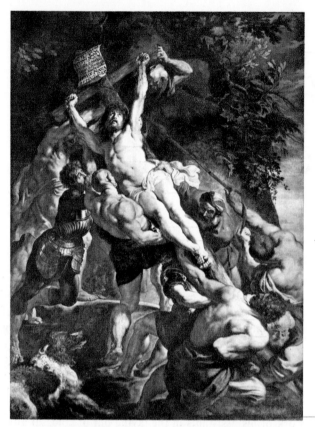

284. PETER PAUL RUBENS. *Raising of the Cross* (center panel of triptych). 1609–10. 15'2" x 11'2". Cathedral of Antwerp, Belgium

Italian art, beginning with ancient Rome and skipping to the High and Late Renaissance. He made hundreds of drawings and scores of copies after Roman sculpture, and paintings by Leonardo (see fig. 129), Raphael, Michelangelo, Correggio, Titian, Tintoretto, and Veronese, not to speak of the Carracci and Caravaggio, then still working busily in Rome; of all the masters of the Early Renaissance, apparently only Mantegna caught his attention. He commissioned assistants to make hundreds more drawings, many of which he retouched. From this comprehensive record of the ideas and compositions of the Italian masters, he evolved a personal style characterized by abundant physical energy and splendid color; the seventeenth-century critic Giovanni Pietro Bellori spoke of his "fury of the brush."

An early work in Antwerp Cathedral, the *Raising of the Cross* (fig. 284), a panel more than fifteen feet high, painted in 1609–10, shows the superhuman energy with which Rubens attacked his mighty concepts. The central panel of a triptych, the picture is, nonetheless, complete in itself. Interestingly enough, there is no hint of Caravaggio's psychological interests. The executioners, whose muscularity recalls Michelangelo's *Last Judgment* (see fig. 181), heave and tug the Cross upward, forming a colossal pyramid of struggling figures, an enriched version of the characteristic High Renaissance interfigural composition transformed into a Baroque climax. The

sheer corporeal force of the painting makes it hard to realize that at this very moment in Spain El Greco was painting his most disembodied and mystical visions.

As his style matured, Rubens' characteristic spiral-into-the-picture lost the dark shadows of his early work and took on an always more Titianesque richness and translucency of color. His *Rape of the Daughters of Leucippus*, of about 1616–17 (fig. 285), recalls forcibly Titian's *Rape of Europa* (see fig. 167), which Rubens carefully copied while in Spain. Although the figures have been made to fit into Rubens' mounting spiral, such is the buoyancy of the composition that the result does not seem artificial. The act of love by which Castor and Pollux, sons of Jupiter, uplift the mortal maidens from the ground draws the spectator upward in a mood of rapture not unrelated to that Bernini was soon to achieve in the *Saint Theresa* (see fig. 239). The female types, even more abundant than those of Titian, are traversed by a steady stream of energy, and the material weight of all the figures is lightened by innumerable fluctuations of color running through their pearly skin, the tanned flesh of the men, the armor, the horses, even the floods of golden hair. The low horizon increases the effect of a heavenly ascension, natural enough since this picture like the ceiling of the Farnese Gallery (see colorplate 36) is a triumph of divine love; the very landscape heaves and flows in response to the excitement of the event.

The power of Rubens can be seen at its greatest in the *Fall of the Damned* (fig. 286), painted about 1614–18, a waterspout of hurtling figures—Rubens' spiral in re-

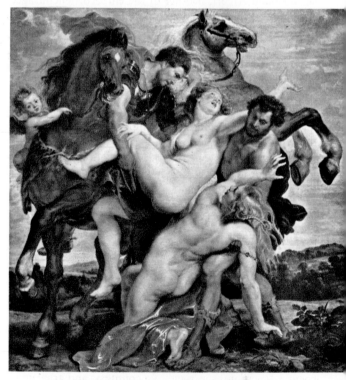

285. PETER PAUL RUBENS. *Rape of the Daughters of Leucippus*. c. 1616–17. Oil on canvas. 87½ x 82¼". Alte Pinakothek, Munich

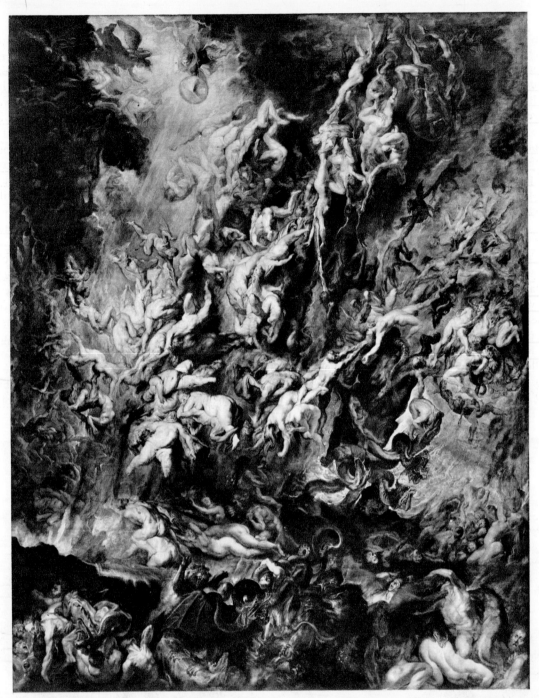

286. PETER PAUL RUBENS. *Fall of the Damned.* c. 1614–18. Oil on panel, 9'4½" x 7'4⅛". Alte Pinakothek, Munich

verse—raining down from Heaven, from which the rebels against divine love are forever excluded. It is hard for English-speaking viewers to avoid thinking of the torrential lines from Milton's *Paradise Lost* (I, 44–49):

> Him the Almighty Power
> Hurld headlong flaming from th' Ethereal Skie
> With hideous ruine and combustion down
> To bottomless perdition, there to dwell
> In Adamantine Chains and penal Fire,
> Who durst defie th' Omnipotent to Arms.

Nor is it difficult to see in Rubens' mighty conception the

origin of the falling figures in Gaulli's ceiling for Il Gesù (see colorplate 38).

In 1621–25 Rubens carried out a splendid commission from Maria de' Medici, dowager queen of France, widow of Henry IV, and regent during the minority of her son Louis XIII. The twenty-one large canvases represent an allegorized version of the queen's checkered career, showing her protected at every point by the divinities of Olympus. The series was originally installed in a ceremonial gallery in the Luxembourg Palace, a Baroque Parisian version of Maria's native Pitti Palace in Florence (see fig. 191). While all the canvases show the magnificence of Rubens' compositional inventiveness and the depth of his Classical learning, they are not of uniform quality in detail. *Henry IV Receiving the Portrait of Maria de' Medici* (colorplate 41) is one of the best, a brilliant achievement not only in composition but also in every detail, surely finished throughout by Rubens' own hand. The aging king, whose helmet and shield are purloined by Cupids, is advised by Minerva to accept as his second bride the Florentine princess, whose portrait is presented by Mercury, as Juno and Jupiter, caught in a rare moment of marital harmony, smile upon the proposed union. The happy promise of divine intervention; the radiant health of the youthful nude figures; the sage grandeur of the armored king; the splendor of the coloring of flesh, metal, drapery, clouds, even Juno's gorgeous peacocks; and the opulence of the distant landscape render this one of the happiest of Rubens' allegorical works. Parenthetically, he decided to abandon a second series, the *Life of Henry IV*, because the first was never paid for, but when the queen, driven out of France by her former protégé Cardinal Richelieu, took refuge in Flanders, it was Rubens who helped to support her during her twelve years of impecunious exile—a remarkable tribute not only to the generosity of a great

man, but also to the position of a Baroque artist who could finance a luckless monarch.

During his second stay in Madrid, in 1628–29, Rubens is reported to have exclaimed that he was "as in love with Titian as a bridegroom with his bride." This was not only an apt simile for the startling rebirth of poetic beauty and coloristic vitality in the artist's later works, founded on his Baroque reinterpretation of Titian, but also a prophecy as well; in 1630, then fifty-three years old and a widower, Rubens married Helena Fourment, a girl of sixteen, who was to bear him five healthy children. Her golden loveliness illuminates a score of pictures, and the artist's radiant happiness during his final decade received its perfect embodiment in the *Garden of Love* (fig. 287), painted about 1638, a fantasy in which seven of the Fourment sisters are happily disposed throughout the foreground, some with their husbands (Rubens himself, somewhat idealized, with Helena at the extreme left), before the fantastic fountain-house in Rubens' own garden at Antwerp. Cupids, emulated from Titian, fly above the scene with bows, arrows, a rose garland, and torches, and on the right sits a statue of Venus astride a dolphin, pressing jets of water from her abundant breasts. All Rubens' love of Titian, all the movement of his color, all

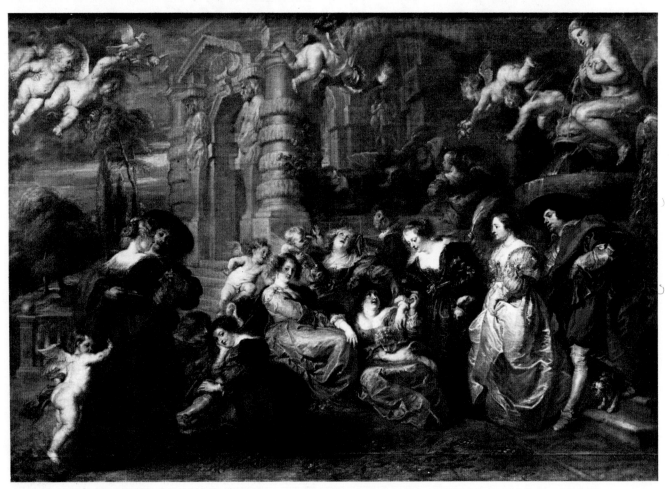

287. Peter Paul Rubens. *Garden of Love.* c. 1638. Oil on canvas. 6'6" x 9'3⅜". Museo del Prado, Madrid

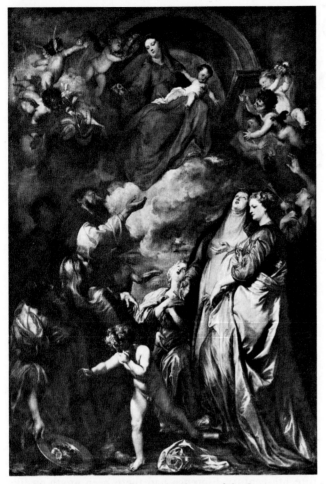

288. ANTHONY VAN DYCK. *Madonna of the Rosary.*
1624–c. 1627. Oratorio della Compagnia del
Rosario di S. Domenico, Palermo

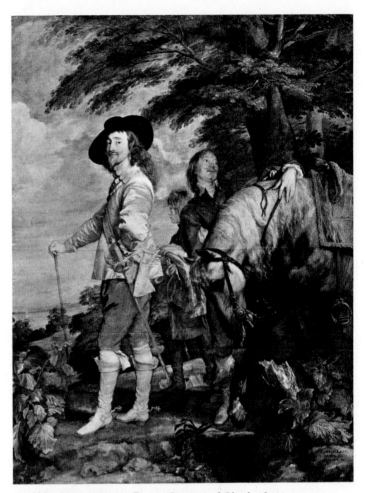

289. ANTHONY VAN DYCK. *Portrait of Charles I in
Hunting Dress.* 1635. Oil on canvas, 8'11" x
6'11½". The Louvre, Paris

the energy of his composition are summed up in the
radiance of this picture, the happiest of Baroque testaments to the redeeming power of love.

VAN DYCK. Rubens' assistant and later a friendly rival in
Flanders, Italy, and England was Anthony van Dyck
(1599–1641), already an accomplished painter in late
adolescence. His extreme sensitivity to color and shape
separates him at once from the more vigorous and robust
Rubens; his only large altarpiece, the *Madonna of the
Rosary* (fig. 288), started in Palermo in 1624 but not
completed until about 1627 in Genoa, shows the unexpected, almost Mannerist attenuation characteristic of
Van Dyck's figures, rivaling the fantastic length and
slenderness of Parmigianino's *Madonna with the Long
Neck* (see colorplate 30). The broad movement of color
and light throughout the picture is influenced by Rubens, whose personality no Flemish artist could escape,
but the exquisite lightness and grace of the figures, not to
speak of the expressions of the yearning saints and benign Virgin floating on clouds under her airborne arch,
are Van Dyck's own.

No seventeenth-century painter could rival his

aristocratic refinement and delicacy, and it is no wonder
that he became famous for his portraits of nobility and
royalty, which generally show the subjects as vastly more
elegant and beautiful than we know them to have been.
Van Dyck enjoyed his greatest success at the court of
Charles I of England (reigned 1625–49), where he occupied a position similar to that of Holbein under Henry
VIII (see Part Four, Chapter 7). From his superb portraits of Charles, we would never guess that in reality the
king was short and undistinguished in appearance; in his
Portrait of Charles I in Hunting Dress (fig. 289), of 1635,
Van Dyck endows him with extraordinary dignity and an
air of romantic melancholy. Despite the relative informality of the costume and moment—the king seems
ready to mount his horse and ride off to the chase—this is
a state portrait; only Van Dyck's inspired ease of composition and of statement prevents it from seeming artificial and posed. The verve of his linear movement and
the sparkle of his color, even to the shimmer of the
horse's mane and the liquid softness of its eyes, render
this one of the most impressive of all official portraits;
Van Dyck, in fact, set the tone for such images in
England for more than a century.

5
Dutch Painting
in the Seventeenth Century

The name *Holland*, which properly belonged to only one of the seven United Provinces of the Netherlands, is now popularly extended to the eleven that make up the modern kingdom; the word *Dutch* (derived from *deutsch*, meaning *German*), is even less appropriate as a name for the inhabitants of the northern part of the former Low Countries; but, like all the other historical misnomers we have seen, these two are by now unavoidable. Democratic and predominantly Calvinist Holland in the seventeenth century offered a spectacle distinct from the general European Baroque scene. Traditional patrons of art were conspicuous by their absence. Calvinism opposed imagery in church buildings. There was no monarchy, and the princes of Orange, whose function in the republic was generally military, turned to Flemish masters or to such Italianate painters as Honthorst for palace decorations. Neither was there any hereditary aristocracy, although toward the close of the century certain wealthy bourgeois families acquired country estates and sought titles of nobility.

As early as the late sixteenth century, the artist was, therefore, for the first time in recorded history thrown entirely on the open market; this, unpredictably, was fertile, and its effect on art enormous. In spite of wars with Spain, France, and England, the country was extremely prosperous. Although New Netherlands was soon lost to the English, the Dutch founded and maintained a large overseas empire and enjoyed worldwide commerce; to protect their trade, they established a powerful navy. Not only did the commercial families suddenly want pictures—so did almost everybody else, down to social levels that never before had been able to afford anything more than a crude wood-block print or a bit of folk art. Peter Mundy, a British visitor to Amsterdam in 1640 at the height of Dutch artistic activity, wrote: "As For the art off Painting and the affection off the people to Pictures, I thincke none other goe beeyond them, . . . All in generall striving to adorne their houses, especially the outer or

street roome, with costly peeces, Butchers and bakers not much inferiour in their shoppes, which are Fairely sett Forth, yea many tymes blacksmithes, Coblers, etts., will have some picture or other by their Forge and in their stalle."

With great skill and industry, and in unbelievable numbers, Dutch painters set about supplying this new demand for paintings (not sculpture, which apparently nobody wanted). That they were able to do so, and to maintain so consistently high a level of quality, is one of the miracles of history; only in Periclean Athens or fifteenth-century Florence had there been anything like this number of good painters in proportion to the general population. Under such circumstances it is not hard to understand that there could be no artistic dictator such as Le Brun, or dominating figures such as Michelangelo, Bernini, or Rubens. On entering the galleries devoted to Dutch painting in any museum, the visitor is struck by the difference between the character and outlook of the Dutch masters and their contemporaries anywhere else in Europe. One would never know that Rubens was working at the same time in Antwerp, less than a hundred miles from Amsterdam. There are few large pictures; almost everything is living-room size. There are no visions or ecstasies of saints, no images of royal power, no allegorized historical events; Classical mythologies are rare, and when they do occur, they are, like biblical scenes, often stated in terms of everyday life.

In preference to such narratives or allegorical scenes, Dutch painters generally concentrated on images of daily life and the immediate environment, and in a sense were the heirs of the early fifteenth-century Netherlandish naturalists. But there is a striking difference; almost never do we find representations of economic activity, like the farming or artisan scenes so vividly presented by the Limbourg brothers (see colorplate 15, fig. 90) and Campin (see fig. 93) or later by Bruegel (see colorplate 34, fig. 221). We are shown upper-middle-class interiors or gardens with or without celebrations, but never the shops, factories, or banks that supported them or the kitchens that prepared food for them; people dressed in silks and satins, but seldom the work of the weavers, tailors, and dressmakers who made their clothes; farmers carousing in taverns, but no scenes of plowing, harvesting, or brewing; still lifes of wine, oysters, tobacco, and exotic fruits, but not the activity of importing these delicacies, and, strangest of all, fertile landscapes whose fat clouds never rain.

In short, what people wanted to see and were willing to pay for were not images of production, in which their days were largely spent, but of leisure-time enjoyment, and for such representations they demanded a workmanly and pleasing style. They got what they wanted in immense profusion, with an optical perfection unequaled in any other country (it is not irrelevant that Amsterdam was the world center of the optical industry). Therefore, although the painters' skill was seemingly unlimited, their variety copious, and their number legion, their productions, exhibited today in endless Dutch galleries in leading museums, tend to become monotonous. No more so, however, than Italian Gothic altarpieces, which were also not intended to be seen at once in large numbers. Viewed two or three at a time, in small rooms like those of the Dutch houses for which they were painted (see fig. 296), Dutch seventeenth-century pictures are deeply satisfying. Nonetheless, only three Dutch masters of the period rise above the general high level of technical excellence into a universal sphere—Hals, Vermeer, and, above all, Rembrandt. It is an apt commentary on the effects of the free market that all three were in severe financial difficulties in their later years—Hals, in fact, throughout his whole life.

THE CARAVAGGESQUES. The new art did not spring like Athena full-grown from the head of Zeus. During the late sixteenth century, Holland underwent strong influences from the final phase of Italian Mannerism. Even the naturalism of the seventeenth century was sparked by Italy, in fact by the same fire from Caravaggio that was at the same time lighting candles in France (La Tour, for example; see fig. 257). The two chief Dutch Caravaggesque painters, HENDRICK TERBRUGGHEN (c. 1588–1629) and GERRIT VAN HONTHORST (1590–1656), made the mandatory pilgrimage to Italy, where they came under the spell of Caravaggio's work. Terbrugghen, in fact, seems to have settled in Rome as an adolescent in 1604 while Caravaggio was still there, and may have known him personally; he returned to the Netherlands in 1614. Honthorst arrived in Rome later, about 1610–12, after Caravaggio's death, and stayed until 1620. Both were from Utrecht (Terbrugghen was probably born at Deventer, but his family moved to Utrecht a few years after his birth), then as now a strong Catholic center; both were Catholics all their lives. Their religious paintings show understanding of Caravaggio's new vision of

ordinary humanity reached by divine love, although they never attain the depth and power of the great Italian innovator.

Honthorst had considerable success in Italy, where he acquired the nickname "Gherardo delle Notti" ("Gerrit of the Nights") because nocturnal pictures were his specialty; many of his works are still on Italian altars and in Italian museums. His *Adoration of the Shepherds*, of 1621 (fig. 290), could almost be taken for an Italian painting; Caravaggio's influence can be seen in the smooth, hard style and in the mysterious background, and there is even a reference to Correggio (see fig. 177) in the light radiating from the Child. But there is something a little trivial in Honthorst's naturalism, and in his too agreeable facial expressions. He distinguishes meticulously between degrees of illumination in terms of nearness to the Child (as had Geertgen tot Sint Jans; see fig. 108) and even

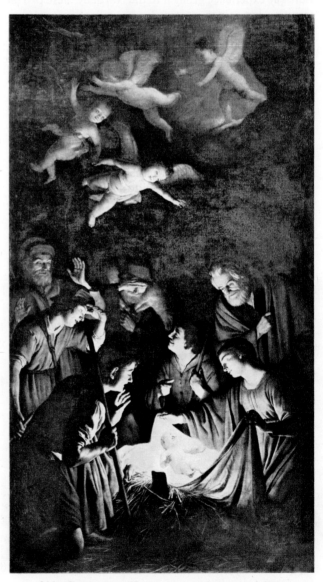

290. GERRIT VAN HONTHORST. *Adoration of the Shepherds.* 1621. Oil on canvas, 51½ x 37¾".
Galleria degli Uffizi, Florence

between the light reflected from the smiling faces and that filtering through the sheet held up by Mary.

Terbrugghen was a different sort of painter, whose work is not to be seen in any Italian church. His *Incredulity of Saint Thomas* (fig. 291), painted after 1614, imitates a composition by Caravaggio, and states the Baroque psychic climax in Caravaggio's physical terms—understanding of the miracle breaking through the resistance of reason by means of direct contact between the finger and the wound. Nonetheless, his painting, for all its Caravaggesque derivation (including the background of nowhere), retains echoes of Dürer, Grünewald, and Bruegel in the very un-Italian faces. Painted several years after the artist's return to Holland, the painting softens considerably the sharp light-and-dark contrasts of Caravaggio. It remained for Rembrandt to open up again, and to deepen immeasurably, the vein of Baroque experience brought to the North by these two interesting but minor masters.

THE "LITTLE MASTERS." The open market system, under which pictures were sold by the artists themselves, by dealers (who might also be painters), or at booths in fairs, tended to produce specialists, each recognizable by his prowess in painting a particular type of subject. There were specialists in landscapes, riverscapes, seascapes, cityscapes, even travelscapes; in skating scenes, moonlight scenes, ships, shipping, and naval battles; in interiors and exteriors, conspicuously scrubbed or conspicuously dirty; in gardens, polite conversations, genteel games, parlor intrigue, light housekeeping, riotous parties, and tavern brawls; in cows, bulls, horses, and hunting scenes; in churches with or without services taking place; and, of course, in still lifes (raised for the first time

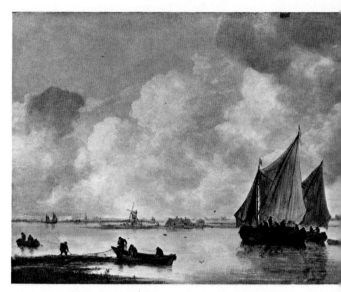

292. JAN VAN GOYEN. *River Scene.* 1656. Oil on canvas, 14⅛ x 24¾". Städelsches Kunstinstitut, Frankfort

to the dignity of independent subjects) and in portraits, single, double, or multiple. At least forty of these "little masters" are of extremely high quality, and any choice among them is sure to be arbitrary.

All Dutch seventeenth-century landscapes were, like those of Annibale Carracci, Poussin, and Claude Lorrain (see fig. 227, colorplate 39, fig. 261), painted in the studio from memory, sketches, or both and constructed not as they were in reality but according to compositional principles that inevitably involved the device of a psychological climax common to much Baroque experience—transferred from the religious, mythological, or historical spheres in which it can easily be isolated and described to the subtler, purely visual realm of space, light, and atmosphere. An early leader of Dutch landscape painting, JAN VAN GOYEN (1596–1656), although a prolific painter, dealer, valuer, and speculator in everything from land to tulip bulbs, died poor. He was one of the first Dutch masters to relegate human figures to a position in which they could no longer determine the mood of a scene but merely establish its scale. Like many of his Dutch contemporaries, Van Goyen was fascinated by water, from which the Dutch had reclaimed much land, against whose incursions they erected dikes, and on whose navigation they founded their prosperity. Even more important than water in Dutch landscape, however, is the celestial architecture of shifting clouds, which towers over the flat land and reduces the works of man to insignificance.

In *River Scene* by Van Goyen (fig. 292), painted in the last year of his life, the horizon has sunk to less than a quarter of the picture's width from the bottom, and the land, with marsh grasses, fishermen's cottages, windmills, and a distant church, is visible only as tiny patches. All else is clouds and water, save for two sloops whose

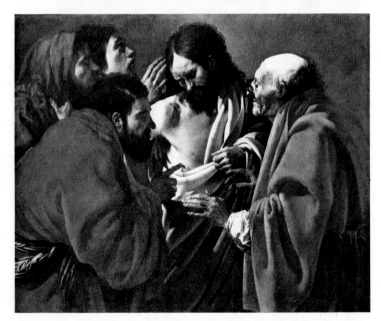

291. HENDRICK TERBRUGGHEN. *Incredulity of Saint Thomas.* c. 1623. Oil on canvas, 42⅛ x 53¾". Rijksmuseum, Amsterdam

slack sails, spread to catch the slight breeze, move slowly into the luminous area of cloud toward the center, reflected in the water below. People are mere spots, as are the low-flying gulls. An almost monochromatic vision, limited to translucent browns in the foreground and gray greens elsewhere, is registered by means of light, sketchy touches of the brush in ground, moving beings, shimmering water, and distant land.

A *View of Haarlem* (fig. 293), of 1670, by the younger painter JACOB VAN RUISDAEL (1628/29–82), opens up an immense prospect from the vantage point of the dunes. The city appears only on the flat horizon, a sparkle of windmills and spires dominated by the mass of the Grote Kerk (Great Church). The immensity of the space is increased by the climax falling in the form of light between clouds on the farmhouses and the linens bleaching in the foreground. The very birds fly higher and the clouds seem more remote than in Van Goyen's picture. One of the grandest of Dutch landscapes is the *Avenue at Middelharnis* (fig. 294), of 1689, by MEYNDERT HOBBEMA (1638–1709), Ruisdael's pupil, who painted little in later life, when he enjoyed a lucrative position levying taxes on wine for the city of Amsterdam. Constructed on the humble theme of a rutted country road plunging into the picture between feathery trees that have long lost their lower branches for use as firewood, the spatial climax is as compelling on a small scale as that of Bernini's colonnade for Saint Peter's (see fig. 243). AELBERT CUYP (1620–91), influenced by Dutch painters who had traveled in Italy, preserves a similar feeling for space in his *Landscape with Cattle and Figures* (fig. 295), of about 1650, intensified by the *repoussoir* effect of the animals and people arranged in the foreground with the precision of a composition by Poussin. Every form is transfigured by the soft, golden light of his favorite river background, rendering solid substance as apparently translucent.

The gentle art of PIETER DE HOOCH (1629–after 1684) celebrates the harmony of the perfect bourgeois household, with everything in its proper place, and respect for cleanliness and order raised to an aesthetic, almost religious level. In the *Linen Cupboard*, of 1663 (fig. 296), De Hooch's Baroque climax, illuminated by an unseen window, is the simple act of counting neatly folded sheets taken from their carved and inlaid cabinet in an interior whose cleanliness matches its perfect perspective and its clear, bright colors; the black-and-white marble

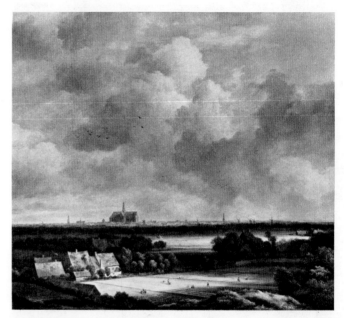

293. JACOB VAN RUISDAEL. *View of Haarlem.* c. 1670. Oil on canvas, 22 x 24⅜". Mauritshuis, The Hague, The Netherlands

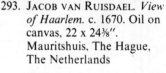

294. MEYNDERT HOBBEMA. *Avenue at Middelharnis.* 1689. Oil on canvas, 40¾ x 55½". National Gallery, London

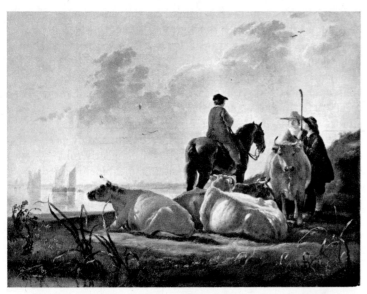

295. AELBERT CUYP. *Landscape with Cattle and Figures.* c. 1650. Oil, 15 x 20″. National Gallery, London

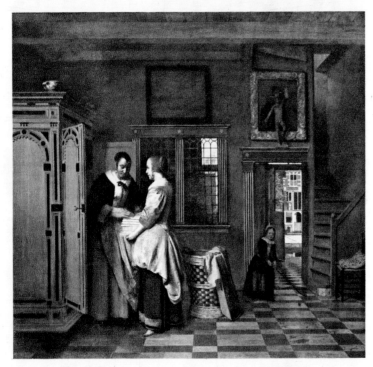

296. PIETER DE HOOCH. *Linen Cupboard.* 1663. Oil on canvas, 28⅜ x 30½″. Rijksmuseum, Amsterdam

floor leads the eye through the door to the view across the street, reminiscent of the backgrounds of van Eyck (see fig. 100) in its rich atmospheric and spatial quality and its reverence for the object. By means of pictures on the wall the painter takes pains to show that art is a part of the ideal daily life.

The exact opposite of De Hooch's religion of order is uproariously extolled by JAN STEEN (1625/26–1679), who revived the humor of the Late Gothic *drôleries*. To

this day a "Jan Steen household" is the Dutch expression for a ménage in which nothing can go right. In fact, nothing does in *The World Upside-Down* (fig. 297), which might well be a parody on De Hooch's linen cupboard and was probably painted in the same year. It was also, doubtless, intended as a moralizing picture in a tradition going back as far as Bruegel. Steen was the son of a brewer, dabbled in brewing, and even kept a tavern; he never tired of representing the effects of his products, shown in this picture as almost universal. Here the scene shifts to the kitchen; the same lady of the house in the same costume as in De Hooch has fallen asleep; beer runs from the keg over a floor strewn with pretzels, a pipe, and a hat; children, a pig, a dog, a duck, and a monkey are where they ought not to be and are doing what they ought not to do. The sodden housemaid, over whose knee an admirer has thrown a possessive leg, hands him absent-mindedly another glass of wine, and nobody pays the slightest attention to an elderly man (doctor or preacher?) reading from a book or to an old woman trying to bring some order into the situation. To make it all the more effective, Steen is at least as good a painter as De Hooch, handling his figures with conviction and power, and has a splendid sense of both composition and color. If his humor can at times be resisted, his children cannot, and his joy of life is infectious.

So indeed is the enthusiasm with which a whole group of Dutch (and Flemish) painters represented scenes several notches lower in the social scale. The best of these artists was a Fleming, ADRIAEN BROUWER (1605/6–1638), who spent the formative years of his brief career in Haarlem in the 1620s, working in the circle of Hals. His peasants drink, rollick, play cards, and fight. Three of them are shown in varying stages of intoxication, all fairly advanced, in his *Boors· Drinking* (fig. 298). One has drowned not only his sorrows but also his face; nothing can be seen of him but his hands holding a tankard up to his hat-covered visage. The dashing brushwork and the strong light-and-dark contrasts that make Brouwer's pictures so lively derive more or less directly from Hals and Rembrandt.

Dutch still lifes were often intended to appeal to the eye and the palate at once. Some are crowded with an unappetizing profusion of fruit or game, but the most tasteful (and tasty) are those restricted to the makings of between-meals snacks (they are traditionally referred to as "breakfast pieces"). White wine, a bit of seafood or ham, lemon, pepper and salt are the subjects, along with polished silver, knobby crystal goblets to keep wine cool, and a rumpled tablecloth. The spectator is tantalized not only by the delicacy with which the carefully selected objects are painted, but also by the expensive carelessness with which a lemon has been left partly peeled and a silver cup overturned (fig. 299). WILLEM CLAESZ HEDA (1599–1680/82) was one of the chief practitioners of this art in which, despite what might seem severe limitations of subject matter, he demonstrates an unexpected elo-

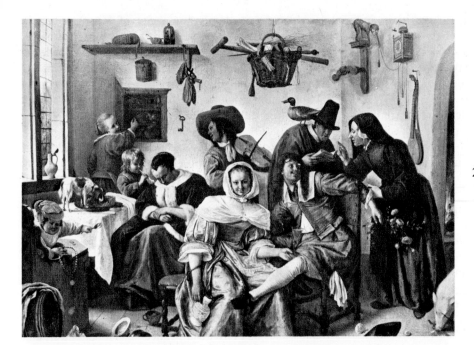

297. JAN STEEN. *The World
Upside-Down.* c. 1663.
Oil on canvas, 41⅜ x
57⅛". Kunsthistorisches
Museum, Vienna

298. ADRIAEN BROUWER.
Boors Drinking. c. 1620s.
Oil on panel, 11½ x 8¾".
National Gallery, London

quence in the rendering of golden light, and sensitivity in establishing the precise relationships between transparent, translucent, reflecting, and mat surfaces—a silent drama of pure sense presented in the style of a Caravaggio religious scene against a background of nowhere, fluctuating between shadow and light.

At the other extreme from such Epicureanism are the Spartan architectural paintings of the period, especially those of PIETER SAENREDAM (1597–1665), a lonely hunchback who found a certain solace in painting the interiors of Dutch Gothic churches, especially whitewashed Protestant ones, stripped of decorations and altars; his works show only enough figures to indicate their scale. Saenredam described his meticulous procedure; he started with exact line drawings made on the spot, then enlarged them to construction drawings in his studio on the basis of measured plans, and finally executed his painting on panel. Predominantly white, austere, apparently inhuman, these quiet pictures, nonetheless, distill their own beauty of form and tone, and an unexpected meditative poetry. The *Church of Saint Bavo*, of 1660 (fig. 300), an interior view of the great

church in Saenredam's home city of Haarlem and in which he was eventually buried, is one of his finest paintings, showing a superb control of space and a knowledge of the relationships of planes, which was not to be attained again until the wholly different but also monochromatic solutions of the Cubists in the twentieth century (see Part Six, Chapter 7).

HALS. Recognized today as one of the most brilliant of all portraitists, Frans Hals (1581/85–1666) was probably born in Antwerp and was brought to Haarlem as a child. Two of his brothers and five of his sons became painters. Interested in little else but the human face and figure, Hals was blessed with an unrivaled gift for catching the individual in a moment of action, feeling, perception, or expression, and recording that moment with tempestuous but unerring strokes. There could hardly be a stronger contrast than that between his electric characterizations of people and the calm, deliberately controlled portraits of the essential person by such great painters of the Renaissance as Piero della Francesca, Titian, Dürer, and Holbein (see colorplates 10, 11, figs. 166, 195, 207).

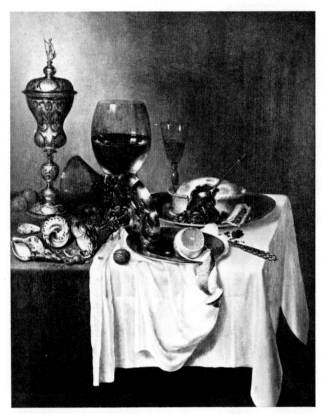

299. WILLEM CLAESZ HEDA. *Still Life.* c. 1648. Oil on panel, 34¾ x 27½". California Palace of the Legion of Honor, San Francisco. Mildred Anna Williams Collection

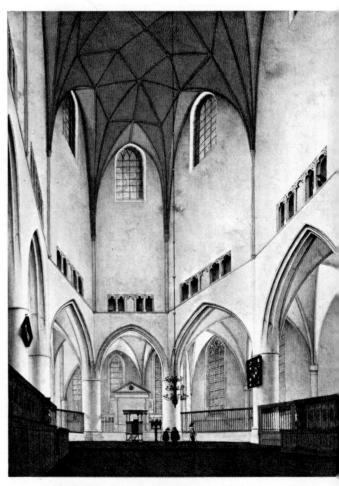

300. PIETER SAENREDAM. *Church of Saint Bavo.* 1660. Oil on panel, 27¾ x 21⅝". Worcester Art Museum, Massachusetts

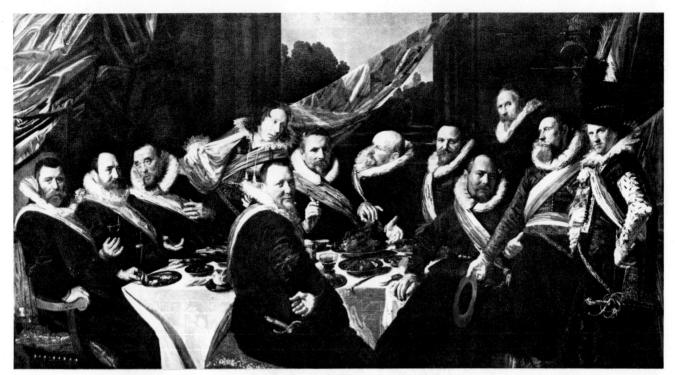

301. FRANS HALS. *Banquet of the Officers of the Saint George Guard Company.* 1616. Oil on canvas,
5'8⅞" x 10'7½". Frans Halsmuseum, Haarlem, The Netherlands

Although tne optical character of Hals' brushwork recalls the Helleno-Roman tradition as preserved in Byzantine painting, and he probably saw works by the great Venetian masters in Dutch collections, there is no indication that Hals had much interest in Mediterranean art of any period; his discoveries about the rendering of light in paint seem to have been almost entirely his own. He owed something to the new naturalism of his Caravaggesque contemporaries (see figs. 290, 291), especially Terbrugghen, who were roughly the same age, but he himself never made the pilgrimage to Italy.

Among his early commissions were group portraits of the militia companies that had been largely responsible for maintaining the very existence of the new Dutch republic in a hostile world; these paintings radiate its self-confidence and optimism. By the 1620s, however, these companies had largely outworn their military function; Hals usually shows the citizen-soldiers in the midst of one of those stupendous banquets that the civic authorities pleaded with them to reduce from a week's duration to three days or at the most four. Such compositions, picturing a dozen or more males, mostly corpulent and middle-aged, each of whom had paid an equal amount for his portrait and expected to be recognizable, were not conducive to imaginative painting. Hals' predecessors generally had composed these group portraits in alignments hardly superior compositionally to a modern class photograph, and it was to take the genius of Rembrandt to raise them to the level of high drama (see fig. 307). But Hals, in his *Banquet of the Officers of the Saint George Guard Company,* of 1616 (fig. 301), has done a superb job within the limitations of the traditional type. The moment is relaxed, the wine and beer have worked their effect, and the gentlemen turn toward each other or toward the painter as if he had been painting the whole group at once, which was certainly not the case. Conviviality is not the only uniting factor; massive Baroque diagonals—the curtain pulled aside, the sashes, the poses, the ruffs—tie the picture together into a rich pattern of white and flashing colors against the shimmering black costumes. Broad brushstrokes indicate the passage of light on color with a flash and sparkle unknown at this moment even to Rubens.

The genial warmth of Hals' early style is seen at its most engaging in an unusually finished portrait, *The Laughing Cavalier* (fig. 302). The date of 1624 and the subject's age of twenty-six are inscribed on the background, and since the cavalier's diagonal shadow also falls on it, it is clearly a wall; the Caravaggesque nowhere is thus converted into a definite here, yet the wall is irradiated with light and seems insubstantial. The amorous proclivities of the young man may be indicated by the arrows, torches, and bees of Cupid and the winged staff and hat of Mercury embroidered in red, silver, and gold on the dark brown of his slashed sleeve. With his glowing complexion, dangerous moustaches, snowy ruff, and dashing hat, the subject is the very symbol of Baroque gallantry; the climax of the painting is the taunting smile on which every compositional force converges.

The opposite of this glittering portrait is the somber *Malle Babbe,* of about 1630–33 (fig. 303). No one knows who the old creature was or the meaning of her probably

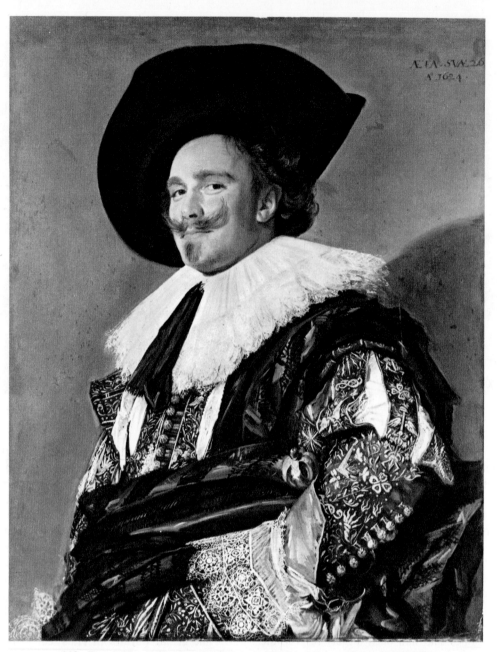

302. FRANS HALS. *The Laughing Cavalier.* 1624. Oil on canvas, 33¾ x 27"
Permission of Trustees of The Wallace Collection, London

uncomplimentary nickname, written in an eighteenth-century hand on the original stretcher. Often called an "old crone," she might be anywhere from forty to sixty years old. She has obviously soaked up the contents of the (two-quart?) tankard she holds, and Hals has caught her in the midst of a fit of insane laughter. Possibly she is the town idiot. The owl on her shoulder is a symbol not of wisdom, as with Minerva, but of foolishness. The astounding expression, seized in a storm of strokes, is rendered with a demonic intensity that shows that Hals, concerned from youth to age with human character as revealed in expression, could plumb depths that repelled even him.

When he was past eighty, about 1664, Hals, already on a pension from the city of Haarlem, showed a still different side of his character and ability in the

Regentesses of the Old Men's Almshouse (fig. 304). Painted almost entirely in black and white and shades of gray, this solemn picture is united by diagonal movements differing in tempo and verve but not in strength from those building up the composition in the *Saint George Guard Company*, even though the painter had only the devastated faces and white collars of the women as component elements. Each of the subjects has reacted in a separate way to age and experience, yet all participate in a calm acceptance of the effects of time. In its simplicity and austerity the composition shows an expressive depth unexpected in the generally ebullient Hals.

REMBRANDT. The greatest of Dutch masters, indeed one of the supreme geniuses in the history of art, is Rembrandt van Rijn (1606–69). The son of a miller, he was born in Leiden, and attended briefly the university in that quiet city. Rembrandt then was trained as a painter by two minor local artists and finally by the Early Baroque history-painter Pieter Lastman in Amsterdam. His rapid success prompted him to move, after five or six years in Leiden, in 1631 or 1632 to Amsterdam, the principal Dutch city, where early in 1632 he was commissioned to paint the *Anatomy Lesson of Dr. Tulp* (fig. 305). Since only the corpses of executed criminals could be used for dissections, such an opportunity was an event for medical research, conducted before distinguished citizens and followed by a dinner of the doctors' guild and a torchlight parade. Conventional representations of public dissections prior to Rembrandt were as stiffly aligned as those of militia companies before Hals. While Rembrandt has painted faces, beards, lace ruffs, and pleated sleeves with all the smooth, meticulous care his patrons could have

desired, he has given the composition a new drama. Against the Caravaggesque wall displaying Rembrandt's signature and the date, he has arranged the composition diagonally in depth, with the corpse foreshortened so that we see the soles of its feet; the open book is used as a *repoussoir*. Dr. Tulp lifts with his forceps the flexors of the cadaver's left hand (which operate from the forearm) and with his own left hand demonstrates how they close the fingers; the freely grouped spectators gaze intently at the stripped human mechanism, at its live counterpart, at the lecturer's face, or inward in contemplation. After a moment an unexpected element begins to dominate —mystery, in the half-shadowed white face and partly open mouth of the corpse, little by little reminding the living of their own inevitable de[...]. Eventually, in Rembrandt's art mystery assumed [...] role, and rendered his message equally diffi[...] contemporaries to accept or for posterity [...]

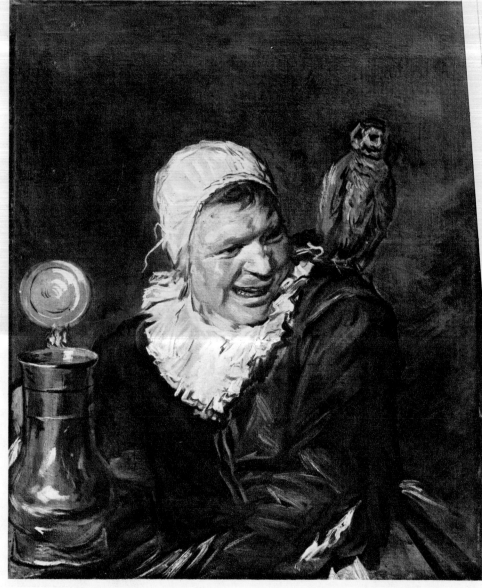

303. FRANS HALS. *Malle Babbe.* c. 1630–33. Oil on canvas, 29½ x 25¼".
Staatliche Museen. Berlin

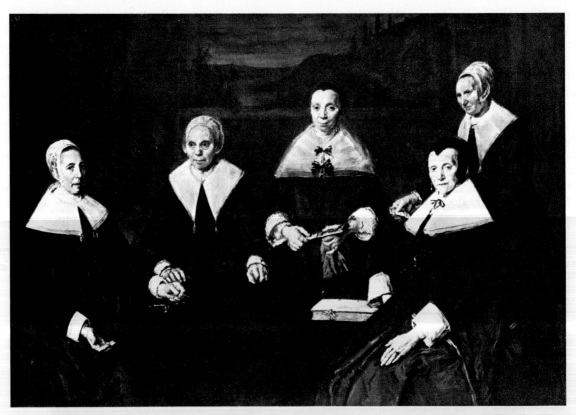

304. FRANS HALS. *Regentesses of the Old Men's Almshouse.* c. 1664. Oil on canvas, 67⅛ x
98⅜". Frans Halsmuseum, Haarlem, The Netherlands

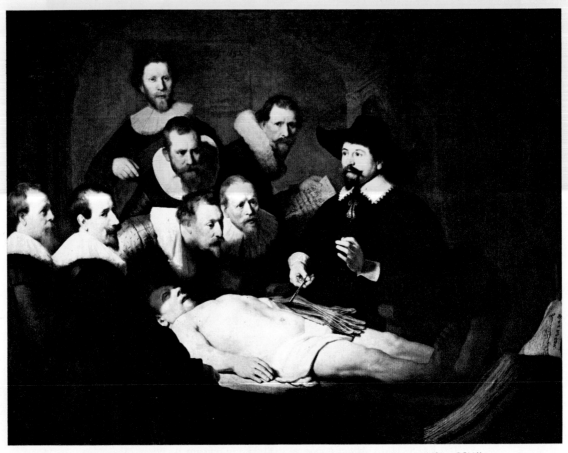

305. REMBRANDT. *Anatomy Lesson of Dr. Tulp.* 1632. Oil on canvas, 66¾ x 85¼".
Mauritshuis, The Hague, The Netherlands

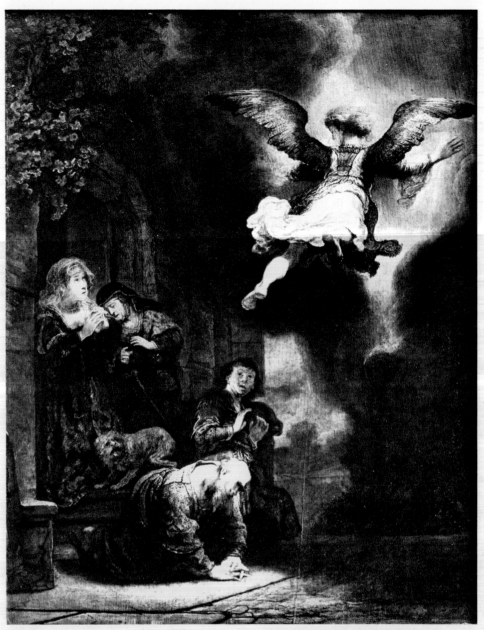

306. REMBRANDT. *Angel Leaving Tobit and Tobias.* 1637. Oil on panel, 26¾ x 20½". The Louvre, Paris

But for the time being his worldly success was assured. He had more commissions and pupils than he could accept; he married Saskia van Uylenburgh, the lovely daughter of a wealthy family; bought a splendid house; started a collection of paintings and rarities; and, in addition to his handsome, lucrative portraits, began to paint in a highly imaginative Baroque style under two combined influences—Caravaggio for sharp light-and-dark contrast and Rubens for spiral composition and speed of execution. A brilliant example is the *Angel Leaving Tobit and Tobias* of 1637 (fig. 306). Rembrandt has followed exactly the Book of Tobit (not included in Protestant Bibles, but available to him in the Apocrypha as a source). The formerly blind Tobit, cured by the Archangel Raphael, prostrates himself in gratitude, while his son

Tobias looks upward in wonder at the departing figure; Anna, the wife of Tobit, and Sarah, Tobias' bride, even the dog mentioned in the text, are shown, yet subordinated to the miracle of the "light of heaven" formerly denied to Tobit and now falling around him in floods. Seen sharply from the back, the angel is taken from their sight into an open cloud in a flash of light. Along with the luminary effects that create this resounding climax goes a new technical freedom. The smooth, detailed early manner is gone; the forms are quickly sketched, although without Hals' virtuosity of the brush, and the light masses are done in a rich impasto against the deep, characteristically brownish glazes used to veil and intensify the shadows.

In 1642, the year of Saskia's untimely death, both the

element of mystery and the technical innovations that accompany and reinforce it began to conquer even commissioned subjects, such as *The Company of Captain Frans Banning Cocq and Lieutenant Willem van Ruytenburch*; this painting, through a misunderstanding natural enough considering its formerly darkened condition, is called the *Night Watch* (fig. 307). The account that the members of the company were dissatisfied with their colossal group portrait is legendary, but Rembrandt's commissions in the 1640s did slacken off, whether or not as a result of this unconventional painting. It was cut down in size in the eighteenth century to fit into a space in the Town Hall of Amsterdam, and it is no longer evident that the group are about to cross a bridge. Even a cleaning, shortly after the close of World War II, which revealed the original brilliance of the color, did not restore any semblance of natural light.

The subject was probably the formation of the militia company for a parade in honor of the state visit of Maria de' Medici, dowager queen of France, to Amsterdam in 1638. Not only through Hals' device of diagonals but also through irrational and wonderfully effective lighting Rembrandt has turned narrative prose into dramatic poetry. We are never really told what is happening; real events are submerged in the symphonic tide of the coloring, dominated by the lemon yellow of the lieutenant's costume and the captain's scarlet sash against shadows that, even after cleaning, are still deep and warm. All the men had paid equally for their portraits, yet some are sunk in shadow; one man is concealed except for his eyes. It was inevitable that Rembrandt would lose popularity as a portrait painter, although not at once.

During the 1640s Rembrandt is believed to have joined the Mennonites, who believed in the sole authority of the Bible and in silent prayer. His luminary visions of scriptural subjects become deeper and more tranquil. The *Supper at Emmaus*, in which Christ reveals himself to two of his disciples on the evening of the first Easter when "the day is far spent" (Luke 24: 30–31) in the breaking of bread is a natural subject for the Baroque, and the climax

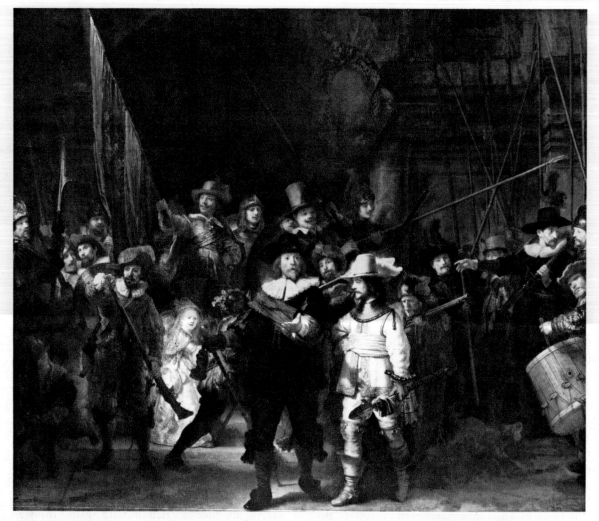

307. REMBRANDT. *The Company of Captain Frans Banning Cocq and Lieutenant Willem van Ruytenburch (Night Watch)*. 1642. Oil on canvas, 11'5¾" x 14'4½". Rijksmuseum, Amsterdam

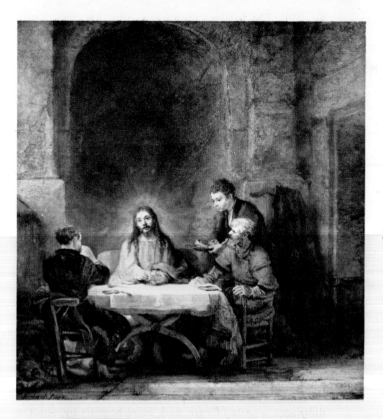

308. REMBRANDT. *Supper at Emmaus.* 1648. Oil on canvas, 26¾ x 25⅝". The Louvre, Paris

is often represented with great psychological intensity, or as a burst of light. In Rembrandt's version of 1648 (fig. 308), all is still. A niche behind Christ becomes an apse, the table an altar, both gently illumined by rays from Christ's head. The servant perceives nothing, and only an involuntary motion of hand to mouth on the part of one disciple and a drawing back of the other betray their sudden recognition of their companion.

In 1655 Rembrandt found himself in the midst of severe financial troubles, which reached disastrous proportions the following year, forcing the eventual sale of his house in 1658 and his collections in two auctions (one in 1657, the other in 1658) in an attempt to satisfy his creditors. His common-law wife, Hendrickje Stoffels, and his only surviving child, Titus, formed a company in 1660 to discharge the master's debts, and to assume him ostensibly as an employee. At the beginning of this unhappy period, about 1655, he painted *The Polish Rider* (colorplate 42). It recalls the *Bamberg Rider*, which it is unlikely that Rembrandt knew, and Dürer's *Knight, Death, and the Devil* (see fig. 198), which he could hardly have escaped knowing. The most thorough investigations have not yet succeeded in uncovering the precise meaning of this painting, but there can be little doubt that in some way it is an allegory of man's earthly journey, its many dangers, and its uncertain destination. One cannot go far wrong to cite the words of Psalm 84: 5–6, on which Rembrandt must often have dwelt: "Blessed is the man whose strength is in thee. . . . Who passing through the valley of Baca[i.e., tears] make it a well; the rain also filleth the pools." In the grim and rocky valley a pool can be seen. Against the dark hill with its

suggestions of habitations—here and there a hut; near the crest a ruined castle—the youth rides in light, alert, his weapons at the ready. The figure and his mount stand forth in a new sculptural grandeur, intensified by the fact that many of the impastos have been laid on not with a brush but with a palette knife, literally carving the pigment, especially in the dark rocks and in the bony forms of the horse and the masses of his mane.

A special role in Rembrandt's vast production is played by his etchings. Etching was a medium known to the Renaissance, but relatively little used. In contrast to copper engraving (see figs. 197, 199), etching exacts little manual tension. The plate is coated with wax on which lines are drawn with a metal stylus, as rapidly as desired, but always firmly enough to penetrate to the copper. The plate, wax and all, is then put in an acid bath; whatever has been uncovered by the stylus is eaten into by the acid. The plate is then heated, the wax runs off, and the bitten lines are ready for printing. Because of the greater flexibility of the process itself and the range of values attainable by sensitive printing, the results are freer and more fluid than engraving. Etching can capture the lightness of a fugitive sketch or the tonal resonance of an oil painting. Rembrandt's etchings deal with every conceivable subject, from landscape and daily life to the Scriptures. Often they went through several phases, known as "states," before Rembrandt was satisfied. In its early states *The Three Crosses* of 1653 depicts in detail an elaborate drama. In the fourth and final state (fig. 309), clusters of lines are so bitten as to flood down in darkness at the right and in rays of light at the center like those that descend upon Bernini's *Saint Theresa* (see

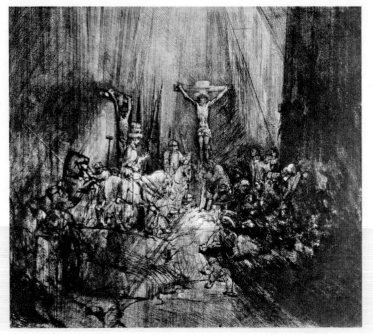

309. REMBRANDT. *The Three Crosses* (fourth state). 1660-61. Drypoint and burin, 15¼ x 17¾". The Metropolitan Museum of Art, New York. Gift of Felix M. Warburg and his Family, 1941

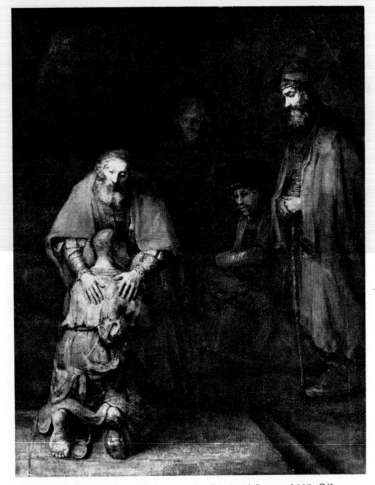

310. REMBRANDT. *Return of the Prodigal Son.* c. 1669. Oil on canvas, 8'8" x 6'8¾". The Hermitage, Leningrad

fig. 239). The penitent thief hangs upon his cross, dimly seen, but many of the other figures sink into shadow. Only a tip of the impenitent thief's cross still appears; the rest is obliterated by the darkness that fell over the land. We are left alone in the tumult with the Crucified, on whom the rays of light fall, and with the centurion, glorifying God and saying, "Certainly this was a righteous man" (Luke 23: 47).

Hendrickje probably died in 1662. Ill, Titus continued to help his lonely father until death claimed him, too, in 1668. Probably in 1669, the year of his own death, Rembrandt painted his *Return of the Prodigal Son* (fig. 310), which stands at the ultimate peak of Christian spirituality, illuminating the relationship of the Self to the Eternal. The parable (Luke 15: 11–32) was a favorite in Baroque art; its meaning, in general, can be discerned in Saint John of the Cross's words about union with divine love: "God communicates himself to the soul in this interior union with a love so intense that the love of a mother who so tenderly caresses her child, the love of a brother, or the affection of a friend bear no likeness to it, for so great is the tenderness and so deep the love with which the infinite Father comforts and exalts the humble and loving soul."

In Rembrandt's dark background one makes out two dim faces, a seated figure, and, more brightly lighted, the eldest son, hurt and uncomprehending because there was never a celebration for him, the lawabiding. In a spontaneous gesture of loving forgiveness, the gentle, aged father comes into the light to press to his bosom the cropped head of his ragged son. Faces have been reduced to little more than the essential angle between forehead and nose, framing the deep eyes. Only the hands of the father and the tired feet of the son—the left bared by its disintegrating shoe—are painted in any detail. The picture is, as Christ intended his parable to be, an allegory of the earthly pilgrimage of man finding rest and meaning in divine redemption. But Rembrandt's language in these late works is almost entirely that of color and texture. Rich tans and ochers in the prodigal's worn garments are inundated by the glowing red of his father's festal cloak against the deep browns of the encompassing dark; solid masses in thick impastos gleam against the translucent glazes.

In paintings, etchings, and drawings, Rembrandt depicted himself, in known examples, nearly a hundred times; all except a few of the earliest lack any trace of vanity. The Baroque was the age of the self-portrait; many a minor artist has left us a self-portrait superior in quality to any of his other works. Such revelations are foreign both to the High Renaissance and to Mannerism. Dürer, for example, shows us a self-possessed, self-contained, self-directed human being (see fig. 195); Parmigianino a congealed self in a distorted world (see fig. 180). Baroque self-portraits generally aim at revealing the artist as open to the world outside and beyond him, sensitive and responsive to higher powers. The Jesuit Cardinal Robert Bellarmine, who taught at Louvain in

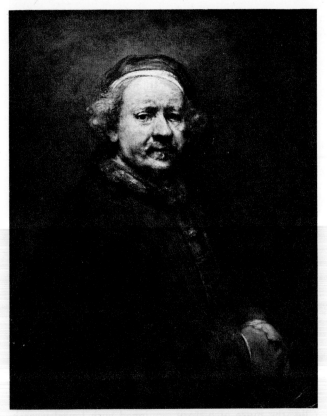

311. REMBRANDT. *Self-Portrait.* 1669. Oil on canvas, 33⅞ x 27¾". National Gallery, London

Flanders and whose work may well have been known to Rembrandt, proclaimed that "he that desires to erect a ladder by which he may ascend so high as to God Almighty, ought to take the first step from the consideration of himself." This is indeed what Rembrandt did, with increasing depth as the difficult and often tragic circumstances of his later life compelled constantly changing self-assessments in relation to God.

In a series of self-portraits painted in the final decade of his life, he attained a spiritual level that can only be compared with that of Michelangelo in his last *Pietà* (see fig. 187). One of the most moving of these last self-portraits (fig. 311) must date from the period of grief over the loss of Hendrickje. Although the face is impassive and the hands folded in resignation, the picture radiates quiet loneliness and the head is surrounded by light as by a halo. The masses of face, hair, and garments are kept as simple as in the *Prodigal Son*—mere blocks of pigment laid on with the knife, or perhaps even with the fingers. In these ultimate self-revelations, one recalls the opening words of Psalm 139, which Rembrandt must often have read, "O Lord, thou hast searched me, and known me," and in the interpenetration of impasto and glaze, mass and space, darkness and light, Verse 12: "Yea, the darkness hideth not from thee; but the night shineth as the day: the darkness and the light are both alike to thee."

VERMEER. In the seventeenth century, Jan Vermeer of Delft (1632–75) must have seemed to be another of the "little masters," hardly different in range and style from De Hooch (see fig. 296), whose domestic interiors those of Vermeer superficially resemble, and one seventeenth-century French traveler recorded that he found Vermeer's paintings vastly overpriced. Contemporary sources either barely mention Vermeer or omit his name entirely from lists of prominent artists. In the eighteenth century Sir Joshua Reynolds (see Chapter 8) considered Vermeer's *Kitchen Maid*, of about 1658 (fig. 312), one of the finest pictures he saw on a trip to Holland, but only in the nineteenth, with the rise of interest in naturalistic color (see Part Six, Chapter 3), were Vermeer's paintings truly appreciated. Today he is universally considered one of the greatest of Dutch painters, second only to Rembrandt. It is not difficult to see why. Although he has none of Rembrandt's mystery or passion, avoids the master's supernatural lighting effects, and indulges in none of the brilliant brushwork of Hals, his message is immediate, deep, and lasting. He was able, as were none of his contemporaries (and none of his predecessors save perhaps van Eyck and Piero della Francesca), to transmute simple actions into eternal symbols through the magic of pure perception and the perfect adjustment of space, tone, and color.

Because of his slow and painstaking methods, Vermeer seems to have painted very few pictures. He earned his living principally from art dealing, at which he lost heavily, due to a French invasion; he left a wife and eleven children in debt. Only about thirty-five of his paintings survive, and all but three represent interiors. When characterized at all, these rooms are modest in size and sparsely furnished. The background wall, when visible, is invariably parallel to the picture plane. All but two of the interiors are lighted strongly from one side—the left in all but three instances. In all but five the source of light is represented as a window; never is the spectator permitted to see through the window to the world outside. No matter what Vermeer may suggest or summarize of the outer world, or invite the spectator to imagine, wisdom begins and ends in the room, conceived as a cube of shining space in which the figures and their transitory actions seem forever suspended in light.

It has been recently suggested that Vermeer utilized for his pictorial compositions and techniques the device of the camera obscura, a darkened enclosure with an opening on one side and a flat, light surface on the other. The normal action of rays of light, reflected from objects outside the camera obscura, passing through the aperture, projects the image on the light surface, upside down, even without a lens. By the interposition of a mirror before the opening the image may be rectified, and the insertion of a lens provides the possibility of focus. The camera obscura without a lens was known to Islamic scientists in the tenth century, and with a lens to Italians in the early sixteenth. Such devices were popular in the seventeenth century throughout Europe. There are two types, one in which the viewer is inside the box, the other in which he looks through a peephole. Only the first, which may be portable like a sedan chair, or supplied with a hood to envelop the viewer, will project an image onto a flat surface on which it may be studied, drawn, or painted.

Vermeer seems to have used the camera obscura at first to unify the planes of light and dark and the patches of color into a coherent image. The camera obscura tends to turn all reflections of light into tiny blobs of white; these are clearly visible in the *Kitchen Maid*, especially on the pointed bread rolls on the table and on the fresh cheese in the basket, but also on the rim of the pitcher and on the puckered hem of the maid's apron. Vermeer has treated them as indications of volume in light, in the manner of the necklace of pearls around the subject's neck in Piero della Francesca's *Battista Sforza* (see colorplate 10). The camera obscura also allowed Vermeer to escape from the conventional coloring of his Dutch predecessors and contemporaries, dominated even in outdoor scenes by grays, greens, and browns, into a world of brighter, purer hues, such as the strong blue of the maid's apron and the bright yellow of her bodice. These colors are seen reflected through the other colors in the room, notably in the bluish shadows on the creamy wall. Although Vermeer depicts a brass brazier and a hamper hanging in the corner, as well as a foot warmer on the floor with a pot of hot ashes inside, with true Dutch naturalism, he concentrates all attention on the nobility of the simple action of the maid pouring milk and the purity of the spherical and cylindrical volumes, producing a composition as monumental as anything that ever issued from High Renaissance Italy.

Vermeer's careful optical studies made it possible for him to paint his rare outdoor scenes with a glowing intensity of color unknown before his time. There is nothing contrived about the composition of the *View of Delft*, of about 1662 (fig. 313). We seem really to be there, and to experience the warm red of the old bricks and tiles with our own eyes. Even the clouds have a sultriness and weight that none of the professional landscapists of the seventeenth century could quite capture, and the characteristic climax of the picture, the sudden stab of light on the distant church spire, seems wholly accidental. Never again until the work of Corot in the nineteenth century were tonal values to be so exquisitely adjusted, or the still figures of ordinary people to be used to induce so quiet a contemplation of the beauty of timeworn structures and vessels in diffused light and moisture-laden air.

Vermeer's art is summed up in his *Allegory of the Art of Painting* (colorplate 43), probably dating from near the end of his brief life. The subject is not entirely clear; the artist—certainly not Vermeer, as he is dressed in late sixteenth-century costume—is painting a model robed as Clio, the muse of history, equipped with laurel wreath, book, and trumpet, according to her description in the *Iconologia*, a treatise on allegorical representations by

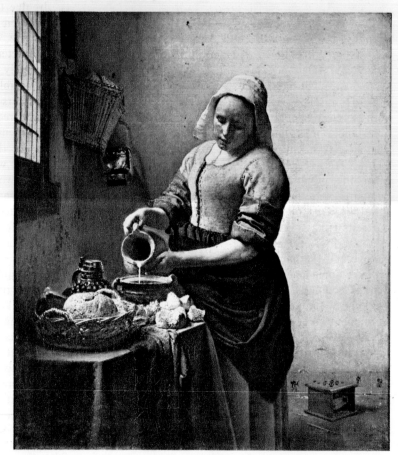

312. JAN VERMEER. *Kitchen Maid*. c. 1658. Oil on canvas, 17⅞ x 16⅛". Rijksmuseum, Amsterdam

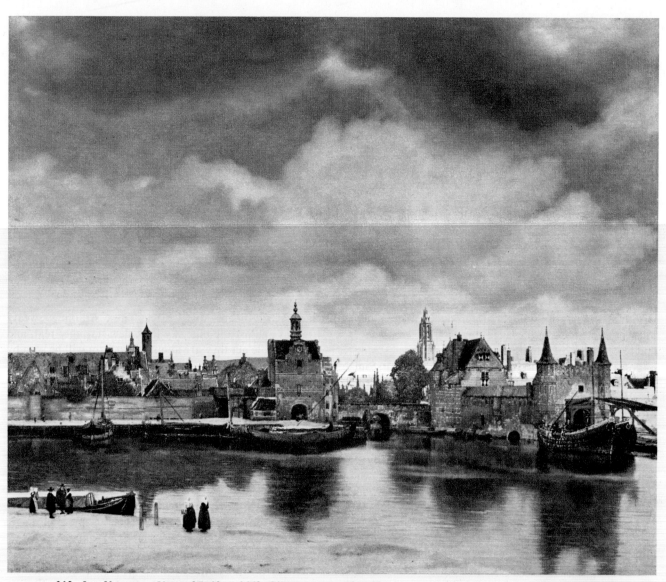

313. JAN VERMEER. *View of Delft.* c. 1662. Oil on canvas, 38½ x 46¼". Mauritshuis, The Hague, The Netherlands

Cesare Ripa, first published in Italy in 1593 and widely read throughout Europe. The painter is making a picture that could hardly be farther from Vermeer's own work. Steadying his right hand on a maulstick, he has already executed the general contours of Clio's pose in white, filling the canvas with her half-length figure, and is now painting the leaves of her crown. She stands in the light of an unseen window, against a huge map representing both northern and southern Netherlands, bordered by views of twenty cities (it appears in several of Vermeer's backgrounds). Thus the outer world is permitted to invade the picture, but only symbolically, along with the muse of history. The map looks as though it could be read in detail, like the open manuscripts in the works of van Eyck; only the largest letters, however, are actually legible, as if Vermeer had interposed a threshold between the object and the viewer that permits only elements of a certain size to be clearly distinguished.

The magic fascination of the picture lies less in the subject than in Vermeer's brilliant perspective contrasts, made possible by his use of the camera obscura, which even exaggerates such phenomena. Compare, for instance, the interior by De Hooch (see fig. 296), which avoids any strong foreground elements, with this painting. In this symbolic image of the artist faced with geography and history, time and space, congealed in planes of clear, bright color in a light-filled room, Vermeer has created a perfect Baroque counterpart to the Early Renaissance interior in the *Arnolfini Wedding* (see fig. 101), which it so strongly suggests.

6
Spanish Painting in the Seventeenth Century

Although Spain, like England, produced writers and musicians of great importance during the Renaissance, and few painters of interest, the country had been strongly impressed by the work of a foreign master of first importance, El Greco. It is surprising that the great creative development of Spanish painting in the seventeenth century owed little or nothing to El Greco's mysticism, which had vibrated in such perfect harmony with Spanish Counter-Reformation thought. Nor did the new art in Spain spring from the central region dominated by El Greco; the painters of the seventeenth century who suddenly established Spain in the forefront of Baroque visual creativity were all southerners.

RIBERA. One of the earliest of these, Jusepe de Ribera (1591–1652), from Valencia province, although not the earliest Spanish master to feel the force of the Caravaggesque revolution, but probably the most important link between Spain and Italy, went to Italy probably shortly after 1610, visited the North and Rome, and then settled in Naples, at the time a Spanish province, where he immediately came under the influence of Caravaggio's numerous Neapolitan followers, known as the *tenebrosi* (*shadowy ones*) because of their exaggeration of Caravaggio's strong light-and-dark contrasts.

Ribera's best-known work, the *Martyrdom of Saint Bartholomew* (fig. 314), probably painted in 1639, shows an obvious reliance on Caravaggio in its emphasis on direct experience; it is surprising after El Greco that this experience is predominantly physical, even when the subject is religious. Bartholomew was flayed alive (see fig. 182 for Michelangelo's personal interpretation). Ribera has spared us the clinical rendering of the event as seen in Netherlandish art, yet the picture is dominated by pain and fear. The almost naked saint is being hauled into position by his executioners, straining gigantically like Rubens' figures in the *Raising of the Cross* (see fig. 284). Ribera has no interest, however, in either Italian physical

beauty or Rubens' spiral surge. These straining, sweaty figures against the blue sky look devastatingly real, and the horrible act they are about to perform will be seen by a very real crowd, including women and children. Such vivid concentration on the immediate is perhaps significant, for Spain's greatest contribution to European art, in the painting of Velázquez at midcentury, is purely optical, without spiritual purpose or overtones. The harsh reality of the scene is a precursor of some of the most powerful Spanish art of later periods, notably that of Goya (see Part Six, Chapter 2).

ZURBARÁN. A translation of the spiritual into direct physical terms communicates a special element of magic to the work of another southerner, Francisco de Zurbarán (1598–1664), who never visited Italy, but settled and worked in Seville. Like La Tour (see fig. 257), with whose poetic work that of Zurbarán has something in common, he experienced the Caravaggesque revolution at second hand, yet his art is closer to the basic message of Caravaggio—the externalization of inner experience—than is the more strident realism of Ribera. In the *Vision of Saint Peter Nolasco*, of 1629 (fig. 315), the Apostle Peter—who had been crucified upside down at his own request to avoid comparison with Christ—appears in a vision to his meditating thirteenth-century namesake in the darkness of his cell. The room has disappeared; bright light reveals vision and visionary, both equally tangible, as if suspended, one surrounded by the darkness of this world, the other revealed by the light of the next.

VELÁZQUEZ. The supreme native master of painting in Spain is universally recognized to be Diego Rodríguez de Silva y Velázquez (1599–1660). Born in Seville, Velázquez studied with a local Mannerist named Francisco Pacheco. In 1623 he was appointed court painter, and the following year settled permanently in Madrid; by 1627 he

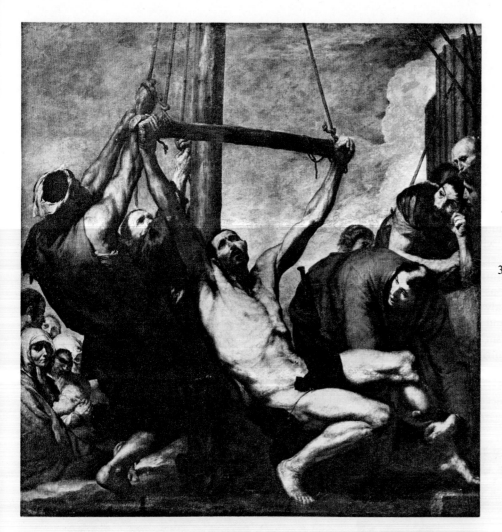

314. JUSEPE DE RIBERA.
*Martyrdom of Saint
Bartholomew.* c. 1639. Oil
on canvas, 92⅛ x 92⅛".
Museo del Prado, Madrid

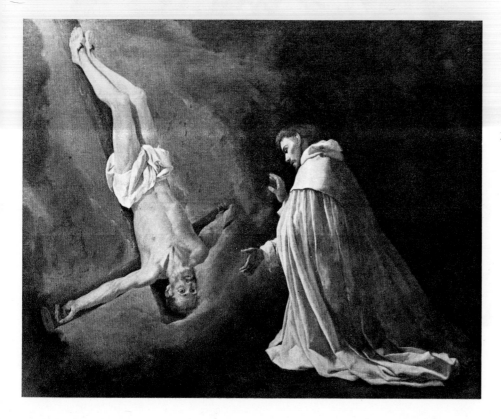

315. FRANCISCO DE ZURBARÁN.
*Vision of Saint Peter
Nolasco.* 1629. Oil on
canvas, 70½ x 87¾". Museo
del Prado, Madrid

was established in the royal household, attaining in 1652 the rank of court chamberlain, which gave him a residence attached to the palace and a studio inside it. For more than thirty years Velázquez painted King Philip IV and members of the royal family and court, yet such was his originality and candor that not one of his paintings can be reproached with being a mere state portrait.

Although a close friend of Rubens at the time of the great Fleming's second visit to Madrid in 1628, Velázquez never deserted the integrity of his own style, and not once did he adopt the characteristic machinery of allegorical figures, columns, curtains, and boiling clouds utilized by most Catholic painters in the seventeenth century. Temperamentally little suited to religious subjects, he painted them rarely, and with varying degrees of success. Like Hals and Vermeer, with whose works he could hardly have been familiar, Velázquez was profoundly attached to nature as revealed through light to human vision. He visited Italy twice, and expressed a frank distaste for Raphael—and thus in all probability for the Classical Italian idealism of which Raphael was the chief exponent—while admiring Titian and copying Tintoretto, doubtless as an exercise in freedom of the brush. Lest one think that Velázquez had no interest in Renaissance ideas on the subject of form, however, it is worthwhile noting that his private library contained the works of the principal Italian architectural theorists, even though their architecture seldom appears in his paintings. Throughout his life he was deeply concerned with the principles of composition and design, no matter how immediate his subject matter.

Caravaggesque realism had already penetrated Spain in the works of Ribera and others, and must have been felt as a liberation by the young Velázquez. His own interpretation of the movement is original and irresistible. His *Triumph of Bacchus,* of about 1628, which has acquired the nickname of *Los Borrachos* (*The Drunkards*) (fig. 316), contains numerous reminiscences of Titian's *Bacchanal of the Andrians* (see fig. 161), reinterpreted in basically Caravaggesque terms. Bacchus is a rather soft Spanish youth, with nothing but a towel and a cloak around his waist, as if he had just climbed out of a neighboring stream, and anything but Classical in appearance. Crowned with vine leaves himself, he mischievously bestows a crown upon a kneeling worshiper, who is a simple Spanish peasant. Other peasants are gathered round; one, with bristling moustache and hat pushed back to show the white forehead of a farmer's grinning, sunburned face, hands a cup of wine toward the spectator, while another tries roguishly to grab it. The genial proletarian invitation to join in the delights of wine is painted with a brilliance unequaled by any other Latin

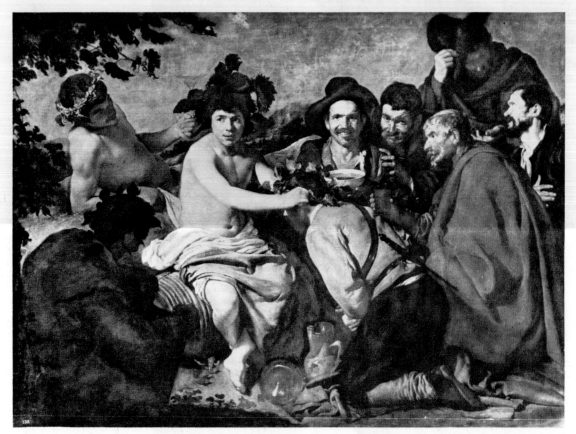

316. DIEGO DE VELÁZQUEZ. *Triumph of Bacchus (The Drunkards).* c. 1628. Oil on canvas, 65 x 88⅝". Museo del Prado, Madrid

painter in the seventeenth century. Yet the crusty surface, and the emphasis on the solidity of flesh, rough clothing, and crockery, show that Velázquez is basically a Mediterranean painter, concerned with substance, and unlikely to indulge in such fireworks of the brush as those of Frans Hals. It is no wonder that this picture excited the admiration of Manet in the nineteenth century (see Part Six, Chapter 4).

At the time of Velázquez's second trip to Italy (1649–51), he fell even deeper under the influence of the great Venetians of the preceding century, but never that of his Italian Baroque contemporaries, nor of the austerely classical Poussin. In the gardens of the Villa Medici, he painted small studies (fig. 317), the earliest examples we know of landscapes not composed in the studio but done outdoors with a directness hitherto restricted to the preliminary sketch in wash (see fig. 262). This great historic step was not to be followed until the English landscape painters of the early nineteenth century (see Part Six, Chapter 2). In his attempt to seize the immediacy of the moment of vision, Velázquez painted with free, light strokes of differing hues—browns, greens, blue greens, and whites. Both the subject and the method were an important step in the direction of nineteenth-century landscape art.

Velázquez's acknowledged masterpiece, and one of the most original paintings of the entire seventeenth century, is *Las Meninas* (*The Ladies-in-Waiting*—its original title was simply *The Portrait of the Family*), of 1656 (colorplate 44). The painter is shown in his studio in the royal palace, at work upon a canvas so large that it can only be this very picture, unique in scale in his entire production. In the center the light falls most strongly on the glittering figure of the five-year-old princess, who has paid the painter a visit, accompanied by two ladies-in-waiting, one of whom kneels to hand her a cup of water. On the right are shown two dwarfs—those playthings of the Spanish court, whom Velázquez always painted with humanity and comprehension—one gently teasing with his foot an elderly and somnolent dog. Through an open door in the background wall, light falls on a court official, pausing for a moment on the steps. Most important of all, the mirror alongside the door reflects the king and queen, who also honor the painter with their presence.

Today the painting prompts speculations on the relationship of reality and image, space within the picture and figures outside it, as in Manet's *A Bar at the Folies Bergère* (see fig. 419). However, it has been recently shown that this picture is connected with Velázquez's attempts to be recognized as a noble, which met with some difficulty at first, but in 1658 were rewarded with the Order of Santiago at the hands of the king, who after the painter's death in 1660 caused the cross of Santiago to be painted on his doublet in this very picture. Since the only obstacle to his admission to the order was his profes-

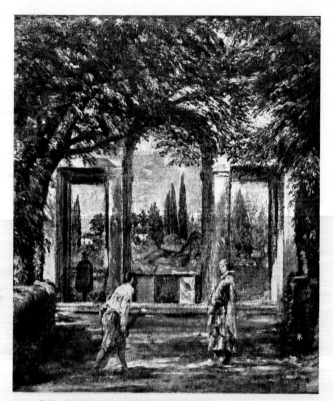

317. DIEGO DE VELÁZQUEZ. *Garden of the Villa Medici, Rome.* c. 1649–51. Oil on canvas, 17⅜ x 15". Museo del Prado, Madrid

sion of painting, then considered a manual trade, the artist demonstrates in this picture the nobility of his art, favored with familiarity by the king, the queen, and the little princess in an allegory all the more effective for being so strikingly real. Despite the apparent ease and informality of the subject, the picture, like all Velázquez's compositions, is carefully balanced, in a series of interlocking pyramids that can be ranked with the greatest designs of the Renaissance.

Totally and dazzlingly new, however, is Velázquez's optical method of painting, paralleled (independently) only by Vermeer's. In light and dark the illusion of the picture is as startlingly real as the intimate and quiet mood. Velázquez's brush suggests convincingly the reality of objects entirely through the sparkles and reflections of light on hair, silks, flowers, and embroidery. We could hardly be further from the linear precision of Holbein (see colorplate 33, fig. 206), let us say; nothing is drawn; nothing has visible edges. Only spots of light and color, set down by dexterous touches of the brush, create an illusion of form, in the last analysis more accurate than Holbein's method because more closely related to the actual phenomena of instantaneous vision. In *Las Meninas* Velázquez demonstrates not only to his contemporaries but also to all time the nobility of his art—a rank that no king can confer.

7
Continental Art in the Eighteenth Century

In European cultural history the eighteenth century is a unique period in that it did not produce a single figure in the visual arts to rank with the universal masters of previous epochs. The seventeenth century can boast Caravaggio, Bernini, Borromini, Rubens, Rembrandt, Vermeer, and Velázquez, all artists of the highest stature. In the eighteenth century the palm passed to music—Bach, Handel, Vivaldi, Haydn, and Mozart. Paradoxically, it was a period of intense creative activity, with countless artists of talent, many delightful, yet all limited. Nothing completely new was created except the Rococo style (see below), and even that was a light-hearted version of Baroque grandiloquence, as if the overinflated Baroque balloon had burst and the floating pieces had alighted wherever they could find a perch. After the grandeur of the Catholic triumph in Rome and the pomposity of the Age of Louis XIV in France, grace, charm, and wit substituted for grandeur and splendor. Yet all the time in the background flowed the strains of classicism and realism, which in the seventeenth century had formed countercurrents to the more outspokenly Baroque styles, and when least expected one or the other could move into the light. Aside from its frequent lack of deep seriousness, the most striking aspect of eighteenth-century art is the contrast between international styles on the continent of Europe and an assertive nationalism in England, where the Rococo was never more than partially accepted no matter how much of it the English lord or wealthy merchant might have absorbed on the Grand Tour.

JUVARRA. In Italy the international dimension of eighteenth-century style emerged in the architecture of Filippo Juvarra (1678–1736), a Sicilian brought to Turin by Vittorio Amedeo II during the brief period when this duke of Piedmont and Savoy reigned as king of Sicily. In and around the Piedmontese capital, already studded with brilliant works by Guarini, Juvarra turned out an astonishing array of churches and royal residences, and from this center he either traveled or sent designs throughout Central and western Europe, from Vienna to Lisbon. A very agreeable phenomenon of the Late Baroque in Italy is the mountaintop sanctuary, intended to bring a vast landscape into focus. The shrine of Superga (fig. 318), commissioned from Juvarra by Vittorio Amedeo in 1715 or 1716 in gratitude to the Virgin for assistance in battle and completed in 1731, looks across Turin to a rampart of glittering Alps. Only the battalions of windows and chimneys relieve the brick mass of the monastery intended to serve the shrine.

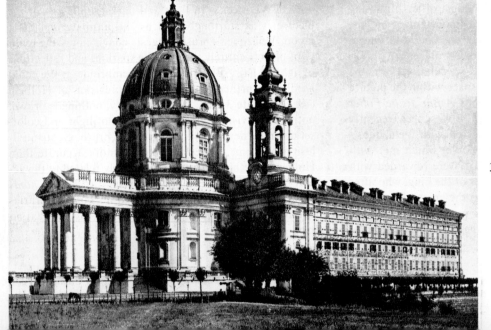

318. FILIPPO JUVARRA. Exterior, Superga (Monastery Church). c. 1715–31. Near Turin, Italy

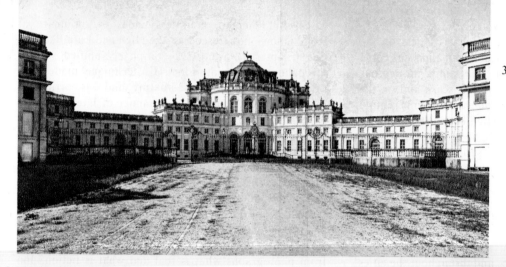

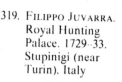
319. FILIPPO JUVARRA. Royal Hunting Palace. 1729-33. Stupinigi (near Turin). Italy

Growing out of the very mountain, the structure comes to its climax in the white stone church, a circular structure on an octagonal core, preceded by a temple portico and crowned by a circular dome, and flanked by a campanile on each side. A somewhat similar arrangement of church and monastic buildings had already been devised at Melk in Austria (see fig. 336). One recalls at once buildings by Michelangelo and Borromini (see figs. 184, 249), yet the general effect is much lighter than their designs. The coupled pilasters and columns are more widely spaced, the latter quite freely grouped in the portico, and the airy campaniles abound in double curvature.

The sprightliness of early eighteenth-century taste finds unexpected expression in Juvarra's fantastic hunting lodge of Stupinigi, outside Turin, of 1729-33 (fig. 319), a brilliant parody of Versailles. The plan of the main block is a flattened X, whose spokes radiate from a central oval hall, its dome crowned by a stag. The Classical orders barely assert themselves in the membrane-like undulation of wall and window.

Among all the Italian schools of painting, only that of Venice survived with real originality and vigor into the eighteenth century; the revived Venetian School was, in fact, the only serious rival to that of France on the Continent. Interestingly enough, the period was one of political stagnation; the thousand-year-old republic ruled by an oligarchy was an anachronism, incapable of competing with the imperialist monarchies to the north and west. The splendid city had become a playground for the rich and great of all Europe, the first tourist center of the modern world. Old themes, transformed in content and lightened in style, remained in the new painting that decorated church and palace interiors in an astonishing burst of creative energy.

PIAZZETTA. The first important master of eighteenth-century Venice was Giovanni Battista Piazzetta (1682–1754), who spent most of his long life in the city of the lagoons. While his pictures often retain something of the darkness of the *tenebrosi* and the drama of the Roman High Baroque, they already show something of the lightness and grace of the eighteenth century. His *Ecstasy of Saint Francis*, of about 1732 (fig. 320), echoes at a dis-

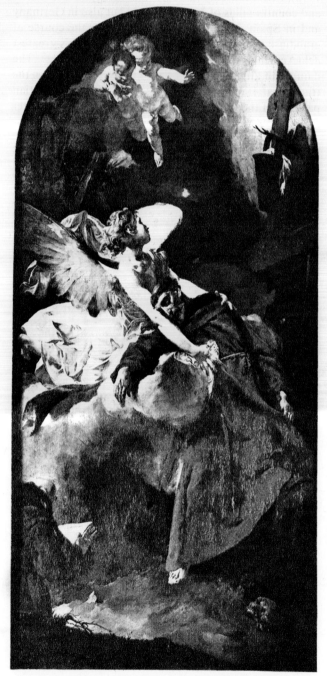
320. GIOVANNI BATTISTA PIAZZETTA. *Ecstasy of Saint Francis*. c. 1732. Oil on canvas, 12'4½" x 6'1⅛". Museo Civico d'Arte e Storia. Vicenza. Italy

tance Bernini's *Ecstasy of Saint Theresa* (see fig. 239), but with far less intensity. The emphasis is less on the climax than on the moment of healing; an angel has come down to stanch the blood from the saint's miraculous wounds, and light plays softly on this scene and on the two child angels above, creating delicate rhythms remote from the powerful forms of the High Baroque, just as the figures are relieved from the weight of Caravaggio and Rubens. As compared with the serious themes of the seventeenth century, the mood is exquisite and almost playful.

TIEPOLO. The supreme Venetian master of the period, and one of the two or three finest painters of the eighteenth century, was Giovanni Battista Tiepolo (1696–1770), active not only in Venice and throughout the cities and country villas of Northern Italy but also in Germany and in Spain; he died in Madrid while in the course of grandiose projects at the royal palace. Tiepolo's greatest achievements were his vast decorative frescoes. The damp, salt air of Venice was not kind to true fresco in the traditional Italian style, and as we have seen Venetian painters of the sixteenth century (see Part Four, Chapter 5) preferred to cover large surfaces with detachable can-

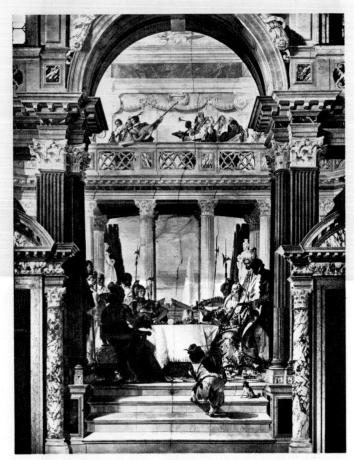

321. GIOVANNI BATTISTA TIEPOLO. *The Banquet of Anthony and Cleopatra.* Fresco. Before 1750. Palazzo Labia, Venice

vases. But Tiepolo, doubtless under the influence of Roman illusionist frescoes of the High and Late Baroque (see Chapter 1), wanted a completely unified surface throughout entire interiors. His technique made considerable use of sand in the mixture, and was carried out *secco su fresco*, much in the manner of late Byzantine painting, at the Kariye Djami, for instance. By these means he was able to cover enormous surfaces, but with a completely new lightness, combined with a mathematical perfection of perspective in no way inferior to that of Pozzo (see fig. 252). The walls and ceiling of the great hall in the Palazzo Labia in Venice (fig. 321), probably finished before Tiepolo's trip to Germany in 1750, are completely painted away with illusionistic architecture of such accuracy that it is often next to impossible to tell from photographs what is real and what is fiction, and difficult even when one is standing in the room. Actually, only the narrow rectangular marble doorframes shown in the illustration are real.

The story of Antony and Cleopatra is treated as a continuous festival surrounding the entire room, like a greatly expanded Veronese supper (see colorplate 29), from which one picks out with difficulty even the figures of the principal actors; drama hardly matters—only the operatic splendor of the conception, the colors of the marbles and the costumes, and the free flow of forms and light. Architecture and figures are bathed in a luminous atmosphere that had not been seen since ancient Roman painting, which Tiepolo must have known at least in engravings (excavations began at Herculaneum in 1738 and at Pompeii in 1748).

Tiepolo showed his magical facility and feather lightness in decorations on an even more ambitious scale in the ceiling frescoes for the archiepiscopal Residenz in Würzburg, finished in 1753 (colorplate 45). The ceilings of the halls and the grand staircase remind one of Pozzo's Sant'Ignazio frescoes (see fig. 252), especially in that the four parts of the world reappear, but shorn of all weight and solemnity. The mighty, upward-boiling geyser of the Baroque pictorial composition, in Cortona or in Rubens, has dissolved into scraps floating in light and color in the pearly immensity of space.

GUARDI. A new category of Venetian eighteenth-century painting was that of views, whether of Venice itself or of Venetian buildings recombined in imaginary landscape settings. These works were generally intended for the wealthy international public who thronged Venice and took them back as mementos to their splendid houses throughout Europe. Some of the view painters were accurate perspective theorists who made wide use of the camera obscura (see pages 267, 268), but in modern eyes the most gifted were several brothers of the Guardi family, whose sister married Tiepolo. Experienced in the painting of altarpieces, the Guardi brought to view painting a special kind of fantasy and a dazzling lightness of touch. Francesco (1712–93) is generally considered the most important, but the situation is still very confused,

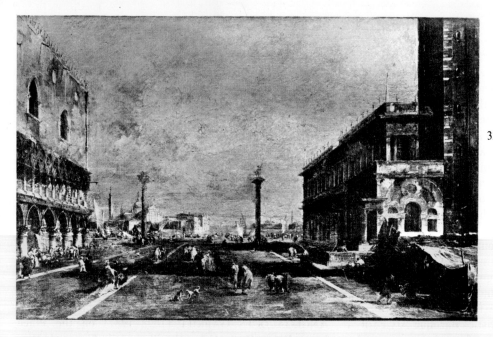

322. FRANCESCO GUARDI. *Piazzetta San Marco*. Date unknown. Oil on canvas, 17¾ x 28⅜". Ca' d'Oro, Venice

and it may never be possible completely to disentangle the styles of the brothers and their assistants; they seem to have worked together in a shop like other skilled Italian artisans.

Not until he reached seventy-two was Francesco elected to the Venetian Academy, in the category of view painter, and then there were two votes against him. One can see why; even for eighteenth-century Venice his technique is so brisk and his vision so unconventional that his work must have been at times hard to digest. To us his paintings seem the very embodiment of the carnival atmosphere of the last century of the republic's life before Napoleon turned Venice over to Austria. Instead of dignified monumentality, the familiar shapes of the Doges' Palace, the Library of San Marco, and the façade of San Giorgio Maggiore (fig. 322) take on a quality of tattered age in the long light of afternoon, with elegant strollers out to enjoy the air and a bit of intrigue, lower classes busy at an awninged shop at the base of the Campanile, and two dogs in the exploratory stage of courtship. Actually, Guardi's fantasy and light touch revive an ancient tradition, that of the freely painted view we have seen in the Fourth Pompeiian style, with the same delightful combination of poetry and wit.

THE ROCOCO AND CLASSICISM. In France the Late Baroque took on a new flavor and lightness after the demise of Louis XIV, which freed the courtiers for a life in Paris considerably more agreeable than their virtual imprisonment at Versailles. A number of *hôtels particuliers* (*town mansions*) were built by the aristocracy in fashionable quarters of the capital. Although their exteriors were designed in a tradition flowing directly from that of the seventeenth century, in the interiors everything was transformed. Nothing was more odious to the eighteenth century than the pomposity of Le Roi-Soleil. The new and delightfully irresponsible style has

won the name Rococo, derived from the word *rocaille* (the fantastic decoration of rocks and shells lining grottoes in Mannerist and Baroque gardens) because of its frequent use of shell forms, combined with scrolls, flowers, ribbons, and other caprices in a decoration that obliterates form and direction and defies analysis.

One of the most brilliant examples of this characteristically intimate and small-scale decoration is the Salon de la Princesse in the Hôtel de Soubise (fig. 323), designed in 1732 by GERMAIN BOFFRAND (1667–1754), a pupil of Hardouin-Mansart, and supplied with paintings by CHARLES-JOSEPH NATOIRE (1700–77). The plan is oval, and the walls so treated that it is impossible to decide where they end and the ceiling begins.

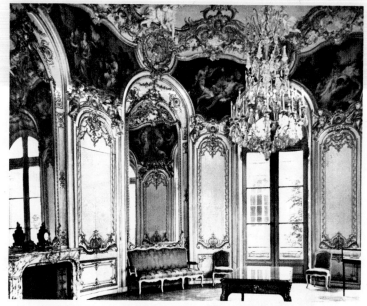

323. GERMAIN BOFFRAND and CHARLES-JOSEPH NATOIRE. Salon de la Princesse. Hôtel de Soubise. 1732. Paris

The room is light and frivolous, a mere bubble of plaster, paint, gold, and glass. The eight openings oscillate between windows and mirrors so arranged as to provide reflections that further confuse one's sense of direction. There are no Classical orders (although there are many on the exterior); the walls are treated as panels, surrounded by gilt moldings whose only straight lines are the verticals. On them scraps of gilt decoration, blown like thistledown, seem to have come momentarily to rest. In frames whose double curvatures elude geometrical definition, the lighthearted paintings unfold the romance of Cupid and Psyche. The central chandelier, its scores of faceted pendants reflecting and multiplying the light of the candles, is an essential element in the fragile web of color and light. In assessing the meaning, purpose, and limitations of such extreme examples of the Rococo, however, it should be borne in mind that Boffrand's more monumental buildings, both exteriors and interiors, derive from the sober, classicistic Baroque style of Hardouin-Mansart (see figs. 272, 274).

The same society that demanded such frivolities as the Salon de la Princesse for aristocratic diversions required a wholly different mode for serious buildings, increasingly Classical—in fact, Augustan—toward the middle of the century. The Panthéon, in Paris (figs. 324, 325), built in 1757–90 after the designs of GERMAIN SOUFFLOT (1713–80) as the Church of Sainte-Geneviève, shows a classicism more thorough and severe than that of Perrault (see fig. 267). Trained in Rome, Soufflot admired High Renaissance architecture and originally planned a Greek-cross structure with a hemispheric dome reflecting Bramante's designs for Saint Peter's. Following the wishes of the clergy, he prolonged his design to its present Latin-cross shape, and the dome consequently

had to be heightened; Soufflot obviously followed Wren's dome for Saint Paul's (see fig. 282), eliminating the niches. The portico is, of course, the pronaos of a Roman temple, especially reminding us of the Maison Carrée at Nîmes, although with a projecting wing on each side. Interestingly enough, Soufflot was an admirer of Gothic constructional principles, and concealed not only a clerestory, but an elaborate system of supports for his interior vaulting behind the lofty screen wall and balustrade, which make the two-story building appear one story high on the exterior. The cold aspect of the blank outer walls is due to the walling up of the windows during the Revolution, in 1791, when the building was converted to its present purpose as a memorial to France's illustrious dead; traces of the original windows can still be seen in the illustration.

A triumph of the new Classical tendency in French monumental architecture is the pair of palaces built by ANGE-JACQUES GABRIEL (1698–1782) on the Place Louis XV in Paris, today the Place de la Concorde (fig. 326). In its handling of space the general idea is still Baroque. The façades were intended to flank the straight street leading to the Church of the Madeleine (eventually built in the nineteenth century on the model of a Roman temple). Inspired by the East Façade of the Louvre (see fig. 267), Gabriel's masterpieces are more strongly Classical in that the columns are single, as in Roman buildings, instead of paired. Widely spaced in a steady parade above rusticated arches, the colonnades uniting the terminal temple fronts produce an impression of extreme elegance and grace. Gabriel was also responsible for the exquisitely proportioned Petit Trianon, of 1762–68 (figs. 327, 328), built in the park of Versailles as a hideaway for the king's reigning mistress, Madame de

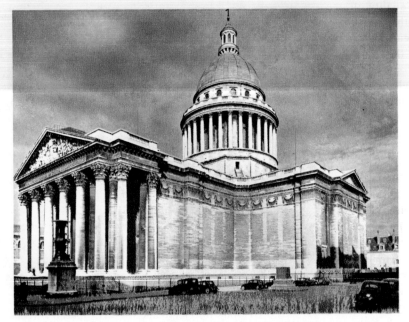

324. GERMAIN SOUFFLOT. Exterior, The Panthéon
(Church of Ste.-Geneviève). 1757–90. Paris

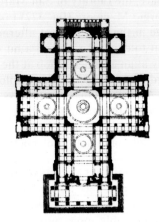

325. GERMAIN SOUFFLOT. Plan of
The Panthéon (Church of
Ste.-Geneviève)

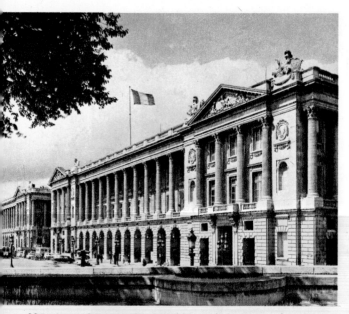

326. ANGE-JACQUES GABRIEL. Place de la Concorde (originally Place Louis XV). 1763. Paris

Pompadour, who, in fact, governed France, and her impetus was responsible for the great upsurge in building activity at midcentury, as her taste was for the Augustan style.

WATTEAU. One of the greatest French painters of the eighteenth century, and one of the two or three anywhere to be ranked with Tiepolo, was Jean-Antoine Watteau (1684–1721), whose paintings embody the interests of the

Rococo raised to the plane of lyric poetry. Born in the Flemish town of Valenciennes, annexed by Louis XIV only six years before his birth, Watteau never forgot his Flemish heritage, especially his allegiance to the Baroque colorism of Rubens. After an impoverished and difficult beginning in Paris, which undermined his health, the young painter rapidly achieved recognition. In 1712 he was invited to join the Academy, and was permitted to write his own ticket for a reception piece. His remaining nine years of life, constantly clouded by illness, were largely devoted to the production of an enchanting series of canvases idealizing the themes of courtship and of outdoor festivals and plays popular during the last years of Louis XIV, and overwhelmingly so during the Regency. His special category was the *fêtes galantes*, which can best be described as festivals attended by exquisitely dressed young ladies and gentlemen in gardens or parks.

The loveliest of these is *A Pilgrimage to Cythera*, the artist's reception piece for the Academy, painted in 1717 (fig. 329), intended to evoke fragile memories of Rubens' *Garden of Love* (see fig. 287). The subject is a day's journey of youthful couples to the island of Cythera, sacred to Venus, whose statue, hung with rose garlands, stands at the right. At its base Cupid has hung his quiver of arrows, and the couples, still exchanging vows in the light of early evening, prepare to embark for the shore in a golden boat attended by clouds of cherubs, not without a mournful look backward at the pleasures of the enchanted isle. This wistful evocation of the transience of love is carried out with an unrivaled grace of drawing and delicacy of color. Watteau usually covered his canvases with a heavy coating of pearly color, shifting from white to blue and sometimes to rose. Once the underpaint was dry, he indicated the trees in swiftly applied washes of

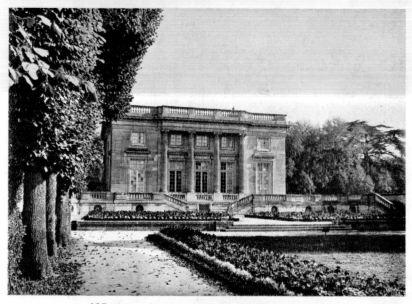

327. ANGE-JACQUES GABRIEL. West façade, Petit Trianon. 1762–68. Versailles, France

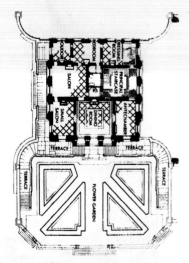

328. ANGE-JACQUES GABRIEL. Plan of the Petit Trianon and flower garden. 1762–68. Versailles, France

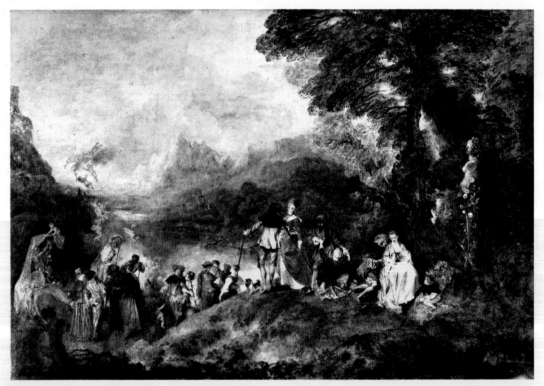

329. JEAN-ANTOINE WATTEAU. *A Pilgrimage to Cythera*. 1717. Oil on canvas, 51 x 76½". The Louvre, Paris

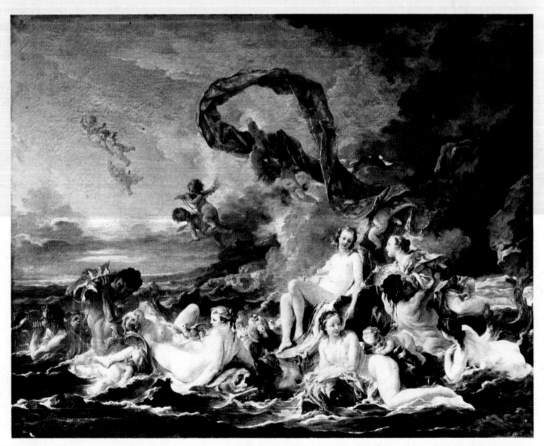

330. FRANÇOIS BOUCHER. *Triumph of Venus*. 1740. Oil on canvas, 51⅛ x 63¾". Nationalmuseum, Stockholm

green, blue green, and golden brown, somewhat in the manner of Van Goyen (see fig. 292), but so transparent that the pearly undercoat shows through. The figures were then touched in with fairly thick impastos, in jewel-like tones predominantly of rose, blue, yellow, and white. The whole was then glazed in the manner of Titian, so that the impastos would gleam richly through an atmosphere determined by the surrounding washes. The figures are generally very small in relation to the space, and invariably based on pointed forms—triangles delicately supported by the toes of shoes, the tips of canes, or the pointed ends of ladies' trains; even the faces are generally conceived in terms of pointed shapes, and all were preceded by scores of preparatory drawings from life in which every facet of form, color, and expression was carefully studied.

It is an art that depends largely on poise for its effect, and on brushstrokes of great accuracy and delicacy. These are being appreciated by buyers in an extraordinary painting, the *Signboard of Gersaint* (colorplate 46), probably painted in the last year of Watteau's life for his friend Gersaint, an art dealer, and intended to be hung outdoors in front of the shop (one would hope only in good weather). The interior is lined with paintings to the ceiling, and frequented by elegant ladies and gentlemen, one of whom goes down on one knee to examine the precise quality of a painter's touch (an observation owed to Meyer Schapiro). There could hardly be more eloquent proof of the importance of touch to artist and public alike, or a more vivid evocation of the circumstances under which pictures were bought and sold in the eighteenth century. Watteau was able to invest even this prosaic scene with excitement and poetry.

BOUCHER. The painter who more than any other epitomizes the pleasure-loving aspect of the Rococo is François Boucher (1703–70), the favorite painter of Madame de Pompadour. There is little in his work of the mystery and poetry of Watteau, but for sheer sensuous charm his paintings, overflowing with voluptuous nudes, are hard to equal. The *Triumph of Venus*, of 1740 (fig. 330), shows the goddess of love half-seated, half-reclining on silks and satins in a huge shell, drawn across the sea by dolphins, accompanied by tritons and sea nymphs, one of whom offers her a shell of pearls, while Cupids race in twos and threes through the trailing clouds, carrying a miraculously graceful salmon-and-silver-striped scarf that resembles a gigantic banner. In contrast to Watteau, Boucher retains Rubens' device of the spiral into the picture, and his colors, reveling in sensuous shades of pink and blue, are richly enameled and dense, with little or no use of glazes. Frivolity, grace, and charm are pushed almost to the point of surfeit, but just when one has had enough sweetness, the authority of Boucher's drawing steps in, and provides unexpectedly solid support for his most unbridled fantasies.

CHARDIN. To modern eyes one of the most impressive French eighteenth-century painters was Jean-Baptiste-Siméon Chardin (1699–1779). Yet his contemporaries held him in somewhat lower esteem, save for Denis Diderot, the encyclopedist and critic of art, literature, and music, whose reports on the Salons (the biennial exhibitions of the Royal Academy) are a major source for our knowledge of eighteenth-century French art, and a barometer of the taste of the intellectuals. In an age when the highest honors went to those who could celebrate, veiled or naked, its fantasies and gratifications, Chardin displayed a disconcerting interest in its realities. His subjects and style celebrate a lifelong allegiance to the Parisian lower-middle class, from which both he and Boucher (though one would hardly have known it in the case of Boucher) had sprung. His early work consists almost entirely of still life, but not of the Dutch epicurean variety; he transferred the scene of his pictures from the gardens of Watteau and the gilded salons or boudoirs of Boucher, and even the bourgeois living room of the Dutch, to the kitchen. It is the more surprising that aristocrats should have bought his work.

His *Copper Cistern*, of about 1733 (fig. 331), presents the cistern as a monumental object, surrounded by a pitcher, a pail, and a dipper as a planet by satellites. To endow such humble objects with nobility required a sense

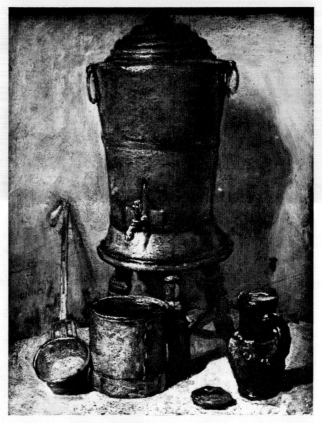

331. JEAN-BAPTISTE-SIMÉON CHARDIN. *Copper Cistern.* c. 1733. Oil on panel, 11¼ x 9¼". The Louvre, Paris

of the density and richness of pigment equal to the artist's respect for their copper and zinc, and for the rough wall, which is the only background. His thick impastos are derived from a study of Rembrandt, and communicate to his subjects a glow as satisfying as that of Watteau's silks and satins. Chardin's figure studies are concerned with Rococo ideals of transience and lightness, but without abandoning his bourgeois loyalty. The *House of Cards*, of 1741 (fig. 332), shows us a simply dressed boy toying with his cards as delicately as a Watteau lady with her suitor, and presents an image as fragile—a breath will blow the house of cards over. Yet for as long as it lasts, the fantasy of a child is set forth as a structure of great dignity.

GREUZE AND FRAGONARD. Chardin's honest devotion to bourgeois subjects was unconsciously parodied by Jean-Baptiste Greuze (1725–1805) and flouted by Jean-Honoré Fragonard (1732–1806), both of whom managed to subsist in relative independence from the Academy. Both had the ill fortune to survive into the revolutionary era, which Greuze limped through, while Fragonard had to flee Paris. Greuze's sentimental and moralizing pictures, on subjects of his own invention, struck the taste of the 1760s and 1770s exactly right; they were warmly praised by Diderot, who condemned Boucher on both moral and stylistic grounds. *The Son Punished*, of 1777–78 (fig. 333), is a sermon on family solidarity. The young man who had braved his father's curse and gone off with the recruiting sergeant so that he might taste the adventures of military life returns to find his father dead and his family plunged in reproachful grief. While the types are supposedly drawn from real life, they actually echo stock Classical poses. The mother gestures like a Roman orator, and the figures move on their narrow stage in a strict relief plane. This type of composition provided the basis for the later Neoclassic formulas of David (see Part Six, Chapter 1, and fig. 366), and also for innumerable nineteenth-century storytelling pictures. A moment's comparison will show the qualitative gulf between Greuze and Chardin in such matters as the handling of furniture and crockery.

Fragonard functioned on a far higher artistic level. After six regrettable months in Chardin's studio, for which he was temperamentally unsuited, he went on to study with Boucher, whose style he was able to imitate with ease. Rapidly, however, he moved forth on his own, and developed a buoyant composition and spontaneous brushwork, both brilliantly original. In *The Bathers* (colorplate 47), of about 1765, he adopted a Rubenesque

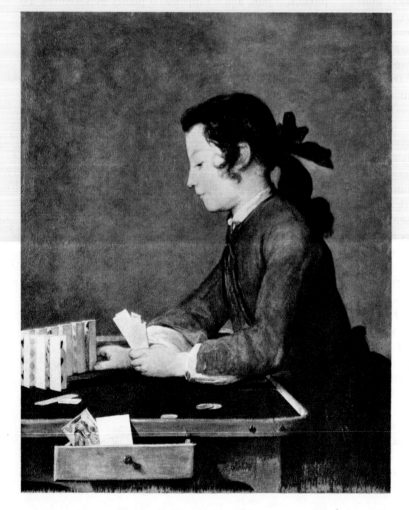

332. JEAN-BAPTISTE-SIMÉON CHARDIN. *House of Cards.* 1741. Oil on canvas, 32⅜ x 26″. National Gallery of Art, Washington, D.C. Andrew W. Mellon Collection

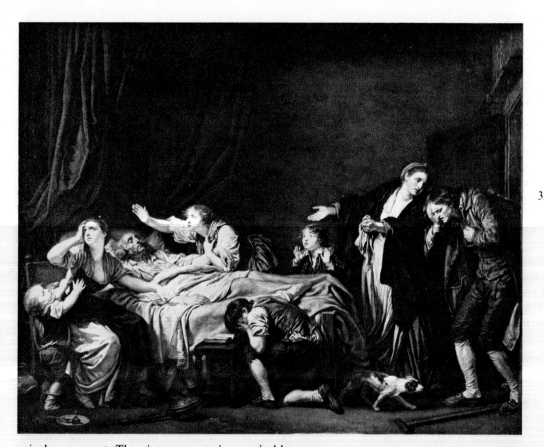

333. JEAN-BAPTISTE
GREUZE. *The Son
Punished.* 1777-78.
Oil on canvas, 51 x
65". The Louvre,
Paris

spiral movement. The picture erupts in a veritable geyser
of nudes, water, clouds, and trees, all apparently composed of much the same soft, sweet substance. In contrast
to the enameled surfaces of Boucher, Fragonard often attacked the canvas with a brushwork even more energetic
than that of Hals (see fig. 303), and discharged with
refreshing effervescence. Despite his attempt to recoup
his lost popularity in later life by exchanging his voluptuous subjects for domestic interiors, farmyards, and
even laundries, and accepting a position as a minor
republican official, this delightful painter died in obscuri-
ty and poverty.

CLODION. In some ways a sculptural parallel to
Fragonard was Claude Michel (1738–1814), known by
his nickname of Clodion. His *Satyr and Bacchante*, of
about 1775 (fig. 334), revives on a miniature scale the immediacy and dynamism of Bernini. His groups of accurately modeled figures in erotic abandon are made all
the fresher and more alluring by his knowing use of
pinkish terra-cotta as if it were actual pulsating flesh,
rendering each incipient embrace "forever warm and still
to be enjoyed." Clodion, too, outlived the popularity of
his subjects, but was able to make the switch to themes
more likely to be approved by the Revolution, and had a
considerable success with heroic Neoclassic groups.

BAROQUE AND ROCOCO IN AUSTRIA AND GERMANY.
In Central Europe the Thirty Years' War, concluded in
1648, left most countries so devastated that construction

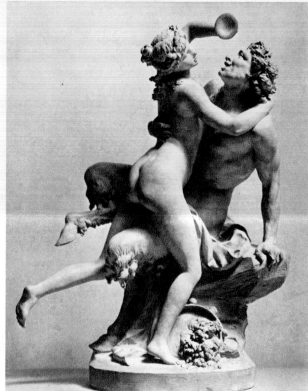

334. CLODION (CLAUDE MICHEL). *Satyr and
Bacchante.* c. 1775. Terra-cotta, height 23".
The Metropolitan Museum of Art, New York.
Bequest of Benjamin Altman, 1913

was next to impossible. Not until later in the seventeenth century did monumental projects really get under way, and the blooming of the Late Baroque at the turn of the century under Italian influence soon collided with a wave of French Rococo. Throughout the Austro-Hungarian Empire works of great brilliance were created in a hybrid style, involving at times the transformation of such medieval cities as Prague, Salzburg, and Warsaw, down even to the houses of the bourgeoisie, into fascinating and constantly changing pictures of Late Baroque imaginative grace. An architect of great importance for the formation of Austrian style was JOHANN BERNHARD FISCHER VON ERLACH (1656–1723), whose career culminated in the majestic Karlskirche in Vienna (fig. 335). Begun in 1716 and finished in 1737, this church was commissioned by the emperor Charles VI in gratitude for the delivery of Vienna from the plague. Fischer was the author of a substantial history of architecture from antiquity to the eighteenth century, at the end of which he not immodestly placed his own signal achievements. While in Rome for years of study, he had enjoyed the unplanned relationship of the Column of Trajan to neighboring Italian Renaissance domed churches. The Karlskirche gave him the opportunity to translate this historical accident into a building whose dramatic effect was increased by its relationship to a wide foreground space outside the fortifications of the city. The broad

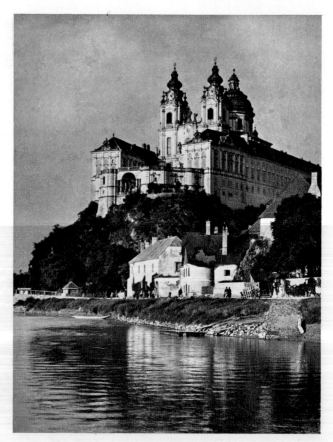

336. JAKOB PRANDTAUER. Benedictine Abbey. Begun 1702. Melk, Austria

façade terminates in arches like those on the façade of Saint Peter's (see fig. 234), supporting low bell towers, hardly more than pavilions. The central portico was imitated from that planned by Michelangelo for Saint Peter's, and is almost contemporary with the design by Juvarra for Superga (see fig. 318). The church itself is a Greek cross intersecting an oval, culminating in a splendid invention of Fischer's, an oval dome, whose drum is richly articulated with paired engaged columns alternating with paired pilasters, flanking the arched windows. Above the drum oval windows crowned by arched pediments and flanked by sculptures erupt into the shell of the dome. The two gigantic columns, whose spiral relief-bands symbolize the victory of faith over disease, are tucked into exedrae between the pavilions and the portico with spectacular results. Their severity is decreased by the eagles that enrich the square corners of the abaci and little domed turrets suggesting minarets.

Meanwhile, a wholly different kind of pictorial effect was being achieved in the Benedictine Abbey at Melk (fig. 336), designed in 1702 by JAKOB PRANDTAUER (1660–1726) for a spectacular site on a rocky eminence above a curve in the Danube and visible to travelers on the river in both directions. The long wings of the monastery burst forth above the river in a climax of giant orders, gables, balustrades, and a great central arch, harboring the façade of the church, with its two bell towers

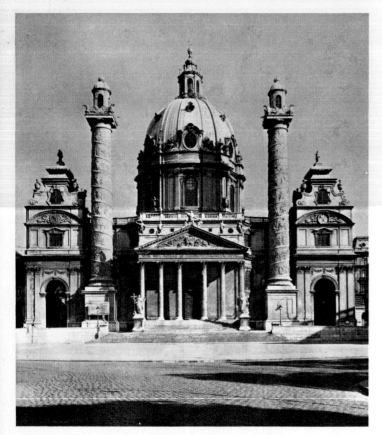

335. JOHANN BERNHARD FISCHER VON ERLACH. Façade, Karlskirche. 1716–37. Vienna

and central dome. The pilasters articulating the surfaces are subordinated to the rich double curvatures of the onion domes, which contrast with the severity of the monastic building, the whole producing the impression of a glittering, heavenly city, reflected in the water below. The interior (fig. 337), continued after Prandtauer's death by his cousin and pupil Joseph Munggenast, suggests the giant pilasters and imposing barrel vault of Maderno's nave for Saint Peter's (see fig. 235), but, in apparent emulation of Borromini's undulating façade of San Carlo alle Quattro Fontane (see fig. 244), the walls between the pilasters belly outward like sails in the breeze. Antonio Beduzzi provided galleries that, with their lighthearted Rococo decorations, look like boxes at the opera, and were indeed intended for nobles and distinguished visitors; sometimes in Austrian churches such boxes were glazed so that aristocratic conversation might continue without disturbing Mass.

One of the most brilliant achievements of the Austrian Late Baroque is the palace of the Upper Belvedere (fig. 338), built in 1721–22 for the victorious commander Prince Eugene of Savoy by JOHANN LUCAS VON HILDE-BRANDT (1663–1745). Situated on a hilltop overlooking the city of Vienna, the palace combines pavilions adopted from French architecture in a graduated succession outward from the center so that its shape suggests an immense bird with wings outstretched. The corner pavilions burst into octagonal domes, and the central mass opens into two superimposed glazed galleries for the enjoyment of the view. Although Hildebrandt was born in Genoa, his architecture shows fewer Italianisms than that of Fischer; as at Melk the Classical orders are scarcely distinguishable until one gets close to the airy structure, which seems just then to have perched on its eminence.

The princely states of South Germany were not long in following the Austrian lead. The principal German architect of the Late Baroque and Rococo was BALTHASAR NEUMANN (1687–1753), who carried out grandiose designs for the palace of the prince bishops of Würzburg from 1719 to 1750, under direct advice from Boffrand (see pages 277, 278). The palace, partly destroyed in World War II but since rebuilt, retains its magnificent staircase (colorplate 48), roofed by a single vault about 62 by 107 feet. From the comparatively dark entrance floor the visitor ascends halfway before the staircase divides in two and doubles back on itself, richly ornamented with balustrades and statues, to arrive at the main floor, brilliantly lighted by windows on both sides to provide a climax of architectural splendor worthy of its ceiling frescoes by Tiepolo (see page 276). On the exterior (fig. 339), as in Austrian structures, the pilasters are absorbed into the decorative scheme so that the capitals seem to dissolve into a general frieze of ornament.

Neumann's exhilarating pilgrimage church of Vierzehnheiligen, 1743–72, is strongly Rococo on the exterior (fig. 340), with its undulating façade, broken pediment, quivering bell towers crowned by onion domes and

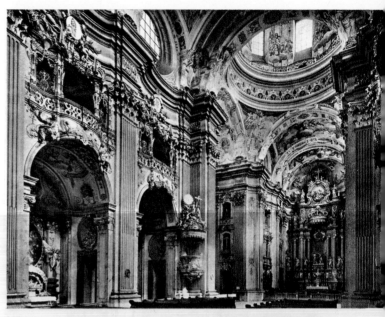
337. JAKOB PRANDTAUER. Interior, Benedictine Abbey. Melk, Austria (Galleries by ANTONIO BEDUZZI)

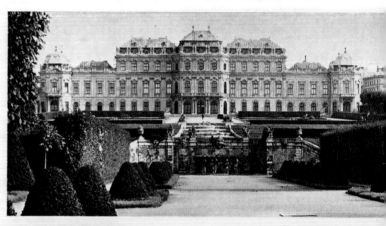
338. JOHANN LUCAS VON HILDEBRANDT. Garden façade, Palace of the Upper Belvedere. 1721–22. Vienna

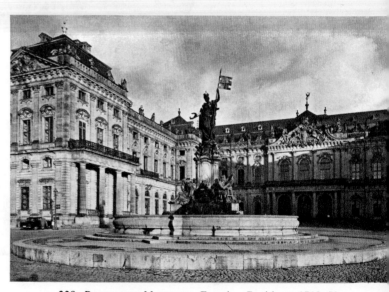
339. BALTHASAR NEUMANN. Exterior, Residenz. 1719–50. Würzburg, Germany

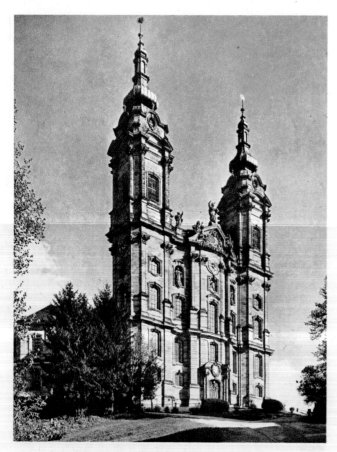

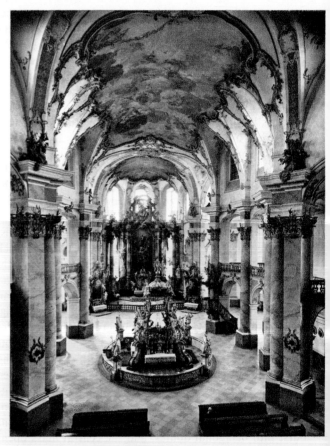

340. BALTHASAR NEUMANN. Exterior, Pilgrimage
Church of Vierzehnheiligen. 1743–72. Near
Staffelstein, Germany

341. BALTHASAR NEUMANN. Interior, Pilgrimage
Church of Vierzehnheiligen

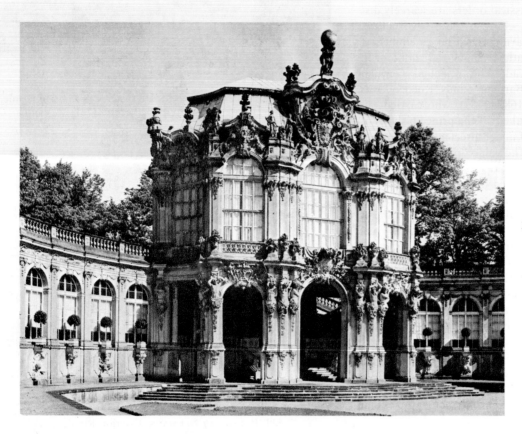

342. MATHAES DANIEL
PÖPPELMANN.
"Wallpavillon," Zwinger.
1711–22. Dresden, Germany

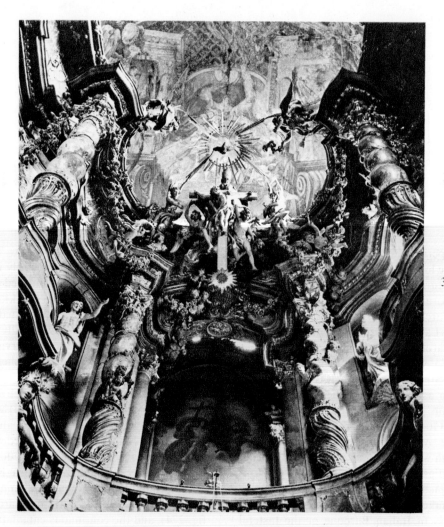

343. COSMAS DAMIAN ASAM
and EGID QUIRIN ASAM.
Holy Trinity.
Polychromed wood.
1733–46. Church
of St. Johannes Nepomuk,
Munich

steeples, and gesticulating statues. The gorgeous interior (fig. 341) is completely Rococo; the plan, based on seven adjacent or interlocking ellipses, is an expansion of that of Sant'Ivo (see fig. 247) without any of Borromini's spirituality. The ceiling, surrounded by a linear Rococo decoration of scrolls, dissolves the vault into an airy fresco so decorative that its subject scarcely attracts attention. With this and the columns and friezes painted to resemble pink marble, and the pulsating high altar with columns, decorations, and apparently dancing statues, the structure recalls the Salon de la Princesse at the Hôtel de Soubise (see fig. 323) more than any Roman seventeenth-century church.

The triumph of secular Rococo architecture in Germany is the Zwinger by MATHAES DANIEL PÖPPEL-MANN (1662–1736), attached to the palace of the electors of Saxony and kings of Poland at Dresden. Erected from 1710–32 (fig. 342), it is a court whose arcades and pavilions were intended to serve as an orangery and as a gallery for the viewing of pageants and tournaments. The building is now largely composed of glass, with the Classical orders barely distinguishable in the wings of the exedra and replaced in the central pavilion by decorative sculpture. The pavilion, in fact, resembles nothing so

much as a huge bouquet of flowers, the vertical straight lines having been suppressed in an insubstantial architecture that recalls forcefully the most extreme phase of Flamboyant Gothic. Devastated in the American bombardment of Dresden in 1945, the Zwinger has been expertly rebuilt.

In Munich EGID QUIRIN ASAM (1692–1750), a sculptor and architect, built at his own expense and endowed the Church of Saint Johannes Nepomuk, 1733–46, next to his own dwelling. His brother, COSMAS DAMIAN ASAM (1686–1742), a painter, assisted in the design of the church and its decoration. The interior (fig. 343), embellished by paintings and sculptures from their hands, pushes the Rococo style to its ultimate limits. The spiral columns of the gallery support an undulating entablature, almost masked by garlands with child angels; the climax is a vision of the Holy Trinity, carved in wood and painted, suspended in midair against ceiling decorations and illuminated from an unseen source; the painting visible below was, unfortunately, substituted in the nineteenth century for a statue of Saint Johannes Nepomuk looking upward at this heavenly vision, and similarly lighted. The Rococo style could be carried no further, and an eventual reaction became inevitable.

8

English Art
in the Eighteenth Century

The immense prosperity of eighteenth-century England, little affected by the loss of her North American colonies in 1776, gave rise to a wave of building unprecedented since Gothic times, and favored the development of a national school of architectural design and also, for the first time since the Late Middle Ages, a national school of painting. The Baroque in England, founded by Wren (see pages 244–246), was continued by his pupils and by another amateur, SIR JOHN VANBRUGH (1664–1726), equally well known as one of the wittiest dramatists of the post-Restoration period. When the grateful Queen Anne decided in 1704 to present her victorious commander, the duke of Marlborough, with a suitable residence, Vanbrugh was called upon to design Blenheim Palace, 1705–22 (figs. 344, 345). The result was impressive, but the picturesque splendor of the building does not entirely make up for its stiff pomposity, lacking the organic richness of Italian Baroque or the tasteful

balance of the French equivalent. The colonnades of Saint Peter's did not take root easily in Oxfordshire, nor were chimneys successfully masked as Classical urns. The impracticality of the plan (the kitchens are a quarter of a mile from the dining salon) netted Vanbrugh ridicule in his own day; he was eventually dismissed by the duchess, who had taken over supervision of the project, and his grandiose dream was finished by a pupil.

The followers of Wren continued building Baroque structures, especially churches, well into the eighteenth century. JAMES GIBBS (1682–1754) was the most gifted of these. Having worked with the Late Baroque architect Carlo Fontana in Rome, he returned with a full repertory of Continental ideas; his superb Radcliffe Library at Oxford, 1739–49 (fig. 346), is like a Roman or Parisian dome grounded; the coupled columns are derived from Michelangelo (see fig. 184) and Hardouin-Mansart (see fig. 274), and the continuous entablature from Bramante

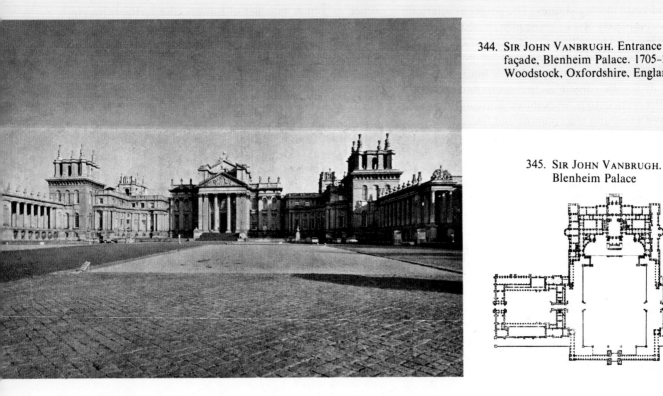

344. SIR JOHN VANBRUGH. Entrance façade, Blenheim Palace. 1705–24. Woodstock, Oxfordshire, England

345. SIR JOHN VANBRUGH. Plan of Blenheim Palace

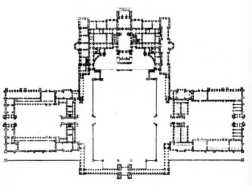

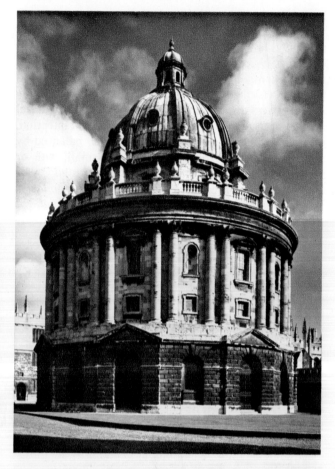

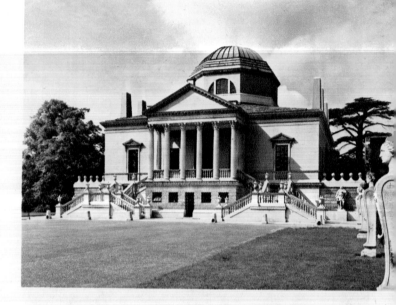

346. JAMES GIBBS. Radcliffe Library. 1739–49. Oxford, England

347. EARL OF BURLINGTON (RICHARD BOYLE). Chiswick House. 1725–29. Middlesex, England

(see fig. 139) by way of Wren (see fig. 282), but the design has a grandeur all its own, enriched by such subtleties as wide bays between the buttresses alternating with narrow ones above, the placing of the buttresses between the paired columns rather than in line with them, and the alignment of the entrances only with the central two columns of each group of four. The building profits especially by its position as the only large dome placed at ground level so one can walk around it rather than having to gaze up at it.

With the accession of George I in 1714, the Baroque became discredited as a leftover from the Stuarts, and the Palladian style of Jones (see page 244) was revived in mansions, town houses, country houses, streets, squares, circles, crescents, and eventually churches. One of the strongest supporters of the Palladian movement was Richard Boyle, third EARL OF BURLINGTON (1695–1753), a widely traveled nobleman of considerable learning and taste, friend of Pope, Swift, Thomson, and Handel, and a gifted architect in his own right. His best-known work is Chiswick House, 1725–29 (fig. 347), in whose elaborate interiors he was assisted by WILLIAM KENT (1685–1748); the exterior, however, is entirely by Burlington. The little cubic structure, intended for receptions and conversation, was connected by means of an unobtrusive wing with a Jacobean manor house (torn

down in 1788). While Burlington obviously emulated the general conception of Palladio's Villa Rotonda, near Vicenza (see fig. 174), the details are sharply different. As the structure was not to be freestanding and had no mountain view, it needed only a single portico. The order was changed from Ionic to Corinthian, the dome from round to octagonal and raised on a drum to admit more light to the central hall. The double staircases with their balustrades and decorative urns were derived from Italian models.

Soon, under the influence of the excavations at Pompeii and Herculaneum (see page 276), a third style made its appearance, a Classicism far more thoroughgoing than its French counterpart, led by ROBERT ADAM (1728–92). At Syon House (fig. 348), remodeled by Adam beginning in 1762 for Sir Hugh Smithson, the entrance hall attempts archaeological correctness. Copies of ancient statues in marble or in bronze are ranged about the walls or set in an apse with an octagonally coffered semidome. Actually, as we have seen (see Vol. 1, Part Two, Chapter 6), Roman interiors were very richly adorned, and the austerity of Adam's design, with its unrelieved wall surfaces and sparing, chaste decoration, was symptomatic of his personal taste.

The fourth eighteenth-century style would be totally unexpected if we did not know that in England the Gothic

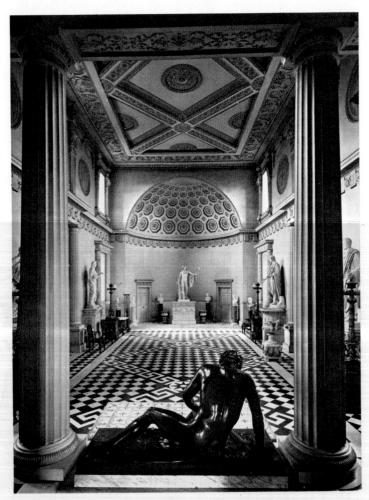

348. ROBERT ADAM. Entrance hall, Syon House.
Remodeling begun 1762. Middlesex, England

had never really died out. Wren and his pupils, as well as Vanbrugh and Kent, all built or extended Gothic structures at one time or another. Usually, these were churches or colleges, deriving from a long Gothic tradition. By the 1740s, however, country houses were being built in Gothic style, and a textbook appeared on how to design them. Needless to say,.the organic principles of Gothic building (see Vol. 1, Part Three, Chapter 9) were little understood save by such masters as Guarini or Soufflot. The usual result was a merely decorative use of motives drawn from Gothic architecture. In addition to the Renaissance revival of Classical antiquity, the eighteenth-century revival of the Renaissance, and the eighteenth-century attempt to revive antiquity independently, a revival of just what the Renaissance had fulminated against—the "barbarous" Gothic taste—now occurred. The eighteenth century found the Gothic interesting in itself—always picturesque and at times sublime. Eighteenth-century Gothicism in art was, of course, connected with contemporary interest in medieval history and the vogue for "Gothic" romances and poems.

At the culmination of this movement, rather than the

beginning, stands Strawberry Hill, built at intervals from 1750–90 (fig. 349), the home of HORACE WALPOLE (1717–97), a wealthy amateur who hired professionals to construct it according to his own ideas. So greatly was the mansion admired by his contemporaries that he had to limit visiting parties to one a day. A completely asymmetrical disposition of elements, which in medieval art had been the result of accident rather than intention, includes a huge round tower in one angle, balanced by nothing elsewhere; windows, large and small, with or without tracery; battlements, buttresses, and other Gothic elements spread over the surface *au petit bonheur*. The library (fig. 350) is decorated with tracery, imitated from Perpendicular churches (such as Gloucester

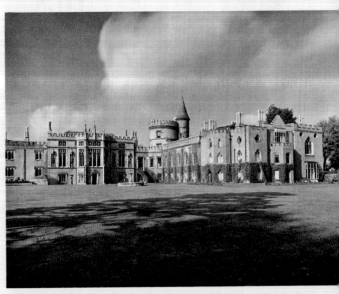

349. HORACE WALPOLE, with WILLIAM ROBINSON and others. Strawberry Hill. 1748–77. Twickenham, Middlesex, England

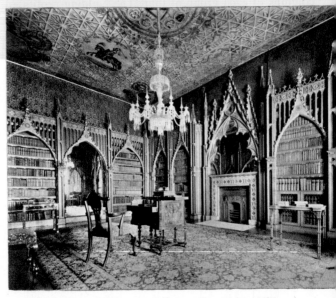

350. HORACE WALPOLE. Library, Strawberry Hill

Cathedral), used as frames for bookcases, and even the rectangular eighteenth-century mantelpiece and the cast-iron forms of the fireplace frame are clothed in Gothic detail.

Fascination with the picturesque led to the construction of sham ruins in the wandering complexities of English parks, whose apparent naturalism was in fact achieved only by great labor and at vast expense. The park surrounding Hagley Hall, laid out for Lord Lyttelton, contains both a ruined Gothic castle (fig. 351), built from scratch in 1749–50 by SANDERSON MILLER (1717–80), a gentleman architect, and a Greek Doric portico (fig. 352), based on the Propylaia at Athens, added in 1758 by JAMES STUART (1713–88). The latter was the

first known attempt to revive in architecture pure Greek principles based on the monuments of Athens, which Stuart, in company with NICHOLAS REVETT (1720–1804), had studied exhaustively and measured on the spot. Their sumptuous engravings were published in a famous work, *The Antiquities of Athens*, the first of four volumes appearing in 1762; the second was not issued until 1790, two years after Stuart's death. A similar study by J.-D. Le Roy also appeared in France. Studies of other Classical monuments, such as Baalbek, Palmyra, and the palace of Diocletian at Split, were also published. Along with these earliest archaeological studies came the theoretical and art historical writings of Johann Joachim Winckelmann, a German art critic, who lived in Rome

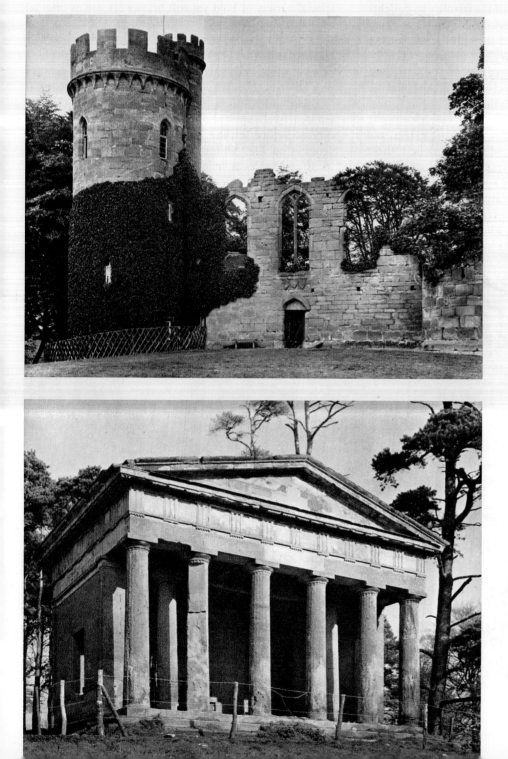

351. SANDERSON MILLER. Sham Gothic castle ruins. 1747. Park, Hagley Hall, Worcestershire, England

352. JAMES STUART. Doric portico. 1758. Park, Hagley Hall

and never visited Greece, but on the basis of Roman copies proclaimed Greek art as the ideal that later periods had only remotely approached. (He detested both the Rococo and the French who had invented it.) As yet, however, both Gothic and Greek buildings were built for dilettantes only; no one seemed to think either mode suitable for monumental civic structures, and no one saw in either any principles useful for political ideology. Therein lies the crucial difference between these mid-eighteenth-century revivals and those of the late eighteenth and the nineteenth century.

HOGARTH. A strikingly original school of painting arose in eighteenth-century England—the first, in fact, since the Gothic period—under limited influence from Continental Rococo, but with little of the frivolity so delightful in French painting of the period. The most engaging of the new English painters and the real founder of the modern British school was William Hogarth (1697–1764), a Londoner whose narrative candor and satiric wit are as effective as his dazzling pictorial skill. Although he tried his hand occasionally at mythological and historical subjects, Hogarth was at his best in quintessentially English portraits and in pungent moralistic cycles, the counterparts of the novels of Fielding and Smollett; these were painted as bases for engravings, which Hogarth sold widely and profitably. The most successful were *A Scene from the Beggar's Opera*, illustrating John Gay's famous work; *A Rake's Progress*; *A Harlot's Progress*; and *Marriage à la Mode*, 1743–45, whose opening episode is

the *Signing the Contract* (fig. 353). The scene is set diagonally in depth for greater theatrical effect. In a room of his London house, lined with Old Masters (which Hogarth professed to hate), the gouty alderman, father of the bride, sits before a table spread with the golden coins of the dowry and expatiates on his family tree, to which he proposes to add the earl. That gentleman, who has exhausted his fortune in building the Palladian mansion seen out the window (Hogarth detested the Palladian style, as well as both Burlington and Kent), admires himself in a mirror. His betrothed, meanwhile, is listening to the blandishments murmured in her ear by the attorney. Clearly, the story will come to a bad end. While the energetic composition owes much to the Rococo, Hogarth's robust handling of poses and his special variety of bold yet soft brushwork are as original as his caustic wit.

GAINSBOROUGH. The most accomplished and in the long run the most influential English painter of the century was Thomas Gainsborough (1727–88), who studied briefly in London with a pupil of Boucher. Until 1774 he painted landscapes and portraits in various provincial centers before settling in London for the last fourteen years of his life. Although the elegant attenuation of his lords and ladies is indebted to his study of Van Dyck, Gainsborough achieved in his full-length portraits a freshness and lyric grace all his own. Occasional objections to the lack of structure in his weightless figures are swept away by the beauty of his color, and the delicacy of

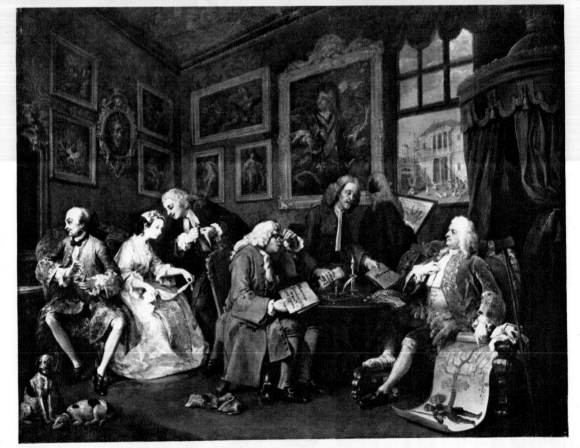

353. WILLIAM HOGARTH. *Marriage à la Mode, Signing the Contract.* 1743–45. Oil on canvas, 28 x 35⅞". National Gallery, London

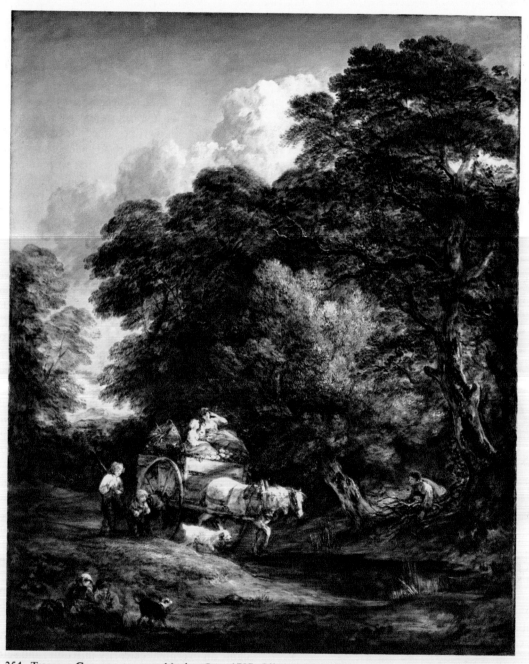

354. THOMAS GAINSBOROUGH. *Market Cart*. 1787. Oil on canvas, 72½ x 60⅝". The Tate Gallery, London

his touch, closer to the deft brushwork of Watteau than to Boucher's enameled surface. The figure in *Mary Countess Howe* (colorplate 49), painted in Bath in the mid-1760s, is exquisitely posed, as usual in front of a landscape background. Gainsborough has expended his uncanny ability on the soft shimmer of light over the embroidered organdy of her overdress and the cascades of lace at her elbows, sparkling in the soft English air; the only solid accents in the picture are her penetrating eyes. Although Gainsborough was country-born, his landscape elements seem artificial, added like bits of scenery to establish a spatial environment for the exquisite play of color in the figure.

In later life Gainsborough painted always more freely and openly. Although his landscapes, which he preferred

to his portraits, exhale a typically English freshness, they were painted in the studio on the basis of small models put together from moss and pebbles, still in the tradition recorded by Cennino Cennini (see page 14). Constructed in the grand manner of such a seventeenth-century Dutch master as Hobbema (see fig. 294), and painted largely with soft strokes of wash like those of Watteau, the *Market Cart* (fig. 354), of 1787, shows an almost rhapsodic abandonment to the mood of nature, which led as surely to the great English landscapists of the early nineteenth century (see Part Six, Chapter 2) as did the nature poetry of James Thomson to the meditative lyricism of Wordsworth. Constable said that Gainsborough's landscapes moved him to tears, and contemplating the freedom and beauty of the painting of the cart

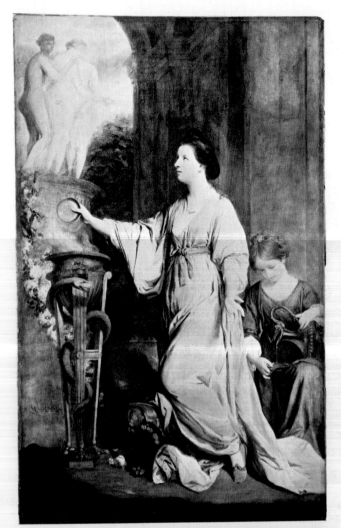

355. SIR JOSHUA REYNOLDS. *Lady Sarah Bunbury Sacrificing to the Graces.* 1765. Oil on canvas. 94 x 60". The Art Institute of Chicago. Mr. and Mrs. W. W. Kimball Collection

do much of the mechanical work. There is inevitably something artificial about the grandiloquence of the Classical or Renaissance poses in which he, without either the humor of Hogarth or the poetry of Gainsborough, painted the very solid English men and women of his own day, investing them with qualities borrowed from a noble past. It is, nonetheless, to his majestic portraits, with their contrived backgrounds of Classical architecture and landscape, that we owe our impression of English aristocracy in the eighteenth century. *Lady Sarah Bunbury Sacrificing to the Graces* (fig. 355), painted in 1765, is a case in point, and speaks eloquently for itself.

COLONIAL AMERICAN PAINTING. The modest beginnings of colonial American painting in the work of self-taught limners achieved a surprising degree of maturity in the style of JOHN SINGLETON COPLEY (1738–1815), son of Irish immigrants to Boston. Whatever Copley may have known of the grand English portrait style of the eighteenth century through engravings, he rapidly evolved an original manner, which concealed occasional deficiencies of drawing under a smooth hardness of surface unexpected and refreshing in the eighteenth century, when dexterity of the brush was so highly prized (see Watteau's *Signboard of Gersaint*, colorplate 46). Copley's *Paul Revere* (fig. 356), of 1768–70, dispenses with the column and red curtain that often seem incongruous in his portraits of stolid Yankee merchants. The firm, unflattering portrait of the eminent silversmith and patriot shows him in shirt-sleeves beside his worktable, strewn with engraving instruments, and holding a glittering silver teapot. The honest provincialism of the work and Copley's inborn sense of form make it more attractive than the accomplished portraits and historical scenes he painted after his emigration to England in 1775.

Copley's fellow American BENJAMIN WEST (1738–1820), from Pennsylvania, left for Europe in 1759, became an overnight celebrity in Rome, and settled in London, where he enjoyed a success to which neither his imagination nor his pictorial skill would seem to have entitled him. He rose, in fact, to become president of the Royal Academy of Arts, and historical painter to the king. Historically, West is an important figure. His paintings of Roman historical subjects are forerunners of the more successful and significant Classical scenes by David (see Part Six, Chapter 1), and his *Death of General Wolfe*, of about 1770 (fig. 357), with its still Baroque lighting and pathos, led directly to the great battle pieces of the nineteenth century (see fig. 381). Characteristically, in spite of his own leanings toward classicism, he resisted the temptation to dress this celebrated event of the French and Indian War in Classical costume, which would certainly have been the recommendation of Winckelmann, his Continental and English disciples, and even the great Sir Joshua.

and the boy gathering brushwood, not to speak of the glow of light seeming to come from within the tree in the center, one can understand why.

REYNOLDS. The third master of the period, Sir Joshua Reynolds (1723–92), while less attractive than the other two, was in his own day a commanding figure, whose authority outlived him and who eventually became a target for Romantic attacks. Neither Hogarth nor Gainsborough traveled outside England (Hogarth once tried to reach Paris but got no farther than Calais), but Reynolds did the Grand Tour, and remained in Rome spellbound by the grandeur of Michelangelo and Raphael. He acquired a respectable knowledge of European painting of the preceding two centuries, and gave at the Royal Academy—which he helped to found in 1768—the famous *Discourses*, which, in published form, remain a formidable body of Classical doctrine and the most extensive attempt at art theory by any Englishman. Reynolds' success as a portraitist was so huge that he had to hire assistants to lay out the canvases for him and to

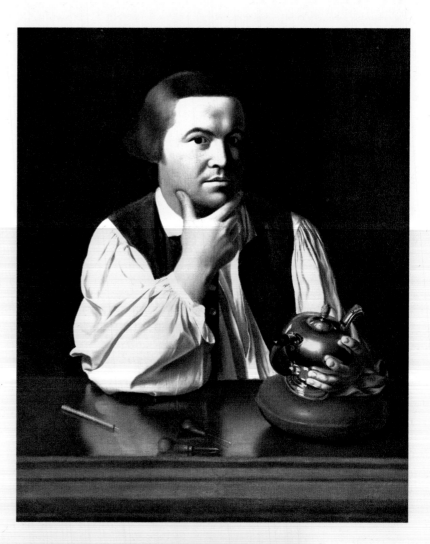

356. JOHN SINGLETON COPLEY.
Paul Revere. 1768–70.
Oil on canvas, 35 x 28½″.
Museum of Fine Arts, Boston.
Gift of Joseph W., William B.,
and Edward H. R. Revere

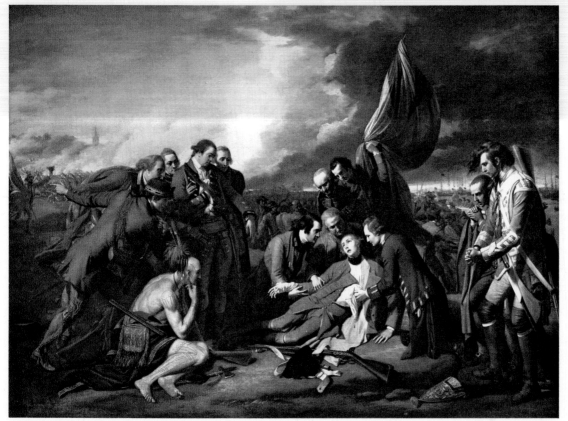

357. BENJAMIN WEST.
*Death of General
Wolfe.* c. 1770. Oil on
canvas, 59½ x 84″.
The National Gallery
of Canada, Ottawa.
Gift of the Duke of
Westminster, 1918

TIME LINE

The numbers in italics refer to illustrations in the text.

	POLITICAL HISTORY	RELIGION, LITERATURE, MUSIC	SCIENCE, TECHNOLOGY
1550		William Shakespeare (1564–1616)	
1575		John Donne (1572–1631)	
			Pope Gregory XIII (1502–85) introduces the Gregorian calendar (1582)
1600	Queen Elizabeth I, Eng. queen, dies (1603) Jamestown, Virginia, founded (1607) Holland's independence recognized by Spain (1609) Maria de' Medici regent of France (1610–17) during minority of Louis XIII Louis XIII, Fr. king (r. 1610–43) Romanov dynasty founded in Russia (1613) Thirty Years' War (1618–48)	Papacy of Pope Paul V (1605–21) Pierre Corneille (1606–84) King James Bible (1611) Molière (1622–73) Pascal (1623–62)	William Gilbert (1540–1603) publishes treatise on magnetism (1600) Dutch lens-grinders in Middleburg construct the first refracting telescope and the compound microscope (c. 1600) Johannes Kepler (1571–1630) announces his first two laws of planetary motion (1609); announces third law (1619) John Napier (1550–1617) invents and describes logarithms (1614)
1625	Cardinal Richelieu, chief minister and adviser (1624–42) to Louis XIII, consolidates power of monarchy Charles I, Eng. king (r. 1625–49) Japan's isolation from Europe begins (1639) Frederick William, Great Elector of Brandenburg (r. 1640–88) Cardinal Mazarin governs France during minority of Louis XIV (1643–61); civil disturbances of the Fronde (1648–53) Louis XIV, Fr. king (r. 1643–1715) Peace of Westphalia (1648) ends Thirty Years' War	Jacques Bossuet (1627–1704) Spinoza (1632–77) John Locke (1632–1704) René Descartes (1596–1650) publishes *Discours de la Méthode* (1637) Racine (1639–99) Papacy of Innocent X (1644–55) Royal Academy of Painting and Sculpture founded in Paris (1648)	William Harvey (1578–1627) describes circulation of the blood (1628) Galileo Galilei (1564–1642) publishes *Dialogo dei due Massimi Sistemi del Mondo* (1632) Evangelista Torricelli (1608–47) discovers principle of the barometer and devises earliest form of the instrument (1643)
1650	Charles I beheaded (1649); Commonwealth under Cromwell (1649–53); Protectorate (1653–59) Charles II, Eng. king (r. 1660–85), restores monarchy in England Louis XIV, assisted by Colbert, assumes absolute rule of France (1661) Great Fire of London (1666)	Thomas Hobbes (1588–1679) publishes *Leviathan* (1651) Papacy of Alexander VII (1655–67) French Academy in Rome founded (1666) Colbert creates Buildings Council—Le Vau, Le Brun, and Perrault—to complete Louvre (1667) Milton publishes *Paradise Lost* (1667) Giovanni Battista Vico (1668–1744) Colbert establishes Royal Academy of Architecture (1671)	Robert Boyle (1627–91) formulates law that the volume of gas varies inversely as the pressure (1660) Charles II charters Royal Society, London (1662); establishes Royal Observatory, Greenwich (1675)
1675	English Parliament passes Habeas Corpus Act (1679) Peter the Great, Rus. czar (r. 1682–1725) westernizes Russia Louis XIV revokes Edict of Nantes (1685) Glorious Revolution against James II of England (1688); Bill of Rights	Antonio Vivaldi (c. 1675–1791) Bunyan publishes *Pilgrim's Progress* (1678) Johann Sebastian Bach (1685–1750) George Frederic Handel (1685–1759) Alexander Pope (1688–1744) Montesquieu (1689–1755) Voltaire (1694–1778)	Isaac Newton (1642–1727) sets forth idea of universal gravitation in *Principia* (1687); publishes *New Theory about Light and Color* (1672) and *Optics* (1704)
1700	English and allies defeat French at Blenheim (1704) Frederick William I, Pr. king (r. 1713–40), lays foundation of future power of Prussia Louis XV, Fr. king (r. 1715–74) Robert Walpole, first prime minister of England (1721–42)	Act passed in England to build 50 new churches (1711) Daniel Defoe (1659?–1731) publishes *Robinson Crusoe* (1719)	G. W. von Leibnitz (1646–1716) discovers new notations of calculus; publishes *Théodicé* (1710) Gabriel Fahrenheit (1686–1736) proposes the Fahrenheit system and a mode of calibrating thermometers (1717)
1725	Frederick II the Great, Pr. king (r. 1740–86), defeats Austria in War of the Austrian Succession (1740–48)	Jonathan Swift (1667–1745) publishes *Gulliver's Travels* (1726) John Gay (1685–1732) writes *The Beggar's Opera* (1728) Wesley brothers found Methodism (1738) David Hume (1711–76) publishes *Treatise on Human Nature* (1739) Edmund Burke (1729–97) Young, *Night Thoughts* (1742)	Charles du Fay (1698–1739) discovers positive and negative electric charge Carol Linnaeus (1707–78) publishes *Systema Naturae* (1737) Excavations begin at Herculaneum; later at Paestum and Pompeii (1738) Antoine Lavoisier (1743–94)

PAINTING	SCULPTURE	ARCHITECTURE	
			1550
			1575
Annibale Carracci, frescoes, Palazzo Farnese, Rome (226, colorplate 36)		Maderno, façade, Sta. Susanna, Rome (233)	
			1600
Caravaggio, *Calling of Saint Matthew; Conversion of Saint Paul; David with the Head of Goliath* (231, 232, colorplate 37)	Bernini, *Apollo and Daphne*; *David*; Baldachin, St. Peter's, Rome (236–238)	Maderno, façade and nave, St. Peter's, Rome (234, 235)	
Annibale Carracci, *Landscape with the Flight into Egypt* (227)		Jones, Banqueting House, Whitehall Palace, London (279)	
Rubens, triptych, Cathedral of Antwerp (284)			
Reni, *Aurora*, ceiling fresco, Casino Rospigliosi, Rome (228)			
Domenichino, *The Hunt of Diana* (228)			
Rubens, *Fall of the Damned; Rape of the Daughters of Leucippus* (285, 286)			
Hals, *Banquet of the Officers of the Saint George Guard Company* (301)			
Guercino, *Aurora*, ceiling fresco, Casino Ludovisi, Rome (230)			
Honthorst, *Adoration of the Shepherds* (290)			
Rubens, *Henry IV Receiving the Portrait of Maria de' Medici* (colorplate 41)			
Terbrugghen, *Incredulity of Saint Thomas* (291)			
Hals, *The Laughing Cavalier* (302)			
Brouwer, *Boors Drinking* (298)			
Van Dyck, *Madonna of the Rosary* (288)			
			1625
Velázquez, *Triumph of Bacchus (Los Borrachos)* (316)	Bernini, *Ecstasy of Saint Theresa*, Cornaro Chapel, Sta. Maria della Vittoria, Rome; nave sculptures, St. Peter's, Rome; *Fountain of the Four Rivers*, Piazza Navona, Rome (239–241)	Longhena, Sta. Maria della Salute, Venice (253, 254)	
Poussin, *Inspiration of the Poet* (259)		Mansart, Orléans Wing, Château de Blois (265)	
Zurbarán, *Vision of Saint Peter Nolasco* (315)		Borromini, S. Carlo alle Quattro Fontane, Rome; Sant'Ivo della Sapienza, Rome (245–248)	
La Tour, *Newborn* (257)			
Hals, *Malle Babbe* (303)			
Rembrandt, *Anatomy Lesson of Dr. Tulp* (305)			
Pietro da Cortona, *The Triumph of the Barberini*, ceiling fresco, Gran Salone, Palazzo Barberini, Rome (251)			
Heda, *Still Life* (299)			
Van Dyck, *Portrait of Charles I in Hunting Dress* (289)			
Poussin, *Rape of the Sabines* (colorplate 39)			
Rembrandt, *Angel Leaving Tobit and Tobias* (304)			
Rubens, *Garden of Love* (287)			
Ribera, *Martyrdom of Saint Bartholomew* (314)			
Louis Le Nain, *The Cart* (258)			
Lorrain, *Embarkation of Saint Ursula* (colorplate 40)			
Rembrandt, *The Company of Captain Frans Banning Cocq and Lieutenant Willem van Ruytenburch (Night Watch)* (307)			
Poussin, *Holy Family on the Steps* (260)			
Rembrandt, *Supper at Emmaus* (308)			
Lorrain, *Marriage of Isaac and Rebecca* (261)			
			1650
Champaigne, *Unknown Man* (263)	Bernini, Cathedra Petri, St. Peter's, Rome (242)	Borromini, Sant'Agnese, Rome (249, 250)	
Cuyp, *Landscape with Cattle and Figures* (295)	Puget, *Milo of Crotona* (278)	Bernini, colonnade of St. Peter's, Rome (243)	
Rembrandt, *The Polish Rider* (colorplate 42)		Le Vau, Le Brun, and Le Nôtre, Château de Vaux-le-Vicomte (266)	
Velázquez, *Las Meninas* (colorplate 44)		Borromini, façade, S. Carlo alle Quattro Fontane, Rome (244)	
Van Goyen, *River Scene* (292)		Perrault, East façade, The Louvre, Paris (267)	
Vermeer, *Kitchen Maid* (312)		Guarini, Chapel of the Holy Shroud, Turin (256)	
Saenredam, *Church of Saint Bavo* (300)		Le Vau and Hardouin-Mansart, Palace of Versailles (268–270)	
Vermeer, *View of Delft* (313)		Le Nôtre, gardens, Versailles (269)	
De Hooch, *Linen Cupboard* (296)			
Steen, *The World Upside-Down* (297)			
Hals, *Regentesses of the Old Men's Almshouse* (304)			
Vermeer, *Allegory of the Art of Painting* (colorplate 43)			
Rembrandt, *Return of the Prodigal Son; Self-Portrait* (310, 311)			
Ruisdael, *View of Haarlem* (293)			
			1675
Baciccio, *Triumph of the Sacred Name of Jesus*, ceiling fresco, Il Gesù, Rome (colorplate 38)	Girardon, *Tomb of Richelieu* (277)	Wren, St. Paul's, London (280–283)	
Le Brun, frescoes, Hall of Mirrors, Palace of Versailles (270)	Raggi, vault, Il Gesù, Rome	Hardouin-Mansart, Church of the Invalides, Paris; Hall of Mirrors, Palace of Versailles (270, 274, 275)	
Hobbema, *Avenue at Middelharnis* (294)	Coysevox, *Portrait Bust of Colbert; Louis XIV on Horseback*, Salon de la Guerre, Palace of Versailles (271, 276)	Guarini, Palazzo Carignano, Turin (255)	
Pozzo, *Missionary Work of the Jesuits*, ceiling fresco, Sant'Ignazio, Rome (252)		Hardouin-Mansart, Grand Trianon, Versailles; Royal Chapel, Palace of Versailles (272, 273)	
			1700
Rigaud, *Portrait of Louis XIV* (264)		Prandtauer, Benedictine Abbey, Melk (336, 337)	
Watteau, *A Pilgrimage to Cythera; Signboard of Gersaint* (329, colorplate 46)		Vanbrugh, Blenheim Palace, Woodstock (344, 345)	
		Pöppelmann, The Zwinger, Dresden (342)	
		Juvarra, Superga, near Turin (318)	
		Fischer von Erlach, Karlskirche, Vienna (335)	
		Neumann, Residenz, Würzburg (339, colorplate 48)	
		Hildebrandt, Palace of the Upper Belvedere, Vienna (338)	
			1725
Piazzetta, *Ecstasy of Saint Francis* (320)		Burlington and Kent, Chiswick House, Chiswick (347)	
Natoire, paintings, Salon de la Princesse, Hôtel de Soubise, Paris (323)		Juvarra, Royal Hunting Palace of Stupinigi, near Turin (319)	
Chardin, *Copper Cistern* (331)		Boffrand, Salon de la Princesse, Hôtel de Soubise, Paris (323)	
Hogarth, *A Scene from the Beggar's Opera; A Rake's Progress; A Harlot's Progress*		Asam brothers, Church of St. Johannes Nepomuk, Munich (343)	
Boucher, *Triumph of Venus* (330)		Gibbs, Radcliffe Library, Oxford (346)	
Chardin, *House of Cards* (332)		Neumann, Vierzehnheiligen, Staffelstein (340, 341)	
Hogarth, *Marriage à la Mode* (353)		Miller, Gothic Castle ruins, Hagley Hall, Worcestershire (351)	
Tiepolo, frescoes, Palazzo Labia, Venice (321)		Walpole and others, Strawberry Hill, Twickenham (349, 350)	

TIME LINE

The numbers in italics refer to illustrations in the text.

	POLITICAL HISTORY	RELIGION, LITERATURE, MUSIC	SCIENCE, TECHNOLOGY
1750	Seven Years' War (1756–63): England and Prussia vs. Austria and France, called French and Indian War in U.S.A.; French defeated in battle of Quebec (1759); England becomes greatest colonial and naval power Catherine the Great (r. 1762–96) extends Russian power to Black Sea Partition of Poland among Russia, Prussia, Austria (1772–95)	Gray, *Elegy* (1750) Diderot, *Encyclopedia* (1751–72) Johnson, *Dictionary* (1755) Macpherson, ''Ossian'' forgeries (1760–63) Rousseau, *Social Contract* and *Émile* (1762) Georg Wilhelm Friedrich Hegel (1770–1831) William Wordsworth (1770–1850) Sir Walter Scott (1771–1832) Goethe, *Sorrows of Young Werther* (1774)	Coke-fed blast furnaces for iron smelting perfected (c. 1760–75) Mechanization of textile spinning (1764–69) Watt perfects modern condensing steam engine (1765–76) Priestley discovers oxygen (1774)

	PAINTING	SCULPTURE	ARCHITECTURE
1750	Tiepolo, ceiling frescoes, Residenz, Würzburg (*colorplate 48*) Stuart and Revett, *The Antiquities of Athens* Fragonard, *The Bathers* (*colorplate 47*) Gainsborough, *Mary Countess Howe* (*colorplate 49*) Reynolds, *Lady Sarah Bunbury Sacrificing to the Graces* (*355*) Copley, *Paul Revere* (*356*) West, *Death of General Wolfe* (*357*)		Soufflot, Panthéon, Paris (*324, 325*) Stuart, Doric portico, Hagley Hall, Worcestershire (*352*) Adam, Syon House, Middlesex (*348*) Gabriel, Petit Trianon, Versailles; Place de la Concorde, Paris (*326–328*)
1775	Guardi, *Piazzetta San Marco* (*322*) Greuze, *The Son Punished* (*333*) Gainsborough, *Market Cart* (*354*)	Clodion, *Satyr and Bacchante* (*334*)	

PART SIX

The Modern World

Modern is an even less accurate period designation than any other we have as yet encountered. The word means "pertaining to the present or very recent past"; its use signifies that in our eyes the period it denotes is still going on, but it tells us nothing more. The term has been in English use since the late sixteenth century, and therefore has already referred to a number of periods. Its inevitable corollary is that as the present moves along inexorably into the past our own period will sooner or later cease to be modern and will undoubtedly be given another name by future generations.

If one judges by the standard of nearness to the present, the modern period probably began in Europe and in America in the late eighteenth century. We feel a sense of kinship with the people of this period, and can easily understand their ideas and accept their customs. This sense of nearness is more apparent than real because the end of the eighteenth century is much closer to its beginning than it is to our own time. Yet the historical figures of the American and French revolutions, for example, seem close to us, although the princes of the Baroque era seem remote. We could settle down comfortably at Monticello but would feel out of place in the grandeur of Versailles or the luxury of the Hôtel de Soubise. We listen easily to the music of Mozart and Beethoven; Bach and Handel require a more difficult type of hearing. We read Keats and Wordsworth with immediate comprehension, but must be very attentive to understand Pope.

The political and social conditions of the late eighteenth century seem akin to those with which we are familiar, if not from the present, at least from the recent past. Religion, for example, while important to many in the eighteenth century as it is today, was no longer a belief that could be legally enforced, or a cause to go to war about. Culture had become strongly secularized by the end of the century in western Europe and in America, and the two basic forces that shape our lives today—the idea of social democracy and the notion of scientific progress—were already clearly in operation. Before long

these two forces influenced each other so strongly as at times almost to fuse. The idea of a universal democracy arose first in France under the influence of the philosophers of the Enlightenment, notably Voltaire and Rousseau, although its earliest successes were in America, insofar as success was permitted by the institution of chattel slavery. Scientific technology first influenced social and economic structure in England during the Industrial Revolution, spreading in the nineteenth century to all Western nations and furnishing the material foundation for modern bourgeois capitalism.

It is in its internationalism that we must seek the basic nature of the modern world, throughout vast areas of the globe, including countries with long and rich historical traditions hitherto hardly touched by Western culture. Capitalism is by nature urban, at the expense of rural areas, which become increasingly devoted to mechanized farming and are often abandoned by their original populations. Unless they are protected by stringent laws, the centers of large cities everywhere come to look more or less alike; modern metropolises have the same utilitarian skyscrapers, the same urban traffic, the same suburban sprawl. The seeds of this new internationalism were planted in the late eighteenth century, and they have brought forth some striking similarities of customs in developed areas of the world.

For example, for the first time in history there arose in the late eighteenth century a sharp distinction in colors and materials between the dress worn by men and that worn by women, and by and large this distinction remains in all countries that have accepted bourgeois capitalism and even in many Marxist societies. Indigenous forms of dress tend to disappear in urban areas. Likewise, cultural activities have begun to resemble each other across wide distances. Japanese musicians play Mozart and Bartók with technical perfection, convincing "westerns" are filmed in Italy, rock concerts take place in Belgrade, and after initial opposition Western forms of abstract art have been shown in Moscow. The phenomenon of the open market for works of art, forcing the artist to rely on dealers, was—as we have seen—first predominant in seventeenth-century Holland; it is now universal. The commissioned work of painting or sculpture, the general rule until the eighteenth century except in Holland, is now the exception.

Although new artistic movements are still being born or devised at single points in time and space, they rapidly spread everywhere. It was not long before Impressionism, invented in Paris and its suburbs, took hold in every country in the Western world. It is in such international movements ("isms") that we must look for the basic artistic phenomena of the modern world. The modern era has found itself independent of its predecessors to a startling degree, and has accordingly developed a perspective from which it can with a sense of detachment regard history as a study of social and cultural movements rather than the story of the deeds of great personages. Beginning in the late eighteenth century and throughout the nineteenth, comprehensive histories of entire civilizations, as well as of art, music, literature, philosophy, and religion, were written; these volumes are still read, and they provide the foundations for today's more limited historical studies. Only in the modern period did it become evident that the forces of ceaseless change were bound to affect the works of man and render antiquated tomorrow what was new yesterday. Soon quality itself became equated with novelty, and it was enough to attack a style as *retardataire* to demolish its validity.

Along with this historical detachment there arose in the late eighteenth and in the nineteenth centuries the ability to appreciate widely different forms and periods of artistic creation, including those of archaic and primitive cultures. This attitude has increased in acceptability until at present the ideal (even, oddly enough, in some Marxist countries) is the person of catholic taste who prides himself on enjoying every good thing from whatever area or period, and feels obliged to apologize for a personal dislike. As a result, museums have proliferated, the past is preserved where it can be protected, and conscious efforts are made to keep works of art from disintegrating, to restore them when possible to their original appearance, to publish correct texts of older authors, and to perform older music on the instruments for which it was composed.

The most surprising concomitant of the historical view of art has been the development of styles that deny the validity of the past search for visual reality, and that exalt as models for the art of today the very arts of remote periods or cultures whose aesthetic significance has been newly discovered. Experimentation beyond the limits of representation has proceeded to such a degree that not only have nature and the object lost their control over the work of art but also such technological innovations as laser beams, taped communications, and microelectric waves have been proclaimed as the province of artistic creation.

The modern period as we have known it may be coming to an end. The collapse of ancient Oriental empires was welcomed in the early twentieth century as heralding the spread of universal democracy. So was the dissolution of the European capitalist empires in Africa and the Far East, not to speak of the smaller American empire in the Pacific. So was the technological emancipation of much of Western man from daily chores and the restrictions of time by mechanical and electronic inventions. To the dismay of the West the two greatest empires, comprising nearly half the population of the globe, are now governed by totalitarian movements that have no use for Western-style democracy. Much more embarrassing, the African nations liberated from European domination and certain previously democratic countries of Latin America have fallen under military dictatorships.

The internal-combustion engine brought freedom from distance, yet it has impoverished the centers of our cities, devastated the landscape, and poisoned both atmosphere and water. Nuclear discoveries threaten universal catastrophe. Chemical innovations menace our environment, our bodies, man's genetic capacity to survive, and the ability of the planet to support him. World leaders are helpless before the economic forces now propelling and undermining society. Global industrial combines threaten the autonomy of the national state.

If we have indeed entered a different era, artistically one thing is certain: the collapse of faith in progress has been accompanied by a lull, at least, in that succession of artistic movements that used to take place every generation, then every ten years, then every year, each declaring its predecessors extinct. No one can tell as yet what this means; one hopeful sign is that so many gifted artists are working well in styles long since consigned to oblivion.

1
Neoclassicism

The forty-year period from 1775 to 1815 marks one of the great upheavals of Western history, comparable in scope only to the barbarian invasions of the fifth century and to the two World Wars of the twentieth. The rebellion of England's North American colonies, the product of tensions that had developed for generations, was rapidly transformed into a genuine revolution (1775–83), resulting in independence from the mother country. Power was transferred to a republic, dominated by landowners and merchants. The success of the American Revolution encouraged the French followers of the eighteenth-century philosophers of the Enlightenment. During the extreme economic and political crisis in France in 1789, a constitutional monarchy was proclaimed, followed in 1792 by a republic. The revolutionary movement culminated in the Reign of Terror in which thousands of aristocrats, relatives of aristocrats, officials of the royal government, and suspected sympathizers of the old order lost their lives. Temporarily, at least, a classless form of government was in control.

Under the Directory (1795–99) the middle classes assumed power; then unexpectedly the Revolution, which was supposed to bring about a new era of freedom for all, fell a victim to its own most successful military leader. Under the dictatorship of Napoleon Bonaparte—the Consulate (1799–1804) and the Empire (1804–14 and 1815)—colossal military force was unleashed upon the continent of Europe, and it swept the Baroque monarchies great and small into the discard, dissolved the thousand-year-old Holy Roman Empire, and, in a series of military exploits unrivaled since the days of Alexander the Great, threatened Russia on the one hand and England on the other. After Napoleon's military collapse many, but by no means all, of the monarchies were restored, but the work of the Revolution and of Napoleon could not be entirely undone; the efficient revolutionary administrative system has been retained in France to this day, and the *Code Napoléon* remains the basis of many western European legal systems. Even more important, monarchy had been exposed as vulnerable, and revolutions were to erupt at intervals throughout the nineteenth century.

It might on the surface have been expected that the American and French revolutions would inspire a generation of inflammatory art. The reverse was the case; not until the Napoleonic slaughters, unprecedented in history in their scale and scope, did an art develop that registered directly the drama of the moment. Revolutionary art was by choice sternly Neoclassical. The distinction between the classicism of the mid-eighteenth century and the Neoclassicism of the revolutionary period may seem subtle, but it is important. Although to Winckelmann classicism was a religion, to most architects and cultivated patrons in the mid-eighteenth century it was a fashion, one that could easily be exchanged for Gothic. To the revolutionary period Neoclassicism was a way of life, affecting not only the arts but also all aspects of existence from religion to the dress of ordinary men and women, and in France even the calendar. Moreover, it was, at least as far as knowledge then extended, not imperial but republican Rome that the revolutionary period attempted to revive. Despite its origins, Neoclassicism survived both the Revolution and Napoleon, and persisted as a fashion throughout the continent and England well into the nineteenth century.

ARCHITECTURE

The well-known shape of Monticello (fig. 358) by THOMAS JEFFERSON (1743–1826) illustrates the process that had taken place. Jefferson intended to reform the Georgian architecture current in colonial Virginia by a thoroughgoing application of the principles he was studying in Palladio's treatise on architecture. As first built from 1770–84, Monticello, commanding from its hilltop a magnificent view of mountains, valleys, and plains, was a two-story structure, adorned with a two-story portico like those on some of Palladio's villas. During his long stay in Europe as minister to France, Jefferson had a chance to study not only the Classical French architecture of the eighteenth century but also the Maison Carrée at Nîmes, which he said he contemplated "as a lover gazes at his mistress." Beginning in 1796, he rebuilt

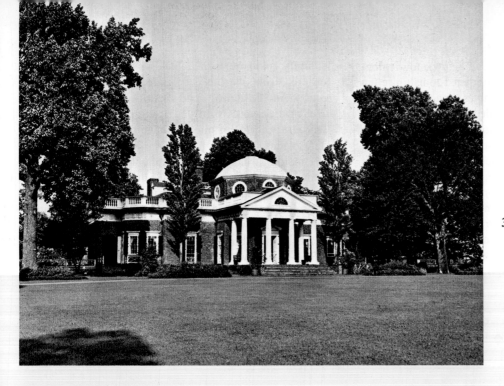

358. THOMAS JEFFERSON.
Monticello. 1770–84; rebuilt
1796–1800. Charlottesville,
Virginia

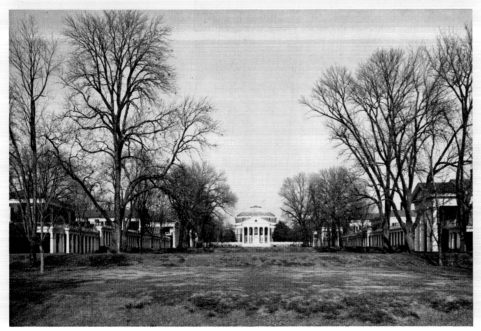

359. THOMAS JEFFERSON,
"Lawn," University of
Virginia. 1817–25.
Charlottesville

Monticello as a Neoclassic temple, apparently one story high, although a second story is concealed behind the entablature and balustrade. Clearly, Jefferson had both Chiswick (see fig. 347) and its ancestor, the Villa Rotonda (see fig. 174), in mind, but his mansion differs from both in being a permanent residence rather than a pleasure-house. It is built, moreover, of local brick rather than stone, with brick columns stuccoed and painted white and with white wood trim.

The octagonal dome is mirrored in semioctagonal shapes at either end of the building. The central portico is treated like a Roman pronaos and united with the ground by a single flight of steps. As the citizen of a republic, Jefferson chose the Doric order, always considered the simplest and most masculine, in preference to the Ionic of the Villa Rotonda or the Corinthian of Chiswick. The illusion of simplicity, in fact, is artfully maintained throughout the building and grounds through the device of hiding the many service elements behind simple brick colonnades under the sides of the lawn terraces.

Jefferson's cherished dream was the University of Virginia, at Charlottesville, which he brought to reality only in his old age. Built from 1817 to 1825, the central "Lawn" (fig. 359) constitutes not only the masterpiece of early Federal architecture in the United States but also one of the finest Neoclassic ensembles anywhere. From the central Pantheon-like Rotunda, planned as the library following a suggestion made by the professional architect Benjamin H. Latrobe (see below), low colonnades on either side in front of student rooms unite ten pavilions—Roman prostyle temples spaced at ever-increasing intervals. These provided lower rooms for the ten "schools" and upper rooms for the professors' living quarters. The colonnades are Tuscan; the pavilions, each different in a deliberate avoidance of symmetry, exploit the varying possibilities of Doric, Ionic, and Corinthian orders drawn from Classical monuments, so that the students could have before them a rich vocabulary of Classical style, the visual counterpart of the humanistic education to which Jefferson was devoted. The Composite, the richest of the orders, was reserved for the interior of the Rotunda. Although the Doric and Tuscan capitals could be turned locally, the others had to be ordered from marble carvers in Carrara, according to plates in Palladio. The result, clearly related to Hellenistic stoas, is an "environment" (to use the contemporary term) of magical harmony, still in daily use. The Neoclassic style became immediately *the* style for the buildings of the new republic and its various states, and reappeared in innumerable variations in Washington and in state capitals into the middle of the twentieth century. It was also used throughout the republic for country houses and town houses, great and small.

An English-born architect, BENJAMIN H. LATROBE (1764–1820), who furnished the self-taught Jefferson with much professional counsel, brought with him to the

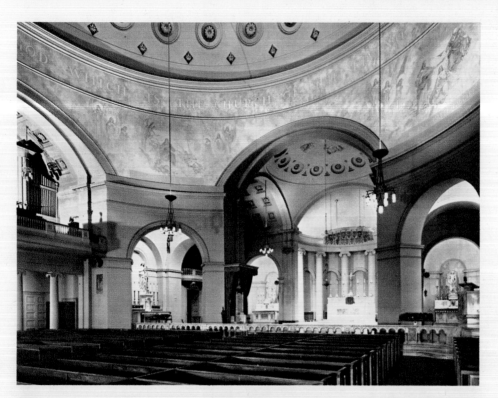

360. BENJAMIN H. LATROBE. Interior, Catholic Cathedral of Baltimore. Begun 1805

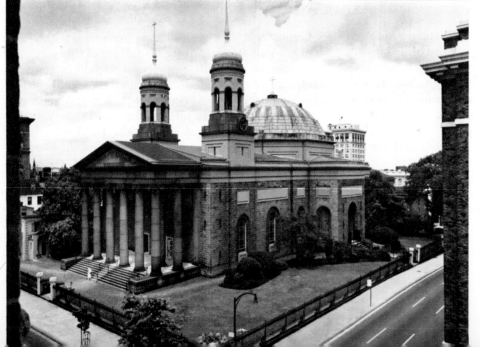

361. BENJAMIN H. LATROBE. Catholic Cathedral of Baltimore

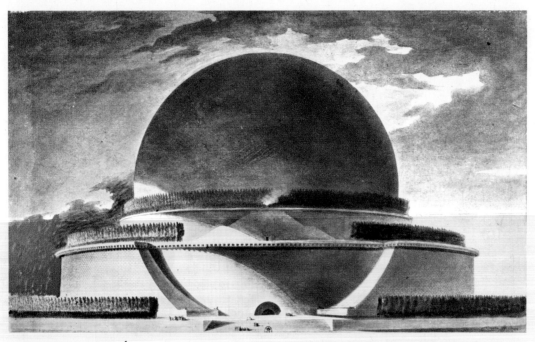

362. ÉTIENNE-LOUIS BOULLÉE. Design for the Tomb of Newton. 1784

United States the capability of building in both Neoclassic and Gothic styles. Only the former was in demand for his work in Washington, where he collaborated for years in the building and rebuilding of the United States Capitol. For the Catholic Cathedral of Baltimore in 1805 he submitted designs in both styles. His rather bleak Gothic design was not accepted. His handsome Neoclassic interior (fig. 360) is roofed by a succession of hemispheric domes, lighted from above like that of the Pantheon. The grandeur of the effect is enhancd by the sparse ornamentation, recalling the austerity of Adam (see fig. 348). The onion domes (fig. 361), added to the towers after Latrobe's death, were not from his design, but the Ionic pronaos, in the tradition of Soufflot (see fig. 324), is substantially as he planned it, although not built until 1863.

During the French Revolution little could be built but much was dreamed, especially by ÉTIENNE-LOUIS BOULLÉE (1728–99), whose visionary plans were intended to establish a new architecture symbolizing the Rights of Man for which the revolution had, presumably, been fought. Nothing could be less practical or less traditional than Boullée's idea for a Monument to Newton (fig. 362). This design, made in 1784, five years before the Revolution got under way, reduced the mass to essential forms of sphere and cylinder, stripped even of the conventional orders. The titanic scale can be deduced from the size of the antlike humans at the base and the groves of trees that encircle the sphere at various levels. The minute entrance was to lead the awestruck visitor through a long, dark tunnel to the interior, lighted only by holes so spaced as to suggest the moon and stars of the night sky.

When architecture could recommence under Napoleon, the Classical orders in their severest form dominated. For forty years ideas for a church of the Madeleine, to head the Rue Royale between the twin palaces by Gabriel (see fig. 326), had been under consideration. When the final competition was held in 1806, Napoleon decreed that the structure should be a Temple of Glory (he renounced the idea in 1813 after his defeat at Leipzig), and chose a Roman peripteral Corinthian temple design by PIERRE VIGNON (1762–1828), the first to be erected since the third century. The colossal structure (fig. 363) took until 1843 to build, and still dominates an entire quarter of Paris, dwarfing even from a distance the delicate masterpieces of Gabriel. Still breathing something of the megalomania of Boullée, the Madeleine is the most thoroughgoing example of the Neoclassic attempt to live in ancient style. Inside, of course, it could not work; a windowless Christian interior is an impossibility, and the nave had to be roofed by domes on pendentives and pierced by skylights.

A strikingly different kind of quotation from the ancient world is the Brandenburg Gate at Berlin (fig. 364), built by KARL LANGHANS (1733–1808) in 1789–94, while Jefferson was in Europe. A direct imitation of the Propylaia at Athens, this is the first public building in Greek rather than Roman style, incongruously enough bearing an imitation of a Roman four-horse chariot as on a triumphal arch. Doubtless the virile Doric order was connected in the minds of both the architect and his patron, King Frederick William II, with the martial vigor of the Prussian kingdom. Neoclassic architecture was carried the length and breadth of Europe from Copenhagen and St. Petersburg (the modern Lenin-

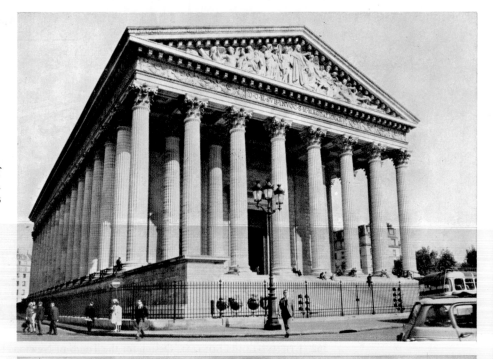

363. PIERRE VIGNON. Church of
the Madeleine. 1806–43.
Paris

364. KARL LANGHANS.
Brandenburg Gate.
1789–94. Berlin

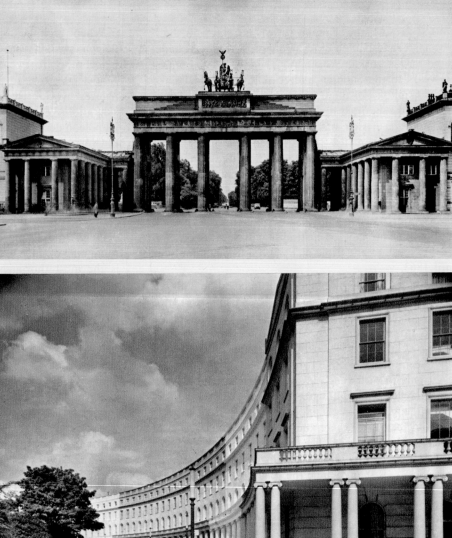

365. JOHN NASH. Park Crescent.
1812–22. Regent's Park,
London

grad)—where the mile-wide stretch of the Neva River was lined on both sides with columned structures, incongruous above the winter ice—as far south as Rome, Naples, and Athens. Greek independence was celebrated in the 1830s by the erection of a host of Greek Revival structures within sight of the Parthenon. The loveliest of all Neoclassic cityscapes, although much of it has been lost to twentieth-century commercialism, is early nineteenth-century London. Cumberland Terrace, Eaton Square, and dozens of enchanting side streets still stand, among them the gracefully colonnaded Park Crescent (fig. 365) by JOHN NASH (1752–1835), begun in 1812 while Jefferson's ideas for the University of Virginia were beginning to mature.

PAINTING

DAVID. The official artist of the French Revolution was Jacques-Louis David (1748–1825), eventually entrusted with commemorative portraits of martyred revolutionary leaders, the design of public pageants, celebrations, and state funerals, and even the designs for the costumes to be worn by the citizens and citizenesses of the republic. At his decree the aristocratic powdered wigs, silk and velvet coats, and lace ruffles worn by men were replaced by natural hair (later worn short and tousled), woolen jackets, and simple linen shirts. Women shed their towering headdresses adorned with ribbons and feathers for a simple style imitated from the ancient Greeks, and their hoopskirts, lace, and furbelows for a muslin tunic belted high above the waist. Yet David's most rigidly doc-

trinaire painting, the *Oath of the Horatii* (see fig. 366), which was the opening salvo in the Neoclassic battle against both the dying Rococo and the nostalgic classicism of the mid-eighteenth century, was commissioned in 1784 for Louis XVI. Nine years later this monarch was to lose his head under the guillotine because of the very forces David had helped to unleash.

Historical circumstances elucidate the apparent paradox. The Royal Academy held, at first in odd-numbered years, much later annually, a large public exhibition known as the Salon. In the nineteenth century this institution became a brake on artistic progress, but in the eighteenth it was a strong stimulus. The great galleries, first in the Louvre and later in the Tuileries, were in a sense a theater, with all Paris as the audience. The more dramatic a picture was and the greater the attention it attracted, the better were the artist's chances of obtaining the portrait commissions that often provided his principal livelihood. In addition, pictures were commissioned by the royal superintendent of buildings, who under Louis XVI was the Comte d'Angiviller, a man with a passion for elevated subjects. Greuze, limited as he seems to us today (see fig. 333), filled the bill nicely; so did an array of minor painters now almost entirely forgotten, who covered the walls with historical pictures intended to demonstrate moral truths. The *Oath of the Horatii*, finished in Rome in 1785, was one of these pictures, but it pointed a message whose implications neither d'Angiviller nor the king, nor probably even David at that moment, understood.

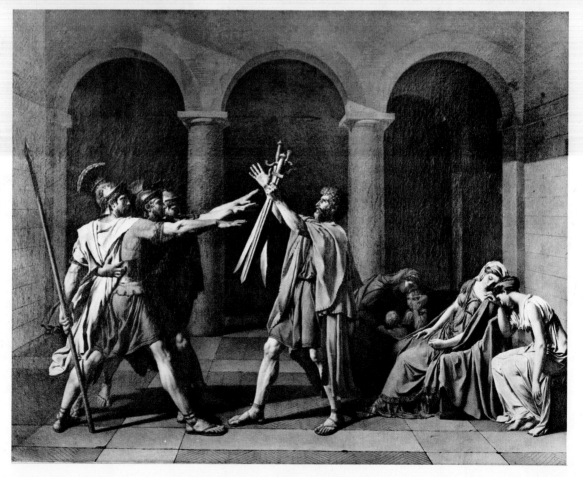

366. JACQUES-LOUIS DAVID. *Oath of the Horatii*. 1784–85. Oil on canvas, 10'8¼" x 14'. The Louvre, Paris

David arrived at the French Academy in Rome in 1775, a thoroughly accomplished Rococo painter in the general tradition of Boucher, but already devoted to the approved moral subjects. When he came in contact with Classical art in its native land, he said that he felt as if he "had been operated on for cataract." This statement not only expresses vividly the new clarity demanded of Neoclassic vision, in contrast to the softness and vagueness of the Rococo, but also characterizes that voluptuous style as a malady demanding surgical removal. The new style was not achieved rapidly; during much of his first year in Rome, David devoted himself to drawing eyes, ears, feet, and hands from the most beautiful statues. Most of his paintings during these formative years are lost, but from all accounts they were drowned in black shadow like those of Caravaggio and the *tenebrosi* (see figs. 231, 232, colorplate 37). But by 1781 the new style was established, and in 1783 David, then thirty-five, was elected to the Academy, which he soon came to detest, along with all royal officials, whom he called *les perruques* (*the wigs*).

The *Oath of the Horatii* (fig. 366) shows the three Horatii brothers, chosen to defend Rome in combat against the three Curiatii, representing neighboring Alba, to one of whom Horatia, sister of the Horatii, was betrothed. The incident was recorded by Roman historians, and although it took place under the kingdom was believed by the French to have been an example of republican patriotism. The oath of the three brothers on the swords held aloft by their aged father appears to be an invention on David's part. As in the compositions of Greuze (see fig. 333), the figures move in a strict relief plane, against a background of what David considered historically correct early Roman architecture, in sharp reaction to the spiral into the picture characteristic of the compositions of Boucher and Fragonard. The martial resolve of the young heroes is displayed in stances as grand as those of statues, although more rigid than most, while Horatia, her sister, her mother, and a tiny niece and nephew mourn the approaching conflict between brothers and lover in attitudes of classical grace. Every form, masculine and feminine, is exactly projected with a hallucinatory clarity going beyond anything demanded by Poussin in the seventeenth century (see colorplate 39); superb male musculature and smooth female arms and legs—even drapery folds—are as hard as the steel of the uplifted swords. The coloring, inert like the surfaces, is restricted to individual areas, without any of the reciprocal exchange of colors typical of Baroque and Rococo traditions.

Although the picture was not recognized as potentially revolutionary in a political as well as an artistic sense, it was the direct forerunner of openly republican political allegories. After several such heroic paintings, David weakened his ties with the Royal Academy. During the Revolution he became a friend of Robespierre and ally of the Jacobins, and he presided briefly over the National Convention. In 1793 he had the satisfaction of seeing the Academy dissolved to be replaced with a society of revolutionary artists. Thereafter, his stern style served as the funnel through which all new talent was poured, and the most important new artists of France were either his pupils or his imitators. In enforcing his sculptural discipline, he is reported to have advised his pupils, "Never let your brushwork show." What a transformation from the days of the *Signboard of Gersaint*!

David's most memorable work is the *Death of Marat* (fig. 367), a painting of tragic grandeur because the subject is presented directly, stripped of allegorical disguise. Marat, one of the leaders of the Revolution, was constrained to work in a medicated bath on account of a skin disease he had contracted while hiding from the royal police in the Paris sewers before the Revolution. His desk was a rough packing box. The young counterrevolutionary Charlotte Corday gained admittance to this unconventional office with a note reading, "It suffices that I am very unhappy to have a right to your benevolence," and then plunged a knife into his chest. David was called in immediately to draw the corpse still in position, and from the drawing the painting was made, the elements slightly rearranged for greater theatricality. It should be recalled that David had arranged the actual funeral of an earlier martyred revolutionary, Le Peletier de Saint-Fargeau, exhibiting the seminude corpse propped up so as to dis-

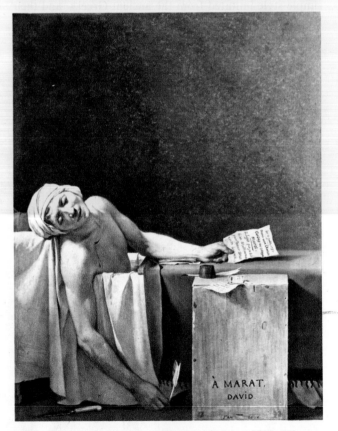

367. Jacques-Louis David. *Death of Marat.* 1793. Oil on canvas, 63¾ x 49⅛". Musées Royaux des Beaux-Arts, Brussels

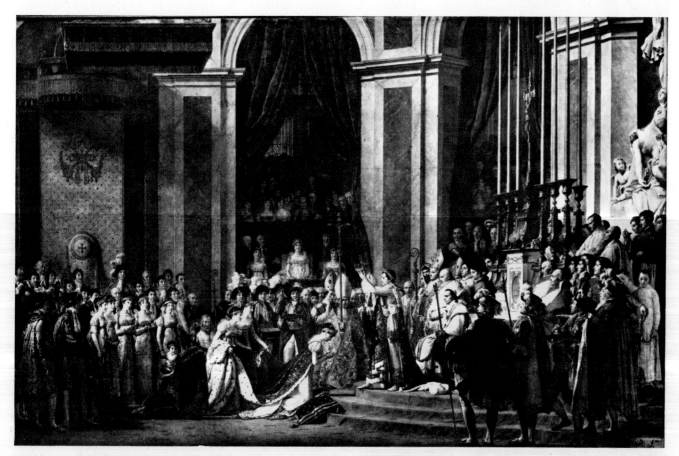

368. JACQUES-LOUIS DAVID. *Coronation of Napoleon and Josephine.* 1805-7. Oil on canvas, 20′ x 30′6½″. The Louvre, Paris

play the wound in imitation of his own painting of the slain Hector.

Not only Classical history is recalled in the *Marat*, but also obviously the traditional rendering of the dead Christ (Michelangelo's *Pietà*, for example; see fig. 132) and the high side lighting of Caravaggio and his followers, with the setting in nowhere (see fig. 231, colorplate 37). The box, the bloodstained towel, and the tub were venerated as relics by the populace. David has painted the rough boards as well as Chardin might have, but arranged parallel to the picture plane like a Classical tablet, and supplied with the words (in French): "To Marat, David, Year Two." The stony treatment of head and figure shows an unexpected feeling for impasto in the handling of the flesh, and the rich treatment of the background in a basketwork of tiny, interlocking brushstrokes that endow it with a vibrant texture gives the lie to David's own advice to his students.

A new turn of the Revolution a year later brought Robespierre to the guillotine and David to prison and a narrow escape from death. On his release he became increasingly interested in Napoleon as the man who could bring order out of revolutionary chaos and could offer him the protection he needed. Although by no means the only painter to the emperor, David was entrusted with

such important commissions as the *Coronation of Napoleon and Josephine*, commissioned in 1804 and painted 1805–1807 (fig. 368), a majestic work in which the painter's hard-won Neoclassicism survives only in the projection of individual forms. The stiff solemnity of the courtiers gathered at the ceremony recalls the Ravenna mosaics rather than Roman statues, but the unexpected sparkle of color from gold, jewels, rich velvets, and brocades derives from the Venetian tradition, especially Veronese (see colorplate 29). At the Restoration of the monarchy, the aging painter, who had turned his republican coat once for Napoleon, could not turn it again, and he spent his remaining years in exile in Brussels.

INGRES. Although not only David's followers but also the master himself in later life turned away from the more doctrinaire aspects of Neoclassicism, Jean-Auguste-Dominique Ingres (1780–1867), by far the greatest of David's pupils, remained faithful to Neoclassical ideals to the end of his long life, and eventually formed the center of a conservative group that utilized the principles of Neoclassicism, forged in the Revolution, as a weapon for reaction. Ingres was an infant prodigy, attending art school at eleven, and already

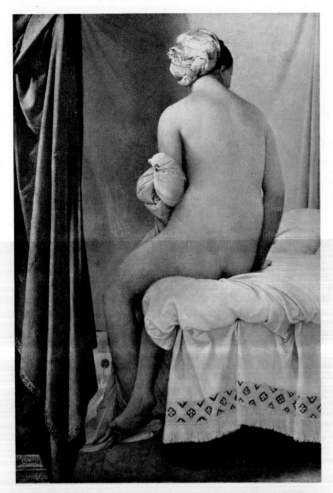

369. JEAN-AUGUSTE-DOMINIQUE INGRES. *Valpinçon Bather.*
1808. Oil on canvas, 56⅝ x 38¼". The Louvre, Paris

a capable performer on the violin. He entered the studio of David at seventeen; although as long as he lived, he never let his brushwork show, neither did he accept the cubic mass of David's mature style, preferring curving forms flowing like violin melody. Winner of the Prix de Rome in 1801, he was not able to leave for the Villa Medici until 1806; he remained in Rome until 1820, and returned there 1835–41, absorbing not only ancient but also Renaissance Rome, especially the art of Raphael. He also stayed four years in Florence (1820–24), where he was one of the first to appreciate not only the Florentine Mannerists but also Fra Angelico. The first pictures he exhibited at the Salon were almost uniformly ridiculed, accused of being everything from Gothic to Chinese, and his special brand of nonpolitical Neoclassicism was worked out in isolation.

In 1808 Ingres did one of his finest paintings, whose pose he revived again and again in later works, the *Valpinçon Bather* (fig. 369), named after the collection it first adorned. While the coolness of this lovely nude may at first sight recall Bronzino (see fig. 192), whom Ingres ad-

mired, it is drawn with a contour line as subtle and as analytic as that perfected by Holbein, but infinitely more musical, gliding in delicate cadences over shoulders, back, and legs. The surface is modeled to porcelain smoothness, but is never hard; Ingres was always at his best with delicate flesh and soft fabrics. His frequent subtle linear distortions have less to do with Raphael than with the attenuated forms of Parmigianino (see colorplate 30), as does his sense of space—for example, the sudden jump between the foreground and the tiny spigot at an unexplained distance, from which water pours into a sunken bath. One could hardly imagine a greater distance than that between this cool, chaste nude and the frolicking ones of Fragonard's *The Bathers* (see colorplate 47).

Ingres fancied himself a history painter, although too many of his narrative pictures are weakened by his inability to project a dramatic situation. A work that embodies his ideal (rather than political) program for Neoclassicism is the huge *Apotheosis of Homer* (fig. 370), a new *School of Athens* (see colorplate 24), painted in 1827 and intended for the ceiling of a room in the Louvre, where it would undoubtedly have been more effective than at its present height on a wall. Ingres made no concessions to the principles of illusionistic ceiling perspective from below, starting with Mantegna (see colorplate 13), continuing with Correggio (see fig. 178), and culminating in the High Baroque (see figs. 251, 252, colorplate 38). Like Poussin he preferred the High Renaissance tradition, as exemplified by Michelangelo (see fig. 138, colorplate 23) and his contemporaries. Before an Ionic temple dedicated to Homer, the blind poet is enthroned, crowned with laurel by the muse of epic poetry. Below him sit two female figures, the one with a sword representing the *Iliad*, the one with a rudder the *Odyssey*. Around are grouped the geniuses from antiquity and later times whom Ingres considered truly Classical; Pindar extends his lyre, Phidias his mallet, Apelles his palette and brushes, and Aeschylus his scroll, in homage. Phidias holds by his hand Raphael, admitted to the upper level but not, alas, to the front row; on the other side Leonardo and Fra Angelico may be discerned. Dante, at the left, is presented by Virgil, and lower down Poussin may be seen, copied from the great master's self-portrait. At the lower right are grouped three French Classical writers, Boileau, Molière, and Racine. Shakespeare and Corneille just make the scene in the lower left-hand corner, and Mozart, a subject of torment to Ingres, who repeatedly put him in and dropped him out, was finally omitted from the company of the immortals. The cool light of an ideal realm binds the figures together in the kind of artificial composition that became definitive for classicizing muralists even into the twentieth century.

Much of the time Ingres was financially obliged to accept portrait commissions, which he considered a waste of time, although today his portraits are accepted

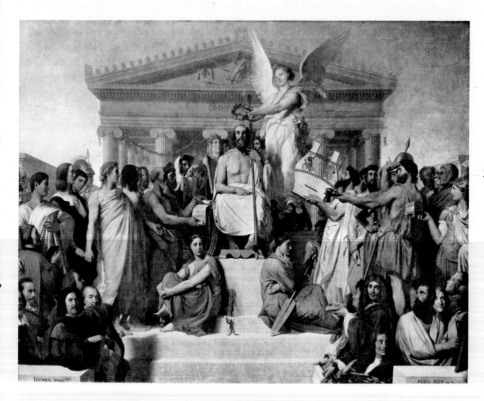

370. JEAN-AUGUSTE-DOMINIQUE INGRES. *Apotheosis of Homer.* 1827. Oil on canvas, 12'8" x 16'11". The Louvre, Paris

as his greatest works. He even drew portraits of visitors to Rome, who trooped to his studio, in such meticulous pencil studies as the *Stamaty Family* of 1818 (fig. 371), which show the exquisite quality of his line. Knowing that lead pencil is disagreeable in excess, he carefully kept it off the paper, only here and there suggesting the darkness of hair or of clothing, but concentrating on the precision of facial delineation and on the interweaving of the folds of the costumes into a fabric of gossamer fineness, as delicate as a pearly roulade from the keys of the piano in the background.

Ingres said, "There is no case of a great draftsman not having found the exact color to suit the character of his drawing." Debatable though the point may be, Ingres' own paintings are almost invariably perfect in color, in a cool range related to that of Holbein or Bronzino or even of Fra Angelico. All the beauty of Ingres' color and the perfection of his form are seen in the portrait of *Comtesse d'Haussonville* (colorplate 50), painted in 1845; she is pensively posed in a corner of her salon, in an attitude that is clearly though unobtrusively derived from Classical art. No Dutch painter ever produced still lifes more convincing than the vases on the mantle, and for all its precision the glow of the color has something in common with that of Vermeer. The reflection in the mirror, going back through Velázquez to van Eyck (see colorplate 44, fig. 102), reappears again and again in nineteenth-century art (see fig. 419, for example), deeply concerned as it was with optical phenomena.

Although many of his subjects were drawn from the medieval history and poetry dear to the Romanticists (see Chapter 2), Ingres was resolutely opposed to their abandonment to emotion, and indeed to the artistic

sources on which they drew. Rubens he called "that Flemish meat merchant." Delacroix, the leader of the Romanticists, was the devil incarnate; at a hanging at the Salon, after Delacroix had left the room, Ingres said to an attendant, "Open the windows, I smell sulfur." Yet his influence later in the century was very great. Degas (see Chapter 4), whose vision was sharpened by his knowledge of Ingres' line, was one of the great innovators of the late nineteenth century, and Matisse, master of twentieth-century line, studied with Gustave Moreau, a pupil of Ingres, and carried his principles in a new transformation well into the twentieth century.

SCULPTURE

HOUDON. Although sculpture would seem to have been predestined for a dominant role in Neoclassicism, that art produced no genius to rank with David or Ingres at their best. The finest French sculptor of the eighteenth century was Jean Antoine Houdon (1741–1828). His life-span overlaps that of David at both ends, but his style was formed in the classicistic period of the eighteenth century, and survived somewhat anachronistically during the revolutionary phase of Neoclassicism, through which he managed to function with a certain agility; the basic honesty of his style won only grudging acceptance from Napoleon. Nonetheless, Houdon pertains to this moment because his work was greatly admired by the philosophers who provided the intellectual basis of the Revolution, many of whom he portrayed with phenomenal accuracy. Houdon was devoted to perfection of naturalness; he studied anatomy with exhaustive care, and did not disdain the use of plaster casts from life and meticu-

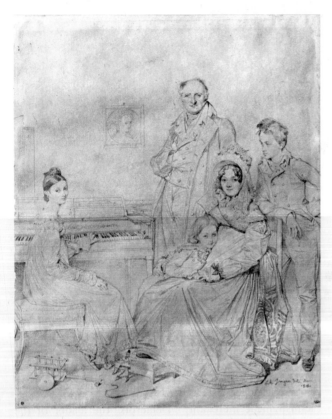

371. JEAN-AUGUSTE-DOMINIQUE INGRES. *Stamaty Family*. 1818. Pencil on paper, 15½ x 11″. The Louvre, Paris

lous measurements. Nonetheless, his scientific precision in no way deadens his work. He declared that his purpose was "to present with all the realism of form and to render almost immortal the image of the men who have contributed the most to the glory or the happiness of their country." Every one of his portraits impresses the contemporary observer with the feeling that across the barriers of time and substance Houdon has made him actually acquainted with the subject, shown in a characteristic pose and in a moment of thought, feeling, or speech.

Houdon's numerous busts and statues of Voltaire sparkle with the aged philosopher's wit. Seated in his armchair, a classicistic piece typical of the taste of Louis XVI, he wears only his dressing gown and the cap donned by eighteenth-century gentlemen at home in place of the wig worn in public (fig. 372). The folds of the gown fall like those of a toga, without sacrificing the intimacy of the moment. Every facet of the papery wrinkled skin, showing the bones beneath, is drawn with delicacy and accuracy, and the eyes twinkle in a wry, half-sad smile. Houdon brought draftsmanship in sculpture to its highest pitch, a kind of accuracy rivaled in painting only by Holbein and Ingres.

Due to his friendship with Franklin and Jefferson, both of whom he portrayed, Houdon was invited to America

in 1785 to measure and study George Washington at Mount Vernon for the superb statue he carved in marble between 1788 and 1792 for the rotunda of Jefferson's State Capitol at Richmond, Virginia, where it still stands (fig. 373). Houdon's brilliant realism was tempered somewhat by the demands of a ceremonial image. Washington, standing in a pose of classical dignity, wears his general's uniform, leans lightly on his baton of command, and rests his left arm upon a fasces (the bundle of rods signifying authority carried before magistrates in Roman processions); attached to it are the sword and the plowshare, indicating the hero's preeminence in war and peace. Seen in the actual space for which it was designed, the statue radiates all the grandeur Houdon desired, and has succeeded in implanting its image of the "Father of His Country" on nearly two centuries of American thought and feeling.

CANOVA. A much stricter adherence to the principles of Neoclassicism is shown by the Italian Antonio Canova (1757–1822), who, after Venetian training, moved to

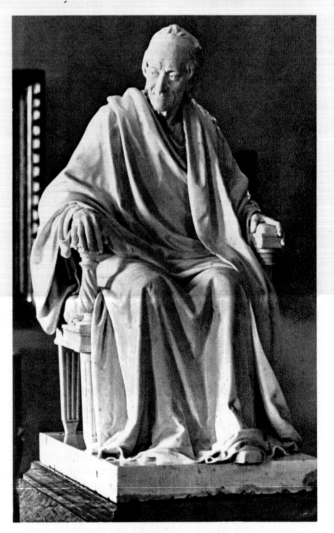

372. JEAN ANTOINE HOUDON. *Voltaire*. 1778. Marble, height c. 65″. The Hermitage, Leningrad

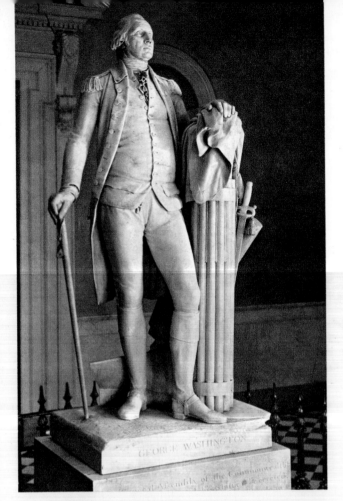

373. JEAN ANTOINE HOUDON. *George Washington.*
1788–92. Marble, height 74". State Capitol,
Richmond, Virginia

Rome in 1779. Revered in his lifetime, he was vilified soon after; more recently, the pendulum has come to rest in an appreciation of Canova as a gifted but limited artist, who combined superb technical ability with reverence for Greek originals. He studied enthusiastically the Parthenon sculptures brought to London by Lord Elgin but declined an invitation to restore them. Canova made no attempt at precise portraiture in the manner of Houdon, but produced idealized images, such as a nude statue of Napoleon as a Greek hero, which still stands in Milan, and one of Washington in Classical garb for the State Capitol in Raleigh, North Carolina, unfortunately destroyed by fire. The alluring lifesize marble statue of Napoleon's sister, Maria Paulina Borghese, as Venus Victrix, 1805–1807 (fig. 374), shows the princess partly nude, reclining in a Classical pose on marble cushions on a gilt bronze couch, holding the apple given the goddess as the prize by Paris in the earliest recorded beauty contest—a triumph to which the subject's not inconsiderable charms clearly entitle her. The chill of Canova's smooth surfaces, which somehow manage to convert the natural translucency of marble into something as opaque as cake frosting, cannot obscure the eventual Baroque derivation of his style. The head is obviously close to that of Apollo in Bernini's *Apollo and Daphne* (see fig. 237), then as now in the Borghese collection, which Canova must have studied with loving care.

Canova managed to transform the character of the dramatic tomb (see the Rossellino tombs, figs. 67, 68) into imagery deprived of any reference to Christianity in his pyramidal monument to Maria Christina, archduchess of Saxe-Teschen (fig. 375), erected to her memory by her husband, Archduke Albert, between 1798–1805. Her portrait is upheld by a soaring Classical figure representing Happiness, while her ashes are borne in an urn by Piety into the open door; to the right the winged genius of Mourning rests upon the lion of Fortitude, and to the left youthful, mature, and aged figures symbolize the Three Ages of Man. The contemporary Italian critic Francesco Milizia declared that a monument should "demonstrate in its simplicity the character of the person commemorated and bear no symbols that are not immediately intelligible." He must have been pleased by this one, although today's viewer requires a few words of explanation. Nonetheless, the mystery of the unknown Beyond is beautifully dramatized by the soaring line of the pyramid, and by the curve of the cloth sweeping the figures inexorably on to the dark and silent door.

374. ANTONIO CANOVA.
*Maria Paulina Borghese,
as Venus Victrix.*
1805–7. Marble,
62⅞ x 78¾"
(including bed).
Galleria Borghese,
Rome

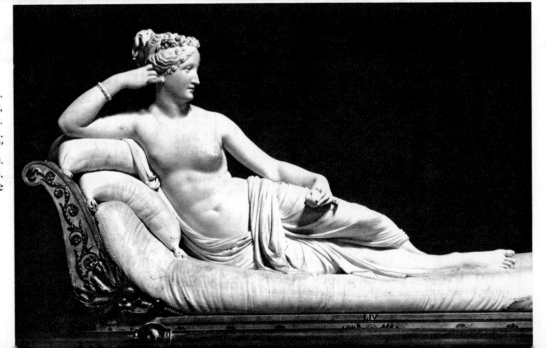

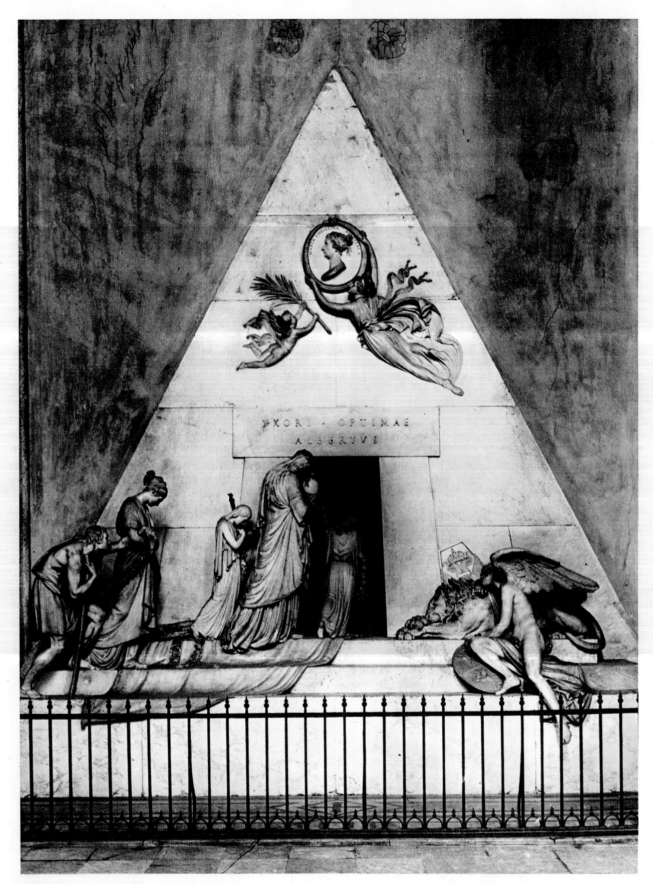

375. ANTONIO CANOVA. *Tomb of the Archduchess Maria Christina.* 1798–1805. Marble, life-size. Augustinerkirche, Vienna

2

Romanticism

In contrast to Neoclassicism, which in its purest form is instantly recognizable, the parallel current of Romanticism is vague indeed. The characterizations of Romanticism, and the lists of artists to be included in the movement—if anything so amorphous can be called a movement—are as numerous as the writers on the subject. The term *Romantic* appears to have originated in the type of narrative, popular in the late Middle Ages, in which the adventures of a legendary hero were spun out to great length, and from the very start, therefore, involved connotations of unreality and of distance, in time or space or both. The Gothicism of Walpole, expressed in architecture in Strawberry Hill (see figs. 349, 350) and in literature in his Gothic novel *The Castle of Otranto* (1764), has often been called Romantic, although *pre-Romantic* might be a better term.

By the middle of the eighteenth century, the term *Romantic* was applied to the natural English garden whose winding walks, pools, and groves—in revolt against the formal planning of the Baroque garden—were in actuality, as we have seen, the result of careful planning and often of enormous cost. Thus, to the literary elements of the exotic and the remote, the ingredient of the natural was added, finding its philosophical support in the writings of Rousseau.

But the culminating aspect of Romanticism is undoubtedly its interest in the sublime, as distinguished from the beautiful, deriving from a tradition that originated in the treatise *On the Sublime*, attributed to Longinus, a Greek Platonic philosopher of the third century A.D. The sublime, which contains elements of pain, terror, majesty, and above all awe before the unknown and the unknowable, constitutes a strong component of ancient art at many times, particularly during the Hellenistic period, notably in the sculptures of Pergamon, in contrast to the clearly defined Classical standards of beauty prevailing in Greek art of the fifth century B.C. The sublime was the object of meditation by the French critic Boileau in the seventeenth century, and almost against his will by the rationalistic Voltaire, who had trouble with the intractable phenomenon of

Shakespeare's greatness in spite of his violation of all classical rules—"a savage who could write."

Although so many of the elements of Romanticism existed in the eighteenth century, like eighteenth-century classicism they may be considered rather as an elegant pose of cultivated society; in fact, the two attitudes could easily coexist. The same English natural garden could contain mock Greek temples and Gothic ruins (see figs. 352, 351), not to speak of Chinese pagodas. Elements imported from China by Jesuit missionaries recur as playthings in Rococo decoration. Not until the great upheaval of the French Revolution and its aftermath did a general Romantic attitude become widespread and definitive for works of art of a very high order. In English poetry the new freedom of Wordsworth, Byron, Keats, Shelley, and Scott differs from the measured cadences of their precursors, Pope, Thomson, Gray, and Cowper; in music the new movement was expressed in the greatly expanded symphonies, concerti, and sonatas of Beethoven and Schubert and in the flowering of Italian tragic opera. Eighteenth-century principles of form were swept away by a new emotionalism that generated its own forms. Like Neoclassicism, Romanticism became a way of life, affecting not only art but also conduct, an elevation of emotion above intellect, content above form, color above line, intuition and passion above judgment, resulting in an entirely new ideal hero—Byron's Childe Harold and Goethe's Werther. While Neoclassicism exalted Poussin, Raphael, and the "antique" (Classical art seen through Roman eyes), Romanticism appealed to the Baroque, especially Rubens and Rembrandt, to Michelangelo, the Middle Ages, and the East.

Except in architecture, Neoclassicism was relatively weak in England; indeed, English Neoclassical architects could just as happily practice in Classical, Gothic, or Oriental styles. In France, however, Romanticism, arising before he knew it in the very studio of David, eventually declared against him and the whole Neoclassical movement. Interestingly enough, Neoclassicism and Romanticism soon changed sides politically. The first allegiance of the Romanticists was to the Napoleonic dream of a united Europe, comparable to Beethoven's original dedication of the "Eroica" Symphony to Napoleon. After his fall the Romanticists often sided with new revolutionary movements, while the late phase of Neoclassicism under Ingres associated itself with the restored Bourbon monarchy, eventually with the Second Empire, and as well with the ever more repressive force of the Academy. The most extreme manifestations of the Romantic spirit are sometimes difficult to accept as works of art, especially those outside France, Spain, and England where the young artist was raised in an already rich professional tradition. The account given here is one-sided in that it attempts to present only works of enduring quality, but they should be recognized as part of a vast movement invading all aspects of nineteenth-century life in every European country as well as in the United States.

GOYA. Hardly known to the French Neoclassicists or—except for his prints—even to the early Romanticists, the greatest artistic genius of the turn of the eighteenth century was a Spaniard, Francisco José de Goya y Lucientes, to give him his full name (1746–1828), whose long lifetime overlaps that of David. One wonders what these two utter opposites could have had to say to each other if fate had ever brought them together. Goya made the required obeisance to Italy, but only briefly,

and seems to have been unimpressed either by antiquity or by the Renaissance. He was a lifelong rebel against artistic or intellectual straitjackets, and could never have tolerated the stern doctrines of David, in fact, he managed to skip the Neoclassical phase entirely, even though one of its most influential practitioners, the German painter Anton Raphael Mengs, friend of Winckelmann, was in a position of authority in Madrid. Goya was certainly more influenced by Tiepolo, who worked in Madrid from 1762 till his death in 1770, and thus passed directly from a personal version of the Rococo, with a strong admixture of Spanish folklore, to a style we can hardly call anything but Romantic.

In 1786 Goya was appointed painter to the king, and in 1799, already more than fifty, first court painter. After 1792, when he suffered a severe illness, Goya was totally deaf, which disability may have been responsible—as it was with his younger contemporary Beethoven—for liberating him from some of the trivialities of life for meditation on its deeper significance. Goya's brilliant portraits of the royal court may have been influenced by the light, free brushwork and diaphanous forms of Gainsborough, whose works were then widely known in accurate engravings. But his characterizations are far more vivid, pervaded by intense humanity and at times biting satire. His supreme achievement in portraiture is the *Family of Charles IV*, painted in 1800 (fig. 376), an inspired parody of Velázquez's *Las Meninas* (see

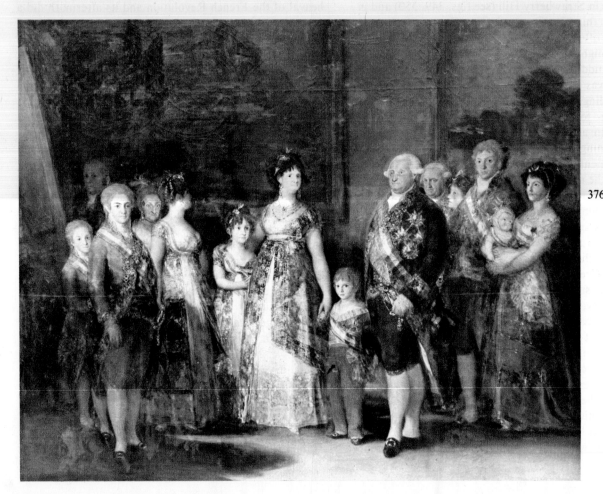

376. FRANCISCO GOYA. *Family of Charles IV*. 1800. Oil on canvas, 9'2" x 11'. Museo del Prado, Madrid

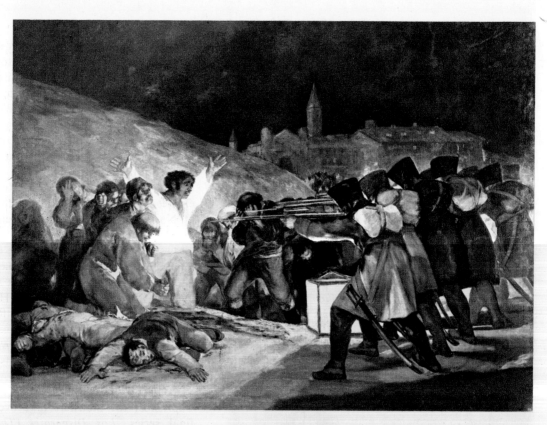

377. FRANCISCO GOYA. *Third of May, 1808*. 1814. Oil on canvas, 8'8¾" x 11'3⅞". Museo del Prado, Madrid

colorplate 44). Thirteen members of the royal family, representing three generations, are assembled in a picture gallery of the palace, with Goya himself painting at a large canvas in the shadows at the left, a sardonic commentator on this parade of insolence and vulgarity. The king, with his red face and with his chest blazing with decorations, and the ugly and ill-natured queen are painted as they undoubtedly were. Daudet called them "the baker's family who have just won the big lottery prize," but Goya's real purpose is deeper than satire: he has unmasked these people as evil. Only some (not all) of the children escape his condemnation. The mystery is that the family were so obtuse as not to realize what Goya was doing to them. Unexpectedly, the result is a dazzling display of color in the lighting, the costumes, and the decorations—brilliant sparkles of impastos against rich, deep glazes—all touched in lightly and swiftly without a hint of the formal construction and composition of the contemporary French Neoclassicists.

A still unexplained picture, probably painted in the same year, is the *Maja desnuda* (colorplate 51)—the word *maja* is untranslatable; *coquette* is an approximation—one of the most delightful paintings of the female nude in history. The pose is an updated and very awake transformation of the sleeping nude in the lower right corner of Titian's *Bacchanal of the Andrians* (see fig. 161), at that time in the Spanish royal collections. There exists a second, much sketchier clothed version of the picture. The nude was formerly explained as an unconventional portrait of the duchess of Alba, a patron and close friend of Goya's, and the clothed replica as an attempt to account for the artist's time, hastily painted

against the duke's return. In any event the seductive pose is entrancing, as is the delicacy of Goya's unusually smooth and polished modeling of the flesh, contrasted with the crisp brushwork of the white satin sheet and pillow slips and lace ruffles and with the intensity of the blue velvet cushions.

The frivolity of the picture hardly prepares us for Goya's indignant denunciations of the inhumanity of warfare, of which the most monumental example is the *Third of May, 1808* (fig. 377), depicting the execution of Madrid rebels by Napoleonic soldiery, commissioned by the liberal government at the artist's request after the expulsion of the French in 1814. This painting, done in 1814, is the earliest explicit example of what has come to be known as "social protest" in art, as distinguished from the allegorical allusions to contemporary events common enough in the Renaissance and the Baroque. Despite written meditations, such as those of Leonardo da Vinci, on the cruelties and terrors of battle, warfare itself had uniformly been depicted as glorious and cruelties as inevitable (see figs. 61, 129). Goya treats the firing squad as a many-legged, faceless monster, before whose level, bayoneted guns are pushed group after group of helpless victims, the first already shattered by bullets and streaming with blood, the next gesticulating wildly in the last seconds of life, the third hiding the horror from their eyes with their hands. A paper lantern gives the only light; in the dimness the nearest houses and a church tower of the city almost blend with the earth against the night sky. The conviction of reality conveyed by the picture, painted so long after the event, is a testament to the extraordinary powers of Goya's imagination and to the depth of his inner participation in human suffering. Through the medium of brushstrokes as broad as those of Tintoretto, he communicates unbearable emotion with thick pigment, which, as if sacramentally, becomes the still living or already rent flesh and streaming blood, achieving at once a timeless universality and an immediacy that bring to mind all too effectively the reality of similar twentieth-century events.

Goya's passionate humanity speaks uncensored through his engravings. These rely for their effect on a combination of traditional etching with the newly invented technique of aquatint, in which rosin is utilized to cover the areas between etched lines. When the plate is heated, the rosin creates a granular surface; ink applied and wiped off then produces a rich, gray tone, greatly expanding the expressive range of the print medium and bringing it close to wash drawing. Goya made several series of etching-aquatints, the earliest of which, *Los Caprichos* (*The Caprices*), of 1796–98, is wildly imaginative. The first section, dealing satirically with events from daily life, is surpassed by the second, devoted to fantastic events enacted by monsters, witches, and

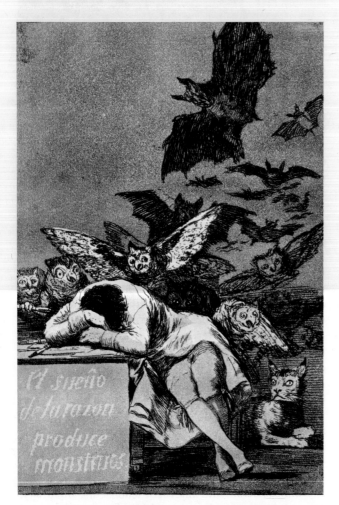

378. FRANCISCO GOYA. *The Sleep of Reason Produces Monsters,* from *Los Caprichos.* 1796–98. Etching and aquatint, 7 x 4¾"

malevolent nocturnal beasts from the demonic tradition of Spanish folklore. The introductory print of the second section (fig. 378) shows the artist asleep at his table loaded with idle drawing instruments, before which is propped a tablet inscribed, "El sueño de la razon produce monstruos" ("the sleep of reason produces monsters") —words significant not only for Romantic art, which as a matter of policy anesthetizes reason, but also for the current of fantastic art to be strongly revived in the twentieth century (see Chapter 8). Reason, the goddess of eighteenth-century philosophers, to whom the Cathedral of Notre-Dame in Paris had been temporarily rededicated during the French Revolution, once put to sleep, allows monsters to arise from the inner darkness of the mind. Goya's menacing cat and the rising clouds of owls and bats glowing in light and dark are lineal descendants of the beasts of medieval art, the Hiberno-Saxon animal interlace, and the hybrid animals that Saint Bernard had so vehemently and futilely condemned and that had reappeared in the marginal *drôleries* of Gothic manuscripts to triumph in the art of Bosch (see colorplate 20, fig. 112).

Instead of merely threatening human life, as in *Los Caprichos*, the monsters take over entirely in Goya's final series, *Los Disparates* (*The Follies*), engraved between 1813 and 1819. In a print entitled *Unbridled Folly* (fig. 379), a wildly rearing horse, resembling a natural force erupting from the ground, carries off a woman whose garments it has seized with its teeth, while at the left the earth turns into a bestial maw devouring humanity. The ultimate horror of Goya's imagination seethes through the series of dark frescoes the artist painted with fierce strokes on the walls of his own house from 1820–22, depicting a universe dominated by unreason and terror, and making cruel mock of humanity. One of his rare references to Classical mythology illustrates the most savage of Greek legends. *Saturn Devouring One of His Sons* (fig. 380) is an allegory of Time, which engulfs us all. The glaring, mindless deity holds with colossal hands the body of his helpless son, from which he has torn and is chewing the head and the right arm—all indicated with brushstrokes of a hitherto unimagined ferocity.

Now nearing eighty, the great painter was not to live long with these creatures of his despairing imagination. After the restoration of a reactionary monarchic government in 1823, he left for France the following year, and, like his complete opposite David, he died in exile. In the formative stages of the Romantic movement in France, Goya's paintings seem to have been unknown; of his engravings, only *Los Caprichos* were published, but even they had a limited effect; it remained for the late nineteenth century to rediscover Goya.

GROS. The transformation of Davidian Neoclassicism into Romanticism was initiated by one of David's own pupils, Antoine Jean Gros (1771–1835), torn between his loyalty to the doctrines of his master and his admiration

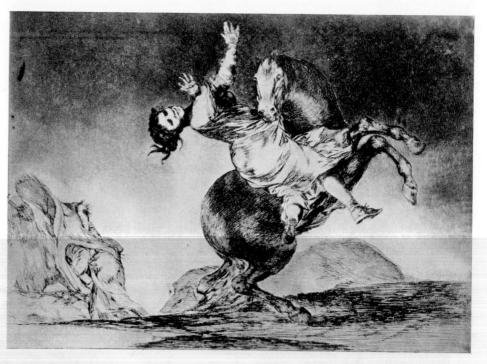

379. FRANCISCO GOYA. *Unbridled Folly*, from *Los Disparates*. 1813–19. Etching and aquatint. 8⅝ x 12⅜"

380. FRANCISCO GOYA. *Saturn Devouring One of His Sons*. 1820–22. Fresco (transferred to canvas), 57⅞ x 32⅜". Museo del Prado, Madrid

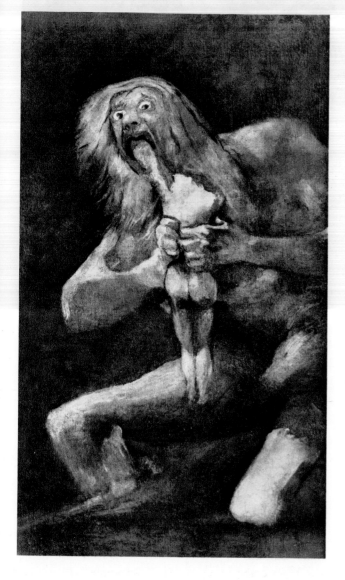

for the color and movement of the hated Rubens. The young Gros actually accompanied Napoleon on his North Italian campaign. Later, he painted colossal canvases commissioned to display the alleged humanitarianism of the emperor rather than his military glory. Such subjects, aptly described as "pious lies," would have nauseated Goya, but Gros' treatment of them is impressive. *Napoleon on the Battlefield at Eylau* (fig. 381), was painted in 1808, according to a fixed program that prescribed the persons, actions, and background to be represented. Among the heaped-up bodies of the dead and dying, after the bloody but indecisive battle, the emperor appears on a white horse as a kind of savior, commanding that proper care be taken of the wounded Russian and Prussian soldiers. Across the snowy fields in the background the imperial armies are arrayed for the triumphal march past the conqueror, while long lines of Russian prisoners are led away. The fact that the commission was intended to counteract public knowledge of the inadequacy of Napoleon's medical services does not weaken the drama of the composition, with its hundreds of near and distant figures. The reference to Roman battle compositions, such as the *Ludovisi Sarcophagus*, in the emperor's gesture and the packed bodies is all that remains of Neoclassicism. The colors of the uniforms are muted by the gray sky and the snow; the latter has sifted onto the greenish-gray faces of the frozen corpses in the foreground. The painter's interest in color and in the sufferings of the wounded opened the way to the passionate outbursts of the Romantic style. Gros himself, however, bitterly criticized by David from Brussels for his contemporary subjects, could never reconcile the opposites in his life and work, and despite his elevation to a barony by the restored Bourbons, he eventually ended his life in the Seine.

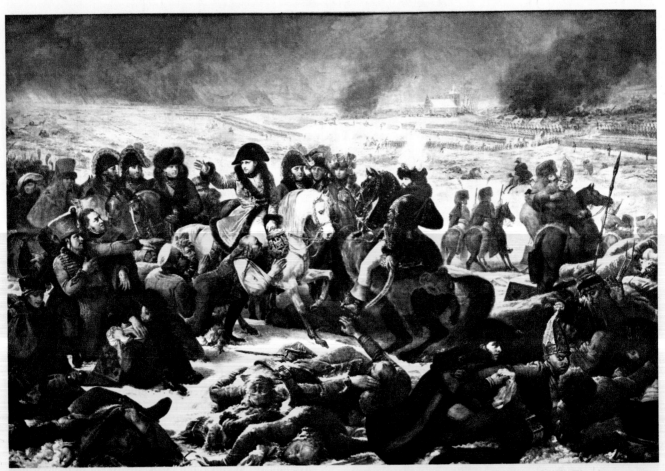

381. ANTOINE JEAN GROS. *Napoleon on the Battlefield at Eylau*. 1808. Oil on canvas, 17'6" x 26'3". The Louvre, Paris

GÉRICAULT. The hero of the formative stage of French Romanticism was Jean Louis André Théodore Géricault (1791–1824), a Romantic figure in his own right in his disdain for his personal safety, his dedication to the life of the emotions, and his espousal of the cause of the down-trodden and rejected. Although only three of his paintings were publicly exhibited during his brief lifetime, he exerted an enormous influence on the whole of the Romantic movement. His *Officer of the Imperial Guard* (fig. 382), shown at the Salon of 1812, is a dazzling performance for a twenty-one-year-old artist, already in full command of pictorial technique in a tradition stemming from the later Titian and Tintoretto. The guardsman is mounted on a rearing horse, which, while resembling that of Marshal Murat to the left of the emperor in the *Napoleon on the Battlefield at Eylau*, was probably also inspired by Leonardo's composition of the *Battle of Anghiari*, known to Géricault from Rubens' imaginative recreation (see fig. 129), not to speak of the spiral composition and the rich colorism of the great Flemish master himself, which have caused Géricault's style to be termed neobaroque. Although he had studied with Pierre-Narcisse Guérin, a follower of David, he lets his brushwork show brilliantly just as David claimed it should not. He wholeheartedly accepted the Napoleonic mystique—indeed in 1815 he took part in the famous Hundred Days of the emperor's meteoric return to power—and in his painting has nothing to say about the sufferings of war; the young officer is a hero, braving not only the smoke and flame of the battle but also attempting to tame the turbulence of nature itself, expressed in the fiery stallion and the surging storm clouds. The theme of man pitted against nature in eternal combat runs through most of Géricault's paintings.

In 1816–17 he lived in Florence and Rome, but paid less attention to antiquity and to Raphael than to Italian street scenes, especially those involving horses, and to the paintings of Michelangelo, whose grandeur and violence thrilled him. Out of his study of the great High Renaissance master came the young artist's only monumental canvas, the huge *Raft of the Medusa* (fig. 383), on which he worked from 1818–19. The subject was an incident that had convulsed all France. The government vessel *Medusa*, bound for Senegal, was wrecked in July 1816. After abandoning ship, 149 passengers were crowded onto a raft in tow by the officers' boats; the cable broke and the raft was cut adrift. Only fifteen passengers were eventually rescued by the brig *Argus*, after they had suffered the torments of thirst and starvation under the equatorial sun.

A political scandal because of the incompetence of the captain, who owed his appointment to his support of the monarchy, the subject seems to have obsessed the artist rather as a supreme instance of the tragic conflict between man and nature. He interviewed the survivors, read the newspaper accounts, even painted corpses and the heads of guillotined criminals in an attempt to achieve the highest fidelity to truth. Yet the final result, achieved after endless sketches and preliminary compositions, was by no means a realistic picture. Géricault chose to depict the moment when the brig was first sighted on the horizon. The composition results from a pyramidal surge of agonized figures, rising higher than the threatening sea, and culminates in two men waving garments against the clouds. In essence, it is a translation into multifigural design of the motive of the *Officer of the Imperial Guard*, the sea substituting for the horse as a symbol of hostile nature. While the rendering of the corpses and the maddened survivors recalls Gros' *Napoleon on the Battlefield at Eylau*, their heroic muscularity and the mood of titanic struggle are clearly affected by the grandeur of Michelangelo's *Last Judgment* (see fig. 181).

The artist was far from pleased by the public reception of this work more as a political than an artistic event, and he accompanied it to London, where he showed it for a year at considerable profit from the admissions. He learned, incidentally, much about color from English painters, especially Constable (see below), and would have seemed destined for a leading role in French painting on his return. Especially impressive are his studies of the insane, done in Paris in 1822–23 at the suggestion of a psychiatrist friend, and given titles that look a little strange to present-day students of psychiatry. The *Madwoman* (fig. 384; actually entitled the *Monomania*

of Envy) discloses in the inner world of thoughts and feelings the same struggle between man and nature that the artist had previously studied in the realm of physical action. It was typical that he should lose the battle. A passionate horseman, he was injured by a fall from a horse, insisted on riding again too soon, fell a second time, and died, probably of his injuries. More than any of

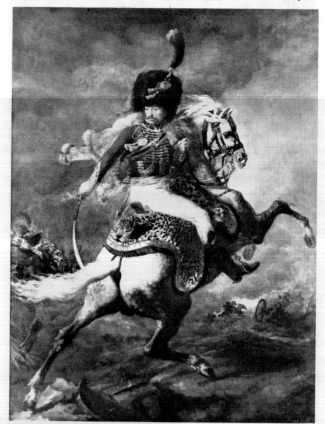

382. THÉODORE GÉRICAULT.
Officer of the Imperial Guard.
1812 . Oil on canvas,
9'7" x 6'4½".
The Louvre, Paris

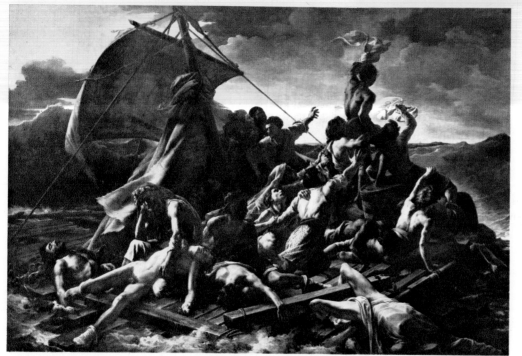

383. THÉODORE GÉRICAULT.
Raft of the Medusa.
1818–19. Oil on canvas,
16'1" x 23'6".
The Louvre, Paris

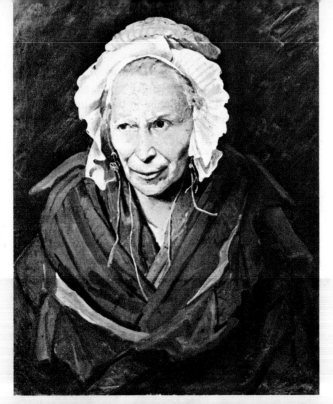

384. THÉODORE GÉRICAULT. *Madwoman (Monomania of Envy)*. 1822–23. Oil on canvas, 27⅝ x 22″. Musée des Beaux-Arts, Lyons, France

professional enmity, the leadership of French and indeed European painting for more than a generation. He seems the archetype of the Romantic—solitary, moody, inexhaustibly imaginative, profoundly emotional. He confided to his *Journal*, the most complete record we have of the thoughts and feelings of any great artist, that he was never without a slight fever. Yet in contrast to Géricault he lived an existence marked by few external events. Although he admired Italian art and said he wanted to go to Italy, he never went there; his journeys were to England, Belgium, Holland, Spain, and North Africa. Save for one youthful adventure, no enduring amorous connections are known, and he remained unmarried. He was haughty toward most other artists ("Vulgarity is in every moment of their conversation"). His real life, of great intensity, was lived on the canvas. "What is most real in me," he wrote, "are the illusions I create with my painting; the rest is shifting sand." In the course of his life he produced literally thousands of oil paintings and watercolors and innumerable drawings, and not long before his death he claimed that "in the matter of compositions I have enough for two human lifetimes; and as for projects of all kinds, I have enough for four hundred years."

At first Delacroix wrote in his *Journal* lists of subjects he wanted to paint, invariably scenes of emotional or physical violence; later, discovering that the creative urge was dissipated in setting down the titles, he abandoned this practice. Often he drew his subjects from English poetry, especially Shakespeare and Byron, and from medieval history. Music enthralled him; he knew Chopin personally and analyzed his music with keen understanding, aware at once of its beauty and its limitations. At first he admired Beethoven, but later found his music

his contemporaries, he may be considered the founder of the veritable religion of emotional violence championed by Delacroix.

DELACROIX. The torch of Romanticism passed from the hands of Géricault to those of his seven-years-younger friend and, in a sense, pupil, Eugène Delacroix (1798–1863), who shared with Ingres, despite their bitter

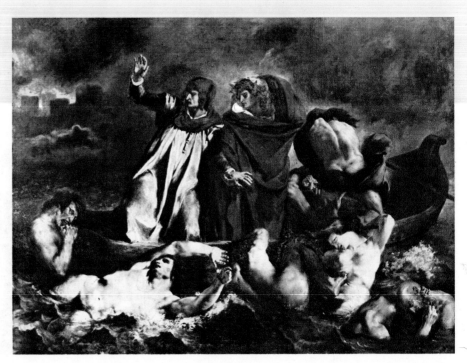

385. EUGÈNE DELACROIX. *Bark of Dante*. 1822. Oil on canvas, 74⅜ x 96⅛″. The Louvre, Paris

noisy and exaggerated. Never, surprisingly, did he betray any taste for the Romantic style of Berlioz, which one would have thought his musical counterpart. From youth to age his one idol in music was "the divine Mozart," which tells us at once much about the fire and imagination of Mozart and about the discipline of Delacroix's art, despite its apparent impetuosity always under firm intellectual control. As a youth, he was drawn to Michelangelo, whose paintings he knew only from engravings and from the accounts of his mentor Géricault. But as Delacroix matured the influence of the great Florentine waned along with that of the departed friend, and his lifelong loyalty to the sixteenth-century Venetians (see Part Four, Chapter 5) and to Rubens (see Part Five, Chapter 4), apostles of colorism, constantly strengthened.

In the *Bark of Dante* (fig. 385), which Delacroix exhibited in 1822 at the age of twenty-four, he illustrates a moment from the *Divine Comedy* in which the poet, accompanied by Virgil, is steered across the dark tides of the lake surrounding the city of Dis, assailed in the sulfurous dimness by damned souls rising from the waves against a background of towers and flames. The obvious Michelangelism of the figures (cf. the *Last Judgment*, fig. 181), not to speak of the frail craft on heaving waters, reminds us of Géricault's *Raft of the Medusa*, exhibited only three years earlier. But there are already significant differences. Delacroix has broken up the pyramidal grouping, and is more concerned with effects of color and of light and dark than with form, however strongly modeled here and there. Some of the drops of water are painted in pure tones of red and green. Throughout his entire career his basic compositional principle is a series of free curves, emanating from the central area but always returning to it, with a responsive logic unshaken even in the moments of greatest violence. Gros praised the picture highly, calling it a "chastened Rubens."

Delacroix's next major effort, however, the *Massacre at Chios* (colorplate 52), which he exhibited in 1824, was not so easily accepted. Like that of the *Raft of the Medusa*, the subject was a cause célèbre, in this case an incident from the Greek wars of liberation against the Turks, which had excited the sympathies of Romantic spirits everywhere, notably Lord Byron. While the foreground strewn with bodies and the panoramic background are related to Gros' *Napoleon on the Battlefield at Eylau* and the Turk on his rearing horse to Géricault's *Officer of the Imperial Guard*, great changes have taken place. The neobaroque composition is diffused in Delacroix's centrifugal curves, which part to display the distant slaughter and conflagration. And although our sympathies are supposed to be enlisted by the sufferings of the Greeks, their rendering lacks the conviction of the *Raft of the Medusa*. Clearly, Delacroix did not investigate the subject with Géricault's reportorial zeal. In fact, the expressions tend to become standardized; the head of the young woman at the lower left almost exactly repeats that of the dead mother at the

lower right. Suffering, violence, emotional excess of all sorts are reveled in rather than lamented.

Gros called this picture the "massacre of painting," and not only because of Delacroix's treatment of the subject. As we see the picture today, the color shows a richness and vibrancy not visible in French painting since the Rococo, but far more powerful than the harmonies of that delicate style. Delacroix saw and was amazed by Constable's *The Hay Wain* (see fig. 392), brought to Paris for the Salon of 1824, and before the exhibition opened he took down his huge picture and in a few days repainted it extensively in tones emulating those he found in Constable.

From here on Delacroix's interest in color was greatly heightened. He recounts in his *Journal* his exhaustive attempts to investigate the relationship of color contrasts through experience of their effects next to each other on the canvas, as well as from visual observation of nature, deriving from these lists a law—"the more the contrast the greater the force." His contrasting hues, set side by side unmixed, caused conservative painters great distress, but marked an important step in the direction of the color effects to be derived from sunlight by the Impressionists (see Chapter 4). In 1847 Delacroix wrote, "When the tones are right, the lines draw themselves," the exact opposite of Ingres' dictum on the same subject (see page 311).

With the *Death of Sardanapalus* (fig. 386), as much a manifesto for Romanticism as was Ingres' *Apotheosis of Homer* (see fig. 370) for Neoclassicism (ironically enough, the two were exhibited at the Salon of 1827), the artist drew down upon himself the execration of conservatives and the disapproval of royal administrators. The legendary subject concerns the last of the Assyrian monarchs, besieged in his palace for two years by the Medes. On hearing that the enemy had at last breached his walls, the king had all his concubines, slaves, and horses slaughtered and his treasures destroyed before his eyes, as he lay upon a couch soon to become his funeral pyre. Abandoning the pretext of humanitarianism that justified the *Massacre at Chios* and other pictures inspired by the Greek struggle for independence, the painting becomes a veritable feast of violence, spread out in glowing colors against the smoke of distant battle. With the brooding king and three excited male servants as focuses, the movement surges about the couch in Delacroix's characteristic curves. Yet the picture is a phantasmagoria in which no real cruelty is exerted. Faces are contorted with destructive fury or paralyzed with fear, but no blood flows from the breast of the naked woman in the foreground into which a dagger has been plunged. Quivering female flesh is heaped in every conceivable position, like flowers or fruit, among the glittering jewels and the fabrics of crimson or turquoise, all brilliantly painted. In this solitary fantasy the artist, identifying himself in imagination with the king and the executioners, discharges all his creative—and destructive—energy in an explosion of tones that foreshadows the Venusberg music of Wagner and the Immolation scene from his *Götterdämmerung*, but is in reality as harmless as a still life.

The Revolution of 1830, which placed on the throne Louis Philippe, the "Citizen King," brought Delacroix major mural commissions and relief from poverty. Early in 1832 he traveled through North Africa with a French delegation. He was the first major painter of modern times to visit the Islamic world, and this was the one real adventure of a lifetime otherwise fairly tranquil—externally, at least. Although he had no opportunity to paint, and sometimes even found drawing dangerous on account of Islamic hostility to representation, he managed to bring back with him hundreds of sketches in pencil or pen, some touched with watercolor. These, his memory of exotic sights and colors, and his vivid imagination provided him with endless material for paintings for the next thirty years.

Delacroix's memories of North Africa were brought to realization in the *Women of Algiers* (fig. 387), a picture of exquisite intimacy and charm, painted and exhibited in 1834. Delacroix had managed to gain entrance to a harem, and was delighted with "the charm of the figures and the luxury of the clothing." The languorous poses, soft flesh, and somnolent eyes of the women, the varying textures and colors of the striped and figured fabrics, the light and luminous shadow of the interior, and the endless arabesques of the tiles form a constantly changing tissue of line and tone. This picture had an enormous influence on the Impressionists of the late nineteenth century and on many painters of the early twentieth, especially Matisse (see fig. 449, colorplate 64). Nothing could have more fully embodied Matisse's ideal of "luxe, calme, et volupté" ("*luxury, calm, and pleasure*").

Most of the pictures of North African subjects painted during Delacroix's later years, however, were by no means so calm. The *Tiger Hunt* (fig. 388), of 1854, is typical, with forms and poses born almost entirely of the artist's unbridled imagination. "When the tones are right, the lines draw themselves," and so they do, in the movements of the raging animals and furious huntsmen, flowing out from the center and back again with passionate intensity and perfect logic. Almost weightless, liberated from matter, these late fantasies of violence carry the artist into a phase of free coloristic movement pointing directly toward the twentieth century.

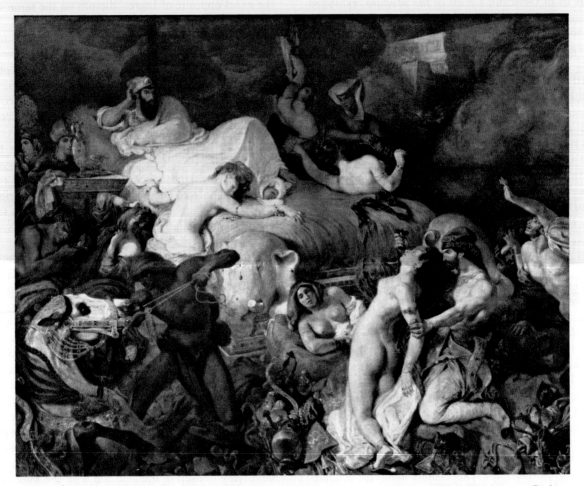

386. EUGÈNE DELACROIX. *Death of Sardanapalus.* 1827. Oil on canvas, 12'1½" x 16'2⅞". The Louvre, Paris

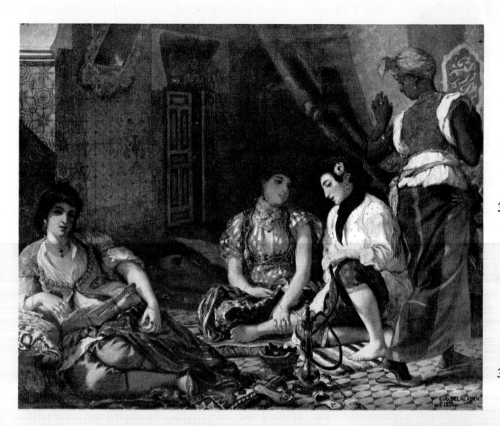

387. Eugène Delacroix.
Women of Algiers.
1834. Oil on canvas,
70⅞ x 90⅛".
The Louvre, Paris

388. Eugène Delacroix.
Tiger Hunt. 1854.
Oil on canvas,
29 x 37".
The Louvre, Paris

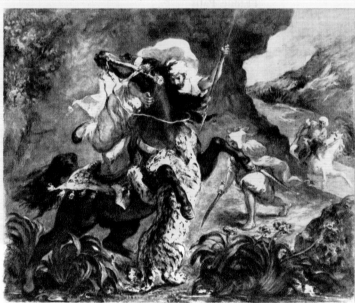

SCULPTURE

Romantic sculpture never quite reached the plane of painting; there were no geniuses to catch the fire of Goya or Delacroix. Nonetheless, some powerful and effective works were conceived and executed in large scale for important Parisian buildings. The grandest of these is *La Marseillaise* (fig. 389; its full title is *The Departure of the Volunteers in 1792*), by FRANÇOIS RUDE (1784–1855). Although the work was done in 1833–36, one can still catch echoes of the *Oath of the Horatii* (see fig. 366) in the bombastic mood and vigorous Classical poses and costumes. Under the thundering folds of Liberty's flying garments, the massed figures, with their rich light-and-dark constrasts, are deployed to great effect against the clifflike surface of the Napoleonic Arc de Triomphe at the Étoile, center of the radiating avenues the emperor designed for a new quarter of Paris. In contrast, the sculpture of JEAN-BAPTISTE CARPEAUX (1827–75) seems almost Rococo in its grace and sensuousness. In spite of its enormous scale, *The Dance* (fig. 390), of 1867–69, reminds one of Clodion (see fig. 334). Its energy and sparkle are seen better in the plaster cast after Carpeaux's original work in clay than in the somewhat more frigid version executed in limestone for the façade of the Paris Opéra. The irresistible verve of the work certainly influenced the sculpture of Rodin (see figs. 429, 431) and even the paintings of Matisse (see fig. 448).

ENGLAND

Romantic art in England lacked the ideological impetus of the Revolution and the Napoleonic wars, and like much of English Romantic poetry was highly personal. The strangest figure of the period was WILLIAM BLAKE (1757–1827), a visionary poet and painter, who was vehemently opposed both to Reynolds and to the teaching of the Academy. Trained in a severe Classical style by drawing from plaster casts of ancient art, and influenced deeply by the art of Michelangelo he knew only from engravings, he was also familiar with medieval churches and steeped himself in the Bible, in Dante, and in Milton. In addition to his own mystical poems, which

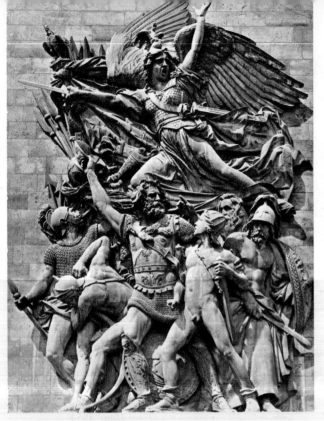

389. FRANÇOIS RUDE. *La Marseillaise (The Departure of the Volunteers in 1792)*. 1833–36. Stone, c. 42 x 26'. Arc de Triomphe, Place de l'Étoile, Paris

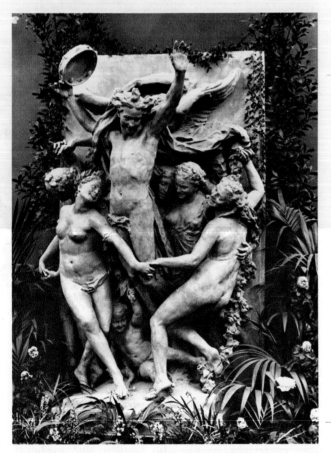

390. JEAN-BAPTISTE CARPEAUX. *The Dance*. 1867–69. Plaster model, c. 15' x 8'6". Musée de l'Opéra, Paris

he illustrated himself, he created an amazing series of illustrations of his favorite literary works both in engravings, which he hand-tinted, and in watercolors, marked by surprising distortions of anatomical reality and by strong abstract movement of form and color. In his *Circle of the Lustful* (fig. 391), of 1824–27, Blake illustrates Canto V of Dante's *Inferno* in which Virgil shows the poet a whirlwind carrying lovers from the past who had abandoned reason for a life of passion and are doomed to be swept along by the tempest for eternity without rest. At Dante's request Virgil beckons nearer Paolo and Francesca, and as they tell their story of guilty love, and as their first kiss appears above in a vision, Dante falls in a swoon. Blake's startling simplifications of the human form derive from its subjection to mystical forces, in this case the mighty spiral that heaves the various lovers up and around in the foreground and off into the distance. A strong believer in genius as a God-given force within the artist, Blake is often cited as a precursor of certain aspects of twentieth-century art; Kokoschka, for example, may have known this watercolor when he painted *Bride of the Wind* (see colorplate 67).

CONSTABLE. The mainstream of English painting in the first half of the nineteenth century was landscape; Constable and Turner, the greatest of the landscapists, approached nature with an excitement akin to that of the poets Wordsworth, Keats, and Shelley. It is not beside the point that nature itself was beginning to be swallowed up by the expanding cities of the Industrial Revolution, then in full swing. The effects of that transformation were lamented by Oliver Goldsmith in his *The Deserted Village* in 1770, and William Blake had deplored the "dark Satanic mills." John Constable (1776–1837), son of a miller on the River Stour in Suffolk, celebrated all that was natural and traditional, including the age-old occupations of farmer, miller, and carpenter, close to the land whose fruits and forces they turned to human use. As we have seen (page 293), he loved the poetic landscapes of Gainsborough, but he also studied the constructed compositions of the Baroque, especially those of Claude Lorrain, then considered the standard for all landscape painting, and of Ruisdael, whose skies he particularly admired (see figs. 261, 293). Rebelling against the brown tonality then fashionable in landscape painting—actually the result of discolored varnish darkening the Old Masters—he supplemented his observations of nature with a study of the vivacity of Rubens' color and brushwork (see colorplate 41).

As early as 1802, Constable had started to record the fugitive aspects of the sky in rapid oil sketches made outdoors, the earliest series of outdoor paintings of which we have any record. "It will be difficult to name a class of landscape in which sky is not the keynote, the standard of scale, and the chief organ of sentiment," he wrote. His systematic studies of cloud formations, done in 1821–22,

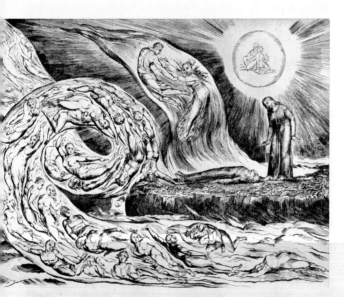

391. WILLIAM BLAKE. *Circle of the Lustful*, illustration for Dante's *Inferno*. 1824–27. Ink and watercolor. 14¾ x 20⅞". City Museum and Art Gallery, Birmingham, England

were influenced by the scientific research on cloud types and formations conducted by the contemporary Englishman Luke Howard. But even more important than their devotion to actual appearances, Constable's studies show an abandonment to the forces of nature, a passionate self-identification with sunlight, wind, moisture, and light. One is reminded of Shelley's invocation to the west wind, "Make me thy lyre, even as the forest is . . . ." Constable allowed nature to play upon his sensibilities as on an instrument. At first, he made dutiful sketching tours through regions of acknowledged scenic beauty (he never left England), but before long came to the conclusion that "it is the business of the painter . . . to make something of nothing, in attempting which he must

almost of necessity become poetical." He returned to the quiet landscape of his native Stour Valley with a special delight. "The sound of water escaping from mill-dams, etc.," he wrote, "willows, old rotten planks, slimy posts, and brickwork—I love such things."

His superb *The Hay Wain* (fig. 392) of 1821 sums up his ideals and his achievements. No longer contrived but composed as if accidentally—though on the basis of many preliminary outdoor studies—the picture, painted in the studio, shows Constable's beloved Stour with its trees, a mill, and distant fields, and all the slimy posts his heart could desire. In his orchestra of natural color the solo instrument and conductor at once is the sky. The clouds sweep by, full of a light and color not even the Dutch had ever attained, and their shadows and the sunlight dapple the field with green and gold. As the stream ripples, it mirrors now the trees, now the sky, breaking blues and greens into many separate hues, including touches of white when direct sunlight sparkles back. The trees themselves, in fact, are made up of many shades of green, set side by side, and patches of light reflect from their foliage. These white highlights were incomprehensible to many contemporary viewers, who called them "Constable's snow."

This comment is one of the first of the adverse reactions that became common in the nineteenth century on the part of a public that resented being shown what it actually saw, instead of what it had been taught by tradition and Old Masters it ought to see. Under Impressionism in the 1870s (see Chapter 4), the detachment between artist and public was to become extreme, but enough people appreciated Constable's new vision of nature that his work could be exhibited at the Royal Academy, of which he was belatedly made a member in 1829. Géricault saw and was impressed by Constable's painting during his

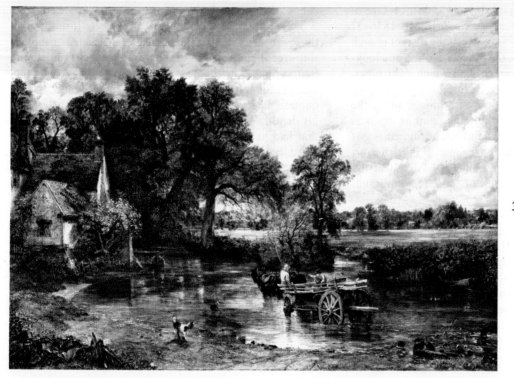

392. JOHN CONSTABLE. *The Hay Wain*. 1821. Oil on canvas, 50½ x 73". National Gallery, London

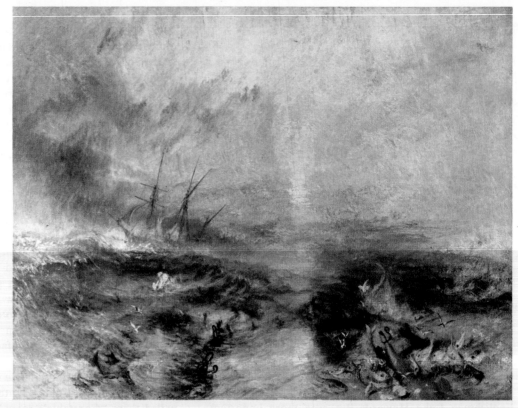

393. JOSEPH MALLORD
WILLIAM TURNER.
The Slave Ship.
1840. Oil on canvas,
35¾ x 48″.
Museum of Fine Arts,
Boston. Henry Lillie
Pierce Fund (Purchase)

English trip, and *The Hay Wain* was, as we have seen (page 323), triumphantly exhibited at the Salon of 1824, where Constable's broken color and free brushwork were a revelation to Delacroix. Although the later Impressionists were not directly influenced by Constable, he may be said to have set in motion a new current in French landscape art, which later culminated in the Impressionist movement.

In later life, after the death of his wife, Constable entered a period of depression in which his passionate communion with nature reaches a pitch of semimystical intensity, which competes with the visions of El Greco (see fig. 225, colorplate 35) in vibrancy and force. One of these late pictures is *Stoke-by-Nayland* of 1836–37 (colorplate 53), a large canvas in which the distant church tower, the wagon, the plow, the horses, and the boy looking over the gate are instruments on which light plays. The symphonic breadth of the picture, and its crashing chords of color painted in a rapid technique using the flexible steel palette knife to apply the paint as much as the brush, bring to the finished painting the immediacy of the color sketch. Such pictures are equaled in earlier art only by certain landscape backgrounds in Titian (see fig. 167) or by the mystical reveries of the late Rembrandt (see colorplate 42).

TURNER. Constable's contemporary, Joseph Mallord William Turner (1775–1851), who outlived him by more than a decade, was like Hogarth a Londoner, and had none of Constable's mystical attachment to nature. Nor did he remain fixed in England, but for many years made frequent trips throughout the Continent, especially Germany, Switzerland, and Italy, reveling in mountain landscapes, gorgeous cities (especially Venice), and the most extreme effects of storms, fires, and sunsets. Once he even had himself tied to a mast during a storm at sea so that he could experience the full force of the wind, waves, and clouds swirling about him. Although he made beautiful and accurate color notes on the spot in watercolors—a traditionally English medium that he pushed to its utmost limits of luminosity—he painted his pictures in the studio in secrecy, living under an assumed name and accepting no pupils. He was the first to abandon pale brown or buff priming, still used by Constable, in favor of white, against which his brilliant color effects could sing with perfect clarity.

Turner often painted historical subjects, usually like those of Delacroix, involving violence as well as shipwrecks and conflagrations, in which the individual figures appear as scarcely more than spots in a seething tide of humanity. He liked to accompany the labels with quotations from poetry, often his own. Nonetheless, at his death a great many unfinished canvases were found that had no identifiable subject or representation at all. What he really enjoyed and painted first was the pure movement of masses of color without representational meaning, although natural forces and effects are often suggested—a kind of color music, strikingly relevant to Abstract Expressionism of the 1950s (see Chapter 10). Shortly before the opening of an exhibition at the Royal Academy, the aging Turner would send such unfinished works, and on varnishing day paint in the details to make the pictures exhibitable to a nineteenth-century public.

The Slave Ship, of 1840 (fig. 393), represents an incident all too common in the days of slavery, when entire human cargoes were pitched into the sea, either because of epidemics or to avoid arrest. The ship itself, the occasional figures, and the fish feasting on the corpses in the foreground were obviously painted at great speed only after the real work, the movement of fiery waves of red, brown, gold, and cream, had been brought to completion.

Rain, Steam, and Speed, of 1844 (colorplate 54), is one of the very first paintings of a railway train, and its Romantic idealization of "progress"—man conquering nature by utilizing its forces—should be compared with the more objective, visual approach of Monet in 1874 (see fig. 417). The train with its lighted carriages (preceded by a speeding rabbit) moving across the high bridge is enough of a subject already, but Turner lifts it to an almost unearthly realm in which insubstantial forces play through endless space. The veils of blue and gold are the real subject of the picture, and it was Turner's heightened and liberated color sense that proved as much of a revelation to those Impressionists (especially Monet) who took refuge in London in 1870 as had Constable's *The Hay Wain* to Delacroix nearly half a century before.

GERMAN ROMANTICISM

FRIEDRICH. A complete survey of Romanticism, like a thorough treatment of any other artistic style, would inevitably take in many phenomena of limited aesthetic interest. Even more than Neoclassicism, Romanticism was enthusiastically accepted in Germany, predisposed by the poetry of Goethe and Schiller and the music of the great Romantic composers. Unfortunately, no consistent pictorial tradition had existed in Germany since the sixteenth century, and many of the dreams of German Romantic painters were beyond their powers of execution, and immeasurably below the level of contemporary German music. A conspicuous exception is the art of Caspar David Friedrich (1774–1840), a North German painter whose landscapes are of high artistic quality and

great poetic depth. Friedrich was as deeply imbued with love of nature as his English contemporaries, but shared neither Constable's rhapsodic self-identification with natural forces nor Turner's desire to project his own emotions into natural lights and spaces. Friedrich was by inclination melancholy, even pessimistic, and his landscapes are always concerned with an immense and impersonal world, responsive to no human emotion save sadness. Meditations on solitude, alienation, and death predominate in his pictures; not surprisingly, his style shows none of the spontaneity of color and freedom of brushwork so impressive in his English contemporaries. "You shall keep holy every pure emotion of your soul," he said; "you shall esteem holy every pious presentiment. In an exalted hour it will become visible form and this form is your work."

Friedrich's mystical doctrines are set forth with great precision of form and surface. In his meticulously painted *Abbey Graveyard Under Snow*, of 1819 (fig. 394), the ruined Gothic choir of a monastic church near his native town of Greifswald combines with the trunks of leafless, wintry trees to define a space suggesting profound desolation. Since the shattered church had long been abandoned when Friedrich painted it, and since funerals do not take place in ruins, the procession of monks moving two by two, following a coffin through the portal in the snow, is clearly intended as a visionary evocation of the vanished past. The intensity of the mood and the clarity of the surface rendering foreshadow aspects of Surrealism in the twentieth century (see below, Chapter 8). Unfortunately, this painting was destroyed during World War II.

ARCHITECTURE

Like Romantic sculpture, the architecture of the Romantic movement is often of uncertain and irregular quality,

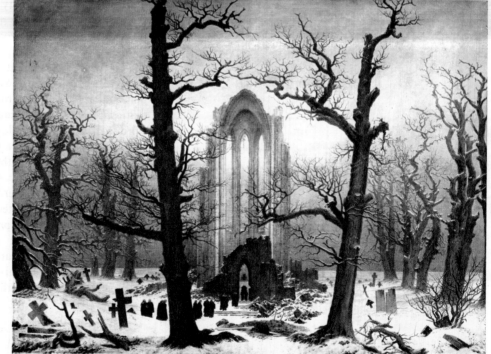

394. CASPAR DAVID FRIEDRICH. *Abbey Graveyard Under Snow.* 1819. Oil on canvas, 47⅝ x 66⅞". Formerly Nationalgalerie, Staatliche Museen, Berlin (destroyed, 1945)

yet it can be extremely successful in its picturesqueness: like Romantic painting, Romantic architecture seeks above all to establish a mood. Some architects entrusted with Romantic schemes had already carried out major Neoclassical projects. John Nash, for instance, the architect of Park Crescent (see fig. 365) in 1812, was asked in 1815 to begin the remodeling and enlargement of the Royal Pavilion at Brighton (fig. 395), a pleasure dome for the prince regent, later George IV, with forms imitated from Islamic architecture in India. This kind of thing is a lineal descendant of the Chinese pagodas that often rose in eighteenth-century gardens, but it is one of the earliest instances of a pseudo-Oriental building intended for habitation. The interiors are derived from a variety of sources—Greek, Egyptian, and Chinese—but the exterior with its tracery and onion domes, and its chimneys masquerading as minarets, is a delightful bit of Oriental fantasy, whose changing forms and surfaces are calculated for the soft sea light of Brighton.

To the English Gothic architecture was an indigenous style (notwithstanding its French origin), and it is hardly accidental that Gothic was adopted for the Houses of Parliament, begun in 1836 and completed only after 1860. The immense structure adjoins the older, truly Gothic Westminster Hall, and from many points of view can be seen together with the Gothic Westminster Abbey. Two architects of diverse tastes, SIR CHARLES BARRY (1795–1860), a Neoclassicist, and A. WELBY PUGIN (1812–52), a Gothic revivalist, collaborated on the design. At first sight (fig. 396) Gothic irregularity seems to predominate, especially in view of the asymmetrical placing of the major towers, but it soon becomes apparent that in Barry's plan around a central octagon, and especially the handling of the masses along the river front, the building is as symmetrical as any Renaissance or Baroque palace. In its linearity and abundance Pugin's

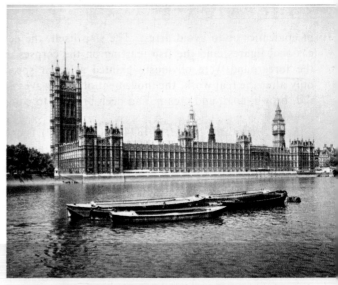

396. SIR CHARLES BARRY and A. WELBY PUGIN. Houses of Parliament. 1836–c. 1860. London

detail is derived from the Perpendicular, especially such monuments as Gloucester Cathedral and Henry VII's Chapel.

Although in England the Gothic style could be used for anything from public buildings to distilleries and sewage plants, in France it appeared suitable only for churches, often built in imitation of High Gothic cathedrals. For other structures classicism continued well into the nineteenth century, gradually modified by a revival of the French Renaissance. The city of Paris itself is the triumphant result of this revival. Napoleon I had designed a system of avenues radiating outward from the Arc de Triomphe de l'Étoile, and connected this monument to imperial glory with the Louvre by a prolongation of the Champs Élysées, so that artillery could, if necessary, rake a considerable area of the city. His nephew Napoleon III (reigned 1852–71) employed the engineer GEORGES EUGÉNE BARON HAUSSMANN (1809–91) to interconnect these radiating avenues with new boulevards in order to ring the city after the destruction of the medieval walls, and with new broad avenues cut through older quarters. This network of stately thoroughfares was bordered by trees and lined with limestone façades whose design, while not absolutely uniform, was controlled in the interests of consistency, and imposed upon owners and builders alike. Generally, the houses consisted of six stories; the first was occupied by shops, the second and third were united by pilasters delicately projected like those of Lescot's Square Court of the Louvre (see fig. 211), the fourth above the entablature remained plain like a Renaissance attic story, and the fifth and sixth were tucked into a towering, bulbous roof known as a mansard (after the architect François Mansart; see page 237). The regulations prevented the construction of buildings of any great individuality, but created a homogeneous urban picture unequaled in known history, which remained intact until the tragic depredations under the Pompidou regime in the 1970s. The long avenues and

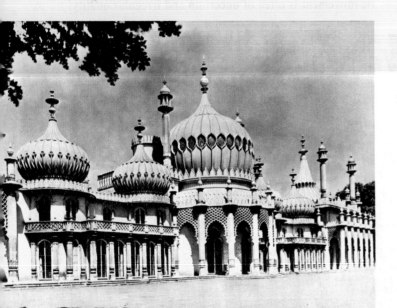

395. JOHN NASH. Royal Pavilion. Remodeling begun 1815. Brighton, England

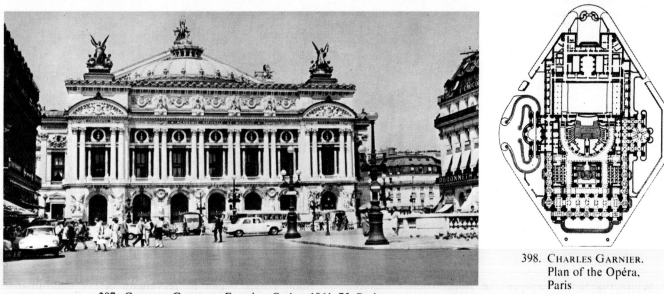

397. CHARLES GARNIER. Exterior, Opéra. 1861–75. Paris

398. CHARLES GARNIER. Plan of the Opéra, Paris

gently curving boulevards provided airy, luminous vistas extremely important for the Impressionists, who found in them a new and vital subject for their paintings (see figs. 420, 421).

Here and there in the Haussmann plan loomed monumental structures, some preexistent, such as Notre-Dame, the Panthéon (see fig. 324), and the Madeleine (see fig. 363), some extended under Napoleon III, such as the Louvre, and some entirely new, such as the Opéra (figs. 397, 398), designed in 1861 by CHARLES GARNIER (1825–98) and intended as the focus of the new Paris. Actually, the structure was detested by the Empress Eugénie, who would have preferred a less ostentatious building, but it epitomized the taste of the new industrial bourgeoisie who had supported King Louis Philippe, become stronger yet under Napoleon III, and dominated the Third Republic (1871–1940); it was completed only in 1875, four years after the collapse of Napoleon III and his Second Empire. With its giant order of coupled Corinthian columns supported by an arcade and connecting two terminal pavilions, the façade is clearly derived from the twin palaces by Gabriel on the Place de la Concorde (see fig. 326), but immensely enriched with sculptural ornament (including Carpeaux's *The Dance*, see fig. 390). The low bulbous dome with its sculptured lantern and the allegorical groups imitated from Classical Victories create a rich, neobaroque profile sharply different from the compact masses favored by eighteenth-century classicism.

The barely tolerable splendor of the exterior becomes offensive to modern eyes in the Grand Staircase (fig. 399), a grandiose setting for the display of wealth and luxury, which encloses approximately as much space as the auditorium itself. With its cascading flights of steps, ponderous sculptural decorations—including even the light fixtures (intended for gaslight)—and veined marble columns, the Grand Staircase is the swan song of neobaroque magnificence, the kind of aberration against

which architects in that very period were beginning to react (see figs. 409, 410), later to be jettisoned entirely by the progressive designers of the late nineteenth and twentieth centuries. It is, however, the direct ancestor of many pompous buildings throughout the world, including the movie palaces that rose in cities everywhere in the 1920s and 1930s to gratify a different sort of collective fantasy. To be understood, the Grand Staircase, like the Hall of Mirrors at Versailles, must be peopled in our imagination with the classes for whom it was intended—men in black tailcoats and women in gorgeous fabrics, bustles, and trains, representing the old nobility; the new Bonapartist aristocracy; the industrialists; and, surprisingly enough, a wholly new class of prosperous courtesans that battened on all three.

399. CHARLES GARNIER. Grand Staircase, Opéra, Paris

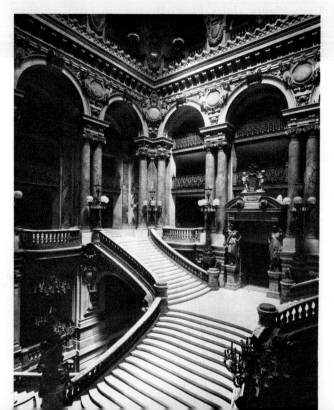

3
Realism

While the battle between the Neoclassicists and the Romanticists was reaching its height, a third group of artists was at work, inconspicuously at first, then more and more vocally, for whom the struggle had no meaning; for them, both sides were wide of the mark. The term *Realism*, applied to the new movement only in the 1840s and grudgingly accepted by its protagonists, can be extended to cover its beginnings two decades or more earlier. For the entire group, history had no artistic importance. Courbet, its most powerful champion, declared that Realism was a "human conclusion which awakened the very forces of man against paganism, Greco-Roman art, the Renaissance, Catholicism, and the gods and demigods, in short against the conventional ideal." The Realist revolt was even directed against the rendering of any contemporary events, military or political, in which the artist had not actually taken part.

To the Realists the only worthy forebears were the Dutch and Flemish naturalists of the seventeenth century, the study of whom was led by one of the principal apologists of Realism, Théophile Thoré (1807–69), who may be said to have rediscovered Vermeer. In 1850 Champfleury (Jules Fleury-Husson, 1821-89), another theorist of the movement, wrote the first appreciation of the Le Nain brothers, expanded into a book in 1862, *Les peintres de la réalité sous Louis XIII: Les frères Le Nain.*

Soon critics began to reevaluate earlier naturalists—some of the neglected Venetian minor painters, for example—and the great Netherlandish and Italian masters of the fifteenth century. Chardin and other eighteenth-century naturalists were at last fully understood.

It is hardly surprising that most of the Realists were staunch republicans, dedicated along with their literary friends to the establishment of a new social order founded on justice for the working class. Artists, politicians, economists, critics, and philosophers met and exchanged ideas in the Andler Keller, a Parisian *brasserie* (a type of restaurant serving food at all hours, characteristically washed down with beer), which became known as the "temple of Realism." Significantly enough, the Realists ran afoul of organized authority. Courbet's paintings were refused by the director of the imperial museums, Count Nieuwerkerke, at the Universal Exposition of 1855, and eventually the split between progressive artists and conservative power became so great that in 1863 a Salon des Refusés was organized, which exhibited the works of those who are now recognized as the best painters of the period. As a consequence of their participation in social movements, two of the greatest Realist masters, Daumier and Courbet, were actually forced to serve prison sentences.

The break between new and accepted art, which seems

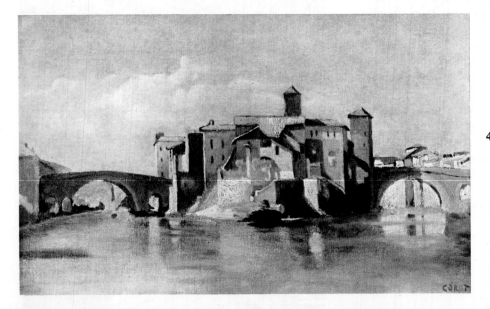

400. JEAN-BAPTISTE-CAMILLE COROT. *Island of San Bartolomeo.* 1825. Oil on canvas, 10½ x 17". Museum of Fine Arts, Boston. Harriet Otis Cruft Fund (Purchase)

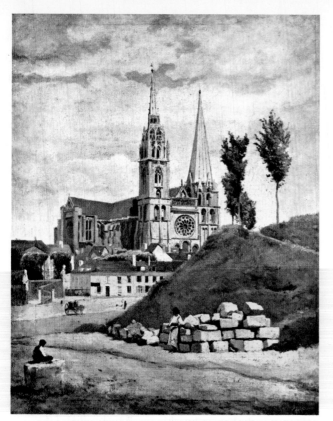

401. JEAN-BAPTISTE-CAMILLE COROT. *Chartres Cathedral.* 1830. Oil on canvas, 25⅝ x 19⅝".
The Louvre, Paris. Moreau-Nélaton Collection

to have been heralded by the refusal of two of Caravaggio's paintings by the patrons who had commissioned them, and by the declining material success of the late Rembrandt, reached crisis stage in the mid-nineteenth century. From our present vantage point it is a little hard to understand why, for to twentieth-century eyes Realist painting looks eminently conservative. On leaving a gallery devoted to Neoclassicism and Romanticism, one is instantly aware of a lowering of the general tonality of color, as well as of action and emotion, in Realist painting. For the realists the brightly tinted linear constructions of Ingres and the rich chromatic fantasies of Delacroix were equally luxurious, even self-indulgent. One had to begin again, with the sensations of actual existence, the brown of the earth, the blue of the sky, the green of foliage, the gray of stone, the drab colors of everyday garments. This resolute, almost puritanical concentration on fact instead of fancy was a shock to Parisians, and by no means universally accepted. They preferred not only the work of Ingres, Delacroix, and their followers, but also meticulously painted storytelling pictures of a quality too low to permit illustration in this book; the artists of these works were the recipients of medals and membership in the Academy. Yet many critics, notably the poet Baudelaire, found something deeply satisfying in the solidity of the matter-of-fact Realists, who could and did discover poetry and even drama of a high order in the prosaic facts of existence as revealed by sight. Their concentration on visual reality, moreover, was to stimulate the Impressionists, all of

whom began as Realists and continued to call themselves such in their later revolutionary exploration of the perception of light.

COROT. The new objective style becomes apparent first in the quiet landscapes of Jean-Baptiste-Camille Corot (1796–1875). Son of a moderately prosperous businessman, Corot was enabled by a paternal allowance to leave business for the study of painting at the unusually late age of twenty-six. After three years of study, he made his first trip to Italy in 1825, remaining until 1828. It is typical of his attitude toward Italian art that not until his third visit to Italy in 1843 did he pay what he termed a "courtesy call" on the Sistine Chapel. What interested him was not the long Italian artistic tradition from the ancient world, the Middle Ages, the Renaissance, and the Baroque, but the harmony of man and nature in the Italian landscape and the beauty of Italian light, which erases differences of time and unifies all objects, natural or man-made, in the serenity of vision. Visitors of the author's age remember Italy when it still looked much as it does in Corot's paintings, before the automobile clogged the cities, burdened the roads, and muddied the air.

Although he occasionally painted pictures on religious or mythological themes for exhibition at the Salon or on commission, the figures in these paintings are usually quite small, and the artist's primary concern is the landscape. Corot's little landscape studies done out of doors, like the contemporary oil sketches of Constable, were sometimes used as themes for larger, finished works painted in the studio; in the twentieth century these studies are valued for their own sake, as tiny miracles of color, form, and light. In fact not since Piero della Francesca (see figs. 65, 66, colorplates 10, 11), whose work Corot probably never saw, had form been so beautifully constructed through the play of light. Looking at such a masterpiece as the *Island of San Bartolomeo*, of 1825 (fig. 400), it is hard to believe that Corot had only begun to paint three years before. No matter what their age or historical importance, the buildings and bridges of Rome were to him cubes bounded by planes, revealed by delicate changes of hue and value. Corot claimed that he could distinguish no fewer than twenty gradations between pure white and black, but in his landscape restricts himself generally to the upper and middle ranges; there are seldom any deep shadows. Pearly tones of blue-gray, blue, tan, and rose establish the existence of forms in clear Italian air, and prolong them in reflections on the surface of the river, disturbed only here and there by ripples. It is typical of Corot's detachment that in these early cityscapes not a human or animal can be seen. The timelessness of these meditations on form and light anticipates in many ways the art of Cézanne toward the close of the nineteenth century (see Chapter 5) and that of the Cubists in the early twentieth (see Chapter 7).

Corot's keen powers of visual analysis reached their fullest expression in his *Chartres Cathedral*, of 1830 (fig. 401). In spite of the fact that this study was painted during a visit to Chartres in company with the architect P. A. Poirot, Corot quietly suppressed architectural detail and softened the historical differences between the two towers in favor of a unity of broad planes building up masses. He even played off the unequal shapes of the Early Gothic south tower and Flamboyant north tower as reverse, man-made counterparts of the two unequal saplings in the foreground in a reciprocal system of interlocking diagonals in depth. He is reported to have said that the secret of landscape painting lay in knowing where to sit down; certainly, the success of his calm and unedited transcriptions of the essential forms in buildings and in nature depends in large measure on his selection of a perfect point of view. The painting was retouched by the artist in 1872; very likely the quiet figures were added at that time.

Although toward the end of his career Corot returned to the objectivity of his early work, in middle life he took to painting dreamy landscapes in the studio either from memory or imagination. He had a house at Ville d'Avray, a hamlet on the edge of the forest of Fontainebleau, where a group of Realist landscape painters worked, with whose sober productions these lyrical canvases have remarkably little in common. The soft, silvery light of Corot's woodland studies, such as his *Ville d'Avray* (fig. 402), is broken by fugitive touches indicating foliage, in reminiscence of the technique of Constable. The Impressionists found these later landscapes lacking in devotion to reality, and twentieth-century critics have generally preferred the cubic forms

of Corot's earlier work. But the landscapes were immensely popular and widely imitated—even forged—in Corot's own time. Their velvety gray and olive tones, suggesting layers of space seen through superimposed films of light and shade, are very beautiful; so, indeed, is their unique personal poetry.

MILLET. Another painter who settled in the forest of Fontainebleau, at the village of Barbizon, and was not likely to be found among the Realists of the Andler Keller, was Jean François Millet (1814–75). Born in Normandy of a peasant family, he preferred to live like a peasant, with his family of fourteen children, dedicating his life to the painting of peasants in whose attachment to the soil he found a religious quality. Generally, before his time peasants had been portrayed as stupid or even ridiculous, even when Bruegel (see fig. 221, colorplate 34) permitted them to exemplify the blind forces of nature. Millet saw them as pious actors in a divinely ordained drama—a Catholic counterpart to the dominant role peasants and workers were assuming at that very moment in the thought of Karl Marx, who would have had little but contempt for the supine way in which Millet's peasants accept their humble lot. Millet invests the solitary figure in his *Sower*, of about 1850 (fig. 403), with a Michelangelesque grandeur as he strides over the plowed land, and the broad strokes of rich pigment emulate Rembrandt.

DAUMIER. The earthiest of the Realists who met in the Andler Keller was Honoré Daumier (1808–79), known to most Parisians of his day solely as a caricaturist. He worked in the lithograph technique, which involved draw-

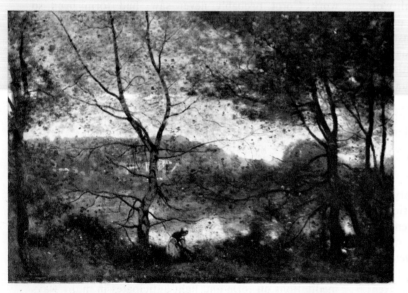

402. JEAN-BAPTISTE-CAMILLE COROT. *Ville d'Avray.* 1870. Oil on canvas, 21⅜ x 31½". The Metropolitan Museum of Art, New York. Bequest of Catherine Lorillard Wolfe, 1887

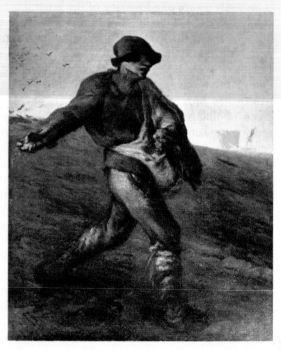

403. JEAN FRANÇOIS MILLET. *Sower.* c. 1850. Oil on canvas, 40 x 32½". Museum of Fine Arts, Boston. Shaw Collection

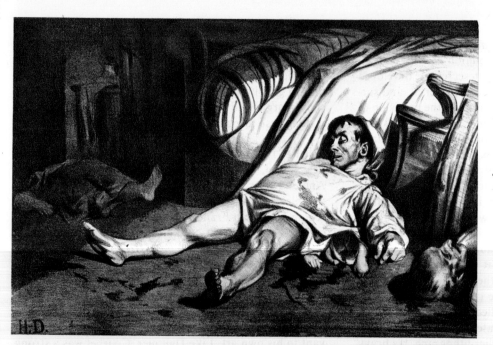

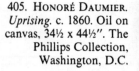

404. HONORÉ DAUMIER. *Rue Transnonain, April 15, 1834*. 1834. Lithograph, 11½ x 17⅝". Bibliothèque Nationale, Paris

ing on porous stone with a fatty pencil; it could be printed easily in large numbers along with blocks of type, which made it ideal for newspaper illustration. Both Géricault and Delacroix had made lithographs, but Daumier poured out more than four thousand of them in the course of some thirty years for such satirical weeklies as *Caricature* and *Charivari*. He was one of the most brilliant and devastating caricaturists who ever lived, satirizing unmercifully the Royalists, the Bonapartists, politicians in general, and lawyers in particular, and mocking somewhat more indulgently the foibles of the bourgeois class on whom the shifting governments of nineteenth-century France depended for their support. He was imprisoned for six months in 1832 for a

caricature of King Louis Philippe as the giant Gargantua, swallowing the earnings of workers and peasants lifted to his maw on an endless belt, and excreting honors, decorations, and political favors for the bourgeoisie and the aristocracy. Even after his imprisonment, Daumier continued his attacks. One of his most powerful lithographs (fig. 404), called simply *Rue Transnonain, April 15, 1834*, depicts an incident during the insurrection of that month in which all the inhabitants of a working-class house were butchered in reprisal for shots fired at a soldier. The masterly sculptural rendering of the figure, the powerful foreshortening, and light and shade are in the tradition of Géricault, but the intense pathos is Daumier's own.

405. HONORÉ DAUMIER. *Uprising*. c. 1860. Oil on canvas, 34½ x 44½". The Phillips Collection, Washington, D.C.

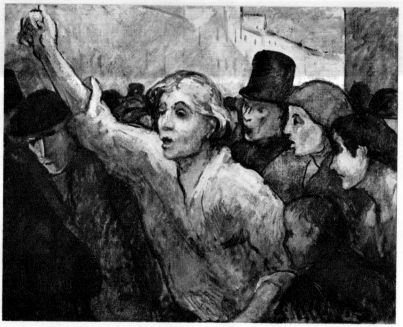

After the suppression of *Caricature* in 1835, he turned to social satire, and after the revolution of 1848 he took up painting in earnest and largely in secret. He developed a style at once individual, simple and powerful, and surprisingly spontaneous when compared to the precision of the early lithographs. His *Uprising*, of about 1860 (fig. 405), depicts no single incident from any one of the many insurrections that rocked Paris in the nineteenth century but is rather a personification of the working class in a roughly dressed and single-minded young hero, who gathers old and young about him in a march through the grim streets. Suggestion works wonders; instead of depicting scores of individuals, as in the massive crowd scenes of the Romanticists, Daumier sketches in only a few heads, just as he hints at hundreds of windows with a touch of dark here and there. Yet the walls tower in shadow and light, and the crowd pushes forward, seemingly irresistible in its collective might. Although Daumier's technique is deliberately rough, when compared to the precision of the earlier lithograph, his heavy impastos convey both the mass and the tension of the figures.

In spite of the fact that he knew Michelangelo's paintings only from engravings, Daumier managed to invest his working people with the grandeur of the Sistine prophets and sibyls (see colorplate 23). His *Third-Class Carriage*, of about 1862 (fig. 406), is the earliest known painting to be concerned with the effect of a modern conveyance on human beings (as distinguished from Turner's hymn to modernity in *Rain, Steam, and Speed*). Ordinary people of both sexes and all ages are brought together physically yet remain spiritually isolated in the cramped interior, which Daumier has painted in Rembrandtesque light and shade. The massive figures are indicated with quick and summary contours even freer than those of the late Delacroix. Not until 1878, a year before Daumier's death, when increasing blindness had forced him to give up painting, did he receive his first one-man show—organized for him by artist friends—bringing him at long last recognition as a great painter.

COURBET. The most aggressive, even noisy apostle of the new school, as well as the most influential habitué of the Andler Keller, was Gustave Courbet (1819–77). Born in the bleak village of Ornans in the mountainous Jura region of eastern France, he came to Paris determined to create a lasting effect on the art of the capital, not only through his devotion to concrete reality but also through his study of the art of the past, which he hoped would place his own in the tradition of the museums. In both respects he reminds us of Caravaggio (see pages 215–218), equally truculent in his insistence on reality and respectful toward those aspects of the past he found relevant to his own art. Like Daumier, Courbet was a strong republican and champion of working-class rights and ideas. A friend and disciple of the Socialist writer Pierre Joseph Proudhon, Courbet wanted his art to embody his ideas concerning society. At the start, at least, he was completely consistent. "The art of painting should consist only in the representation of objects which the artist can see and touch . . ." he declared; "I hold that the artists of a century are completely incapable of reproducing the things of a preceding or a future century. . . . It is for this reason that I reject history painting when applied to the past. History painting is essentially contemporary."

His paintings, therefore, are wholly concerned with events of his own time. *The Stone Breakers*, of 1849 (fig. 407), fully embodies his artistic and social principles, and

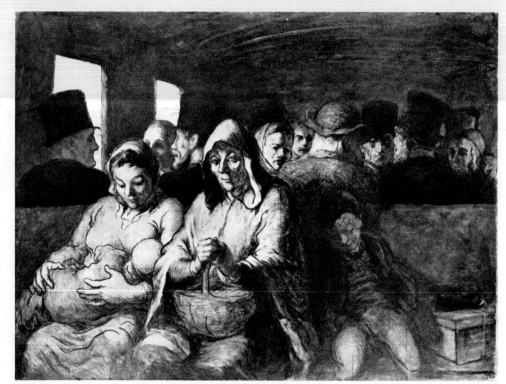

406. HONORÉ DAUMIER. *Third-Class Carriage.* c. 1862. Oil on canvas, 25¾ x 35½". The Metropolitan Museum of Art, New York. Bequest of Mrs. H. O. Havemeyer, 1929. The H. O. Havemeyer Collection

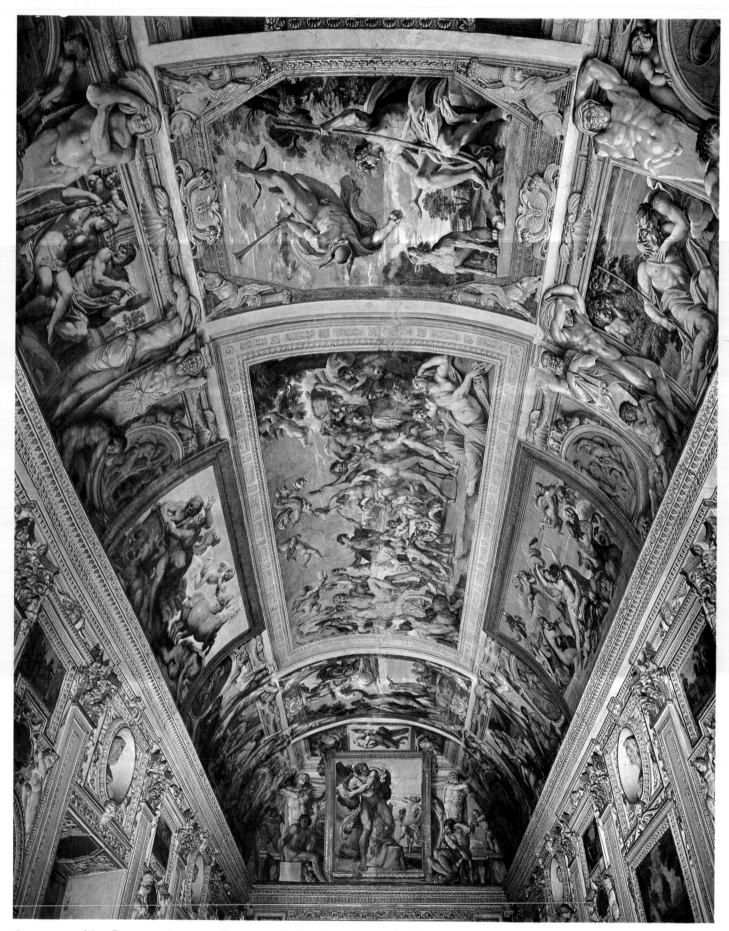

COLORPLATE 36.   Baroque. ANNIBALE CARRACCI. Ceiling fresco (portion). 1597–1600. Palazzo Farnese, Rome

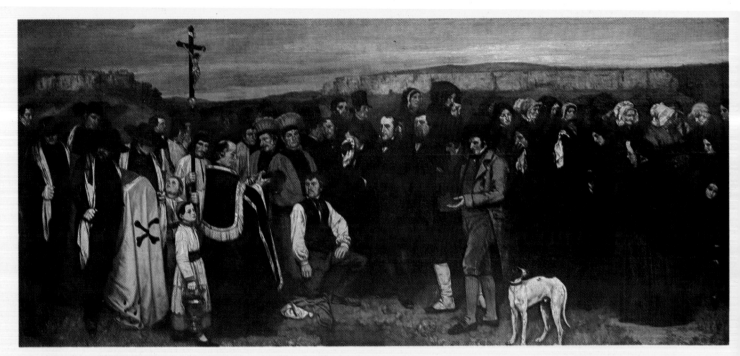

COLORPLATE 55.   Realism. GUSTAVE COURBET. *A Burial at Ornans.* 1849–50. Oil on canvas, 10′3⅜″ x 21′9⅜″. The Louvre, Paris

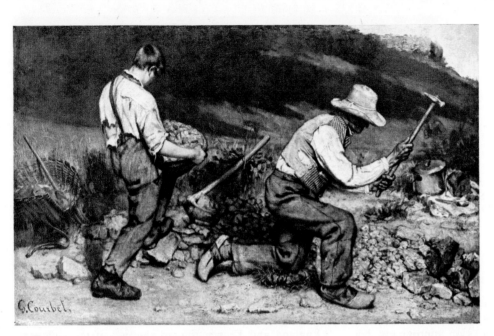

caused a scandal when it was exhibited at the Salon of 1850. A public accustomed to the grandiloquence of the Neoclassicists and the Romanticists, and the trivia of the new official art, had no way of understanding such a direct and hard study of reality. Impressed by a sight he had actually seen, Courbet depicted the dehumanizing labor of breaking stones into gravel for road repairs, undertaken calmly and anonymously—their faces are almost concealed from us—by an old man and a boy, without any of the religious overtones of Millet, yet with perfect dignity. Proudhon called it a parable from the Gospels. The simplicity of the relief-like composition is so deeply Classical, recalling the metopes from Olympia, as to render the *Oath of the Horatii* (see fig. 366) empty in contrast. The everyday, emotionless power of Courbet's compositions was matched by the workmanliness of his methods. His paint was first laid on with the palette knife, which both Rembrandt and Delacroix had used for expressive purposes; Courbet handled it as though it were a trowel and he were laying plaster on a wall. His unfinished works, done entirely in palette knife, are to twentieth-century eyes very beautiful. When the knifework was dry, he worked up the surface effects of light and color with a brush, but it is the underlying palette-knife construction that gives his figures their density and weight.

In the same Salon of 1850 he showed *A Burial at Ornans* (colorplate 55), which fulfilled exactly his requirements for true history painting. The inescapable end of an ordinary inhabitant of the village (the identity of the deceased is unknown) is represented with sober realism and a certain rough grandeur. Accompanied by altar boys and pallbearers, and women in regional costume, the parish priest reads the Office of the Dead before the open grave, around which stand family and friends, some with handkerchiefs to their eyes, and the mayor in his knee breeches and cocked hat, not to speak

of the kneeling gravedigger and the perplexed dog (who always appears in illustrations of the Office of the Dead in Books of Hours). The canvas, about twenty-two feet long, was so large that the artist could not step back in his studio to see the whole work, yet it is thoroughly unified. In a great S-curve in depth, the figures stand with the simple dignity of the Apostles in Masaccio's *Tribute Money* (see colorplate 6). Locked between the rocky escarpment above and the grave beneath, these people realize their destiny is bound to the earth (as securely as that of Bruegel's peasants), yet they seem in contrast to comprehend and to accept their fate. Each face is painted with all of Courbet's dignity and sculptural density, recalling the prophets of Donatello (see fig. 41), yet sometimes unexpectedly beautiful, as the face of the boy looking up in conversation with one of the pallbearers. This is one of the strongest and noblest works of all French painting.

In 1855, as we have seen, Courbet's paintings were rejected by the Universal Exposition, due actually to his publicizing his refusal to provide Count Nieuwerkerke with projects for official approval. These works included not only the *Burial*, which had been accepted by the Salon of 1850, but also a more recent programmatic work, *The Studio: A Real Allegory Concerning Seven Years of My Artistic Life*, painted in 1854–55 (fig. 408). Courbet's friend and patron J. L. Alfred Bruyas helped to finance the construction of a special shed for a large exhibition of Courbet's paintings, including the rejected works; the artist called this building *The Pavilion of Realism*. For the catalogue he wrote a preface setting forth the principles of his art. In the *Studio* the relationship between artist and sitters as seen by Velázquez and Goya (see colorplate 44, fig. 376) is exactly reversed; instead of playing a subsidiary role at one side, painting a canvas seen only from the back, the artist displays himself in the center, at work on a completely visi-

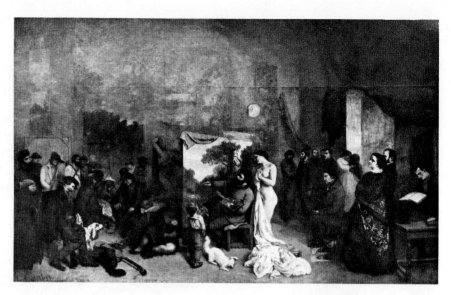

408. GUSTAVE COURBET. *The Studio: A Real Allegory Concerning Seven Years of My Artistic Life*. 1854–55. Oil on canvas, 11'10" x 19'7¾". The Louvre, Paris

ble landscape, similar to those that adorn the walls of the dim studio. A model who has just shed her clothes, probably representing Truth, looks on approvingly, her voluminous figure beautifully revealed in light. In spite of Courbet's lengthy explanation, the group at the left remains, perhaps deliberately, somewhat obscure, but it comprises figures drawn from "society at its best, its worst, and its average," with whom the painter had come in contact. Among the gathering on the right are recognizable the woman novelist George Sand, and the poet and critic Baudelaire, reading a book. Few of the figures look at the artist; all are silent. Interestingly enough, Delacroix called the picture a masterpiece, reproaching the jury for having "refused one of the most remarkable works of our times."

Once Courbet had won material success, however, something of the rude power of his early works vanishes from his portraits of the French aristocracy and his often provocative nudes. After the revolution of 1870 he joined the short-lived Paris Commune, and took part in the commission that decreed the dismantling of the lofty Colonne Vendôme, a Napoleonic monument in central Paris. For this he was condemned under the Third Republic to six months in prison, which he spent in painting still lifes of extraordinary clarity and simplicity. Later, he was charged a huge sum for rebuilding the monument, fled to Switzerland, and died in exile, after all his belongings had been sold by the authorities to pay the debt.

METAL ARCHITECTURE

This is perhaps the best moment to discuss the new forms of architecture made possible by the Industrial Revolution. Metal had been used from time to time in the history of architecture as an adjunct to other materials, such as often the bronze or iron dowels in the centers of Greek columns and the iron frames used to enclose sections of stained-glass windows in Gothic cathedrals. Iron beams had even been inserted in the sixteenth century to strengthen the fragile outer walls of the Uffizi in Florence (see fig. 190). Cast iron came into use on a grand scale in England and France toward the end of the eighteenth century in bridges and for the inner structures of factories, and in the 1830s for railway stations. Almost invariably buildings using cast iron were intended for purely utilitarian purposes. A conspicuous exception was the Royal Pavilion at Brighton (see fig. 395), whose onion domes were carried on iron frames, but when the iron was exposed in the same building in a "Chinese" staircase and in palm-tree columns in the kitchen, it was cast into shapes previously familiar from work in stone or wood. During the 1840s and 1850s, the use of cast iron became widespread, even in Gothic revival churches. The mid-nineteenth-century façades common in office buildings still standing in downtown New York City, and the dome (1850–65) of the U.S. Capitol in Washington, D.C., by Thomas U. Walter (1804–87), are outstanding examples.

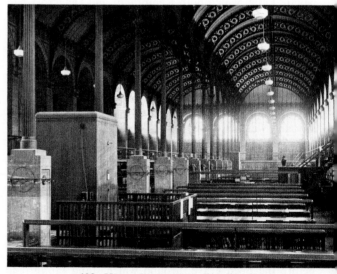

409. HENRI LABROUSTE. Reading Room, Bibliothèque Ste.-Geneviève. 1843–50. Paris

An early and brilliant use of exposed iron for architectural purposes is the reading room of the Bibliothèque Sainte-Geneviève in Paris (fig. 409), built in 1843–50 by HENRI LABROUSTE (1801–75). The exterior of the building is arched like the flanks of the Malatesta Temple (see fig. 32), but the interior is roofed by two parallel barrel vaults of iron plates, resting on iron rivets cast with a perforated vinescroll design of the greatest lightness; these are supported in the center by iron arches springing airily from slender Corinthian colonnettes, recalling the fantastic elements of pictorial architecture at Pompeii. The precast elements made it possible to assemble a large structure in comparatively short time, and seemed a great advantage to the architects of the mid-nineteenth century.

The triumph of iron architecture was the Crystal Palace (fig. 410), built in the astonishing space of nine months in 1850–51 by SIR JOSEPH PAXTON (1801–65), who had learned the principles of construction in iron and glass from building greenhouses. No glass-and-iron structure had ever before been put up on such a scale, however, and the airy interior with its barrel-vaulted transept and multiple galleries all of glass on an iron skeleton showing throughout was the luminous wonder of the London Great Exhibition—the first of a long procession of world's fairs. Its seemingly infinite space, pervaded by light at every point and utterly weightless, doubtless shimmering with color in the rosy glow of good weather, must have been a perfect counterpart to the paintings of Turner. The rapid end of cast-iron architecture was spelled by its unsuspected vulnerability to fire. The Crystal Palace (the first of many in Dublin, New York City, and elsewhere) was reconstructed at Sydenham, south of London, in supposedly permanent shape in 1852–54, but it perished by fire in 1936. However, the utility of metal for architecture had been established, and the material was to be revived for a

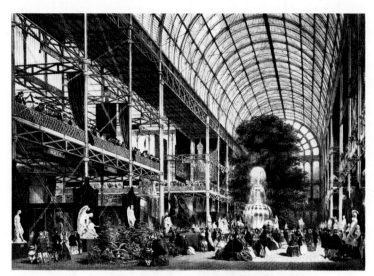

410. SIR JOSEPH PAXTON. Interior (view of transept looking north), Crystal Palace. 1850–51. Cast iron and glass. London (Lithograph by Joseph Nash. Victoria and Albert Museum, London. Crown Copyright Reserved)

somewhat different constructional role, giving rise to strikingly new architectural forms after the invention of a method of making steel in 1855 by Sir Henry Bessemer.

REALISM IN THE UNITED STATES

The influence of realism spread throughout Europe. Gifted American artists arriving in France in the 1860s were deeply impressed by the work of the Barbizon painters, by Corot, and by Courbet. A formidable figure in American nineteenth-century art was WINSLOW HOMER (1836–1910). Self-taught and active as an illustrator and documentary artist during the Civil War, he underwent the influence of Realism during a visit to

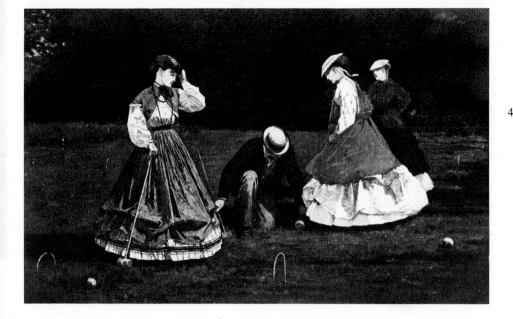

411. WINSLOW HOMER. *The Croquet Game.* 1866. Oil on canvas, 16 x 26″. The Art Institute of Chicago

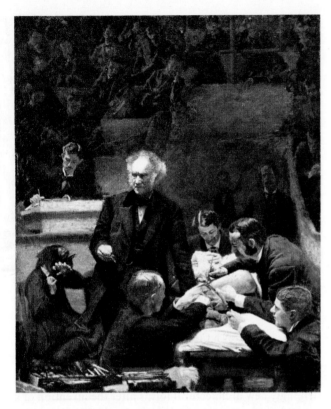

412. THOMAS EAKINS. *The Gross Clinic.* 1875.
Oil on canvas, 96 x 78".
Jefferson Medical College, Philadelphia

France in 1866–67, at which time his early style crystallized. A typically early work is *The Croquet Game* (fig. 411), of 1866, in which the clarity of forms and spaces and the beautiful adjustment of tones betray the influence of Corot, while the density of substance and of pigment reflects an indebtedness to Courbet. In later life Homer developed a strongly individual style as a marine painter, in relative isolation on the Maine coast, with trips to the Caribbean.

An even more important figure, considered by many to have been America's greatest native-born artist, is THOMAS EAKINS (1844–1916). After early study at the Pennsylvania Academy, he, like Homer, visited France in 1866. He also went to Spain, where he was profoundly affected by Velázquez, and returned to America in 1870 to paint powerful works uncompromisingly founded on fact. His insistence on posing a nude male model before female students forced his resignation from the directorship of the Pennsylvania Academy, and his honest realism cost him fashionable portrait commissions. Fortunately, he enjoyed a small independent income, and was able to continue doing portraits of friends —searching psychological analyses of great depth and emotional intensity, dryly painted, without the richness

of pigment in which Corot and Courbet delighted. Eakins was fascinated by the new art of photography, and used it as an aid in his researches into reality.

Eakins' masterpiece is a monumental painting called *The Gross Clinic* (fig. 412), painted in 1875 for the Jefferson Medical College in Philadelphia, where Eakins had studied anatomy. The lifesize group represents an actual operation being performed by an eminent surgeon and his staff in an operating theater before medical students. The composition was undoubtedly influenced by Rembrandt's *Anatomy Lesson of Dr. Tulp* (see fig. 305). Like that great painting, Eakins' work deals with an inherently repulsive subject not only in a direct and analytical manner, but also with a certain reverence for the mystery of human existence. He goes far beyond the seventeenth-century prototype in his depiction of the drama of the moment; the careful portraiture of the surgeons, absorbed in their task, is unforgettable, as is the compulsive gesture of the female relative of the patient, who draws her arm before her face. The noble and seemingly spontaneous grouping, enriched by strong contrasts of light and shade, is one of the most powerful pictorial compositions of the nineteenth century, worthy to be set alongside *A Burial at Ornans* (see colorplate 55).

4

Impressionism

Rapidly and unexpectedly the new Realist movement gave rise in the mid-1860s and throughout the 1870s to the first complete artistic revolution since the Early Renaissance in the fifteenth century, and to the first universal style to originate in France since the birth of the Gothic in the twelfth century. The new style almost immediately became known as Impressionism, and although it lasted only about fifteen years in its purest form, it determined in one way or another nearly every artistic manifestation that has taken place since. In fact, the consequences of Impressionism are still apparent in contemporary art more than a hundred years later. "Nothing is seen without light," wrote Ghiberti (see Part Four, Chapter 1), and while that master and his Florentine contemporaries were aware, as had been the ancient Greeks before them (see Vol. 1, Part Two, Chapter 4), of the role of light in establishing the existence of objects and determining their forms and colors, it had never occurred to Renaissance artists that light might also function in the opposite way to deform, denature, or dissolve objects.

Starting on the basis of Courbet's solid realism and the graduated light effects of Corot, the Impressionist artists, working from start to finish out-of-doors, became fascinated by the transformations wrought by light on natural objects, surfaces, and atmospheric spaces. It soon became clear to them that color, for example, is not the property of the object itself but of the moment of perception of light, and thus changes constantly with the times of day, the movement of the sun, and the density of the atmosphere. Baroque artists, especially Rubens and Vermeer (see Part Five, Chapters 4 and 5), followed in the nineteenth century by Delacroix, had studied the effect colors have on each other when juxtaposed, and the reflection of one color in another, observations sternly rejected by Classical tradition from Poussin to Ingres. Even earlier, in the High Renaissance, Leonardo da Vinci (see Part Four, Chapter 3) had noted that if a person clothed in white passed through a sunlit field the white clothing would appear green.

Yet neither he nor any other Renaissance artist had deemed such a scientific curiosity worthy of painting. In the twentieth century, due chiefly to the Impressionists, we take such phenomena for granted. No one needs proof

that when he drives toward the western sun the glare on an asphalt road will turn it white, or that stage lighting converts the local color of objects on the stage to any desired color merely by interposing a transparent sheet of the proper hue between the light source and the object. Neither do we require proof that an object can be so transformed or rendered contourless by mist or haze that neither its size nor its material composition can be grasped. Nonetheless, in the 1860s and 1870s such facts, if realized at all by the general public or by most artists, were automatically discounted, and were compensated by readjustment of tones and contours in favor of the known rather than the seen qualities. It was this habitual compensation that the Impressionists stubbornly refused to accept, and we are eternally in their debt for a brilliant new vision of the world about us. They were the first to render the full intensity of natural light and the glow of natural colors. If the general tone of a gallery hung with Realist paintings seems dark to us after experiencing the rich colors of the Romantics and the delicate tints of the Neoclassicists, that of an Impressionist gallery is keyed up to such a degree that we feel as though we had suddenly stepped from a dim interior into the full glare of sunlight. To quote Paul Signac, a painter who helped to transform the Impressionist style in the 1880s, "the entire surface of the [Impressionist] painting glows with sunlight; the air circulates; light embraces, caresses and irradiates forms; it penetrates everywhere, even into the shadows which it illuminates." It was light, perceived in a flash too quick to permit the eye to focus on detail, judge contours, enumerate elements, and assess weights and densities, that the Impressionists tried to capture. Claude Monet, leader of the movement, called his goal "instantaneity." It is far from irrelevant that at this very moment instantaneity was also the aim of photographers who, although their art had been invented in the 1820s, had long been bound to lengthy time exposures.

It is now our task to trace how the Impressionist movement came about, how it spread, and how it became rapidly transformed into a radically different style. The well-nigh unanswerable question is why the revolution in vision occurred when and where it did. It is not enough to point out that much of what the Impressionists achieved in the perception of color in painting had already been

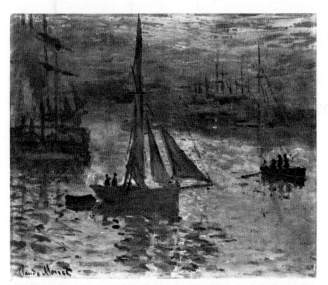

413. CLAUDE MONET. *Impression—Sunrise, Le Havre.* 1872. Oil on canvas, 19½ x 25½". Musée Marmottan, Paris

particles in an endless web of color, subject to the changes of light in the soft, moisture- and smoke-laden air of Paris, in which no form is clear and all elements tend to be reduced to particles of more or less the same size (see figs. 417, 420). The most striking aspect of the rapid development of Impressionism is that it was in no way retarded by the defeat of France in the Franco-Prussian War of 1870–71, the devastation of Paris by Prussian shelling during the siege, and the disorders of the brutally repressed Commune of 1871. As if nothing had happened, the Impressionist friends, with few exceptions temporarily dispersed from the capital, returned to it immediately, and heightened their dazzling colors and intensified their perceptions of the light of the metropolis and its surrounding country.

MANET AND MONET. The use of the name Impressionism to characterize the new style came from the first exhibition of members of the group at the studio of the photographer Nadar in 1874—significantly enough, since photography is produced by the action of light, the chief interest of the Impressionists. Claude Monet (1840–1926) exhibited among others an extraordinary painting entitled *Impression—Sunrise, Le Havre*, painted two years earlier (fig. 413). The title gave rise to the name applied to the entire movement, one that its members soon adopted. The exhibition was greeted with public derision, the like of which had never been experienced in Paris. A newspaper story recounted solemnly how a visitor was driven mad by the paintings, and rushed out onto the Boulevard des Capucines where he started biting innocent passersby. Every tradition of European painting seemed to have been thrown aside. Not only form but also substance itself has vanished. The

formulated scientifically in research conducted during the 1820s, and embodied in a book published in 1839 by the French chemist Michel Eugène Chevreul (1786–1889); the Impressionists were not influenced by Chevreul's work, which was not systematically studied by painters until the days of Seurat in the 1880s (see Chapter 5). One important factor in Impressionist experience may well have been the spectacle of Haussmann's Paris, which had taken shape around them, with its seemingly infinite perspectives of straight avenues and curving boulevards lined with almost identical structures. Buildings and all their details, trees, carriages, pedestrians—all became

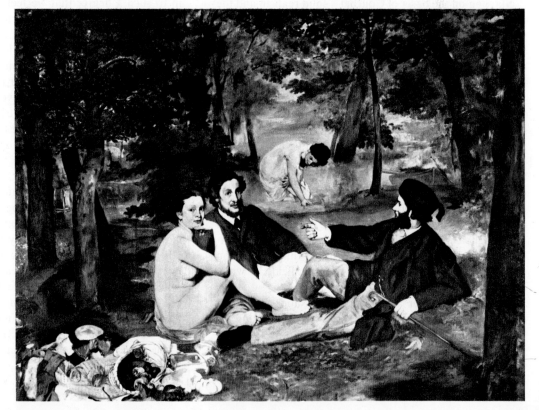

414. EDOUARD MANET. *Luncheon on the Grass (Déjeuner sur l'herbe).* 1863. Oil on canvas, 6'9⅛" x 8'10¼". Musée du Jeu de Paume, Paris

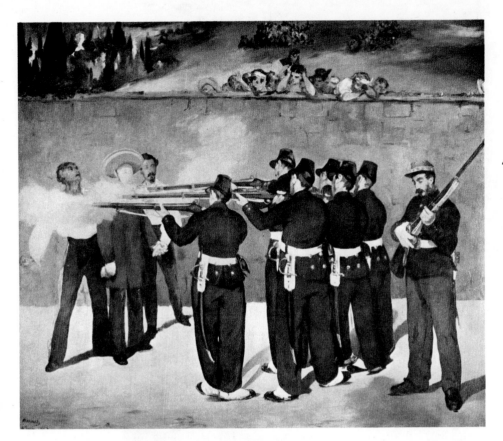

415. EDOUARD MANET.
*Execution of the Emperor
Maximilian of Mexico.*
1867. Oil on canvas, 8'3¼" x
12'⅛". Städtische
Kunsthalle, Mannheim,
Germany

picture was a mere collection of colored streaks and blobs on a light blue ground. Today observers have no difficulty recognizing a sailboat and a rowboat in the foreground, distant masts and rigging, haze, and smoke, all reflected in the rippled surface of the water. This revolutionary image, intended to correspond to the image the eye sees in an instantaneous glimpse of the port of Le Havre at sunrise, summed up the beliefs of the school. In retrospect, the name Impressionism seems one of the few appropriate names in the history of art.

The beginnings of the movement, from which no one, least of all the artists themselves, could have predicted its culmination, seem light-years earlier. The germs of the new perception are apparent in the art of Édouard Manet (1832–83), the similarity of whose surname to that of Monet causes confusion today and at first distressed Manet, who thought it was a bad joke. Scion of a well-to-do and elegant Parisian family, the young Manet was trained for a naval career, but then permitted to enter the studio of the conservative painter Thomas Couture, where he received a thorough training in drawing and painting. Trips to Italy, the Netherlands, Germany, and Austria in the 1850s brought him into contact with the work of the Old Masters, through careful copying. He was particularly impressed by the optical art and brilliant brushwork of Velázquez (see Part Five, Chapter 6), whose work he saw during a brief visit to Spain in 1865, and to whom he remained permanently indebted. He also admired Goya, and among the artists of his own time preferred Courbet and Daumier.

In 1863 Manet exhibited at the Salon des Refusés a canvas entitled *Luncheon on the Grass* (*Déjeuner sur l'herbe*) (fig. 414), which created an uproar. The nonchalant grouping of a nude female figure and two fully clothed men in what appears to be a public park shocked the Parisians as the height of immorality. In actuality Manet had wittily adapted the composition and the poses from a sixteenth-century engraving after a design by Raphael; Giorgione also had painted a similar theme. Manet simply modernized the clothing, surroundings, and accessories. Even Courbet joined the chorus of denunciation, finding the painting formless and flat. This flatness, however, was just what Manet was striving for. He discarded Courbet's characteristic lighting from one side and strong modeling in favor of delicately modeled areas silhouetted in light and dark. Illumination seems to come from the direction of the observer, and eliminates mass. It is as though Manet were using the "indecent" subject for its shock value to point up his belief that the important thing about a picture is not what it represents but how it is painted. The erasure of form allows him to concentrate on the luminosity of the green grass and foliage, the sparkling remains of the picnic, and the glowing flesh of the nude. By posing an insoluble enigma of subject, he has, in effect, transformed a group of figures into a still life.

Manet soon went even farther; in 1867 he painted a subject from contemporary history, the *Execution of the Emperor Maximilian of Mexico* (fig. 415), which records an event that had deeply shocked the French public and

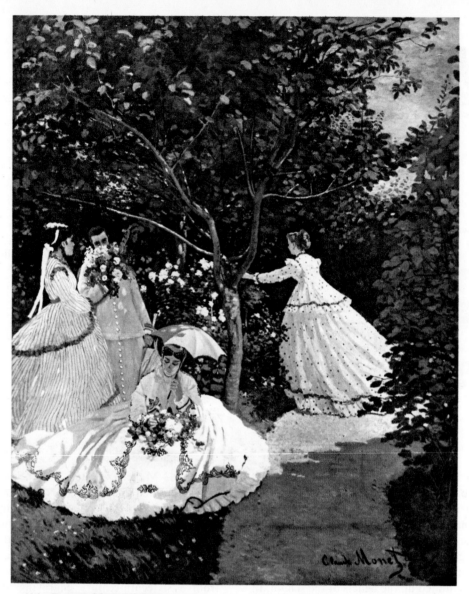

416. CLAUDE MONET. *Women in the Garden*. 1866–67. Oil on canvas, 8'4½" x 6'8¾".
Musée du Jeu de Paume, Paris

for which Napoleon III and his government, who had in-stalled Maximilian, were generally blamed. Manet treated the incident in a totally unexpected way, almost as a reaction against such elaborately staged protest compositions as Géricault's *Raft of the Medusa* (see fig. 383) and Goya's *Third of May, 1808* (see fig. 377). He made a close study of newspaper accounts of the execution, and even of portrait photographs of the slain emperor, but rather than arranging the figures for max-imum emotional effect seems almost to have taken a snapshot of the scene. One can scarcely make out the ex-pressions of the doomed men. No longer the embodiment of mechanized cruelty as in Goya, the soldiers are merely doing their job. If any figure receives special attention it is the officer preparing his rifle for the coup de grace. The onlookers peering over the wall are merely curious. The picture consists largely of colored uniforms, a briskly painted background, and puffs of smoke. Another traditional subject, this time a tragic one, has been modernized in terms of immediate vision.

At first Manet maintained a certain distance from the members of the Impressionist group; he went to chat with them at the Café Guerbois, but never exhibited with them. His younger contemporary, Monet, came from an utterly different background. Although he also was born in Paris, his father was a grocer, and the family soon moved to Le Havre on the coast of Normandy, where the father became a ship chandler, and the boy could con-stantly observe ships and the sea. This circumstance was not unimportant for his later preoccupation with light, water, and human experience in relation to the unending stream of time. After starting as a caricaturist, the young artist was introduced to landscape painting in 1858 by a gifted outdoor painter, Eugène Boudin. In 1867 he sub-mitted to the Salon a revolutionary work, the huge *Women in the Garden* (fig. 416), painted the preceding year. The model for all the figures was the artist's mis-tress, whom he later married, Camille Doncieux. But the entire picture, more than eight feet high, was painted out-doors. Monet had already developed in the direction of instantaneity, and the picture required him to devise new methods in order to record the immediate impression of light on the muslin dresses, the flowers, and the trees. To the astonishment of Courbet, he refused to paint at all when the sun went under a cloud. And since in order to paint the upper portions of the picture he would have had to climb a ladder, thus altering his view of the subject, he dug a trench and built a device for lowering and raising the canvas so that all parts of it could be painted from the same point of view. The feeling of sunlight is warm and rich, but the colors are still local, though soft blue shadow does reflect into the faces of the women from their flowing dresses. The leaves are colored in varying shades of green, which means that Monet had not really gone farther than Constable in his perception of the makeup of any given color. But the general impression is far brighter than anything Manet had achieved in the *Luncheon on the Grass* of only three years before. Already Monet has begun to divide the entire surface into patches of color of roughly uniform size. Even more important, now that Manet had demolished the emotional drama as a subject, Monet in this and other pictures established the new Impressionist subject—the moment of pleasure in light.

However successful from an artistic and historical point of view, like most of the artist's early works the painting was a worldly failure. Not only was it rejected from the Salon of 1867, but also when it was shown in a shopwindow, Manet poked fun at it. Interestingly enough, a few years later, when he had come to understand Monet's style and adopted his brilliant coloring, Manet bought the picture for himself.

Although Manet remained in Paris during the disorders of 1870–71, Monet fled, first to London, where he experienced a different kind of light and studied the art of Constable and Turner, then to Holland and Belgium, where he seems to have been interested chiefly in landscape. On his return to France his style changed rapidly and radically. *Impression—Sunrise, Le Havre*, which we can now see in its place in the perspective of the Impressionist movement, marks very nearly the apogee of Monet's attempt to seize instantaneity. The canvas must have been already covered with a monochrome underpaint before Monet began the picture, but the actual visual impression he rendered was of such brief duration that the touches of color on the surface, indicating the water, the boats and rigging, and their reflections, could hardly have taken more than an hour. In the *Women in the Garden*, he had proclaimed the Impressionist subject as the moment of experience of light; in *Impression—Sunrise, Le Havre*, he demonstrated that color belongs not to the object but to the moment of visual experience.

This was hard for his contemporaries to accept. Monet explained his method to an American lady: "When you go out to paint, try to forget what objects you have before you, a tree, a house, a field or whatever. Merely think, here is a little square of blue, here an oblong of pink, here a streak of yellow, and paint it just as it looks to you, the exact color and shape, until it gives your own naive impression of the scene before you." What Monet achieved in the 1870s was the dissolution of the object. Substance itself becomes permeated with air and light. The difference between his approach and that of Turner (of whose art Monet never entirely approved) was that Turner began with the subjective experience of color and painted reality into it as he went, while Monet began with reality and made it entirely subservient to the objective perception of color.

As early as 1873 Monet had set up a floating studio in a boat on the Seine, an idea he borrowed from the Barbizon painter Charles-François Daubigny. If to Corot the art of painting consisted in knowing where to sit down, to Monet it lay in judging where to drop anchor. The world passing before his eyes at any one spot formed a continuous stream of experience, from which he singled out moments, recorded in series. For example, at the financially disastrous third Impressionist exhibition of 1877 he showed seven canvases in which he had studied from his own objective point of view the theme of the railway. But it was neither the idea of man's victory over nature that fascinated him as it did Turner (see colorplate 54) nor sympathy with the plight of the common man trapped in his own machine as in Daumier (see fig. 406), but the simple spectacle of a locomotive drawing cars into a station, as depicted in the *Gare Saint-Lazare in Paris*, painted in 1877 (fig. 417)

The iron-and-glass train shed offered to him a tissue of changing light and color, dominated by blue and silver in this instance, but touched unexpectedly on the ground with tan, green, rose, and gold. The shadows and the

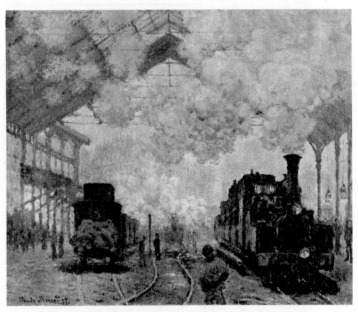

417. CLAUDE MONET. *Gare Saint-Lazare in Paris.* 1877. Oil on canvas, 32½ x 39¾". Fogg Art Museum, Harvard University, Cambridge, Massachusetts. Maurice Wertheim Collection

massive black locomotive were painted in deeper shades of these hues, chiefly blue, for the Impressionists had eliminated black from their palette. Black is the absence of color, a circumstance they would not admit; their work shows what from experience we know to be true, that black absorbs and to a degree reflects colors in the surrounding atmosphere. The people in Monet's picture are spots of blue, their faces rose and gold; the puffs of steam are bubbles of blue and pearl, whose dissolution we can watch under the glass roof. The only local color remaining is the bright red of the locomotive's bumper, necessary as a foil to the myriad blues. Just as instantaneity was the basic principle of Monet's vision, accidentality produced his compositions, yet in every case they show extraordinary power and consistency.

It will be obvious that the evanescent effects that absorbed Monet's attention could not pause long enough for him to paint them. A picture like this one, therefore, was inevitably the product of several sessions. Various layers of superimposed strokes can be distinguished in Monet's mature and late canvases, in contrast to the fresh and sketchy touches of *Impression—Sunrise, Le Havre*. It seems clear, therefore, that Monet's instantaneity carried within itself the seeds of its own dissolution. The moment of experience had become a palimpsest of several similar but not identical moments isolated from the stream of experience and blended and overlaid upon each other in various stages of completion. Monet was now constrained to work systematically in series. By the 1890s, still faithful to Impressionist principles when other advanced artists had long deserted them, Monet brought with him daily in a carriage, to the place chosen to paint, stacks of canvases on each of which he had begun the study of a certain light effect at a given moment of the day. He would select the canvas that corresponded most closely to the moment before him and recommence painting—not without periods of desperation when the desired light effects in the landscape before him refused to reappear.

Monet painted a series each of cliffs, of haystacks, of poplars bordering a river, of the Thames at London, and the Grand Canal at Venice. But the most impressive was the series of views of Rouen Cathedral. During the winters of 1892 and 1893, when he could not easily paint outdoors, Monet, now critically accepted and financially successful, rented a second-story window in a shop opposite the façade of the Cathedral, an extreme example of Flamboyant Gothic dematerialization of stone, which doubtless appealed to him as an analogue of his own Impressionist insubstantiality. Systematically, he studied the effects of light and color on the lacy façade in the dimness of dawn, in the morning light, at noon, in the afternoon, at sunset. In 1895 he exhibited eighteen views of the façade and two other views of the Cathedral, an occasion that brought forth paeans of praise and torrents of condemnation. But Monet's moments had, in the very process of being painted, become the work of art, and were at once superimposed and suspended in time. Sky and ground were all but eliminated. The façade was coextensive with the canvas, covered with a tissue of spots of

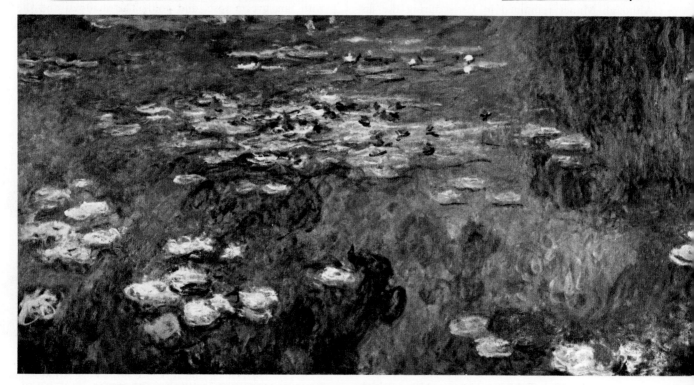

418. CLAUDE MONET. *Nymphéas (Water Lilies)*. c. 1920. Oil on canvas, 6'8½" x 19'9¼". Museum of Art, Carnegie Institute, Pittsburgh. Purchased through the generosity of Mrs. Alan M. Scaife

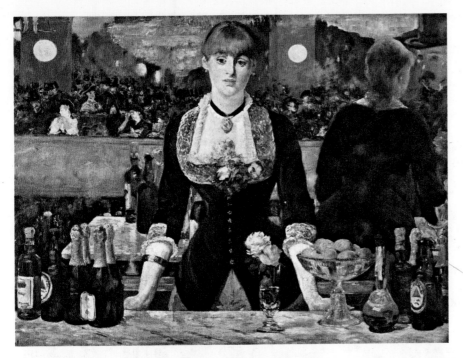

419. EDOUARD MANET.
A Bar at the Folies-Bergère.
1881–82. Oil on canvas,
37½ x 51". Courtauld
Institute Galleries,
University of London

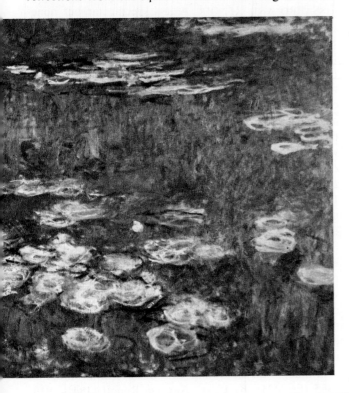

contrasting colors, a kind of cloth of gold embroidered in silver and studded with diamonds and sapphires. The light permeating the shadows and the stone had now obviously become the object of intense emotional involvement on the part of the artist.

The painting known as *Rouen Cathedral: The Façade at Sunset* (colorplate 56) must, in fact, represent the moment just about noon when the low winter sun is still striking the southern flanks of the masses of masonry, and has not yet entered the west portals, illuminated by reflections from the square in front. Dazzling as the ca-

thedral paintings are, Monet himself was so discouraged by the impossibility of registering with his hand what he saw with his eyes that he thought of abandoning them. However, he took them all back to his home at Giverny, between Paris and Rouen, and worked on them, significantly enough, *away from* the object, with only his memories of light to guide him and his constantly deepening and intensifying knowledge of the poetry of color.

In 1899 Monet began a series of water landscapes that were to occupy him till his death twenty-seven years later. In some ways these late pictures are the most magical of all. At Giverny, dissatisfied with painting experiences chosen from the chaotic stream of the outside world, he constructed an environment that he could control absolutely, a water garden filled with water-loving trees and flowers, and crossed at one point by a Japanese footbridge. Here, in canvases as gigantic as any by David, Gros, or Géricault, he submerged himself in the world of changing color, a poetic fabric in which visual and emotional experience merge. Eventually abandoning the banks entirely, the aged artist gazed into the water, and these paintings (fig. 418) show a surface in which the shimmering reflections of sky and trees blend between the floating water lilies. Two series of these canvases were designed to join, in ellipses that envelop entire rooms, without beginning or end. In Monet's last works the stream of experience has become timeless without renouncing its fluidity; despite his failing vision and his sense that he had attempted the impossible, Monet had, symbolically at least, conquered time.

In the early 1870s Manet, at the height of his career, suddenly gave up his flat style, and adopted both the brilliant palette and the broken brushwork of the Impressionists. Some of his later pictures are well-nigh indistinguishable from theirs. But the most memorable of these, *A Bar at the Folies-Bergère* (fig. 419), painted in

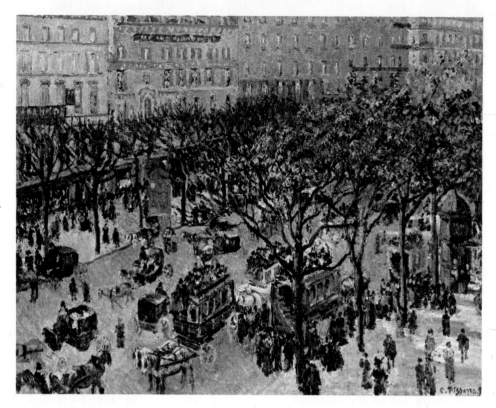

420. CAMILLE PISSARRO. *Boulevard des Italiens, Paris—Morning Sunlight.* 1897. Oil on canvas, 28⅞ x 36¼". National Gallery of Art, Washington, D.C. Chester Dale Collection

1881–82 only two years before the artist's premature death at the age of fifty-one, is a brilliant restatement—in Impressionist terms—of Manet's earlier interest in the human figure.

The entire foreground is constituted by the marble bar, laden with fruit, flowers, and bottles of champagne and liqueurs. As the nearer edge of the bar is cut off by the frame, we have the illusion that its surface extends into our space, and that we as spectators are ordering a drink from the stolid barmaid who leans her hands on the inner edge. This illusion is reinforced by the reflection in the mirror, which fills the entire background of the picture. We can make out clearly a back view of the barmaid, who is in conversation with a top-hatted gentleman who, by elimination, must be identical with the spectator. Manet was certainly remembering Velázquez's *Las Meninas* (see colorplate 44), in whose background mirror appear the king and queen. But his extension of the mirror beyond the frame at top and sides substitutes for the expected space within the picture the reflected interior of the cabaret, which is behind the spectator and, therefore, *outside* the picture. Spatially, this is the most complex image we have seen thus far in the history of art. In his early works Manet had modernized the subject. Monet in the 1870s had dissolved the object. It remained for Manet in this painting to eliminate the last vestiges of that Renaissance pictorial space that Alberti (see Part Four, Chapter 1) had defined as a vertical section through the pyramid of sight. Manet's masterpiece is painted with a brushwork that combines memories of Velázquez's virtuosity with the most brilliant achieve-

ments of the Impressionists. Paradoxically, the imposing dignity of the figure and the straight lines of the bar and the crowded balcony make this work his most monumental achievement.

PISSARRO AND RENOIR. A less spectacular but nonetheless extremely gifted member of the Impressionist group was Camille Pissarro (1830–1903), whose father, a Portuguese Jew living in the West Indies, had become a French citizen. From the very first Pissarro exhibited with the Impressionists. He was the most careful and craftsmanly of them all, and it was his companionship and advice that provided a much needed technical foundation for the most impetuous Cézanne (see Chapter 5), who called him (very appropriately) "humble and colossal." He is both in the scrupulously painted *Boulevard des Italiens, Paris—Morning Sunlight,* of 1897 (fig. 420). With infinite care he recorded the innumerable spots of color constituted by people, carriages, omnibuses, trees, windows, and kiosques in this view of one of the great metropolitan thoroughfares, whose activities provided the subject for so many Impressionist paintings. In fact, Impressionist artists often worked side by side painting the same view of a street, a café, or a riverbank at the same moment of light and atmosphere, and it is often only the special sensibility and personal touch of each painter that makes it possible to tell their works apart.

Although the sparkling *Les Grands Boulevards,* of 1875 (fig. 421), by Pierre Auguste Renoir (1841–1919) was not such a collaborative venture, it shows us how much latitude remained for individuality in treating a similar subject at the height of the collective phase of the Impressionist movement. Renoir, the most sensuous and effervescent of the group, has not bothered with the detail that occupied Pissarro. Rather he has captured a moment of high excitement as we look across a roadway from the shadow of the trees to the trotting white horse pulling a carriage filled with people in blazing sun. Warmth, physical delight, and intense joy of life are the perpetual themes of Renoir; as a painter his touch is correspondingly both silkier and more spontaneous than that of Pissarro. Trained at first as a painter on porcelain, he later studied with the academic painter Charles Gabriel Gleyre, and soon made the acquaintance of the Impressionist group, with whom he exhibited until 1886.

The most exuberant image from the Impressionist heyday is Renoir's *Le Moulin de la Galette*, of 1876 (colorplate 57), depicting a Sunday afternoon in a popular outdoor *café dansant* on Montmartre. Young couples, bewitching in their freshness, are gathered at tables under the trees, or dancing happily through the changing interplay of sunlight and shadow. Characteristically, there is not a trace of black; even the coats and the shadows turn to blue, delicious as a foil to the higher tones of pearly white and soft rose. One could scarcely imagine a more complete embodiment of the fundamental theme of Impressionist painting, the enjoyment of the moment of light and air. Although he later turned toward a Post-Impressionist style (see Chapter 5), Renoir never surpassed the beauty of this picture, which sums up visually the goal he once expressed in words: "The earth as the paradise of the gods, that is what I want to paint."

DEGAS. There could be no more complete opposite to Renoir than Hilaire Germain Edgar Degas (1834–1917).

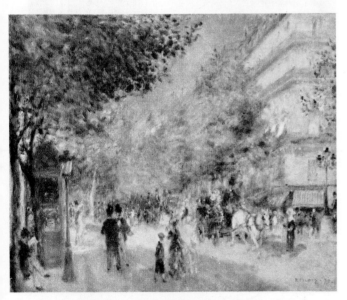

421. PIERRE AUGUSTE RENOIR. *Les Grands Boulevards.* 1875. Oil on canvas, 20½ x 25″. Collection Henry P. McIlhenny, Philadelphia

Although Degas exhibited with the Impressionists, he did not share their interest in landscape, and his version of their cult of instantaneity concerned itself solely with people, in a detached way; as a person, Degas was apt to be remote and difficult. His apparent haughtiness concealed a profound sense of his own limitations and a continuing reverence for the Old Masters. Partly Italian by ancestry, he made several trips to Italy, and both there and in the Louvre copied Italian paintings and, particularly, Italian drawings, including those of Pontormo (see Part Four, Chapter 4), not then generally appreciated. Taught by a disciple of Ingres, he was a deep admirer of the great Neoclassicist's linear perfection, and learned much from his analytic style. An amateur photographer himself, he studied the work of the British-American pioneer photographer Eadweard Muybridge (1830–1904), who collaborated with Eakins in an attempt to analyze accurately the motion of human beings and horses through photographs of stages of their actions.

Degas defined the goal of his own style succinctly as "bewitching the truth." There could be no more apt phrase for his art, at once brilliantly real and magically beautiful. Like Monet, Degas worked in series; a subject that fascinated him, and that he explored for decades, was the dance. He had no interest in such allegorical groupings as those of Carpeaux (see fig. 390), but in real dancers and in every facet of their activities from their grueling workouts at the bar to their rehearsals and their triumphant performances. His dancers are never idealized; they are little, sometimes scrawny women in tulle skirts, either working hard to produce an illusion of exquisite lightness and ease or merely lounging about on stage, stretching, yawning, or scratching, as in *The Rehearsal*, of 1874 (fig. 422). The view of the stage is not that enjoyed by most of the audience, but is located far forward in a box at one side, giving an informal and diagonal aspect. Although Degas never adopted the Impressionist color fleck, this and all of his mature pictures were conceived according to the same principles of accidentality and instantaneity that govern Monet's *Gare Saint-Lazare.* Each painting is a kind of snapshot of a moment of action, with nothing edited out, not even the paunchy impresario at the right, his top hat down on his forehead and the back of the chair between his knees. The surfaces are indicated in soft, rather dry washes of tone over drawing of uncanny accuracy.

Like many artists of the last decades of the nineteenth century, Degas was fascinated by café life, including its seamier aspects. His *The Glass of Absinthe*, of 1876 (fig. 423), shows a sodden couple, beyond communication, merely tolerating each other's presence. Dominated by the central glass of milky green liqueur, the picture is a superb composition of apparently accidental diagonals in depth, composed of the tables, the bench, and even the diagonal relationship between the couple and their reflections in the mirror. The same kind of closed-in space, extending forward into that of the spectator in the manner

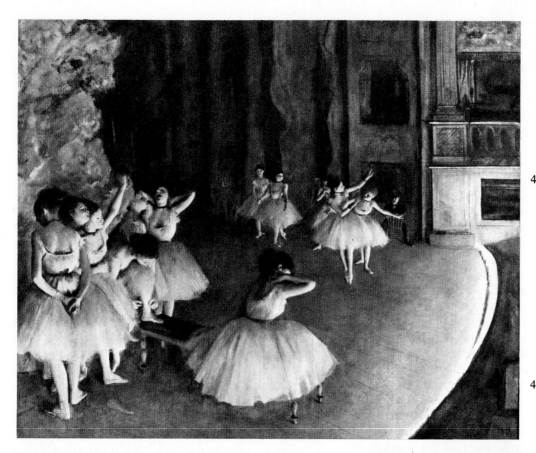

422. EDGAR DEGAS. *The Rehearsal.* 1874. Oil on canvas, 26 x 32¼". The Louvre, Paris

423. EDGAR DEGAS. *Glass of Absinthe.* 1876. Oil on canvas, 36¼ x 26¾". The Louvre, Paris

of Manet's *A Bar at the Folies-Bergère*, is exploited in *Two Laundresses* (fig. 424), of about 1884, one of a series. The exhausting pressure on the flatiron and the sleepiness of the workers in the steam of the stuffy interior are rendered with sovereign authority. Degas composes these figures as powerfully as had Courbet in his *The Stone Breakers* (see fig. 407), but with a more arresting immediacy.

In later life Degas made extensive use of the medium of pastel (powdered color compressed into sticks so it can be applied almost like chalk), which had been employed for delicate effects by French portraitists of the Rococo. Degas' experiments with this medium, combining it at times with water so it could be worked into a paste, and holding it to the paper surface with a special fixative varnish, gave him at once great resonance of color and bloomlike freshness. Casting aside all allusions to Classical poses (which linger on even in Courbet's *The Studio*, see fig. 408), he painted a strikingly original series of female nudes, seen, as he put it, "through a keyhole." To the disgust of the Parisians, whose taste in nudes had been nourished on Ingres and the Italian Renaissance tradition, he depicted "the human beast occupied with herself. Until now," he claimed, "the nude has always been represented in poses that presuppose an audience. But my women are simple, honest people, who have no other thought than their physical activity." *After the Bath*, of about 1889–90 (fig. 425), concentrates all the forces of the composition on the simple activity of drying

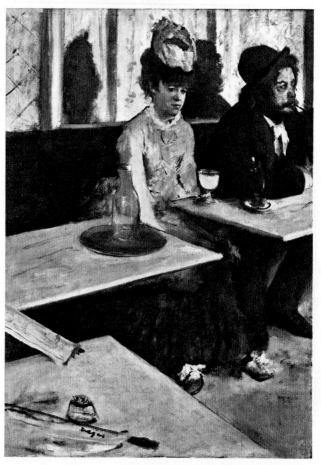

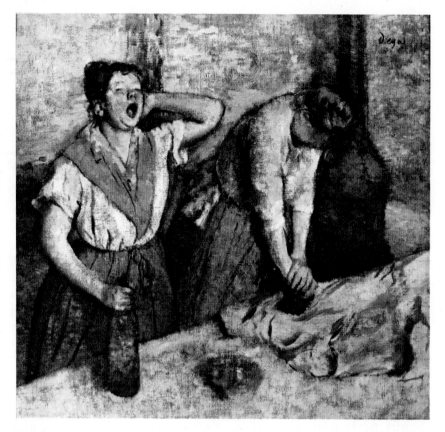

424. EDGAR DEGAS. *Two Laundresses.* c. 1884. Oil on canvas, 29⅞ x 32¼". The Louvre, Paris

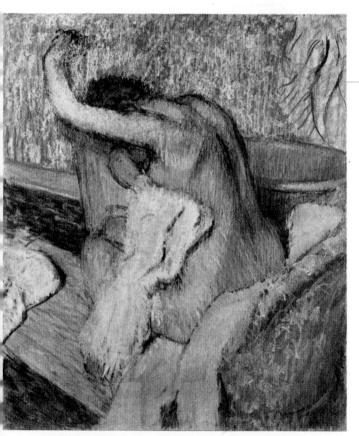

425. EDGAR DEGAS. *After the Bath.* c. 1889–90. Pastel and watercolor, 29⅛ x 22⅞". Courtauld Institute Galleries, University of London

oneself with a towel; not even the face is shown. Unclassical though the figure may at first sight appear in its proportions and attitudes, Renoir recognized the sculptural power of Degas' nudes when he said that one of them looked like a fragment from the sculptures of the Parthenon. Tragically, like Piero della Francesca (see Part Four, Chapter 1), an earlier apostle of the poetry of sight, Degas was destined to spend his last years in near blindness and inactivity. During World War I he caused his friends great anxiety by walking about the streets of Paris when he was scarcely able to find his way.

WHISTLER. The Impressionist movement attracted quite early the partial allegiance of a young American, James Abbott McNeill Whistler (1834–1903), who had been living in Paris since 1855. Whistler admired the work of Courbet in the famous Pavilion of Realism at the Universal Exhibition in that year (see Chapter 3). For a while he worked with Courbet, and came in contact with the major figures of the Impressionist movement. He never really joined the group, although his *Portrait of Thomas Carlyle: Arrangement in Gray and Black, No. 2* (fig. 426), painted in England in 1872 but first shown in Paris at the Salon of 1884, is still reminiscent of the flattened style of Manet. Whistler never emulated Manet's vigorous brushwork, however, but developed his own method of sensitive gradations and adjustments of tone. He was strongly influenced by Japanese prints, which Degas admired for their originality of viewpoint and subject, but whose systematic silhouetting was adopted only by Whistler.

In an ostensible attempt to win for art the freedom from natural resemblances always accorded to music, Whistler called his paintings harmonies, symphonies, nocturnes, or arrangements (*Arrangement in Gray and Black, No. 1* is actually the famous portrait of his mother). *Nocturne in Black and Gold: Falling Rocket* (fig. 427), painted in England about 1874 and exhibited there in 1876, was attacked in an article by the English critic John Ruskin—a supporter of "truth" in art and of craftsmanship in what he believed to be the medieval sense—as "a pot of paint [flung] in the public's face." Any apparent prophetic resemblance between this daring picture and the Abstract Expressionist works of the 1950s (see fig. 555, colorplate 78), especially the "drip style" of Jackson Pollock, however, is dismissed by the subtitle. In brilliant and witty testimony during a lawsuit he brought against Ruskin, Whistler claimed that his art was "divested from any outside sort of interest . . . an arrangement of line, form and color first." The last word in the sentence discloses its true substance, however, because even if Whistler felt that his pictures were arrangements *first*, there is nothing by his hand that is not at the same time thoroughly representational. He never attempted to break the tie connecting the work of art with the visual image of the object. Even the picture at

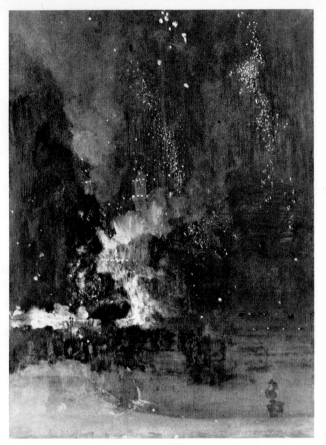

427. James Abbott McNeill Whistler. *Nocturne in Black and Gold: Falling Rocket*. c. 1874. Oil on panel, 23¾ x 18⅜". The Detroit Institute of Arts

issue is in fact a realistic portrayal of the clouds of sparks from a falling rocket, as much the record of an instantaneous impression as the railway stations of Monet or the ballet dancers of Degas.

RODIN. During the eighteenth and nineteenth centuries, sculpture had lagged behind both painting and architecture as a medium of artistic expression. Among all the sculptors of this period the only one who could be compared in quality with his contemporaries among the painters was Houdon. Nonetheless, public squares throughout Europe and America were populated by large-scale monuments, topped by galloping generals or frock-coated dignitaries, and loaded with allegorical figures and attributes, supplying in sheer volume what they too often lacked in aesthetic interest or even good taste. The most original sculptor of the mid-nineteenth century was the painter Daumier, whose little caricatures in clay were hardly known before his death, and only afterward evaluated and cast in bronze. Likewise, Degas produced hundreds of small sculptures of figures in action poses, few of which were known in his day. It would hardly seem likely that Impressionism, in its beginnings so strongly opposed to form—in fact dissolving it utterly in the paintings of Monet, Renoir, and Pissarro—could possibly be accompanied by a comparable current in sculpture, seemingly by definition the art of form. Yet a backward glance at the history of sculpture, particularly

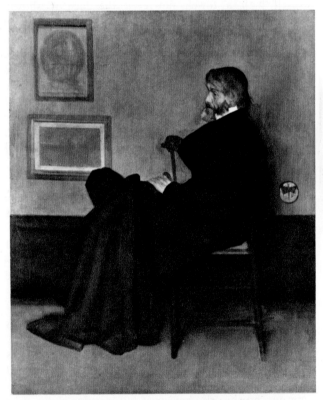

426. James Abbott McNeill Whistler. *Portrait of Thomas Carlyle: Arrangement in Gray and Black, No. 2*. 1872. Oil on canvas, 67⅜ x 56½". Glasgow Art Gallery and Museum

during the Hellenistic period, the Early Renaissance, and the Baroque, shows that at moments sculpture could and did rival the effects of painting without sacrificing quality.

It should not, therefore, be surprising that the first sculptor of universal importance since Bernini, Auguste Rodin (1840–1917), would be able to parallel the basic principles of Impressionism—accidentality and immediacy—in masterpieces of a sculptural power not seen since Michelangelo. In fact, Rodin is one of the few truly great sculptors of Western tradition since the Middle Ages (in addition to the two just named, one would have to count Donatello and Claus Sluter and, in the twentieth century, Brancusi). Yet although Rodin had single-handedly revived sculpture as a leading art, his style was so strongly personal that he attracted no major followers. All the leading sculptors of the early twentieth century moved in directions opposed to those he had so thoroughly explored.

Impressionist subject matter (chiefly landscape or cityscape seen in light) and technique (the floating spot of pure color) were, of course, denied to sculpture. Rodin

428. AUGUSTE RODIN. *The Age of Bronze.* 1876. Bronze, height 71″. The Minneapolis Institute of Arts. John R. Van Derlip Fund

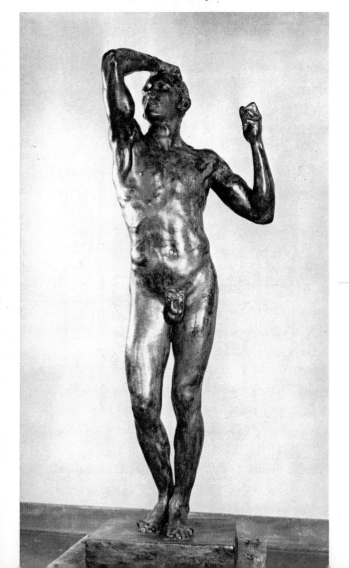

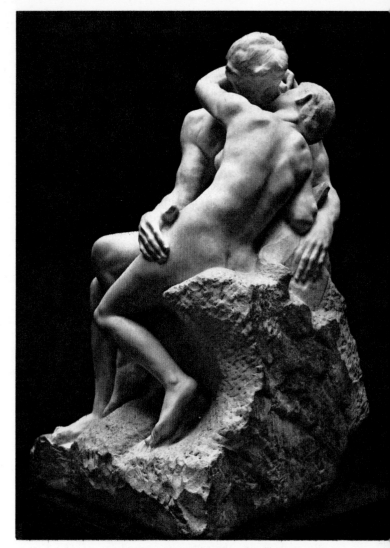

429. AUGUSTE RODIN. *The Kiss.* 1886. Marble, over-lifesize. Musée Rodin, Paris

was almost exclusively concerned with the human figure. Like those few Impressionist painters who treated the figure, he saw it in action and in light, but unlike them in moments of great physical and emotional stress. He is, therefore, closely related to both Donatello and Michelangelo, whose works he studied with a passion, and whose expressive intensity he was the first sculptor of modern times to revive and the only one to rival. His art was always controversial. At the Salon of 1877 he exhibited *The Age of Bronze* (fig. 428), a superb statue he had created the preceding year. Its realism as compared to the idealized nudes then found palatable, produced a storm of indignation and the accusation that he had passed off a cast from a living figure as an original work. (Interestingly enough, this was actually done in the late twentieth century with no protest whatever; see fig. 556).

What Rodin had in fact done, and what he was to continue to do throughout his long career, was to experiment with transient poses and accidental effects, without predetermined compositions and often without preestablished meaning, much in the manner of Monet's paintings of railway stations and Degas' studies of dancers. In this instance he was modeling in clay from a young Belgian soldier of exceptionally harmonious physique, and had posed him with a pole in his left hand as a support, according to the custom of life classes, while his right rested on his head in an attitude reminiscent of Michelangelo's *Dying Slave* (see fig. 135) in reverse. He then noticed that by omitting the pole from his statue he left the figure in a state of unexplained tension, which, combined with the closed eyes and partly open mouth, seems to communicate some nameless anguish. Rodin thought up the mystifying title for the work only as it approached completion. In consequence no satisfying interpretation has ever been advanced.

The patches of clay, sometimes smoothed, sometimes left rough, produce in the final bronze a shimmer that is the sculptural counterpart of Monet's sunlight effects. Rodin found that he could similarly exploit the luminous properties of marble, as in *The Kiss*, of 1886 (fig. 429), whose first version dates from 1880–82. In the nineteenth century the actual cutting of marble was done by stonecutters, working from plaster casts of the sculptor's original models in clay. Rodin was fascinated by the unfinished portions of many of Michelangelo's statues (see fig. 131), and stopped the stonecutter when he found a roughly carved mass that had expressive possibilities. Generally, but not always, he finished the smooth portions himself, avoiding both Michelangelo's sharp undercuttings and high polish. He preferred a softly blurred surface in the manner of Desiderio da Settignano (see fig. 70), so that light, absorbed and reflected by the crystals of the marble, would create a glow around the figures, analogous to the atmospheric effects of Impressionism. By such means the sensuous immediacy of *The Kiss* is greatly intensified.

This and many other statues in marble and bronze by Rodin originated in a large-scale commission he received in 1880 for the doors of the Museum of Decorative Arts in Paris. Still unfinished at the sculptor's death, the *Gates of Hell* (fig. 430)—an obvious counterpart to Ghiberti's *Gates of Paradise* (see figs. 47, 48)—is the most ambitious sculptural composition of the nineteenth century, and one of the great imaginative conceptions of modern times. In its cosmic scope the work was clearly indebted to Michelangelo's *Last Judgment* (see fig. 181) and to Rubens' *Fall of the Damned* (see fig. 286). Rodin admits us to a world of flame and smoke, through whose gusts tormented spirits are propelled in poses and groups of the greatest originality and expressive power. Always intensely interested in the figure in motion, Rodin used to ask his models to move at random through his studio, running, jumping, squatting as they wished; when he spotted an unusual attitude, he would signal for an immediate freeze, and then capture the essence of the pose in a few split-second lines and touches of wash. Many of the startling poses in the *Gates of Hell* originated in this manner.

Revolted by the (to him) hypocritical conventionality of most nineteenth-century commemorative sculpture, Rodin tried to make his monuments as arresting and immediate as possible. *The Burghers of Calais* (fig. 431) was commissioned in 1884 as a memorial to the six heroic citizens who in 1347 came before the conquering King Edward III of England in sackcloth with halters around their necks, offering their own lives that the city might be spared. The work, finished two years later, after arduous labors, is a testament to Rodin's greatness as a bronze sculptor. The roughness of the drapery surfaces is masterfully exploited, in heavy folds and masses, against which the twisted gestures, taut limbs, and tragic faces communicate heroism, self-sacrifice, and the fear and inevitability of death. No sculptural figures of such rugged honesty had been created since Donatello's *Lo Zuccone* (see fig. 41). The apparent accidentality of the grouping, nonetheless, builds up to noble masses from every point of view. It is typical of the expressive intent of Rodin, as well as the immediacy of Impressionist art in general, that he wanted the monument to be placed at street level among the cobblestones so that the observer could participate as directly as possible in the emotional and physical tensions of the figures. Rodin's wishes, at first disregarded, were finally carried out in 1924.

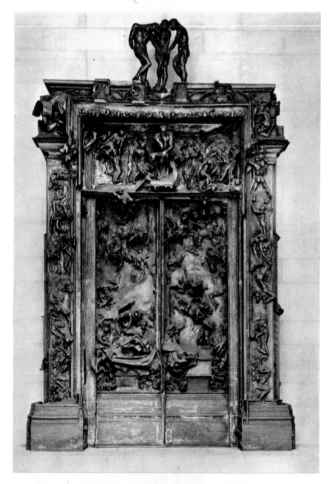

430. AUGUSTE RODIN. *Gates of Hell.* 1880–1917.
Bronze, 18 x 12'. Rodin Museum, Philadelphia

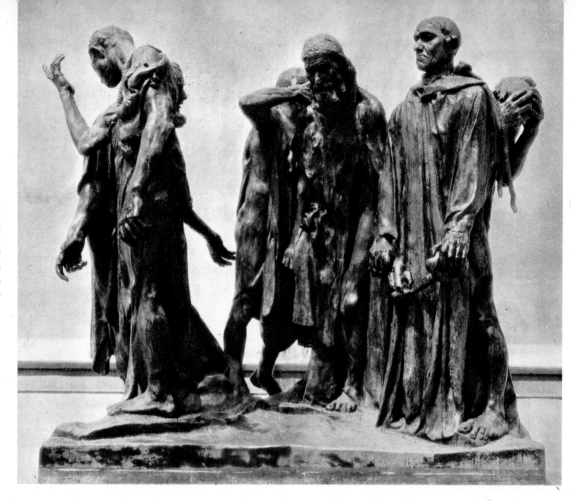

431. AUGUSTE RODIN. *The Burghers of Calais.* 1884–86. Bronze, 82½ x 95 x 78". Hirshhorn Museum and Sculpture Garden, Smithsonian Institution, Washington, D.C.

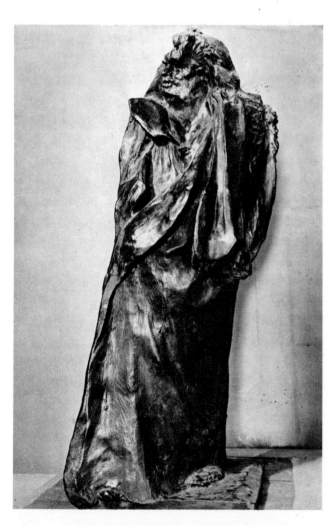

Few of Rodin's monuments reached completion, and some were rejected by the patrons, including one of his greatest late works, the *Balzac* of 1893–97 (fig. 432), not actually set up, at a Paris intersection, until 1939. Condemned as a menhir, the statue is actually an attempt to convey in sculptural masses of the greatest harshness the intensity of the very moment of artistic creativity. Rodin has shown the great novelist wrapped in his bathrobe, stalking through his house as the characters of his novels have seized upon him like demons and possessed him utterly. The throes of creative emotion have never before or since been so convincingly portrayed, and the rude resulting form, with its drastic simplifications and distortions, brings Rodin to the brink of contemporary sculpture.

432. AUGUSTE RODIN. *Balzac.* 1893–97. Bronze, height 9'3". The Museum of Modern Art, New York

5

Post-Impressionism

During the 1870s Impressionism came as close to being a collective style as any in Western art since the Gothic. The painters met frequently in the evenings, first at the Café Guerbois and then at the Café de la Nouvelle-Athènes, exhibited together periodically, and as we have seen sometimes even worked side by side painting the same view under identical conditions of light and air. This happy state of affairs did not outlast the decade.

During the 1880s the Impressionist movement rapidly fell apart. The exhibitions continued, but one after another the original members ceased to send their paintings to the group shows. Renoir visited Italy and found a new stylistic direction based partly on his study of Raphael. Monet himself had come to realize that what he was really creating was a prolonged moment, the palimpsest of many similar moments—a horizontal

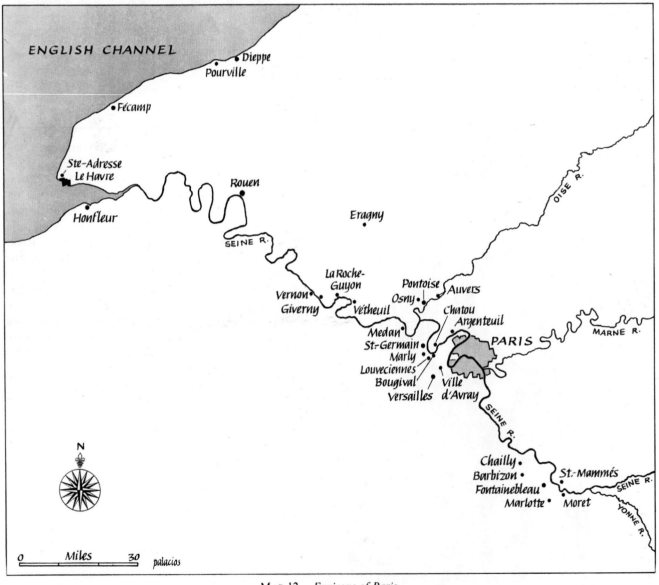

MAP 12. *Environs of Paris*

rather than a vertical section through the stream of time. One member of the original group, Cézanne, who had been considered by many a minor painter and whose works had been especially derided by the public at the Impressionist exhibitions and regularly refused at the Salons, dropped out of the Impressionist group even before the end of the 1870s—in fact, left Paris to work out a new style in isolation.

So indeed did others. The separate tendencies, which we now group loosely together under the general title of Post-Impressionism, had little in common save the derivation of all of them from the Impressionist aesthetic establishing the moment of the experience of light as the foundation of artistic vision. All retained the bright Impressionist palette and even to some extent the Impressionist color patches, although these acquired a new shape and a new function, in keeping with the personal artistic goal of each painter. In a negative sense, however, the Post-Impressionists were united in regarding Impressionism as too fugitive in its aspirations to achieve an art of lasting value. Each Post-Impressionist artist created a sharply individual style, which could no longer be mistaken for that of any of his contemporaries or former associates, in subject matter, content, or technique.

Among the variety of Post-Impressionist styles we can distinguish two major tendencies. One, led by Cézanne and Seurat, sought permanence of form; the other, represented chiefly by Van Gogh and Gauguin, gave primacy to emotional or sensuous expression. Both worked first of all with color. These two trends may be considered in a sense as heirs, respectively, of Neoclassicism and Romanticism, which had divided the first half of the nineteenth century into opposite and hostile camps. Among innovating artists there was no true equivalent for Realism, the third nineteenth-century tendency, which became a stylistic backwater. Instead, a new art arose here and there that owed little or nothing to Impressionism, but aimed at liberating fantasy from the shackles of realistic observation. From these three general trends, clearly distinguishable by the late 1880s, spring the principal currents of twentieth-century art.

CÉZANNE. The leading painter of the late nineteenth century in France, indeed one of the most powerful artists in the history of Western painting, was Paul Cézanne (1839–1906). Son of a prosperous banker in the southern French city of Aix-en-Provence, Cézanne experienced none of the financial difficulties that plagued Monet and Renoir during the formative period of Impressionism. He received some artistic training in Aix, and although he arrived in Paris for the first time in 1861, he never set up permanent residence there; after visits of varying duration, he always returned to his Provençal home. At first he was interested in the official art of the Salons, but soon achieved an understanding of Delacroix and Courbet, and before long of Manet as well. His early works are still Romantic, thickly painted in a palette limited to black, white, tans, and grays, and an oc-

casional touch of bright color. Not until the early 1870s, during two years spent at Pontoise and Auvers, in the Île-de-France not far from Paris, did he adopt the Impressionist palette, viewpoint, and subject matter under the tutelage of Pissarro. He showed at the first Impressionist exhibition in 1874 at Nadar's and at the third in 1877. Only in 1882 was one of his paintings exhibited at the Salon.

During most of his independent career, save for visits to Paris, its environs, and to the Mediterranean village of L'Estaque, as well as a trip to Switzerland, Cézanne remained in Aix. His isolation from other artists he considered essential for his intense concentration on the formation of a new style of painting. His great pictorial achievements date from those lonely middle and later years. His mature style is often interpreted in the light of two celebrated sayings: "I want to do Poussin over again, from nature," and "I wish to make of Impressionism something solid and durable, like the art of the museums." Less often quoted but equally important is his remark to the painter Emile Bernard: "Drawing and color are not distinct . . . . The secret of drawing and modeling lies in contrasts and relations of tones."

Among the subjects Cézanne studied repeatedly was Mont Sainte-Victoire, the rugged mass that dominates the plain of Aix. The version illustrated (fig. 433) was painted about 1885–87. In contrast to the momentary glimpses Monet was painting, none of Cézanne's landscapes indicate the time of day or even the season. In this he was assisted by the fact that in Provence there are many evergreens and winter wheat is green in December. It neither rains nor snows in his landscapes, and there are seldom any recognizable clouds. Time is defeated by permanence, even in the subject. In this picture Cézanne has not even informed us clearly where we stand. A bit of rock in the foreground could be near or at a little distance. We do not know where the tree is rooted. At no point in the picture are objects described even as much as in a Monet. Some objects are identifiable as houses, trees, fields, and the arches of a viaduct, but Cézanne's visual threshold is high, and below that level nothing is defined. The effect of durability and massiveness is produced by a new use of the Impressionist color spots. These assume in his art definite directions, either horizontal, vertical, or diagonal, and are grouped to form planes. The planes, in turn, are used to bound the smaller masses, even the facets of the tree trunk and the passages of white and blue in the sky. The landscape becomes a colossal rock crystal of color—a cubic cross section of the world, as it were, its foreground and background planes established by the branches and by the mountain whose rhythms they echo, its floor by the valley, its ceiling by the sky. The constituent planes embrace an astonishing variety of subtly differentiated hues of blue, green, yellow, rose, and violet, and it is the delicate differentiation between these hues that produce the impression of three-dimensional form.

To put it simply, Cézanne has used to construct form

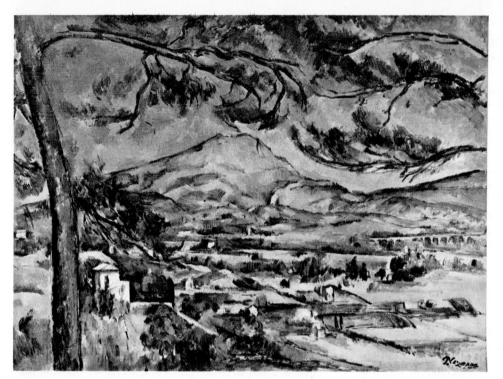

433. PAUL CÉZANNE. *Mont Sainte-Victoire*. 1885–87. Oil on canvas, 25½ x 32". Courtauld Institute Galleries, University of London

the very color patch the Impressionists had employed ten years before to dissolve it. He has indeed achieved from nature a construction and intellectual organization analogous to that Poussin had derived from the organization of figures, and made of Impressionism something durable, reminding us inevitably of the stable world of Piero della Francesca (see colorplates 10, 11, figs. 65, 66) and even of the airless backgrounds of Giotto (see colorplate 2, fig. 8). In so doing, however, he has created a world remote from human experience. A road appears for a few yards, but we cannot walk on it; there are houses, but few windows. There are in fact no people, animals, or birds in Cézanne's landscapes, nor any moving thing. The beauty of his color constructions is abstract, and it is no wonder that many artists of the early twentieth century, especially the Cubists, claimed him as the father of modern art.

Still life was to Cézanne second only to landscape, the principal subject for his analyses of form through color, for his drawing and modeling in contrasts and

434. PAUL CÉZANNE. *Still Life with Apples and Oranges.* 1895–1900. Oil on canvas, 28¾ x 36¼". The Louvre, Paris

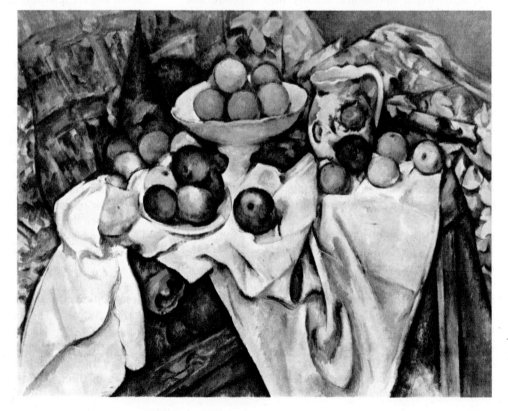

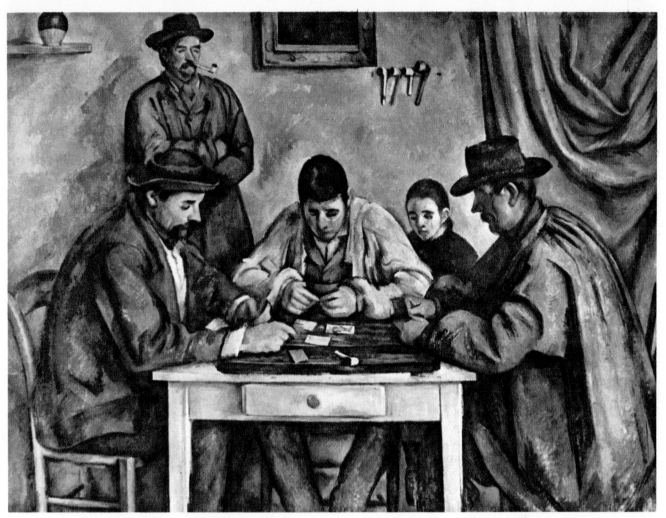

435. PAUL CÉZANNE. *Card Players.* c. 1890-92. Oil on canvas, 52¾ x 71¼". © The Barnes Foundation, 1976, Merion Station, Pennsylvania

relationships of tones. They owe little to Dutch still lifes (see fig. 299) or to those of Chardin (see fig. 331). *Still Life with Apples and Oranges* was painted between 1895 and 1900 (fig. 434). His arrangements of fruits, bottles, plates, and a rumpled cloth on a tabletop never suggest the consumption of food or drink; they are spheroid or cylindrical masses, and the planes of color that build them up are solely responsible for their revolution in depth. Often the appearance of reality is neglected; the table, for example, has a tendency to disappear under the tablecloth at one level and emerge from it at another, and the two sides of a bottle or a carafe can be sharply different. Whether Cézanne did not notice such discrepancies in his search for just the right color to make a form go round in depth, or whether he decided on deformations consciously in the interests of abstract relationships of design, has never been convincingly determined. What is certain is that he cared for the subject only as arrangements of form and color. His procedure was so time-consuming that apples and oranges began to rot before a painting could be completed, and had to be replaced by wax ones.

For his rare figure pieces, Cézanne chose during the 1890s—the great decade for his classical constructions of pure form—subjects as quiet, impersonal, and remote as his still lifes. The *Card Players,* of about 1890–92 (fig. 435), shows three men, two of whom are clad in the blue smock of the farmer or country laborer, sitting around a table, while a fourth gazes downward, arms folded. The card game had been a favorite subject among the followers of Caravaggio, and was usually set forth dramatically with strong light-and-dark contrasts underscoring suspicious expressions; one player is often shown cheating. Nothing could be farther from Cézanne's timeless and immobile scene, which recalls in its symmetrical disposition parallel to the picture plane Rembrandt's *Supper at Emmaus* (see fig. 308). The quiet figures contemplate the cards, themselves (like Cézanne's paintings) planes of color on white surfaces. No expression can be distinguished; the downcast eyes are mere planes of color. The Giotto-like tubular folds of the smock of the man on the right echo in reverse those of the hanging curtain, locking foreground and background in a single construction. Yet the background wall fluctuates at an indeterminable distance like the sky in one of Cézanne's landscapes, and the pipes on their rack seem to float against it. These perfect constructions of Cézanne's maturity were painted very lightly as compared to the heavy pigment of his early Romantic style; the planes are indicated in veils of color so thin as to be almost transparent.

The full beauty of Cézanne's developed style is seen in his *Woman with the Coffeepot*, of about 1895 (colorplate 58). Cézanne's planes of varying hues of blue and blue-violet have built majestic cylinders from the arms and a fluted column from the body. Yet even at this most classical moment of Cézanne's career stability is something imposed by his demand for total coherence upon a fundamentally unstable arrangement. For example, the door panels in the background tilt slightly to the left, compensating for the turn of the head toward the right, and the placing of the coffeepot and cup. So exquisitely are these adjustments calculated that the removal of any element deals the whole picture a fatal blow. The reader can experiment with this principle by covering up the coffeepot and cup, whose blue-and-white cylinders are an indispensable element in the whole, toward which the movement of all the planes is directed. Beautiful as its elements still are, the composition loses something essential. It will be noticed that any small section of the picture contains the same blues, whites, and rose tones as the painting as a whole, although in different arrangements and different gradations. The rose of the woman's cheeks, for example, turns up in her skirt and in the door, while the blue of the dress is reflected throughout the painting. Cézanne's search for the exact plane of color to fit into his structure at any given point was so precise that at times the plane eluded him. Here and there in the hands and in the dress, for in-stance, some of the white priming shows through. Surprising elements are the mysteriously vertical spoon, and the cylinders of cup and pot, definitely out of drawing.

Toward the very end of his life, Cézanne's development toward abstraction became more and more evident. The large *Bathers*, of 1898–1905 (fig. 436), is the culmination of a series of nude compositions that had occupied Cézanne's imagination again and again. These nudes were never painted from life, nor in the open air. The subject, of course, is as unlikely as that of the bubbly *Bathers* of Fragonard (see colorplate 47), of which this carefully constructed picture is the exact opposite. Women in the eighteenth and nineteenth centuries did not bathe naked in streams and sun themselves on the banks. But the fantasy gave Cézanne the materials with which to build a grand imaginary architecture, composed of strikingly simplified figures, overarching tree trunks, blue sky, and white clouds—a modern cathedral of light and color. Many areas of the figures are still in the white priming stage, because Cézanne had not yet found the right planes of color. But it is safe to say that even if he had, the bold, sometimes multiple contour lines of the figures and heads would have remained as schematic as they now are; features are suppressed and mouths omitted entirely so as not to break the ovoid forms of the heads. Within the context of Impressionist accidentality—the women are, after all, strewn about in relaxed poses, or engaged in spreading a luncheon cloth on the ground—the figures are organized as closely as any in a composition by Poussin (cf. colorplate 39). The end result, perhaps as much to Cézanne's surprise as to our own, is a simplification of the human figure that had not been seen since the sculpture of Romanesque portals.

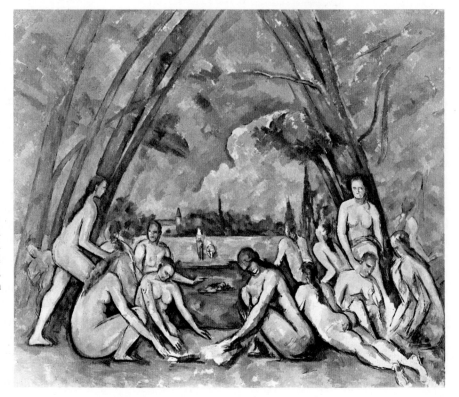

436. PAUL CÉZANNE. *Bathers.* 1898–1905. Oil on canvas, 82 x 98". Philadelphia Museum of Art. The W. P. Wilstach Collection

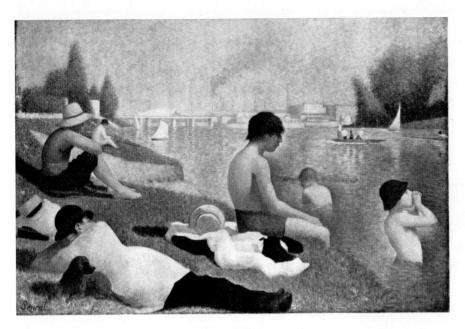

437. GEORGES SEURAT. *Bathers at Asnières.*
1883–84. Oil on canvas, 79⅛ x 9'10⅛".
The Tate Gallery, London

SEURAT AND NEOIMPRESSIONISM. While Cézanne was pursuing his lonely search for a new monumentality based on Impressionist discoveries, a younger but almost equally gifted painter, Georges Pierre Seurat (1859–91), was working toward similar goals but with radically different methods and results. During his tragically brief career (he died before reaching thirty-two, at an earlier age than any other major painter in the Western tradition save Masaccio), Seurat attempted to embody in a quasi-scientific style the results of his close study of Delacroix's theory and of the research of Chevreul (see pages 357, 358), as well as that of Hermann von Helmholz and Ogden N. Rood, into the physical nature of color and the chromatic structure of light.

His first major achievement in this direction was the *Bathers at Asnieres,* of 1883–84 (fig. 437), which shows still another possibility for the traditional bather composition. This is not an ideal bathing scene, like those of Cézanne, but a real one, taking place along the Seine just to the northwest of Paris, with working-class people in the foreground and boats, a bridge, and factory chimneys in the background. The picture is as completely dedicated to the enjoyment of sunlight as any by Monet. But instead of that master's instantaneity, it communicates a mood of quiet permanence, and has often been compared in this respect to the calm compositions of Piero della Francesca (see colorplates 10, 11, figs. 65, 66), whom Seurat admired, although he could have known the originals only from photographs and copies. He prepared for this composition by careful preliminary figure drawings done in conté crayon, a rich black drawing stick that, rubbed on roughgrained white paper, gives a luminous effect, and by tiny color sketches on wood panels, which look very like Impressionist paintings in their immediacy and brightness.

The final picture, however, painted in the studio in a return to traditional practice, achieves a kind of compositional grandeur absent from French painting between David and Cézanne. In contrast to the style of Monet, Renoir, and Pissarro, contours are strongly in evidence, very simple ones, outlining forms reduced to the appearance of cylinders or spheroids. These are not the drawn lines one finds in some late Cézannes, but rather hard, clear edges between darker and lighter areas. Along these edges contrasts of color and light and shade intensify abruptly, as happens in nature and can be verified in photographs. Even in the black-and-white illustration in conté crayon it can be seen that the water becomes lighter near the shadowed side of a figure and darker near the lighter one. In the original these are changes of hue as well as of value. Within the firm, unbroken contours, which establish a dense pattern of masses and spaces, the brushstrokes resemble a slow, methodical stippling of the surface rather than the quick strokes of the Impressionists. Also, each touch of the brush represents a separate color, set down at full intensity and contrasting with its neighbor to mix not on the palette but in the eye. This effect, drawn from the scientist's analysis of light, was called divisionism by Seurat's friend Paul Signac. The method won for Seurat and his associates the title of Neoimpressionists. It has been pointed out by Meyer Schapiro that the extraordinary sense of restful horizontality in this picture is produced partly by psychological means. The few actual horizontals in the background are reinforced by the implied horizontal gazes of the figures, although in only two cases is an eye actually indicated.

In many ways the culmination of Seurat's mature style is the huge *Sunday Afternoon on the Island of La Grande Jatte* (colorplate 59), on which Seurat worked from 1884–86. About forty preliminary color studies were necessary, all done outdoors. On the basis of these accurate studies and his thorough, scientific knowledge of color, Seurat was able to paint the magically sunny picture not only in his studio but also at night, by gaslight. When it was first

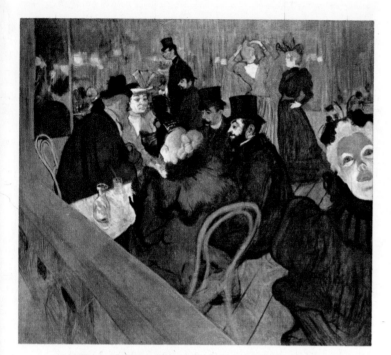

438. HENRI DE TOULOUSE-LAUTREC. *At the Moulin Rouge.*
1892. Oil on canvas, 48⅜ x 55¼". The Art Institute
of Chicago. Helen Birch Bartlett Memorial Collection

shown at the eighth and last Impressionist exhibition in
1886, the work was denounced by some critics and
praised by others as being "Egyptian." The customary
Impressionist theme is indeed treated with almost Egyptian formalism and rigidity. The foreground figures are
arranged as if in a frieze, but their movement back in
depth on the sunny lawn, with light and shadow coor-
dinated with the cylindrical figures, recalls the Italian
Quattrocento, especially the space of Masaccio, Uccello,
and again Piero della Francesca (see colorplates 10, 11,
figs. 65, 66). In his own theoretical way Seurat has done
just what Cézanne was doing empirically—he has converted Impressionism into something as durable as the
art of the museums.

By now, however, his divided touch has become
systematized into tiny round particles, which are generally and not inaccurately compared to the tesserae of
Classical and medieval mosaics. Although Seurat could
not have known even of the existence of the Sinai mosaic,
it is interesting how strong an analogy his simplification
of form and his analysis of light bear to that early Byzantine work. Each patch of light, each area of shadow, is
composed of countless such particles, of almost identical
size and shape. From close up, their colors appear absolutely pure, the quality of shading or color transition
being controlled by the numerical proportion of colors of
varying value or hue. Although these are intended to mix
in the observer's eye, the mixture is never complete, and
the little spots retain their autonomy, like the notes in
music, giving the picture even at a distance a grainy texture. The mock solemnity of Seurat's composition is
lightened by many touches of wit and whimsy, such as the

details of costumes and accessories, and the drama
between the pug-dog and the ringtail monkey at the lower
right. It is amazing that a revolutionary work of such
skill and brilliance could have been completed by Seurat
at the age of only twenty-seven. The history of modern
painting might well have been different had he lived an
ordinary life-span. As it was, even Pissarro, the oldest of
the Impressionists, was for a while won over by the style
of this twenty-nine-years-younger genius, and joined the
Neoimpressionists; the art of the Fauve painters in the
early twentieth century (see Chapter 6) was profoundly
indebted to Seurat's discoveries.

TOULOUSE-LAUTREC. A maverick on the Parisian art
scene at the end of the century was Henri de Toulouse-
Lautrec (1864–1901). Born to one of the oldest noble
families in France, he broke both legs in early
adolescence, and they never developed properly. For the
rest of his brief existence he remained a dwarf, alienated
from his family's fashionable life. He learned to paint,
and took refuge in the night life of Paris, which he
depicted with consummate skill—scenes of cafés,
theaters, and cabarets, and even a witty series of bordello
interiors to set against the poplars and cathedrals of
Monet. All of his portrayals are prompted by the same
uncritical acceptance of the facts of Parisian night life
that he wished for his own deformity and found only in
this shadowy world. *At the Moulin Rouge*, of 1892 (fig.
438), was strongly influenced by Degas, whom he deeply
admired (see especially fig. 423). Toulouse-Lautrec's line
was sure, almost as much so as that of his idol, but his
tolerant humanity was entirely his own. The little artist
can be made out toward the top of the picture in profile,
alongside his towering cousin and constant companion. It
is significant that, to reinforce the psychological impact
of the picture, Toulouse-Lautrec extended it on all four
sides, particularly at the bottom and at the right. The
plunging perspective of a balustrade in the added section
pushes the little group huddled about the table into the
middle distance, while it forces toward us with startling
intensity the face of a heavily powdered entertainer, so
lighted from below that the shadows are green. Toulouse-
Lautrec's smart and vivid drawing style, his brilliant
patterning, and his surprising color contrasts were the
dominant influence in Paris when in 1900, eight years
after this picture was painted, the young Pablo Picasso
arrived from Spain.

GAUGUIN. A more imaginative but often unequal
approach to the problems of a new art was that of Paul
Gauguin (1848–1903). Although without formal artistic
training, this successful businessman became intensely
interested in art, and began painting as an amateur.
Under strong influence from Pissarro, he rapidly absorbed Impressionist ideas and techniques, and from
1879 to the last Impressionist exhibition in 1886 exhibited regularly with the group. In 1881 he came in contact with Cézanne, and bought some of the great

painter's work. But there was a streak of the drifter in Gauguin, and rapidly, to the great gain of art but the consternation of his family, this tendency became dominant. He was partly of Peruvian (Indian) extraction, had spent four years of his childhood in Peru, six years of his youth as a sailor, and was incurably drawn to the exotic and the faraway.

Gradually, painting itself became identified with his wanderlust, and drew him away from all his daily associations. In 1883 he gave up his business career, and in 1885 he abandoned his wife, his children, and his bourgeois existence to devote his life to art. Convinced that European urban civilization and all its works were incurably sick, he spent less and less time in Paris. Henceforward, his life was nomadic; he moved back and forth between villages in Brittany (because it was the most remote and "backward" of French regions), the island of Martinique, Brittany again, Arles (where for a brief and stormy period he lived with Van Gogh), Brittany for a third time, Tahiti, Brittany for a fourth time, Tahiti again, and finally—impoverished, terminally ill, and in trouble with the law—the Marquesas Islands, where he died.

Gauguin's departure from Western artistic tradition was prompted by the same rebellious attitude that impelled his break from middle-class life. He renounced not only the instantaneity and formlessness of Impressionist vision but also Western devotion to naturalistic effects, which had been carried to its final flowering in Impressionism. Instead, he recommended a return to archaic and, for the first time in the history of art, "primitive" styles as the only refuge for art. What he sought, however, was still immediacy of experience, but intensified. "A powerful sensation," he said, "may be translated with immediacy; dream on it and seek its simplest form." This is just what Gauguin did in his brilliant *Vision After the Sermon* (fig. 439), painted in 1888 during his second stay in Brittany. In the background Jacob is shown wrestling with the angel (Gen. 32: 22–31). It has recently been demonstrated that this event forms the lesson in the Breton rite for the eighth Sunday after Trinity (August 5 in 1888). On the preceding day took place the blessing of horned beasts, followed by wrestling contests and a procession with red banners, and at night fireworks, a bonfire that turned the fields red with its glow, and an angel descending from the church tower.

Gauguin has shown in the foreground at the extreme right the head of a priest, and next it those of praying women in Breton costume, whose vision fuses the events of the preceding day and night with the lesson on Sunday morning. The apparently arbitrary intense red of the ground is an immediate translation, in Gauguin's terms, of the powerful sensations of the folk festival. Although the figures are outlined with the clarity that Gauguin derived from his study of Oriental, medieval, and primitive arts, the contrast between the large foreground

heads and the sharply smaller groups in the distance still presupposes Western perspective, and is drawn from theater subjects developed by Daumier, Degas, Renoir, and Toulouse-Lautrec.

In Oceania Gauguin was influenced only to a limited degree by the art of the natives with whom he lived (see Vol. 1, Part One, Chapter 5). In point of fact, he took his flattened style with its emphasis on brilliant color to the South Seas with him, and fitted into it the people whose folkways and personalities attracted him. The accidental attitudes in which he drew and painted them still derive from Impressionist vision. In *The Day of the God*, for instance (colorplate 60), painted in 1894, a happy nude woman and her two children relax at the water's edge, below the towering image of the god in the background. But while the poses are free in the Western tradition, the contours have been restored, as continuous and unbroken as in Egyptian or Archaic Greek art. And the contour is brilliant, arbitrary, and intense, bearing in the free-form shapes seen in the water in the foreground little or no relationship to visible reality. Just before his death, Gauguin said, "I wanted to establish the right to dare everything . . . . The public owes me nothing, since my pictorial *oeuvre* is but relatively good; but the painters who today profit from this liberty owe me something." So indeed they did, especially Matisse and the Fauves (see Chapter 6), but no more than Cubism and abstract movements since owe to the pioneer researches of Cézanne.

VAN GOGH. It is with a special reverence that one approaches the art of Vincent van Gogh (1853–90), as surely the champion of those late nineteenth-century artists who identified art with emotion as Cézanne was the

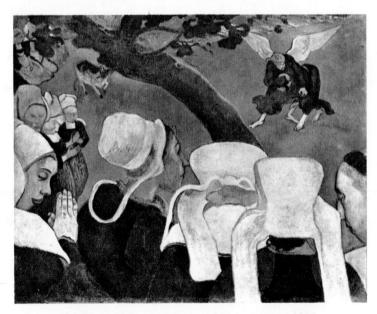

439. PAUL GAUGUIN. *Vision After the Sermon.* 1888. Oil on canvas, 28¾ x 36¼". National Gallery of Scotland, Edinburgh

leader of those who sought spiritual ultimates in form. The son of a Protestant Dutch minister, the young Van Gogh was by turns the employee of a firm of art dealers in The Hague, London, and Paris; a language teacher in Ramsgate and Isleworth, England; a student of practical evangelism in Brussels; and a missionary to the downtrodden coal miners of a village in southern Belgium. Through these fragmentary careers, and indeed through his personal relationships, including several impossible love affairs and his disastrous friendship with Gauguin, runs the same theme—a love of humanity, of life, and of things, whose inevitable corollary was a sense of failure and betrayal. This love was the theme of his art as well, and was to produce one of the most intensely personal witnesses in the spiritual history of mankind. Even Van Gogh's mental illness, severe enough to bring about his frequent hospitalization and his untimely death, did not prevent him from becoming the only Dutch painter whose stature could set him on a level with the three great Dutch masters of the seventeenth century (see Part Five, Chapter 5).

Van Gogh's earliest drawings and paintings date from his association with the Belgian miners and from a later stay among the peasants of northern Holland. Only in 1881 did he embark on formal study of art, but remained in a somewhat provincial Dutch tradition, out of touch with the new coloristic discoveries of Impressionism. In 1886 he came to Paris for a two-year stay with his brother Theo, and under the joint influences of Impressionism and Japanese prints freed his palette and worked out a fresh, new sense of pattern in contour not unrelated to Seurat, but already highly original. Having shown

signs of depression and emotional instability, he left the North early in 1888, hoping to find a happier and more healthful existence at Arles, in Provence (not far from Cézanne's home at Aix, although there seems to have been no contact between these two great masters of Post-Impressionism). During the next two years, which were all that remained of life to Van Gogh, he painted at white heat—often a canvas a day—his series of masterpieces in a style without precedent in European art. He showed little interest in the Roman and Romanesque antiquities of Arles, but was enraptured by the beauty of the landscape and above all by the clear southern light, utterly different from that of northern France with its mists and rain. Disturbingly, he noted that the intense sunlight could drive a man mad.

A superb example of this brief period of gladness is his *A View of La Crau* (fig. 440), painted in June, 1888, with its almost Renaissance perspective of fields and farms, a surprising revival of the principles that had been swept aside by the Impressionists and Gauguin. To Van Gogh, however, space construction became an expressive device, propelling the observer forcefully toward the distant mountains. The whole picture is colored in the red-gold and blue that were his own colors—hair, beard, and eyes (see fig. 442)—and whose dominance in his work invariably betokens at least temporary mental equilibrium. The thick pigment, blazing color, and strong, straight strokes are Van Gogh's personal transformation of Impressionist technique.

Alas, the happy period did not last long. In September of the same year, a month before the eagerly awaited arrival of Gauguin to share his house, Van Gogh painted

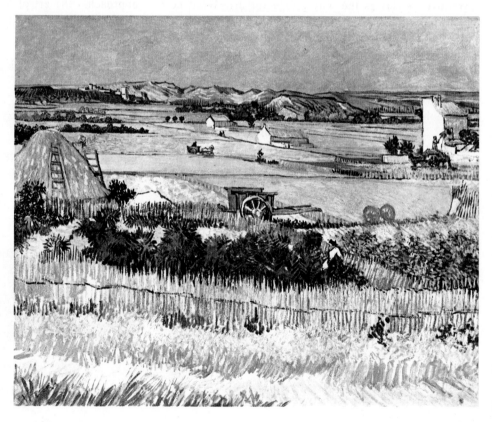

440. VINCENT VAN GOGH. *A View of La Crau.* 1888. Oil on canvas, 28½ x 36¼". Rijksumuseum Vincent van Gogh, Amsterdam

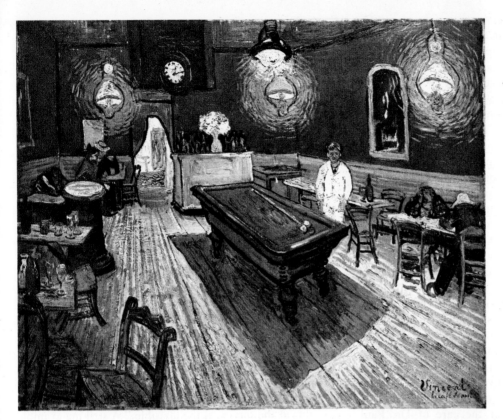

441. VINCENT VAN GOGH. *The Night Café.* 1888. Oil on canvas, 28½ x 36¼". Yale University Art Gallery, New Haven, Connecticut. Bequest of Stephen C. Clark

442. VINCENT VAN GOGH. *Self-Portrait.* 1889. Oil on canvas, 22½ x 17¼". Private collection, New York

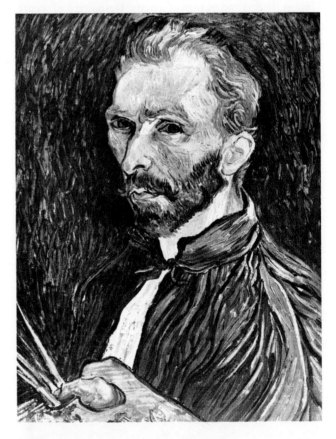

the first of his disturbing pictures, *The Night Café* (fig. 441), which cannot be better described than in Van Gogh's own words:

> I have tried to express the terrible passions of humanity by means of red and green.
>
> The room is blood red and dark yellow with a green billiard table in the middle; there are four lemon yellow lamps with a glow of orange and green. Everywhere there is a clash and contrast of the most alien reds and greens in the figures of little sleeping hooligans, in the empty dreary room . . . . The white coat of the *patron*, on vigil in a corner of this furnace, turns lemon yellow, or pale luminous green.
>
> I have tried to express the idea that the café is a place where one can ruin one's self, run mad or commit a crime. So I have tried to express as it were the powers of darkness in a low drink shop . . . .

The harsh green ceiling completes the fierce contrasts of the picture, and the perspective, used for such a happy effect in the *View of La Crau*, is here so strongly exaggerated that it seems to catapult the observer into the end wall, in which the red-and-green contrast is insoluble. In late December of the same year Van Gogh hurled a knife at Gauguin; then he cut off one of his own ears and gave it to a prostitute; consequently, Gauguin fled Arles. Cared for at first in the hospital at Arles, then in the asylum at nearby Saint-Rémy, he was allowed to paint, and produced some of his most beautiful and moving works. His *Self-Portrait* (fig. 442), painted in the asylum

in September, 1889, betrays the period of desperation through which the artist had passed. The brushstrokes are now curved, and vibrate intensely throughout the picture. In a mood of renewed confidence, the artist has again endowed the painting with his own physical coloring, and his ivory face, gold hair, and red-gold beard float in tides of ever deeper and more sonorous blue, carving out as it were a haven for the soul in the sky itself, the color of the artist's piercing eyes. Only in the greatest self-portraits of Rembrandt do we find such intense self-revelation, or such a triumph over sorrow.

In the fields near the asylum, by day or even at night, Van Gogh drew and painted the wonders of the earth and sky, for which he felt a kind of pantheistic reverence, no longer explicable in terms of conventional religion. Yet these pictures communicate a mood of self-identification with the infinite, which is the mark of religious ecstasy in Van Gogh as much as in the visions of the Counter-Reformation mystics (see Part Five, Chapter 1). In *The Starry Night* (colorplate 61), painted in June, 1889, he shows us not the stars he observed but exploding masses of gold fire, expanding against the blue. Two of these swirl through the sky in a kind of cosmic embrace, un-imagined by the denizens of the sleeping town below, but attainable through the intermediary of the dark-green cypresses that swirl upward into their visionary midst.

In May, 1890, Van Gogh went to Paris for a three-day stay with his brother, then to Auvers, which had sheltered many of the Impressionists and Post-Impressionists, where he placed himself under the care of Dr. Paul Gachet, friend and patron of artists. Despairing of a cure, he shot himself on July 27, and died two days later. For all the tragic circumstances of his life, Van Gogh won a spiritual victory in opening a new path to artistic vision and expression.

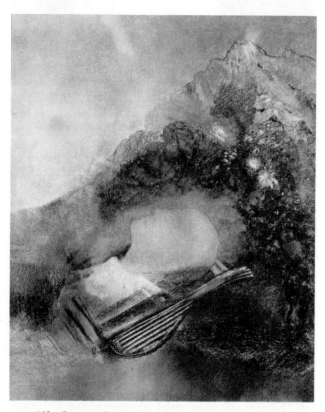

443. ODILON REDON. *Orpheus.* 1903. Pastel, 27½ x 22¼". The Cleveland Museum of Art. Gift of J. H. Wade

SYMBOLISM. As we have seen in the art of Gauguin and Van Gogh, the anti-Impressionist reaction of the 1880s was directed not only against the formlessness of Impressionism, which had disturbed Cézanne and Van Gogh, but also against its objectivity. A tendency to penetrate beyond the surface of visible reality into the world of folklore, mythology, fantasy, and dreams (beloved by many Romanticists) soon began to make its presence felt in the French art scene. The individual artists, and the shifting groups to which they belonged, can be loosely classified under the term Symbolism. A solitary apostle of this tendency—and in many ways the most gifted—was ODILON REDON (1840–1916), whose activity parallels that of Monet in time but could scarcely have been more different. After training in architecture and painting, he studied anatomy and microscopic biology. Throughout the 1870s and 1880s, calling black "the prince of colors," he turned out series after series of fantastic lithographs, often based on such poets of the imagination as Baudelaire and Poe. In the 1890s he burst forth with a steady succession of brilliantly colored works in oil and in pastel in which, according to his own words, he desired "to make improbable beings live, like human beings . . . by putting insofar as possible the logic of the visible at the service of the invisible." A striking example of his later art is *Orpheus*, of 1903 (fig. 443). The Greek legend tells us how the great musician, after the death of his wife Eurydice, wandered the earth, lamenting her loss in song, and refused to submit to the blandishments of the Maenads, female followers of Dionysos, who in revenge tore him to bits and threw the pieces in a stream. The frightful legend is muted by Redon into the magic of a waking dream. There is no blood. The head shines in an opalescent dusk, floating with a fragment of the singer's lyre, and sparkling flowers cluster about it. Intended to evoke the magical power of music to transfigure violence and tragedy, the picture also provides the solace of a retreat into fantasy. Redon's rich imagination and his glowing color made him the immediate precursor of a major current of twentieth-century art (see Chapter 8) in which the private fantasy of the artist has free rein in escaping from the increasingly onerous restrictions of modern urban society.

We have already seen how the Realists and the Impressionists exchanged ideas during informal meetings at Parisian cafés. The phenomenon of the independent exhibition, beginning with Courbet's Pavilion of Realism in 1855 and continuing with the officially sponsored Salon des Refusés of 1863, became increasingly important as the gulf between radical artists and conservative public and critics widened and deepened. The eight group exhibitions of the Impressionists from 1874 to 1886 are a case in point. In 1884 Seurat and Redon were instrumental, along with a number of other artists, in organizing the Société des Artistes Indépendants, as a counterforce to the all-powerful Salon, and it was at the exhibitions of this society that the innovators showed their work.

At various moments during the nineteenth century,

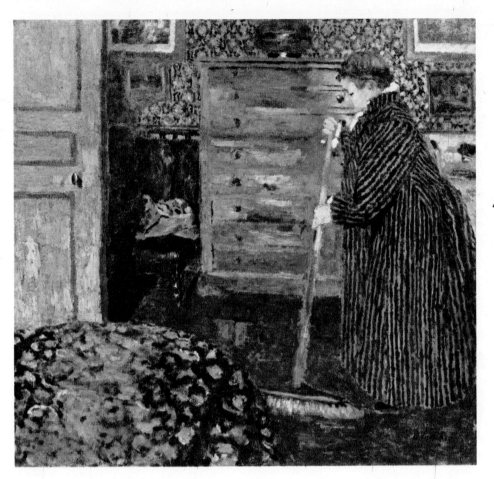

444. EDOUARD VUILLARD. *Woman Sweeping in a Room*. 1892–93. Oil on composition panel, 18 x 19". The Phillips Collection, Washington, D.C.

veritable brotherhoods of artists were formed, fewer in France than in England and in Germany. During the last two decades of the nineteenth century, these brotherhoods began to include more and more of the most gifted artists. Van Gogh dreamed of such a brotherhood, through which he and Gauguin could lead the reform of European art. A small group of Symbolist artists, starting at Pont-Aven in Brittany around the dominant figure of Gauguin, continued to meet in Paris. The most vocal members of the Pont-Aven group, although by no means the most talented, were Émile Bernard (1868–1941) and Maurice Denis (1870–1943). Bernard claimed more influence on Gauguin than the facts justify, and even priority in the invention of a linear, bright-colored, and flattened style. The lasting value of the Symbolist movement in its Pont-Aven phase is found less in the works of these two artists than in Denis' dictum in 1890 that a picture is first of all "an arrangement of colored shapes." The Pont-Aven artists, especially Gauguin with his arbitrary forms and colors, came much closer to this principle than had Whistler to his similar pronouncement. Some of the group joined a new brotherhood of Symbolists, which met weekly for discussions in Paris, beginning in 1888, and monthly for semisecret ceremonial dinners in costume. The group called themselves the Nabis, a name derived from a Hebrew word for *prophet*, and included not only Denis but also such far more gifted artists as ÉDOUARD

VUILLARD (1868–1940), and Aristide Maillol, then a painter but better known for his later work in sculpture (see Chapter 7).

Interestingly enough, the mystical doctrines of the Nabis, allied to Rosicrucianism, included a strong devotion to home life, including the artistic decoration of domestic interiors, in spite of the group's supposed opposition to bourgeois values. The most eloquent paintings of the Nabis are those of Vuillard, who never married, lived with his mother until her death, and produced intimate paintings of interiors unrivaled in their delicacy and charm in spite of the airless and crowded nature of their subjects. In *Woman Sweeping in a Room*, of about 1892–93 (fig. 444), every inch is packed with domestic detail, which by his own personal magic Vuillard is able to translate into exquisite pattern, relying on the juxtaposition of areas of great richness and constant variety. Sometimes his technique recalls that of Seurat and the Neoimpressionists in its use of tiny dots; at other moments parallel lines or stripes and decorative opposition of softly painted flat surfaces foretell the work of Matisse (see colorplate 64), who was deeply indebted to Vuillard's acute sensibility to the relationship of the most ordinary objects.

FORERUNNERS OF EXPRESSIONISM. Toward the end of the nineteenth century, a number of artists outside of France, notably in Brussels, Oslo (then named

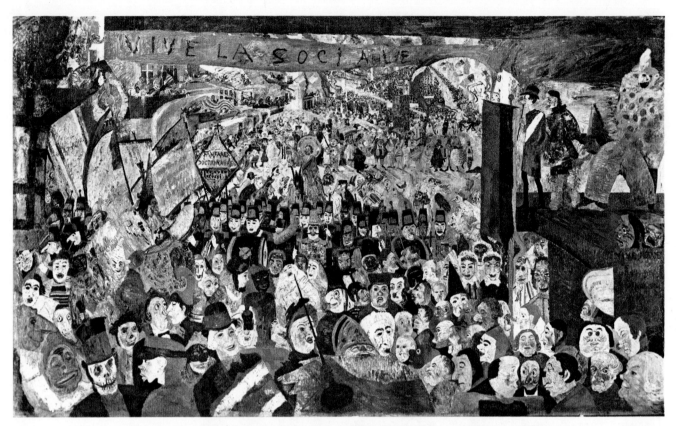

445. JAMES ENSOR. *The Entry of Christ into Brussels in 1889.* 1886. Oil on canvas, 8'5" x 12'5".
Collection Louis Franck, London. On loan to Koninklijk Museum voor Schone Kunsten, Antwerp

Christiania), and Vienna, attempted the direct expression of emotion in pigment with relatively little care for the Impressionist aesthetic, considering style, color, form, and surface as subservient to the prime necessity of emotional expression. JAMES ENSOR (1860–1949), a Belgian born of an English father, absorbed Impressionist style and method, but soon turned to the most daring treatment of unexpected and shocking themes, and to the sharp, often horrifying contrast of colors and shapes. Interestingly enough, there seems to be no evidence that, at the moment of his most revolutionary works, Ensor had any knowledge of the roughly parallel development of Van Gogh. His mother kept a souvenir shop, selling among other wares the masks used at Flemish carnivals, and these obsessed Ensor as symbols of the basic evil of contemporary existence. His huge canvas entitled *The Entry of Christ into Brussels in 1889* (fig. 445; ironically, the work was painted in 1886) so shocked his contemporaries that even The Twenty, a group of radical Belgian artists to which Ensor belonged, refused to exhibit it. Under a broad, red banner inscribed "VIVE LA SOCIALE," Christ, who can barely be distinguished at the upper center, enters the streets of Brussels, which are filled with a tide of masked figures in a cacophonous combination of brilliant reds, greens, yellow, and blues—a Christ as powerless as in a painting by Bosch (see fig. 109).

In Norway a similar tendency is seen in the art of ED

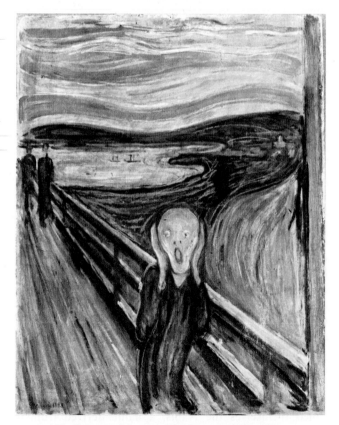

446. EDVARD MUNCH. *The Scream.* 1893. Oil on canvas, 36 x 29". Nasjonalgalleriet, Oslo

VARD MUNCH (1863–1944), whose work had little in common with the academic current of Norwegian art, but showed quite early an understanding of the bright palette of the French Impressionists. Munch was associated with the great Norwegian psychological dramatist Henrik Ibsen, for whom he designed stage sets, but he went past Ibsen in his treatment of themes involving obsession with sex and death. *The Scream* (fig. 446), painted in 1893, is a work one can hardly contemplate without horror. A person walking along a seashore promenade puts his hands to his head, bursting with anguish, while the very landscape about him heaves in waves as if vibrating along with his intolerable inner conflict, intensified by the arbitrary use of red, yellow, and green throughout the background. Munch's paintings created such an uproar when shown in Berlin in 1892 that the authorities forced the closing of a group exhibition in which he participated. Both he and Ensor were strongly influential in the development of the German Expressionist movement of the early twentieth century (see Chapter 6).

Unexpectedly enough, England in the 1890s saw the flowering of a movement that prided itself on its "decadence," centering around the controversial figure of the poet and dramatist Oscar Wilde. The short-lived and highly imaginative draftsman AUBREY BEARDSLEY (1872–98) illustrated a number of literary works, including Wilde's *Salome*, with drawings matchless in their brilliant handling of flowing line and surprising contrasts of black and white areas and scale. Such a drawing as his *John the Baptist and Salome* (fig. 447), with its strong erotic content, is also allied to the Continental current known as Art Nouveau, which found its richest expression in architecture and decoration (see Chapter 9).

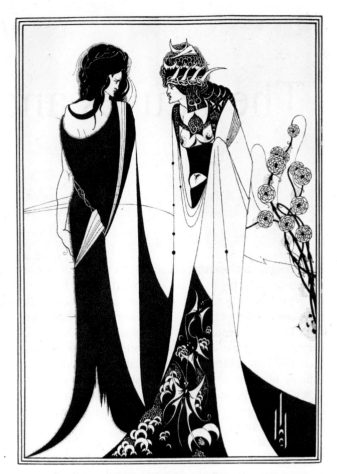

447. AUBREY BEARDSLEY. *John the Baptist and Salome.* c. 1894. Pen and brush, black ink, and black chalk on paper, 9⅛ x 6½". Fogg Art Museum, Harvard University, Cambridge, Massachusetts. Grenville L. Winthrop Bequest

ROUSSEAU. An utterly unexpected and delightful apparition on the Parisian art scene at the close of the nineteenth century was the self-taught painter Henri Rousseau (1844–1910). Having earned his living in the prosaic calling of toll collector, Rousseau retired early on a small pension and devoted himself entirely to painting. His combination of straight-faced whimsy, imagination, poetry, and real artistic sensitivity caused his work to be rapidly known and appreciated in the most advanced artistic circles. As early as 1886, he exhibited at the Société des Artistes Indépendants, to the universal derision of the public. Yet, although the artists of his day never took him quite as seriously as he took himself, for a quarter of a century, from the days of Degas to those of Picasso,

Rousseau was received everywhere. He is the first untutored, "primitive" artist to be highly valued in modern times; his naïve style is a product of imagination and visual experience rather than of visual analysis in the Western tradition that culminated in Impressionism. *The Sleeping Gypsy* (colorplate 62) shows an entirely new style in its smooth surfaces with no visible brushstrokes, its immense night sky, and its delightful air of mystery. Only recently has it been discovered that both the sleeping gypsy in her coat of many colors and the sniffing, harmless lion were modeled from children's toys on sale in Parisian shops; while painting them with utter literalness, Rousseau distilled from these toys his own delicate poetry. His art of the enigma was as important an element as the poetic fantasy of Redon in the development of the fantastic current in twentieth-century art.

6

The Fauves and Expressionism

In retrospect the opening decade of the twentieth century impresses us today as an era of revolution, in the course of which fundamental changes transformed the relationship between art and nature that had been traditionally accepted ever since the end of the Gothic period. To a great extent this impression is founded on fact; the innovators of this crucial decade did indeed achieve often unforeseeable and strikingly new results, which amounted at times to a sharp break with the past and were largely to determine the course of twentieth-century art up to the present.

Nonetheless, two other considerations should be borne in mind. First, the Impressionist and Post-Impressionist movements had already deprived visual reality of what could be recognized as permanent and autonomous properties of color, shape, and space. The artist himself now assumed the prerogative of determining these qualities, either as his eye saw them (Impressionism) or as his ideas, emotions, or fantasy might dictate (Post-Impressionism). Thus the path had already been prepared, to a certain extent, for even the most radical of twentieth-century artists.

Second, the vast majority of painters and sculptors at the opening of the twentieth century were still working in diluted versions of styles whose basic principles had been laid down by the Neoclassicists, the Romanticists, or the Realists at least two generations earlier. Yet these conservative artists controlled the Salon and dictated public taste. Even Impressionism, led by Monet who was still painting with great vigor, had by that time attracted wide admiration and many followers all over the globe, and was in the process of becoming itself a conservative tendency.

The innovators of the first heroic decade of the twentieth century were a hardy band, with every official, critical, and financial force arrayed against them. But the precedent had long been established. At least since Gros called Delacroix's *Massacre at Chios* (see colorplate 52) the "massacre of painting" at the Salon of 1824, every new tendency in modern art has had to establish itself as an avant-garde movement by a revolutionary exhibition

or even, in the twentieth century, by provocative actions. Courbet's Pavilion of Realism at the Universal Exposition of 1855, Manet's pictures at the Salon des Refusés of 1863, and the Impressionist group exhibitions beginning in 1874 are examples of those gestures of defiance that appear to have been considered by artistic innovators as necessary to the success of their movements.

The artistic scandals inevitably excited by such gestures, while hardly conducive to profitable sales in the initial stages of a new movement, always drew public attention to its contributions, and inevitably—such is the combative nature of man—tended to nourish the artist's courage and self-esteem. Early in the twentieth century such new movements often required explanatory writings or manifestos, and a rich literature of aggressive art criticism arose in defense of revolutionary tendencies, paralleling the provocative writings that generally attended contemporary political and social tendencies. By the early 1970s the phenomenon of the self-proclaimed avant-garde and its inescapable uproars and manifestos had become so generally accepted that its significance and effects were reversed—an artist could hardly hope to win critical acclaim *unless* he could demonstrate that his work truly belonged to the avant-garde. Since the possibilities available to artistic revolution are now beginning to show signs of running out, it is by no means certain whether the phenomenon of the avant-garde still has a productive future in the remaining quarter of the century.

In the early 1900s, however, the avant-garde was real enough; so indeed were the financial hardships inflicted on its members. The first unmistakable avant-garde event of the new century was the exhibition of an extraordinary roomful of pictures at the Salon d'Automne of 1905. According to a still not absolutely verified story, the critic Louis Vauxcelles gazed about the room in horror and, seeing in the center a work of sculpture in Renaissance tradition, exclaimed, "Donatello au milieu des fauves!" ("Donatello among the wild beasts!"). The name Fauves immediately stuck to the new movement. While today its joyous productions hardly seem to show

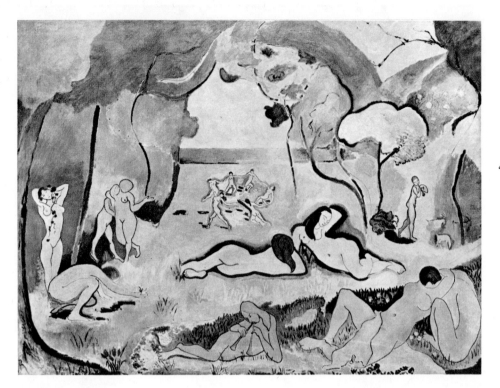

448. HENRI MATISSE. *Joie de vivre (Joy of Life)*. 1905–6. Oil on canvas, 68½ x 93¾". © The Barnes Foundation, 1976, Merion Station, Pennsylvania

the ferocity implied by the nickname, it is not hard to understand that to an academic critic in 1905 such explosions of brilliant color, not to speak of the rough brushstrokes and antinaturalistic drawing and perspective, seemed bestial indeed. Interestingly enough, only two of these revolutionaries of 1905, Matisse and Rouault, were eventually to achieve major artistic stature.

MATISSE. When the twentieth century opened, Henri Matisse (1869–1954) was already past thirty. He was a competent painter in a modified Impressionist style, and had executed an impressive series of copies of Old Masters, some quite literal, others delicately altered to bring out those aspects that interested him the most. Yet he had not shown signs of exceptional talent or originality, nor any awareness of the innovations of the Post-Impressionists. Soon after the turn of the century, however, he began experimenting with figures so simplified that their masses could be stated in bold areas of pigment. Rapidly he turned to the divided touches of bright color introduced by the Neoimpressionists. Then in 1905 came the Fauve explosion. Matisse burst upon the art world with an astonishing series of paintings in which masses of brilliant color—reds, greens, deep blues, bright blues, rose, yellow, and lavender—were applied in full intensity and juxtaposed with jarring results. His *The Green Stripe*, of 1905 (colorplate 63), exhibited in the celebrated group of Fauve pictures in the Salon d'Automne of that year, excited especial horror because this blazing bouquet of colors was applied not only to the arbitrarily divided background and the dress and collar but also, only slightly diluted by flesh tones, to the face,

dominated by the intense green stripe through the center of the forehead and down the nose. Not even Gauguin had dreamed of such apparent distortions of natural appearances. Nonetheless, all Matisse had really done was to intensify the differentiation of hues already analyzed by the Impressionists in order to produce a strong emotional effect.

The triumphant affirmation of Matisse's Fauve period is the huge *Joie de vivre* (*Joy of Life*) of 1905–1906, nearly eight feet long (fig. 448). A forest glade, reduced to stage drops, is inhabited by a happy company of nudes, male and female, embracing, playing pipes, picking flowers, draping garlands about their bodies, or dancing in a ring, all indicated with an unbroken contour of the utmost flexibility. The sudden jumps in scale between one figure and the next can no more be explained in naturalistic terms than can the broad, thinly brushed areas of arbitrary color. Matisse's new scale and color were both in a sense prepared for by Gauguin (see fig. 439, colorplate 60), but Matisse has gone much farther, especially in his heightening of color to intensify the fluidity of contour. The primitivism desired by Gauguin has here been achieved without reference to exotic cultures; Matisse's figures abandon themselves to nature physically as the Impressionist painter and viewer had visually.

In 1908 Matisse published his *"Notes d'un peintre,"* in which he explained: "What I am after, above all, is expression. . . . Expression to my way of thinking does not consist of the passion mirrored upon a human face or betrayed by a violent gesture. The whole arrangement of my pictures is expressive. The place occupied by figures or objects, the empty spaces around them, the propor-

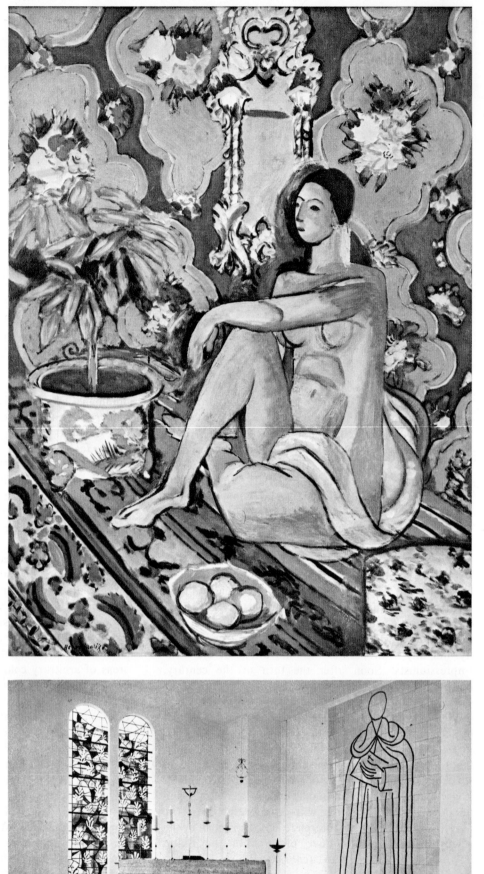

449. HENRI MATISSE. *Decorative Figure Against an Ornamental Background (Nude with the Straight Back).* 1925. Oil on canvas, 51½ x 38⅜". Musée National d'Art Moderne, Paris

450. HENRI MATISSE. Chapel of the Rosary of the Dominican Nuns, Vence, France. 1948–51 (Consecrated June 25, 1951)

tions, everything plays a part. . . . What I dream of is an art of balance, of purity and serenity devoid of troubling or depressing subject matter. . . ." His *Red Studio*, of 1911 (colorplate 64), sums up his art and his philosophy. Walls and floor are colored the same strong yet surprisingly airy brownish red. Against the walls hang or lean recognizable canvases by Matisse—a veritable gallery of his Fauve works of the preceding five years or so. Among the furniture contoured in wavering yellow lines are modeling stands bearing small sculptured nudes by Matisse; a figure on the table in the foreground is draped in a frond of ivy emerging from a green wine flask. Whistler's idea of the picture as an arrangement in color has been perfectly fulfilled, but in Matisse's terms of the expressive relationship between objects apparently scattered at random. His recapitulation of his artistic achievements becomes a delicate web of line and color, in which Renaissance perspective survives only as an echo.

For more than forty years longer Matisse continued to paint the relaxed themes he loved. Save for a brief flirtation with Cubism (see Chapter 7), he never deserted his basic Fauve message of linear and coloristic freedom, calm, and beauty. In 1921 he took up residence at Nice on the Riviera, where he turned out an unbroken series of masterpieces, large and small. Typical of his Nice period is *Decorative Figure Against an Ornamental Background*, of 1925 (fig. 449; nicknamed *Nude with the Straight Back*). The strongly modeled, grandly simplified forms of the nude are played off against the movement of the Rococo shapes in the wallpaper and the mirror. Between the browns, rose tones, blues, and yellows of the Oriental rug and the wallpaper the richness of color is almost overwhelming.

In 1943 Matisse moved to the Riviera hill-town of Vence, where during a serious illness he was cared for by Dominican nuns. In gratitude he designed and financed a wonderful chapel for them—he created architecture, murals, stained glass, vestments, even the altar, its candlesticks, and crucifix, between 1948–51 (fig. 450). Innumerable preparatory drawings are preserved, often complex at the start, but in final definition starkly simple. The murals, surprisingly, are devoid of color, painted in Dominican black and white on ceramic tile. The color of the interior is provided entirely by the vestments and the stained glass, which bathe the interior in yellow, blue, and green light as if it were an enchanted glade. Despite the fact that Matisse professed no formal religion, his labor of love is one of the few great works of religious art done in the twentieth century, and provides for the prayers and liturgies of the nuns an environment of untroubled beauty.

Although in old age Matisse was confined to his bed, the scope and freedom of his art miraculously widened. Unable to paint at an easel, he imagined lyric compositions often unexpectedly large. These were done entirely in colored papers, which he could paint and cut out while working in bed, and pinned to enormous paper surfaces on which they were later pasted. *Zulma* of 1950 (fig.

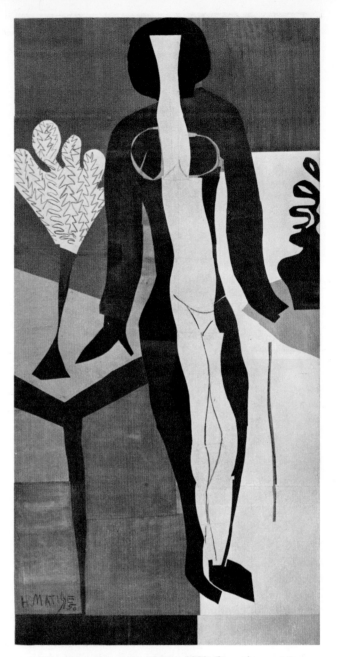

451. HENRI MATISSE. *Zulma.* 1950. Gouache on cut and pasted paper, 93¾ x 52⅜". Statens Museum for Kunst, Copenhagen

451), dominated by blue, green, and pink, is an example of the spontaneous verve of these *gouaches découpées*, whose pulsating contours, flat surfaces, and brilliant color revive on a new scale the energy of Matisse's *Joy of Life*, painted nearly half a century before. To many critics Matisse remains, from a purely pictorial standpoint, the most sensitive painter of the twentieth century.

ROUAULT. At the same Salon d'Automne of 1905 when the works of the Fauves first astonished Paris, there were also exhibited paintings by a companion of Matisse in student days, Georges Rouault (1871–1958). The intensely Catholic Rouault could not accept the hedonistic view of existence so delightful throughout the work of

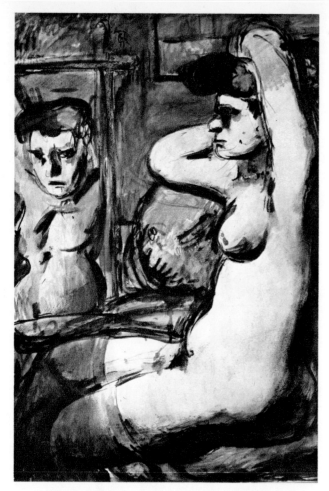

452. GEORGES ROUAULT. *Prostitute at Her Mirror.*
1906. Watercolor on cardboard, 27⅝ x 20⅞".
Musée National d'Art Moderne, Paris

Matisse. Rouault's early paintings embody an attitude of
rebellion against the life around him. His sympathies are
reserved, strangely enough, for circus performers, whom
he sees as tragic figures; he condemns violently a mixed
population of criminals, prostitutes, and judges. In contrast to the gentle, cynical acceptance of prostitutes by
Toulouse-Lautrec ten years earlier, Rouault paints them
with savage fury. Expression to him is just what Matisse
said it was not: "the passion mirrored upon a human face
or betrayed by a violent gesture." The fierce contours of
Prostitute at Her Mirror, of 1906 (fig. 452), describe
volumes of surprising force. This malevolent woman, exposed as an incarnation of evil, takes on a strange
rhythmic beauty as if Rouault, like Bosch but without his
fantasy (see Part Four, Chapter 2), was fascinated by
what he most condemns. Like many of Rouault's early
works, this one is painted in oil on cardboard, which gives
a quality at once mat and translucent to the blue contours
and shadows. The violence of such paintings relates
Rouault less to the French Fauves than to contemporary
German Expressionists, especially the Blaue Reiter (see
below).

Rouault's later work shows a transformation of his
early moral indignation into a gentler mysticism in some
ways reminiscent of Rembrandt (see Part Five, Chapter
5). *The Old King*, of 1937 (colorplate 65), could be any

monarch from the Old Testament—one thinks especially
of David or Solomon—laden with a twin burden of
prophecy and sorrow, which Rouault has successfully
transmuted into glowing color. His early training as a
stained-glass maker is doubtless influential in the way he
bounds the masses of brilliant impasto with broad, black
lines recalling the lead separations between the pieces of
glass in medieval windows.

DIE BRÜCKE. The name Expressionism is generally
applied to the movements that dominated avant-garde
painting in Germany in the early twentieth century, recalling at times the emotional violence of Grünewald in
the sixteenth (see Part Four, Chapter 7). A rebel group
called Die Brücke (*The Bridge*) was formed in Dresden in
1905, the very year the Fauves first showed in Paris. This
was a brotherhood, not unlike those that had appeared in
France and England at various moments in the
nineteenth century, and especially close to what Van
Gogh had envisioned in Arles. The most gifted member
of the group was EMIL NOLDE (1867–1956), who belonged to the organization only briefly. In masses of pigment unfettered by any structural contours like those of
Rouault, he expressed themes of equally fierce intensity,
all the more shocking on account of the unexpected content he discovered in such traditionally Christian themes
as that of the *Doubting Thomas*, painted in 1912 (fig.
453; cf. an example from the Baroque, fig. 291). The
Apostles gathered around Christ in Nolde's picture seem
to be engaged in some barbaric ritual; an emaciated
Thomas gazes gloatingly at Christ's wounds, below a row
of Apostles' heads that recall Ensor's masks (see fig.
445). All are painted in barbarically bright color.

DER BLAUE REITER. Among the constantly dissolving
and recombining artist groups formed in Germany just
prior to the outbreak of World War I, only Der Blaue
Reiter (*The Blue Rider*) surpasses Die Brücke in importance. This group did not share Die Brücke's
revolutionary attitude of social protest, nor did it comprise a brotherhood; in the end Der Blaue Reiter was far
more influential in the development of the most imaginative tendencies in twentieth-century art. In fact,
three painters of first importance, the German Franz
Marc, the Russian Wassily Kandinsky, and the Swiss
Paul Klee (see Chapter 8), were the leaders in the group
of exceptional talents who exhibited together in Munich
in the winter of 1911–12 (including, oddly enough,
Rousseau, as well as other artists). FRANZ MARC (1880–
1916) was probably the best animal painter since the
prehistoric men who painted caves. His romantic, poetic
art sought liberation from the conventions of human existence in the world of animals, thus—whether or not he
was consciously aware of it—reviving a tradition that had
originated in the art of the migrations, had played an important part in that of the Late Middle Ages, and,
although generally submerged during the Renaissance,

had surfaced from time to time in such manifestations as the fantasies of Bosch (see figs. 110, 111, 112, colorplate 20). A brilliant example is Marc's *Deer in the Wood, No. 1,* of 1913 (fig. 454). Under a certain amount of influence from both Cubism and Futurism (see Chapter 7), Marc crisscrosses the enchanted glade with the verticals of the trees, diagonals being derived from the slopes of the hills and curves suggested by the flight of the hawk at the upper left; in this woodland interior nestle four deer (apparently does or fawns—certainly no antlered stags), resting or moving in poses of unconscious grace. Marc's coloring is brilliant and arbitrary, in hues generally of symbolic significance to him, and is carefully applied without the explosive roughness of the Brücke artists. The loss of Marc, killed in World War I, cut short one of the most promising careers of the twentieth century.

WASSILY KANDINSKY (1866–1944) has been credited with the first entirely abstract paintings. Whether or not this is true may never be determined, but in his book *Concerning the Spiritual in Art,* written in 1910 and published in 1912, Kandinsky warned specifically against total abstraction, which he feared might degenerate into pure decoration. As early as 1909 he had begun to paint his series called *Improvisations,* referring as had Whistler's titles to those of musical compositions. But Whistler had always implied the intervention of conscious choice and planning in his harmonies, symphonies, arrangements, and the like. Improvisations are, of course, unplanned, and Kandinsky wrote that his were "largely unconscious, spontaneous expressions of inner character, non-material in nature." *Improvisation 30 (Cannon),* of 1913 (colorplate 66), at first sight seems to be a meaningless assortment of shapes and colors of astonishing brilliance. Then one begins to notice not only the cannons at the lower right but also what appear to be hills and houses moving at odd angles and clouds in the sky. Kandinsky suggested that the cannons might be explained by the war talk that had been commonplace during the year, but that the name was selected by him purely for convenience and did not refer to any meaning in the picture, "painted rather subconsciously in a state of strong inner tension."

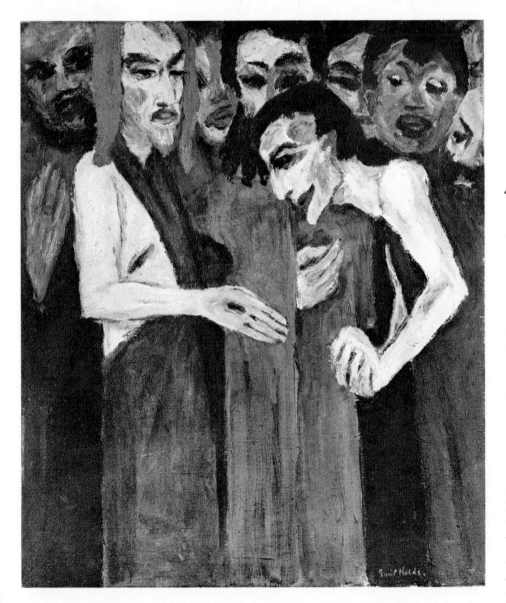

453. EMIL NOLDE. *Doubting Thomas.* 1912. Oil on canvas, 39⅜ x 33⅞". Nolde-Museum, Seebüll, Germany

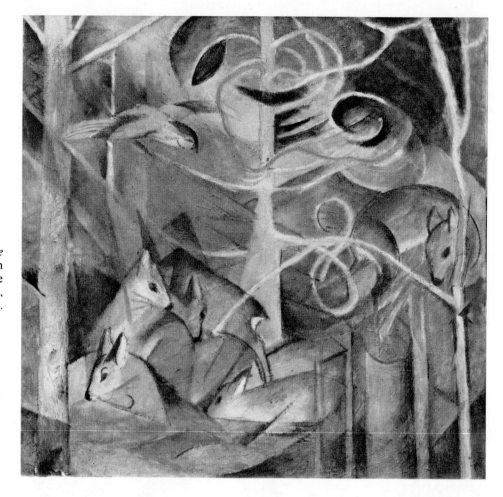

454. FRANZ MARC. *Deer in the Wood, No. I.* 1913. Oil on canvas, 39¾ x 41″. The Phillips Collection, Washington, D.C.

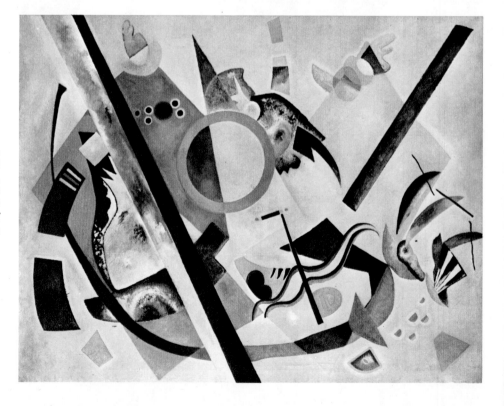

455. WASSILY KANDINSKY. *Composition 238: Bright Circle.* 1921. Oil on canvas, 54½ x 70⅞″. Yale University Art Gallery, New Haven, Connecticut. Gift of the Société Anonyme

The year it was painted the picture was exhibited in London, and accepted as "pure visual music" by the critic Roger Fry, who also discerned a kind of logic in the apparently spontaneous oppositions of shapes and colors. In a strange combination of Russian mysticism, theosophy, and a feeling that Impressionism had destroyed the object and atomic research dissolved all substance, Kandinsky had, in fact, proposed a completely subjective, symbolic meaning for colors, as had Marc, and also a new theory of abstract structural relationships. At some moment during the creation of the *Improvisations*, possibly during 1910, Kandinsky happened to see one of them upside down, and was impressed by its beauty when nothing in it could any longer be recognized. But not until late in 1913 did he completely desert representation. After his return to Russia in 1914, where he was in touch with the Constructivist movement, whose members had arrived at abstraction by a different route (see Chapter 7), Kandinsky's wholly abstract paintings began to assume considerable dimensions. *Composition 238: Bright Circle*, painted just before his return to Germany in 1921 (fig. 455), shows the influence of El Lissitzky in the ruled lines and geometrical shapes, but the intensity of feeling that drives the freely associated shapes is pure Kandinsky. The painting is a kind of celestial explosion in which we seem to be present at the formation of new astronomical configurations. From 1922–23 Kandinsky taught at the Bauhaus in Weimar (see page 438), and from 1933 until his death lived in the Paris suburb of Neuilly-sur-Seine. The true heirs of Kandinsky's imaginative legacy of form inflamed by emotion were the American progenitors of the Abstract Expressionist movement after World War II (see Chapter 10).

The forces unleashed by Die Brücke were, however, by no means forgotten. The movement had exalted individual emotional experience to the plane of the ultimate determinate of moral as well as artistic values. The Austrian painter OSKAR KOKOSCHKA (1886–) continued the Expressionist freedom of statement and technique until long after World War II without ever abandoning his loyalty to the visible world. In his early portraits Kokoschka had absorbed much from his study of Van Gogh. A haunting testament of his rebellious youth is the *Self-Portrait*, of 1913 (fig. 456), clearly reminiscent of Van Gogh in its intense emotional avowal and heavy application of pigment, and recalling El Greco in its elongated distortion. It seems hard to believe that this "talented terror," after the production of two wildly sadistic dramas he had written and produced in 1909, was obliged to leave Vienna for a more sympathetic atmosphere in Berlin, where Expressionist artists from all over Central and Eastern Europe were gathering.

Kokoschka's glorious *Bride of the Wind*, of 1914 (colorplate 67), is one of the rare unabashed celebrations of romantic love in the twentieth century. The artist and his mistress, like Dante's Paolo and Francesca in Blake's illustration (see fig. 391), are swept in a whirlwind above

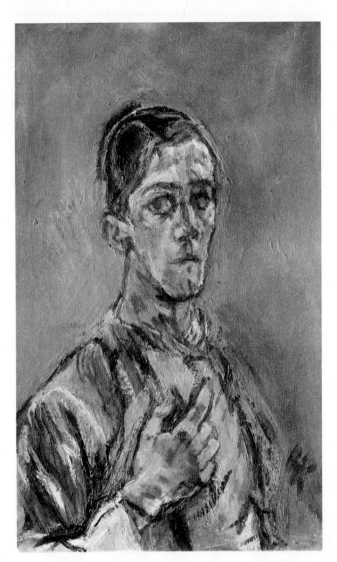

456. OSKAR KOKOSCHKA. *Self-Portrait*. 1913. Oil on canvas, 32⅛ x 19½". The Museum of Modern Art, New York. Purchase

a blue mountain valley before glittering crags illuminated by a crescent moon, lost in their emotion like the ecstatic saints in the depths of an El Greco cloud (see fig. 223).

MAX BECKMANN (1884–1950), a somewhat lesser figure than Kokoschka but still a powerful artist, picked up the legacy of Die Brücke after World War I and carried it to midcentury. Trained and successful as an academic painter, Beckmann was spiritually devastated by the wave of disillusionment in Germany after World War I. *The Night*, of 1918–19 (fig. 457), is a terrifying indictment of official cruelty, difficult to connect with any specific incident save possibly the fierce repression of the Communist "Spartacus" attempt to seize power in Germany in January, 1919. The tortures and the powerful, jagged forms are reminiscent of Grünewald in their horror, yet the coloring is unexpectedly thin and almost monochromatic. In retrospect the picture seems prophetic of Nazism, which designated Beckmann, like all modern artists in Germany, "degenerate." He fled to

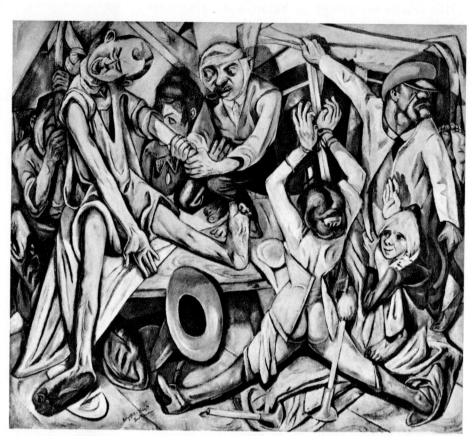

457. MAX BECKMANN. *The Night.*
1918–19. Oil on canvas, 52⅜
x 60¼″. Kunstsammlung
Nordrhein-Westfalen,
Düsseldorf

458. MAX BECKMANN.
Blindman's Buff (triptych).
1945. Oil on canvas, side
panels each 42½ x 74½″;
center panel 90 x 80″. The
Minneapolis Institute of
Arts. Gift of Mr. and Mrs.
Donald Winston

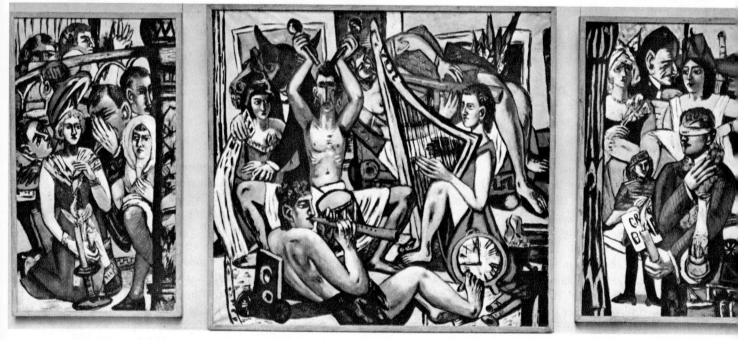

Amsterdam and, after the German occupation of the Netherlands, went into hiding. The last three years of his life Beckmann spent in the United States.

His majestic triptychs, painted during the 1930s and 1940s, preserve the angular figural composition of the earlier works, reinforced now by strong black contours reminiscent of Rouault and by brilliant coloring. Still tormented and full of enigmatic symbols insoluble by any known iconographic method, and never fully deciphered even by Beckmann himself, these paintings are as effective as if they had been planned for mural decoration. *Blindman's Buff*, painted in Amsterdam in 1945 (fig. 458), apparently reduces life, haunted by memories of both a Classical and a barbaric past, to a terrible game.

7

The Search for Form— Cubism and Abstract Art

Almost parallel in time to the Expressionist outburst of emotion, yet equally instrumental with Expressionism in eventually dissolving all ties with visual reality, was a succession of movements that attempted to explore pure form instead of feeling. As the Fauves and the Expressionists derived in large measure from the pioneer explorations of Gauguin and Van Gogh, so the formalist movements of the early twentieth century entered the field under the banner of Cézanne. Yet Cézanne had achieved form through careful integration of color, while the formalist painters of the early twentieth century invariably restricted the free movement of color by strong contour, often reduced its intensity severely, and sometimes denied color altogether. Since sculpture is by identity the art of form, it is useful to begin our account of twentieth-century formalism with sculpture rather than painting.

At one time or another Daumier, Degas, Renoir, Gauguin, and Matisse had all made use of sculpture, either as an aid to the creation of form in painting or as an end in itself. But the sculpture of the late nineteenth century had been dominated, as we have seen, by the towering genius of Rodin, who often exploited his art for what purists might—and indeed did—denounce as nonsculptural purposes.

The return to form begins in the early twentieth century with the sculpture of ARISTIDE MAILLOL (1861-1944), who had been for a while a painter allied to the Nabis (see page 383). Not until a dangerous eye disease forced him to renounce painting did Maillol commence his career as a sculptor. His *Mediterranean*, of about 1901 (fig. 459), then known simply as *Crouching Woman*, was exhibited at the Salon d'Automne of 1905,

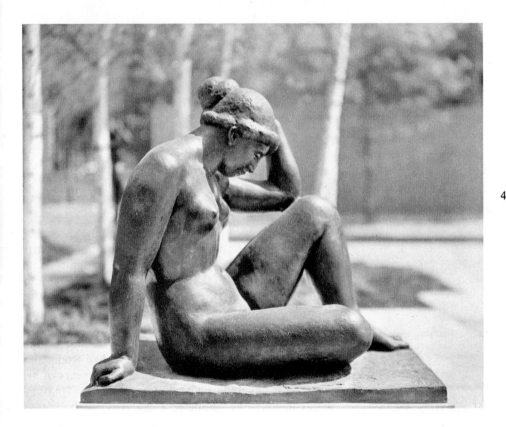

459. ARISTIDE MAILLOL. *Mediterranean (Crouching Woman).* c. 1901. Bronze, height 41". The Museum of Modern Art, New York. Gift of Stephen C. Clark

renowned for the Fauve scandal. Rodin had greatly admired a slightly later work of Maillol in much the same style, saying that he knew of nothing "so absolutely beautiful, absolutely pure, absolutely a masterpiece . . . in all modern sculpture." This comment is the less expected in that Maillol's style seems in every respect opposed to that of Rodin. The transformation Maillol brought about is as sudden and as far-reaching as that between the Rococo and David (see Chapter 1), but without any hint of political motivation.

The accidentality, immediacy, and strong emotion of Rodin are replaced in Maillol's statue with the revived classical values of balance, repose, and restraint. The simple masses of the figure recall the nobility of the Severe Style in the sculpture of fifth-century Greece and even the simple grandeur of that of Old Kingdom Egypt, which Maillol had admired with Gauguin in the Louvre. The quiet, understated forms of the body, the limbs, and the head of Maillol's reposeful figure reveal to a greater degree than had Cézanne's own paintings the cylinder, the cone, and the sphere that the great leader of Post-Impressionism sought in the natural world. Although Maillol occasionally experimented with more dynamic poses and dramatic contrasts of direction, in general he was content to the end of his long life to continue in much the same vein as this early work. He often reused an earlier figure, or removed head and limbs to reduce it to a

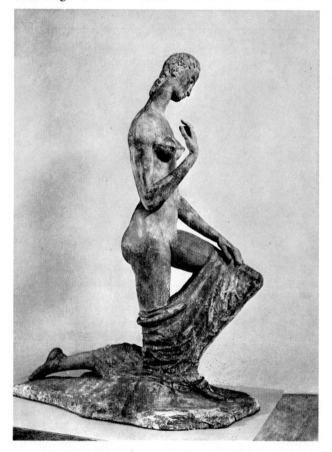

460. WILHELM LEHMBRUCK. *Kneeling Woman.* 1911. Cast stone, height 69½". The Museum of Modern Art, New York. Abby Aldrich Rockefeller Fund

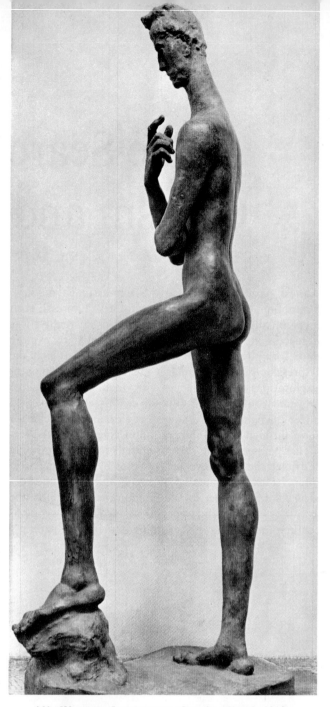

461. WILHELM LEHMBRUCK. *Standing Youth.* 1913. Cast stone, height 92". The Museum of Modern Art, New York. Gift of Abby Aldrich Rockefeller

torso fragment, thus imitating deliberately the effect produced by time and accident on works of ancient art.

The twenty-years-younger German sculptor WILHELM LEHMBRUCK (1881–1919) was deeply influenced at first by Rodin and then, on his arrival in Paris in 1910, by Maillol. Although he was acquainted with the most advanced sculptors of the time, notably Brancusi (see figs. 474, 475), Lehmbruck remained faithful to the human figure and continued to work, as had Rodin and Maillol, in clay. Only during the last eight years of his brief and haunted life did he produce the series of masterpieces in which he combined a classicism derived from

Maillol with an extraordinary elongation recalling that of the Royal Portal figures of Chartres Cathedral. Lehmbruck's strange combination of touching, bony awkwardness and Botticellian grace was influenced by the Renaissance sculpture he had seen in Italy. His almost emaciated *Kneeling Woman*, of 1911 (fig. 460), and his *Standing Youth*, of 1913 (fig. 461), show less concern with mass than Maillol had felt and more with space. The directions of the weary glances of these figures and the strong projections of their bony limbs extend movement, real and implied, into the surrounding atmosphere. Although he never carved directly, as other sculptors were beginning to do, Lehmbruck was interested in a stony surface. In order to produce a stone effect, he used cast stone—an amalgam of pulverized stone and cement—which gives a velvety blend with the consistency of stone and the plasticity of clay. Profoundly depressed by the tragedy of World War I, and in ill health, he took his own life, truncating one of the most promising careers in twentieth-century sculpture.

PICASSO, BRAQUE, AND THE CUBIST STYLE

The long career of PABLO RUIZ Y PICASSO (1881–1974) cast across the twentieth century a shadow as long as those of Michelangelo and Titian across the sixteenth. He created, along with his associate Georges Braque, one of the most important movements of the century, participated in many others, and influenced every phase of artistic activity throughout the world in one way or another until his extreme old age. Throughout his entire life he showed an incredible range of ideas and styles, and though in later years he did not expand his imagination as Matisse did, he remains a towering figure. The best works among his prodigious output have taken their place among the masterpieces of twentieth-century art.

A fully trained painter at the age of only nineteen, the Spanish-born Picasso took up residence in France in 1900, and thereafter returned only for brief stays to his native land. In Paris he fell under the spell of Toulouse-Lautrec, an influence that he soon managed to absorb and convert into a highly original style. He became concerned with the lives of those who lived, as he did, on the periphery of society, identifying his misery with theirs. He saw prostitutes, beggars, street musicians, and blind people from within, and was able to project their moods with overpowering intensity. The woman in his *Absinthe Drinker*, of 1902 (fig. 462; cf. Degas, fig. 423), sits lost in the stupefying liqueur, enveloped in self-pity and helplessness, a figure of extraordinary sculptural simplicity and beauty. The entire painting is colored by an all-pervading and corrosive blue—the proverbial color of melancholy—which has given its name to this period in Picasso's evolution, lasting about four years (1901–1904). For the young painter it was a period of hopeless maladjustment to the art world of Paris, punctuated by frequent, dejected returns to Barcelona.

In this picture, as throughout all the chameleon changes of Picasso's long career, the frame is definitive. For Matisse, as for the Impressionists, the frame was, with few exceptions, a finder held up to nature, which appears to extend beyond it. For Picasso, even at this early stage, form was all in all; the masses are composed with an eye to the frame, which they do not transgress or even approach; rather they are built up within it like a box within a box.

By late 1904 Picasso's mood of depression had lightened, and so also had his palette. A briefer Rose Period (1904–1906) ensued, in which his concerns were less with the tragic aspects of poverty than with the nostalgic charm of itinerant circus performers and the solace of make-believe. The wonderful *Les saltimbanques*, of 1905 (fig. 463), shows a family of these strolling players grouped together physically—but emotionally detached—before a mysterious desert landscape in which they appear almost to float. Figures and costumes, surely and deftly drawn and modeled, blend with the ground and the sunny haze in tones of softly grayed blue, rose, and beige, creating mother-of-pearl effects of the greatest delicacy. This, one of the loveliest pictures of the twentieth century, hardly prepares us for the astonishing out-

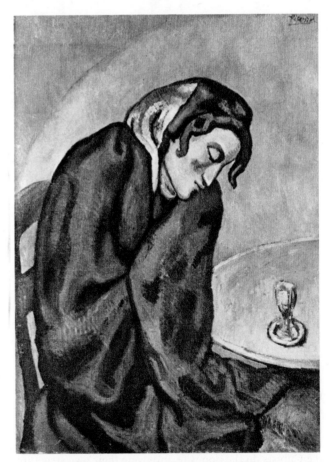

462. PABLO PICASSO. *Absinthe Drinker.* 1902. Oil on canvas, 31½ x 23⅝". Collection Othmar Hüber, Glarus, Switzerland

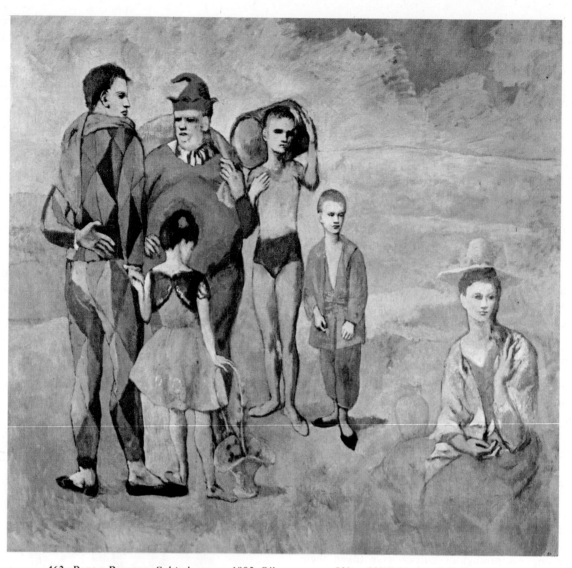

463. PABLO PICASSO. *Saltimbanques.* 1905. Oil on canvas, 83¾ x 90⅜″. National Gallery of
Art, Washington, D.C. Chester Dale Collection

burst that followed in *Les demoiselles d'Avignon*, in 1907
(fig. 464), which heralds the beginning of Cubism. But
these sudden oscillations between moods that verge
perilously on sentimentality and those of great violence
are typical of Picasso's career.

In the art of Matisse and the Expressionists, including
the most abstract phases of the early Kandinsky, the
progression from visual reality to a total concern with the
independent movement of color and shape can be clearly
traced, and is made all the easier to understand and to
justify by the forces of sensation in Matisse and emotion
in Rouault and the Expressionists that obviously propel
this evolution. But the attitude and methods of the
Cubists are not so easy to explain. Cézanne had found
planes in real objects (see Chapter 5) and had used them
to establish a structure of form seen by means of color;
the Cubists do the opposite, imposing their own structure
of largely monochromatic planes upon the object. How
and, above all, why were a small group of artists in 1908-

10—comprising at first just Picasso and Braque—
obsessed by such an extraordinary concern? And why did
their new ideas take such instant hold on the imagination of others, and spread to influence all aspects of vision and design in the twentieth century? These questions
have never been satisfactorily answered, and in fact are
seldom even posed. Considering the unique position of
Cubism in twentieth-century intellectual and artistic life,
this dilemma is strange indeed.

Certainly, one contributing factor was the gallery
devoted to Cézanne's paintings in the Salon d'Automne
of 1906, the year of the great master's death, and also the
posthumous retrospective of his work at the Salon
d'Automne of 1907. But such external circumstances
hardly account for the transformation that took place,
totally unrelated to Cézanne's lifelong search for form
through color. Originally, to judge from the sketches, the
composition of *Les demoiselles d'Avignon* was derived
from a small bather composition by Cézanne (for a mon-

umental treatment of the same theme, see fig. 436). The scene was at first intended to be the parlor of a brothel on the Carrer d'Avinyó (Avignon Street) in Barcelona. In the center foreground of the preliminary sketches was seated a sailor in the midst of five nude women. A student with a skull in his hand was to the left. But in the final picture, painted in the spring of 1907 before the Cézanne retrospective, the sailor and student disappear, and the women are presented to the observer in unexplained poses suggesting violent action, with faces transfixed as if with horror at some cataclysm. Insofar as possible for a

Picasso composition, constructed as always with total respect for the frame, the poses suggest a revelation of sexuality that is a demonic counterpart of El Greco's religious visions (see fig. 223, colorplate 35), and are traversed by sharp diagonal and twisting movements that convert the background from an interior to a kind of jungle. The intensity of the partially decomposed figures contrasts strangely with a serene little still life in the foreground (a pear, an apple, a slice of melon, a bunch of grapes). Instead of the lovely roses, blues, and greens of Cézanne, the figures are largely buff, their anatomy in-

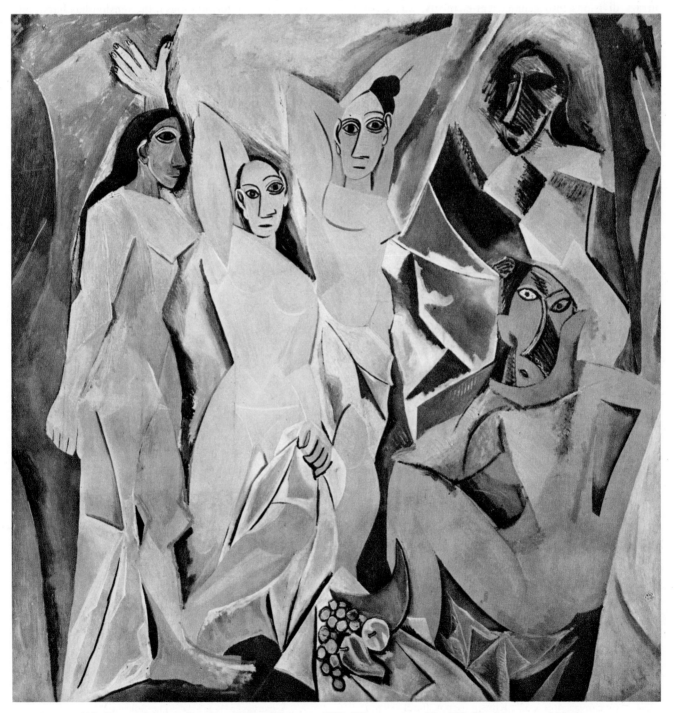

464. PABLO PICASSO. *Les demoiselles d'Avignon*. 1907. Oil on canvas, 96 x 92″. The Museum of Modern Art, New York. Lillie P. Bliss Bequest

dicated by jagged white or black contours, but one takes on the cinnamon tone of the background at the left. A harsh blue, as if a sudden glimpse of sky, surrounds the figure at the upper right.

Strangest of all, the staring expressions of the central figures give way at the sides to faces simplified in obvious emulation of the spoon faces and flangelike bosses in African sculpture, which Fauve painters had already started to collect as objects of aesthetic value. Since Picasso has claimed that in the spring of 1907 he had not yet seen any African sculpture, these heads must have been repainted by him in the new style a few months later. But the influence of African sculpture, with its arbitrary divisions into geometrical elements, was second only to that of Cézanne in the development of Cubist style.

The final product, however, differs essentially from both Cézanne and African sculpture. Heads, busts, still lifes, and occasional landscapes form the subject matter of early Cubist painting. These are deformed by sharp separation into planes, reminding one of the torso of the Magdalene in Rosso's *Descent from the Cross* (see fig. 158), a picture probably unknown to the Cubists. These planes are often traversed by a strong vertical twist.

producing a tension that, it appears, must inevitably burst the connection between the planes, although in such pictures as the *Seated Woman*, of 1909 (colorplate 68), the equipoise of forces produces a strikingly beautiful effect. The individual forms—the characteristic swelling and distortion of the neck muscles, for instance, or the reduction of the eyes to trapezoids—can in no way be derived from nature. And the strong, harsh coloring of *Les demoiselles d'Avignon* has given way in early Cubist pictures to soft tans and olive tones, remarkably cool and serene.

By 1911, in the phase known to art historians as Analytical Cubism (the artists, it must be emphasized, never used such terminology), the tension has burst, and so has the object. The entire foreground is filled with its formerly component planes, floating as if in a thick mist. The planes are, moreover, no longer opaque; one seems to see through them, and a great deal of the effect of an Analytical Cubist picture is derived from the delicacy of the intersection of these planes. They are rendered with a divided touch that recalls that of Impressionism. Gradually, as one watches, these planes build up a pervasive structure, often pyramidal, superseding the structure of observed reality.

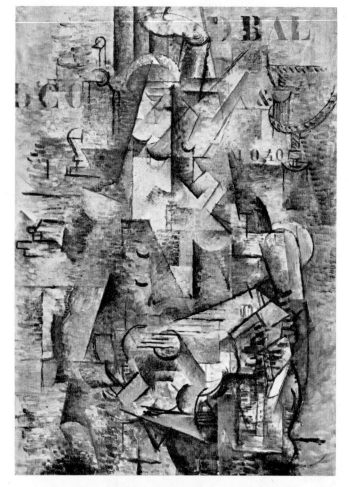

465. GEORGES BRAQUE. *The Portuguese.* 1911. Oil on canvas, 46⅛ x 32″. Kunstmuseum, Basel

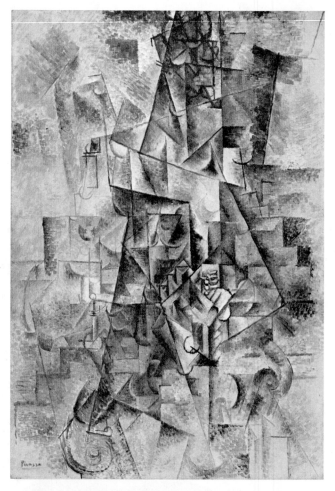

466. PABLO PICASSO. *The Accordionist.* 1911. Oil on canvas, 51¼ x 35¼″. The Solomon R. Guggenheim Museum, New York

The subjects, it has been emphasized, are now placed close to the observer, and generally pertain to café life—a performer; his instrument; a page of music; a tabletop; glasses; letters drawn from posters, programs, or newspapers; and everywhere cigarette smoke. It is as if the subject had been disintegrated into its component planes by the relaxed, nonfocused attentiveness of a café patron. The more intense the process of decomposition into planes becomes the less color remains—generally only occasional hints of tan, gray blue, or olive dominated by grays and touched with black and white. To follow the simile we have used earlier, walking from an Impressionist, Post-Impressionist, or Fauve gallery into one filled with Cubist pictures is like moving from brilliant sunlight into a smoke-filled, dim café. Or, to use a metaphor, the Cubist painters have substituted for the full orchestra of Impressionism the soft tones of a clavichord. Like Impressionism, Cubism rapidly became a common style.

Working in nearby studios in 1911 and 1912, GEORGES BRAQUE (1882–1963) and Picasso turned out paintings remarkably similar in contour and even in touch. It would be a hardy critic who could be sure of telling the difference between the two artists in such works as *The Portuguese* by Braque (fig. 465) and *The Accordionist* by Picasso (fig. 466), both painted in 1911. Often the artists themselves could not. In both pictures the ostensible subjects are reduced to afterimages, definitely secondary to the new geometrical structures formed by the floating planes.

During 1912 the Cubist artists began to turn to a new series of interests and a new kind of experience, responsible for the phase known generally as Synthetic Cubism, since the painters no longer sought to disintegrate the object but to reassert it. In Synthetic Cubism, in fact, the barrier between reality and representation is unexpectedly broken, as it had been from time to time in earlier periods. We recall that at Jericho actual skulls had been overlaid with plaster. Spanish Baroque sculptors often had supplied their plaster or wood saints with gruesomely lifelike glass eyes and porcelain teeth, and Degas dressed one of his bronze ballet dancers in an actual costume. Now bits of the real object make their entrance into the picture: newspaper clippings, lengths of rope (in the paintings of Braque, simulated strips of veneering), and similar "found objects." Picasso's *The Bottle of Suze*, of 1913 (fig. 467), is an epitome of this synthetic phase; newspaper clippings, used as opaque equivalents of the floating planes in Analytical Cubism, are held in a structure of lines, and dominated by the bright blue label of the bottle of aperitif. Such bits, stuck to the surface of the canvas as elements in a design and echoes of the object, gave rise to the term collage, from the French word *coller* (*to glue* or *paste*).

Once established, the Cubist mode of vision and construction continued vital for many years. Its emphasis on the supremacy of the plane had far-reaching effects not only in painting but also in sculpture, architecture, and

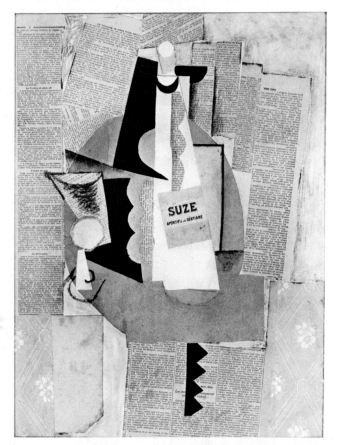

467. PABLO PICASSO. *The Bottle of Suze.* 1913. Collage and charcoal on canvas, 25¼ x 19⅝". Washington University, St. Louis

every aspect of commercial and industrial design. Every major current in abstract art during the period from the 1920s to the present owes a major debt to Cubism; some important tendencies, such as Futurism, Constructivism, and Purism (see pages 409–410, 412–414), were outgrowths of Cubist theory and practice. Picasso, one of the two inventors of Cubism, continued for the rest of his life to make use of Cubist forms and ideas, to a greater or less degree corresponding to his interests at any given moment, but the presence of Cubism can be felt in the styles of all his later work.

During the years immediately after World War I, it is no longer possible to talk of "periods" in Picasso's work; two sharply different styles, superficially opposed but in reality strongly related to each other, coexist in his production. The gorgeous *Three Musicians*, of 1921 (fig. 468), is still basically a Synthetic Cubist picture in that the planes are now locked into a total design governed by the recognizable image. We have no doubt that the three incongruous musicians are there—a Pierrot and a Harlequin drawn from the tradition of the Italian commedia dell'arte of the seventeenth and eighteenth centuries, and a Franciscan monk. But the planes into which they have been divided proceed according to their own laws and not those of natural appearances. No found objects remain, but the coloring is now as brilliant as that of any Fauve painting. Its hard, clear tones (Picasso said at one time

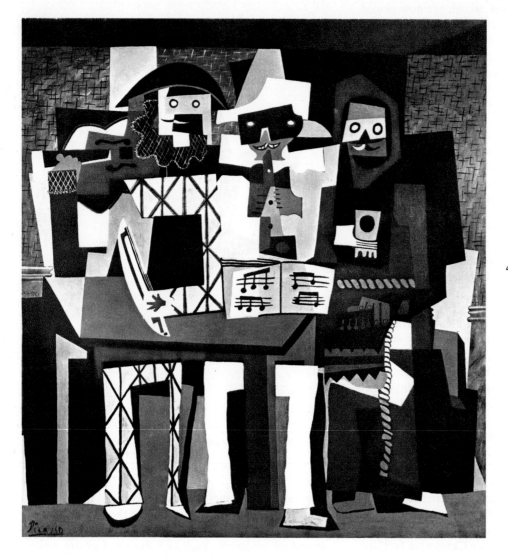

468. PABLO PICASSO. *Three Musicians.* 1921. Oil on canvas, 80 x 74". Philadelphia Museum of Art. The A. E. Gallatin Collection

that any bright color would do), together with its astonishing size—the picture is nearly seven feet high—create a splendid decorative effect reminding us that in 1917 Picasso had had considerable experience in stage designs. Although the figures are set on a narrow space like that of a stage, their surfaces function as sub-divisions of a total surface. The background plane is as severely parallel to the pictorial surface as is that of David's *Oath of the Horatii* (see fig. 366). The freshness, smartness, and gaiety of the *Three Musicians* are infectious, rendering it one of the few completely joyous large-scale compositions of the generally troubled twentieth century.

While Picasso was in Italy in 1917 preparing stage designs for the Ballets Russes, he had been greatly impressed by the grandeur of the Italian past, especially Roman sculpture and the mural paintings of Giotto and Piero della Francesca. Quite unexpectedly he developed, parallel with the brilliantly colored late Cubism of the *Three Musicians*, a monumental and largely mono-chromatic Classical style with complete figures heavily modeled as if they were statues. He experimented with

every aspect of Classical style, from imitations of Etruscan painting and Greek vases to the pencil line of Ingres, but his most imposing Classical creations are the majestic compositions involving seated giantesses seem-ing to derive from a legendary past. The best of them are overpowering in their cylindrical mass and stony im-placability. In *Three Women at the Spring*, of 1921 (fig. 469), Picasso has deliberately made the figures graceless, emphasizing the bulk and weight of their hands and feet, and intensifying the impersonality of their stony faces. For several years this modeled, Classical style coexisted in Picasso's production with the flat, well-nigh abstract phase of late Cubism.

The lightning changes of style that characterize Picasso's post-Cubist work are too many to record here. Sometimes seemingly incompatible styles appear side by side in the same painting. Although during the 1930s Picasso took an active part in the Surrealist movement (see Chapter 8), his finest work of this decade, and in many ways the greatest of all social protest pictures, is the *Guernica* (fig. 470). Picasso executed this enormous painting to fulfill a commission for the pavilion of the

Spanish republican government at the Paris Exposition of 1937, while the Civil War was still going on in Spain. Intended as a protest against the destruction of the little Basque town of Guernica in April, 1937, by Nazi bombers in the service of the Spanish Fascists, the picture has become in retrospect a memorial to all the crimes against humanity in the twentieth century. The painting is not a literal narration in the tradition of Goya, which would have been foreign to Picasso's nature and principles, nor even an easily legible array of symbols. As he worked, Picasso seems to have decided, perhaps subconsciously, to combine images drawn from Christian iconography, such as the Slaughter of the Innocents, with motives from Spanish folk culture, especially the bullfight, and from his own past. Actual destruction is reduced to fragmentary glimpses of walls and tiled roofs, and flames shooting from a burning house at the right. A bereft mother rushes screaming from the building, her arms thrown wide. Agonized heads and arms emerge from the wreckage. At the left a mother holding her dead child looks upward, shrieking. The implacable bull above her, the adversary in Spanish popular experience, is sure-

ly related to the dread Minotaur, adopted by the Surrealists, as an embodiment of the irrational in man, for the title of their periodical in Paris, to which Picasso had contributed designs. If the bull then signifies the forces of Fascism, the dying horse, drawn also from the bullfight ritual, suggests the torment of the Spanish people, and the oil lamp held above it the resistance of humanity against the mechanized eye, whose iris is an electric bulb. The spiritual message of combined terror and resistance is borne, unexpectedly, by the Cubist aesthetic means. An explosion of shattered planes of black, white, and gray reforms as one watches into the shape of a giant pyramid, as if triumphant even in destruction. Picasso never again reached this height, and though he continued painting with great energy for thirty-six years, with occasional remarkable achievements, much of his later work is a recapitulation of motives he had invented earlier.

THE INFLUENCE OF CUBISM

Although Picasso and Braque remained aloof from group exhibitions, their principles were avidly adopted by

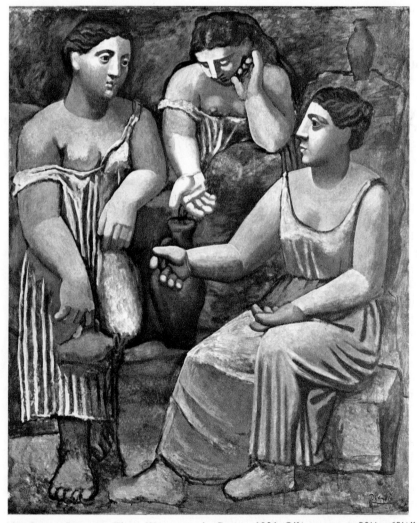

469. PABLO PICASSO. *Three Women at the Spring.* 1921. Oil on canvas, 80¼ x 68½".
The Museum of Modern Art, New York. Gift of Mr. and Mrs. Allan D. Emil

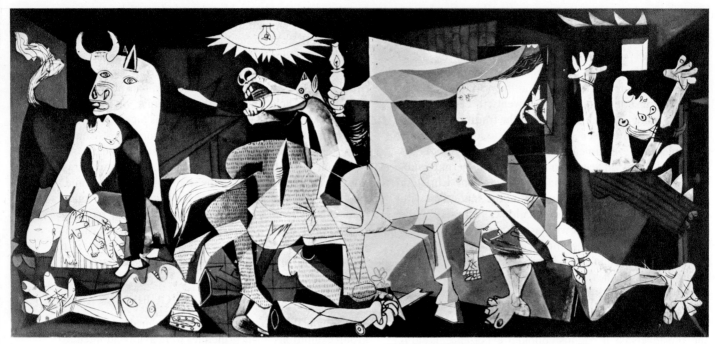

470. PABLO PICASSO. *Guernica.* 1937. Oil on canvas, 11'5½" x 25'5¾". On extended loan to The Museum of Modern Art, New York, by the estate of the artist

a host of lesser masters. Treatises on Cubism soon appeared, notably that by the painters Albert Gleizes and Jean Metzinger in 1912, which went through fifteen editions in less than a year and was published in English in 1913. Cubist principles influenced painters and sculptors everywhere, even for a while Matisse and certainly Kandinsky and Marc (see figs. 454, 455). Cubist principles also exercised a formative influence on new styles, especially that of FERNAND LÉGER (1881–1955), who applied the notion of fragmentation to his vision of an industrialized world. Léger was delighted by certain severely formal arts of the past, such as those of Egypt and Sumeria, and had little use for European painting since Giotto. His *Disks*, of 1918 (fig. 471), shows circles and arcs suggesting dynamos dominating the grid of a city, punctuated here and there (the man lifting a hammer at the extreme left, for instance) by the form of a human being. The hard, geometrical forms and mechanically inert surfaces of machinery, which were interchanged and recombined from one of Léger's pictures to the next, control the composition, just as the bright, crude colors of illuminated signs determine the color. In this machine world, ironically enough, is at last realized the dictum of the humanistic David, "Never let your brushwork show."

Whirring disks had, however, already appeared in the art of ROBERT DELAUNAY (1885–1941), who found in the industrialized world an imaginative excitement completely opposed to the stern order of Léger. Disks of brilliant color and constantly changing size and speed interlock and fuse, while never losing motion or atmospheric resonance, in Delaunay's *Homage to Blériot*, of 1914 (fig. 472), which celebrated the first flight by a

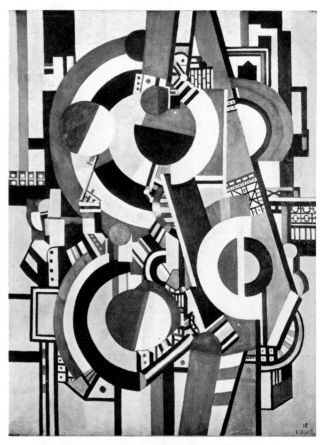

471. FERNAND LÉGER. *Disks.* 1918. Oil on canvas, 94½ x 71". Musée d'Art Moderne de la Ville de, Paris

heavier-than-air craft across the English Channel in 1909. Above the tumult of form and colors a biplane and the Eiffel Tower can be seen at the upper right.

The greatest French painting inspired by Cubist principles of fragmentation is the *Nude Descending a Staircase, No. 2* (fig. 473), painted in 1912 on the basis of a study done the preceding year, by MARCEL DUCHAMP (1887–1968), a still controversial artist whose major contributions will be studied in Chapter 8. The almost Botticellian grace of the forms seems so obvious today that it is hard to understand the uproar the picture created at the comprehensive Armory Show of modern art in New York in 1913, when it was singled out above all others for a torrent of outraged abuse from public and critics alike. The picture was not influenced by Futurism, of which Duchamp knew little at the time of the preparatory study, but was suggested, in part at least, by books of photographs, popular at the time, that showed stages of movement succeeding each other so rapidly that one could flip the pages and obtain the effect of a motion picture. Duchamp's painting superimposes the images of such a series, so that the descending nude is seen in many successive moments simultaneously. As a result, they fuse to form a web of movement in which time is at once affirmed and denied, and thus forever suspended, just as it was at the same moment in the water-lily series (see fig. 418) in which Monet was prolonging to infinity the instantaneity of Impressionist vision. Paradoxically, the exquisite resiliency of the figural movement is, if anything, enhanced by the apparent substitution for flesh and bones of tubes of celluloid pierced by flexible steel rods. In the course of the fluid motion all forms fuse into a magical shimmer of golden tan and brown rhythms in space.

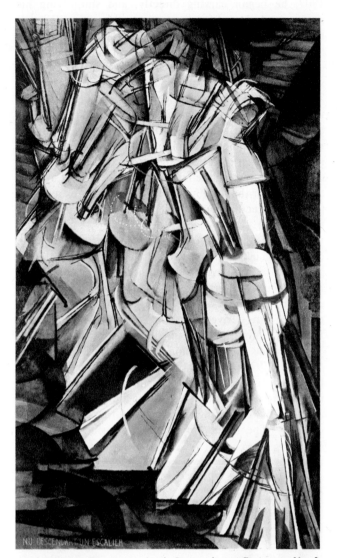

473. MARCEL DUCHAMP. *Nude Descending a Staircase, No. 2.* 1912. Oil on canvas, 58 x 35". Philadelphia Museum of Art. Louise and Walter Arensberg Collection

CUBISM AND THE FIRST ABSTRACT SCULPTURE

BRANCUSI. Despite the crucial importance of Cubism for many modern movements including some in sculpture, the earliest abstract sculpture was an independent if parallel development. The leading pioneer, indeed one of the two or three greatest sculptors of the twentieth century, was a Rumanian, Constantin Brancusi (1876–1957), who, after thorough academic training in Bucharest, arrived in Paris in 1904 and was at first strongly influenced by Rodin, and emulated the great master's atmospheric dissolution of mass with brilliant success. Brancusi had, however, been once apprenticed to a cabinetmaker, and his intense love of craftsmanship seems to have prompted him to abandon the by then universal practice of turning the actual execution of a work of sculpture over to a professional stonecarver working from the sculptor's clay model cast in plaster. As early as

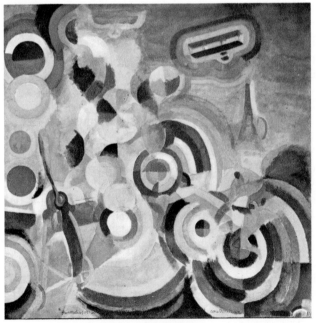

472. ROBERT DELAUNAY. *Homage to Blériot.* 1914. Tempera on canvas, 98½ x 99". Kunstmuseum, Basel

1907, he began carving directly, and simplifying his shapes to elemental forms of universal beauty. "What is real," he said, "is not the external form but the essence of things," and this essence he found in subtle shapes of deceptive simplicity, approaching those of the egg, the wave-worn pebble, and the blade of grass. Some traces of African sculpture may be discerned in the bulging eyes of the bust of *Mademoiselle Pogany*, of 1912 (fig. 474), but the spiral of the composition is derived from a delicate study of the inner rhythm of the dancer's pose. The mouth has been resorbed into the ovoid of the head, and the shapes caressing the face might be the subject's hands and wrists or the long folds of a scarf. Their exact identity no longer matters—only the delicate suggestion of movement.

The fact that a work like *Mademoiselle Pogany*, originating in marble carefully selected for its coloring and texture and lovingly smoothed by Brancusi's own hands, could be further refined in other materials and even cast in bronze or brass to take a high polish shows that the forms derived from universal ideas originating in Brancusi's mind and not in the nature of the material. The extreme of abstraction in his style is the *Bird in Space*, of 1928 (fig. 475), which began in more representational form, but through constant refinement evolved into a marvelous symbol suggesting the shape of a bird or a feather but conveying the purity, swiftness, and solitude of flight. The beauty of Brancusi's surfaces caters ir-

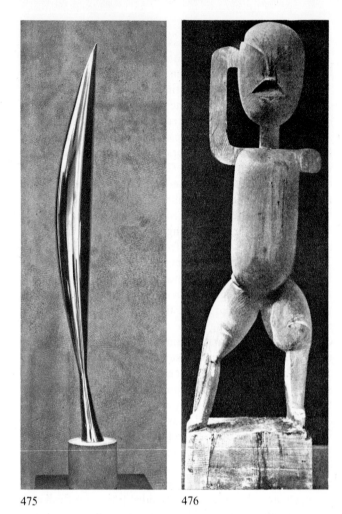

475   476

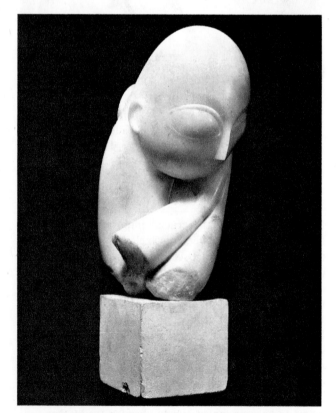

474. CONSTANTIN BRANCUSI. *Mademoiselle Pogany*. 1912. Marble, height 17½" (without base). Philadelphia Museum of Art. Gift of Mrs. Rodolphe M. de Schauensee, 1933

resistibly to the desire to touch, which he gratified by creating a series of so-called sculptures for the blind. Along with his exquisitely finished works in harder materials, Brancusi also carved in wood, with a certain heroic roughness, utilizing forms derived from the highly imaginative porch pillars and corbels of Rumanian peasant houses. In *The First Step*, of 1912–13 (fig. 476), done in rudely chiseled oak, the elongated shapes suggest with disarming humor a little girl about to stagger forth into the world.

After a period of considerable indebtedness to the simplifications of early Cubism, RAYMOND DUCHAMP-VILLON (1876–1918) gave promise of the highest originality. If his career had not been cut short by World War I, he might well have been one of the leading sculptors of the twentieth century. His *Horse*, of 1914 (fig. 477), is an extraordinary work. Its shapes suggest the elemental fury of a rearing horse only through their spirited curvilinear rhythms. As in the *Nude Descending a Staircase, No. 2*, by Duchamp-Villon's younger brother, Marcel Duchamp, the forms are mechanized; the elements of equine anatomy are already translated into the metal parts of turbines and pistons.

Although by no means an artist of the power of Duchamp-Villon, ALEXANDER ARCHIPENKO (1887–1964) absorbed the principles of Cubism in regard to the

475. CONSTANTIN BRANCUSI. *Bird in Space.* 1928. Bronze, 54". The Museum of Modern Art, New York

476. CONSTANTIN BRANCUSI. *The First Step.* 1913. Wood, height c. 44". Musée National d'Art Moderne, Paris. (All but the head now destroyed)

477. RAYMOND DUCHAMP-VILLON. *Horse.* 1914. Bronze, 39⅜ x 24". The Art Institute of Chicago. Gift of Miss Margaret Fisher

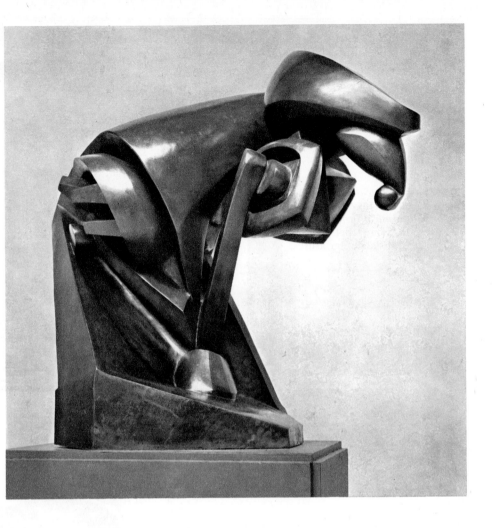

478. ALEXANDER ARCHIPENKO. *Walking Woman.* 1912. Bronze, height 26⅜". Collection Mme Alexander Archipenko, Hollywood, California

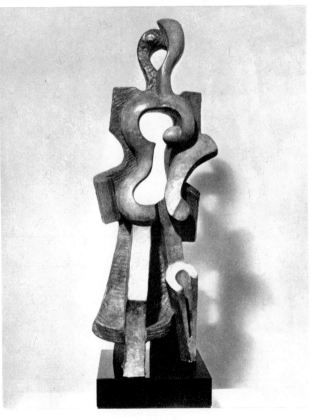

fragmentation of figures, and produced a series of Cubist sculptures of remarkable originality and brilliance. Often these were painted to resemble pictures, or executed in contrasting materials to produce a pictorial effect. His *Walking Woman*, of 1912 (fig. 478), exploits for the first time deliberately the principle of empty spaces in sculpture, which had appeared as a by-product of Baroque movement in such works as Bernini's *Apollo and Daphne* (see fig. 237). The holes are now as much a part of the composition as are the solids. It remained for the Constructivists (see pages 412–414) to take the next step by substituting directly assembled flat, folded, or carved sheets of material enclosing compartments of space for the modeled or carved masses of traditional sculpture.

Another sculptor of great ingenuity and, fortunately, a long and productive career was the Lithuanian-born JACQUES LIPCHITZ (1891–1973), who worked in Paris beginning in 1909, formed acquaintanceships with Cubist artists, and after 1941 lived and worked in the United States. Lipchitz declared that there was "no difference between painting and sculpture," and was for a while drawn totally into the Cubist orbit. Much of his early work, such as the *Still Life with Musical Instruments*, of 1918 (fig. 479), is a direct sculptural counterpart of Synthetic Cubist painting. The flat planes are organized much as in Cubism in a limited foreground space, but

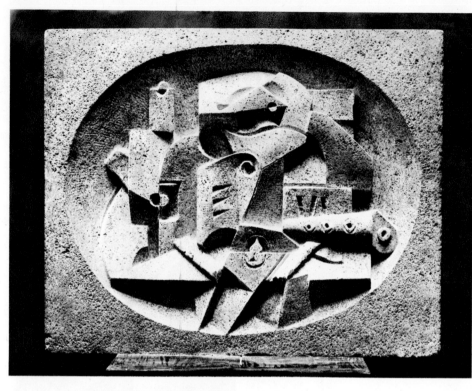

479. JACQUES LIPCHITZ. *Still Life with Musical Instruments.* 1918. Stone relief, 23⅝ x 29½". Estate of the artist

480. JACQUES LIPCHITZ. *Figure.* 1926–30. Bronze, height 85¼". The Museum of Modern Art, New York. Van Gogh Purchase Fund

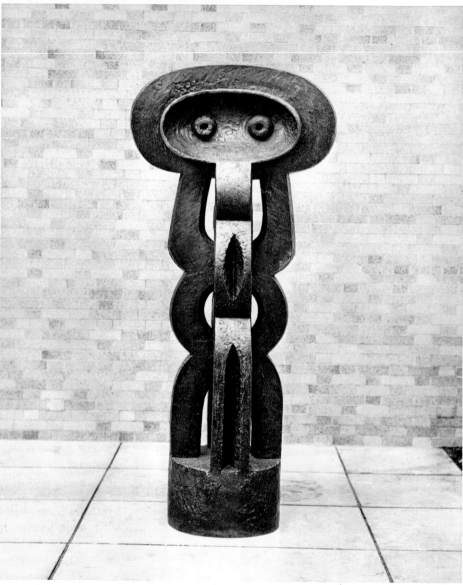

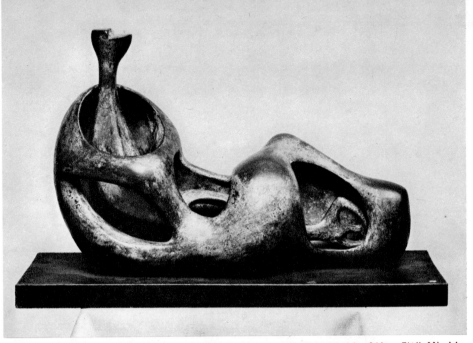

481. HENRY MOORE. *Interior-Exterior Reclining Figure.* 1951. Bronze, 14 x 21⅜ x 7½". Hirshhorn Museum and Sculpture Garden, Smithsonian Institution, Washington, D.C.

tilted here and there so as to produce a play of light and shadow analogous to the vibrant pictorial surfaces of Picasso and Braque. Lipchitz never worked directly in hard materials as did Brancusi, and preferred to the clay used by Rodin the synthetic material plasticine, which when cast in bronze can produce a rich pictorial surface. Monumental as is the disturbing *Figure,* of 1926–30 (fig. 480), whose eyes stare outward over a body composed of two opposed systems of links that interlock but never touch, the shimmer of light and shade still remains within the Cubist tradition.

Although the English sculptor HENRY MOORE (1898–) was never a Cubist in the strict sense and came to international prominence only after World War II, he has continued to the present certain tendencies that found their origin in Brancusi, Archipenko, and Lipchitz. His work is uneven, but the best of it, such as *Interior-Exterior Reclining Figure,* of 1951 (fig. 481), shows his original adaptation of the empty spaces and interlocking shapes of Cubist sculpture.

FUTURISM

In Italy in the first decade of the twentieth century was born a movement violently opposed to the character of that ancient land as a vast museum of the past. At first Futurism was a literary movement, conceived and championed by the writer Filippo Tommaso Marinetti as early as 1908, and proclaimed in a series of manifestos in 1909, 1910, 1911, and later. Impelled by the growing industrialization of the great cities of Northern Italy, the Futurists launched an ideological program that raised the machine-Romanticism of Léger and Delaunay to the status of a religion, attacking the past, advocating the destruction of academies, museums, and monumental

cities as barriers to progress, extolling the glories of industrial achievement and even of modern war, and leading, alas, in the direction of Italian Fascism. The aesthetic derivation of the Futurist artists inspired by Marinetti's ideas came from a variety of sources, chiefly Neoimpressionism and Cubism. The latter is dominant in the *Funeral of the Anarchist Galli* by CARLO CARRA (1881–1966); it is a brilliant work (fig. 482) of 1910-11, in which the cinematic aspects of Duchamp's *Nude Descending a Staircase, No. 2* are paralleled in a vast crowd composition, composed of a multitude of superimposed simultaneous images. The fragmented and shuffled views, stated as Cubist planes, are pervaded by an irresistible surge of motion, as crowds of enraged anarchists intersect with attacking police, and lifted weapons with floating banners, in a tempest of red and black planes.

The most gifted member of the Futurist group was UMBERTO BOCCIONI (1882–1916), who lost his life in World War I, ingloriously enough by a fall from a horse far from the scene of battle. His immense *The City Rises,* of 1910–11 (colorplate 69), is a panegyric to "modern" industrialism, a tidal wave of rearing draft horses and laborers hauling cables, above which rise the scaffolding and unfinished walls of a modern city in the process of building, and factory chimneys belching smoke into the air. The movement is achieved by means drawn from Géricault (see fig. 382), but the color is stated in terms of the divided palette of Seurat. Boccioni's finest achievement was in sculpture. His *Unique Forms of Continuity in Space,* of 1913 (fig. 483), is a tour de force the like of which had not been seen since Bernini. A charging male figure is preserved in any number of superimposed views, each miraculously expressed in solid form as far as form could be carried without disappearing.

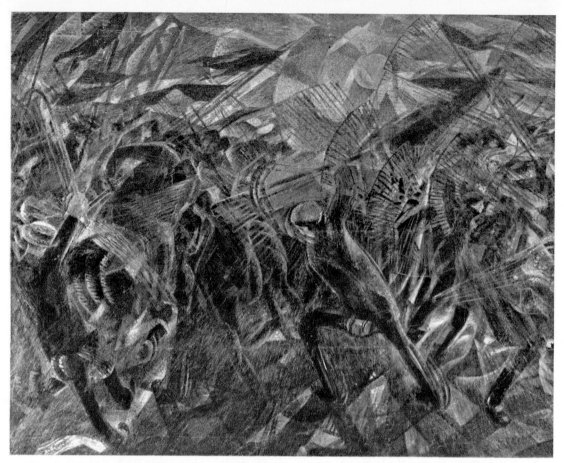

482. CARLO CARRÀ. *Funeral of the Anarchist Galli.* 1910–11. Oil on canvas, 6'6" x 8'6". The Museum of Modern Art, New York. Lillie P. Bliss Bequest

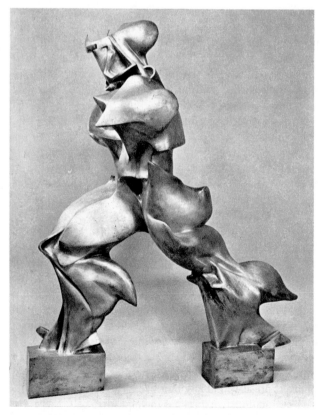

483. UMBERTO BOCCIONI. *Unique Forms of Continuity in Space.* 1913. Bronze, height 43½". The Museum of Modern Art, New York. Lillie P. Bliss Bequest

One of the last exponents of Futurism was JOSEPH STELLA (1877–1946), who came to the United States to live at the age of twenty-five, but revisited his native Italy during the formative period of Futurism. Stella's cinematic vision in the *Brooklyn Bridge*, painted in 1917–18 (fig. 484), celebrates a structure that had become for the late nineteenth and twentieth centuries a symbol of industrial and engineering triumph. Towers, cables, lights and beams of light, distant skyscrapers, tunnels, water, and night are woven into a symphonic structure of interpenetrating form, space, light, and color. Exhilaration in man's engineering victories had found its first artistic expression in Turner's *Rain, Steam, and Speed* (see colorplate 54), but voices of doom had already been raised in the eighteenth century by Goldsmith and Blake; the latter's vision of "dark Satanic Mills" was paralleled in nineteenth-century France by the prison-like constraint of Daumier's *Third-Class Carriage* (see fig. 406). Never again after Joseph Stella would it be possible to view in a positive sense industrial life, universally experienced in later twentieth-century art as dehumanizing.

SUPREMATISM AND CONSTRUCTIVISM

The modern movement, in which the Russian Kandinsky

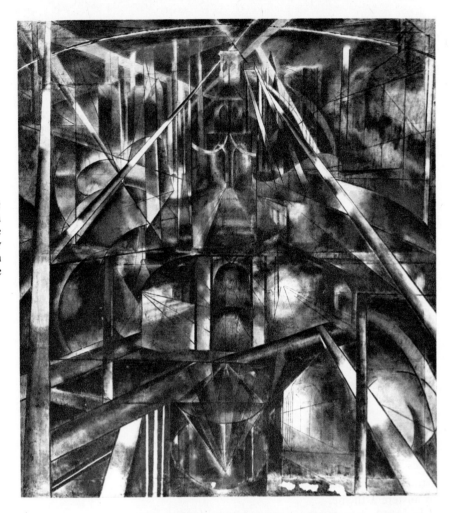

484. JOSEPH STELLA. *Brooklyn Bridge.* 1917–18. Oil on bedsheeting, 84 x 76″. Yale University Art Gallery, New Haven, Connecticut. Collection Société Anonyme

played such a crucial role, enjoyed a magnificent Russian chapter just before and just after World War I. In the early work of KASIMIR MALEVICH (1878–1935), especially *The Knife Grinder*, of 1912 (fig. 485), the principles of Cubism and Futurism merge. The mechanized geometrical shapes of Léger are multiplied by the cinematic multiple vision of the Futurists; as the knife grinder sits on the balustraded steps before a town house, his left foot pumps the treadle, his hands move back and forth with the wheel and the knife, and his head bobs up and down, producing a delightful set of simplified simultaneous images in bright red, yellow, blue, and white. We are hardly prepared by such a picture for Malevich's most original invention, a style practiced by him alone, which he entitled Suprematism. At first he dealt with constellations of soaring rectangles or trapezoids, which may have influenced the later airborne visions of Kandinsky (see fig. 455). Malevich's process of simplification culminated in the reduction, about 1918, of the whole pictorial field to a single white square floating delicately and freely on an ever so slightly different white ground (fig. 486). The *White on White* series, even at this early stage of twentieth-century art, represents very nearly the ultimate in abstraction. Yet contemplating a series of these ascetic pictures hung side by side, one is

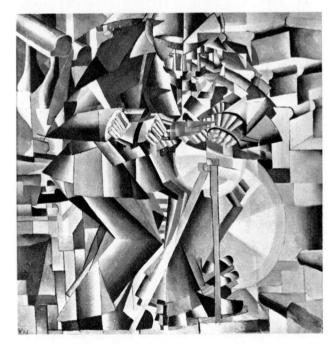

485. KASIMIR MALEVICH. *The Knife Grinder.* 1912. Oil on canvas, 31⅜ x 31⅜″. Yale University Art Gallery, New Haven, Connecticut. Collection Société Anonyme

486. KASIMIR MALEVICH. *Suprematist Composition: White on White.* c. 1918. Oil on canvas, 31¼ x 31¼". The Museum of Modern Art, New York

487. VLADIMIR TATLIN. *Monument to the Third International.* Model. 1919–20. Wood, iron, and glass. (Re-created in 1968 for the Tatlin Exhibition, Moderna Museet, Stockholm)

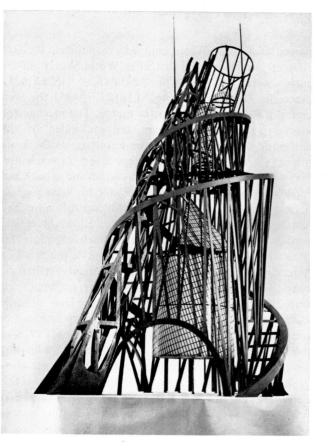

astonished at the range and variety Malevich can find in so austere a theme.

In 1913 VLADIMIR TATLIN (1895–1956) visited France, and was fascinated by the constructions Picasso was making as a by-product of his synthetic concern with the object. When he returned to Russia, Tatlin put together a series of reliefs (now destroyed and known only from photographs) from a wide range of improbable materials; these abstractions involve the principles of suspension and motion. In the early years after the revolution, Tatlin, excited by the vision of a new society, translated his abstract forms to almost inconceivable dimensions in order to praise socialism. His ambitious *Monument to the Third International*, for which only the model (fig. 487) was ever carried out, in 1919–20, would have been about 1300 feet in height, the tallest colossus ever imagined up to that time. As much architecture as sculpture, its three glass units inside a metal frame (a cylinder, a cube, a cone), housing assembly halls and meeting rooms, were intended to revolve at separate speeds, one daily, one monthly, and one yearly.

Two brilliant brothers, ANTON PEVSNER (1886–1962) and NAUM GABO (1890–), who changed his surname to avoid confusion with his older brother, carried Constructivism, as the new style came to be called, to a high pitch of intellectual and formal elegance. Gabo was the more inventive of the two, and was producing Constructivist sculpture based on the human form but exe-

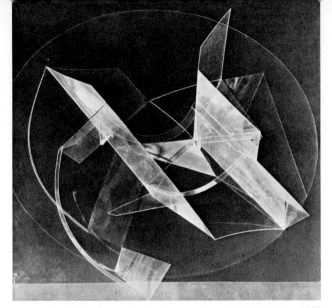

488

488. NAUM GABO. *Space Construction C.* c. 1922.
Plastic, 39 x 40″. (Whereabouts unknown.)
Photograph of the work, Yale University Art
Gallery, New Haven, Connecticut. Collection
Société Anonyme. Bequest of Katherine S. Dreier

489. ANTON PEVSNER. *Portrait of Marcel Duchamp.*
1926. Celluloid on copper, 37 x 25¾″. Yale
University Art Gallery, New Haven,
Connecticut. Collection Société Anonyme

490. EL LISSITZKY. *Proun 99.* 1924–25. Oil on
canvas. 50¾ x 39″. Yale University Art
Gallery, New Haven, Connecticut. Collection
Société Anonyme

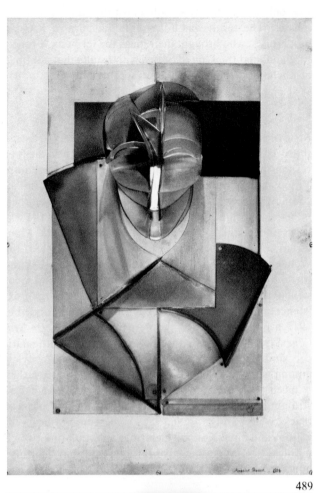

489

cuted in sheets of metal and cardboard, thus abandoning
entirely the concept of sculpture as mass, as early as 1915
in Norway. After the 1917 revolution he returned to
Moscow, where he was inspired by Tatlin's constructions, and began to create completely abstract works,
some even containing motors to produce vibrations. His
Space Construction C, of about 1922 (fig. 488), done entirely in transparent plastic, suggests volumes without
delimiting them, and produces endlessly changing
relationships of spaces as the observer moves around it.
Pevsner, trained as a painter, developed under his
brother's influence a somewhat weightier and more static
version of the volume style. The *Portrait of Marcel
Duchamp* (fig. 489), of 1926, commissioned by Katherine
S. Dreier, cofounder with Duchamp and Man Ray of the
Société Anonyme, suggests the brooding intellectuality
of the great innovator by means of abstract volumes
enclosed by translucent or opaque planes.

The achievements of the Constructivist sculptors were
paralleled in painting by EL LISSITZKY (1890–1956) in a
series that he called *Proun,* a fabricated word. *Proun 99,*
of 1924–25 (fig. 490), is a beautiful play on perspective
lines and a cube, which float in abstract space before a
slightly offcenter strip anchored by semicircles at top and
bottom. The freedom accorded to the ideas of the Constructivists in the early days of the revolution came to a
sudden end in 1920, when the Soviet government decided

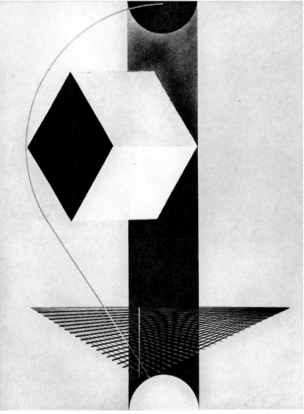

490

that only a realistic style could enlist the adherence of the masses. The result was a veritable diaspora of Russian modernists, who brought their ideas to Germany, France, England, and the United States with results that continue in unchecked vitality to the present day.

DE STIJL

MONDRIAN. World War I disrupted the lives of artists in those countries involved in the conflict. The war was responsible for the early deaths of Marc and Duchamp-Villon and, indirectly, that of Boccioni. It also cut off all contact between the groups of artists who had owed their intellectual origin to Cubism. In Holland during the war years the painters Theo van Doesburg and Piet Mondrian, the Belgian sculptor Georges Vantongerloo, the architect J.J.P. Oud, and others formed a group that had certain points of similarity with Suprematism and Constructivism, although without any knowledge of their existence, much less their ideas. The Dutch circle founded in 1917 a periodical called simply if pretentiously *De Stijl* (*The Style*), consecrated to the exaltation of mathematical simplicity in opposition to all "baroque" styles, among which they included Impressionism. Sternly, they reduced all formal elements to flat surfaces bounded by straight lines intersecting at right angles, and all colors to black, white, and gray and the three primary hues, red, yellow, and blue. Not only paintings and sculpture (which needless to say excluded all representation) but also houses, interiors, furniture, and all forms of design were

subjected to this principle. The leading theorist and finest artist of the movement, indeed one of the most sensitive, imaginative, and influential painters of the twentieth century, was Piet Mondrian (1872–1944).

Mondrian arrived at his point of view through a rapid evolution, in which he recapitulated the various stages of Modernism we have already seen, including Realism, Impressionism, Post-Impressionism, and Cubism. His development was guided by a mystical Calvinist philosophy, according to which art helped him to attain spiritual absolutes through the balance of opposites in the Cross. He stated that "(a) in plastic art reality can be expressed only through the equilibrium of *dynamic movements* of form and color; (b) pure means afford the most effective way of attaining this [equilibrium]." In such early, still Post-Impressionist works as *The Red Tree*, of 1908 (fig. 491), Mondrian reduced a leafless tree in bright winter sun to rhythms of brilliant red partly contoured in black, and reflected in red touches throughout the intense blue of ground and sky. Although strongly indebted to Van Gogh, Mondrian has already negated distance and emphasized the division of the plane of the canvas into colors united by movement. The intense excitement of this early work is maintained undiminished in his apparently ascetic later creations.

In 1911 Mondrian came under the influence of Cubism in Paris, and rapidly developed on the basis of Cubist segmentation a style that reduced Cubist planes to an almost entirely rectilinear grid covering the entire surface, through which floated still rather soft colors indebted to

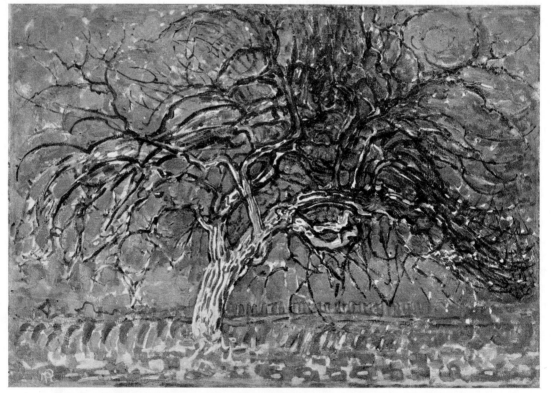

491. PIET MONDRIAN. *The Red Tree.* 1908. Oil on canvas, 27½ x 39″. Gemeentemuseum, The Hague, The Netherlands

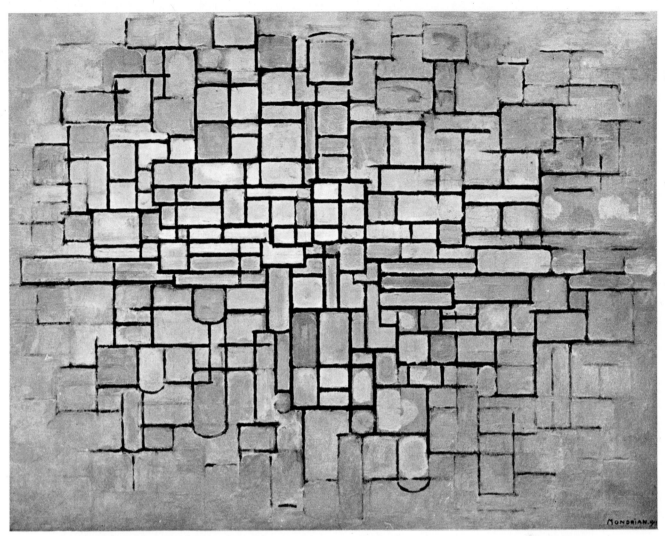

492. PIET MONDRIAN. *Composition in Line and Color.* 1913. Oil on canvas, 34⅝ x 45¼". Rijksmuseum Kröller-Müller, Otterlo. The Netherlands

Cubist limitations of hue. In such paintings as *Composition in Line and Color*, of 1913 (fig. 492), Mondrian has obeyed the implications of his title, as Whistler did not (see fig. 426), and all reference to natural appearances has vanished. It is important for the understanding of Mondrian's style that none of the scores of rectangles in the painting are identical, that each functions (as in the cityviews of the Impressionists, see fig. 420) like a single individual subject to the crosscurrents of an urban conglomeration. The opening or narrowing of the intervals in the grid produces the impression of surge, flow, constriction, impulses of varying speeds.

Contending that Cubism "did not accept the consequences of its own discoveries," Mondrian by 1919 had identified the picture firmly with the foreground plane. In his *Composition with Red, Yellow, and Blue*, of 1921 (colorplate 70), a system of broad black lines intersecting at right angles rules the field into rectangles of white, red, yellow, and blue. The effect is unexpectedly intense and lyrical. The white frame, designed by Mondrian himself,

is set back from the canvas, and does not appear to limit the movement of colors and lines, which run to the edge and appear to continue beyond it. No two rectangles are the same size or shape. Even the whites are not absolutely equal; those of the external rectangles are ever so slightly grayed. The color surfaces are delicately brushed, and never appear inert like those of Léger. The red, yellow, and blue are exquisitely weighted so that a system of poise and counterpoise emerges. The result is, as Mondrian intended it to be, a dynamic rather than a static expression, yet it establishes a serene harmony the like of which had not been seen in art since the subtle refinements and counterpoises of the Parthenon. In all the welter of twentieth-century styles, Mondrian's is the only one to achieve such a perfect state of rest.

If imitation is the sincerest flattery, Mondrian might possibly have been pleased by the spread of his ideas throughout all forms of twentieth-century art. He would have been less gratified by the popularization of his notions, misunderstood and caricatured, in advertising

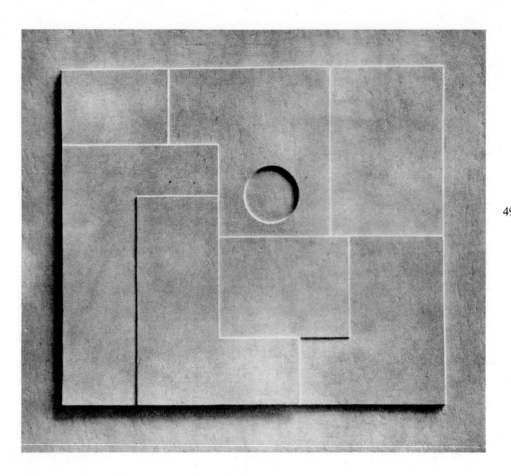

493. BEN NICHOLSON. *White Relief.* 1936. Oil on carved board, 8 x 9¼". Collection Naum Gabo, Middlebury, Connecticut

and even costume design. One reserved and sensitive artist who has always admired Mondrian, but knows how to put his principles to use in a highly original style, is the English painter-sculptor BEN NICHOLSON (1894–), who spent his adolescent years from 1911–13 in France and Italy. Out of the planes of Cubism he produced a system of subtly projected surfaces, rectangular and strictly vertical-horizontal as in Mondrian, but sometimes interlocking, and retaining the circle to great effect. Nicholson's delicate equipoise of white or softly tinted forms, as in *White Relief*, of 1936 (fig. 493), is more an emulation than an imitation of the great Mondrian.

8

Fantastic Art, Dada, and Surrealism

Throughout history fantasy and imagination have always underlain the most apparently rational thought processes, as witness the preposterous myths believed by the rational Greeks and embodied by them in images of ideal clarity, or the unbuildable architectural mirages that decorated the walls of the Romans, who were the most accomplished and practical architectural engineers of ancient times. A rich heritage of demons and monsters was bequeathed by the barbarian invaders to the collective experience of western Europe, and only partially endowed with Christian meaning in Hiberno-Saxon art. Time and again the undercurrent of demonic folklore has surfaced in European art, as in the Romanesque monsters denounced by Saint Bernard, or the phantasmagoria that haunted Bosch. The serenity of the eighteenth-century Enlightenment is jarred by the fantasy of Blake and Goya. And while the Impressionists were absorbed with the moment of optical reality, Redon, Ensor, Munch, and Rousseau in individual ways were exploring the world of the unreal.

During the twentieth century, despite severe attempts to rationalize human behavior, even to control it by totalitarian systems, the stubbornly irrational inner life of individuals and societies has been illuminated by Freud and his followers. Throughout this superficially scientific century, the current of fantasy has been fully as productive and important as those tendencies that seek an outlet in emotional expression or exalt the ideal of pure form. The first representatives of this fantastic tendency in the twentieth century were, like their precursors in the nineteenth, isolated individuals, but soon groups arose, notably Dada and the Surrealists, at least as cohesive as the Impressionists or the Cubists and far more vocal.

CHAGALL. A pioneer of twentieth-century fantastic art, and in a sense the heir of Rousseau, is the Russian painter Marc Chagall (1889–   ). From the treasury of Russian and Jewish folklore remembered from his youth in the western Russian city of Vitebsk, he has created a personal mythology of childlike directness and intimacy.

After a brief training in Vitebsk and St. Petersburg, in 1910—the year of Rousseau's death—he was drawn inevitably to Paris, artistic capital of the world. There in 1912 he painted his *Self-Portrait with Seven Fingers* (fig. 494), in which the brilliant colors and delightful imagery of Russian-Jewish folk tradition and the fragmented forms of Cubism are combined with an overflowing richness of imagination. The artist's quite normal right hand holds his brushes and his palette dotted with bright colors as if studded with jewels, while his left, with the inexplicable seven fingers, indicates the canvas he has just painted, representing a pink cow standing by a pail, attended by a soaring milkmaid, near a little Russian

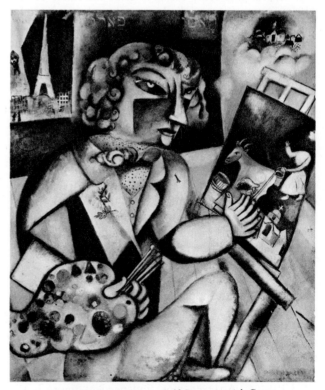

494. MARC CHAGALL. *Self-Portrait with Seven Fingers.* 1912. Oil on canvas, 50⅜ x 42⅛". Stedelijk Museum, Amsterdam

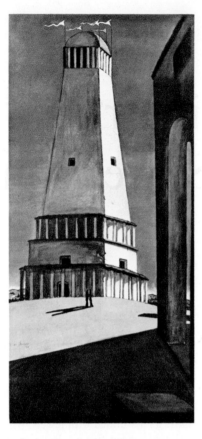

495. GIORGIO DE CHIRICO. *The Nostalgia of the Infinite.* c. 1913–14? (signed 1911). Oil on canvas, 53¼ x 25½". The Museum of Modern Art, New York. Purchase

church. Another vision of Russia appears in the clouds above the painting on the easel, while out the studio window searchlights comb the sky beside the Eiffel Tower. This visionary personal disclosure takes place in a studio with a yellow floor shaded here and there with red, and bright red walls curving like those in the distorting mirror in Parmigianino's *Self-Portrait* (see fig. 180). Lest we be enticed into hazardous interpretations of this and other Chagall pictures, the artist himself has said of his works, "I do not understand them at all. They are not literature. They are only pictorial arrangements of images which obsess me. . . . The theories which I make up to explain myself and those which others elaborate in connection with my work are nonsense. . . . My paintings are my reason for existence, my life, and that's all." During the exciting artistic developments after the Russian revolution, Chagall was as active as his other great compatriots, Kandinsky and the Constructivists, and later joined them in the general exodus of modern artists from Russia after 1920. In 1923 he settled in Paris, moved to New York City during World War II, and in 1948 to Vence in southern France. For more than half a century he has continued to pour out a prodigious series of paintings, stage designs, murals, etchings, lithographs, and the finest stained glass of the twentieth century, all in much the same personal idiom.

DE CHIRICO. An even more independent figure is the Greek-born Italian Giorgio De Chirico (1888–), of the utmost importance to the Surrealists, who deeply ad-

mired his early work. His youthful training in Athens and his adolescent years in Munich brought him in contact with Classical antiquity and German philosophy, particularly that of Nietzsche, who had disclosed his "foreboding that underneath this reality in which we live and have our being, another and altogether different reality lies concealed." In Paris from 1911–15, De Chirico had little interest in Impressionism, whose concern with sunlight seemed to him superficial, nor even in the Cubists or Fauves, then at the height of their fame. He produced a disturbing series of barren cityscapes, as monolithic as if carved from cliffs, lighted from the side so that long shadows fall across squares deserted save for occasional tiny figures. His *The Nostalgia of the Infinite* (fig. 495), painted about 1913–14 in Paris, shows a mysterious tower at the summit of a gently rising square, flags flying triumphantly from its domed top, unapproachable and frightening. The inert surfaces deny completely the Impressionist tradition. The subconscious significance of De Chirico's paintings is often easy to interpret in Freudian terms. In this less transparent instance, the tower may be a paternal symbol. Along with Carrà, whom he met when he was in the military hospital in Ferrara in 1917, and the painter Giorgio Morandi, De Chirico formed a short-lived group of "metaphysical artists." Soon he deserted his earlier manner in favor of a softer, pseudo-Classical style of considerably less interest and, later, imitations of Baroque painting. He even disowned some of his more psychoanalytically revealing early paintings, made copies of others, and in general played little part in the later development of contemporary art.

KLEE. The most intimate, poetic, and resourceful of the independent fantastic artists was Paul Klee (1879–1940), born in Switzerland of a German father, an organist. Klee, himself a trained violinist, studied in Munich and considered himself German. Early trips to Italy and North Africa broadened his artistic horizons. In 1911 he settled in Munich, where he formed a friendship with Marc and exhibited with Der Blaue Reiter. In straitened circumstances, he had no studio, and worked on the kitchen table while preparing meals for his wife, a piano teacher. His work was of necessity on a small scale—drawings, watercolors, and etchings. From 1921–31 he taught at the Bauhaus in Weimar (see Chapter 9), where he had his first studio, and lived in a two-family house, the other half of which was occupied by Kandinsky. The two artists respected each other's work greatly, yet exerted surprisingly little reciprocal influence. Both wrote important theoretical works while at the Bauhaus.

Klee was deeply interested in the art of children, which he felt could reveal much about the mysteries of creativity. This insight he combined with a wholly adult sophistication of wit in a uniquely personal poetic way. *Dance, Monster, to My Soft Song!*, of 1922 (fig. 496), shows a tiny pianist and singer, whose music compels a floating creature, consisting largely of an inflated head with a purple nose, to dance in the air, much to its surprise. The delicacy of the apparently spontaneous scratchy line and the softness of the tone are characteristic of much of Klee's work, which has been likened to a letter or a poem to be read in the hand, rather than a picture to be hung on a wall. *Ad Parnassum*, of 1932 (fig. 497), a painting on canvas, is apparently based on the celebrated series of piano exercises known as *Gradus ad Parnassum* (*Steps to Parnassus*), whose endlessly repeated notes merge as in the mind of a patiently practicing child into a mystical mountain of musical achievement, soaring higher than the sun.

After Klee was forced into exile in Switzerland by the Nazi regime in 1933, his art grew more intense and solemn and the scale of his forms larger and more powerful. *Death and Fire* (colorplate 71), painted in 1940, the last year of the artist's life, is one of the most intense of a series dealing with messages of ultimate spiritual significance in terms of hieroglyphs. The person, the sun, the death's head in the center, the background of brown and red, the ghostly character of the entire picture may well refer to the disaster that had befallen western Europe in that dreadful year of the fall of France, the Low Countries, and much of Scandinavia before Nazi Germany's onslaught.

DADA

As early as 1915, it became apparent that the static trench warfare of World War I was unlikely to produce any result more decisive than continuing mass slaughter. A number of young intellectuals, notably the German writers Hugo Ball and Richard Huelsenbeck and the Alsatian artist Jean (Hans) Arp, sought refuge in Zurich, in neutral Switzerland, where they were soon joined by others, especially the Rumanian poet Tristan Tzara. In Zurich in 1916 Ball founded the Cabaret Voltaire, named after the great French skeptic of the eighteenth century, as a center for protest against the entire fabric of European society, which could give rise to and condone the monstrous destruction of the war. At first the evenings were literary, musical, or both. "Noise-music," a phrase

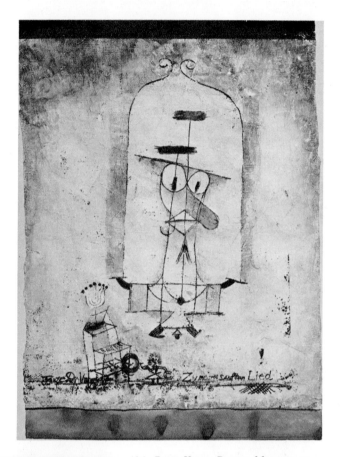

496. PAUL KLEE. *Dance, Monster, to My Soft Song!* 1922. Mixed mediums on gauze, mounted on paper, 17¾ x 12⅞". The Solomon R. Guggenheim Museum, New York. © Cosmopress, Geneva

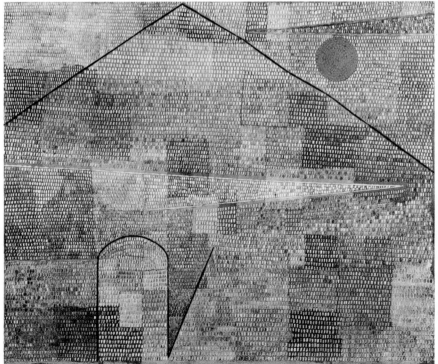

497. PAUL KLEE. *Ad Parnassum.* 1932. Casein and oil on canvas, 39⅜ x 49⅝". Kunstmuseum, Bern, Switzerland

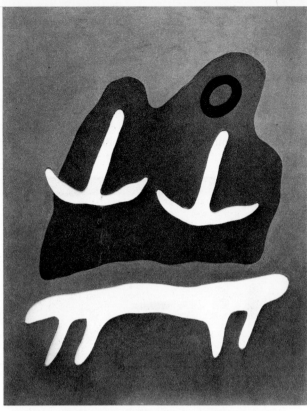

498. JEAN (HANS) ARP. *Mountain Table Anchors Navel*. 1925. Oil on cardboard with cutouts, 29⅝ x 23½". The Museum of Modern Art, New York. Purchase

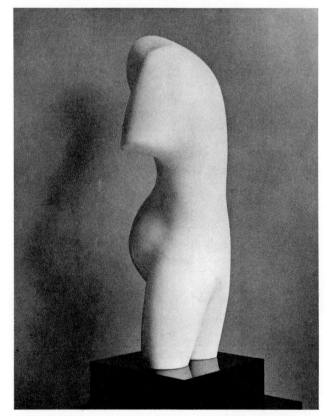

499. JEAN (HANS) ARP. *Torso*. 1953. White marble on polished black stone base, height (including base) 37"; base 4½ x 12 x 12". Smith College Museum of Art, Northampton, Massachusetts. Gift of Mr. and Mrs. Ralph F. Colin, 1956

the group borrowed from the Futurists (with whom they had little in common) alternated with readings of poems in several languages simultaneously, or with abstract poetry composed of meaningless syllables chosen purely for their acoustic interest. Public reaction at times approached actual violence, which was just what the group wanted. They attacked every cultural standard and every form of artistic activity, including even what had been avant-garde a decade earlier. It is characteristic of the movement that there should be several contradictory explanations of how its name, *Dada*, arose, but all agree that the title was intended as nonsense, and it was accepted by acclamation.

Dada soon became international. A group was promptly organized in New York by Marcel Duchamp (see page 405), together with the Cuban artist Francis Picabia, centering around the Gallery 291, which had been founded by the eminent photographers Alfred Stieglitz and Edward Steichen. Huelsenbeck returned to Germany in 1917 from Zurich when defeat seemed only a matter of time, and early in 1918 launched Dada in Berlin, largely as a literary movement. After the close of hostilities, Dada burst out in Cologne, instigated by the arrival of Arp, and sparked by the highly imaginative activity of Max Ernst, a local painter. Independently, Kurt Schwitters, also a painter, began his long Dada activity in Hanover. With the convergence of Tzara, Picabia, and Duchamp on Paris, Dada enjoyed a brief life there from 1919 until its dissolution in 1923.

There was always a certain mad logic about even the most perverse and apparently destructive manifestations of Dada humor, but it was hardly to be expected that new art forms would arise from it. Nonetheless, the very ferocity of the Dada offensive unleashed a remarkable amount of creativity, manifesting itself in spontaneous expressions that exalted artistic activity or chance occurrences.

JEAN ARP (1887–1966), born in Strasbourg, which was then a German city, was the most gifted artist of the Zurich group. According to a perhaps apocryphal story, he discovered accidentally by tossing on the floor pieces of an unsatisfactory drawing he had torn up a very interesting pattern. Soon he experimented with arrangements of torn paper produced by chance, just as Tzara was at the same moment making collage-poems out of words and phrases clipped at random from newspapers.

Arp then began to experiment with pieces of wood cut out freely in curvilinear shapes with a band saw, suggesting amoebas or other primitive forms of life. Later, he used cutout cardboard, tastefully mounted and painted, in vaguely biomorphic shapes or configurations echoing nature as seen through moving water or a distorting glass. *Mountain Table Anchors Navel*, of 1925 (fig. 498), all in white, brown, black, and sky-blue, is a particularly engaging example of Arp's whimsy. In their freedom from such restrictions as the straight lines of table legs or anchor shafts, these collapsed shapes, direct

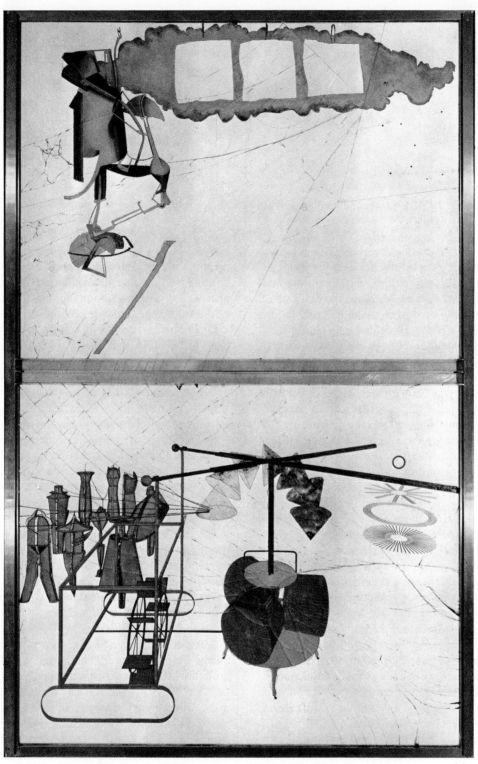

500. MARCEL DUCHAMP. *The Bride Stripped Bare by Her Bachelors, Even (The Large Glass).* 1915–23. Oil, lead foil, and quicksilver on plate glass, 9'1¼" x 5'9⅛". Philadelphia Museum of Art. Louise and Walter Arensberg Collection

ancestors of the soft machines of Oldenburg in the 1960s (see fig. 563), exert a special charm. After the dissolution of Dada, Arp continued to work as a sculptor in the free forms he had invented, promoting his earlier silhouettes to three-dimensional shapes melting into each other with exquisite grace. *Torso*, of 1953 (fig. 499), swells and contracts as subtly as if the velvety marble were breathing.

The leading spirit of Dada was Marcel Duchamp, whom we have already encountered in the wake of Cubism. Duchamp, nonetheless, kept a certain distance from Dada, as Michelangelo had from his Mannerist adulators. His greatest work, *The Bride Stripped Bare by Her Bachelors, Even*, executed between 1915–23 (fig. 500), is an immense construction, made up of two

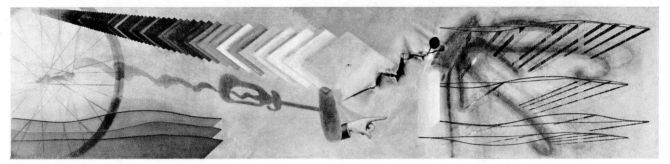

501. MARCEL DUCHAMP. *Tu m'*. 1918. Oil and graphite on canvas, with bottle brush, safety pins, and nut and bolt, 2'3½" x 10'2¾". Yale University Art Gallery, New Haven, Connecticut. Collection Société Anonyme. Bequest of Katherine S. Dreier

superimposed double layers of plate glass. The painting, if it can be called that, is generally done on the inside of one layer and protected by the other, like the filling in a sandwich, and executed in paint, lead foil, and quicksilver by techniques generally used to apply images and lettering to shop windows. The work deliberately eludes final interpretation, but insofar as it can be explained it depicts erotic frustration. The "bachelors" are the nine machine molds at the lower left, united by a "bachelor-machine" to a water mill and a chocolate grinder, all rendered with the precision of an engineering diagram, and in perspective so that they seem to float. Especially delicate are the three designs of rays or concentric circles in quicksilver. The "bride" is the mechanized creature at the upper left, an obvious descendant of the *Nude Descending a Staircase, No. 2* (see fig. 473). She grasps a cloud (suggesting the Milky Way), pierced by windows whose quivering outlines were studied from those of squares of gauze in a crossdraft. The transparency and reflectivity of the glass were intended to include the environment and the observer in the work of art. In 1926 the work was accidentally shattered; Duchamp was delighted, welcoming the cracks (which he meticulously repaired) as important elements in his work of art. The end result of deliberate planning, mechanical draftsmanship, imagination, and accident is a work of indefinable magic. Although its fragility has generally prevented it from traveling, and although during the years when it was in the collection of Katherine S. Dreier it was seen only by permission, this amazing creation has exercised an enormous influence on later art, up to and including the 1970s.

Duchamp's ingenuity produced visual machines, such as whirling blades of glass that fuse to produce floating circles, and visual gramophone records of cardboard that convert to spatial images through the revolution of the turntable. His spirit of raillery caused him to exhibit a photograph of the *Mona Lisa* supplied with a moustache and goatee and the title *L.H.O.O.Q.*, which pronounced in the French manner results in a mildly obscene pun. He exhibited such ordinary objects as a bicycle wheel, a snow shovel, a rack for drying bottles, and a urinal, to which he gave titles, calling them his "ready-mades." Whether or not these manufactured objects were in themselves beautiful (and some undoubtedly were), and although he

had not in any way altered their appearance, Duchamp certainly placed a new dimension on artistic creation by limiting it to the sole act of choice. His ready-mades have provoked lively discussion among artists, critics, and historians for nearly two generations.

One of his last paintings was *Tu m'*, of 1918 (fig. 501), long installed in the library of Katherine S. Dreier's home. Shadows of ready-mades—a bicycle wheel, a corkscrew, and a coatrack—float on the canvas, penetrated by a procession of what appear to be color cards, but are actually painted. Seen in perspective, they seem to be rushing out of the picture, but are restrained by a *real* bolt. Duchamp hired a professional sign painter to paint the pointing hand, then *painted* a jagged rip in the canvas apparently made by the protrusion through it of a *real* bottle brush and fastened by *real* safety pins. The enigma suggested by the incomplete but probably insulting title and the interpenetration of reality, illusion, and shadows make this one of the most disturbing paintings of the twentieth century. Except for producing miniature reproductions of his glass works, Duchamp claimed to have abandoned art for chess; actually, he was producing in secret for many years an elaborate peep show of a nude woman in a vegetation-lined box, whose existence was revealed only after his death.

A kindred spirit is MAX ERNST (1891–   ), a self-taught Cologne painter. The barren world of De Chirico probably influenced Ernst's magical *The Elephant of the Celebes*, of 1921 (fig. 502). The entire foreground is filled with a mechanical monster, towering above a floorlike plain, which ends in a distant range of snowcapped mountains. The creature is composed of a washboiler fitted with various attachments, including a hose that serves as both neck and trunk, leading to a mechanical head sprouting horns; a pair of tusks emerges from the creature's rear. In the foreground a headless female mannequin gestures with a gloved hand next to a perilous tower of coffeepots.

In Hanover, meanwhile, a lonely and sensitive spirit, KURT SCHWITTERS (1887–1948), was producing marvelous pictures out of ordinary discards rescued from the wastebasket or the gutter—tags, wrappers, tram tickets, bits of newspapers and programs, pieces of string. In a sense they resemble Cubist collages, and are as well put together as the best of them, but they lack the unifying temporal experience of the café. Only the detritus of society interested Schwitters, a kind of poetic scavenger who could create beauty from what is ordinarily considered less than nothing—aided from time to time with a few strong touches of a color-laden brush. His *Picture with Light Center*, of 1919 (fig. 503), is typical of what he called his *merz* pictures. This nonsense syllable was drawn from the word *Commerzbank* (*bank of commerce*), and he used *Merzbau* to describe the fantastic structure of junk he erected that eventually filled two stories of his house in Hanover. After the destruction of this concretion by the Nazis, Schwitters began another in Norway and yet a third in England. His *merz* pictures, often tiny and jewel-like in their delicacy and brilliance, continued some of the principles of Dada until the middle of the century.

SURREALISM

By 1923 the iconoclasm and the nihilism of Dada had begun to fade, and most artists had deserted the movement. Nonetheless, Dada had performed a valiant service in liberating the creative process from logical shackles. Surrealism took the next step—that of exploring illogic on Freudian principles in an endeavor to uncover and utilize for creative purposes the "actual" (as opposed to the logical) processes of thought. In 1924 the French author André Breton launched his first Surrealist manifesto. At the outset Surrealism was a thoroughly

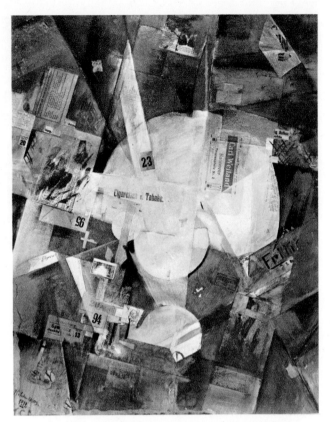

503. KURT SCHWITTERS. *Picture with Light Center.* 1919. Collage of paper with oil on cardboard, 33¼ x 25⅞". The Museum of Modern Art, New York. Purchase

literary movement, based on the free association of mental images through automatic writing, uncontrolled by conscious thought, thus putting in lasting form the fleeting configurations that occur ordinarily through subconscious activity only in dreams or waking reverie. Goya had already shown the way in his celebrated print *The Sleep of Reason Produces Monsters* (see fig. 378). Methodical, even doctrinaire, as was Breton's approach, the resulting combinations of images could and often did exert a commanding power or even a poetic charm, as in a striking simile borrowed by the Surrealists from the nineteenth-century writer Lautréamont: "As beautiful as the chance encounter on a dissecting table of a sewing machine and an umbrella."

Although Breton was at first hostile to painting, artists were not slow in seeing the possibilities inherent in his emphasis on subconscious association. In 1925 the first Surrealist group exhibition took place at the Galerie Pierre in Paris; among the exhibiting artists, Arp, De Chirico, Ernst, Klee, and Picasso are already familiar to us; of these only Ernst would today be classified as a true Surrealist. A brilliant new name was that of Joan Miró. René Magritte joined the group in 1927, and in 1929 Salvador Dali became a member, although he was formally read out of the party by Breton only five years later.

Ernst at first studied the possibilities offered by recom-

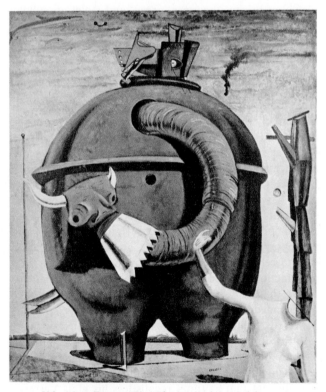

502. MAX ERNST. *The Elephant of the Celebes.* 1921. Oil on canvas, 51⅛ x 43¼". Collection The Elephant Trust, London

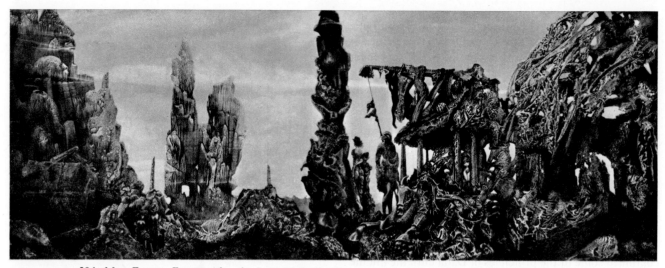

504. MAX ERNST. *Europe After the Rain.* 1940-42. Oil on canvas, 21½ x 58⅛". Wadsworth Athenaeum, Hartford, Connecticut

bining figures, backgrounds, and accessories cut out of nineteenth-century wood-engraved illustrations, assembling them—or so he claimed—only as dictated by free association and pasting the results into illustrations for a subconscious collage "novel." The continuous pseudo-narrative thus produced resembles a continuous dream that at times becomes a nightmare. Ernst also discovered accidentally the effects obtainable by laying a piece of paper over a rough surface, such as wood, stone, leaves, or sackcloth, and rubbing the paper with soft pencil; in the variegated flow of tones thus produced he discovered imagery, which he then exploited in painting. He called this technique frottage (from *frotter*, meaning *to rub*). Later, he spread paint on canvas, and compressed it while still wet, forming free shapes analogous to those produced by frottage. Since conscious choice could be involved in the selection of the surfaces to be used, and in the placing of the image on canvas, it may be questioned whether the frottage technique was a true analogue of Breton's unconscious writing. Ernst used frottage in the production of his most compelling Surrealist works, a series of fantastic views suggesting jungles or underwater or lunar landscapes, among whose seemingly animate accretions figures can at times be discerned. A terrifying example is *Europe After the Rain*, of 1940–42 (fig. 504), done while the artist was in hiding from the Germans during the occupation of Paris, and suggesting the desolation of a collapsed civilization.

MIRÓ. In contrast to the nightmare world of Ernst, the Catalan painter Joan Miró (1893–) revels in a fantasy as unbridled as that of the other Surrealists, and in a wit sharper than that of any other of them. His *Harlequin's Carnival*, of 1924–25 (fig. 505), depicts in sparkling colors a room furnished only with a table, but inhabited by a delightful menagerie of improbable beasts, some resembling cats, some insects, and others serpents. All are as flat as paper cutouts and painted black, white, red, yellow, and blue in irresponsible combinations. One ser-

pent is headless, another terminates in a boxing glove. All are celebrating happily with the exception of an anthropoid creature at the left, whose eyes cross in a face half-red and half-blue, while a serpent winds around what appears to be a horn. A black-and-blue comet joins in the festivities, and a view out the window discloses a black pyramid, a tongue of red flame, and a black-and-blue star. Less uproarious, equally witty, and in a strange way monumental is *Painting, 1933* (colorplate 72), in which biomorphic shapes reminiscent of Arp's are elegantly silhouetted in black, white, or red, or rendered in pure outline; they float in an atmosphere softly divided into planes of brown, tan, rose, green, and violet, dissolving into each other.

DALI. The flat, unmodeled shapes of Miró offer a total contrast to the work of his compatriot Salvador Dali (1904–), who in the minds of many, especially in the United States, typifies in his art, his writing, and his deliberately outrageous public behavior the Surrealist movement at its height in the 1930s. After his visit to Paris in 1928 Dali experimented briefly with semi-abstract forms, as he was then under the influence of Picasso and Miró. Soon Dali set out on his individual path, based on his study of Freud, which seemed to clarify to him his personal fantasies and obsessions. Dali began producing what he called "hand-colored photographs of the subconscious," based as he put it, on the "three cardinal images of life: blood, excrement, and putrefaction." Needless to say, if Dali had limited his subject matter to these three substances he would have commanded only transitory attention. What he called his desire to "materialize images of concrete irrationality with the utmost imperialist fury of precision" resulted in pictures of a quality and brilliance that cannot be ignored, done in bright enameled color, with an exactitude of statement that at times recalls less his idols Vermeer and Velázquez than the technique of the Netherlandish masters of the fifteenth century. Sometimes Dali's sexual symbolism is so explicit as to render the exhibition or publication of his works difficult. Usually, however, it is veiled, but the terrifying images are always brought home with tremendous force by the magical virtuosity of his draftsmanship and color.

The Persistence of Memory, of 1931 (fig. 506), is one of Dali's most striking and best-known early Surrealist paintings. Dali said the idea for the work occurred to him while he was eating ripe Camembert cheese. Actually, the softening of hard objects had already appeared, as we have seen, in the work of Arp (see fig. 498). Whatever their origin, the "wet watches," as they were promptly termed by the astonished, horrified, and fascinated New York public when the picture was first exhibited at The Museum of Modern Art, are disturbing in their destruction of the very idea of time. Three watches lie or hang limply, and a fourth is devoured by ants, while a severed, chinless head—its tongue hanging from its nose, its enormous eyelashes extended on its cheek—lies equally limp on a barren plain reminiscent of De Chirico or early Ernst (see figs. 495, 502). In the background, rendered with hallucinatory clarity, are the rocky cliffs of a Catalan bay.

A contrast to this small picture is the larger and overpowering *Soft Construction with Boiled Beans: Premonition of Civil War*, painted in 1936 (colorplate 73). Monstrous fragments of humans—arms, a breast being squeezed by a clawlike hand, a convulsed and screaming

head—tower against a desolate sky partly covered with filmy clouds. The rocky terrain in the foreground pullulates with beans, while above one clenched fist a tiny bearded man gazes disconsolately at the scene. One of the most frightful images in the entire history of art, this picture is, nonetheless, endowed by Dali's astonishing skill with an unexpected and terrible beauty. After considerable activity in the fields of stage design, jewelry design, and even shop window decoration, Dali moved to Christian art. While he lost none of his technical brilliance, the evaporation of his magical fantasy is regrettable. From a religious standpoint his recent work shows neither the depth of Rouault, let us say, nor the graceful poetry of Matisse.

OTHER SURREALIST PAINTERS. A far less intense Surrealist, but delightful within his self-imposed limitations, is the Belgian RENÉ MAGRITTE (1898–1967), who emerged as a Surrealist in 1926. For the next forty years he continued producing his own quiet, witty versions of the Surrealist style, based on the absurd found in everyday life—double images, vanishing people, opaque objects suddenly become transparent, people and things suddenly transformed into incompatible materials. Magritte hints at nothing sinister, and his surprises offer an irresistible combination of poetry and humor. A late work, the *Delusions of Grandeur*, of 1961 (fig. 507), shows the amount of fun he can extract from nearly

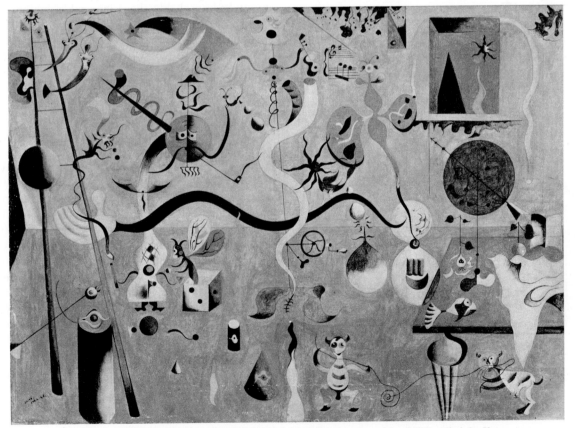

505. JOAN MIRÓ. *Harlequin's Carnival*. 1924–25. Oil on canvas, 26 x 36⅝". Albright-Knox Art Gallery, Buffalo, New York. Room of Contemporary Art Fund

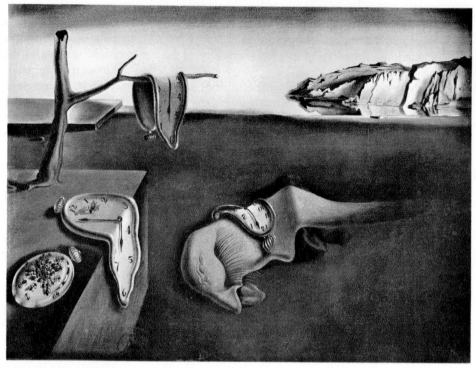

506. SALVADOR DALI. *The Persistence of Memory.* 1931. Oil on canvas, 9½ x 13". The Museum of Modern Art, New York

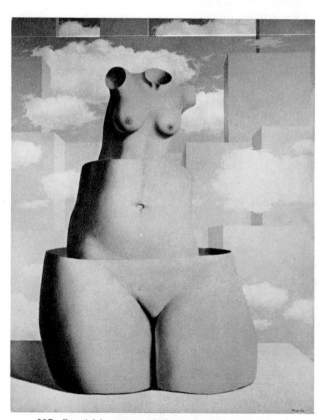

507. RENÉ MAGRITTE. *Delusions of Grandeur.* 1961. Oil on canvas, 39⅜ x 31⅞". Alexandre Iolas Gallery, New York

nothing. A cast of a Classical female torso is divided into three sections, each miraculously smaller than the one below, the last seeming to soar into a cloud-filled blue sky, itself improbably sliced into cubic sections. But we have no right to object; in the deadpan world of Magritte, anything goes.

A latecomer to the Surrealist movement, the Chilean painter Sebastian Antonio Matta Echaurren, generally known as MATTA (1912–   ), formed a historical link between European Surrealism and the American Abstract Expressionist movement (see Chapter 10). But Matta's real importance is far greater than this. His work, especially during the period shortly after his arrival in the United States in 1939, is intensely beautiful in itself. Matta's enormous ability during these exciting years lay, first of all, in his skill in rendering entirely imaginary, abstract shapes with the same convincing accuracy Dali devoted to his images based on reality, and, second, in the fierce energy that surges through his paintings. His brilliant images—opaque, transparent, translucent, pearly, sparkling, milky, in succession or all at once—seem to be driven by some unrestrainable energy, such as a fire storm or a tornado. *Listen to Living,* of 1941 (colorplate 74), with its glowing color and volcanic fury of movement, was a revelation when it was first exhibited to the New York public.

9

Modern Architecture

Architecture has been characterized as the "indispensable art," and rightly so. Mankind could survive physically without images or ornaments of any sort, but in most climates would perish without shelter. Inevitably, the practical functions shelters are designed to fulfill play a strong role in determining their appearance and thus, in part, their artistic character. So, indeed, do the methods of construction available and practicable at any given moment. For example, the revolutionary forms and spaces of Roman architecture can scarcely be understood without knowledge of their purpose in Roman urban society, nor could they have been built without the newly devised Roman technique of concrete construction. Similarly, the forms and spaces of Gothic architecture arose to meet the religious needs of late medieval European society, and were a product of the ribbed vault and its elaborate system of internal and external supports. The strikingly new forms of architecture that appeared in the late nineteenth and in the twentieth centuries were built to meet the needs of industry and of commerce based on industry, in a society whose essential character and internal relationships had been sharply transformed by the Industrial Revolution. Few new palaces were built for the nobility or monarchies, for example; the characteristic new structures were industrial or commercial buildings, and the techniques invented to fulfill the new functions were, in turn, adopted for such traditional types as dwellings and churches.

THE LATE NINETEENTH-CENTURY COMMERCIAL BUILDING

About the middle of the nineteenth century, mechanized industrial production began to demand large, well-lighted interiors in which manufacturing could be carried on. The administration of giant industrial and commercial concerns required office buildings of unprecedented size, containing suites of offices easily accessible to employees and to those of other organizations. The marketing of industrial products necessitated large-scale storage spaces, and enormous shops selling under one roof a wide variety of items. Industrial and commercial pressures drew increasing populations to urban centers, and traditional housing was no longer adequate to contain them. Mechanized transportation of industrial products and industrial and business personnel was essential. Leisure-time entertainment and cultural activities for the vast new urban populations required still a different kind of structure. Hence, the characteristic new architectural forms of the late nineteenth and twentieth centuries have been the factory, the multistory office building, the warehouse, the department store, the apartment house, the railway station (eventually superseded by the air terminal), the large theater, and the gigantic sports stadium. None of these could have been built on the desired scale by traditional constructional methods.

Unfortunately, as a glance around any modern metropolis will show, only a small fraction of these new structures could be described as artistically interesting. And many that can have nostalgically masked their new constructional methods under a veneer of columns, arches, towers, and ornament drawn from the architecture of earlier periods. Worse, the immense demand for economically "viable" new constructions has already swept out of existence considerable numbers of really fine late nineteenth- and twentieth-century structures that were revolutionary when they were built, and completely satisfied the commercial demands of the time. The present account will be limited almost entirely to revolutionary structures that deliberately broke with architectural tradition in one way or another.

Since the Gothic period no truly revolutionary practical techniques of construction arose until the late eighteenth century, when cast iron came into use for bridges. As we have seen (pages 354, 355), cast iron was employed in the mid-nineteenth century also for large interiors, especially for industrial structures and for temporary exhibition buildings (see fig. 410). When used for more traditional architectural types, such as churches and libraries (see fig. 409), cast iron was generally restricted to roofs and their internal supports, and from the exterior the building presented itself as a masonry

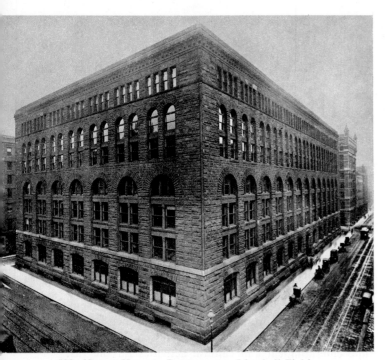

508. HENRY HOBSON RICHARDSON. Marshall Field
Wholesale Store (demolished 1930). 1885–87.
Chicago. Courtesy Chicago Historical Society

structure. Mid-nineteenth-century commercial buildings in some American cities did, however, exhibit cast-iron façades whose elements were imitated from the columns and arches of Italian Renaissance *palazzos*.

Cast iron had its faults as a construction material. Its tensile strength was low, and so was its melting point; hence, it was prone to collapse and to conflagration. The invention of a process for the manufacture of steel by Sir Henry Bessemer in the 1850s led to steel's first widespread use in building in response to the new necessities. Only structural steel could have made possible the characteristic multistory structure of the modern city. A concomitant invention, the power elevator, rendered such buildings practicable by freeing the vertical transportation of persons and objects from endless stairs. Hoists of one sort or another, operated manually, have been known since antiquity, but the first power elevator, driven by steam, made its appearance only after the middle of the nineteenth century. By the 1870s steam had given way to hydraulic power as the motive force for elevators, and during the 1890s electricity took over this job. The modern city was on its way, with all its seemingly insoluble problems of space and transportation, increased manyfold by the invention of the internal-combustion engine.

Early commercial structures in most nineteenth-century metropolitan centers were not essentially distinguishable from any other kind of secular building—houses or hotels, let us say—save by their extent. The development of the multistory structure, and eventually the skyscraper, was immeasurably assisted by the great fire of 1871 that virtually destroyed the center of

Chicago, which was built largely of wood. A number of pioneer multistory buildings were constructed during the ensuing period of chaotic rebuilding. An early attempt to face the necessities of the commercial building and express them artistically was the Marshall Field Wholesale Store (fig. 508), built in 1885–87 by HENRY HOBSON RICHARDSON (1838–86), who died before its completion. Richardson recognized that, although the ground story of a tall business building might have a real reason for being higher than the others, the needs of subsequent floors were essentially identical. In his seven-story structure, therefore, he kept the heights of the six upper stories uniform, but treated them as if they diminished by grouping them under massive, rusticated arches imitated from those of Roman aqueducts. The first arcade embraces the second, third, and fourth stories. The second arcade, with arches half as wide as those below them, contains the fifth and sixth stories. The windows of the seventh story, above a stringcourse, are rectangular, and half the width of those of the lower floors.

Out of sheer commercial necessity the immense number of windows was determined not by the external design of the building, as in many Renaissance and Baroque structures (some of which have false windows for symmetry's sake), but by the requirements of the interior. Internally, the floors were supported by an iron skeleton, as was general at the time, but the grand exterior arches and walls did bear weight. Unfortunately, the building had a life of little more than forty years; it was demolished in 1930 to make way for a parking lot. At the moment of its construction, however, the essential characteristic of the American multistory structure, the steel frame, was already in use elsewhere in Chicago in the artistically uninteresting Home Insurance Building, built in 1883–85 by William Le Baron Jenney (1832–1907). The steel frame, composed of vertical and horizontal beams riveted together, created a structure that stood almost independent of the laws of gravity, holding together not by downward thrust but by the tensile strength of the steel. When the Home Insurance Building was demolished in 1929, the walls were found to have been supported entirely by steel shelving protruding from the frame and to have been constructionally useless.

SULLIVAN. The steel-frame structure is a rectangular grid in which walls are reduced to curtains, and have in the twentieth century often been replaced entirely by glass (see figs. 533, 534). Hence, the impression of massiveness and of superimposed elements of constantly decreasing weight, which in the Marshall Field structure corresponded to fact, was doomed to be replaced by emphasis on an allover rectangular pattern, well-nigh universal in twentieth-century multistory buildings. Post and lintel, arch and vault were reduced to anachronistic ornaments. An early building in whose design this essential fact was recognized from the start is the Wainwright Building in St. Louis, of 1890–91 (fig. 509), a masterpiece by Louis Sullivan (1856–1924), rescued from demolition in 1975 by enlightened governmental action. Sullivan grouped the first and second stories together as a pedestal, then handled the next seven as absolutely identical. He emphasized the verticality of the structure by treating the walls between the windows as slender shafts, running up seven stories, with delicate capitals and bases, achieving the effect that the building looks much taller than it really is. For the spaces between the windows, corresponding to the floors supported by horizontal beams, and for a splendid band at the top, he used a rich system of ornamentation devised by himself. The final cornice (to hide chimneys and water tower) gives the building a blocklike effect not unlike that of a Renaissance palace

(see fig. 31). But if its massive appearance recalls Renaissance tradition, for its basic design the building depends entirely on frank recognition of its steel frame.

A still more revolutionary work, remarkably prophetic of much twentieth-century architecture, is the Carson Pirie Scott Department Store, built in Chicago by Sullivan in 1899–1901 and enlarged in 1903–1904 (fig. 510). Here he recognized for the first time the basic identity between vertical and horizontal directions implicit in the very nature of the steel frame. In his design any reference to columns is reduced to the slender shafts running up ten stories between the windows at the rounded corner of the building. The areas between the windows on both façades are left flat and smooth, so that verticality

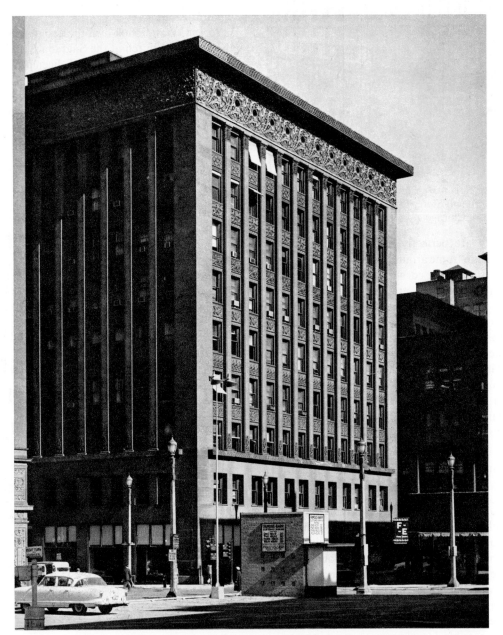

509. LOUIS SULLIVAN. Exterior, Wainwright Building (view from the southeast). 1890–91. St. Louis

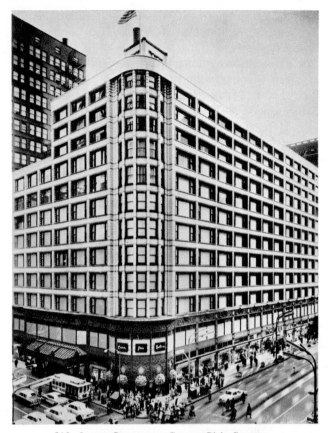

510. Louis Sullivan. Carson Pirie Scott Department Store. 1899–1901; enlarged 1903–4. Chicago

and horizontality are perfectly balanced. Ornament is reduced to a delicate frame around each window, and to a gorgeous outburst over the corner entrance to the store. Such ornamental passages are the only aspect of Sullivan's style that ties him to the work of his European contemporaries discussed below. The crowning cornice, as compared to that of the Wainwright Building, is greatly reduced in height and projection. Despite innumerable reversions to Gothic tracery or Classical columns at the bases and summits of American steel-frame structures during the first three decades of the century—embellishments now abandoned as useless luxuries—Sullivan had set the stage for modern architecture.

ART NOUVEAU AND EXPRESSIONIST ARCHITECTURE

In sharp contrast to the rational criteria that guided the work of the architects who have come to be known as the Chicago School, a very different set of principles was evolving in Europe, related to those of the Nabis and the Symbolists (see pages 382, 383), and to the movement in interior design and the decorative arts at the turn of the century known as Art Nouveau. European designers seem to have held the straight line in horror, substituting for it wherever possible (or where not, enriching it) exuberant curves recalling those of the Rococo (see figs. 323, 341) but surpassing them in freedom because of their emancipation from the rules of symmetry. The fresh naturalism of Art Nouveau and its related movements was often expressed in such characteristic modern materials as metal and glass.

GAUDÍ. In the last two decades of the century the new style appeared in Barcelona, and then just before the turn of the century burst forth in Paris, Brussels, Munich, Vienna, and even the traditionalist Italian cities. The greatest innovator, whose works are still astonishing in the liberty and scope of the imagination they disclose, was the Catalan architect and designer Antoni Gaudí (1852–1926). His work is limited to Barcelona, but his buildings are so richly scattered throughout the modern sections of the metropolis as to constitute one of its principal attractions.

In 1883 Gaudí took over the design and construction of the colossal Church of the Sagrada Familia in Barcelona (fig. 511), which had previously been projected and partly built as a rigorously neo-Gothic edifice. Although Gaudí worked on the Sagrada Familia off and on until his death, the church remains a fragment; only the crypt is

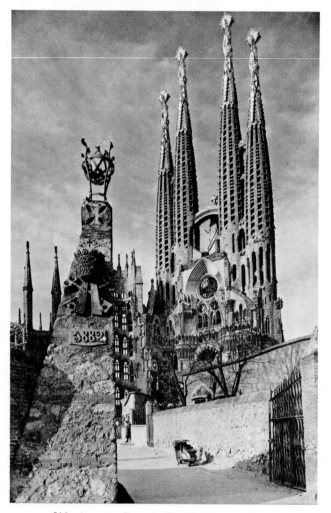

511. Antoni Gaudí. Church of the Sagrada Familia. 1883–1926. Barcelona

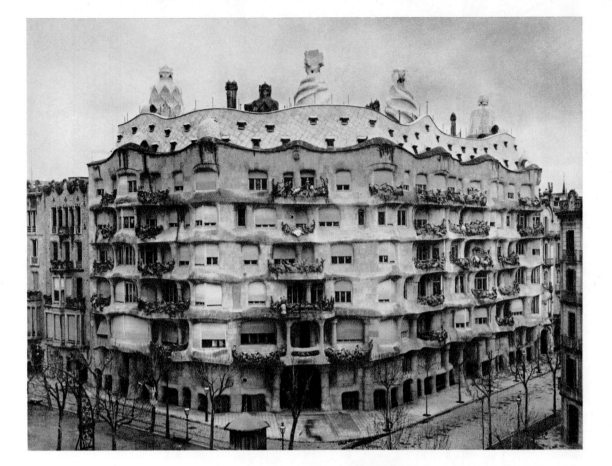

512. ANTONI GAUDÍ. Casa Milá. 1905–7. Barcelona

513. ANTONI GAUDÍ. Plan of a typical floor, Casa Milá

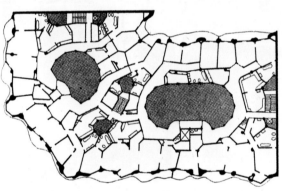

usable. The four bottle-shaped spires of one transept, pierced by unbelievably irregular spiral fenestration, tower above the earlier Gothic windows of the façade and the unprotected nave floor in shapes so fantastic that they seem to have grown there rather than to have been built.

Gaudí's masterpiece is the Casa Milá of 1905–1907 (figs. 512, 513), an apartment house, in whose plan and design, aside from the window mullions and transoms and some inner partitions, not a straight line remains. The building is convulsed as if it were gelatin. Balconies ripple and flow, bulge and retract in a constant turmoil; windows reject vertical alignment. Rich vegetable ornament in wrought iron drips from the balconies like flowering vines or Spanish moss. The chimneys—all different, of course—are spiral or imprinted with ir-

regular lozenge shapes or freely conoid. Inner courtyards and corridors move with the random patterns of natural caverns, and the interior walls and partitions are so arranged that few are parallel and none meet at right angles. Although one might have expected so fluid a building to have been constructed of a plastic material such as concrete, the façade is actually made of cut stone, the pulsating roof of marble slabs, and the chimneys of marble fragments. (In much of his work in houses, chapels, and parks, Gaudí included bits of broken ceramics or glass, embedded in free-form mosaics.) Could Dali have had the Casa Milá in mind when he painted his "wet watches"? Neglected and even condemned during the heyday of the International Style (see figs. 527, 532), Gaudí has recently taken his place as one

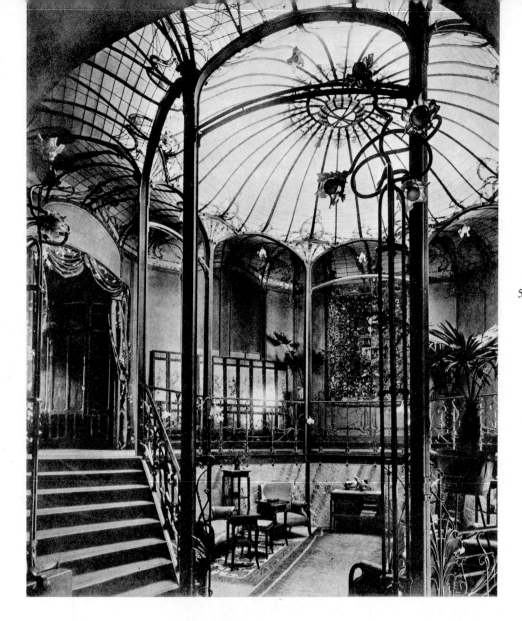

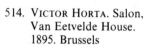

514. VICTOR HORTA. Salon,
Van Eetvelde House.
1895. Brussels

515. MAX BERG. Interior,
Centenary Hall.
1912–13. Wroclaw,
Poland (formerly
Breslau, Germany)

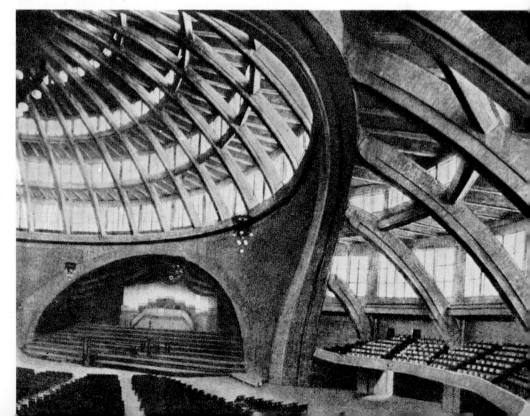

of the great creative minds of modern architecture, and his ideas have influenced immeasurably the work of such recent architects as Eero Saarinen, Nervi, and Soleri (see figs. 539, 540, 537, 546).

HORTA. A less vigorous but even more refined architect of the turn of the century, the true founder of Art Nouveau, was the Belgian Victor Horta (1861–1947). Horta studied with care the principles of Baroque and Rococo architecture and the structural ideas of the French nineteenth-century neo-Gothic architect and theoretician Eugène Viollet-le-Duc (1814–79), who was responsible for the excessive restoration of many French Gothic buildings. In Horta's Salon for the Van Eetvelde House in Brussels, built in 1895 (fig. 514), the only straight lines are the verticals of the columns and the horizontals of the floors, steps, and balustrades, although even these are curved in plan. Every line flows with the grace of natural growth, the lampstands curl like flowering vines, the light bulbs form the centers of huge flowers, and the framework that holds in place the glass of the central dome expands in natural curves like the ribs of a gigantic leaf.

EXPRESSIONIST ARCHITECTURE. Parallel with the development of Expressionism in German painting, early twentieth-century German architecture took on new and freer shapes, all strongly influenced by the structural innovations and imaginative fluidity of Art Nouveau. A brilliant example, displaying daring structural techniques, is the interior of the Centenary Hall at Wroclaw, Poland (formerly Breslau, Germany), built in 1910–12 by MAX BERG (1870–1948). Although the exterior is conventional and unimpressive in design, the vast interior space, based on an almost Leonardesque design with four apses radiating from a central circular space, is unexpectedly original (fig. 515). The four colossal arches supporting the dome on pendentives are curved even in plan, and the vaulting of the dome and the semidomes over three of the four apses (the fourth is a stage) consists of nothing but ribs, open to views of seemingly endless tiers of windows. The thrilling effect of lightness and free space is clearly related to the inventions of Guarini (see fig. 256), which were built in masonry; Berg's new design could have been executed only in the material for which it was intended, reinforced concrete, which has been used with great advantage in Europe and adopted somewhat more reluctantly in the United States. Berg's vision was the starting point for the even more dramatic recent creations of Pier Luigi Nervi (see fig. 537).

Another milestone in Expressionist architecture was the Einstein Tower at Potsdam, outside Berlin, built in 1919–21 by ERICH MENDELSOHN (1887–1953) and now destroyed (fig. 516). While a soldier in the trenches during World War I, Mendelsohn occupied many dreary hours by jotting down with a heavy stub pen in tiny sketchbooks hundreds of imaginative building designs, of which the idea for the Einstein Tower was one. He

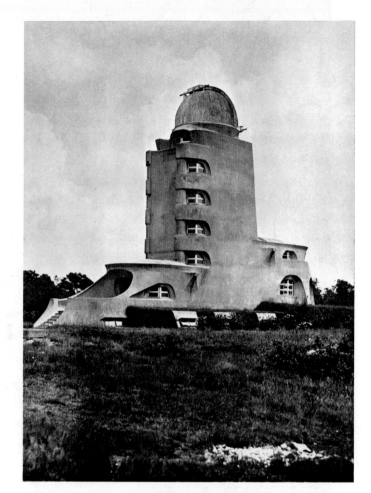

516. ERICH MENDELSOHN. Einstein Tower (destroyed). 1920–21. Potsdam, Germany

designed it to be constructed of poured concrete, for which its fluid forms were obviously intended, but for technical reasons it had to be built in brick covered with stucco. All the forms, including staircase, entrance, walls, windows, and dome, flow smoothly into one another with the utmost freedom and to great expressive effect, obliterating all straight lines other than, as in the Casa Milá by Gaudí, the inescapable window mullions and transoms.

FRANK LLOYD WRIGHT

A period and a law unto himself was Frank Lloyd Wright (1867–1959), one of the greatest American artists in any medium. Praise for him must be tempered by recollection of his weaknesses—his more than occasional lapses of taste, and the egoism that made it difficult for him to admit into his interiors any object he had not designed himself (an obvious impediment to the success of his designs for the Solomon R. Guggenheim Museum in New York City, and a torment to its staff since before the building was erected). But when all is said and done, Wright was an extraordinary man, a prophet of a new freedom and at the same time of a new discipline in architecture, a molder of form and space, and a genius

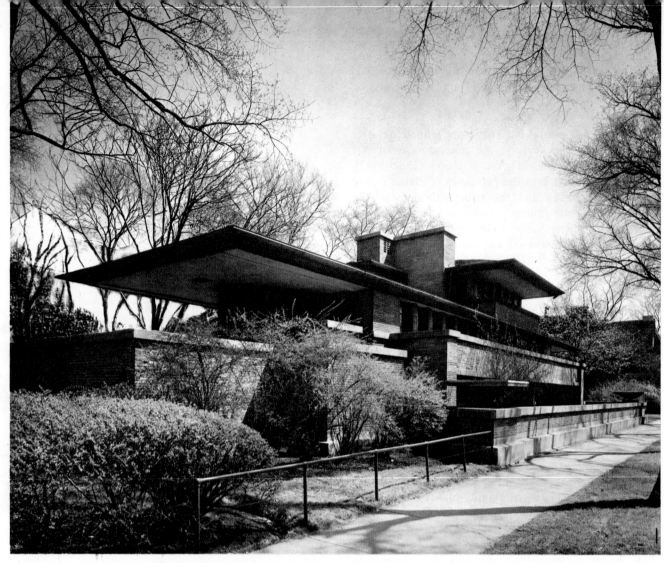

517. FRANK LLOYD WRIGHT. Exterior, Robie House. 1909. Chicago

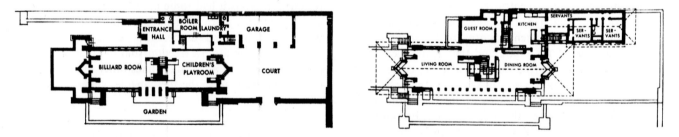

518. FRANK LLOYD WRIGHT. Plan of the ground floor and first floor, Robie House

who experienced the relationship between architecture and surrounding nature as has perhaps no other architect in history, so that his buildings seem literally to grow out of their environments.

Wright's first success, which brought him international recognition, was in the field of private residences, his "prairie houses," such as the revolutionary Robie House in Chicago, built in 1909 (fig. 517). As is visible in the plan (fig. 518), Wright has to a considerable extent departed from the Western tradition of enclosed, self-sufficient spaces opening into each other by means of doors. His rooms are partially enclosed subdivisions of a common space, which in itself is felt as a concentration of motives and forces outside the building. In plan and in elevation the house is at once invaded by outside space and reaches back dramatically into it. The influence on Wright of the Japanese Pavilion at the Chicago World's Fair of 1893 has often been pointed out, but it should also be recalled that as early as the 1870s American houses bristled irregularly with verandas at all levels, and interior spaces did indeed flow into one another (with room divisions often no more formidable than curtains or beaded dowel screens) off a central staircase hall utilized as the main living space. Wright's individual contribution lay in the daring of his assault on the outer world through cantilevered roofs projecting without vertical supports, seeming to float freely, and the purification of vertical and horizontal masses, as if by some sixth sense he had realized what was about to happen in Analytical Cubism in France. The Robie House combines cubic forms and projecting planes with a mastery never before seen in architecture.

More than a quarter of a century later, in 1936, Wright built one of his most original conceptions, the Kaufmann House at Bear Run, Pennsylvania, suspended over a waterfall (fig. 519). The idea did in a sense have a prototype in the French Renaissance château of Chenonceaux built on a bridge across the River Cher. But Wright seems to have derived the masses of Falling Water from the very rock ledges out of which it springs. A central mass of rough-cut stone masonry blossoms forth in cantilevered concrete terraces, colored beige so as not to disrupt the tonal harmony of their woodland environment—a house really at one with the rocks, the trees, the sky, and the rushing water.

Wright could work only with sensitive, discerning, and (be it admitted) fairly submissive patrons, and thus was destined never to receive the great commissions to which his genius entitled him. American cities are filled with monstrous fifty-story caskets of steel and glass, and American suburbs with miles of identical shoe boxes or even less attractive attempts at variations in "town houses" plastered with split pediments and unnecessary mansards. Yet Wright's dream of a mile-high skyscraper for Chicago, and his Broadacre City, an imaginative combination of industrial plants with houses and gardens for factory personnel, went unbuilt. One supremely beautiful commercial structure by Wright is his Administration Building for S.C. Johnson and Son, Inc., at Racine, Wisconsin (fig. 520), built in 1936–39 and extended in 1950. The central tower, although only seven stories high (four of which appear in the illustration), is treated as an envelope of translucent rather than transparent glass interrupted by strips of brick but without external verticals, wrapped around a core of space. The corners are rounded in response to the myriad circles of the interior, whose ceilings are supported by columns tapering downward like those of Minoan architecture (fig. 521), while their capitals become immense disks like lotus leaves, between which the light filters.

THE INTERNATIONAL STYLE

After the close of World War I, a new architectural style arose almost contemporaneously in Holland, France, and Germany, and has thus received the name the Inter-

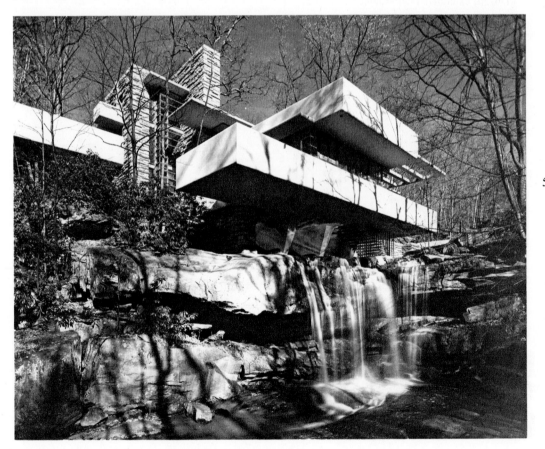

519. FRANK LLOYD WRIGHT. Kaufmann House ("Falling Water"). 1936. Bear Run, Pennsylvania

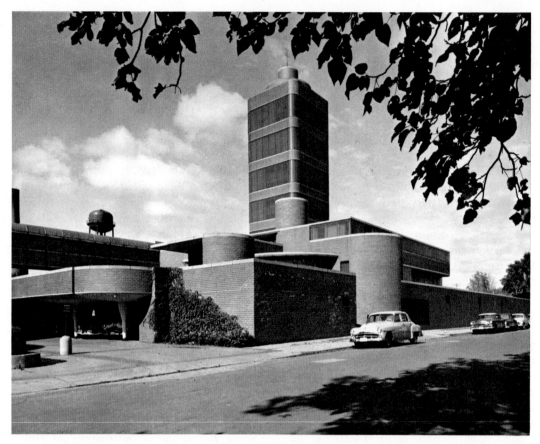

520. FRANK LLOYD WRIGHT. Administration Building, S. C. Johnson and Son, Inc.
1936–39: extended 1950. Racine, Wisconsin

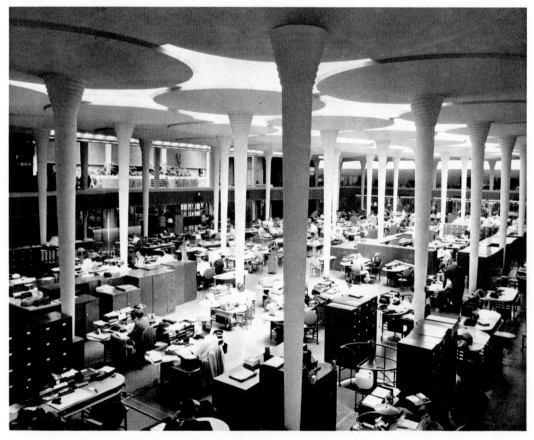

521. FRANK LLOYD WRIGHT. Interior, Administration Building, S. C. Johnson and Son, Inc.

national Style. Its consequences, for good or ill, are still with us today. The International Style is responsible for some of the most austerely beautiful creations of twentieth-century art, and once it became apparent to patrons and builders alike that the principles of the International Style could be used for cheap construction, these principles were eventually welcomed commercially. What began in the 1920s as a revolutionary ideal for a new architecture has become in the 1960s and 1970s the cliché of mass-produced building.

The International Style rejected ornament of any sort. It also denied the traditional concept of the building as a mass. Finally, it prohibited the use of such "natural" materials as stone or wood. This was no wonder, since the open planes and spaces of the International Style could only have been created with the use of modern materials, especially steel and reinforced concrete. These were used to form absolutely flat surfaces, kept as thin as possible, and almost invariably white, alternating only with areas of glass, to enclose volumes rather than to create masses. The result is a boxlike appearance, reminding one less of architecture as it had been conceived in the West since antiquity (with the sole exception of the Gothic interlude) than of the cabin block on a steamship. Models for traditional European buildings were usually carved from wood, and some were modeled in clay and cast in plaster. A model for an International Style building could be, and often was, constructed of light cardboard and cellophane. Not even in the gravity-defying structures of the High Gothic had there been anything so utterly weightless as the buildings of the International Style.

Clearly, the principles of Cubism, with its exaltation of the plane to a position of supreme importance, played a part in the creation of the International Style. So did the new architecture of Wright, widely known in Europe after his Berlin exhibition of 1910. Especially important was the aesthetic of De Stijl (see pages 414, 415, and fig. 492, colorplate 70), which in Holland had already reduced both the subject and the elements of art to flat planes, right angles, black, gray, white, and the three primary colors—with white predominating. One of the earliest buildings of the International Style is the Schröder House at Utrecht, Holland (figs. 522, 523), built in 1924 by GERRIT RIETVELD (1888–1964). In this extraordinary building the appearance of weightlessness characteristic of the International Style is first proclaimed, but in full conformity with the principles of De Stijl. The Schröder House, in fact, is the three-dimensional equivalent of a painting by Mondrian. Nothing weighs, thrusts, or rests; all planes are kept as slender as possible, as external surfaces bounding internal volumes. Some of the planes connect at the corners, some appear to slide over each other in space. The cantilevered roof and balconies, doubtless influenced by those of Wright, are restricted to concrete slabs instead of Wright's massive forms. Windows are

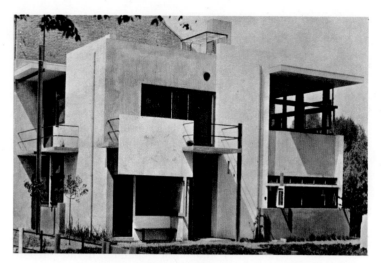

522. GERRIT RIETVELD. Schröder House. 1924. Utrecht, The Netherlands

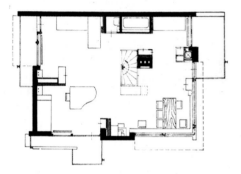

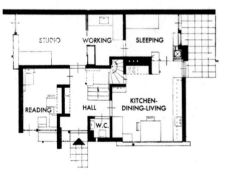

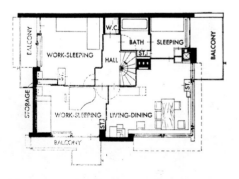

523. GERRIT RIETVELD. Plans of the Schröder House

continuous strips of glass. The only details are the mullions and the simple steel pipes used as railings.

As early as 1911, the principles of the International Style had been foreshadowed in industrial architecture by WALTER GROPIUS (1883–1969), who had used continuous glass sheathing as a substitute for walls, even at the corners of the building, whose supports, entirely internal, were not visible on the exterior. Gropius' great opportunity, however, came in the building of the famous Bauhaus, an international center for design in all its forms. Originally called the Weimar Schools of Arts and Crafts and located at Weimar, Germany, the institution came under the direction of Gropius in 1919, who reorganized and renamed it. Bauhaus, derived from the German words for *building* (in the figurative as well as the literal sense) and *house*, epitomized the purpose Gropius saw in the organization. It was to comprise instruction not only in the traditional arts of painting, sculpture, and architecture, but also in the crafts, from weaving to printing; instruction was to be directed toward industrial design, and dominated by rational, up-to-date principles employing and directing mechanized techniques. As we have seen (page 418), both Klee and Kandinsky came to the Bauhaus as professors; so did a number of other artists, designers, and architects, and a large group of gifted students. From the Bauhaus the new ideas radiated to all parts of the globe, with consequences that are still visible in many countries.

In 1925 Gropius moved the Bauhaus to Dessau, where he was building new quarters for the school from his own designs. In the workshop wing (fig. 524), constructed in 1925–26, Gropius carried out systematically the principles of the International Style. The building is a huge glass box, with panes as large as they could be economically manufactured held in a uniform steel grid. The four stories of the interior receive no external expression in this uninterrupted glass exterior, being separately supported on their own reinforced concrete columns. Walls are reduced to narrow, white strips at top and bottom. According to a principle of the International Style—as defiant of climate as its constructional principles are of gravity—the roof is completely flat. Such vast expanses of glass remained in fashion up to the energy crisis of the 1970s, and buildings utilizing them require enormous heating, ventilating, and cooling mechanisms, not to speak of death-defying external window-washing teams.

LE CORBUSIER. Meanwhile, in France the principles of the International Style were being brilliantly exploited by the Swiss painter-architect Charles-Edouard Jeanneret (1887–1965), known by the pseudonym of Le Corbusier, who competes with Wright for the leadership in the formation of twentieth-century architecture. Le Corbusier had already built several International Style houses when he undertook in 1928–30 the masterpiece of his early period, the Villa Savoye at Poissy, France, even more severe and revolutionary in its appearance than the Schröder House. At first sight the building, supported on stiltlike reinforced-concrete poles, seems to have no ground story; actually, there is one, recessed deeply under the overhanging second story, and containing entrance hall, staircase, servants' quarters, and carport (fig. 525).

Le Corbusier called his houses "machines for living in," and this one fulfills his designation to perfection. The second floor, dominated by a staircase tower that suggests the funnel of a steamship, is a box bounded by perfectly flat, continuous planes, acknowledging no possibility of overlap, and punctuated by windows reduced to unbroken horizontal strips of glass panels, sustained by slender mullions. The window strips not only light the interior rooms of the second floor, but also provide outlook for a sunny, interior terrace, open to the sky and

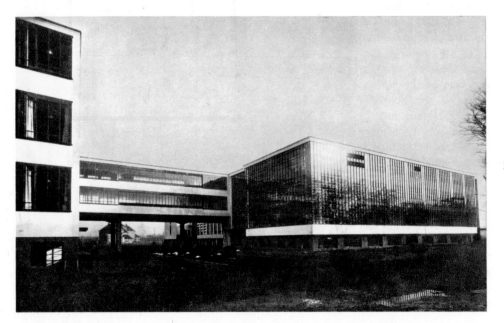

524. WALTER GROPIUS. Workshop wing, Bauhaus. 1925–26. Dessau, Germany

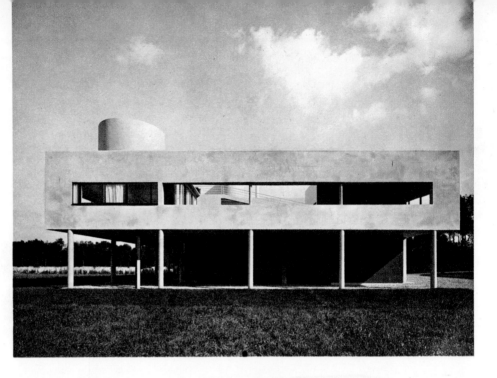

525. LE CORBUSIER. Villa Savoye. 1928–30. Poissy, France

separated from the living room only by floor-to-ceiling panels of plate glass (fig. 526). Revolutionary in Le Corbusier's day, this method of creating a free interchange has become a commonplace of residential (and motel!) design since the 1950s. Electric lighting is confined to a long, chrome-plated fixture.

Le Corbusier did not restrict his revolutionary architectural ideas to single structures, but, as Wright had—although on a far larger scale—dreamed of urban planning as well. He envisioned, designed, and theorized about a *ville radieuse* (*radial city*) of three million people, with interrelated factories, office buildings, apartment blocks both high and low, and cultural and amusement centers, all connected by means of elevated highways and punctuated by green areas for recreation. As we contemplate our choked and polluted present-day urban agglomerations, we can only regret that, in spite of his designs for the administrative center of Chandigarh in India, Le Corbusier never had a chance to demonstrate the potentialities of his dream of an organic metropolis.

Under the initial influence of Gropius, the German architect LUDWIG MIES VAN DER ROHE (1886–1969) developed a new and purified personal version of the International Style, alongside which the work of Gropius and even of Le Corbusier seems heavy. The German Pavilion at the Barcelona International Exposition in

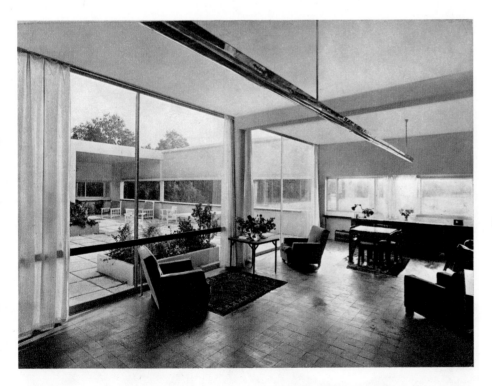

526. LE CORBUSIER. Interior (view of living room toward terrace), Villa Savoye

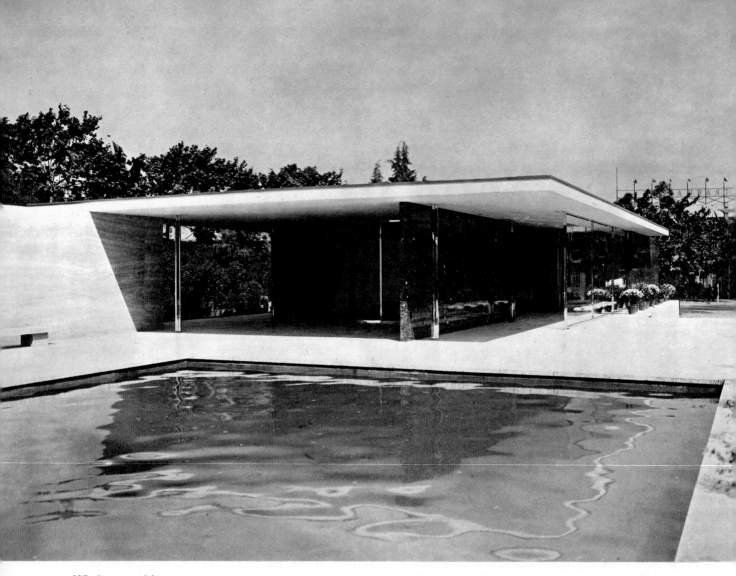

527. Ludwig Mies van der
Rohe. German Pavilion
(dismantled), Barcelona
International Exposition,
1929

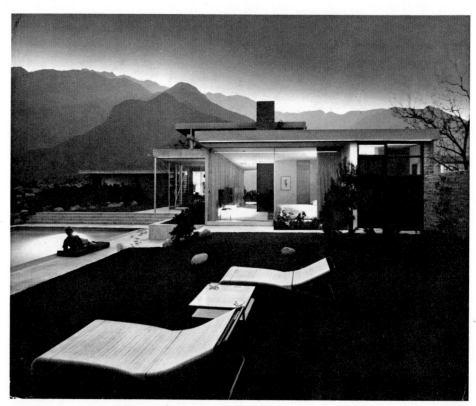

528. Richard Neutra.
Kaufmann House. 1947.
Palm Springs, California

1929 delicately reinstated the use of such natural materials as veined marble and travertine (fig. 527). Mies' famous dictum, "less is more," is expressed here in his extraordinary refinement of space, plane, and proportion, all reduced to absolute essentials. The eye moves serenely from interior to exterior spaces, unified by the movement of planes and separated only by plate glass. Marble, concrete, chrome, water, and air are formed into a harmony as delicately adjusted as a white-on-white painting by Malevich (see fig. 486). The Austrian-born RICHARD NEUTRA (1892–) exploited a spectacular site in the California mountains in 1947 in his Kaufmann House, built of fluid, glass-enclosed areas moving easily into each other along Miesian principles (fig. 528).

THE INTERNATIONAL STYLE AND THE SKYSCRAPER

The history of the American skyscraper after Sullivan is colored by recollections of the past rather than by premonitions of the new era, of which that amazing American invention would have seemed to be the perfect herald. Skyscrapers went up apace in the first two decades of the century, and created a delightful Dolomitic skyline in downtown New York and Chicago, but each individual building, however picturesque, attempted to clothe the steel frame with elements drawn from the past. In 1922 Gropius submitted a strongly International Style design (in association with Adolf Meyer) in the competition for the Chicago Tribune Tower, clearly related to the ideas of Sullivan and the Chicago School of twenty years before. His project was not selected; the choice went instead to a neo-Gothic design by RAYMOND HOOD (1881–1934). Ironically enough, in his later buildings Hood shook off all historic ornament and began to adopt some of the principles of the International Style.

Architects of the 1930s in New York City were bound by the conventions of the building code, including the so-called setback law, to terrace their structures progressively back from the street in order to allow sunlight to penetrate into what were becoming dark canyons. The result was a number of commercial buildings designed so as to profit from every cubic inch allowable under the law, and promptly nicknamed "ziggurats." Imaginative architects had, nonetheless, to satisfy their materialistic clients. Hood discarded all reference to the historic past in the Daily News Building (fig. 529), which he designed with John Mead Howells for New York in 1930; he was constrained to set the building back in steps from the street, and attempted to compensate for this enforced irregularity of contour by corresponding irregularities within planes composing the sides. Otherwise, he concentrated on unbroken strips of white masonry between the windows to accent the verticality of the steel frame. This innovation, marking a considerable advance in skyscraper design, was greeted by attacks from conservative architects and derision from the general public.

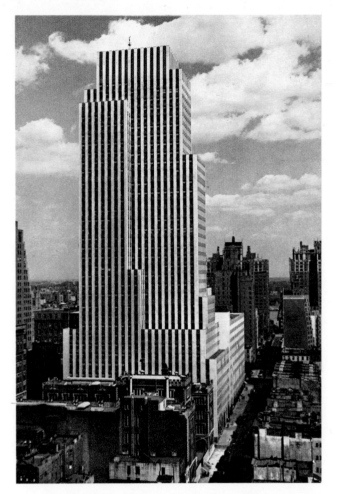

529. RAYMOND HOOD and JOHN MEAD HOWELLS. Daily News Building. 1930. New York

A year later GEORGE HOWE (1886–1955) and WILLIAM LESCAZE (1896–1969) designed the Philadelphia Savings Fund Society Building (fig. 530), finished in 1932, a structure that does not attract the attention it deserves because it can so easily be thought of as a building designed only today. The grid character of the steel frame is recognized in every aspect of the structure. Along the narrow sides of the building the windows are treated as strips of glass wrapped around the cantilevered corners. But the first skyscraper whose tower was conceived as a simple shaft without changes from top to bottom, a design that brings about its own economies in construction even if it "wastes" a bit of airspace, was the Secretariat Building of the United Nations, built in New York in 1947–50 by a team of architects led by WALLACE K. HARRISON (1895–). Such teams, employing armies of draftsmen, had in fact become essential to the execution of the vast skyscrapers that rose in cities throughout the world after World War II. The slab shape of the Secretariat Building (fig. 531), with a grid of glass and steel on the wide sides and unbroken marble end panels, was the idea of Le Corbusier, who was a consultant. While the shape is not wholly successful

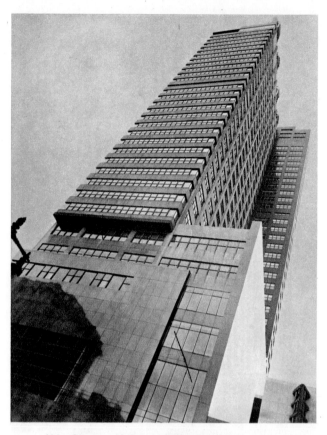

530. GEORGE HOWE and WILLIAM LESCAZE.
Philadelphia Savings Fund Society Building.
1931–32

aesthetically, it does mark the first total escape from historic tradition and from the consequences of the setback law. The necessary service units (water tanks and machinery for elevators, window cleaning, and air conditioning) are subsumed within a separate grid at the top. The rest of the tower is broken by doubled strips into four superimposed panels of unequal height.

Mies van der Rohe, who had made a model (now lost) for an all-glass tower as early as 1919, constructed in 1951 the Lake Shore Drive Apartments in Chicago (fig. 532) as pure International Style structures whose harmony resides in their exquisite subtlety of proportion. The two buildings, placed at right angles to each other, look absolutely uniform in fenestration, until one discovers that, after every fourth window, as after every fourth beat in four-four time, comes a sort of bar line in the form of a slightly wider vertical. The next development was the all-glass Lever House, of 1951–52, in New York, one of the few really thrilling skyscraper designs in that metropolis, erected by the firm of Skidmore, Owings and Merrill, but largely the idea of their associate GORDON BUNSHAFT (1909–   ). The building (fig. 533) consists of horizontal and vertical units, both elevated on pylons above the street so that the passerby can move directly into a partially shaded and open court. The tower is a shaft of glass, totally without masonry, tinted to avoid excessive glare, and the floors are marked by panels of dark-green glass. To preserve the total unity of the building, the light fixtures, visible from the outside, are

531. WALLACE K. HARRISON, and others. Secretariat Building of the United Nations. 1947–50. New York

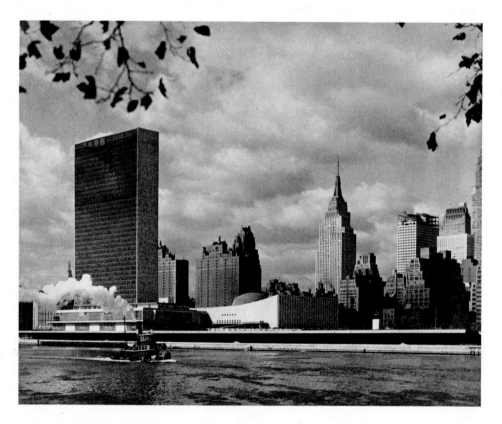

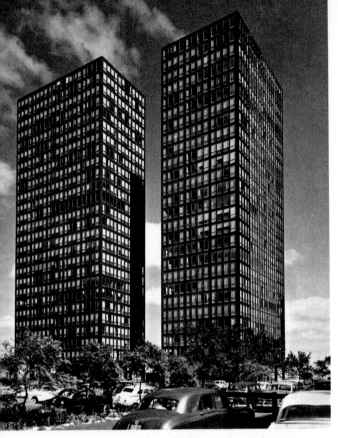

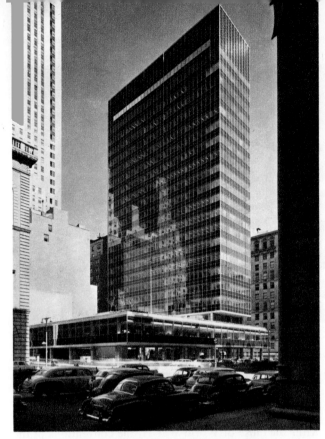

532. LUDWIG MIES VAN DER ROHE. Lake Shore Drive Apartments. 1951. Chicago

533. GORDON BUNSHAFT, and Skidmore, Owings and Merrill (New York). Lever House. 1951–52. New York

534. PHILIP JOHNSON and JOHN BURGEE, with Edward F. Baker Associates (Minneapolis). I. D. S. Center. Completed 1972. Minneapolis

identical throughout. The result is one of the most delicately harmonious of all modern buildings, whose beauty is only enhanced by many unsuccessful attempts to imitate it.

In recent years the convention of the all-glass exterior has been modified by flaring the glass sheath sharply outward at the bottom and by tilting it inward so that the structure rises in the form of a pyramid. One of the most imaginative variations is the I.D.S. Center in Minneapolis, Minnesota, finished in 1972 (fig. 534), the work of PHILIP JOHNSON (1906–) and John Burgee of New York in association with the Edward F. Baker firm in Minneapolis. The glass shaft is molded toward the sides in vertical rather than horizontal setbacks with brilliant effect. Since glass structures inevitably both blend with and mirror the sky and clouds, this shaping produces a very delicate spatial harmony around the building. The glass-and-steel-covered courtyard, connecting the tower with a hotel, piles up pyramidally at the base like a giant wasps' nest. Doubtless, the all-glass skyscraper, which requires ventilation and lighting and either heating or air conditioning day and night, winter and summer—a colossal waste of energy—will soon become a thing of the past. Energy restrictions will certainly produce sharp changes in skyscraper design, with the natural orientation of structures and restitution of the wall.

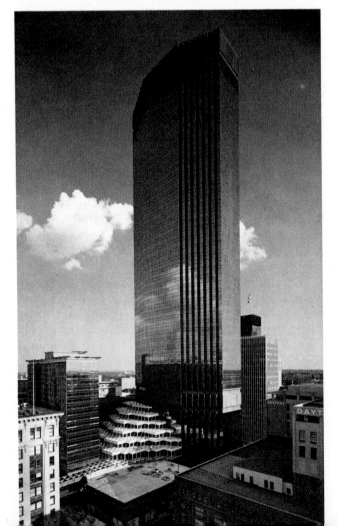

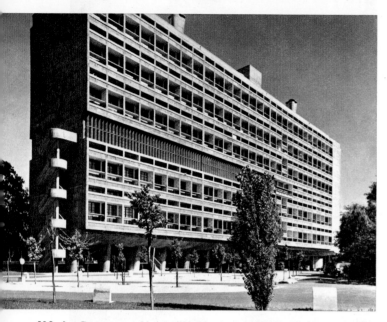

535. LE CORBUSIER. Unité d'Habitation. 1947–52. Marseilles

COUNTERCURRENTS

After the close of World War II, the conventions of the International Style, appropriate to the multistory business building, seemed unnecessarily confining to a number of gifted architects, including even Le Corbusier, who had been one of the pioneers of that very style. His Unité d'Habitation, built on a hilltop in Marseilles from 1947–52 (fig. 535), treats his favorite material, reinforced concrete, in a new and monumental fashion. The building seems a gigantic piece of abstract sculpture, with the surface of the concrete left in its rough state just as it emerges from the wooden molds, and uncolored so that it turns a soft gray. The windowless end walls (which, as we have seen, Le Corbusier imposed upon the United Nations Secretariat Building) can scarcely be called functional, but they are, nonetheless, an outgrowth of the concept of the building, which is made up of a large number of identical living units, each with a bedroom on an inner balcony above kitchen and bath, overlooking a high living room, and each having access to a continuous outer balcony, with wall breaks between units. The structure, held aloft on massive columns rather than the slender shafts of the Villa Savoye, contains a restaurant and shops so that its inhabitants hardly need to leave the premises except to go to work.

When Dali was asked by Le Corbusier what he thought his new architecture should look like, he replied, "soft and hairy." This is very nearly what happened in the most extraordinary of Le Corbusier's late works, the pilgrimage Chapel of Notre-Dame-du-Haut on a hilltop at Ronchamp, France, built in 1950–54 (fig. 536). Every convention of the International Style has been abandoned. The very plan is irregular, and the forms are modeled in the most surprising way into wall and roof shapes flaring, curving, and twisting as if organic and

alive. Le Corbusier had visited the island of Mykonos in the Cyclades east of mainland Greece, and had been impressed by the beauty of its simple buildings, chiefly the tiny churches and windmills. These structures have sloping, rounded walls in order to offer less resistance to the constant wind, and are whitewashed every year, so that in time they develop a kind of fur coat formed by successive layers of whitewash. Le Corbusier emulated the sloping walls and the softness and richness of these shapes of folk-architecture in a highly imaginative way. Even the fenestration of the chapel is irregular, openings scattered at random over the curving walls. The effect in the interior is magical because the windows are also of different sizes and proportions, their stained glass differs from window to window in color and design, and their embrasures slope at different angles, as if each corresponded to the experience of an individual worshiper approaching in his own way the mystery of the altar.

An immensely influential constructional genius, the Italian engineer-architect PIER LUIGI NERVI (1891–   ), has produced some of the most beautiful forms in modern architecture. In order to span vast interiors he abandoned traditional concepts separating walls and roof, and devised new methods of working with concrete, as in the interior of the Exhibition Hall, of 1948–49 (fig. 537), built appropriately enough at Turin, the city that boasts so many triumphs of Nervi's great predecessor as a constructional innovator, Guarino Guarini (see page 230, figs. 255, 256). The entire structure of the Exhibition Hall is formed by gigantic ribs that start from the floor in sweeping curves, united by boomerang-shaped elements, leaving countless window spaces for illumination. To facilitate rapid construction, all elements were precast and assembled on the spot. The design produces an inspiring effect of organic growth according to repeated geometrical patterns, whose soaring rhythms recall,

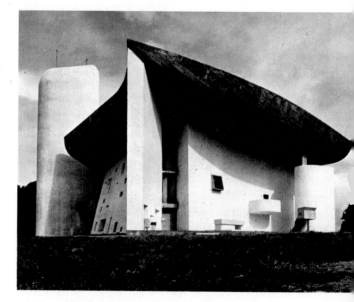

536. LE CORBUSIER. Notre-Dame-du-Haut.
1950–54. Ronchamp, France

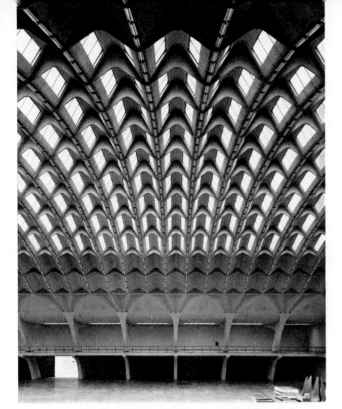

537. PIER LUIGI NERVI. Interior, Exhibition Hall. 1948–49. Turin, Italy

without in any way imitating, those of High Gothic cathedrals.

Another architect of vast influence at midcentury was LOUIS I. KAHN (1901–74), who after thorough study of Le Corbusier turned to contemporary design problems in a highly individual and often intuitive manner, producing brilliant solutions that have been widely emulated. His Richards Medical Research Building at the University of Pennsylvania, Philadelphia (fig. 538), built in 1957–61, compresses all the service elements—stairs, elevators, air and heating ducts—into rectangular shafts rising like the towers of some medieval fortification. From these masonry masses, as from central trunks, radiate the floors (branches) containing laboratories, glass-enclosed.

In countries throughout the world the problem of the air terminal has been thrust into extreme prominence by the lightning growth in air travel. How seldom it has yet been rationally faced thousands of weary air travelers can daily testify. Two of the all-too-few imaginative solutions are due to the same gifted architect, EERO SAARINEN (1910–61), son and pupil of the equally celebrated Finnish-American architect Eliel Saarinen. Eero Saarinen's untimely death prevented him from seeing either of his great air-terminal designs completed. His beautiful Trans World Airlines Terminal, finished in 1962, with its curves flowing like air currents (fig. 539), as pure in its lines as a sculpture by Brancusi, is the only bright spot in the hopeless confusion of New York's Kennedy Airport. And his magnificent terminal for Dulles Airport, in rural Virginia outside Washington, D.C. (fig. 540), built in 1961–62, solves on a grand scale one of the major problems of airports—how to get passengers painlessly to and from planes, which must of

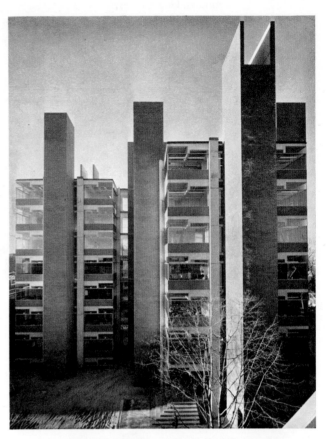

538. LOUIS I. KAHN. Richards Medical Research Building. 1957–61. University of Pennsylvania, Philadelphia

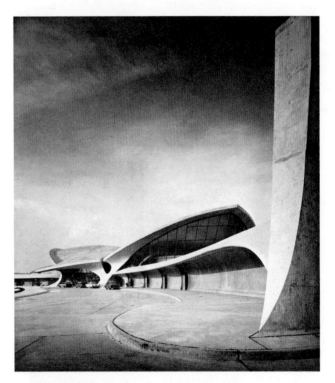

539. EERO SAARINEN. Trans World Airlines Terminal. Completed 1962. John F. Kennedy International Airport, New York

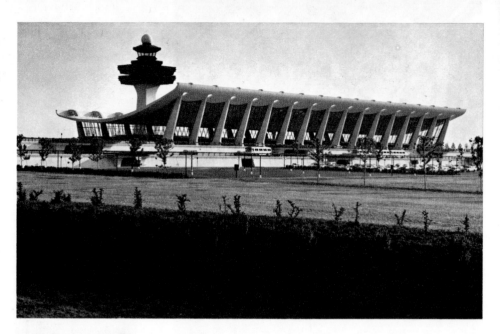

540. EERO SAARINEN. Terminal, Dulles Airport. 1961–62. Chantilly, Virginia (outside of Washington, D.C.)

541. MARCEL BREUER. Whitney Museum of American Art. Completed 1966. New York

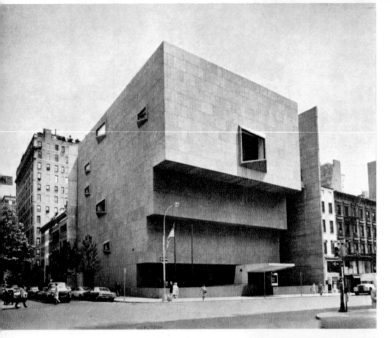

necessity be widely separated on the ground—by the device of mobile lounges. At Dulles little of traditional building design is left. The sharply raking concrete columns form a kind of cradle, piercing the roof, which is concave like a colossal hammock, and is suspended from them. Even the windows are canted outward. In both his air-terminal designs, each a highly original and unique solution, Saarinen suggested the principles of aircraft construction and of aerodynamics in the lightness, buoyancy, and rounded edges of his forms.

The insistent problem of the design of the art museum has received in recent years a number of strikingly different yet effective solutions. An extremely impressive one is the building for the Whitney Museum of American Art (fig. 541), completed in 1966 in New York by the veteran Hungarian-born American architect MARCEL BREUER (1902–). The immense, blank masses of the building, constructed of raw concrete blocks and granite, are cantilevered outward in three stages alongside Madison Avenue. Since the building depends on artificial

542. MARCEL BREUER. Third-floor gallery, Whitney Museum of American Art

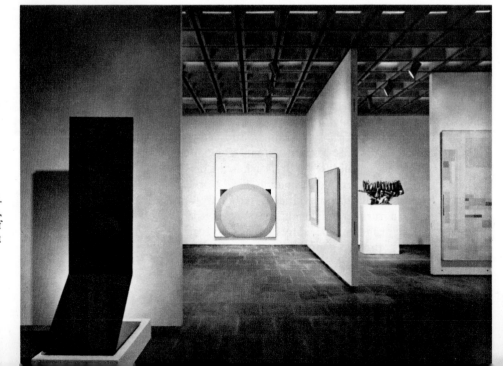

illumination, there are few windows, and these are scattered and differently shaped as in Le Corbusier's chapel at Ronchamp. The vast interiors are simple and flexible; the partitions are movable but solid, attachable at any point under the ceiling grid, and the lighting system is extremely effective—one of the best in any New York museum (fig. 542).

A totally different solution was offered by Louis I. Kahn in his last major work, the Kimbell Museum in Fort Worth, Texas, completed in 1972 (fig. 543). In order to utilize the abundant natural light, Kahn devised a system of semielliptic concrete vaults, pierced by long skylights concealed by elaborate baffles. The combination of concrete and travertine provides a sympathetic and resonant background for works of art of all periods,

and the magical illumination fills the interior with a pearly radiance that brings out the paintings' colors with great accuracy, yet prevents direct glare, and belies the somewhat ponderous appearance of the interior in photographs.

A third and highly dramatic solution appears in the museum building designed by I.M. PEI (1917–   ) to house the contemporary collections of the National Gallery of Art in Washington, D.C. (fig. 544). The triangular shape of the structure is dictated by the site, which is one of the many residual triangles created by Pierre Charles L'Enfant's design for Washington, carried out in the 1790s. There have been in the past a few other triangular-building designs, also for residual spaces. Michelangelo had planned, but never built, a triangular

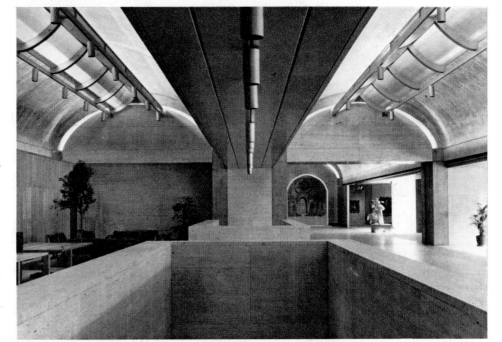

543. Louis I. Kahn. Kimbell Art Museum. Completed 1972. Fort Worth, Texas

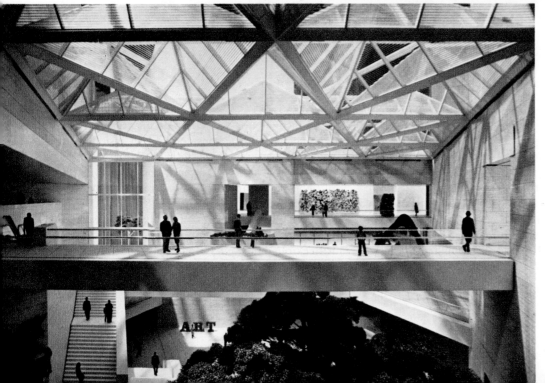

544. I. M. Pei. Central Court, East Building (Contemporary Art), National Gallery of Art. Model. Proposed completion date 1977–78. Washington, D.C.

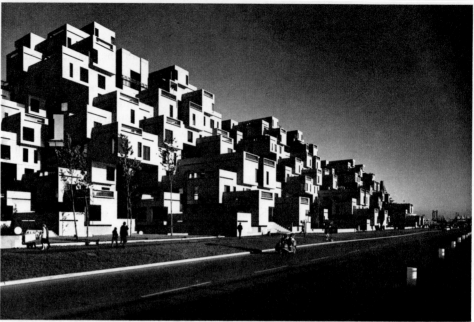

545. MOSHE SAFDIE. Habitat
(built for EXPO 67). 1967.
Montreal

546. PAOLO SOLERI. Elevation,
Arcology "Babel II C"
Design for a Mushroom City

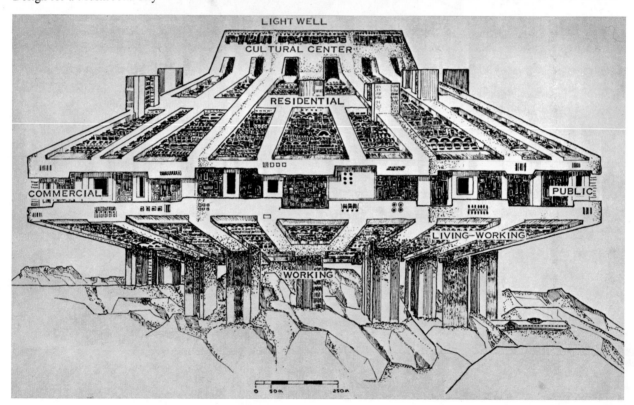

rare book room for the Laurentian Library in Florence
(see fig. 155), and New York boasts the Flatiron Building
and the Times Tower (only the former still intact), both
of which rise from areas shaped by the diagonal path of
Broadway across the early nineteenth-century gridiron
plan of Manhattan. Pei's structure exploits the triangle in
every major space of the interior, as well as in the powerful exterior shapes, a daring solution considering the conservative nature of most of the surrounding buildings,
including the Neoclassical structure of the National
Gallery.

An introduction to modern architecture should fitting-
ly conclude with a consideration of visionary designs,
some eminently practical, others that have yet to prove
their merit. The first is an ingenious idea for a new kind
of housing complex by the Israeli architect MOSHE
SAFDIE (1938–   ). In his Habitat for EXPO 67 in Montreal, Safdie devised a completely original solution for
urban design, which combined ease of mass production
with extreme flexibility of plan (fig. 545). Habitat is composed of a theoretically infinite series of precast, one-
piece concrete housing units, each a complete apartment,

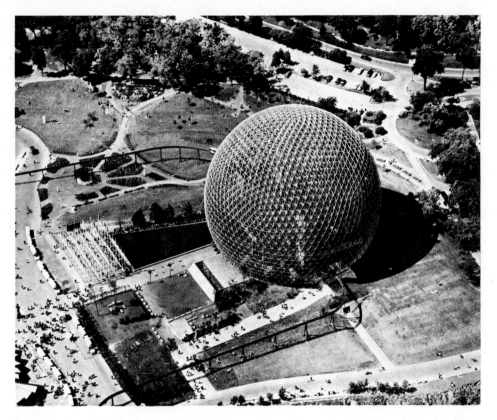

547. R. BUCKMINSTER
FULLER. American
Pavilion (Biosphere),
built for EXPO 67. 1967.
Montreal

transported to the site and set in place in a preformed frame, which can also be extended in any direction and to any height. A great amount of individuality has been allowed each tenant in the shape and size of his dwelling, in the relationships of form and space, and in the constantly changing views of the outer world and the approaches, which, on each story, include play space for children. The result is dramatic in its freedom from the uniformity of previous concepts for multiple housing, as, for example, Le Corbusier's Unité d'Habitation. Perhaps the most astonishing thing about Habitat is its uncanny exterior resemblance to one of the earliest urban complexes we know, the town of Çatal Hüyük, which dates from the seventh millennium B.C. In our history of architectural development we seem to have come full circle.

Equally imaginative, but less susceptible to actual realization, are the mushroom-shaped cities (fig. 546) envisioned by PAOLO SOLERI (1920–), which tower above the surrounding landscape and contain within themselves facilities for all the necessities of modern life from manufacturing to living. Finally, the uninhibited and fearless pioneer designer R. BUCKMINSTER FULLER (1895–) has been preaching and practicing for nearly half a century a totally new approach to architecture in terms of prefabricated, centrally planned units. His universal solution is the geodesic dome, a spheroid structure composed of mutually sustaining polyhedral elements, which can be constructed anywhere and of any material, including opaque or transparent panels, and at extremely low cost. Previously, Fuller's domes had been realized only in greenhouses and sheds, but the American Pavilion at EXPO 67 (fig. 547), the first large-scale realization of Fuller's eminently practical ideas, may really give us a view into the architectural future.

10

American Art of the Twentieth Century and Recent Movements Elsewhere

Throughout the eighteenth and nineteenth centuries, American art remained largely provincial in spite of the original ideas of a small number of gifted individual artists. As we have seen, the most imaginative architect of the early Republic, Thomas Jefferson, was deeply indebted to the Palladian tradition and turned for technical criticism to the Englishman Latrobe. Copley, West, and Whistler emigrated to England. The painters John Singer Sargent and Mary Cassatt (not discussed in this book) settled, respectively, in London and Paris. After the turn of the century, many American painters gathered near Giverny in the orbit of Monet. Every current of European nineteenth-century painting continued to flow in the United States, and the most vigorous American movement of the early twentieth century, the "Ash Can School" (also known as "The Eight"), was a group of Neorealists indebted largely to Courbet and the early Manet.

But in the twentieth century American art at last came into its own. Several young artists absorbed European modernism through trips to France and Germany, and returned to develop their newly acquired ideas in the United States, chiefly in New York, centering around the gallery at 291 Fifth Avenue, managed by the great photographer Alfred Stieglitz. Then came the Armory Show, or to give it its full title, the International Exhibition of Modern Art, held at the New York National Guard's 69th Regiment Armory in 1913, and including all the important masters of Post-Impressionism and the Fauve movement, but relatively few works of German Expressionism and none of Italian Futurism. The works of many American pioneers were also shown. Important sections of the exhibition traveled to Chicago and to Boston. Hundreds of thousands of Americans received their first exposure to the new art through the Armory Show, and at first only a few liked what they saw. Many adverse reactions in the press and in art schools were violent.

Nonetheless, the ice had been broken, and galleries devoted to modern art sprang up in many cities, especially New York. Katherine S. Dreier, one of the first American abstract painters, and a sensitive and foresighted collector of modern art, founded with Marcel Duchamp and Man Ray the Société Anonyme: Museum of Modern Art 1920 (as it was first called), in 1920, using rented quarters or sometimes her own apartment for exhibitions of American and European avant-garde artists. Before her death in 1952 the bulk of the Société Anonyme collection was given to Yale University. In 1927 A.E. Gallatin lent his collection to New York University under the title of The Gallery of Living Art, and in 1929 The Museum of Modern Art first opened its doors in temporary quarters in a New York skyscraper. The new movements could no longer be ignored or ridiculed in New York without effective reply. The collection of Dr. Albert C. Barnes, at Merion Station, Pennsylvania, was not so fortunate. Although Barnes had acquired a magnificent collection, including the finest group of Cézannes, Renoirs, and early Matisses then in public or private possession anywhere in the world, his pictures were refused by the University of Pennsylvania and held up to scorn in Philadelphia. The Barnes Foundation has, nonetheless, continued educational work on the basis of its unrivaled treasures ever since. Courses in the history of contemporary art, pioneered at Columbia University by Meyer Schapiro, have found their way into the curriculum of well-nigh every department of the history of art in the country.

World War II resulted in the emigration of important European painters and sculptors to the United States (Ernst, Mondrian, Beckmann, Lipchitz, and for a while Léger). European art never fully recovered from the catastrophe of the war and Nazi occupation, and although many of the leading masters resumed their activity (some, indeed, had never stopped), few new figures of importance appeared, and none of first rank.

Astonishingly, quite the opposite took place in the United States. Some artists of European birth and training—but many more native Americans—participated in new movements, generally centering in New York, which replaced Paris in the 1950s, 1960s, and 1970s as the artistic capital of the world. Important local schools also grew up in Boston, Washington, D.C., and San Francisco.

Although by the mid-1970s some of the force of American modernism seems to have spent itself, and no new movements of great significance have appeared for several years, the achievements of American twentieth-century art can be rated very high; they are at least on a par with those of Germany and Russia in the first three decades of the century, and superior to those of any other country save France. Choices in a field so recent are inevitably subject to individual bias, and the author admits from the start the impossibility of a totally fair estimate. But whatever the omissions from the following account, it can at least be claimed that all the artists included are of cardinal importance for the art of our own time.

THE PIONEERS

The earliest American painter to break with the tradition of naturalism was MARSDEN HARTLEY (1878–1943), who came in contact with Der Blaue Reiter group in Berlin in 1912. In the years just before World War I

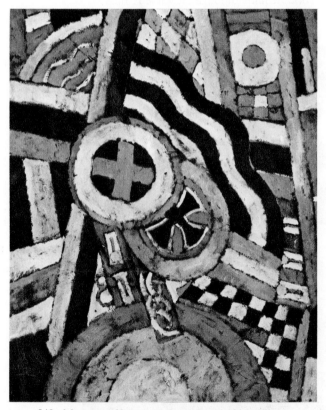

548. MARSDEN HARTLEY. *Iron Cross.* 1914. Oil on canvas, 39½ x 31¾". Whitney Museum of American Art, New York. Anonymous gift

Hartley painted a remarkable series of pictures based on German military symbols. Although the elements of his *Iron Cross*, of 1914 (fig. 548), are all derived from that celebrated Prussian decoration and from regimental flags, this and the other pictures in the series can certainly be termed abstractions, and are the first in American history. As masses of brilliant color arrayed against black backgrounds, they are extremely effective. This series did not, however, lead to a career in abstract art. For nearly a generation more, Hartley continued to paint Maine landscapes, whose elements are vigorously simplified for expressive purposes.

JOHN MARIN (1870–1953) spent the years 1905–11 in Europe. He was deeply impressed by the later work of Cézanne, and then by early Cubism, especially the dynamic art of Delaunay (see fig. 472). Marin's career was spent principally in painting watercolors; among the best are those in which, like Joseph Stella (see fig. 484), he tried to embody the energy and vitality of New York City. *Lower Manhattan (Composition Derived from Top of the Woolworth Building)*, of 1922 (fig. 549), surveys a panorama of skyscrapers in the clashing and intersecting views typical of Cubism, yet painted with an almost Expressionist vigor of brushwork and color.

ARTHUR G. DOVE (1880–1946) began his contact with Parisian movements in 1907, and soon moved to paintings he called abstractions, but which were in reality based on landscape forms. A relatively late example, *That Red One*, of 1944 (fig. 550), show the great staring eye that often appears in Dove's paintings, looming across powerful stripes of brilliant color with the effect of a cosmic apparition. A totally original American painter, whose work is unconnected with any European movement, is GEORGIA O'KEEFFE (1887–). Throughout her immensely long creative life, O'Keeffe's imagery was derived from an infinite variety of objects surrounding her, from the magnified forms of flowers to driftwood and animals' skulls. Her *Blue and Green Music*, of 1919 (colorplate 75), may be based on the aurora borealis, or is perhaps a complete invention. In either case, the free flow of rhythmic shapes against the massive diagonals moves, as the title suggests, with the quality of visual music; this kind of melodic flow is never absent from her work.

Along with these early distinguished modernists, a number of gifted American artists turned after World War I to new forms of realism, focusing on the dreariness and banality of much of American urban and rural life. One of the best of these so-called American Scene painters was EDWARD HOPPER (1882–1967). It is a bleak world he presents to us, made up of dreary streets, gloomy houses, comfortless rooms, and unattractive restaurants—such as in *Automat*, of 1927 (fig. 551). Yet the apparent hopelessness of his subjects, and their total lack of aesthetic or spiritual rewards, is mysteriously compensated by an austere beauty of form, space, and especially of light, whether by day or night, which transforms the dullest scene into a harmonious construction of planes and spaces. By no means unaware of the

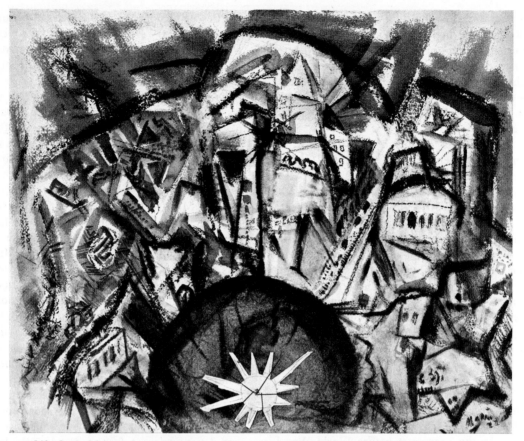

549. JOHN MARIN. *Lower Manhattan (Composition Derived from Top of the Woolworth Building).* 1922. Watercolor and charcoal, and paper cutout attached with thread, 21⅝ x 26⅞". The Museum of Modern Art, New York. Acquired through the Lillie P. Bliss Bequest

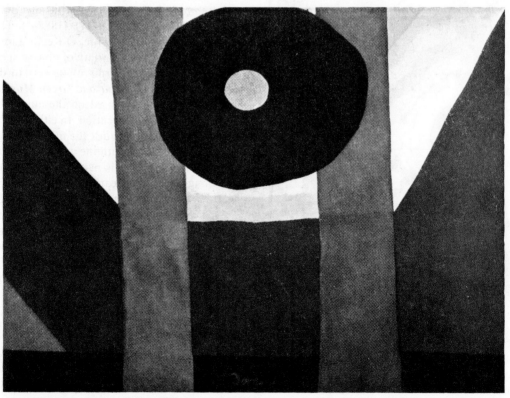

550. ARTHUR G. DOVE. *That Red One.* 1944. Oil on canvas, 27 x 36". William H. Lane Foundation, Leominster, Massachusetts

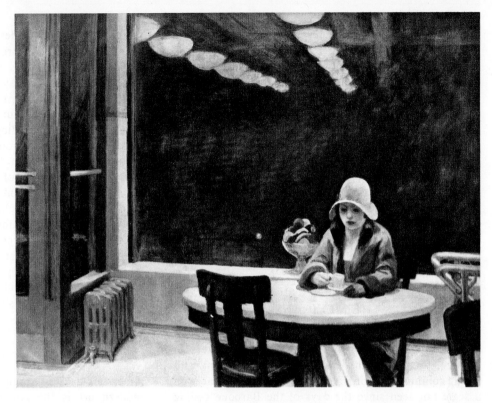

551. EDWARD HOPPER. *Automat.* 1927. Oil on canvas, 28 x 36". Des Moines Art Center, Iowa. Edmundson Collection

formal conquests of abstract art, Hopper is a precursor of the more recent Photorealists (see pages 489–491).

The American scene appears in a different guise in the painting of STUART DAVIS (1894–1964), who was for decades the leader of American abstract painting. As a nineteen-year-old art student, Davis exhibited five watercolors in the Armory Show. During the 1920s, he developed a personal manner by imposing the techniques of late Cubism on American Scene subject matter with an impudence that foretells the irreverent wit of Pop Art (see pages 460–464). His *House and Street*, of 1931 (fig. 552), treats a subject similar to those of Hopper with a fragmented flatness recalling the impersonal paintings of Léger (see fig. 471), but with an intensely personal smartness and decorativeness. The elements are drawn from the inescapable ugliness of an American city—win-

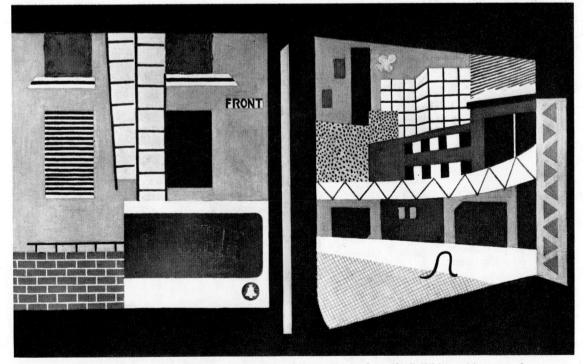

552. STUART DAVIS. *House and Street.* 1931. Oil on canvas, 26 x 42¼". Whitney Museum of American Art, New York. Purchase

dows from a nineteenth-century row house, a street sign, loft buildings, the elevated railroad, even a little Bell Telephone insignia. But during and after World War II, Davis' style moved into an abstract manner in which the bits and pieces of industrial society were reduced to brilliant ornaments. *Owh! In San Pão*, of 1951 (colorplate 76), is a superb example. Disjointed words, often drawn from signs or billboards, float against a strong yellow background, among blue, violet, orange, and green rectangles, parallelograms, and trapezoids, penetrated by forms suggesting factory chimneys and rooftops, and a field of red dots surely prompted by the coarse "net" of newspaper illustrations. The grand inventions of Davis were clearly precursors of the even more austere art of Frank Stella, Noland, and Indiana (see figs. 571, 572, colorplate 84, fig. 565).

THE MEXICANS

The decade of the 1920s saw the rise of a vigorous and inventive school of strongly Marxist mural painters in Mexico, favored by the revolutionary government with public commissions for frescoes covering vast surfaces on a scale not seen since the days of the Baroque ceiling painters. The least interesting of the leading triumvirate of Mexican muralists was Diego Rivera (1886–1957), who from 1909 to 1921 lived in Europe, and was a marginal adherent of Cubism. With limited success, Rivera attempted to create an easily understood popular style based on Mexican folk art and a study of Italian fourteenth-century fresco techniques. Far more impressive was Rivera's pupil and collaborator, JOSÉ CLEMENTE OROZCO (1883–1949), who, after a massive series of mural commissions in Mexico, was invited to paint a cycle of frescoes at Dartmouth College, Hanover, New Hampshire, in 1932. *The Departure of Quetzalcoatl* (fig. 553) from the Dartmouth frescoes, executed between 1932 and 1934, verges dangerously on bombast, and is unnecessarily crude in detail, but its strength and sincerity are, nonetheless, impressive. In the midst of his sacred serpents the god leaves his pyramid temple, while the Aztecs recoil in dismay. DAVID ALFARO SIQUEIROS (1896–1974) is blatantly propagandistic in his *Portrait of the Bourgeoisie*, a mural of 1939 in the Electrical Workers' Union Building in Mexico City (fig. 554), covering more than a thousand square feet with hundreds of figures and symbols. The temple of Liberté, Égalité, Fraternité (the motto of the French Revolution) is on fire. An eagle with jointed metal wings dominates the scene; factory chimneys and steel towers rise against the sky; hordes of marching soldiers are harangued by political leaders in bourgeois dress on the left, and on the right by others in Fascist uniforms, wearing helmets and gas masks, while money pours out of a huge machine. The spectator is overwhelmed, as Siqueiros intended that he should be, by the sheer volume of his descriptive rhetoric.

ABSTRACT EXPRESSIONISM

America's greatest single contribution to the history of modern art is the Abstract Expressionist movement, which dominated the New York scene for about fifteen years after the end of World War II. Official recognition of the movement came in a major exhibition at The Museum of Modern Art in 1951. Through the medium of modern communications, the work of the pioneers was rapidly transmitted throughout the world, and everywhere imitations of the new art grew up with far greater speed than those of Impressionism in the late nineteenth century. Abstract Expressionist exhibitions were soon organized from London to Tokyo. It is somewhat easier to explain what Abstract Expressionism is not than what it is. No consistent mode of vision or way of applying paint united the artists of the movement in the way that the Impressionists and the Cubists were

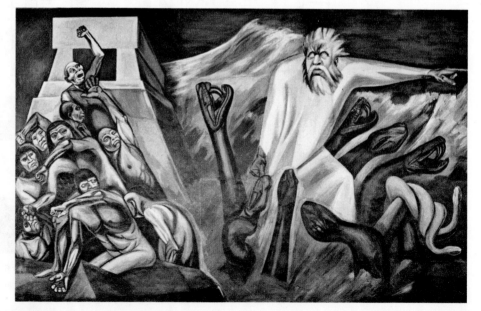

553. JOSÉ CLEMENTE OROZCO. *The Departure of Quetzalcoatl* (detail). 1932–34. Fresco mural. Baker Library, Dartmouth College, Hanover, New Hampshire

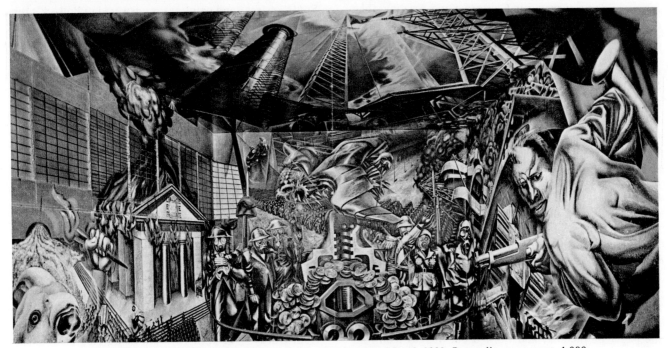

554. DAVID ALFARO SIQUEIROS. *Portrait of the Bourgeoisie.* Mural. 1939. Pyroxylin on cement, 1,000 square feet. Electrical Workers Union Building, Mexico City

united, but they were all opposed to the strict formalism that had characterized much of abstract art until that time, culminating in the painting of Mondrian, physically present and highly influential in New York from 1940 until his death in 1944.

The roots of Abstract Expressionism can be found in the early work of Kandinsky, who had been described as an "abstract expressionist" as early as 1919. But the automatism preached by the Surrealists was also of extreme importance. The sharp difference between the personal styles of the Abstract Expressionist leaders is implicit in the very nature of the movement, which exalted individualism and the unfettered expression of the inner life through the free application of paint. It can truly be said of all the best Abstract Expressionist painters that no one before them had ever painted abstract pictures of such emotional intensity on such a scale.

Clearly, Abstract Expressionism corresponded to the psychological necessities of a historic moment in American, indeed world, experience. It is perhaps of importance that the movement, which owed its existence to a new evaluation of the individual, arose and spread immediately after the defeat of totalitarianism in World War II, and the victory of the democracies—and equally important that it was strongly opposed in authoritarian Communist countries at a time when a new vision of the possibilities open to humanity was fired by the presence in New York of the United Nations, then still considered a Messianic institution. It is also far from accidental that Abstract Expressionism disintegrated as the Cold War intensified, and disappeared almost entirely as faith in man's future weakened under the impact of catastrophic political events in the 1950s. And it is striking that, of the

seven Abstract Expressionist leaders considered here, only De Kooning and Still survived to the mid-1970s; Gorky, Rothko, and Kline each ended his life, and Pollock perished under conditions that suggest a death wish.

GORKY. The earliest painter of the American Abstract Expressionist movement is the Armenian-born Arshile Gorky (1904–48). At first a realist working in a belated Impressionist tradition, Gorky fell under the influence of Picasso, then that of Miró and Matta. By 1944 he was painting in a new style, strongly automatic, gaining an intense poetic effect from the movement of clearly contoured biomorphic shapes against freely brushed tides of color. In such works as *Golden Brown Painting,* of 1947 (colorplate 77), the regularity and surface precision of the Surrealists have vanished, and the often erotically suggestive shapes move, swell, and turn with the greatest abandon, yet with a distinct rhythmic relationship to the delicate calligraphy of the brushwork. The haunting mood of Gorky's paintings from 1944 to 1948, their disturbing combination of linear delicacy and implicit violence, and, alas, their rarity have rendered them the jewels of Abstract Expressionism.

POLLOCK. In the minds of most observers the hero of the Abstract Expressionist drama is Jackson Pollock (1912–56). His short and turbulent existence seems in retrospect to have been dedicated to violence, and his death in a frightful automobile crash (he was driving) to be tragically appropriate. Born in Wyoming, Pollock passed most of his childhood in Arizona and his nomadic youth in California. In high school his rebellious spirit kept him in constant trouble, resulting in his expulsion. He worked for a while as a surveyor in California and Arizona, then moved to New York in 1930, where he studied at the Art Students League with the American Scene muralist Thomas Hart Benton. While still an adolescent, Pollock made powerful drawings after Tintoretto, El Greco, and Michelangelo, and his paintings showed the influence of the Mexicans, especially Orozco. As early as 1933, he was working in a semiabstract manner with recognizable fragments of the human image, reflecting Picasso and Miró. In a labored, turgid fashion, with color often muddy and uncertain, he began to construct paintings in the broad curves that later became his signature. Many of the strokes show a strong tendency toward automatism.

If he had died in 1944 rather than in 1956, Pollock would today be remembered only as a gifted, unusual, but somewhat chaotic minor painter. In 1944, however, he began the free motion of the arm that characterized his mature style, and in 1946 he began to exploit the drip. Whether Pollock knew it or not, he had predecessors during the Southern Sung Period in China (1127–1279), the so-called ink flingers, who dipped their caps in ink, struck the paper or the silk, and worked out images from the shapes thus produced. As we have seen, the accident had been pursued by Duchamp, Arp, and others, and in *Guernica* (see fig. 470) there are many passages where the artist allowed the paint to drip freely after application with great expressive effect. Pollock knew well and admired the sand paintings of the Southwestern Indians, which held magical significance and were executed rhythmically as part of a religious rite.

In 1946 the curving shapes began to show big gobs of color, freely dripped. In 1947 commenced the series of immense canvases, tacked to the floor unstretched, which Pollock declared made him feel "nearer, more a part of the painting, since this way I can walk round it, work from the four sides and literally be *in* the painting." At last Pollock was liberated from the obstacle of the brush and the necessity of mixing his colors. With a can of Duco or other commercial paint in his hand, he moved freely, dripping, spilling, throwing the color, apparently with total abandon as he performed a kind of pictorial dance whose choreography is recorded on the canvas. Soon dubbed "action painting," this activity Pollock allowed to be photographed, even filmed. Nonetheless, he said, "When I am painting I have a general notion as to what I am about. I *can* control the flow of the paint: there is no accident, just as there is no beginning and no end."

A completed Pollock of this period is almost infinitely complex. *Blue Poles*, of 1953 (colorplate 78), is one of the most monumental—sixteen feet in length—and shows layer upon layer of seething, swirling, spitting, snarling paint, reviving in a new and modern way the interlace of Hiberno-Saxon manuscripts, and the ferocity of Scythian animal art, which Pollock knew and admired. White, gray, black, orange, yellow, and aluminum are intertwined in deadly conflict, resolved only by the forceful superimposition of the immense blue poles that go swaying across the scene. The religious content of the

Southwestern sand paintings is answered in Pollock's turbulent psyche by a mystic and undirected intensity of feeling (he had, for a while, been interested in Oriental religions). More than any other modern painter, with the possible exception of Van Gogh, Pollock achieved in his work—rather than in his chaotic, pugnacious, alcohol-soaked life—a sense of unity with forces he conceived to be operating in the universe. Tragically enough, these were forces that eventually defeated him, as they had Van Gogh. Nevertheless, *Blue Poles* is one of the greatest paintings of the twentieth century, and one of the noblest achievements of American art.

DE KOONING. An entirely different direction was taken by the Dutch-born painter Willem de Kooning (1904–), who shares with Pollock preeminence among the Abstract Expressionists. At first a realist painter who could draw like Ingres, De Kooning painted in New York, from 1926 on, in a modern delicate, figurative manner, based partly on Picasso but with elements drawn from Gorky. Not until 1948 did he develop an Abstract Expressionist style, in pigments at first limited to black and white house paints because he could not afford colors. A superb, large-scale work of 1950 is *Excavation* (fig. 555). At first sight there seems to be no image at all—only masses of paint randomly applied. Yet, rubbed out, scraped off, repainted, and repainted again, the surface builds up a cumulative effect like monumental sculpture, composed of many centers of implied action.

During the 1950s De Kooning's Abstract Expressionist style reached its height in a group of pictures that, for all their apparent spontaneity and freshness of surface handling, were in fact the result of intensive labor and continual reworking. In consequence of this method relatively few major works could be produced each year in spite of their limited dimensions. An intense and enigmatic series was dedicated to images of almost demonic women, terrifying in their hostility and ferocity. Even more important, however, were the paintings in which no shred of visual reality can any longer be recognized. In each picture, generally dominated by reds, greens, and yellows, but with strong passages of black and white, the eye moves from vortex to vortex, always more passionate and more intense, as if from crater to seething crater.

In *The Time of the Fire*, of 1956 (colorplate 79), the energy of any given section is not only volcanic but overflowing. De Kooning's lava is a thick pigment applied in brisk, sometimes explosive strokes, but traces of previous flows show through from below. Since many of the strokes are either vertical or horizontal, an allover sense of structure begins to emerge from the very opposition of directions between one passage and the next. The result is an allover compositional texture of tremendous strength, utterly different from the myriad overlapping spirals of Pollock. In later work De Kooning enlarged each vortex to embrace an entire canvas, working,

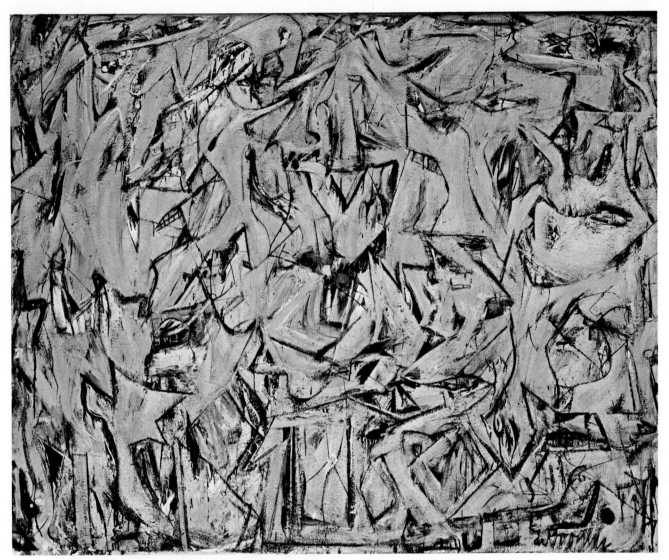

555. WILLEM DE KOONING. *Excavation.* 1950. Oil and enamel on canvas, 80⅛ x 100⅛". The Art Institute of Chicago. Mr. and Mrs. Frank G. Logan Purchase Prize; Gift of Edgar Kaufmann, Jr., and Mr. and Mrs. Noah Goldowsky

therefore, with greater speed. But he has never surpassed the magnificence of his great decade, the 1950s.

HOFMANN. An unexpected apparition on the New York scene was Hans Hofmann (1880–1966), who belonged to a wholly different generation than most of the Abstract Expressionists. Born in Bavaria, he lived and worked in Paris from 1903 to 1914. His surviving works from this period show the influence of Delaunay and of Matisse, but most of his early paintings perished in a studio fire. When he arrived in New York in 1932, his reputation was that of an extremely successful European teacher, and he continued to teach in the United States, exerting a great influence on younger artists. In 1940 Hofmann began experimenting with a drip technique that in a modest way prefigured some aspects of Pollock's work, but he is best known for his canvases in which areas of brilliant color assert themselves with magical intensity. Characteristic of Hofmann's Abstract Expressionist style at its height is

The Gate, of 1960 (colorplate 80), with its great rectangles of yellow and red floating against a background whose colors change in more softly brushed rectangular areas from yellow through green to intense violet, suggesting distant space. In contradistinction to the violence that is the principal theme of De Kooning and Pollock, Hofmann's lyrical paintings achieve a serene equilibrium of mass, space, and color.

KLINE. Until 1949 Franz Kline (1910–62) was a representational painter with little connection with any advanced movement. His work, nonetheless, showed a highly individual sense of pigment and surface, and bold brushwork. Then in 1949, while looking at enlarged projections of some of his black-and-white sketches, he discovered that small sections of them would make powerful abstract configurations. The evolution in his style was immediate. He abandoned representation and, for the moment, even color, and proceeded to work on a huge

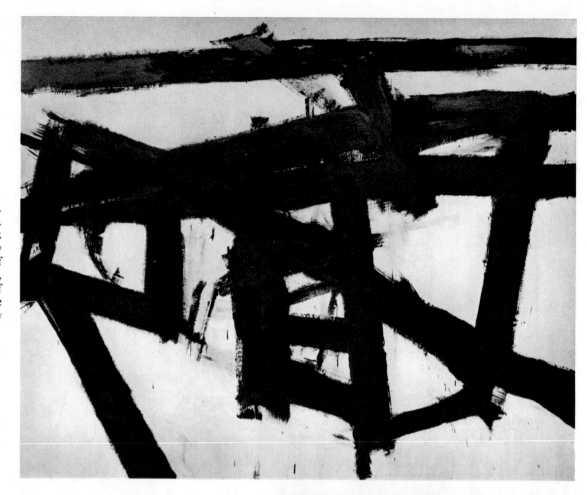

556. FRANZ KLINE. *Mahoning*. 1956. Oil on canvas, 80 x 100″. Whitney Museum of American Art, New York. Gift of the Friends of the Whitney

scale—*Mahoning*, of 1956 (fig. 556), is more than eight feet long—with powerful strokes of black laid rapidly on the white canvas with a house painter's brush. Although Chinese and Japanese calligraphy had no direct influence on Kline's style, his massive strokes, building up entirely abstract images with the greatest freedom, have often been compared to the Far Eastern freely brushed characters known as grass writing. But the fact that Kline preferred to tack his unstretched canvases to the wall for painting gives them a special hardness that is important for the often almost architectural quality of the great stripes. Before his premature death Kline was already varying his severe style by including masses of smoldering color between the black strokes. Energies have seldom been released to function as effectively as in the best of Kline's monumental paintings.

STILL. A remote, secretive, and yet tremendously influential figure in the development of Abstract Expressionism in new directions was Clyfford Still (1904–   ). For the qualities that Still exerts, it was essential for him to work on a considerable scale. He covers immense canvases, such as *Painting, 1951* (fig. 557), with areas of color that move slowly, like ocean currents. Restricted generally to two or three basic hues, these streams of color ebb and flow in such a manner that the observer seems engulfed in their action, almost to the point of

557. CLYFFORD STILL. *Painting, 1951*. 1951. Oil on canvas, 93¼ x 75¾″. The Detroit Institute of Arts. Purchase, The W. Hawkins Ferry Fund

abandoning his connection with the solid earth. In a sense Monet had tried to exert a similar effect with his enormous late works (see fig. 418), but on a representational basis. In executing his vast fields of color, Still places no special emphasis on the individual brushstroke, the discharge of psychic energy at the canvas, which had been so important for the paintings of Pollock, De Kooning, and Kline. One is hardly aware of the movement of the painter's hand or arm, only of the independent motion of the color masses. In this sense the art of Still leads beyond Abstract Expressionism to the color-field painting of the 1960s (see pages 481–484).

ROTHKO A much more expressive manner of exploiting the psychic, even spiritual, effects of color was worked out slowly by Mark Rothko (1903–70). Long an abstractionist, Rothko was painting in the late 1940s in a biomorphic abstract style close to that of Gorky. Gradually, he began to eliminate contours, leaving only color areas somewhat resembling those of Hofmann, but without clear-cut edges. Through soft, blotlike borders these color areas seem to dissolve into each other as if emulating in oil the effects of watercolor allowed to spread on wet paper. Finally, in the 1950s Rothko began a majestic series of canvases in which, with a finality suggesting that of Malevich or of Mondrian, he abandoned all suggestions of form in favor of the two or three superimposed rectangular shapes with cloudy edges that constitute his dominant theme. These shapes float as if in a continual misty sunset at sea and produce a strongly meditative effect.

White and Greens in Blue, of 1957 (colorplate 81), is typical of Rothko at his greatest. As with Still, scale is extremely important in Rothko's pictures (this one is more than eight feet high). The observer seems less to be enveloped in the colors than to be enticed to float outward into them, as if in some enchanted celestial voyage. The effect of several Rothkos together in the same room amounts to a mystical experience; one's voice is automatically hushed in their brooding presence. Rothko was commissioned during the 1960s to produce several murals, the most effective of which is a series of panels for a chapel at St. Thomas University in Houston, Texas, which form a unity somewhat like the water-lily series of Monet, provoking intense meditation on timeless essences and truths.

An offshoot of the colorism of both Still and Rothko is the work of RICHARD DIEBENKORN (1922–   ), who was brought up and continues to work in the San Francisco Bay area, where both Still and Rothko had painted and taught in the late 1940s. As in *Ocean Park, No. 40*, of 1971 (fig. 558), with its simplified elements drawn from a beach landscape, Diebenkorn has anchored his softly brushed, at times almost translucent, planes to clear suggestions of actual interior or exterior spaces in a manner recalling that of Matisse (see colorplate 64), but still reflecting the lessons of Abstract Expressionism. Often, he has included figures, generally as accents in his

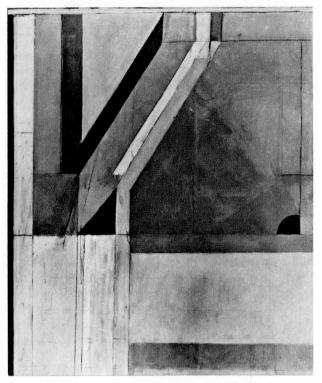

558. RICHARD DIEBENKORN. *Ocean Park, No. 40.* 1971. Oil on cotton duck, 93 x 81″. Collection Mr. and Mrs. S. I. Newhouse, New York

colored spaces, without any sort of implied drama and as focuses for the directional energies of his compositions.

THE REACTION AGAINST ABSTRACT EXPRESSIONISM

It was perhaps implicit in the intensely emotional nature of the Abstract Expressionist movement that it would soon play itself out. Furthermore, the ground swell of optimism that had given rise to the movement was no longer a real force as the disaster of the Korean War moved toward the tragedy of American involvement in Indochina. Considering the intensity and speed of twentieth-century life as compared with the more relaxed pace of the late nineteenth, it is perhaps more to be wondered at that Abstract Expressionism remained dominant as long as it did before the inevitable reaction set in—a period of about fifteen years, which corresponds more or less to the duration of the Impressionist movement prior to the emergence of the first Post-Impressionist countercurrents. Most of the greater and lesser survivors among the Abstract Expressionists, especially De Kooning, continued to paint in much the same vein in the late 1960s and 1970s, although with greatly diminished intensity, conviction, and influence. But an opposing force was already being sought even in the late 1950s, with the anxious refrain, "After Abstract Expressionism, what?" The opposition was not long in coming, and with bewildering speed and multiplicity. A new movement began to appear every few years, then every year—Pop Art, Op Art, Color Field, Hard Edge, Minimal Art, Postminimal Art, Environments, Happenings, Body Art, Earth Art, Kinetic Art, Conceptual Art, and Photorealism—to name only a few. The variety and complexity of the new artistic movements of the 1960s and early 1970s can only be suggested here through their most important achievements.

POP ART. Although to most observers Pop Art, in its exaltation of the most aggressively banal aspects of a plastic civilization, seems peculiarly American, it actually owes its start to a small group of artists working in London in the mid-1950s. Nevertheless, the most commanding figures among the Pop artists are all Americans, and the movement reached its height in the United States during the 1960s. It should be recalled that Marcel Duchamp was then still active in New York, and exerted a widespread influence on the new generation. It is no accident that Pop owes much to Dada, born in a similar period of frustration. Pop, like Dada, functions on a basis of devastating wit, antiaestheticism, and—if one may use so contradictory a phrase—positive nihilism.

As early as 1955, one of the leading American Pop artists, ROBERT RAUSCHENBERG (1925–), was including found objects in his paintings—not fragments of an object, as in the collages of Picasso and Schwitters, but the entire object, including such diverse flotsam and jetsam as Coca-Cola bottles, old wall clocks, a quilt made up as a bed, and an entire stuffed ram with an automobile tire around its middle. Often, he incorporated in his paintings silk-screen photographic prints of famous works of art, such as Rubens' *Venus with a Mirror* in *Trapeze*, of 1964 (fig. 559). While these bits of extraneous reality suggest collage as we have seen it among the Cubists and in Dada and Surrealism, they are painted into the overall texture of a picture with a richness and abandon, at times even a splash, that derive directly from Abstract Expressionism. The result is invariably challenging, sometimes harrowing in its intensity.

Many echoes of Abstract Expressionist colorism also linger on in the work of another Pop pioneer, JASPER JOHNS (1930–), who like Rauschenberg emerged on the art scene in New York in 1955. However, Johns' imagery is entirely different. His paintings were characteristically done in encaustic, a technique, using melted wax as a vehicle, that results in a peculiarly rich surface. In contrast to this pictorial quality, often very seductive, Johns' subjects have been rigidly serialized. One series was devoted to the American flag, either identified with the actual surface of the canvas, or built up in superimposed flags of progressively diminishing scale, or painted entirely in mottled white or entirely in green. Another series consists of targets; a particularly disturbing example is the *Target with Four Faces*, of 1955 (fig. 560), which combines the suggestion of gunfire (the bull's-eye) with that of a firing squad (the eyeless, implacable faces ranged above). In his later work Johns in-

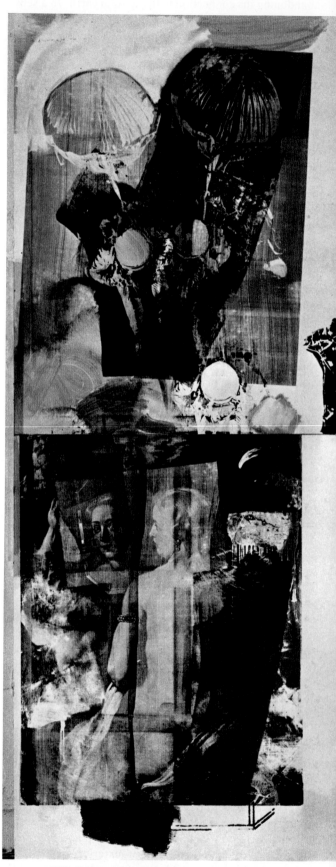

559. ROBERT RAUSCHENBERG. *Trapeze*. 1964. Oil on canvas with silkscreen. 10 x 4'. Private collection. Turin. Italy

troduced a freedom of surface and a combination of found objects not unlike those of Rauschenberg's "combine" paintings.

ROY LICHTENSTEIN (1923–) founded his art exclusively on the comic strip and the mechanical technique of reproducing it; he enlarges such images to billboard size by purely mechanical means. The rich pictorial surface of Abstract Expressionism, still retained by Rauschenberg and Johns, is entirely rejected by Lichtenstein in favor of a stenciled imitation of the hard contours and characteristic net of coarse dots used in the newspaper reproduction of comic strips. A deliberately heartless rendering of an air combat, entitled *Whaam*, of 1963 (fig. 561), is more than thirteen feet long, and brings the harshness of the comic-strip adventure series—needless to mention, an imitation, not an actual comic strip—to the scale of mural painting. Interestingly enough, Lichtenstein deliberately chooses all the tawdriest aspects of the comic strip to emulate—never, for example, does he imitate the gentle *Peanuts*. JAMES ROSENQUIST (1933–) actually was a billboard artist for a while; perched on a height overlooking Broadway, he painted colossal faces with cheap smiles. In his huge wraparound mural of 1965, named *F-111* after the American fighter-bomber (fig. 562), a painting ten feet high and eighty-six feet long, Rosenquist has created an endless composition juxtaposing in space photographic images of the trivial aspects of American life with those of appalling atomic or other military destruction, even at times intersecting the two extremes, just as they are often juxtaposed in time on television screens.

The wittiest of the Pop artists is assuredly the painter-sculptor CLAES OLDENBURG (1929–), who has taken ordinary mass-produced objects from American life and reproduced them in three dimensions, at first in actual size in painted plaster, later immensely enlarged in can-

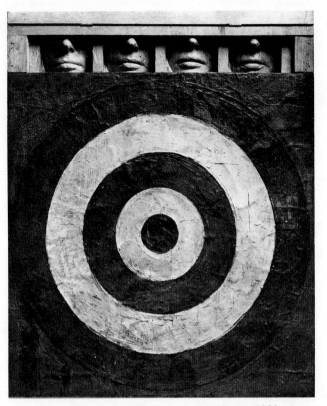

560. JASPER JOHNS. *Target with Four Faces*. 1955. Encaustic and newspaper on canvas with plaster casts, 30 x 26″. The Museum of Modern Art, New York. Gift of Mr. and Mrs. Robert C. Scull

vas, stuffed with kapok, and painted. Hamburgers oozing with catsup and onions were expanded to five feet in thickness. Then it occurred to Oldenburg that these standard objects on which we rely—lipsticks, musical instruments, toilets—could be made soft, as if collapsing, in a three-dimensional parody of Dali's "wet watches"

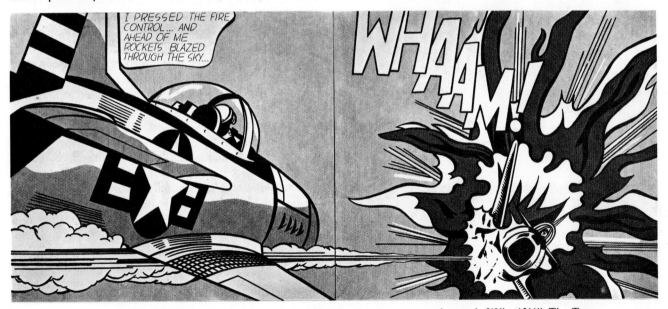

561. ROY LICHTENSTEIN. *Whaam* (2 panels). 1963. Magna on canvas, entire work 5′8″ x 13′4″. The Tate Gallery, London

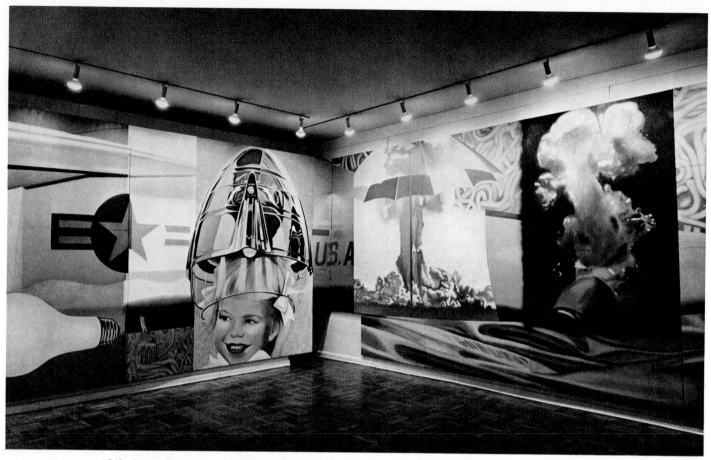

562. JAMES ROSENQUIST. *F-111* (portion). 1965. Oil on canvas with aluminum, entire work 10 x 86'. Collection Robert C. Scull, New York

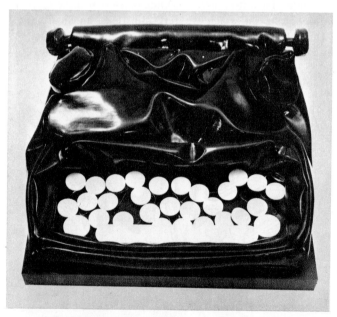

563. CLAES OLDENBURG. *Soft Typewriter*. 1963. Vinyl, kapok, cloth, and Plexiglas, 27½ x 26 x 9". Collection Alan Powers, London

(see fig. 506). *Soft Typewriter*, of 1963 (fig. 563), is one of the most amusing of these works, if it can really be found amusing that objects that must retain their consistency in order to function are suddenly discovered—as in a nightmare—to be soft. Oldenburg also projected colossally enlarged cigarette butts, peeled bananas, toilet floats, and Teddy bears with mock seriousness as monuments for the center of some hapless metropolis, such as London or New York. In the long run the power of an Oldenburg image remains after the laugh is over. His work is, in reality, a searing commentary on the triviality of modern mechanized existence, drained not only of spiritual qualities but also of genuine physical satisfactions.

Through his flamboyant personality and the films he has directed, as well as the later ones directed by others under Warhol's name, ANDY WARHOL (1930–   ) has become something of a household word. He specializes in the boring. One film shows nothing but the Empire State Building from one camera position and lasts for eight hours. Warhol burst upon the public consciousness with his endless arrays of Campbell's tomato soup cans and his false three-dimensional Brillo boxes, as if, on the principle of Duchamp's ready-mades, the mere finding of such objects made them works of art. (Ironically enough, the designer of the *actual* Brillo box was an Abstract Expressionist.) The deadly impersonality of Warhol's mechanized sameness has its own cumulative, if far from cheerful, emotional effect. He has had enormous success with his silk-screen prints in garish colors from photographs of American sex goddesses, such as *Marilyn Monroe*, of 1962 (fig. 564), as well as those done after pictures of such horrors as automobile crashes and the electric chair, infinitely repeated like frames in a motion picture. Following the lead of Stuart Davis, ROBERT INDIANA (born Robert Clark, 1928–) takes words from American signs (or other words treated as if they came from such sources)—EAT, LOVE, DIE—as artistic themes. Unlike Davis, he does not alter and recombine these words but leaves them inert with all their mechanical hardness of lettering intact, so that they function on the consciousness like hammerblows delivered by a robot. After many painted versions of these words in garish colors, Indiana expanded some of the words, as in *Love*, of 1966 (fig. 565), to three-dimensional metal sculpture.

Among the host of sculptors affected in one way or another by the Pop movement, the most haunting is GEORGE SEGAL (1924–). Although Segal started as a painter under the tutelage of Hofmann, and demonstrated an exceptional ability to handle brilliant color, he abandoned color entirely in his sculptural treatment of the human figure. He proceeds by making direct molds of living figures with surgical plaster bandages. Reconstituted as complete figures, these images are unsettling in their ghostly white. These personages inhabit, in varying attitudes of dejection, the grisly environments Segal constructs for them out of actual rejected furniture

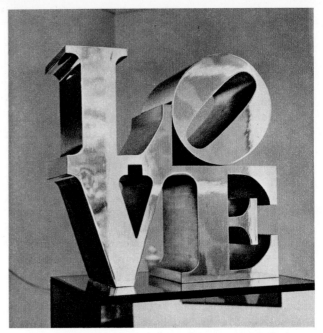

565. ROBERT INDIANA. *Love*. 1966. Aluminum. 12 x 12 x 6". Denise René Galerie, New York

and equipment. For his scenes Segal concentrates deliberately on the run-down and shabby periphery of modern society rather than its jazzy, aseptic mainstream exalted by Lichtenstein and Rosenquist. In a sense, Segal's groups are three-dimensional versions of the type of subjects Hopper painted, and they are far more disturbing. In his *The Bus Riders*, of 1964 (fig. 566), as in Daumier's *Third-Class Carriage* (see fig. 406), people are enclosed in and subjected to a thing over which they have

566. GEORGE SEGAL. *The Bus Riders*. 1964. Plaster, metal, and vinyl, 69 x 40 x 76". Hirshhorn Museum and Sculpture Garden, Smithsonian Institution, Washington, D.C.

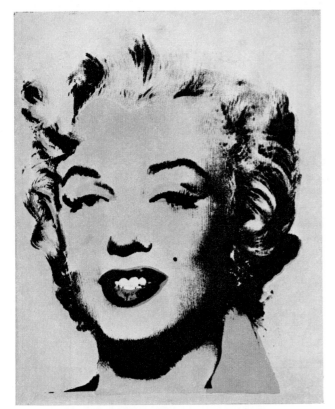

564. ANDY WARHOL. *Marilyn Monroe*. 1962. Oil, acrylic, and silkscreen enamel on canvas, 20 x 16". Collection Jasper Johns, New York

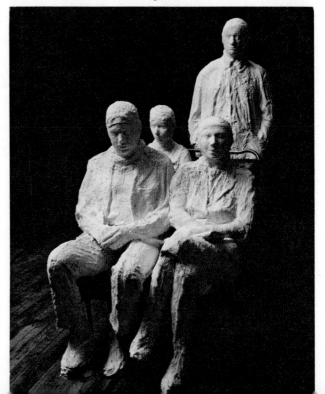

no control and that, at the same time, they cannot do without.

In a sense an offshoot of Pop is the work of the Bulgarian-born CHRISTO (born Christo Javachef, 1935–), who attempts to dominate his surroundings by the modern device of packaging them. He has wrapped in sheets of various kinds of plastic any number of inert objects: bicycles, machines, a skyscraper, and even one million square feet of the coast of Australia. *Wrapped Coast, Little Bay, Australia*, of 1969 (fig. 567), shows beautiful effects of drapery movement, perhaps a by-product of the original idea. Alas, Christo's valiant attempt to string a vast curtain across a mile-wide canyon in the Rocky Mountains must be set down as a failure. The sculpture of the Greek-born LUCAS SAMARAS (1936–) can best be considered at this point, although his connections with Pop are tenuous. Along with objects of furniture or boxes studded with dangerous points from pins to razor blades, crawling with hair, or streaming with rope fringes, Samaras has done work of great imaginative brilliance. His rooms entirely lined with squares of mirror—all four walls, ceiling, and floor—in which hangs a single electric light bulb over a single mirror-covered table, as in *Room No. 2*, of 1966 (fig. 568), are at once dazzling and dizzying. They are, of course, exploitations of the commonplace phenomenon of multiple reflections to be seen in many old-fashioned barbershops and restaurants; but as they prolong Renaissance perspective recessions to the nth power, they produce a fantastic vision of infinity that suggests cosmic implications, and literally lift the observer (who is inside the room and can see nothing else but its diminishing reflections in every direction) out of himself and his world.

OP ART. Optical Art (Op, for short) rapidly succeeded the first outburst of Pop as a new fad in the early 1960s. It had, however, been quietly germinating for many years. Op differs basically from the subject-oriented Pop in that it denies representation altogether, but it is no less firmly opposed to individual emotional expression than is Pop. Historically, Op has sought to produce by a variety of means strong optical illusions of depth, mass, and motion. Often the materials used are synthetic, and absolute regularity of production is always emphasized, so that several important Op artists have limited their own personal participation to the initial study and bequeathed the actual execution to assistants, working largely by mechanical means.

The leader of the Op movement is the Hungarian-born VICTOR VASARELY (1908–), who worked much of his life in Paris. Vasarely studied carefully the theory of

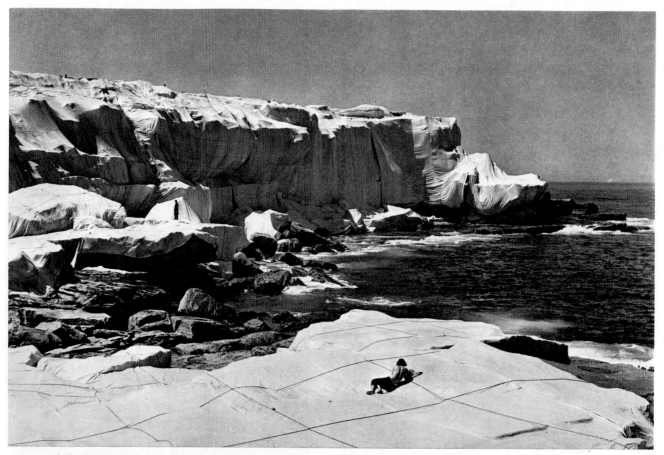

567. CHRISTO. *Wrapped Coast, Little Bay, Australia.* 1969. Surface area of entire projct 1,000,000 square feet

color perception and the writings of Mondrian and Kandinsky. He has stated, "Painting and sculpture become anachronistic terms: it is more exact to speak of a bi-, tri-, and multidimensional plastic art. We no longer have distinct manifestations of a creative sensibility, but the development of a single plastic sensibility in different spaces." In the manipulation of variations in parallel lines, Vasarely was able to give the illusion of space where none exists, as if perspective had suddenly become rubbery and could be stretched out of shape, only to bounce back again. Superimposed layers of transparent glass or plastic with linear configurations on them give striking illusions of actual space constructions. It should be noted at this point that these ideas, like so many others in recent art, had been pioneered by Marcel Duchamp in his machines, visual gramophone records, and the perspectives of *The Bride Stripped Bare by Her Bachelors, Even* (see fig. 500). In the 1950s Vasarely's designs were restricted to black and white, but in the 1960s he began working with brilliant color to resounding effect. For all their apparent impersonality and their reliance on optics and other branches of mathematics, the creations of Vasarely (one ought not to betray his stated aim by calling them paintings) project the observer into new and perfect worlds of pure experience, as do the mirror rooms of Samaras. Vasarely's true artistic ancestors are the great perspectivists of the Renaissance and the Baroque, especially Uccello and Pozzo. Such works as *Arcturus II*, of 1966 (colorplate 82), with its splendid colors and concave-convex forms, are often carried out on a considerable scale, and exert a real poetic excitement. Architectural murals are the true realm for Vasarely's activity, although he has seldom been commissioned to do them. The visionary world he presents to us has possibilities as limitless as the mathematics he relies on.

Among the other leading Op artists the American RICHARD ANUSZKIEWICZ (1930–) should be singled out for special mention. Anuszkiewicz works by means of constantly reversing illusions of depth and mass, as in *Trinity*, of 1970 (colorplate 83), so that the same configuration may at one moment appear concave, at the next convex. His pictures are painted in colors so closely adjusted as to form sharp dissonances, or so exactly complementary as to establish contrasts of well-nigh intolerable intensity; yet in the final analysis all conflicts are resolved, and Anuszkiewicz's art is one of brilliance, harmony, poise, and beauty.

COLOR FIELD AND HARD EDGE. It is less easy to label some of the other movements that arose to participate in the general assault on the Abstract Expressionist fortress. In the 1940s BARNETT NEWMAN (1905–70) was working with rectangular areas, and in the early 1950s arrived at a simple statement in terms of one or two fields of color, seldom very bright, comprising the entire canvas, usually quite large. These fields are separated from

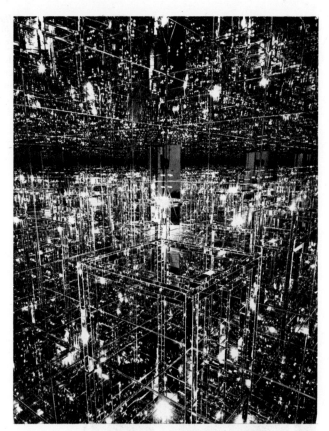

568. LUCAS SAMARAS. *Room No. 2.* 1966. Wood and mirrors, 8 x 10 x 8'. Albright-Knox Art Gallery, Buffalo, New York. Room of Contemporary Art Fund

each other by one or two narrow color stripes, whose edges are purposely left a little fuzzy to suggest space. Newman was a well-read intellectual and a pioneer in insisting that the picture consist entirely of itself so that the artist's work resides solely in dividing and coloring the actual canvas. In the memorial exhibition of his work held at The Museum of Modern Art, New York, in 1973 it was evident that Newman had not always succeeded, but when he had his achievement was brilliant. His *Stations of the Cross: Twelfth Station*, of 1965 (fig. 569), shows that he worked entirely by balancing areas against each other, with the crucial, but never central, stripe or stripes as the fulcrum. Newman was a seminal figure, influential in the development of a movement favoring the supremacy of the canvas itself over all illusion or expression and especially over the emotion-loaded brush, which had been all-important for the Abstract Expressionists.

At the end of the 1950s, it became apparent that a distinct group of painters had formed around the concept of the dominant canvas, led by MORRIS LOUIS (1912–62) and KENNETH NOLAND (1924–), both of whom worked in Washington, D.C., isolated from the New York scene. Louis based his images entirely on the literally physical movement of color across the raw, unprimed canvas. He poured the color on the canvas, and by means of delicate tilting let it run until it produced

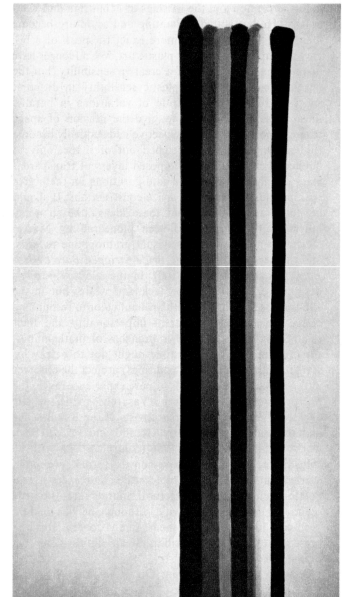

570. Morris Louis. *Pillar of Hope*. 1961. Acrylic resin on canvas, 85 x 48¼". Collection Robert H. Shoenberg, St. Louis

569. Barnett Newman. *Stations of the Cross: Twelfth Station*. 1965. Acrylic polymer on canvas, 78 x 60". Collection Annalee Newman, New York

fluid patterns, superimposed veils of hue. Toward the end of his life, he poured from near the top of the canvas down, let each color run off the canvas, then poured the next stripe, as in *Pillar of Hope*, of 1961 (fig. 570). These clusters of broad stripes, usually of very rich and sonorous color, move against the mat surface of the canvas with great effect. Noland started with concentric circles of bright color painted on unprimed canvas, reminiscent of Johns' targets, and seeming to float. He then moved to immense inverted chevrons of bright color, each made up of several stripes, against the now primed canvas; at first, these were centered on the bottom edge, but later they were directed to one side or the other, as in *Bridge*, of 1964 (colorplate 84). With its powerful blues, yellow, orange, and red against white, it is a vivid example of Noland's work at its best. The execution is deliberately precise and inert. More recently, Noland has painted canvases of immense length entirely

in horizontal clustered stripes of brilliant color floating against a vast field of white, producing the effect of landscapes inspired by the Great Plains. A still different possibility for color-field painting was explored by Ellsworth Kelly (1923–), whose *Red White*, of 1961 (colorplate 85), suggests remotely the free forms of Arp or the cut-paper compositions of the late Matisse. Always with great clarity of vision and execution, Kelly simplified his image so that during the early 1970s he placed large, smooth, rectangular panels, each a different and very bright color, side by side to produce color progressions with the regularity of a color chart, and with a certain loss of effect, considering the clear, rhythmic beauty of the contours in such works as *Red White*.

The name *hard edge* has been applied to such color-field paintings as those of Noland and Kelly—not without some confusion because the term could equally well designate the work of abstractionists as different from each other as Léger, Mondrian, Malevich, and Davis, to name only a few. But the phrase seems peculiarly apt as a description of the work of FRANK STELLA (1936–), the youngest of all the influential American artists of the moment. Only forty years old in 1976, Stella was just twenty-four when his first shaped canvases appeared on the New York art scene. *Ophir*, of 1960–61 (fig. 571), is a striking example of Stella's brilliant and implacable early style, whose hardness, coldness, and total impersonality seemed a sword aimed directly at the heart of the Abstract Expressionist movement. Pictures had, of course, not always been of the rectangular shape customary since the eighteenth century. A backward glance over the illustrations in this volume will turn up every kind of shape from the gables and pointed arches of Gothic altarpieces, to Renaissance round arches, ovals, and circles, to the irregular, pulsating areas left for paintings by Rococo architects. As early as the 1920s, some artists had experimented with new shapes. But Stella's systematic exploitation of a total shape derived entirely from the action of the stripes within the canvas was an achievement of the highest originality, and by itself establishes his place in the history of modern art.

At first, Stella's color was restricted to grays and browns—a shock after the gorgeous abandon of Abstract Expressionist color—and then he began to work in copper and aluminum paints. He restricted himself severely to a single theme—absolutely straight, parallel, monochrome stripes, separated by narrow white lines. If the stripes changed their course, so did the shape of the

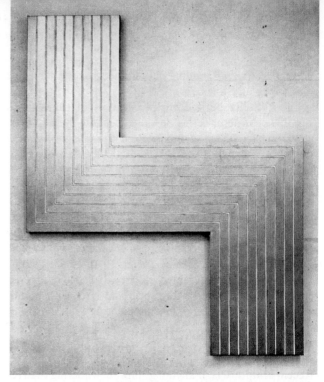

571. FRANK STELLA. *Ophir*. 1960–61. Copper paint on canvas, 90 x 84". Collection James Holderbaum, Smith College, Northampton, Massachusetts

canvas, in forms resembling V's, W's, and horseshoes. The strange fact is that these shapes have impressed no observer as ornamental. Their very austerity and hardness have given them a kind of totemic significance unsupported by the faintest hint of either representation

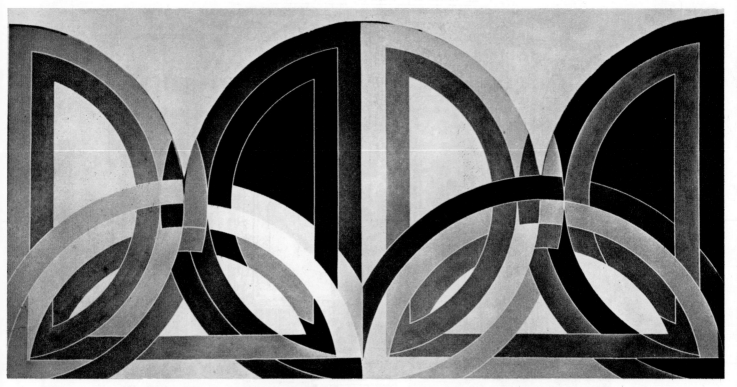

572. FRANK STELLA. *Tahkt-I-Sulayman I*. 1967. Polymer and fluorescent paint on canvas, 10'¼" x 20'2¼". Pasadena Art Museum, California. Gift of Mr. and Mrs. Robert A. Rowan

or expression, but residing only in the hypnotic power of the stripes and lines.

Later, Stella burst forth in canvases of tremendous size, his protractor series, so called because their component forms, whose composite contours establish the shape of the picture, are systematically derived from superimposed and intersecting arcs. These are no longer restricted to the reserved, metallic tones of his early style, but painted in the teeth-jarring fluorescence of Da-glo. *Tahkt-I-Sulayman I*, of 1967 (fig. 572), is a brilliant example of this phase, ten feet across, and unexpectedly lyrical in its circles and half circles of yellow, two tones of red, and two tones of blue. After 1970, Stella's color calmed down considerably, and he worked out layered constructions covered with fabric and later with metal, which are as much sculpture as painting.

ABSTRACT SCULPTURE
SINCE WORLD WAR II

Recent sculpture is, if anything, more bewildering than recent painting in the richness of its development and the multifarious shapes of its creations. A complete survey of sculpture in the third quarter of the twentieth century would far exceed the scope of this book. The tendency toward working directly in metal, which we have seen as early as Archipenko, Gabo, and Pevsner, found a new ex-

pression in the metal junk culled from automobile graveyards and made into assemblages by John Chamberlain and Richard Stankiewicz; these works responded in tortured surfaces and sometimes brilliant color to the pictorial richness of Abstract Expressionism. The most eloquent assemblages are those created by LOUISE NEVELSON (1900–   ), who ranks as one of the finest women artists of the twentieth century and one of the best American sculptors. Nevelson works with overpowering effect by putting together found objects—boxes, pieces of wood, bits of furniture, ornamental fragments from demolished Victorian buildings. Her towering, wall-like structures share at once the echoes of haunted houses and glimmers of a new perfection. For years these assemblages were painted in a solemn, allover black; later, they gleamed in white, then in gold. Nevelson's brilliantly harmonized *An American Tribute to the British People*, of 1960–65 (fig. 573), is a monumental, gold-painted, abstract successor to Ghiberti's *Gates of Paradise* and Rodin's *Gates of Hell*. In the late 1960s Nevelson worked with great success in such luminous materials as aluminum and Lucite without sacrificing her innate sense of structure.

The most impressive American sculptor of the last quarter century is DAVID SMITH (1906–65), an artist of extraordinary power and originality. Starting with welded

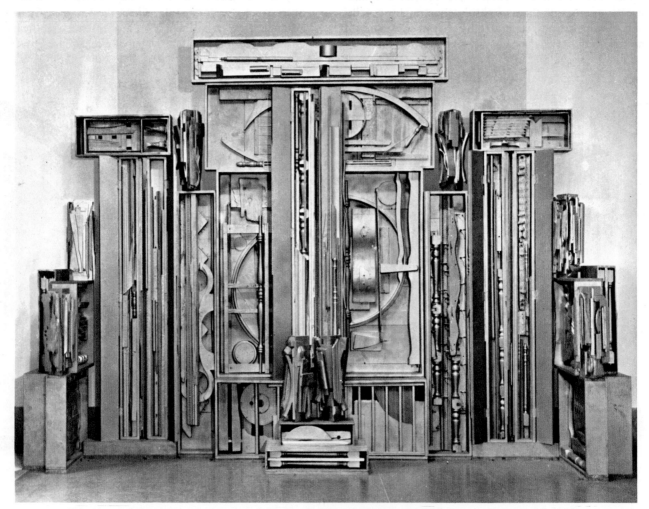

573. LOUISE NEVELSON. *An American Tribute to the British People*. 1960–65. Wood painted gold, 10'2" x 14'3". The Tate Gallery, London

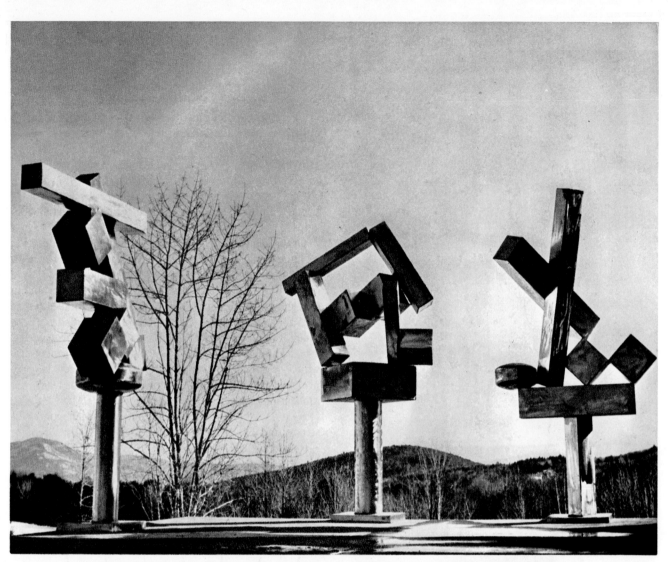

574. DAVID SMITH. Left: *Cubi XVIII*. 1964. Stainless steel, height 9'8". Museum of Fine Arts, Boston.
Anonymous gift. Center: *Cubi XVII*. 1963. Stainless steel, height 9'. Dallas Museum of Fine Arts
Right: *Cubi XIX*. 1964. Stainless steel, height 9'5". The Tate Gallery, London

steel constructions, Smith proceeded to put together wagons and chariots recalling those of the Bronze Age, then to make superb abstract masses built from superimposed blocks of steel. Smith did all the mechanical work himself on the basis of his experiences in an automobile plant and a locomotive factory. His triumphant period came just before his tragic death in an automobile accident. In the late 1950s and early 1960s, Smith turned out constructions of imposing grandeur and yet astonishing lightness of poise and balance in the *Cubi* series, fabricated in the studio on his farm at Bolton's Landing, New York. Three of these sculptures (*Cubi XVIII*, *Cubi XVII*, and *Cubi XIX*), with their openness, lightness, and elemental power, compete in beauty with the surrounding landscape (fig. 574).

Minimal Art came into being in the mid-1960s as the most impersonal form of all. The work of art was a simple object, shorn of all suggestions of meaning or of human receptiveness. There have been many manifestations of minimal art, ranging from simple bathroom shelves fixed to a gallery wall, to sheets of steel laid on a gallery floor, to smoothly lacquered planks leaning against anything. The most impressive of the minimalists is DONALD JUDD(1928–   ), whose art is based on pure proportion. Seven identical, quadrangular, cubic masses of galvanized iron make up his *Untitled*, of 1965 (fig. 575). Judd also works in steel and plexiglass; his constructions are beautifully polished, and some of them are enameled. The relationship between their masses is as subtle as the coloring. Judd, unlike Smith, creates only the design, leaving the execution to skilled industrial craftsmen. The nobility of his work is a living witness to Alberti's claim (see page 33) that beauty is that quality to which nothing can be added and from which nothing can be taken away without destroying it. One also recalls Edna St. Vincent Millay's celebrated sonnet beginning, "Euclid alone has looked on Beauty bare." With forms as perfect and relationships as absolute as those Judd gives us, we can dispense with decoration.

Some recent sculpture has renounced substance entirely, and exploited the effects of light in ways impossible to reproduce adequately in photographs. RICHARD

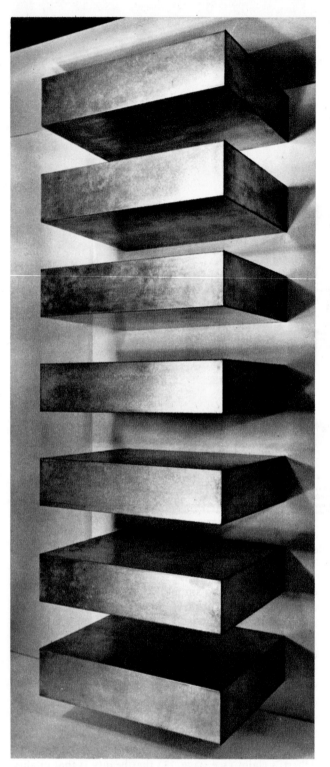

LIPPOLD (1915–   ) has, beginning in the 1940s, arranged gold-filled wires, rods, and thin slabs in enormous spaces in constructions so ephemeral that they appear to consist of light rays; they are reminiscent in effect of such visionary apparitions as the gold rays emanating from an angel's head in the background of an altarpiece by Fra Angelico (see colorplate 8), or those streaming from the Holy Spirit in a Baroque revelation (see fig. 242). *Variation Within a Sphere, No. 10: the Sun*, of 1953–56 (fig. 576), twenty-two feet in length, shows the extreme intricacy and delicacy of Lippold's radial interrelationships.

Other sculptors have turned toward the manipulation of light itself. Gothic artists had in a sense worked with light in their stained glass windows, and—as we have seen—Bernini was a pioneer in this respect in arranging and shaping the concealed sources of light in his *Ecstasy of Saint Theresa* (see fig. 240) and his *Cathedra Petri*, much as he had modeled water in his fountains (see fig. 241). Thomas Wilfred (1889–1968) invented a new art, which he called Lumia; a "color organ" projects lengthy programs of constantly changing luminous forms onto a motion-picture screen. The Argentinian JULIO LE PARC (1928–   ), who works in Paris, contrived such wonderful structures of light and movement as *Continuel Lumière Formes en Contorsion*, of 1966 (fig. 577), in effect not unlike some aspects of Wilfred's Lumia. The Greek-born CHRYSSA (1933–   ) works with the familiar elements of the neon sign, already imitated in the paintings of Davis and Indiana, which she places in layers in depth, producing patterns of ornamental repetition in space. In

575. DONALD JUDD. *Untitled.* 1965. Galvanized iron, seven boxes, each 9 x 49 x 31″ (9″ between each box). Locksley-Shea Gallery, Minneapolis

576. RICHARD LIPPOLD. *Variation Within a Sphere, No. 10: the Sun.* 1953–56. Gold-filled wire, c. 11 x 22 x 5½″. The Metropolitan Museum of Art, New York. Fletcher Fund, 1956

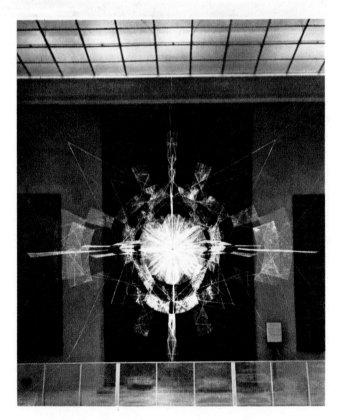

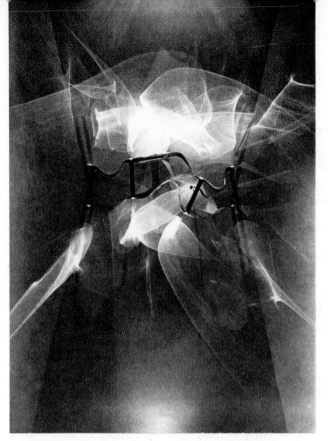

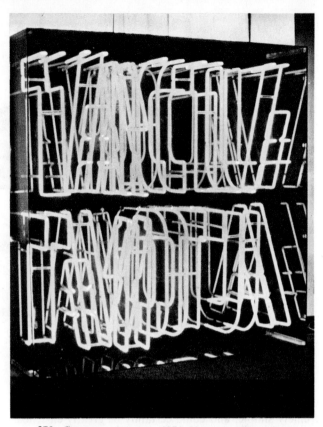

577. JULIO LE PARC. *Continuel Lumière Formes en Contorsion*. 1966. Motorized aluminum and wood, 80 x 48½ x 8″. Howard Wise Gallery, New York

578. CHRYSSA. *Automat*. 1971. Neon and Plexiglas, 68½ x 68½ x 20″. The Harry N. Abrams Family Collection. New York

Automat, of 1971 (fig. 578), she has created majestic and seemingly durable forms out of these ubiquitous elements of modern urban society. ROCKNE KREBS (1938–) works with colossal laser beams traced against the night sky of an urban center, as in the clusters bursting miraculously forth above the staid Neoclassical pediment of the Philadelphia Museum of Art in his *Study for Laser Project, Philadelphia Festival, May, 1973* (fig. 579).

The latest gesture of the sculptor in space has been Earth Art, a movement led by ROBERT SMITHSON (1938–73), who met a tragic death while exploring from the air a site for one of his gigantic projects.

579. ROCKNE KREBS. *Study for Laser Project, Philadelphia Festival, May, 1973*. 1973. Mixed mediums, 18⅞ x 24¾″. Philadelphia Museum of Art. Purchase, The Marie Kimball Fund

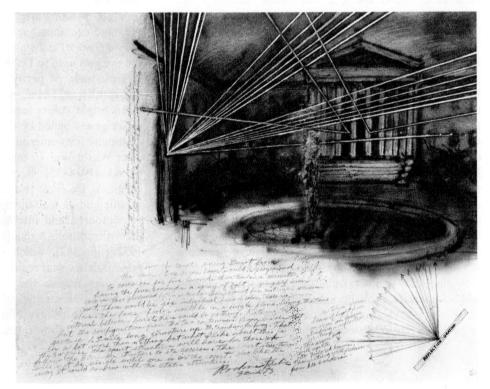

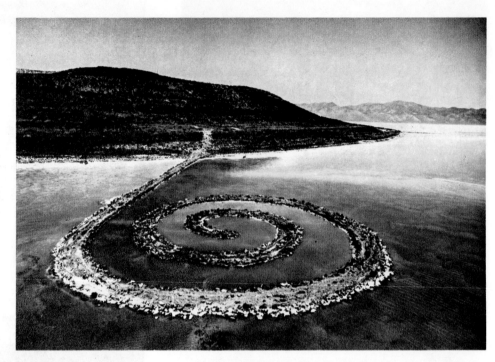

580. ROBERT SMITHSON. *Spiral Jetty*. Rocks, salt crystals, earth, and algae. 1970. Coil, length 1,500'; width c. 15'. Great Salt Lake, Utah

Characteristically enough, the forms of Earth Art are extremely simple, and could certainly be greatly enriched; often, they are no more than trenches. Parenthetically, such projects demand both considerable financial expenditure and rather selfless patrons who often cannot see the works they pay for and who must content themselves with photographs and glory. Smithson's most successful work is the colossal *Spiral Jetty*, of 1970 (fig. 580), constructed of rocks, which jut into Great Salt Lake in Utah. The whole process of earthmoving, with standard mechanical equipment, was recorded by Smithson in a film, which is in itself a work of art. Only Christo's wrappings and curtains rival Smithson's earthworks in their defiance of space, but it is worthwhile recording that Earth Art had its predecessors in the activities of the pre-Columbian Mound Builders of North America.

EUROPEAN MOVEMENTS SINCE WORLD WAR II. Although a considerable number of artists of interest have made their appearance in various European countries since the close of World War II, it is safe to say from the present vantage point, a generation after the war, that none can rival such great European innovators of the first half of the twentieth century as Matisse, Picasso, Kandinsky, Mondrian, and Brancusi. A surprising number, in fact, either derive from or more or less closely parallel American contemporary artists, and they cannot really be compared in stature with such figures as Pollock, Rauschenberg, or Frank Stella. The most original personality of the postwar period in France is JEAN DUBUFFET (1901–), whose first one-man show took place only in 1944. Dubuffet's activity is prodigious and his interests, probably sparked by his study of Klee, range over every variety of what he called *art brut* (*rough* or *raw art*). He relentlessly collected and studied thou-

sands of examples of the art of children and that of the insane—as well as the graffiti that appeared on Parisian buildings, scratched on layer over layer of posters—in a ceaseless attempt to discover how the uncensored and untutored human animal draws and paints. His own paintings could be and were made of anything from cement to ashes, and the message was generally one of profound pessimism. In the mid-1960s he emerged with a gloriously irresponsible new series, for which he coined the word *Hourloupes*. On a principle suggesting the endless relief compositions of the Aztecs, he covered many surfaces (some enormous—one painting is twenty-seven feet long) with countless tiny figures, producing a jigsaw-puzzle effect. The red and blue contours, often raised in relief, separate writhing irregular areas of white striped with blue and occasional yellows. A small example is *Legendary Figure of a Tap*, of 1965 (fig. 581), in which, once the eye gets used to Dubuffet's tricks, one can descry tiny figures, nude or partly clothed, locked in a continual mass embrace. The absolute uniformity of accent and the clean bright colors lend these pictures a sense of decorative gaiety belied by the licentiousness of the subjects.

Among the numerous gifted artists of the Paris School after World War II, one of the leaders was NICOLAS DE STAËL (1914–55), born in Russia and brought up in Belgium. De Staël worked in rich masses of pigment usually laid on with the palette knife in broad areas firmly contoured and interlocking, still within a generally Cubist tradition. A relatively late work, *Le Lavandou*, of 1952 (fig. 582), which shows the artist beginning to reassimilate visual reality into the framework of abstraction, also reveals the sensitivity of his color and the delicacy of his sense of pattern. The broad, vertical stripes of color suggest furniture, curtains, and a view out of a window. A considerable feeling of deep recession is achieved entirely by juxtaposition of color tones. In a mood of despair at having reached what he considered a blind alley in his work, de Staël committed suicide.

A delightfully outrageous figure of the Paris School was YVES KLEIN (1928–62), who experimented with almost anything, and seems to have been the first to exhibit the bare walls of an art gallery as his own creative work. His favorite color was ultramarine blue, with which he impregnated everything from sponges to plaster casts of his friends' nude bodies. The inventor of Body Art, Klein covered nude models with blue paint and let them roll on canvas to leave prints of their entire anatomies. He painted canvases blue, exposed them to rain, and exhibited the results. But his best works were certainly his fire paintings, such as *Fire Painting*, of 1961–62 (colorplate 86), produced by the application of flame to painted asbestos, with a frequently gorgeous effect. Had it not been for Klein's untimely death, there is no telling what other directions this enfant terrible of modernism would have taken.

The most successful of the European artists who moved in a direction parallel to Abstract Expressionism is the Dutch KAREL APPEL (1921–), a coformer of the international expressionist group CoBrA (a word made from *Copenhagen, Brussels,* and *Amsterdam,* where its members reside). Nothing could be further from the CoBrA intent than the purity of the De Stijl tradition. Appel reacts against it with the coloristic equivalent of a

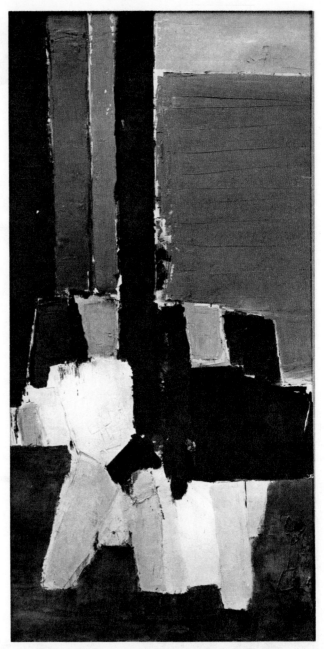

582. NICOLAS DE STAËL. *Le Lavandou.* 1952. Oil on canvas, 76¾ x 38⅛″. Musée National d'Art Moderne, Paris

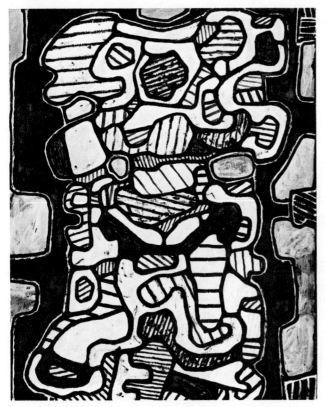

581. JEAN DUBUFFET. *Legendary Figure of a Tap.* 1965. Vinyl on canvas, 39⅜ x 31⅞″. Collection the artist

howl, directed against the unfortunate canvas in great swatches of discordant tone. The areas are as bold as the colors themselves are harsh, with an effect of frightening barbarity. *Angry Landscape,* of 1967 (fig. 583), is done in blocks of strong red, yellow, and blue, interspersed with dark blue, violet, and dirty greenish-yellow, and through its bold masses one can make out an occasional malevolent mask, reminiscent of Ensor.

PHOTOREALISM. In the early 1970s, another strong artistic movement, Photorealism, made its appearance. Born in California, the movement struck New York in

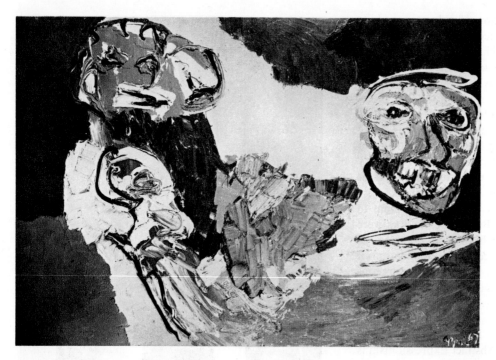

583. KAREL APPEL. *Angry Landscape.* 1967. Oil on canvas, 51½ x 76¾". Collection Jimmy J. Younger, Houston

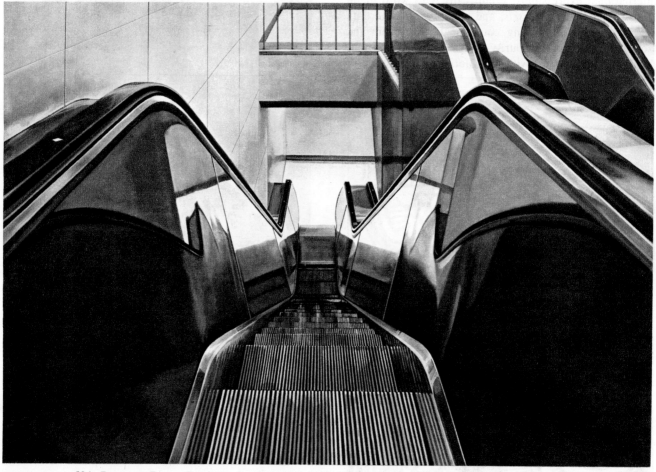

584. RICHARD ESTES. *Escalator, Bus Terminal.* 1969. Oil on canvas, 42 x 60". Collection Mr. and Mrs. Robert P. Kogod, Bethesda, Maryland

force in 1971. Its practitioners, who vary greatly among themselves in subject and in style, agree on two principles: first, that the picture should be painted, unaltered, with an airbrush from a photographic slide projected on the actual canvas; and, second, that the subject be as banal as possible. In this latter respect the Photorealists clearly derive from the tradition of such American Scene painters as Hopper, a style continued by the Pop movement of the 1960s. In the former they derive wholly from Pop's frequent insistence on mechanical methods. The undisputed leader of the group is RICHARD ESTES (1936–), whose dreary subjects are presented with stunning brilliance. The apparent impersonality of the Photorealists is belied by the fact that, after all, they take the photographs from which they work, so a considerable latitude of choice is available. How Estes manages to photograph public places without a human being in them, such as is the case in his *Escalator, Bus Terminal*, of 1969 (fig. 584), is a secret known only to himself, but in his beautiful barrenness of surface and in his strong sense of mass and depth, he shows that he has learned all the lessons of abstract art. Strongly related to Estes is the sculptor DUANE HANSON (1925–), who produces lifesize, colored models of human beings provided with actual accessories and painted in so lifelike a fashion that gallery-goers inevitably titter, especially when a waggish curator places an apparently real house painter complete with wet brush and full pail in the middle of a doorway through which everyone must pass. But as soon as the initial laughter dies down, such a group as the truly dreadful *Tourists*, of 1970 (fig. 585), betrays its essentially tragic content. The two fat, aging people, whose goodwill is equaled only by their total lack of taste and understanding, are a devastating appraisal of Americans let loose on the world. Even less cheerful are Hanson's down-and-out characters—the dog-tired worker with a can of beer, the exhausted middle-aged shopper, the stoned junkie—who, as the dregs of civilization, can only ap-

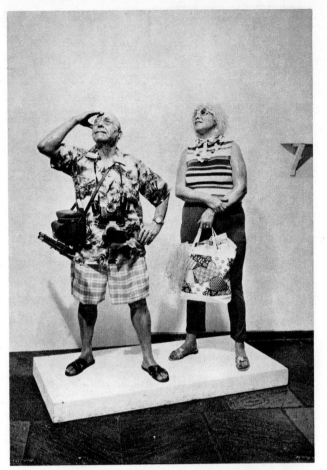

585. DUANE HANSON. *Tourists.* 1970. Fiberglas and polychromed polyester. 64 x 65 x 47″. Private collection

pear the human counterparts of the rags and scraps put together by Schwitters and Rauschenberg.

What direction art will turn to next is anyone's guess. This writer has no crystal ball. But even if we seem in the mid-1970s to have reached a temporary lull in inventiveness, it may be the calm before some new expression of what has proved to be one of the most inexhaustible of natural phenomena—the human imagination.

TIME LINE

The numbers in italics refer to illustrations in the text

POLITICAL HISTORY	RELIGION, LITERATURE, MUSIC	SCIENCE, TECHNOLOGY
1775		
American Revolution (1775–85); Declaration of Independence (1776); U.S. Constitution adopted (1789)	Gibbon, *The History of the Decline and Fall of the Roman Empire* (1776–88)	Adam Smith, *Wealth of Nations* (1776)
First British governor general of India appointed (1784)	Kant, *Critique of Pure Reason* (1781)	First aerial crossing of English Channel, in hydrogen-filled balloon (1785)
French Revolution (1789–97); Louis XVI beheaded, Reign of Terror under Robespierre (1793)	Paine, *The Rights of Man* (1790)	Power loom (1785); cotton gin (1792)
	Percy Bysshe Shelley (1792–1822)	Hutton, *Theory of the Earth* (1795)
	John Keats (1795–1821)	Laplace postulates nebular hypothesis (1796)
	Wordsworth and Coleridge, *Lyrical Ballads* (1798)	Jenner discovers smallpox vaccine (c. 1798)
Consulate of Napoleon (1799)	Honoré de Balzac (1799–1850)	
1800		
Louisiana Purchase (1803)	Victor Hugo (1802–85)	Volta invents electric battery (1800)
Napoleon crowns himself emperor (1804); fails in Russian campaign (1812); beaten at Leipzig, exiled to Elba (1814); defeated at Waterloo, banished to St. Helena (1815)	Beethoven, *Fidelio* (1803–1805)	Cuvier publishes work on paleontology (1800)
	Wordsworth, *The Prelude* (1805)	First voyage of Fulton's steamship *Clermont* (1807); first Atlantic crossing (1819)
	Hegel, *Phenomenology of Mind* (1807)	Stephenson builds first locomotive (1814)
Spanish War of Independence (1808–14); return of Spanish king, Ferdinand VII, to throne (1814)	Goethe, *Faust* (Part I) (1808)	Faraday discovers principle of electric dynamo (1821)
	Edgar Allan Poe (1809–49)	
Congress of Vienna (1814–15)	Madame de Staël, *De l'Allemagne* (1810)	
Germanic Confederation founded (1816)	Byron, *Childe Harold's Pilgrimage* (1812–18)	
Revolution in Latin America gains independence for Spanish colonies (1817–25)	Sören Kierkegaard (1813–55)	
	Saint-Simon's ideas for the reorganization of European society (1814)	
Napoleon dies on St. Helena (1821)	Rossini, *The Barber of Seville* (1816)	
Beginning of Greek War of Independence against the Turks (1821); declaration of Greek independence (1822)	Goethe, *Italian Journey* (1816–17)	
	Shelley, *Prometheus Unbound* (1820)	
	Charles Baudelaire (1821–67)	
Monroe Doctrine proclaimed (1823)	Gustave Flaubert (1821–80)	
1825		
Andrew Jackson becomes U.S. president (1829–37)	Manzoni, *The Betrothed* (1827)	Erie Canal opened (1825)
July Revolution in France (1830)	Henrik Ibsen (1828–1906)	First railway completed (England, 1825)
Whigs in England end Tory rule (1830); political and social reforms (1832–35)	Stendhal, *The Red and the Black* (1830)	McCormick invents reaper (1831)
	Pushkin, *Boris Godunov* (1831)	Babbage develops "analytical" engine (1833)
Start of revolutionary movements and uprisings throughout Europe	Goethe, *Faust* (Part II) (1832)	Daguerreotype process of photography introduced (1839)
	Pushkin, *Eugene Onegin* (1832/33)	
France conquers Algeria (1830–47)	Goethe, *Dichtung und Warheit* (final vol. pub. 1833)	Chevreul, *De la Loi du Contraste Simultané des Couleurs* (1839)
Quadruple Alliance: treaty between England, France, Spain, and Portugal to protect liberalism (1834)	Dickens, *Oliver Twist* (1838)	Morse perfects telegraph (1844)
	Émile Zola (1840–1902)	Joule formulates First Law of Thermodynamics (1847)
Victoria, Eng. queen (r. 1837–1901)	Carlyle, *On Heroes, Hero-Worship, and the Heroic in History* (1841)	
Chartist movement in England (1839)	Adam's ballet, *Giselle* (1841)	
British win Hong Kong (1841)	Verdi, *Nabucco* (1842)	
Boers found Orange Free State in South Africa (1842)	Stéphane Mallarmé (1842–89)	
U.S. treaty with China opens Chinese ports (1844)	Henry James (1843–1916)	
The Weavers' Rising in Silesia (1844)	Kierkegaard, *Either/Or* (1843)	
U.S. annexes Western land areas (1845–60)	Paul Verlaine (1844–96)	
Famine in Ireland, mass emigration (1845)	Dumas, *The Count of Monte Cristo* (1845)	
British Parliament repeals Corn Laws (1846)	Proudhon develops anarchist theory (1846)	
February Revolution in Paris; March Revolution in Berlin and other cities; October Revolution in Austria (1848)	Thackeray, *Vanity Fair* (1848)	
	Marx, *Communist Manifesto* (1848)	
Risorgimento in Italy	J. K. Huysmans (1848–1907)	
France sets up Second Republic (Louis Napoleon); restores papal supremacy in Rome (1848)	Ruskin, *Seven Lamps of Architecture* (1849); *Stones of Venice* (1851)	
1850		
Prussia receives constitution (1850)	Dickens, *David Copperfield* (1850)	Lord Kelvin states Second Law of Thermodynamics (1851)
Louis Napoleon's coup d'état (1851); proclaimed emperor as Napoleon III (1852)	Melville, *Moby Dick* (1851)	First International Exhibition of Industry, New York (1853)
	Verdi, *Rigoletto* (1851); *Il Trovatore* and *La Traviata* (1853)	
Independent state of Transvaal set up (1852)		First transatlantic cable (1858–66)
Crimean War (1853–56); England and France halt Russia's advance into Balkans; Treaty of Paris ends Crimean War (1856)	Wagner begins composition of *The Ring of the Nibelung* (1853; completed 1874)	Darwin publishes *On the Origin of Species by Means of Natural Selection* (1859)
	Oscar Wilde (1854–1900)	First oil well drilled (Pennsylvania, 1859)
Perry's visit ends Japan's isolation (1854)	Whitman, *Leaves of Grass* (1855)	Bessemer patents tilting converter for turning iron into steel (1860)
Treaty of Tientsin (1858); China agrees to respect embassies of the Western powers	G. B. Shaw (1856–1950)	Pasteur develops germ theory (1864)
	Baudelaire, *Les Fleurs du Mal* (1857)	Mendel publishes first experiments in genetics (1865)
German National Union founded (1859)	Anton Chekhov (1860–1904)	Nobel invents dynamite (1867)
Unification of Italy (1860–70)	Turgenev, *Fathers and Sons* (1862)	First transcontinental railroad completed in America (1869)
Lincoln becomes U.S. president (1861–65)	Tolstoy, *War and Peace* (1864–69)	
Russia abolishes serfdom (1861)	Lewis Carroll, *Alice in Wonderland* (1865)	Suez Canal opened (1869)
American Civil War (1861–65)	W. B. Yeats (1865–1939)	Schliemann starts excavations at Troy (1870)
The First International (1864)	Dostoyevsky, *Crime and Punishment* (1866)	Maxwell, *Electricity and Magnetism* (1873)
Emperor Maximilian of Mexico executed (1867)	Marx, *Das Kapital* (1867–94)	
Russia sells Alaska to U.S.A. (1867)	André Gide (1869–1951)	
Canada granted dominion status (1867)	Pius IX convenes first Vatican Council (1871–1922)	
Third Republic established in France (1870)	Marcel Proust (1869–70)	
Franco-Prussian War (1870–71)	Zola begins the series of novels *Les Rougon-Macquart* (1871; completed 1893)	
Bismarck made chancellor of German Empire (1871)	First performance of Mussorgsky's *Boris Godunov* (1874)	
Three Emperors' League (Germany, Austria, and Russia) (1873)		
Disraeli, Br. p.m. (1874–80)		
1875		
High tide of European colonialism (1876–1914)	First performance of Bizet's *Carmen* (1875)	Wundt establishes first Institute of Experimental Psychology in Leipzig (1875)
Queen Victoria becomes Empress of India (1876)	Tolstoy, *Anna Karenina* (1875–77)	Bell patents the telephone (1876)
Russo-Turkish War (1877)	Mark Twain, *The Adventures of Tom Sawyer* (1876)	Edison invents phonograph (1877)
Great Britain annexes Transvaal (1877)	Tchaikovsky, *Fourth Symphony* (1878)	Albert Einstein (1879–1955)
Germany becomes colonial power (1884)	Ibsen, *A Doll's House* (1879)	Edison invents electric light bulb (1879)
Bismarck signs "Reinsurance Treaty" with Russia (1887)	First performance of Tchaikovsky's *Eugene Onegin* (1879)	Pasteur and Koch prove germ theory of disease (1881)
Brazil abolishes slavery, the last state to do so (1888)	Guillaume Apollinaire (1880–1918)	First internal combustion engines for gasoline (1885)
Internationalization of the Suez Canal (1889)	Dostoyevsky, *The Brothers Karamazov* (1880)	Roentgen discovers X-rays (1895)
Luxembourg secedes from the Netherlands (1890)	James Joyce (1882–1941)	Marconi invents wireless telegraphy (1895)
Japan defeats China (1894–95)	Sinclair Lewis (1885–1951)	Edison invents motion picture (1896)
Spanish-American War (1898): U.S. gains Philippines, Guam, Puerto Rico; annexes Hawaii	Ezra Pound (1885–1972)	The Curies discover radium (1898)
	D. H. Lawrence (1885–1930)	
War between Greece and Turkey (1897)	Rimbaud, *Illuminations* (1886)	
Boer War (1899–1902)	Eugene O'Neill (1888–1953)	
	T. S. Eliot (1888–1964)	
	Ludwig Wittgenstein (1889–1951)	
	First performance of Mascagni's *Cavalleria Rusticana* (1890)	
	First performance of Leoncavallo's *Pagliacci* (1892)	
	André Malraux (b. 1895)	
	William Faulkner (1897–1962)	
	Rostand, *Cyrano de Bergerac* (1897)	
	André Breton (1898–1966)	
	Ernest Hemingway (1898–1961)	
	Bertolt Brecht (1898–1956)	
	World of Art periodical issued (1898)	
	Ibsen, *When We Dead Awaken* (1899)	

PAINTING	SCULPTURE	ARCHITECTURE	
			1775
David, *Oath of the Horatii; Death of Marat (366, 367)* Goya, *Los Caprichos (378)*	Houdon, *Voltaire; George Washington (372, 373)*	Boullée, Design for the Tomb of Newton *(362)* Langhans, Brandenburg Gate, Berlin *(364)* Jefferson, Monticello *(358)*	
			1800
Goya, *Family of Charles IV; Maja desnuda* *(376, colorplate 51)* David, *Coronation of Napoleon and Josephine (368)* Ingres, *Valpinçon Bather (369)* Gros, *Napoleon on the Battlefield at Eylau (381)* Géricault, *Officer of the Imperial Guard (382)* Goya, *Third of May, 1808; Los Disparates (377, 379)* Géricault, *Raft of the Medusa (383)* Friedrich, *Abbey Graveyard Under Snow (394)* Goya, *Saturn Devouring One of His Sons* from murals, Quinta del Sordo, Madrid *(380)* Constable, *The Hay Wain (392)* Géricault, *Madwoman (Monomania of Envy) (384)* Delacroix, *Bark of Dante; Massacre at Chios* *(385, colorplate 52)* Blake, illustrations for Dante's *Inferno (391)*	Canova, *Tomb of the Archduchess Maria Christina;* *Maria Paulina Borghese, as Venus Victrix* *(374, 375)*	Latrobe, Roman Catholic Cathedral, Baltimore *(360, 361)* Vignon, Church of the Madeleine, Paris *(363)* Nash, Park Crescent, London; Royal Pavilion, Brighton *(365, 395)* Jefferson, University of Virginia, Charlottesville *(359)*	
			1825
Corot, *Island of San Bartolomeo (400)* Ingres, *Apotheosis of Homer (370)* Delacroix, *Death of Sardanapalus (386)* Corot, *Chartres Cathedral (401)* Delacroix, *Women of Algiers (387)* Constable, *Stoke-by-Nayland (colorplate 53)* Turner, *The Slave Ship; Rain, Steam, and Speed* *(393, colorplate 54)* Ingres, *Comtesse d'Haussonville (colorplate 50)* Courbet, *The Stone Breakers; A Burial at Ornans* *(407, colorplate 55)*	Rude, *La Marseillaise (The Departure of the* *Volunteers in 1792) (389)*	Barry and Pugin, Houses of Parliament, London *(396)* Labrouste, Bibliothèque Ste.-Geneviève, Paris *(409)*	
			1850
Millet, *Sower (403)* Delacroix, *Tiger Hunt (388)* Courbet, *The Studio: A Real Allegory Concerning* *Seven Years of My Artistic Life (408)* Daumier, *Uprising; Third-Class Carriage (405, 406)* Manet, *Luncheon on the Grass (414)* Monet, *Women in the Garden (416)* Homer, *The Croquet Game (411)* Manet, *Execution of the Emperor Maximilian of* *Mexico (415)* Corot, *Ville d'Avray (402)* Whistler, *Arrangement in Gray and Black, No. 1, the* *Artist's Mother; Portrait of Thomas Carlyle:* *Arrangement in Gray and Black, No. 2 (426)* Monet, *Impression-Sunrise, Le Havre (413)* Degas, *The Rehearsal (422)* Whistler, *Nocturne in Black and Gold: Falling* *Rocket (427)*	Carpeaux, *The Dance (390)*	Haussmann, city planning, Paris Paxton, Crystal Palace, London *(410)* Walter, dome, U.S. Capitol, Washington, D.C. Garnier, Opéra, Paris *(397–399)*	
			1875
Eakins, *The Gross Clinic (412)* Renoir, *Les Grands Boulevards; Le Moulin de la* *Galette (421, colorplate 57)* Degas, *Glass of Absinthe (423)* Monet, *Gare Saint-Lazare in Paris (417)* Manet, *A Bar at the Folies-Bergère (419)* Seurat, *Bathers at Asnières; Sunday Afternoon on the* *Island of the Grande Jatte (437, colorplate 59)* Degas, *Two Laundresses (424)* Cézanne, *Mont Sainte-Victoire; Still Life with Apples* *and Oranges (433, 434)* Ensor, *The Entry of Christ Into Brussels in 1889 (445)* Gauguin, *Vision After the Sermon (439)* Van Gogh, *View of La Crau; The Night Café; Self-* *Portrait; The Starry Night (440–442, colorplate 61)* Degas, *After the Bath (425)* Cézanne, *Card Players (435)* Toulouse-Lautrec, *At the Moulin Rouge (438)* Vuillard, *Woman Sweeping in a Room (444)* Monet, *Rouen Cathedral: The Façade at Sunset* *(colorplate 56)* Munch, *The Scream (446)* Gauguin, *The Day of the God (colorplate 60)* Cézanne, *Woman with the Coffeepot (colorplate 58)* Pissarro, *Boulevard des Italiens, Paris–Morning* *Sunlight (420)* Rousseau, *The Sleeping Gypsy (colorplate 62)* Cézanne, *Bathers (436)*	Rodin, *The Age of Bronze; Gates of Hell; The Kiss;* *Burghers of Calais; Balzac (428–432)*	Gaudí, Church of the Sagrada Familia, Barcelona *(511)* Jenney, Home Insurance Building, Chicago Richardson, Marshall Field Wholesale Store, Chicago *(508)* Sullivan, Wainwright Building, St. Louis *(509)* Horta, salon, Van Eetvelde House, Brussels *(514)*	

TIME LINE

The numbers in italics refer to illustrations in the text

	POLITICAL HISTORY	RELIGION, LITERATURE, MUSIC	SCIENCE, TECHNOLOGY
1900			
	T. Roosevelt, Amer. pres. (1901–1909) proclaims Open Door policy; promotes Panama Canal (opened 1914)	Thomas Wolfe (1900–38)	Planck formulates quantum theory (1900)
	Japan defeats Russia (1904–1905)	Louis Sullivan, *Kindergarten Chats* (1902)	Freud, *Interpretation of Dreams* (1900)
	Internal strife, reforms in Russia (1905)	Alfred Stieglitz founds Photo-Secession group, New York (1902); opens the Photo-Secession gallery at 291 Fifth Avenue, New York (1905)	Pavlov's first experiments with conditioned reflexes (1900)
	Triple Entente: Great Britain, France, Russia (1907)	Jean-Paul Sartre (b. 1905)	Wright brothers make first flight with power-driven airplane (1903)
	Revolution in China establishes republic (1911)	Samuel Beckett (b. 1906)	Einstein formulates theory of relativity (1905)
	World War I (1914–18); U.S. enters war 1917	Claude Lévi-Strauss (b. 1908)	Ford begins assembly-line automobile production (1909)
	Bolshevik Revolution (1917); Russia signs separate peace with Germany (1918)	Jean Genet (b. 1910)	Russell and Whitehead, *Principia Mathematica* (1910–13)
	Wilson presents 14 Points (1918); armistice signed in West	First Futurist manifesto (1910)	Rutherford formulates theory of positively charged atomic nucleus (1911)
	Paris Peace Conference (1919); League of Nations founded	Eugene Ionesco (b. 1912)	First radio station begins regularly scheduled broadcasts (1920)
	Gandhi conducts campaign of civil disobedience for Indian independence after World War I	Albert Camus (1913–60)	
	Irish Free State established (1921)	Armory Show, New York (1913)	
	Mussolini's Fascists seize Italian government (1922)	Sant'Elia, *Manifesto dell'Architettura Futurista* (1914)	
	Turkey becomes republic (1923)	Joyce, *Ulysses* (1914–21); published in U.S.A. (1933)	
		Deutsche Werkbund Exhibition, Cologne (1914)	
		Cabaret Voltaire founded, Zurich (1916)	
		De Stijl and journal (1917–31) founded (1917)	
		Das Staatliche Bauhaus founded in Weimar (1919)	
		Gabo and Pevsner, *Realistic Manifesto* (1920)	
		Wittgenstein, *Tractatus Logico-philosophicus* (1921)	
		Constructivist International founded (1922)	
		Alain Robbe-Grillet (b. 1922)	
		Le Corbusier, *Vers un Architecture* (1923)	
		First Surrealist Manifesto (1924)	
1925			
	Chiang Kai-shek unites China (1927–28)	*La Revolution, Surréaliste*, journal founded by André Breton (1925)	First regularly scheduled TV broadcasts in U.S. (1928), in England (1936)
	Stalin expels Bukharin and other members of Rightist opposition (1928); starts Five-Year Plan	Weissenhof Housing Exhibition, Stuttgart (1927)	Invention of radar (1935)
	Stock-market crash in U.S. (1929); worldwide depression	Breton, *Nadja* (1928)	Atomic fission demonstrated on laboratory scale (1942)
	Japan invades Manchuria (1931)	Henry Russell Hitchcock, Philip Johnson, *The International Style* (1932)	First large-scale atomic explosion (Los Alamos, 1943)
	Spain becomes republic (1931)	*Le Minotaure*, journal founded by Albert Skira and E. Teriade (1933)	Penicillin discovered (1943)
	Hitler seizes power in Germany (1933)	Peggy Guggenheim opens the Art of this Century Gallery in New York (1942)	Computer technology developed (1944)
	F.D. Roosevelt proclaims New Deal (1933)	The Architects Collaborative (TAC) founded (1945)	
	Purge of the Communist Party in Russia (1933)		
	Mussolini conquers Ethiopia (1936)		
	Spanish Civil War (1936–39); won by Franco		
	Hitler annexes Austria (1938); seizes Czechoslovakia (1939); signs nonaggression pact with Russia		
	World War II (1939–45)		
	Atomic bomb dropped on Hiroshima (1945)		
	United Nations Charter (1945)		
	Fourth Republic founded in France (1946); Germany divided into occupation zones		
	British rule ends in India (1947)		
	U.S. starts Marshall Plan (1947)		
	Tito breaks with Stalin (1948)		
	Israel becomes independent (1948)		
	NATO founded (1949)		
	West Germany becomes a federal republic (1949)		
	Communists under Mao win in China (1949)		
	Soviets explode atomic bomb (1949)		
1950			
	Korean War (1950–53)	Wittgenstein, *Philosophical Investigations* (1953)	Genetic code cracked (1953)
	Japan and U.S. sign peace treaty (1951)	John Cage composes *Imaginary Landscape No. 4* (1953); publishes *Silence* (1961)	First hydrogen bomb (atomic fusion) exploded (1954)
	Death of Stalin (1953)	Alan Kaprow, *18 Happenings in 6 Parts*, Reuben Gallery, New York (1959)	Sputnik, first satellite, launched (1957)
	U.S. Supreme Court outlaws racial segregation in public schools (1954)	Robert Venturi, *Complexity and Contradiction in Architecture* (1966)	First manned space flight (1961)
	British evacuate Suez Canal zone (1954)	Lévi-Strauss, *The Raw and the Cooked* (1969)	Discovery of quasars (1963) and pulsars (1968)
	West Germany admitted to NATO (1955)	Buckminster Fuller, *Synergetics* (1975)	First manned landing on the moon (1969)
	Warsaw Pact (1955)	Mother Seton canonized (1975)	First orbiting laboratory (Skylab, 1973)
	Khrushchev denounces Stalin (1956); Russia crushes Hungarian revolt		
	Egypt seizes Suez Canal (1956)		
	Common Market established in Europe (1957)		
	U.S. tests first ICBM (1957)		
	African colonies gain independence after 1957		
	Fifth Republic, France (De Gaulle) (1958)		
	John F. Kennedy assassinated (1963)		
	Johnson begins massive U.S. intervention in Vietnam (1965)		
	Six Day War (1967)		
	Martin Luther King, Jr., assassinated (1968)		
	Russia invades Czechoslovakia (1968)		
	The People's Republic of China replaces Nationalist China in United Nations (1971)		
	People's Republic of Bangladesh gains independence from Pakistan (1972–73)		
	Vietnam War ends (1974)		
	Nixon first American president forced to resign (1974)		
	Coup in Ethiopia deposes Haile Selassie (1974)		
	Death of Franco (1975)		

PAINTING	SCULPTURE	ARCHITECTURE	
			1900
Picasso, *Absinthe Drinker (462)*	Maillol, *Mediterranean (Crouching Woman) (459)*	Sullivan, Carson Pirie Scott Department Store, Chicago *(510)*	
Redon, *Orpheus (443)*	Lehmbruck, *Kneeling Woman (460)*	Gaudí, Casa Milá, Barcelona *(512, 513)*	
Matisse, *The Green Stripe (Madame Matisse): Joie de vivre (448, colorplate 63)*	Brancusi, *Mademoiselle Pogany (474)*	Wright, Robie House, Chicago *(517, 518)*	
Picasso, *Saltimbanques (463)*	Archipenko, *Walking Woman (478)*	Berg, Centenary Hall, Wroclaw *(515)*	
Rouault, *Prostitute at Her Mirror (452)*	Lehmbruck, *Standing Youth (461)*	Mendelsohn, Einstein Tower, Potsdam *(516)*	
Picasso, *Les demoiselles d'Avignon (464)*	Brancusi, *The First Step (476)*	Hood, Chicago Tribune Tower, Chicago	
Mondrian, *The Red Tree (491)*	Boccioni, *Unique Forms of Continuity in Space (483)*	Rietveld, Schröder House, Utrecht *(522, 523)*	
Picasso, *Seated Woman (colorplate 68)*	Duchamp-Villon, *Horse (477)*		
Carrà, *Funeral of the Anarchist Galli (482)*	Duchamp, *The Bride Stripped Bare by Her Bachelors, Even (The Large Glass) (500)*		
Boccioni, *The City Rises (colorplate 69)*	Lipchitz, *Still Life with Musical Instruments (479)*		
Matisse, *Red Studio (colorplate 64)*	Tatlin, *Monument to the Third International (487)*		
Picasso, *The Accordionist (466)*	Gabo, *Space Construction C (488)*		
Braque, *The Portuguese (465)*			
Nolde, *Doubting Thomas (453)*			
Duchamp, *Nude Descending a Staircase, No. 2 (473)*			
Malevich, *The Knife Grinder (485)*			
Chagall, *Self-Portrait with Seven Fingers (494)*			
Marc, *Deer in the Wood, No. 1 (454)*			
Kandinsky, *Improvisation 30 (Cannon) (colorplate 66)*			
Picasso, *The Bottle of Suze (467)*			
Kokoschka, *Self-Portrait (456)*			
Mondrian, *Composition in Line and Color (492)*			
De Chirico, *The Nostalgia of the Infinite (495)*			
Kokoschka, *Bride of the Wind (colorplate 67)*			
Delaunay, *Homage to Blériot (472)*			
Hartley, *Iron Cross (548)*			
Stella, *Brooklyn Bridge (484)*			
Léger, *Disks (471)*			
Duchamp, *Tu m' (501)*			
Beckmann, *The Night (457)*			
Malevich, *White on White* series *(486)*			
Schwitters, *Pictures with Light Center (503)*			
O'Keeffe, *Blue and Green Music (colorplate 75)*			
Kandinsky, *Composition 238: Bright Circle (455)*			
Mondrian, *Composition with Red, Yellow, and Blue (colorplate 70)*			
Picasso, *Three Musicians; Three Women at the Spring (468, 469)*			
Ernst, *The Elephant of the Celebes (502)*			
Klee, *Dance, Monster, to My Soft Song! (496)*			
Marin, *Lower Manhattan (Composition Derived from Top of the Woolworth Building) (549)*			
			1925
Lissitzky, *Proun 99 (490)*	Arp, *Mountain Table Anchors Navel (498)*	Gropius, Bauhaus, Dessau *(524)*	
Miró, *Harlequin's Carnival (505)*	Pevsner, *Portrait of Marcel Duchamp (489)*	Le Corbusier, Villa Savoye, Poissy; *Ville radieuse (525, 526)*	
Matisse, *Decorative Figure Against an Ornamental Background (449)*	Lipchitz, *Figure (480)*	Mies van der Rohe, German Pavilion, Barcelona International Exposition *(527)*	
Hopper, *Automat (551)*	Brancusi, *Bird in Space (475)*	Hood and Howells, Daily News Building, New York *(529)*	
Dali, *The Persistence of Memory (506)*	Nicholson, *White Relief (493)*	Howe and Lescaze, Philadelphia Savings Fund Society Building, Philadelphia *(530)*	
Davis, *House and Street (552)*		Wright, Kaufmann House, Bear Run, Pa.; Administration Building, S. C. Johnson and Son, Racine *(519–521)*	
Klee, *Ad Parnassum (497)*		Neutra, Kaufmann House, Palm Springs *(528)*	
Orozco, *The Departure of Quetzalcoatl*, fresco mural, Baker Library, Dartmouth College, Hanover, New Hampshire *(553)*		Harrison, Secretariat Building of the United Nations, New York *(531)*	
Miró, *Painting 1933 (colorplate 72)*		Le Corbusier, Unité d'Habitation, Marseilles *(535)*	
Dali, *Soft Construction with Boiled Beans: Premonition of Civil War (colorplate 73)*		Nervi, Exhibition Hall, Turin *(537)*	
Picasso, *Guernica (470)*		Matisse, Chapel of the Rosary of the Dominican Nuns, Vence *(450)*	
Siqueiros, *Portrait of the Bourgeoisie*, mural, Electrical Workers Union Building, Mexico City *(554)*			
Klee, *Death and Fire (colorplate 71)*			
Ernst, *Europe After the Rain (504)*			
Matta, *Listen to Living (Écoutez Vivre) (colorplate 74)*			
Dove, *That Red One (550)*			
Beckmann, *Blindman's Buff (458)*			
Davis, *Owh! In San Pão (colorplate 76)*			
Gorky, *Golden Brown Painting (colorplate 77)*			
			1950
De Kooning, *Excavation (555)*	Moore, *Interior-Exterior Reclining Figure (481)*	Le Corbusier, Notre-Dame-du-Haut, Ronchamp *(536)*	
Matisse, *Zulma (451)*	Arp, *Torso (499)*	Mies van der Rohe, Lake Shore Drive Apartments, Chicago *(532)*	
Still, *Painting, 1951 (557)*	Lippold, *Variations Within a Sphere, No. 10: the Sun (576)*	Bunshaft and Skidmore, Owings and Merrill, Lever House, New York *(533)*	
De Staël, *Le Lavandou (582)*	Oldenburg, *Soft Typewriter (563)*	Kahn, Richards Medical Research Building, University of Pennsylvania, Philadelphia *(538)*	
Pollock, *Blue Poles (colorplate 78)*	Smith, *Cubi XVII; Cubi XVIII; Cubi XIX (574)*	Saarinen, Trans World Airlines Terminal, Kennedy Airport, New York; Terminal, Dulles Airport, Virginia *(539, 540)*	
Johns, *Target with Four Faces (560)*	Segal, *The Bus Riders (566)*	Breuer, Whitney Museum of American Art, New York *(541, 542)*	
De Kooning, *The Time of Fire (colorplate 79)*	Nevelson, *An American Tribute to the British People (573)*	Safdie, Habitat, EXPO 67, Montreal *(545)*	
Kline, *Mahoning (556)*	Judd, *Untitled (575)*	Fuller, American Pavilion, EXPO 67, Montreal *(547)*	
Rothko, *White and Greens in Blue (colorplate 81)*	Samaras, *Room No. 2 (568)*	Johnson and Burgee, I.D.S. Center, Minneapolis *(534)*	
Hofmann, *The Gate (colorplate 80)*	Le Parc, *Continuel Lumière Formes en Contorsion (577)*	Kahn, Kimbell Art Museum, Fort Worth *(543)*	
Stella, *Ophir (571)*	Indiana, *Love (565)*	Pei, East building (Contemporary Art), National Gallery of Art, Washington D.C. *(544)*	
Kelly, *Red White (colorplate 85)*	Christo, *Wrapped Coast, Little Bay, Australia (567)*		
Louis, *Pillar of Hope (570)*	Smithson, *Spiral Jetty (580)*		
Klein, *Fire Painting (colorplate 86)*	Hanson, *Tourists (585)*		
Warhol, *Marilyn Monroe (564)*	Chryssa, *Automat (578)*		
Lichtenstein, *Whaam (561)*	Krebs, *Study for Laser Project, Philadelphia Festival, May, 1973 (579)*		
Dubuffet, *Hourloupes* series			
Rauschenberg, *Trapeze (559)*			
Noland, *Bridge (colorplate 84)*			
Rosenquist, *F-111 (562)*			
Newman, *Stations of the Cross: Twelfth Station (569)*			
Dubuffet, *Legendary Figure of a Tap (581)*			
Stella, *Tahkt-I-Sulayman I (572)*			
Vasarely, *Arcturus II (colorplate 82)*			
Appel, *Angry Landscape (583)*			
Estes, *Escalator, Bus Terminal (584)*			
Anuszkiewicz, *Trinity (colorplate 83)*			
Diebenkorn, *Ocean Park, No. 40 (558)*			

Glossary

ABACUS (pl. ABACI). In architecture, the slab that forms the uppermost member of a CAPITAL and supports the ARCHITRAVE.

ACADEMY. The word, meaning a *place of study* or a *learned society*, is derived from the name of the grove near Athens where Plato and his followers held their philosophical conferences during the fifth and fourth centuries B.C. Modern academies of fine arts have as their purpose the fostering of the arts through instruction, financial assistance, and exhibitions; the first was the Accademia di Disegno founded by Giorgio Vasari in Florence in 1563; the two most influential have been the Académie Royale de Peinture et de Sculpture founded in 1648 in Paris by Louis XIV, and the Royal Academy of Arts founded in London in 1768.

ACOLYTE. In the Roman Catholic Church, an altar attendant of a minor rank.

AERIAL PERSPECTIVE. See PERSPECTIVE.

AISLE. See SIDE AISLE.

ALTARPIECE. A painted and/or sculptured work of art that stands as a religious image upon and at the back of an altar, either representing in visual symbols the underlying doctrine of the MASS, or depicting the saint to whom a particular church or chapel is dedicated, together with scenes from his life. Examples from certain periods include decorated GABLES and PINNACLES, as well as a PREDELLA. See MAESTÀ.

AMBULATORY. A place for walking, usually covered, as in an ARCADE around a cloister, or a semicircular passageway around the APSE behind the main altar. In a church or mosque with a centralized PLAN, the passageway around the central space that corresponds to a SIDE AISLE and that is used for ceremonial processions.

AMPHORA (pl. AMPHORAE). A storage jar used in ancient Greece having an egg-shaped body, a foot, and two handles, each attached at the neck and shoulder of the jar.

APOCALYPSE. The Book of Revelation, the last book of the New Testament, in which are narrated the visions of the future experienced by Saint John the Evangelist on the island of Patmos.

APOCRYPHA. A group of books included at one time in authorized Christian versions of the BIBLE (now generally omitted from Protestant versions).

APOSTLES. In Christian usage the word commonly denotes the twelve followers or disciples chosen by Christ to preach his GOSPEL, though the term is sometimes used loosely. Those listed in the Gospels are: Andrew; James, the son of Zebedee, called James the Major; James, the son of Alphaeus, called James the Minor; Bartholomew; John; Judas Iscariot; Matthew; Philip; Peter; Simon the Canaanite; Thaddeus; and Thomas (Matt. 10:1–4; Mark 3:13–19).

APSE. A large semicircular or polygonal niche. In a Roman BASILICA it was frequently found at both ends of the NAVE; in a Christian church it is usually placed at one end of the nave after the CHOIR; it may also appear at the ends of the TRANSEPT and at the ends of chapels.

AQUATINT. A print produced by the same technique as an ETCHING except that the areas between the etched lines are covered with a powdered resin that protects the surface from the biting process of the acid bath. The granular appearance that results in the print aims at approximating the effects and gray tonalities of a WATERCOLOR drawing.

AQUEDUCT. From the Latin for *duct of water*. An artificial channel for conducting water from a distance, which, in Roman times, was usually built overground and supported on ARCHES.

ARCADE. A series of ARCHES and their supports. Called a *blind arcade* when placed against a wall and used primarily as surface decoration.

ARCH. An architectural construction, often semicircular, built of wedge-shaped blocks (called VOUSSOIRS) to span an opening. The center stone is called the KEYSTONE. The weight of this structure requires support from walls, PIERS, or COLUMNS, and the THRUST requires BUTTRESSING at the sides. When an arch is made of overlapping courses of stone, each block projecting slightly farther over the opening than the block beneath it, it is called a CORBELED ARCH.

ARCHBISHOP. The chief BISHOP of an ecclesiastical province or archbishopric.

ARCHITRAVE. The main horizontal beam and the lowest member of an ENTABLATURE; it may be a series of LINTELS, each spanning the space from the top of one support to the next.

ARCHIVOLT. The molding or moldings above an arched opening; in Romanesque and Gothic churches, frequently decorated with sculpture.

ARRICCIO, ARRICCIATO. The rough coat of coarse plaster that is the first layer to be spread on a wall when making a FRESCO.

ARTE (pl. ARTI). See GUILDS.

A SECCO. See FRESCO.

ATMOSPHERIC PERSPECTIVE. See PERSPECTIVE.

ATRIUM. The open entrance hall or central hall of an ancient Roman house. A court in front of the principal doors of a church.

ATTIC. The upper story, usually low in height, placed above an ENTABLATURE or main CORNICE of a building, and frequently decorated with PILASTERS.

BACCHANTE. See MAENAD.

BALDACHIN. From Italian *baldacchino*, a rich silk fabric from Baghdad. A canopy of such material, or of wood, stone, etc., either permanently installed over an altar, throne, or doorway, or constructed in portable form to be carried in religious processions.

BALUSTRADE. A row of short pillars, called *balusters*, surmounted by a railing.

BAPTISTERY. Either a separate building or a part of a church in which the SACRAMENT of Baptism is administered.

BARREL VAULT. A semicylindrical VAULT that normally requires continuous support and BUTTRESSING.

BAR TRACERY. See TRACERY.

BASE. The lowest element of a COLUMN, temple, wall, or DOME, occasionally of a statue.

BASILICA. In ancient Roman architecture, a rectangular building whose ground PLAN was generally divided into NAVE, SIDE AISLES, and one or more APSES, and whose elevation sometimes included a CLERESTORY and GALLERIES, though there was no strict uniformity. It was used as a hall of justice and as a public meeting place. In Christian architecture, the term is applied to any church that has a longitudinal nave terminated by an apse and flanked by lower side aisles.

BAY. A compartment into which a building may be subdivided, usually formed by the space bounded by consecutive architectural supports.

BEATO (fem. BEATA). Italian word meaning *blessed*. Specifically, beatification is a papal decree that declares a deceased person to be in the enjoyment of heavenly bliss *(beatus)* and grants a form of veneration to him. It is usually a step toward canonization.

BIBLE. The collection of sacred writings of the Christian religion that includes the Old and the New Testaments, or that of the Jewish religion, which includes the Old Testament only. The versions commonly used in the Roman Catholic Church are based on the Vulgate, a Latin translation made by Saint Jerome in the fourth century A.D. An English translation, made by members of the English College at Douai, France, between 1582 and 1610, is called the Douay. Widely used Protestant translations include Martin Luther's German translation from the first half of the sixteenth century, and the English King James Version, first published in 1611.

BISHOP. A spiritual overseer of a number of churches or a DIOCESE; in the Greek, Roman Catholic, Anglican, and other churches, a member of the highest order in the ministry. See CATHEDRAL.

BLESSED. See BEATO.

BLIND ARCADE. See ARCADE.

BOOK OF HOURS. See HOURS.

BOTTEGA. Italian word for *shop*, used to describe an artist's atelier in which assistants and apprentices worked with an artist on his commissions, and in which works were displayed and offered for sale.

BRACKET. A piece of stone, wood, or metal projecting from a wall and having a flat upper surface that serves to support a statue, beam, or other weight.

BREVIARY. A book containing the daily offices or prayers and the necessary psalms and hymns for daily devotions. Frequently illustrated and generally intended for use by the clergy.

BROKEN PEDIMENT. See PEDIMENT.

BURIN. See ENGRAVING.

BUTTRESS. A masonry support that counteracts the lateral pressure, or THRUST, exerted by an ARCH or VAULT. See FLYING BUTTRESS and PIER BUTTRESS.

CALLIGRAPHY. In a loose sense, handwriting, but usually refers to beautiful handwriting or fine penmanship.

CALVARY. See GOLGOTHA.

CAMERA. Italian word for *room* or *chamber.*

CAMPAGNA. Italian word for *countryside*. When capitalized it generally refers to the area outside Rome.

CAMPANILE. From the Italian word for *bell (campana)*. A bell tower, either attached to a church or freestanding nearby.

CAMPO. Italian word for *field;* used in Siena, Venice, and other Italian cities to denote certain public squares. See PIAZZA.

CANONICAL HOURS. In the Roman Catholic Church, certain hours of each day set aside for prayer and devotion; the seven periods are: matins, prime, tierce, sext, nones, vespers, and compline. These are strictly observed only in monastic establishments.

CANON OF THE MASS. The part of the Christian MASS between the Sanctus, a hymn, and the Lord's Prayer; the actual EUCHARIST, or sacrifice of bread and wine, to which only the baptized were admitted.

CANOPY. An ornamental rooflike projection or covering placed over a niche, statue, tomb, altar, or the like.

CANTILEVER. A projecting BRACKET that supports a balcony, CORNICE, or the like, or a projecting beam or slab of great length attached at one end only.

CAPITAL. The crowning member of a COLUMN, PIER, or PILASTER on which rests the lowest element of the ENTABLATURE. See ORDER.

CARDINAL. A member of the ecclesiastical body known as the Sacred College of Cardinals, which elects the pope and constitutes his chief advisory council.

CARDINAL VIRTUES. See VIRTUES.

CARTHUSIAN ORDER. An eremitic ORDER founded by Saint Bruno (c. 1030–1101) at Chartreuse, near Grenoble, in 1084. The life of the monks was, and still is, one of prayer, silence, and extreme austerity.

CARTOON. From the Italian word *cartone*. A full-scale preparatory drawing for a painting.

CARTOUCHE. An ornamental SCROLL-shaped tablet with an inscription or decoration, either sculptured or drawn.

CARVING. The shaping of an image by cutting or chiseling it out from a hard substance such as stone or wood, in contrast to the additive process of MODELING.

CARYATID. A figure, usually female, used as a COLUMN.

CASSOCK. A long close-fitting garment with sleeves and a high neck worn under the SURPLICE by clergymen, choristers, etc., at church services or as ordinary clerical costume.

CASTING. A method of reproducing a three-dimensional object or RELIEF by pouring a hardening liquid or molten metal into a mold bearing its impression.

CATHEDRAL. The principal church of a DIOCESE, containing the BISHOP's throne, or cathedra.

CELLA. The body of a temple as distinct from the PORTICO and other external elements, or an interior structure built to house an image.

CERTOSA. Italian word for *Carthusian monastery (Chartreuse* in French). Adopted from the name of the town Chartreuse, where Saint Bruno founded a monastery in 1084. See also CARTHUSIAN ORDER.

CHALICE. Generally, a drinking cup, but specifically, the cup used to hold the consecrated wine of the EUCHARIST.

CHANCEL. In a church, the space reserved for the clergy and the CHOIR, between the APSE and the NAVE and TRANSEPT, usually separated from the latter two by steps and a railing or a screen.

CHARTREUSE. See CARTHUSIAN ORDER and CERTOSA.

CHÂTEAU (pl. CHÂTEAUX). A French castle or large country house.

CHERUB (pl. CHERUBIM). One of an order of angelic beings ranking second to the SERAPH in the celestial hierarchy, often represented as a winged child or as the winged head of a child.

CHEVET. The eastern end of a church or CATHEDRAL consisting of the AMBULATORY and a main APSE with secondary apses or chapels radiating from it.

CHIAROSCURO. From the Italian *chiaro (light)* and *oscuro (dark)*. Used to describe the opposition of light and shade.

CHOIR. A body of trained singers, or that part of a church occupied by them. See CHANCEL.

CHOIR SCREEN. A partition of wood or stone, often elaborately carved, that separates the CHOIR from the NAVE and TRANSEPT of a church. In Byzantine churches, the choir screen, decorated with ICONS, is called an ICONOSTASIS.

CHRISTUS MORTUUS. Latin phrase for *dead Christ.*

CHRISTUS PATIENS. Latin phrase for *suffering Christ*. A cross with a representation of the dead Christ, which in general superseded representations of the CHRISTUS TRIUMPHANS type.

CHRISTUS TRIUMPHANS. Latin phrase for *triumphant Christ*. A cross with a representation of the living Christ, eyes open and triumphant over death. Scenes of the PASSION are usually depicted at the sides of the cross, below the crossarms.

CLAUSURA. Latin word for *closure*. In the Roman Catholic Church, the word is used to signify the restriction of certain classes of nuns and monks prohibited from communication with outsiders to sections of their convents or monasteries. Those living within these restrictions are said to be *in clausura* or CLOISTERED.

CLERESTORY. The section of an interior wall that rises above adjacent rooftops, having a row of windows that admit daylight. Used in Roman BASILICAS and Christian basilican churches; in Christian churches, the wall that rises above the nave ARCADE or the TRIFORIUM to the VAULTING or roof.

CLOISTER. Generally, a place of religious seclusion; a monastery, nunnery, or convent. Specifically, a covered walk or AMBULATORY around an open court having a plain wall on one side and an open ARCADE or COLONNADE on the other. It is commonly connected with a church, monastery, or other building, and is used for exercise and study. See CLAUSURA.

CLOSED DOOR or CLOSED GATE. Ezekiel's vision of the door or gate of the SANCTUARY in the temple that was closed because only the Lord could enter it (Ezekiel 44:1–4). Interpreted as a prophecy and used as a symbol of Mary's virginity.

CLOSED GARDEN. "A garden enclosed is my sister, my spouse; a spring shut up, a fountain sealed" (Song of Solomon 4:12). Used like CLOSED DOOR as a symbol of Mary's virginity.

COFFER. A casket or box. In architecture, a recessed panel in a ceiling.

COLLAGE. From the French verb *coller*, meaning *to glue*. A composition made by pasting various scraps of materials (such as newspaper, cloth, or photographs onto a flat surface.

COLONNADE. A series of COLUMNS spanned by LINTELS.

COLONNETTE. A small COLUMN.

COLOR. See HUE, SATURATION, and VALUE.

COLUMN. A vertical architectural support, usually consisting of a BASE, a rounded SHAFT, and a CAPITAL. When half or more of it is attached to a wall, it is called an *engaged column*. Columns are occasionally used singly for a decorative or commemorative reason. See also ORDER.

COMPANY. See SCUOLA.

COMPOUND PIER. A PIER with COLUMNS, PILASTERS, or SHAFTS attached to it, which members usually support or respond to ARCHES or RIBS above them.

CONTÉ CRAYON. A rich black drawing stick.

CONFRATERNITY. See SCUOLA.

CONSOLE. A BRACKET, usually formed of S-shaped SCROLLS, projecting from a wall to support a LINTEL or other member.

CONTRAPPOSTO. Italian word for *set against*. A device introduced in late Greek art that freed representations of the figure from the rigidity present in Egyptian and Archaic Greek painting and sculpture; used to express the shift in axes when contrasting actions set parts of the body in opposition to each other around a central vertical axis.

COPE. A semicircular cloak or cape worn by ecclesiastics in procession and on other ceremonial occasions.

CORBEL. An overlapping arrangement of stones, each course projecting beyond the one below, used to construct a VAULT or ARCH, or as a support projecting from the face of a wall.

CORBEL TABLE. A horizontal piece of masonry used as a CORNICE or part of a wall and supported by CORBELS.

CORNICE. The crowning, projecting architectural feature, especially the uppermost part of an ENTABLATURE. It is frequently decorated. When it is not horizontal, as above a PEDIMENT, it is called a *raking cornice*.

COURSED MASONRY. Masonry in which stones or bricks of equal height are placed in continuous horizontal layers.

CROSSHATCHING. See HATCHING.

CROSSING. That part of a church where the TRANSEPT crosses the NAVE; it is sometimes emphasized by a DOME or by a tower over the crossing.

CROSS SECTION. See SECTION.

CRUCIFIX. From the Latin word *crucifixus*. A representation of a cross with the figure of Christ crucified on it. See CHRISTUS MORTUUS, CHRISTUS PATIENS, and CHRISTUS TRIUMPHANS.

CRYPT. A VAULTED chamber, usually beneath the raised CHOIR of a church, housing a tomb and/or a chapel. Also, a vaulted underground chamber used for burial as in the catacombs.

CUPOLA. A rounded, convex roof or VAULTED ceiling on a circular BASE, requiring BUTTRESSING. See DOME.

CUSP. The pointed projection where two curves meet.

CYCLOPS. A member of a mythological race of giants with one round eye in the center of the forehead. The Cyclopes were believed to have forged Zeus' thunderbolts and to have built massive prehistoric walls.

DALMATIC. An ecclesiastical vestment with wide sleeves and two stripes, worn in the Western church by DEACONS and BISHOPS on certain occasions.

DEACON. A lay church officer or a subordinate minister. In the Roman Catholic, Anglican, and Episcopal churches, the cleric ranking next after the priest.

DEËSIS. The Greek word for *supplication*. A representation of Christ Enthroned between the Virgin Mary and Saint John the Baptist, who act as intercessors for mankind, it appears frequently in Byzantine MOSAICS and in later depictions of the Last Judgment.

DIOCESE. See BISHOP.

DIPTYCH. A pair of wood, ivory, or metal plaques usually hinged together, with the interior surfaces either painted or CARVED with a religious or memorial subject, or covered with wax for writing.

DOME. A large CUPOLA supported by a circular wall or DRUM, or, over a noncircular space, by corner structures. See PENDENTIVE.

DOMINICAN ORDER. A preaching ORDER of the Roman Catholic Church founded by Saint Dominic in 1216 in Toulouse. The Dominicans live austerely, believe in having no possessions, and subsist on charity. It is the second great mendicant order, after the FRANCISCAN.

DONOR. The patron or commissioner of a work of art, often represented in the work.

DORMER. A vertical window projecting from a sloping roof and having vertical sides and a flat or sloping roof.

DOUAY VERSION. See BIBLE.

DRÔLERIES. French word for *jests*. In art, designs interlaced with animals and small fanciful figures; found primarily in the margins of Gothic manuscripts, but also occasionally in decorative wood CARVINGS of the same period.

DRUM. One of several sections composing the SHAFT of a COLUMN. Also, a cylindrical wall supporting a DOME.

ELEVATION. One side of a building, or a drawing of the same.

EMBRASURE. A door or window frame enlarged at the interior wall by beveling or splaying the sides of the frame.

ENCAUSTIC. A method of painting on wood panels and walls with colors dissolved in hot wax.

ENGAGED COLUMN. See COLUMN.

ENGRAVING. A means of ornamenting metal objects, such as suits of armor, or stones, by incising a design on the surface. In pictorial arts, the technique of reproducing a design by incising it on a copper plate with a steel instrument called a *burin,* which digs up a continuous shaving of the metal, leaving a groove. The plate is inked and the ink wiped off except for that remaining in the groove. Then, by subjecting the plate to great pressure on a moistened piece of paper, the image is reproduced and is called an *engraving.*

ENTABLATURE. The upper part of an architectural ORDER, usually divided into three major parts: the ARCHITRAVE, FRIEZE, and CORNICE.

EPISTLE. In Christian usage, one of the apostolic letters that constitute twenty-one books of the New Testament. See also MASS.

ETCHING. The technique of reproducing a design by coating a metal plate with wax and drawing with a sharp instrument called a *stylus* through the wax down to the metal. The plate is put in an acid bath, which eats away the incised lines; it is then heated to dissolve the wax and finally inked and printed on paper. The resulting print is called an *etching.* The plate may be altered between printings, and the prints are then differentiated as *first state, second state,* etc.

EUCHARIST. From the Greek word for *thanksgiving.* The SACRAMENT of the Lord's Supper; the consecrated bread and wine used in the rite of Communion, or the rite itself.

EVANGELISTS, FOUR. Matthew, Mark, Luke, and John, generally assumed to be the authors of the GOSPELs in the New Testament. They are usually represented with their symbols, which are derived either from the four mysterious creatures in the vision of Ezekiel (1:5) or from the four beasts surrounding the throne of the Lamb in Revelation (4:7). Frequently, they are referred to by the symbols alone: an angel for Matthew, a lion for Mark, a bull for Luke, and an eagle for John, or by a representation of the four rivers of Paradise.

EXEDRA (pl. EXEDRAE). A semicircular PORCH, chapel, or recession in a wall.

FAÇADE. The front or principal face of a building; sometimes loosely used to indicate the entire outer surface of any side.

FAIENCE. Glazed earthenware or pottery used for sculpture, tiles, and decorative objects.

FASCES. Latin plural of *fascis* (*bundle*). A bundle of rods containing an ax with the blade projecting, borne before Roman magistrates as a symbol of power.

FATES, THREE. In Greek and Roman mythology, the goddesses Clotho, Lachesis, and Atropos, who were believed to determine the course of human life.

FATHERS OF THE CHURCH. Early teachers and defenders of Christianity from the third to the sixth century A.D. Eight in number, they include the four Latin Fathers: Saint Jerome, Saint Ambrose, Saint Augustine, and Saint Gregory; and the four Greek Fathers: Saint John Chrysostom, Saint Basil the Great, Saint Athanasius, and Saint Gregory Nazianzen. See BIBLE.

FERROCONCRETE. See REINFORCED CONCRETE.

FINIAL. An ornament terminating a spire, PINNACLE, GABLE, etc.

FLUTING. The shallow vertical grooves in the SHAFT of a COLUMN that either meet in a sharp edge as in Doric columns, or are separated by a narrow strip as in Ionic columns.

FLYING BUTTRESS. An ARCH that springs from the upper part of the PIER BUTTRESS of a Gothic church, spans the AISLE roof, and abuts the upper NAVE wall to receive the THRUST from the nave VAULTs; it transmits this thrust to the solid pier buttress.

FONT. A receptacle in a BAPTISTERY or church for the water used in Baptism; it is usually of stone and frequently decorated with sculpture.

FORESHORTENING. In drawing, painting, etc., a method of reproducing the forms of an object not parallel to the

PICTURE PLANE so that the object seems to recede in space and to convey the illusion of three dimensions as perceived by the human eye.

FORUM (pl. FORA). In ancient Rome, the center of assembly for judicial and other public business, and a gathering place for the people.

FOUR RIVERS OF PARADISE. See EVANGELISTS.

FRANCISCAN ORDER. The first great mendicant ORDER. Founded by Saint Francis of Assisi (Giovanni di Bernardone, 1182?–1226) for the purpose of ministering to the spiritual needs of the poor and imitating as closely as possible the life of Christ, especially in its poverty; the monks depended only on alms for subsistence.

FRESCO. Italian word for *fresh.* A painting executed on wet plaster with pigments suspended in water so that the plaster absorbs the colors and the painting becomes part of the wall. *Fresco a secco,* or painting on dry plaster (*secco* is the Italian word for *dry*), is a much less durable technique; the paint tends to flake off with time. The *secco su fresco* method involves the application of color in a vehicle containing some organic binding material (such as oil, egg, or wax) over the still damp plaster.

FRIEZE. The architectural element that rests upon the ARCHITRAVE and is immediately below the CORNICE; also, any horizontal band decorated with MOLDINGS, RELIEF sculpture, or painting.

GABLE. The vertical, triangular piece of wall at the end of a ridged roof, from the level of the eaves or CORNICE to the summit; called a PEDIMENT in Classical architecture. It is sometimes used with no roof, as over the PORTALs of Gothic cathedrals, and as a decorative element on ALTARPIECES.

GALLERY. An elevated floor projecting from the interior wall of a building. In a BÁSILICAN church it is placed over the SIDE AISLES and supported by the COLUMNS or PIERS that separate the NAVE and the side aisles; in a church with a central PLAN, it is placed over the AMBULATORY; in an ancient Roman basilica, it was generally built over each end as well as over the side aisles.

GARDEN. See CLOSED GARDEN.

GENIUS (pl. GENII). In Classical and Renaissance art, usually the guardian spirit of a person, place, thing, or concept; often purely decorative, genii are represented in human form, frequently seminude and winged.

GENRE PAINTING. The representation of scenes from everyday life for their own sake, usually with no religious or symbolic significance.

GESSO. A mixture of finely ground plaster and glue spread on a surface in preparation for painting.

GILDING. Coating paintings, sculptures, and architectural ornament with gold, gold leaf, or some gold-colored substance, either by mechanical or chemical means. In panel painting and wood sculpture, the gold leaf is attached with a glue sizing that is usually a dull red in color.

GLAZE. In pottery, a superficial layer of molten material used to coat a finished piece before it is fired in a kiln. In OIL PAINTING, a transparent film of the vehicle, customarily linseed oil mixed with turpentine, in which a small amount of pigment is dissolved, so as to change the appearance of the color beneath.

GLORY. The circle of light represented around the head or figure of the Savior, the Virgin Mary, or a saint. When it surrounds the head only, it is called a *halo.* See MANDORLA.

GOLGOTHA. From the Aramaic word for *skull;* thus, *the Place of the Skull.* The name of the place outside Jerusalem where Christ was crucified (Matthew 27:33). *Calvary,* from *calvaria* meaning *skull* (Luke 23:33), is the Latin translation of the Aramaic word.

GOSPEL. In Christian usage, the story of Christ's life and

teaching, as related in the first four books of the New Testament, traditionally ascribed to the Evangelists Matthew, Mark, Luke, and John. Also used to designate an ILLUMINATED copy of the same; sometimes called a Gospel lectionary. See MASS.

GREEK CROSS. A cross with four equal arms.

GROIN. The sharp edge formed by two intersecting VAULTS.

GROIN VAULT. A VAULT formed by the intersection at right angles of two BARREL VAULTS of equal height and diameter so that the GROINS form a diagonal cross.

GROUND PLAN. See PLAN.

GUILDS. *Arti* (sing. *Arte*) in Italian. Independent associations of bankers and of artisan-manufacturers. The seven major guilds in Florence were: *Arte della Calimala*—refiners of imported wool; *Arte della Lana*—wool merchants who manufactured their own cloth; *Arte dei Giudici e Notai*—judges and notaries; *Arte del Cambio*—bankers and money changers; *Arte della Seta*—silk weavers, to which the sculptors in metal belonged; *Arte dei Medici e Speziali*—doctors and pharmacists, to which painters belonged; *Arte dei Vaiai e Pellicciai*—furriers. Other important guilds were: *Arte di Pietra e Legname*—workers in stone and wood; *Arte dei Corazzai e Spadai*—armorers and sword makers; *Arte de Linaioli e Rigattieri*—linen drapers and peddlers.

HALL CHURCH. See HALLENKIRCHE.

HALLENKIRCHE. German word for *hall church*. A church in which the AISLES are as high, or almost as high, as the NAVE; especially popular in the German Gothic style.

HALO. See GLORY.

HARPY (pl. HARPIES). From the Greek word for *snatcher*. A female monster that carries souls to Hell; often represented with a woman's head and body, and a bird's wings, legs, claws, and tail. She occasionally appears as a more benign spirit that carries souls to another world.

HATCHING. In drawing or engraving, the use of parallel lines to produce the effect of shading. When crossing sets of parallel lines are used the technique is called *crosshatching*.

HIEROGLYPHS. Characters (pictures or symbols representing or standing for sounds, words, ideas, etc.) in the picture-writing system of the ancient Egyptians.

HORTUS CONCLUSUS. Latin phrase for CLOSED GARDEN.

HOST. From the Latin word for *sacrificial victim* (*hostia*). In the Roman Catholic Church it is used to designate the bread or wafer, regarded as the body of Christ, consecrated in the EUCHARIST.

HÔTEL. A large private residence in a town or a city.

HOURS, BOOK OF. A book for private devotions containing the prayers for the seven CANONICAL HOURS of the Roman Catholic Church. It sometimes contains a calendar, and often elaborate ILLUMINATION. The most famous examples are now known by the names of their original owners.

HUE. That attribute of a color that gives it its name. The spectrum is usually divided into six basic hues: the three primary colors of red, yellow, and blue, and the secondary colors of green, orange, and violet.

ICON. Literally, any image or likeness, but commonly used to designate a panel representing Christ, the Virgin Mary, or a saint venerated by Orthodox (Eastern) Catholics.

ICONOCLASM. Breaking or destroying of images, particularly those set up for religious veneration. Many paintings and statues were destroyed in the Eastern Church in the eighth and ninth centuries as a result of the Iconoclastic Controversy. In the sixteenth and seventeenth centuries, especially in the Netherlands, the Protestants also destroyed many religious images.

ICONOSTASIS. In Eastern Christian churches, a screen separating the main body of the church from the SANCTUARY; it is usually decorated with ICONS whose subject matter and order were largely predetermined.

ILLUMINATED MANUSCRIPTS. Codices or SCROLLS decorated with illustrations or designs in gold, silver, and bright colors.

IMPASTO (pl. IMPASTOS). Pigment applied very thickly to a panel or canvas.

IMPERATOR. Freely translated from the Latin as *emperor*, but in Roman times it literally meant *army commander*.

IMPOST BLOCK. A block placed between the CAPITAL of a COLUMN and the ARCHES or VAULTS it supports.

JESUIT ORDER. Founded as the Society of Jesus in 1540 by Saint Ignatius Loyola (1491–1556) for the purpose of achieving the spiritual perfection not only of its members but also of all men. It became a leading factor in the struggle of the Counter-Reformation to support the Catholic faith against the Protestant Reformation. It also became a teaching ORDER that was responsible for the propagation of the faith in Africa, Asia, and the Americas, as well as in Europe.

KEEP. The innermost central tower of a medieval castle, which served both as a last defense and as a dungeon and contained living quarters, a prison, and sometimes a chapel; or a tower-like fortress, square, polygonal, or round, generally built on a mound as a military outpost.

KEYSTONE. See ARCH.

KING JAMES VERSION. See BIBLE.

LABORS OF THE MONTHS. Representations of occupations suitable to the twelve months of the year; frequently CARVED around the PORTALS of Romanesque and Gothic churches together with the signs of the ZODIAC, or represented in the calendar scenes of ILLUMINATED MANUSCRIPTS.

LANTERN. In architecture, a tall, more or less open structure crowning a roof, DOME, tower, etc., and admitting light to an enclosed area below.

LAPIS LAZULI. A deep blue stone or complex mixture of minerals used for ornamentation and in the making of pigments.

LATIN CROSS. A cross whose vertical member is longer than its horizontal one.

LIBERAL ARTS, SEVEN. Derived from the standard medieval prephilosophical education, they consisted of the trivium of Grammar, Rhetoric, and Logic, and the quadrivium of Arithmetic, Music, Geometry, and Astronomy. During the Middle Ages and the Renaissance, they were frequently represented allegorically.

LIGHT. A pane or compartment of a window.

LINEAR PERSPECTIVE. See PERSPECTIVE.

LINTEL. See POST AND LINTEL.

LITANY. A form of group prayer consisting of a series of supplications by the clergy with responses from the congregation.

LITHOGRAPH. A PRINT made by drawing with a fatty crayon or other oily substance on a porous stone or a metal plate. Greasy printing ink applied to the moistened stone adheres only to the lines of the drawing; the design can be transferred easily to a damp sheet of paper.

LITURGY. A collection of prescribed prayers and ceremonies for public worship; specifically, in the Roman Catholic, Orthodox, and Anglican churches, those used in the celebration of the MASS.

LOGGIA (pl. LOGGIE). A GALLERY or ARCADE open on at least one side.

LUNETTE. A semicircular opening or surface, as on the wall of a VAULTED room or over a door, niche, or window. When it is over the PORTAL of a church, it is called a TYMPANUM.

LUTHER, MARTIN. See BIBLE.

MADRASAH. Arabic word meaning *place of study*. An Islamic theological college providing student lodgings, a prayer hall, lecture halls, and a library. Perhaps first established in the tenth century by the Ghaznavids to combat the influence of dissenting sects, such as the Shi'ites; by the fourteenth century madrasahs were located in all great cities of the Muslim world. Usually consists of an open quadrangle bordered by VAULTED CLOISTERS called *iwans*.

MAENAD. An ecstatic female follower of the wine god Dionysos (Greek) or Bacchus (Roman); hence, also called a *bacchante* (pl. *bacchae*).

MAESTÀ. Italian word for *majesty*, and in religion signifying the Virgin in Majesty. *Virgin in Majesty.* A large ALTARPIECE with a central panel representing the Virgin Enthroned, adored by saints and angels.

MAGUS (pl. MAGI). A member of the priestly caste in ancient Media and Persia traditionally reputed to have practiced supernatural arts. In Christian art, the Three Wise Men who came from the East to pay homage to the Infant Jesus are called the *Magi*.

MAJOLICA. A kind of Italian pottery, heavily glazed and usually decorated in rich colors.

MANDORLA. The Italian word for *almond*. A large oval surrounding the figure of God, Christ, the Virgin Mary, or occasionally a saint, indicating divinity or holiness.

MANSARD ROOF. A roof with two slopes, the lower steeper than the upper; named after the French architect François Mansart (1598–1666).

MASS. The celebration of the EUCHARIST to perpetuate the sacrifice of Christ upon the Cross, plus readings from one of the GOSPELS and an EPISTLE; also, the form of LITURGY used in this celebration. See CANON OF THE MASS.

MENDICANT ORDERS. See DOMINICAN and FRANCISCAN.

MENHIR. A prehistoric monument consisting of an upright monumental stone, left rough or sometimes partly shaped, and either standing alone or grouped with others.

MINARET. A tall slender tower attached to a mosque and surrounded by one or more balconies from which the MUEZZIN calls the people to prayer.

MINOTAUR. In Greek mythology, a monster with the body of a man and the head of a bull, who, confined in the labyrinth built for Minos, king of Crete, in his palace at Knossos, fed on human flesh and who was finally killed by the Athenian hero Theseus.

MITER. A tall cap terminating in two peaks, one in front and one in back, that is the distinctive headdress of BISHOPS (including the pope as bishop of Rome) and abbots of the Western Church.

MODELING. The building up of three-dimensional form in a soft substance, such as clay or wax; the CARVING of surfaces into proper RELIEF; the rendering of the appearance of three-dimensional form in painting.

MOLDING. An ornamental strip, either depressed or projecting, that gives variety to the surface of a building by creating contrasts of light and shadow.

MONSTRANCE. An open or transparent receptacle of gold or silver in which the consecrated HOST is exposed for adoration.

MOSAIC. A type of surface decoration (used on pavements, walls, and VAULTS) in which bits of colored stone or glass (*tesserae*) are laid in cement in a figurative design or decorative pattern. In Roman examples, colored stones, set regularly, are most frequently used; in Byzantine work, bits of glass, many with gold baked into them, are set irregularly.

MUEZZIN. In Muslim countries, a crier who calls the people to prayer at stated hours, either from a MINARET or from another part of a mosque or high building.

MULLION. A vertical element that divides a window or a screen into partitions.

MURAL. A painting executed directly on a wall or done separately for a specific wall and attached to it.

MUSES. The nine sister goddesses of Classical mythology who presided over learning and the arts. They came to be known as Calliope, muse of epic poetry; Clio, muse of history; Erato, muse of love poetry; Euterpe, muse of music; Melpomene, muse of tragedy; Polyhymnia, muse of sacred song; Terpsichore, muse of dancing; Thalia, muse of comedy; and Urania, muse of astronomy.

NARTHEX. A PORCH or vestibule, sometimes enclosed, preceding the main entrance of a church; frequently, in churches preceded by an ATRIUM, the narthex is one side of the open AMBULATORY.

NAVE. From the Latin word for *ship*. The central aisle of an ancient Roman BASILICA or a Christian basilican church, as distinguished from the SIDE AISLES; the part of the church, between the main entrance and the CHANCEL, used by the congregation.

NEOPLATONISM. A philosophy, developed by Plotinus of Alexandria in the third century A.D., founded mainly on Platonic doctrine, Oriental mysticism, and Christian beliefs, in an effort to construct an all-inclusive philosophical system. Neoplatonism was of special interest to Italian humanists of the fifteenth century.

OBELISK, A tapering four-sided SHAFT of stone, usually monolithic, with a pyramidal apex, used as a freestanding monument (as in ancient Egypt) or as an architectural decoration.

OCULUS (pl. OCULI). Latin word for *eye*. A circular opening in a wall or at the apex of a DOME.

OFFICE OF THE DEAD. The burial service of the Christian Church.

OIL PAINT. Pigments mixed with oil; usually applied to a panel covered with GESSO, or to a stretched canvas that has been PRIMED with a mixture of glue and white pigment.

ORATORY. In the Roman Catholic Church, a religious society of priests who live in a community, but are not bound by vows (as are monks). In architecture, a place of prayer; more specifically, a chapel or separate structure for meditation and prayer by a small group of people.

ORATORY OF DIVINE LOVE. A confraternity, founded in Rome, which by 1517 had the grudging approval of Pope Leo X. Its goals were the reform of the Church from within, the cultivation of the spiritual life of its members by prayer and frequent Communion, and the performance of charitable work. When it was dissolved in 1524, its members expanded their original work into the Theatine ORDER, which was founded in 1524 by Saint Cajetan. See SCUOLA.

ORDER (architectural). An architectural system based on the COLUMN (including BASE, SHAFT, and CAPITAL) and its ENTABLATURE (including ARCHITRAVE, FRIEZE, and CORNICE). The five classical orders are the Doric, Ionic, Corinthian, Tuscan, and Composite.

ORDER (monastic). A religious society or confraternity whose members live under a strict set of rules and regulations, such as the Benedictine, Cistercian, DOMINICAN, FRANCISCAN, CARTHUSIAN, Cluniac, JESUIT, and THEATINE.

ORTHOGONALS. Lines that are at right angles to the plane of the picture surface, but that, in a representation using one-point PERSPECTIVE, converge toward a common vanishing point in the distance.

PAGODA. In the Far East, a sacred tower or temple usually pyramidal in shape and profusely decorated. Also, a small, ornamental structure built to imitate such a temple.

PALAZZO (pl. PALAZZI). Italian word for a *large town house;* used freely to refer to large civic or religious buildings as well as to relatively modest town houses.

PALETTE. A thin, usually oval or oblong tablet, with a hole for the thumb, upon which painters place and mix their colors.

PALETTE KNIFE. A small knife with a thin flexible blade, used for mixing painters' colors and sometimes for applying the paint directly to the picture surface.

PANTHEON. From the Greek words meaning *all the gods;* hence, a temple dedicated to all the gods. Specifically, the temple built about 25 B.C. in Rome and so dedicated.

PAPYRUS. A tall aquatic plant formerly very abundant in Egypt. Also, the material used for writing or painting upon by the ancient Egyptians, Greeks, and Romans. It was made by soaking, pressing, and drying thin strips of the pith of the plant laid together. Also, a manuscript or document of this material.

PARAPET. A low protective wall or barrier at the edge of a balcony, roof, bridge, or the like.

PARNASSUS. A mountain in Greece, anciently sacred to Apollo and the MUSES; hence, used allusively in both painting and poetry.

PASSION. In the Christian Church, used specifically to describe the sufferings of Christ during his last week of earthly life; or the representation of his sufferings in narrative or pictorial form.

PASTEL. A crayon made of ground pigments mixed with gum water, or a picture drawn with such crayons.

PAVILION. A projecting subdivision of a building, usually distinguished from the main structure by greater height or more elaborate decoration. Also, a light, ornamental building or pleasure-house.

PEDESTAL. An architectural support for a COLUMN, statue, vase, etc.; also, a foundation or BASE.

PEDIMENT. A low-pitched triangular area, resembling a GABLE, formed by the two slopes of a roof of a building (over a PORTICO, door, niche, or window), framed by a raking CORNICE, and frequently decorated with sculpture. When pieces of the cornice are either omitted or jut out from the main axis, as in some late Roman and Baroque buildings, it is called a *broken pediment.* See TYMPANUM.

PENDENTIVE. An architecutral feature, having the shape of a spherical triangle, used as a transition from a square ground PLAN to a circular plan that will support a DOME. The dome may rest directly on the pendentives or on an intermediate DRUM.

PERIPTERAL. Having a COLONNADE or PERISTYLE on all four sides.

PERISTYLE. A COLONNADE or ARCADE around a building or open court.

PERSPECTIVE. The representation of three-dimensional objects on a flat surface so as to produce the same impression of distance and relative size as that received by the human eye. In one-point *linear perspective,* developed during the fifteenth century, all parallel lines in a given visual field converge at a single vanishing point on the horizon. In *aerial* or *atmospheric perspective* the relative distance of objects is indicated by gradations of tone and color, and by variations in the clarity of outlines. See ORTHOGONALS and TRANSVERSALS.

PIAZZA (pl. PIAZZE). Italian word for *public square.* See CAMPO.

PICTURE PLANE. The actual surface on which a picture is painted.

PIER. An independent architectural element, usually rectangular in section, used to support a vertical load; if used with an ORDER, it often has a BASE and CAPITAL of the same design. See COMPOUND PIER.

PIER BUTTRESS. An exterior PIER in Romanesque and Gothic architecture, BUTTRESSING the THRUST of the VAULTS within.

PIETÀ. Italian word meaning both *pity* and *piety.* Used to designate a representation of the dead Christ mourned by the Virgin, with or without saints and angels. When the representation is intended to show a specific event prior to Christ's burial, it is usually called a *Lamentation.*

PIETRA SERENA. Italian for *clear stone.* A clear gray Tuscan limestone used for building chiefly in Florence and its environs.

PILASTER. A flat vertical element, having a CAPITAL and BASE, engaged in a wall from which it projects. It has a decorative rather than a structural purpose.

PINNACLE. A small ornamental turret on top of BUTTRESSES, PIERS, or elsewhere; mainly decorative, it may also have a structural purpose, as in Reims Cathedral.

PLAN. The general arrangement of the parts of a building or group of buildings, or a drawing of these as they would appear on a plane cut horizontally above the ground or floor.

PODIUM (pl. PODIA). In architecture, a continuous projecting BASE or PEDESTAL used to support COLUMNS, sculptures, or a wall. Also, the raised platform surrounding the arena of an ancient amphitheater.

POLYPTYCH. ALTARPIECE or devotional picture consisting of more than three wooden panels joined together.

PORCH. An exterior structure forming a covered approach to the entrance of a building.

PORPHYRY. A very hard rock having a dark purplish-red base. The room in the Imperial Palace in Constantinople reserved for the confinement of the reigning empress was decorated with porphyry so that the child would be "born to the purple," or "Porphyrogenitus."

PORTA CLAUSA. Latin phrase for CLOSED DOOR or CLOSED GATE.

PORTAL. A door or gate, especially one of imposing appearance, as in the entrances and PORCHES of a large church or other building. In Gothic churches the FAÇADES frequently include three large portals with elaborate sculptural decoration.

PORTICO. A structure consisting of a roof, or an ENTABLATURE and PEDIMENT, supported by COLUMNS, sometimes attached to a building as a PORCH.

POST AND LINTEL. The ancient but still widely used system of construction in which the basic unit consists of two or more upright posts supporting a horizontal beam, or LINTEL, which spans the opening between them.

PREDELLA. PEDESTAL of an ALTARPIECE, usually decorated with small narrative scenes that expand the theme of the major work above it.

PRIMING. A preparatory layer of paint, size, or the like applied to a surface, such as canvas or wood, that is to be painted.

PRINT. A picture, design, or the like reproduced from an engraved or otherwise prepared block or plate from which more than one copy can be made. See ENGRAVING, ETCHING, AQUATINT, WOODCUT, and LITHOGRAPH.

PRONAOS. The vestibule in front of the doorway to the SANCTUARY in a Greek or Roman PERIPTERAL temple.

PROPYLAION (pl. PROPYLIA). Generally, the entrance to a temple or other sacred enclosure. Specifically, the entrance gate to the Acroplis in Athens.

PROSTYLE. Used to describe a temple having a PORTICO across the entire front.

PYLON. Greek word for *gateway.* In Egyptian architecture, the monumental entrance to a temple or other large edifice, consisting of two truncated pyramidal towers flanking a central gateway. Also, applied to either of the flanking towers.

QUATREFOIL. A four-lobed form used as ornamentation.

QUATTROCENTO. Italian term for *four hundred,* meaning the fourteen hundreds or the fifteenth century.

RAKING CORNICE. See CORNICE.

REFECTORY. From the Latin verb meaning *to renew* or *restore.* A room for eating; in particular, the dining hall in a monastery, college, or other institution.

REGISTER. One of a series of horizontal bands used to differentiate areas of decoration when the bands are placed one above the other as in Egyptian tombs, medieval church sculpture, and the pages of a manuscript.

REINFORCED CONCRETE. Poured concrete with iron or steel mesh or bars imbedded in it to increase its tensile strength.

RELIEF. Sculpture that is not freestanding but projects from the background of which it is a part. *High relief* or *low relief* describes the amount of projection; when the background is not cut out, as in some Egyptian sculpture, the work is called *incised relief.*

RELIQUARY. A casket, COFFER, or other small receptacle for a sacred relic, usually made of precious materials and richly decorated.

REPOUSSOIR. From the French verb meaning *to push back.* A means of achieving PERSPECTIVE or spatial contrasts by the use of illusionistic devices such as the placement of a large figure or object in the immediate foreground of a painting to increase the illusion of depth in the rest of the picture.

RETARDATAIRE. From the French meaning *to be slow* or *behind time.* Said of an artist (or work) whose style reflects that of the past rather than that of the present.

RIB. A slender projecting ARCH used primarily as support in Romanesque and Gothic VAULTS; in late Gothic architecture, the ribs are frequently ornamental as well as structural.

RIBBED VAULT. A compound masonry VAULT, the GROINS of which are marked by projecting stone RIBS.

ROSARY. A series of prayers primarily to the Virgin Mary, or a string of beads invented by the DOMINICANS as an aid to memory in the recitation of these prayers. During the recitation the worshiper meditates on the five Joyful, the five Glorious, or the five Sorrowful Mysteries of the Virgin.

ROTUNDA. A circular building or interior hall usually surmounted by a DOME.

RUSTICATION. Masonry having indented joinings and, frequently, a roughened surface.

SACRAMENT. A rite regarded as an outward and visible sign of an inward and spiritual grace. Specifically, in the Roman Catholic Church, any one of the seven rites recognized as having been instituted by Christ: Baptism, confirmation, the EUCHARIST, penance, matrimony, holy orders, and extreme unction.

SACRISTY. See VESTRY.

SALON. A reception room or drawing room in a large house. Also, the exhibition of work by living painters, held in Paris at first biennially and since the mid-eighteenth century annually; so called because it was formerly held in the Salon Carré of the Louvre.

SANCTUARY. A sacred or holy place. In architecture, the term is generally used to designate the most sacred part of a building.

SARCOPHAGUS. From the Greek words meaning *flesh-eating.* In ancient Greece, a kind of limestone said to reduce flesh to dust; thus, the term was used for coffins. A general term for a stone coffin often decorated with sculpture or bearing inscriptions.

SATURATION. The degree of intensity of a HUE and its relative freedom from an admixture with white.

SATYR. One of the woodland creatures thought to be the companions of Dionysos and noted for lasciviousness; represented with the body of a man, pointed ears, two horns, a tail, and the legs of a goat.

SCRIPTURE. See BIBLE.

SCROLL. A roll of paper, PARCHMENT, or the like, intended for writing upon. In architecture, an ornament resembling a partly unrolled sheet of paper or having a spiral or coiled form, as in the VOLUTES of Ionic and Corinthian COLUMNS.

SCUOLA (pl. SCUOLE). Italian word for *school.* In Venetian Renaissance terms, a fraternal organization under ecclesiastical auspices, dedicated to good works, but with no educational function. Called a *company* elsewhere in Italy, except in Tuscany where it was sometimes called a *confraternity.*

SECCO SU FRESCO. See FRESCO.

SECTION. A drawing or diagram of a building showing its various parts as they would appear if the building were cut on a vertical plane.

SERAPH (pl. SERAPHIM). A celestial being or angel of the highest order, usually represented with six wings.

SHAFT. A cylindrical form; in architecture, the part of a COLUMN or PIER between the BASE and the CAPITAL.

SHOP. See BOTTEGA.

SIBYL. Any of various women of Greek and Roman mythology who were reputed to possess powers of prophecy and divination. In time, as many as twelve came to be recognized, some of whom Michelangelo painted in the frescoes adorning the Sistine Chapel ceiling because they were believed to have foretold the first coming of Christ.

SIDE AISLE. One of the corridors parallel to the NAVE of a church or BASILICA, separated from it by an ARCADE or COLONNADE.

SILKSCREEN. A printmaking technique in which a design is blocked out on a piece of stretched silk gauze by means of a stencil, glue sizing, etc. Paint is then forced through the untreated spaces in the silk onto a piece of paper.

SINOPIA (pl. SINOPIE). An Italian term taken from *Sinope,* the name of a city in Asia Minor famous for its red earth. Used to designate the preliminary brush drawing, executed in red earth mixed with water, for a painting in FRESCO; usually done on the ARRICCIO of the wall.

SINS, SEVEN DEADLY. See VICES.

SLIP. Potter's clay reduced with water to a semiliquid state and used for coating or decorating pottery, cementing handles, etc.

SOCLE. A square block supporting a COLUMN, statue, vase, or other work of art, or a low BASE supporting a wall.

SPANDREL. An area between the exterior curves of two adjoining ARCHES, or, enclosed by the exterior curve of an arch, a perpendicular from its springing and a horizontal through its apex.

SPHINX. In Egyptian mythology, a creature with the body of a lion and the head of a man, a bird, or a beast; the monumental sculpture of the same. In Greek mythology, a monster usually having the winged body of a lion and the head of a woman.

STANZA (pl. STANZE). Italian word for *room.*

STATE. See ETCHING.

STIPPLING. In painting, drawing, and ENGRAVING, a method of representing light and shade by the use of dots.

STOA. In Greek architecture, a PORTICO or covered COLONNADE, usually of considerable length, used as a promenade or meeting place.

STRINGCOURSE. A horizontal MOLDING or band of stone, usually projecting and sometimes richly carved, that runs across the face of a building.

STUCCO. Any of various plasters used for CORNICES, MOLDINGS, and other wall decorations. A cement or concrete for coating exterior walls in imitation of stone.

STYLUS. A pointed instrument used in ancient times for writing on tablets of a soft material, such as clay. Also, an etcher's tool. See ETCHING.

SUPERIMPOSED ORDERS. One ORDER on top of another on the face of a building of more than one story. The upper order is usually lighter in form than the lower.

SURPLICE. A loose, broad-sleeved white vestment, properly of linen, worn over the CASSOCK by clergymen, choristers, and others taking part in church services.

TABERNACLE. The portable SANCTUARY used by the Israelites in the wilderness before the building of the Temple. Generally, any place or house of worship. In architecture, a canopied niche or recess, in a wall or a pillar, built to contain an image.

TABLES OF THE LAW. The stone slabs on which the Ten Commandments were inscribed.

TEMPERA. Ground colors mixed with yolk of egg, instead of oil, as a vehicle; a medium widely used for Italian panel painting before the sixteenth century.

TENEBROSI. Italian word for *shadowy ones.* A group of Neapolitan followers of Caravaggio who exaggerated his strong contrasts of light and dark.

TERRA-COTTA. Italian words for *baked earth.* A hard glazed or unglazed earthenware used for sculpture and pottery or as a building material. The word can also mean something made of this material or the color of it, a dull brownish red.

TERRA VERDE. Italian words for *green earth.* The color used for the underpaint of flesh tones in TEMPERA painting.

TESSERA (pl. TESSERAE). See MOSAIC.

THEATINE ORDER. See ORATORY OF DIVINE LOVE.

THEOLOGICAL VIRTUES. See VIRTUES.

THOLOS. In Greek and Roman architecture, a circular building derived from early Greek tombs and used for a variety of purposes.

THRUST. The outward force exerted by an ARCH or VAULT that must be counterbalanced by BUTTRESSING.

TIARA (papal). The pope's triple crown, surmounted by the orb and cross. It is the emblem of sovereign power, but has no sacred character; at LITURGICAL functions the pope always wears a MITER.

TOGA. A loose outer garment consisting of a single piece of material, without sleeves or armholes, which covered nearly the whole body, worn by the citizens of ancient Rome when appearing in public in times of peace.

TONDO. Italian term for a *circular work of art:* painting, RELIEF sculpture, or the like.

TRACERY. Ornamental stonework in geometric patterns used primarily in Gothic windows as support and decoration, but also used on panels, screens, etc. When the window appears to be cut through the solid stone, the style is called *plate tracery;* when slender pieces of stone are erected within the window opening, the style is called *bar tracery.*

TRANSEPT. In a BASILICAN church, the crossarm, placed at right angles to the NAVE, usually separating the latter from the CHANCEL or the APSE.

TRANSVERSALS. Horizontal lines running parallel to the PICTURE PLANE and intersecting the ORTHOGONALS.

TRAVERTINE. A tan or light-colored limestone used in Italy, and elsewhere, for building. The surface is characterized by alternating smooth and porous areas.

TREE OF LIFE. A tree in the Garden of Eden whose fruit gave everlasting life and was thus equated with Christ in medieval theology (Gen. 2:9; 3:22). Also, according to a vision of Saint John the Evangelist, a tree in the heavenly city of Jerusalem with leaves for the healing of nations (Rev. 22:2).

TREE OF THE KNOWLEDGE OF GOOD AND EVIL. A tree in the Garden of Eden bearing the forbidden fruit, the eating of which destroyed Adam's and Eve's innocence (Gen. 2:9; 3:17).

TREFOIL. A three-lobed form used as ornamentation or as the basis for a ground PLAN.

TRIFORIUM. The section of the wall in the NAVE, CHOIR, and sometimes in the TRANSEPT above the ARCHES and below the CLERESTORY. It usually consists of a blind ARCADE or a GALLERY.

TRIPTYCH. ALTARPIECE or devotional picture consisting of three panels joined together; frequently hinged so that the center panel is covered when the side panels are closed.

TRITON. In Classical mythology, a son of Poseidon and Amphitrite, represented as having the head and trunk of a man and the tail of a fish, and carrying a conch shell that he blows to raise or calm the waves. Later, one of a race of subordinate sea gods.

TRIUMPHAL ARCH. In ancient Rome, a freestanding monumental ARCH or series of three arches erected to commemorate a military victory, usually decorated with sculptured scenes of a war and its subsequent triumphal procession. In a Christian church, the transverse wall with a large arched opening that separates the CHANCEL and the APSE from the main body of the church, and that is frequently decorated with religious scenes executed in MOSAIC or FRESCO.

TROPHY. A memorial erected by the ancient Greeks and Romans in commemoration of a victory. It usually consisted of arms and spoils taken from the enemy and hung on a tree or pillar. Also, the representation of such a memorial as an allegory or simply as decoration.

TUNIC. In ancient Greece and Rome, a knee-length garment with or without sleeves, usually worn without a girdle by both sexes.

TYMPANUM (pl. TYMPANA). In Classical architecture, the vertical recessed face of a PEDIMENT; in medieval architecture, the space between an ARCH and the LINTEL over a door or window, which was often decorated with sculpture.

VALUE. The degree of lightness or darkness of a HUE.

VAULT. An ARCHED roof or covering made of brick, stone, or concrete. See BARREL VAULT, GROIN VAULT, RIBBED VAULT, CORBEL.

VELLUM. A fine kind of PARCHMENT made from calfskin and used for the writing, ILLUMINATING, and binding of medieval manuscripts.

VESTRY. A room in or a building attached to a church where the vestments and sacred vessels are kept; also called a *sacristy.* Used, in some churches, as a chapel or a meeting room.

VICES. Coming from the same tradition as the VIRTUES, and frequently paired with them, they are more variable, but usually include Pride, Avarice, Wrath, Gluttony, and Unchastity. Others such as Folly, Inconstancy, and Injustice may be selected to make a total of seven.

VICTORY. A female deity of the ancient Romans, or the corresponding deity the ancient Greeks called NIKE. The representation of this deity, usually as a winged woman in windblown draperies and holding a laurel wreath, palm branch, or other symbolic object.

VILLA. From the Latin and Italian *villa.* Originally a country house of some size and pretension, but now also used to designate a rural or suburban residence or a detached house in a residential area.

VIRTUES. Divided into the three Theological Virtues of Faith, Hope, and Charity, and the four Cardinal Virtues of Prudence, Justice, Fortitude, and Temperance. As with the VICES, the allegorical representation of the Virtues derives from a long medieval tradition in manuscripts and sculpture, and from such literary sources as the *Psychomachia* of Prudentius and the writings of Saint Augustine.

VOLUTE. An ornament resembling a rolled SCROLL. Especially prominent on CAPITALS of the Ionic and Composite ORDERS.

VOUSSOIR. See ARCH.

VULGATE. See BIBLE.

WASH. Used in WATERCOLOR painting, brush drawing, and occasionally in OIL PAINTING to describe a broad thin layer of diluted pigment or ink. Also refers to a drawing made in this technique.

WATERCOLOR. Paint in which the pigment is mixed with water as a solvent, or a design executed with this paint.

WOODCUT. A PRINT made by cutting a design in RELIEF on a block of wood and printing only the raised surfaces.

ZIGGURAT. From the Assyrian-Babylonian word *ziqquratu (mountaintop).* A staged, truncated pyramid of mud brick, built by the Sumerians and later by the Assyrians as a support for a shrine.

ZODIAC. An imaginary belt encircling the heavens within which lie the paths of the sun, moon, and principal planets. It is divided into twelve equal parts called *signs,* which are named after twelve constellations: Aries, the ram; Taurus, the bull; Gemini, the twins; Cancer, the crab; Leo, the lion; Virgo, the virgin; Libra, the balance; Scorpio, the scorpion; Sagittarius, the archer; Capricorn, the goat; Aquarius, the water-bearer; and Pisces, the fishes. Also, a circular or elliptical diagram representing this belt with pictures of the symbols associated with the constellations.

Bibliography

PART FOUR

THE RENAISSANCE

SOURCES

ALBERTI, LEONE BATTISTA, *On Painting and On Sculpture* (tr. C. Grayson), Phaidon, New York, 1972
———————, *Ten Books on Architecture* (ed. J. Rykwert, tr. J. Leoni), Tiranti, London, 1955
CASTIGLIONE, BALDASSARE, *The Book of the Courtier* (tr. C. S. Singleton), Doubleday, Garden City, N.Y., 1959
CELLINI, BENVENUTO, *Autobiography* (ed. J. Pope-Hennessy), Phaidon, London, 1960
CENNINI, CENNINO, *The Craftsman's Handbook* (tr. D. V. Thompson, Jr.), Dover, New York, 1954
FILARETE (ANTONIO AVERLINO), *Treatise on Architecture* (tr. J. R. Spencer), 2 vols., Yale University Press, New Haven, Conn., 1965
HOLT, ELIZABETH, ed., *Literary Sources of Art History*, Princeton University Press, 1947
LEONARDO DA VINCI, *Treatise on Painting* (tr. A. P. McMahon), 2 vols., Princeton University Press, 1956
The Notebooks of Leonardo da Vinci (tr. E. MacCurdy), 2 vols., Harcourt Brace, New York, 1938
VASARI, GIORGIO, *The Lives of the Painters, Sculptors, and Architects* (tr. J. W. Gaunt), 4 vols., Dutton, New York, 1963

GENERAL

ANTAL, FREDERICK, *Florentine Painting and Its Social Background*, Kegan Paul, London, 1948
BERENSON, BERNARD, *The Drawings of the Florentine Painters*, 2d ed., 3 vols., University of Chicago Press, 1938
———————, *Italian Painters of the Renaissance*, 2d ed., Phaidon, London, 1952
———————, *Italian Pictures of the Renaissance*, 7 vols., Phaidon, London, 1957-68
BERGSTRÖM, INGVAR, *Revival of Antique Illusionistic Wall Painting in Renaissance Art*, Elanders, Göteborg, 1957
BLUNT, SIR ANTHONY, *Artistic Theory in Italy 1450-1600*, Clarendon Press, Oxford, 1940
BORSOOK, EVE, *The Mural Painters of Tuscany*, Phaidon, London, 1960
BURCKHARDT, JAKOB C., *The Civilization of the Renaissance in Italy* (tr. S. G. C. Middlemore), 4th ed., Phaidon, London, 1960
CHAMBERS, DAVID S., comp., *Patrons and Artists in the Italian Renaissance*, University of South Carolina Press, Columbia, 1971
CHASTEL, ANDRÉ, *The Age of Humanism: Europe 1480-1539* (tr. K. M. Delavenay and E. M. Gwyer), McGraw-Hill, New York, 1964
———————, *The Crisis of the Renaissance, 1520-1600* (tr. P. Price), Skira, Geneva, 1968
———————, *The Myth of the Renaissance, 1420-1520* (tr. S. Gilbert), Skira, Geneva, 1969
———————, *Studios and Styles of the Italian Renaissance* (tr. J. Griffin), New York, Odyssey, 1966
CUTTLER, CHARLES D., *Northern Painting: From Pucelle to Bruegel*, Holt, Rinehart & Winston, New York, 1968
DECKER, HEINRICH, *The Renaissance in Italy: Architecture, Sculpture, Frescoes*, Viking, New York, 1969
DE WALD, ERNEST, *Italian Painting 1200-1600*, Holt, Rinehart & Winston, New York, 1961
GILBERT, CREIGHTON, *History of Renaissance Art (Painting, Sculpture, Architecture) Throughout Europe*, Abrams, New York, 1973
GOMBRICH, ERNST H., *Norm and Form: Studies in the Art of the Renaissance*, Phaidon, London, 1966
———————, *Symbolic Images: Studies in the Art of the Renaissance*, Phaidon, London, 1972
HARTT, FREDERICK, *History of Italian Renaissance Art*, Abrams, New York, 1969
KELLER, HARALD, *The Renaissance in Italy: Painting, Sculpture, Architecture* (tr. R. E. Wolf), Abrams, New York, 1969
KEUTNER, HERBERT, *Sculpture: Renaissance to Rococo*, New York Graphic Society, Greenwich, Conn., 1969
LOWRY, BATES, *Renaissance Architecture*, Braziller, New York, 1962
MARLE, RAIMOND VAN, *The Development of the Italian Schools of Painting*, X-XIX, Nijhoff, The Hague, 1923-38
MURRAY, LINDA, *The Late Renaissance and Mannerism*, Praeger, New York, 1967
MURRAY, PETER, *The Architecture of the Italian Renaissance*, Schocken Books, New York, 1966
———————, *Architecture of the Renaissance*, Abrams, New York, 1971
PANOFSKY, ERWIN, *Idea* (tr. J. J. S. Peake), University of South Carolina Press, Columbia, 1968
———————, *Meaning in the Visual Arts*, Doubleday, Garden City, N.Y., 1955
———————, *Renaissance and Renascences in Western Art*, 2d ed., 2 vols., Almqvist & Wiksell, Stockholm, 1965
———————, *Studies in Iconology: Humanistic Themes in the Art of the Renaissance*, Oxford University Press, New York, 1939
POPE-HENNESSY, SIR JOHN, *An Introduction to Italian Sculpture*, 2d ed., 3 vols., Phaidon, New York, 1970-71
———————, *The Portrait in the Renaissance*, Pantheon, New York, 1966
SEZNEC, JEAN, *The Survival of the Pagan Gods* (tr. B. Sessions), 3d ed., Harper & Row, New York, 1961
SIMPSON, LUCIE, *The Greek Spirit of Renaissance Art*, Ettrick Press, Edinburgh, 1953
SMART, ALASTAIR, *The Renaissance and Mannerism in Italy*, Harcourt Brace Jovanovich, New York, 1971
———————, *The Renaissance and Mannerism in Northern Europe and Spain*, Harcourt Brace Jovanovich, New York, 1972
TURNER, ALMON R., *The Vision of Landscape in Renaissance Italy*, Princeton University Press, 1966
VENTURI, LIONELLO, *Italian Painting*, 3 vols., Skira, New York, 1950-51
WIND, EDGAR, *Pagan Mysteries in the Renaissance*, 2d ed., Barnes & Noble, New York, 1968
WITTKOWER, RUDOLF, *Architectural Principles in the Age of Humanism*, Random House, New York, 1965

1. THE EARLY RENAISSANCE IN ITALY: THE FIFTEENTH CENTURY

GENERAL

BAXANDALL, MICHAEL, *Painting and Experience in Fifteenth Century Italy*, Clarendon Press, Oxford, 1972
LENGYEL, ALFONZ, *The Quattrocento*, Kendall/Hunt, Dubuque, Iowa, 1971
POPE-HENNESSY, SIR JOHN, *Italian Renaissance Sculpture*, Phaidon, London, 1958
———————, *Sienese Quattrocento Painting*, Oxford University Press, New York, 1947
SEYMOUR, CHARLES, JR., *Sculpture in Italy, 1400-1500*, Penguin, Baltimore, 1966
VAVALÀ, EVELYN SANDBERG, *Sienese Studies: The Development of the School of Painting of Siena*, Olschki, Florence, 1953
———————, *Uffizi Studies: The Development of the Florentine School of Painting*, Olschki, Florence, 1948

MONOGRAPHS

ARGAN, GIULIO C., *Fra Angelico: Biographical and Critical Study* (tr. J. Emmons), Skira, Cleveland, 1955

BAXANDALL, MICHAEL, *Giotto and the Orators (1350–1450)*, Clarendon Press, Oxford, 1971

BERTI, LUCIANO, *Masaccio*, Pennsylvania State University Press, University Park, 1967

BOTTARI, STEFANO, *Antonello da Messina* (tr. G. Scaglia), New York Graphic Society, Greenwich, Conn., 1955

CLARK, KENNETH (Lord Clark of Saltwood), *Piero della Francesca*, Phaidon, New York, 1951

GILBERT, CREIGHTON, *Change in Piero della Francesca*, J. J. Augustin, Locust Valley, N.Y., 1968

HARTT, FREDERICK, et al., *The Chapel of the Cardinal of Portugal, 1434–1459, at San Miniato in Florence*, University of Pennsylvania Press, Philadelphia, 1964

—————, and FINN, D., *Donatello: Prophet of Modern Vision*, Abrams, New York, 1973

HENDY, PHILIP, *Masaccio: Frescoes in Florence*, New York Graphic Society, Greenwich, Conn., 1956

—————, *Piero della Francesca and the Early Renaissance*, Macmillan, New York, 1968

JANSON, H. W., *The Sculpture of Donatello*, 2 vols., Princeton University Press, 1957

KRAUTHEIMER, RICHARD, and KRAUTHEIMER-HESS, T., *Lorenzo Ghiberti*, 2d ed., 2 vols., Princeton University Press, 1970

LAUTS, JAN, ed., *Carpaccio*, Phaidon, New York, 1962

MARTINDALE, ANDREW, ed., *The Complete Paintings of Mantegna*, Abrams, New York, 1967

PASSAVANT, GÜNTER, *Verrocchio* (tr. K. Watson), Phaidon, London, 1969

POPE-HENNESSY, SIR JOHN, *The Complete Work of Paolo Uccello*, 2d ed., 2 vols., Phaidon, London, 1969

—————, *Fra Angelico*, Phaidon, London, 1952

PRAGER, FRANK, and SCAGLIA, G., *Brunelleschi: Studies of His Technology and Inventions*, MIT Press, Cambridge, Mass., 1970

RICHTER, GEORGE M., *Andrea del Castagno*, University of Chicago Press, 1943

ROBERTSON, GILES, *Giovanni Bellini*, Clarendon Press, Oxford, 1968

ROTONDI, PASQUALE, *The Ducal Palace of Urbino*, Tiranti, London, 1969

SALVINI, ROBERTO, *All the Paintings of Botticelli* (tr. J. Grillenzoni), 4 vols., Hawthorn, New York, 1965

SEYMOUR, CHARLES, JR., *Jacopo della Quercia: Sculptor*, Yale University Press, New Haven, Conn., 1973

—————, *The Sculpture of Verrocchio*, New York Graphic Society, Greenwich, Conn., 1971

SINDONA, ENIO, *Pisanello* (tr. J. Ross), Abrams, New York, 1961

TIETZE-CONRAT, ERICA, *Mantegna: Paintings, Drawings, Engravings*, Phaidon, New York, 1955

VENTURI, LIONELLO, *Botticelli*, Phaidon, London, 1961

WILENSKI, REGINALD H., *Mantegna (1431–1506) and the Paduan School*, Faber & Faber, London, 1947

2. THE EARLY RENAISSANCE IN NORTHERN EUROPE

SOURCES

STECHOW, WOLFGANG, *Northern Renaissance Art 1400–1600: Sources and Documents*, Prentice-Hall, Englewood Cliffs, N.J., 1966

GENERAL

CHÂTELET, ALBERT, and THUILLIER, J., *French Painting from Fouquet to Poussin* (tr. S. Gilbert), Skira, Geneva, 1963

COREMANS, PAUL, ed., *Flanders in the Fifteenth Century: Art and Civilization*, Detroit Institute of Arts, 1960

DELAISSÉ, L. M. J., *A Century of Dutch Manuscript Illumination*, University of California Press, Berkeley, 1968

EVANS, JOAN, *English Art, 1307–1461*, Clarendon Press, Oxford, 1949

FRIEDLANDER, MAX J., *Early Netherlandish Painting* (tr. H. Norden), 14 vols., Praeger, New York, 1967- (in progress)

—————, *Early Netherlandish Painting from Van Eyck to Bruegel*, Phaidon, London, 1956

HIND, ARTHUR M., *History of Engraving and Etching*, 3d ed. (repr.), Dover, New York, 1963

—————, *An Introduction to a History of Woodcut*, 2 vols., Dover, New York, 1963

HOLLSTEIN, F. W. H., *Dutch and Flemish Etchings, Engravings, and Woodcuts*, 19 vols., Menno Hertzberger, Amsterdam, 1949–74

LASSAIGNE, JACQUES, *Flemish Painting* (tr. S. Gilbert), I, Skira, New York, 1956

MATĚJČEK, ANTONIN, and PEŠINA, J., *Czech Gothic Painting: 1350–1450* (tr. J. C. Houra), Melantrich, Prague, 1950

MÜLLER, THEODOR, *Sculpture in the Netherlands, France, Germany and Spain: 1400 to 1500*, Penguin, Baltimore, 1966

PANOFSKY, ERWIN, *Early Netherlandish Painting*, 2 vols., Harvard University Press, Cambridge, Mass., 1953

PORCHER, JEAN, *Medieval French Miniatures*, Abrams, New York, 1960

RING, GRETE, *A Century of French Painting*, Phaidon, London, 1949

STANGE, ALFRED, *German Painting: XIV–XVIth Centuries* (ed. A. Gloeckner), Hyperion, New York, 1950

VAN PUYVELDE, LEO, *Flemish Painting from the Van Eycks to Metsys* (tr. A. Kendall), McGraw-Hill, New York, 1970

—————, *The Flemish Primitives* (tr. D. I. Wilton), Continental Book Center, New York, 1947

WHINNEY, MARGARET, *Early Flemish Painting*, Faber & Faber, London, 1968

MONOGRAPHS

ALEXANDER, J. J. G., ed., *The Master of Mary of Burgundy*, Braziller, New York, 1970

BALDASS, LUDWIG, *Jan van Eyck*, London, Phaidon, 1952

BLUM, SHIRLEY N., *Early Netherlandish Triptychs*, University of California Press, Berkeley, 1969

DAVIES, MARTIN, *Rogier van der Weyden*, Phaidon, London, 1972

DENIS, VALENTIN, *All the Paintings of Jan van Eyck* (tr. P. Colacicchi), Hawthorn, New York, 1961

FRIEDL, ANTONIN, *Magister Theodoricus* (tr. I. R. Gottheiner), Artia, Prague, 1956

GIBSON, WALTER S., *Hieronymus Bosch*, Praeger, New York, 1973

MEISS, MILLARD, ed., *The Belles Heures of Jean, Duke of Berry*, Braziller, New York, 1974

—————, *French Painting in the Time of Jean de Berry: The Boucicaut Master*, Phaidon, New York, 1968

—————, *French Painting in the Time of Jean de Berry: The Late Fourteenth Century and the Patronage of the Duke*, 2 vols., Phaidon, London, 1967

—————, *French Painting in the Time of Jean de Berry: The Limbourgs and Their Contemporaries*, 2 vols., Braziller, New York, 1974

—————, and THOMAS, M., eds., *The Rohan Master*, Braziller, New York, 1973

—————, ed., *The Très Riches Heures of Jean, Duke of Berry*, Braziller, New York, 1969

—————, ed., *The Visconti Hours*, Braziller, New York, 1972

MORAND, KATHLEEN, *Jean Pucelle*, Clarendon Press, Oxford, 1962

PHILIP, LOTTE BRAND, *The Ghent Altarpiece and the Art of Jan van Eyck*, Princeton University Press, 1971

RASMO, NICOLÒ, *Martin Pacher* (tr. P. Waley), Phaidon, New York, 1971

SHERMAN, CLAIRE R., *The Portraits of Charles V of France*, New York University Press, 1970

SHESTACK, ALAN, ed., *Master E. S.*, Philadelphia Museum of Art, Philadelphia, 1967

STERLING, CHARLES, ed., *The Hours of Étienne Chevalier by Jean Fouquet*, Braziller, New York, 1971

THOMAS, MARCEL, ed., *The Grandes Heures of Jean, Duke of Berry*, Braziller, New York, 1971

TOLNAY, CHARLES DE, *Hieronymus Bosch* (tr. M. Bullock and H. Mins), Reynal, New York, 1966

WESCHER, PAUL, *Jean Fouquet and His Time*, Reynal & Hitchcock, New York, 1947

3. THE HIGH RENAISSANCE IN FLORENCE AND ROME

SOURCES

KLEIN, ROBERT, and ZERNER, H., *Italian Art 1500–1600: Sources and Documents*, Prentice-Hall, Englewood Cliffs, N.J., 1966

GENERAL

FREEDBERG, SYDNEY J., *Painting in Italy: 1500–1600*, Penguin, Baltimore, 1970
_____, *Painting of the High Renaissance in Rome and Florence*, 2 vols., Harvard University Press, Cambridge, Mass., 1961
LEE, RENSSELAER W., *Ut Pictura Poesis*, Norton, New York, 1967
MURRAY, LINDA, *The High Renaissance*, Praeger, New York, 1967
POPE-HENNESSY, SIR JOHN, *Italian High Renaissance and Baroque Sculpture*, 3 vols., Phaidon, London, 1963
TIETZE, HANS, and TIETZE-CONRAT, E., *The Drawings of the Venetian Painters in the 15th and 16th Centuries*, Augustin, New York, 1944
WÖLFFLIN, HEINRICH, *Classic Art*, 2d ed., Phaidon, London, 1953

MONOGRAPHS

ACKERMAN, JAMES S., *The Architecture of Michelangelo*, 2 vols., Viking, New York, 1961–64
CHIERICI, GINO, *Donato Bramante* (tr. P. Simmons), Universe, New York, 1960
CLARK, KENNETH (Lord Clark of Saltwood), *Leonardo da Vinci*, 2d ed., Penguin, Baltimore, 1967
DE TOLNAY, CHARLES, *Michelangelo*, 2d ed., 5 vols., Princeton University Press, 1969–71
DOUGLAS, ROBERT LANGTON, *Piero di Cosimo*, University of Chicago Press, 1946
DUSSLER, LUITPOLD, *Raphael: A Critical Catalogue*, Phaidon, New York, 1971
FISCHEL, OSKAR, *Raphael* (tr. B. Rackham), 2 vols., Kegan Paul, Trench, Trubner, London, 1948
GOLDSCHIEDER, LUDWIG, *Leonardo da Vinci*, 8th ed., Phaidon, London, 1967
_____, *Michelangelo: Paintings, Sculpture, and Architecture*, 4th ed., Phaidon, London, 1964
HARTT, FREDERICK, *Michelangelo*, 3 vols., Abrams, New York, 1965–71
POPE-HENNESSY, SIR JOHN, *Raphael*, New York University Press, 1970

4. THE MANNERIST CRISIS

GENERAL

BOSQUET, JACQUES, *Mannerism: The Painting and Style of the Late Renaissance* (tr. S. W. Taylor), Braziller, New York, 1964
BRIGANTI, GIULIANO, *Italian Mannerism* (tr. M. Kunzle), VEB Edition, Leipzig, 1962
FRIEDLÄNDER, WALTER F., *Mannerism and Anti-Mannerism in Italian Painting*, Columbia University Press, New York, 1957
SHERMAN, JOHN K. G., *Mannerism*, Penguin, Baltimore, 1967
SMYTH, CRAIG H., *Mannerism and Maniera*, J. J. Augustin, Locust Valley, N.Y., 1963

MONOGRAPHS

CLAPP, FREDERICK M., *Jacopo Carucci da Pontormo*, Yale University Press, New Haven, Conn., 1916
FREEDBERG, SYDNEY J., *Andrea del Sarto*, 2 vols., Belknap Press, Cambridge, Mass., 1963
REARICK, JANET COX, *The Drawings of Pontormo*, 2 vols., Harvard University Press, Cambridge, Mass., 1964
SHEARMAN, JOHN, *Andrea del Sarto*, Clarendon Press, Oxford, 1965

5. HIGH RENAISSANCE AND MANNERISM IN VENICE AND NORTHERN ITALY

GENERAL

MURRAY, LINDA, *The Late Renaissance and Mannerism*, Praeger, New York, 1967
RICCI, CORRADO, *Architecture and Decorative Sculpture of the High and Late Renaissance in Italy*, Brentano, New York, 1923
WÜRTENBERGER, FRANZSEPP, *Mannerism: The European Style of the Sixteenth Century* (tr. M. Heron), Holt, Rinehart & Winston, New York, 1963

MONOGRAPHS

ACKERMAN, JAMES S., *Palladio*, Penguin, Harmondsworth, England, 1966
_____, *Palladio's Villas*, J. J. Augustin, Locust Valley, N.Y., 1967
BALDASS, LUDWIG VON, *Giorgione* (tr. J. M. Brownjohn), Abrams, New York, 1965
BERENSON, BERNARD, *Lorenzo Lotto*, 2d ed., Phaidon, London, 1956
BIANCONI, PIERO, *All the Paintings of Lorenzo Lotto* (tr. P. Colacicchi), 2 vols., Hawthorn, New York, 1963
CIARDI DUPRE, MARIA G., *Small Renaissance Bronzes* (tr. B. Rose), Hamlyn, Feltham, England, 1970
FREEDBERG, SYDNEY J., *Parmigianino: His Works in Painting*, Harvard University Press, Cambridge, Mass., 1950
GIBBONS, FELTON, *Dosso and Battista Dossi*, Princeton University Press, 1968
HARTT, FREDERICK, *Giulio Romano*, 2 vols., Yale University Press, New Haven, Conn., 1958
NEWTON, ERIC, *Tintoretto*, Greenwood Press, Westport, Conn., 1972
PANOFSKY, ERWIN, *The Iconography of Correggio's Camera di San Paolo*, Warburg Institute, London, 1961
_____, *Problems in Titian*, New York University Press, 1969
PIGNATTI, TERISIO, *Giorgione*, Phaidon, London, 1971
POPHAM, ARTHUR E., *Correggio's Drawings*, Oxford University Press, London, 1957
_____, *The Drawings of Parmigianino*, 3 vols., Yale University Press, New Haven, Conn., 1971
QUINTAVALLE, AUGUSTA GHIDIGLIA, *Correggio: The Frescoes in San Giovanni Evangelista at Parma* (tr. O. Ragusa), Abrams, New York, 1964
SCHULZ, JUERGEN, *Venetian Painted Ceilings of the Renaissance*, University of California Press, Berkeley, 1968
TIETZE, HANS, *Tintoretto: The Paintings and Drawings*, Phaidon, New York, 1948
_____, *Titian: Paintings and Drawings*, 2d ed., Oxford University Press, New York, 1950
VALCANOVER, FRANCESCO, *All the Paintings of Titian* (tr. S. J. Tomalin), 4 vols., Hawthorn, New York, 1964
WALKER, JOHN, *Bellini and Titian at Ferrara: A Study of Style and Taste*, Phaidon, London, 1957
WETHEY, HAROLD, *The Paintings of Titian*, 2 vols., Phaidon, New York, 1969–71

6. MICHELANGELO AND LATER MANNERISM IN CENTRAL ITALY (SEE ALSO 3, *supra*)

MONOGRAPHS

McCOMB, ARTHUR K., *Agnolo Bronzino: His Life and Works*, Harvard University Press, Cambridge, Mass., 1928
POPE-HENNESSY, SIR JOHN, *Samson and a Philistine by Giovanni Bologna*, HMSO, London, 1954
SMYTH, CRAIG H., *Bronzino as Draughtsman: An Introduction*, J. J. Augustin, Locust Valley, N.Y., 1971
WILES, BERTHA H., *The Fountains of Florentine Sculptors*, Harvard University Press, Cambridge, Mass., 1933

7. HIGH AND LATE RENAISSANCE OUTSIDE ITALY

GENERAL

AUERBACH, ERNA, *Tudor Artists*, Athlone Press, London, 1954
BENESCH, OTTO, *The Art of the Renaissance in Northern Europe*, 2d ed., Phaidon, London, 1965

_____, *German Painting, from Dürer to Holbein* (tr. H. S. B. Harrison), Skira, Geneva, 1966

BLUNT, SIR ANTHONY, *Art and Architecture in France: 1500 to 1700*, 2d ed., Penguin, Baltimore, 1970

GOMEZ-MORENO, MANUEL, *The Golden Age of Spanish Sculpture*, New York Graphic Society, Greenwich, Conn., 1964

KUBLER, GEORGE, and SORIA, M., *Art and Architecture in Spain and Portugal . . . 1500 to 1800*, Penguin, Baltimore, 1959

LASSAIGNE, JACQUES, and DELEVOY, R., *Flemish Painting, II: From Bosch to Rubens* (tr. S. Gilbert), Skira, New York, 1958

LEYMARIE, JEAN, *Dutch Painting* (tr. S. Gilbert), Skira, New York, 1956

POST, CHANDLER R., *History of Spanish Painting*, 14 vols., Harvard University Press, Cambridge, Mass., 1930–66

SAXL, FRITZ, and WITTKOWER, R., *British Art and the Mediterranean*, Oxford University Press, New York, 1948

SUMMERSON, SIR JOHN, *Architecture in Britain: 1530 to 1830*, 4th ed., Penguin, Baltimore, 1963

VON DER OSTEN, GERT and VEY, H., *Painting and Sculpture in Germany and the Netherlands: 1500 to 1600*, Penguin, Baltimore, 1969

WATERHOUSE, ELLIS K., *Painting in Britain: 1530 to 1730*, 2d ed., Penguin, Baltimore, 1962

MONOGRAPHS

APPLEBAUM, STANLEY, ed., *The Triumph of Maximilian I: 137 Woodcuts by Hans Burgkmair and Others*, Dover, New York, 1964

AUERBACH, ERNA, *Nicholas Hilliard*, Routledge & Kegan Paul, London, 1961

BÄCKSBACKA, INGJALD, *Luis de Morales*, Societas Scientiarum Fennica, Helsinki, 1962

BLUNT, SIR ANTHONY, *Philibert de l'Orme*, Zwemmer, London, 1958

DE TOLNAY, CHARLES, *The Drawings of Pieter Brueghel the Elder* (tr. C. R. Sleeth), London, Zwemmer, 1952

DOS SANTOS, REYNALDO, *Nuno Gonçalves* (tr. L. Norton), Phaidon, London, 1955

GANZ, PAUL, *Hans Holbein, the Younger*, Phaidon, London, 1950

_____, *The Paintings of Hans Holbein the Younger*, Phaidon, London, 1956

GOLDSCHIEDER, LUDWIG, *El Greco*, 3d ed., Phaidon, New York, 1954

GORIS, JAN-ALBERT, and MARLIER, G., eds., *Albrecht Dürer: Diary of His Journey to the Netherlands* (tr. P. Troutman), New York Graphic Society, Greenwich, Conn., 1971

GROSSMANN, FRITZ, *Pieter Breughel: Complete Edition of the Paintings*, 3d ed., Phaidon, New York, 1973– (in progress)

GUDIOL I RICART, JOSIP, *Domenikos Theotokopoulos, El Greco, 1541–1614* (tr. K. Lyons), Viking, New York, 1973

KELEMEN, PÁL, *El Greco Revisited: Candia, Venice, Toledo*, Macmillan, New York, 1961

KNAPPE, KARL-ADOLF, *The Complete Engravings, Etchings and Woodcuts of Albrecht Dürer*, Abrams, New York, 1965

KOSCHATZKY, WALTER, *Albrecht Dürer: The Landscape Water-Colours* (tr. P. McDermott), St. Martin's Press, New York, 1973

LAVALLEYE, JACQUES, *Pieter Brueghel the Elder and Lucas van Leyden: The Complete Engravings, Etchings, and Woodcuts*, Abrams, New York, 1967

MARIJNISSEN, R. H., *Brueghel*, Putnam, New York, 1971

MÜNZ, LUDWIG, *Pieter Brueghel the Elder: The Drawings*, Phaidon, New York, 1961

PANOFSKY, ERWIN, *The Life and Art of Albrecht Dürer*, 4th ed., Princeton University Press, 1955

PARKER, KARL T., *The Drawings of Hans Holbein . . . at Windsor Castle*, Phaidon, London, 1945

PEVSNER, NIKOLAUS, and MEIER, M., *Grünewald*, Abrams, New York, 1958

ROSENTHAL, EARL E., *The Cathedral of Granada*, Princeton University Press, 1961

RÜHMER, EBERHARD, *Cranach* (tr. J. Spencer), Phaidon, London, 1963

_____, *Grünewald: Drawings* (tr. A. R. Cooper), Phaidon, London, 1970

SCHOENBERGER, GUIDO, *The Drawings of Mathis Gothart Nithard called Grünewald*, Bittner, New York, 1948

SMITH, ALLISON, *The Complete Paintings of Dürer*, Abrams, New York, 1968

STECHOW, WOLFGANG, *Pieter Brueghel the Elder*, Abrams, New York, 1969

STRAUSS, WALTER L., *The Complete Drawings of Albrecht Dürer*, 6 vols., Abaris, New York, 1974

TRAPIER, ELIZABETH, *El Greco: Early Years at Toledo, 1576–86*, Hispanic Society of America, New York, 1958

_____, *Luis de Morales and Leonardesque Influences in Spain*, Hispanic Society of America, New York, 1953

WAETZOLDT, WILHELM, *Dürer and His Times*, Phaidon, New York, 1950

WETHEY, HAROLD E., *El Greco and His School*, 2 vols., Princeton University Press, 1962

ZERNER, HENRI, *The School of Fontainebleau: Etchings and Engravings* (tr. S. Baron), Abrams, New York, 1969

PART FIVE

THE BAROQUE

GENERAL

ADHÉMAR, JEAN, *Graphic Art of the Eighteenth Century* (tr. M. I. Martin), McGraw-Hill, New York, 1964

ANDERSEN, LISELOTTE, *Baroque and Rococo* (tr. B. Berg), Abrams, New York, 1969

ARGAN, GIULIO CARLO, *The Europe of the Capitals, 1600–1700* (tr. A. Rhodes), Skira, Geneva, 1965

BAZIN, GERMAIN, *The Baroque* (tr. P. Wardroper), New York Graphic Society, Greenwich, Conn., 1968

BUSCH, HARALD, and LOHSE, B., eds., *Baroque Europe* (tr. P. George), Macmillan, New York, 1962

CANNON-BROOKES, P. and C., *Baroque Churches*, Hamlyn, New York, 1969

DUPONT, JACQUES, and MATHEY, F., *The Seventeenth Century* (tr. S. J. C. Harrison), Skira, New York, 1951

HARTT, FREDERICK, *Love in Baroque Art*, J. J. Augustin, Locust Valley, N.Y., 1964

HELD, JULIUS S., and POSNER, D., *17th and 18th Century Art*, Abrams, New York, 1971

KAUFMANN, EMIL, *Architecture in the Age of Reason*, Harvard University Press, Cambridge, Mass., 1955

KITSON, MICHAEL, *The Age of Baroque*, McGraw-Hill, New York, 1966

LEE, RENSSELAER W., *Ut Pictura Poesis: The Humanistic Theory of Painting*, Norton, New York, 1967

LEVEY, MICHAEL, *Rococo to Revolution*, Praeger, New York, 1966

MILLON, HENRY A., *Baroque and Rococo Architecture*, Braziller, New York, 1961

NORBERG-SCHULZ, CHRISTIAN, *Baroque Architecture*, Abrams, New York, 1972

PEVSNER, NIKOLAUS, *An Outline of European Architecture*, 6th ed., Penguin, Baltimore, 1960

PIGNATTI, TERISIO, *The Age of Rococo* (tr. L. Andrade), Hamlyn, New York, 1969

ROSENBLUM, ROBERT, *Transformations in Late Eighteenth Century Art*, Princeton University Press, 1967

SCHÖNBERGER, ARNO, and SOEHNER, H., *The Rococo Age* (tr. D. Woodward), McGraw-Hill, New York, 1960

SCHWARZ, MICHAEL, *The Age of the Rococo* (tr. G. Onn), Praeger, New York, 1971

SEWTER, A. C., *Baroque and Rococo*, Harcourt Brace Jovanovich, New York, 1972

STERLING, CHARLES, *Still Life Painting from Antiquity to the Present Time*, Universe, New York, 1959

TAPIÉ, VICTOR-LUCIEN, *The Age of Grandeur: Baroque Art and Architecture*, 2d ed., Praeger, New York, 1966

WÖLFFLIN, HEINRICH, *Principles of Art History* (tr. M. D. Hottinger), Holt, New York, 1932

1. THE SEVENTEENTH CENTURY IN ITALY

SOURCES

BELLORI, GIOVANNI PIETRO, *The Lives of Annibale and Agostino Carracci* (tr. C. Enggass), Pennsylvania State University Press, University Park, 1968

BROWN, JONATHAN, *Italy and Spain, 1600–1700: Sources and Documents*, Prentice-Hall, Englewood Cliffs, N.J., 1969

GENERAL

BLUNT, SIR ANTHONY, and COOKE, H. L., *Roman Drawings of the XVII and XVIII Centuries . . . at Windsor Castle*, Phaidon, London, 1960
—————, *Sicilian Baroque*, Macmillan, New York, 1968
—————, and CROFT-MURRAY, E., *Venetian Drawings of the XVII and XVIII Centuries . . . at Windsor Castle*, Phaidon, London, 1957
CHARPENTRAT, PIERRE, *Living Architecture: Baroque, Italy and Central Europe* (tr. C. Brown), Grosset & Dunlap, New York, 1967
FOKKER, TIMON H., *Roman Baroque Art: The History of a Style*, 2 vols., Oxford University Press, London, 1938
GODFREY, FREDERICK M., *A Student's Guide to Later Italian Painting, 1500–1800*, Tiranti, London, 1958
HASKELL, FRANCIS, *Patrons and Painters: A Study in the Relations Between Italian Art and Society in the Age of the Baroque*, Knopf, New York, 1963
HEMPEL, EBERHARD, *Baroque Art and Architecture in Central Europe*, Penguin, Baltimore, 1965
KURZ, OTTO, *Bolognese Drawings of the XVII and XVIII Centuries . . . at Windsor Castle*, Phaidon, London, 1955
LEES-MILNE, JAMES, *Baroque in Italy*, Batsford, London, 1959
McCOMB, ARTHUR K., *The Baroque Painters of Italy*, Harvard University Press, Cambridge, Mass., 1934
MAHON, DENIS, *Studies in Seicento Art and Theory*, Warburg Institute, London, 1947
MANNING, ROBERT L. and B. S., *Genoese Painters: Cambiaso to Magnasco, 1550–1750*, Dayton Art Institute, Ohio, 1962
NISSMAN, JOAN, and HIBBARD, H., *Florentine Baroque Art*, Metropolitan Museum of Art, New York, 1969
PANOFSKY, ERWIN, *Idea: A Concept in Art Theory* (tr. J. J. S. Peake), University of South Carolina Press, Columbia, 1968
PORTOGHESI, PAOLO, *Roma Barocca: The History of an Architectonic Culture*, MIT Press, Cambridge, Mass., 1970
SITWELL, SACHEVERELL, *Baroque and Rococo*, Putnam, New York, 1967
SPEAR, RICHARD, *Caravaggio and His Followers*, Cleveland Museum of Art, 1972
WATERHOUSE, ELLIS K., *Italian Baroque Painting*, 2d ed., Phaidon, London, 1969
WITTKOWER, RUDOLF, *Art and Architecture in Italy: 1600 to 1750*, 3d ed., Penguin, Baltimore, 1973
—————, *Gothic v. Classic: Architectural Projects in Seventeenth-Century Italy*, Braziller, New York, 1974

MONOGRAPHS

BOSCHLOO, A. W. A., *Annibale Caracci in Bologna: Visible Reality in Art After the Council of Trent* (tr. R. R. Symondal), 2 vols., Government Pub. Office, The Hague, 1974
ENGGASS, ROBERT, *The Painting of Baciccio*, Pennsylvania State University Press, University Park, 1964
FRIEDLÄNDER, WALTER F., *Caravaggio Studies*, Princeton University Press, 1955
HIBBARD, HOWARD, *Bernini*, Penguin, Baltimore, 1965
—————, *Carlo Maderno and Roman Architecture, 1580–1630*, Pennsylvania State University Press, University Park, 1971
HINKS, ROGER P., *Michelangelo Merisi da Caravaggio*, Faber & Faber, London, 1953
KITSON, MARTIN, ed., *The Complete Paintings of Caravaggio*, Abrams, New York, 1969
MARTIN, JOHN RUPERT, *The Farnese Gallery*, Princeton University Press, 1965
MOIR, ALFRED, *The Italian Followers of Caravaggio*, 2 vols., Harvard University Press, Cambridge, Mass., 1967
POSNER, DONALD, *Annibale Carracci*, 2 vols., Phaidon, London, 1971
WITTKOWER, RUDOLF, *The Drawings of the Carracci . . . at Windsor Castle*, Phaidon, London, 1952
—————, *Gian Lorenzo Bernini: The Sculptor of the Roman Baroque*, 2d ed., Phaidon, London, 1966

2. THE SEVENTEENTH CENTURY IN FRANCE

GENERAL

BLUNT, SIR ANTHONY, *Art and Architecture in France: 1500 to 1700*, 2d ed., Penguin, Baltimore, 1970
—————, *The French Drawings at Windsor Castle*, Phaidon, London, 1945
LAVEDAN, PIERRE, *French Architecture*, Penguin, Baltimore, 1956
SAVAGE, GEORGE, *French Decorative Art, 1638–1793*, Praeger, New York, 1969
The Splendid Century: French Art, 1600–1715, Metropolitan Museum of Art, New York, 1960–61
THUILLIER, JACQUES, and CHÂTELET, A., *French Painting from Le Nain to Fragonard* (tr. S. Gilbert), Skira, Geneva, 1964

MONOGRAPHS

BECHTEL, EDWIN DE T., *Jacques Callot*, Braziller, New York, 1955
BERGER, ROBERT W., *Antoine Le Pautre*, New York University Press, 1969
BLUNT, SIR ANTHONY, *François Mansart*, Warburg Institute, London, 1941
—————, *Nicolas Poussin*, 2 vols., Pantheon, New York, 1967
CRELLY, WILLIAM R., *The Painting of Simon Vouet*, Yale University Press, New Haven, Conn., 1962
FOX, HELEN M., *André Le Nôtre*, Crown, New York, 1962
FRIEDLÄNDER, WALTER F., et al., *The Drawings of Nicolas Poussin*, 4 vols., Warburg Institute, London, 1939–63
—————, *Nicolas Poussin: A New Approach*, Abrams, New York, 1965
FURNESS, S. M. M., *Georges de la Tour of Lorraine, 1593–1652*, Routledge & Kegan Paul, London, 1949
RÖTHLISBERGER, MARCEL, *Claude Lorrain: The Drawings*, University of California Press, Berkeley, 1969
—————, *Claude Lorrain: The Paintings*, Yale University Press, New Haven, Conn., 1961

3. THE SEVENTEENTH CENTURY IN ENGLAND

GENERAL

DOWNES, KERRY, *English Baroque Architecture*, Zwemmer, London, 1966
LEES-MILNE, JAMES, *The Age of Inigo Jones*, Batsford, London, 1953
SUMMERSON, SIR JOHN, *Architecture in Britain: 1530–1830*, 4th ed., Penguin, Baltimore, 1963
WHINNEY, MARGARET D., and MILLAR, O., *English Art 1625–1714*, Clarendon Press, Oxford, 1957

MONOGRAPHS

FÜRST, VIKTOR, *The Architecture of Sir Christopher Wren*, Lund Humphries, London, 1956
SUMMERSON, SIR JOHN, *Inigo Jones*, Penguin, Harmondsworth, England, 1966
WHINNEY, MARGARET D., *Christopher Wren*, Praeger, New York, 1971

4. FLEMISH PAINTING IN THE SEVENTEENTH CENTURY

SOURCES

MAGURN, RUTH S., ed., *The Letters of Peter Paul Rubens*, Harvard University Press, Cambridge, Mass., 1955

GENERAL

GERSON, HORST, and TER KUILE, E. H., *Art and Architecture in Belgium, 1600–1800*, Penguin, Baltimore, 1960
VAN PUYVELDE, LEO and THIERRY, *Flemish Painting: The Age of Rubens and Van Dyck* (tr. A. Kendall), McGraw-Hill, New York, 1971

MONOGRAPHS

FLETCHER, JENNIFER, *Peter Paul Rubens*, Phaidon, New York, 1968

HELD, JULIUS S., *Rubens: Selected Drawings*, 2 vols., Phaidon, London, 1959

JAFFÉ, MICHAEL, *Van Dyck's Antwerp Sketchbook*, 2 vols., Macdonald, London, 1966

STECHOW, WOLFGANG, *Rubens and the Classical Tradition*, Harvard University Press, Cambridge, Mass., 1968

5.   DUTCH PAINTING IN THE SEVENTEENTH CENTURY

GENERAL

BERGSTRÖM, INGVAR, *Dutch Still Life Painting in the Seventeenth Century* (tr. C. Hedström and G. Taylor), Yoseloff, New York, 1956

ROSENBERG, JAKOB, SLIVE, S., and TER KUILE, E. H., *Dutch Art and Architecture, 1600–1800*, 2d ed., Penguin, Baltimore, 1972

STECHOW, WOLFGANG, *Dutch Landscape Painting of the Seventeenth Century*, Phaidon, London, 1966

MONOGRAPHS

GERSON, HORST, *Rembrandt Paintings*, Reynal, New York, 1968

GOWING, LAWRENCE, *Vermeer*, Harper & Row, New York, 1970

HAAK, BOB, *Rembrandt: His Life, His Work, His Time*, Abrams, New York, 1969

HELD, JULIUS S., *Rembrandt's Aristotle and Other Studies*, Princeton University Press, 1969

JUDSON, JAY R., *Gerrit van Honthorst*, Nijhoff, The Hague, 1959

MULLER, JOSEPH-ÉMILE, *Rembrandt*, Abrams, New York, 1969

NICOLSON, BENEDICT, *Hendrick Terbrugghen*, Lund Humphries, London, 1958

ROSENBERG, JAKOB, *Rembrandt*, 2d ed., Phaidon, London, 1964

SLIVE, SEYMOUR, *Frans Hals*, 2 vols., Phaidon, London, 1970

SWILLENS, P. T. A., *Johannes Vermeer, Painter of Delft, 1632–1675* (tr. C. M. Bruening-Williamson), Spectrum, New York, 1950

TRIVAS, NUMA S., *The Paintings of Frans Hals*, Oxford University Press, New York, 1941

WHITE, CHRISTOPHER, *Rembrandt as an Etcher*, 2 vols., Pennsylvania State University Press, University Park, 1969

6.   SPANISH PAINTING IN THE SEVENTEENTH CENTURY

GENERAL

BAIRD, JOSEPH A., *The Churches of Mexico, 1530–1810*, University of California Press, Berkeley, 1962

BEVAN, BERNARD, *History of Spanish Architecture*, Scribner's, New York, 1939

BOTTINEAU, YVES, *Living Architecture: Iberian-American Baroque* (tr. K. M. Lemke), Macdonald, London, 1971

KELEMEN, PÁL, *Baroque and Rococo in Latin America*, Macmillan, New York, 1951

KUBLER, GEORGE, and SORIA, M., *Art and Architecture in Spain and Portugal and Their American Dominions, 1500 to 1800*, Penguin, Baltimore, 1959

————————, *Portuguese Plain Architecture*, Wesleyan University Press, Middletown, Conn., 1972

LEES-MILNE, JAMES, *Baroque in Spain and Portugal, and its Antecedents*, Batsford, London, 1960

SITWELL, SACHEVERELL, *Baroque and Rococo*, Putnam, New York, 1967

WEISBACH, WERNER, *Spanish Baroque Art*, Cambridge University Press, England, 1941

WETHEY, HAROLD E., *Colonial Architecture and Sculpture in Peru*, Harvard University Press, Cambridge, Mass., 1949

MONOGRAPHS

BROWN, JONATHAN, *Zurbarán*, Abrams, New York, 1973

LÓPEZ-REY, JOSÉ, *Velázquez: A Catalogue Raisonné of His Oeuvre*, Faber & Faber, London, 1963

————————, *Velázquez' Work and World*, New York Graphic Society, Greenwich, Conn., 1968

PROSKE, BEATRICE, *Juan Martínez Montañés*, Hispanic Society of America, New York, 1967

SORIA, MARTIN, *The Paintings of Zurbarán*, 2d ed., Phaidon, London, 1955

TRAPIER, ELIZABETH DU G., *Ribera*, Hispanic Society of America, New York, 1952

————————, *Valdés Leal*, Hispanic Society of America, New York, 1960

————————, *Velázquez*, Hispanic Society of America, New York, 1948

WETHEY, HAROLD E., *Alonso Cano*, Princeton University Press, 1955

7.   CONTINENTAL ART IN THE EIGHTEENTH CENTURY

GENERAL

BLAZICEK, OLDRICH J., *Baroque Art in Bohemia* (tr. S. Kadečka), Hamlyn, Feltham, England, 1968

BOURKE, JOHN, *Baroque Churches of Central Europe*, 2d ed., Faber & Faber, London, 1962

CHARPENTRAT, PIERRE, *Living Architecture: Baroque, Italy and Central Europe* (tr. C. Brown), Grosset & Dunlap, New York, 1967

DE GONCOURT, EDMOND and JULES, *French XVIII Century Painters* (tr. R. Ironside), Phaidon, New York, 1948

HITCHCOCK, HENRY RUSSELL, *Rococo Architecture in Southern Germany*, Phaidon, London, 1968

KALNEIN, WEND GRAF, and LEVEY, M., *Art and Architecture of the Eighteenth Century in France*, Penguin, Baltimore, 1972

KIMBALL, SIDNEY FISKE, *The Creation of the Rococo*, Philadelphia Museum of Art, 1943

LEVEY, MICHAEL, *Painting in XVIII Century Venice*, Phaidon, London, 1959

MAXON, JOHN, ed., *Painting in Italy in the Eighteenth Century: Rococo to Romanticism*, Art Institute of Chicago, 1970

PAULSSON, THOMAS, *Scandinavian Architecture*, L. Hill, London, 1958

POMMER, RICHARD, *Eighteenth Century Architecture in Piedmont*, New York University Press, 1967

POWELL, NICOLAS, *From Baroque to Rococo*, Faber & Faber, London, 1959

ROSSEN, SUSAN F., ed., *The Twilight of the Medici: Late Baroque Art in Florence, 1670–1743*, Wayne State University Press, Detroit, 1974

SAVAGE, GEORGE, *French Decorative Art, 1638–1793*, Praeger, New York, 1969

SUTTON, DENYS, *France in the Eighteenth Century*, Royal Academy, London, 1968

————————, *French Drawings of the Eighteenth Century*, Pleiades Books, London, 1949

THUILLIER, JACQUES, and CHÂTELET, A., *French Painting from Le Nain to Fragonard* (tr. S. Gilbert), Skira, Geneva, 1964

MONOGRAPHS

AURENHAMMER, HANS, *J. B. Fischer von Erlach*, Allen Lane, London, 1973

CONSTABLE, WILLIAM G., *Canaletto*, 2 vols., Oxford University Press, London, 1962

D'ANCONA, PAOLO, *Tiepolo in Milan: The Palazzo Clerici Frescoes* (tr. L. Krasnik), Edizione del Milione, Milan, 1956

McINNES, IAN, *Painter, King, and Pompadour: François Boucher at the Court of Louis XV*, F. Muller, London, 1965

MAYOR, A. HYATT, *Giovanni Battista Piranesi*, H. Bittner, New York, 1952

MILKOVICH, MICHAEL, *Sebastiano and Marco Ricci in America*, University of Kentucky, Lexington, 1966

MONTAGNI, E. C., *The Complete Paintings of Watteau*, Abrams, New York, 1971

MORASSI, ANTONIO, *G. B. Tiepolo*, Phaidon, New York, 1955

OLSEN, HARALD, *Federico Barocci*, 2d ed., Munksgaard, Copenhagen, 1962

PARKER, K. T., *The Drawings of Antonio Canaletto . . . at Windsor Castle*, Phaidon, London, 1948

PIGNATTI, TERISIO, *Pietro Longhi*, Phaidon, London, 1969

SHAW, J. BYAM, *The Drawings of Domenico Tiepolo,* Faber & Faber, London, 1962

——————————, *The Drawings of Francesco Guardi,* Faber & Faber, London, 1951

THOMAS, HYLTON, *The Drawings of Giovanni Battista Piranesi,* Beechhurst, New York, 1954

THUILLIER, JACQUES, *Fragonard* (tr. R. Allen), Skira, Geneva, 1967

WILDENSTEIN, GEORGES, *Chardin* (tr. D. Wildenstein), New York Graphic Society, Greenwich, Conn., 1969

——————————, *The Paintings of Fragonard* (tr. C. W. Chilton and A. L. Kitson), Phaidon, London, 1960

8.   ENGLISH AND AMERICAN COLONIAL ART IN THE EIGHTEENTH CENTURY

SOURCES

REYNOLDS, SIR JOSHUA, *Discourses on Art* (ed. E. E. Wark), Huntington Library, San Marino, Calif., 1959

GENERAL

SUMMERSON, SIR JOHN, *Architecture in Britain: 1530 to 1830,* 4th ed., Penguin, Baltimore, 1963

WATERHOUSE, ELLIS K., *Painting in Britain: 1530 to 1790,* 2d ed., Penguin, Baltimore, 1962

WRIGHT, LOUIS B., et al., *The Arts in America: The Colonial Period,* Scribner's, New York, 1966

MONOGRAPHS

ANTAL, FREDERICK, *Hogarth,* Routledge & Kegan Paul, London, 1962

EVANS, GROSE, *Benjamin West and the Taste of His Times,* Southern Illinois University Press, Carbondale, 1959

HUDSON, DEREK, *Sir Joshua Reynolds: A Personal Study,* G. Bles, London, 1958

PAULSON, RONALD, *Hogarth: His Life, Art and Times,* 2 vols., Yale University Press, New Haven, Conn., 1971

——————————, comp., *Hogarth's Graphic Works,* 2d ed., 2 vols., Yale University Press, New Haven, Conn., 1970

PROWN, JULES D., *John Singleton Copley,* 2 vols., Harvard University Press, Cambridge, Mass., 1966

WATERHOUSE, ELLIS K., *Gainsborough,* 2d ed., Spring Books, London, 1966

PART SIX

THE MODERN WORLD

SOURCES

DELACROIX, EUGÈNE, *Journal* (tr. and ed. W. Pach), Crown, New York, 1948

EITNER, LORENZ, *Neoclassicism and Romanticism, 1750–1850: Sources and Documents in the History of Art,* 2 vols., Prentice-Hall, Englewood Cliffs, N.J., 1970

HERBERT, ROBERT L., ed., *Modern Artists on Art,* Prentice-Hall, Englewood Cliffs, N.J., 1964

McCOUBREY, JOHN, *American Art, 1700–1960: Sources and Documents in the History of Art,* Prentice-Hall, Englewood Cliffs, N.J., 1965

NOCHLIN, LINDA, *Impressionism and Post-Impressionism, 1874–1904: Sources and Documents in the History of Art,* Prentice-Hall, Englewood Cliffs, N.J., 1966

——————————, *Realism and Tradition in Art, 1848–1900: Sources and Documents in the History of Art,* Prentice-Hall, Englewood Cliffs, N.J., 1966

GENERAL

ARNASON, H. H., *History of Modern Art,* Abrams, New York, 1968

BOWNESS, ALAN, *Modern European Art,* Harcourt Brace Jovanovich, New York, 1972

CANADAY, JOHN, *Mainstreams of Modern Art,* Holt, Rinehart & Winston, New York, 1959

DORIVAL, BERNARD, *Twentieth Century Painters,* 2 vols., Universe, New York, 1958

EVERS, HANS G., *The Art of the Modern Age* (tr. J. R. Foster), Crown, New York, 1970

GERNSHEIM, HELMUT and ALISON, *The History of Photography from the Camera Obscura to the Beginning of the Modern Era,* Thames & Hudson, London, 1969

HAFTMANN, WERNER, *Painting in the Twentieth Century* (tr. R. Manheim), 2d ed., 2 vols., Praeger, New York, 1965

HAMILTON, GEORGE H., *19th and 20th Century Art: Painting, Sculpture, Architecture,* Abrams, New York, 1970

——————————, *Painting and Sculpture in Europe, 1880 to 1940,* Penguin, Baltimore, 1967

HOFFMAN, WERNER, *The Earthly Paradise: Art in the Nineteenth Century* (tr. B. Battershaw), Braziller, New York, 1961

LAKE, CARLTON, and MAILLARD, R., eds., *Dictionary of Modern Painting,* 2d ed., Tudor, New York, 1964

LICHT, FRED S., *Sculpture of the 19th and 20th Centuries,* New York Graphic Society, Greenwich, Conn., 1967

LIPPARD, LUCY R., *Six Years,* Praeger, New York, 1973

MAILLARD, ROBERT, ed., *Dictionary of Modern Sculpture,* Tudor, New York, 1960

NOVOTNY, FRITZ, *Painting and Sculpture in Europe, 1780–1880,* 2d ed., Penguin, Harmondsworth, England, 1971

OZENFANT, AMÉDÉE, *Foundations of Modern Art* (tr. I. Rodker), 2d ed., Dover, New York, 1952

RAYNAL, MAURICE, *Modern Painting* (tr. S. Gilbert), 2d ed., Skira, New York, 1960

READ, SIR HERBERT, *A Concise History of Modern Painting,* 2d ed., Praeger, New York, 1968

——————————, *A Concise History of Modern Sculpture,* Praeger, New York, 1964

SCHUG, ALBERT, *Art of the 20th Century* (tr. B. Berg), Abrams, New York, 1969

SELZ, JEAN, *Modern Sculpture: Origins and Evolution* (tr. A. Michelson), Braziller, New York, 1963

SEMBACH, KLAUS-JÜRGEN, *Into the Thirties* (tr. J. Filson), Thames & Hudson, London, 1972

SMITH, BERNARD W., *European Vision and the South Pacific, 1768–1850: A Study in the History of Art and Ideas,* Clarendon Press, Oxford, 1960

TRIER, EDUARD, *Form and Space (Sculpture of the Twentieth Century),* 2d ed., Praeger, New York, 1968

VENTURI, LIONELLO, *Modern Painters* (tr. F. Steegmuller), 2 vols., Scribner's, New York, 1947–50

VOGT, ADOLF M., *Art of the 19th Century* (tr. A. F. Bance), Universe, New York, 1973

MONOGRAPHS

BALLO, GUIDO, *Modern Italian Painting from Futurism to the Present Day* (tr. B. Wall), Praeger, New York, 1958

BARKER, VIRGIL, *American Painting: History and Interpretation,* Macmillan, New York, 1953

BAUR, JOHN I. H., *Revolution and Tradition in Modern American Art,* Harvard University Press, Cambridge, Mass., 1951

BESSET, MAURICE, *New French Architecture,* Praeger, New York, 1967

BROWN, MILTON W., *American Painting from the Armory Show to the Depression,* Princeton University Press, 1955

CARRIERI, RAFFAELE, *Avant-Garde Painting and Sculpture (1890–1955) in Italy,* Domus, Milan, 1955

FITCH, JAMES MARSDEN, *American Building,* Houghton Mifflin, Boston, 1948

GALARDI, ALBERTO, *New Italian Architecture* (tr. E. Rockwell), Praeger, New York, 1967

GARRETT, WENDELL D., et al., *The Arts in America: The 19th Century,* Scribner's, New York, 1969

GAUSS, CHARLES E., *The Aesthetic Theories of French Artists, 1855 to the Present,* Johns Hopkins Press, Baltimore, 1949

GELDZAHLER, HENRY, *American Painting in the Twentieth Century,* Metropolitan Museum of Art, New York, 1965

GREEN, SAMUEL M., *American Art: A Historical Survey,* Ronald Press, New York, 1966

HAMILTON, GEORGE H., *The Art and Architecture of Russia,* Penguin, Baltimore, 1954

HAMMACHER, ABRAHAM M., *Modern English Sculpture,* Abrams, New York, 1967

HARRIS, NEIL, *The Artist in American Society: The Formative Years, 1790–1860,* Braziller, New York, 1966

HATJE, GERD, ed., *Encyclopedia of Modern Architecture*, Praeger, New York, 1964

HUNTER, SAM, *Modern American Painting and Sculpture*, Dell, New York, 1959

——————, *Modern French Painting, 1855–1956*, Dell, New York, 1956

HUYGHE, RENÉ, *French Painting: The Contemporaries*, French & European Publications, New York, 1939

JANIS, SIDNEY, *Abstract and Surrealist Art in America*, Reynal & Hitchcock, New York, 1944

LEHMANN-HAUPT, HELLMUT, *Art Under a Dictatorship*, Oxford University Press, New York, 1954

LYNES, RUSSELL, *The Art-Makers of Nineteenth Century America*, Atheneum, New York, 1970

MARCHIORI, GIUSEPPE, *Modern French Sculpture* (tr. J. Ross), Abrams, New York, 1963

MEEKS, CARROLL L. V., *Italian Architecture, 1750–1914*, Yale University Press, New Haven, Conn., 1966

MYERS, BERNARD S., *Mexican Painting in Our Time*, Oxford University Press, New York, 1956

ØSTBY, LEIF, *Modern Norwegian Painting*, Mittet, Oslo, 1949

POULSEN, VAGN, *Danish Painting and Sculpture* (tr. J. Mammen), Danske Selskab, Copenhagen, 1955

ROH, FRANZ, *German Art in the 20th Century*, New York Graphic Society, Greenwich, Conn., 1968

ROSE, BARBARA, *American Art Since 1900*, Praeger, New York, 1967

RÖTHEL, HANS K., *Modern German Painting*, Reynal, New York, 1957

ROTHENSTEIN, SIR JOHN, ed., *British Art Since 1900: An Anthology*, Phaidon, New York, 1962

——————, *Modern English Painters*, 2 vols., Eyre & Spottiswoode, London, 1952–56

SALVINI, ROBERTO, *Modern Italian Sculpture*, Abrams, New York, 1962

SAN LAZZARO, GUALTIERI, *Painting in France: 1895–1945* (tr. B. Gilliat-Smith and B. Wall), Philosophical Library, New York, 1949

SLOANE, JOSEPH C., *French Painting Between the Past and the Present*, Princeton University Press, 1951

SOTRIFFER, KRISTIAN, *Modern Austrian Art* (tr. A. Jaffa), Praeger, New York, 1965

WILENSKI, REGINALD H., *Modern French Painters*, Harcourt, Brace, New York, 1949

1. NEOCLASSICISM

GENERAL

FRIEDLÄNDER, WALTER F., *From David to Delacroix*, Harvard University Press, Cambridge, Mass., 1952

HAMLIN, TALBOT F., *Greek Revival Architecture in America*, Oxford University Press, New York, 1944

HONOUR, HUGH, *Neo-Classicism*, Penguin, Harmondsworth, England, 1968

MONOGRAPHS

DOWD, DAVID L., *Pageant-Master of the Republic: Jacques-Louis David and the French Revolution*, Books for Libraries Press, Freeport, N.Y., 1969

HAMLIN, TALBOT F., *Benjamin Henry Latrobe*, Oxford University Press, New York, 1955

ROSENBLUM, ROBERT, *Jean-August-Dominique Ingres*, Abrams, New York, 1967

WILDENSTEIN, GEORGES, *Ingres*, Phaidon, London, 1967

2. ROMANTICISM

GENERAL

BRION, MARCEL, *Art of the Romantic Era*, Praeger, New York, 1966

COURTHION, PIERRE, *Romanticism* (tr. S. Gilbert), Skira, Geneva, 1962

RICHARDSON, EDGAR P., *The Way of Western Art, 1776–1914*, Cooper Square Publishers, New York, 1969

MONOGRAPHS

BERGER, KLAUS, *Géricault and His Work* (tr. W. Ames), University of Kansas Press, Lawrence, 1955

BLUNT, SIR ANTHONY, *The Art of William Blake*, Columbia University Press, New York, 1959

EITNER, LORENZ, *Géricault's Raft of the Medusa*, Phaidon, London, 1972

FERRARI, ENRIQUE L., ed., *Goya: His Complete Etchings, Aquatints, and Lithographs*, Abrams, New York, 1962

FINBERG, ALEXANDER J., *The Life of J. M. W. Turner, R. A.*, 2d ed., Clarendon Press, Oxford, 1961

GAGE, JOHN, *Turner: Rain, Steam, and Speed*, Viking, New York, 1972

GUDIOL, JOSÉ, *Goya* (tr. K. Lyons), 4 vols., Ediciones Poligrafa, Barcelona, 1971

HUYGHE, RENÉ, *Delacroix* (tr. M. Griffin), Abrams, New York, 1963

LESLIE, C. R., *Memoirs of the Life of John Constable*, Phaidon, London, 1951

REYNOLDS, GRAHAM, *Constable: The Natural Painter*, Cory, Adams, & Mackay, London, 1965

——————, *Turner*, Abrams, New York, 1969

THOMAS, HUGH, *Goya: The Third of May, 1808*, Viking, New York, 1972

TRAPP, FRANK ANDERSON, *The Attainment of Delacroix*, Johns Hopkins Press, Baltimore, 1970

3. REALISM

GENERAL

HERBERT, ROBERT L., *Barbizon Revisited*, Boston Museum of Fine Arts, 1962

NOCHLIN, LINDA, *Realism*, Penguin, Harmondsworth, England, 1971

MONOGRAPHS

ADHÉMAR, JEAN, *Honoré Daumier* (English ed.), P. Tisné, New York and Basel, 1954

BOAS, GEORGE, ed., *Courbet and the Naturalistic Movement*, Johns Hopkins Press, Baltimore, 1938

BOUDAILLE, GEORGES, *Gustave Courbet: Painter in Protest* (tr. M. Bullock), New York Graphic Society, Greenwich, Conn., 1970

GOODRICH, LLOYD, *Winslow Homer*, Macmillan, New York, 1944

MACK, GERSTLE, *Gustave Courbet*, Knopf, New York, 1951

NICOLSON, BENEDICT, *Courbet: The Studio of the Painter*, Allen Lane, London, 1973

PORTER, FAIRFIELD, *Thomas Eakins*, Braziller, New York, 1959

4. IMPRESSIONISM

GENERAL

CHAMPA, KERMIT S., *Studies in Early Impressionism*, Yale University Press, New Haven, Conn., 1973

LEYMARIE, JEAN, *Impressionism* (tr. J. Emmons), 2 vols., Skira, Geneva, 1955

REWALD, JOHN, *The History of Impressionism*, 4th ed., New York Graphic Society, Greenwich, Conn., 1973

MONOGRAPHS

BROWSE, LILLIAN, *Degas Dancers*, Faber & Faber, London, 1949

CHAMPIGNEULLE, BERNARD, *Rodin: His Sculpture, Drawings and Watercolors* (tr. J. M. Brownjohn), Abrams, New York, 1967

DE LEIRIS, ALAIN, *The Drawings of Edouard Manet*, University of California Press, Berkeley, 1969

DESCHARNES, ROBERT, and CHABRUN, J.-F., *Auguste Rodin*, Viking, New York, 1967

ELSEN, ALBERT E., ed., *Auguste Rodin: Readings on His Life and Work*, Prentice-Hall, Englewood Cliffs, N.J., 1965

——————, and VARNEDOE, J. K. T., *The Drawings of Rodin*, Praeger, New York, 1973

HAMILTON, GEORGE H., *Manet and His Critics*, Yale University Press, New Haven, Conn., 1954

HANSON, LAWRENCE, *Renoir: The Man, the Painter, and His World*, Dodd, Mead, New York, 1968

MOUNT, CHARLES MERRILL, *Monet*, Simon & Schuster, New York, 1966

ORIENTI, SANDRA, et al., *The Complete Paintings of Manet*, Abrams, New York, 1967

PACH, WALTER, *Renoir*, Abrams, New York, 1950

REWALD, JOHN, *Camille Pissarro*, Abrams, New York, 1963

——————, ed., *Camille Pissarro: Letters to His Son Lucien*, 3d ed., P. P. Appel, Mamaroneck, N.Y., 1972

——————, and MATT, L. VON, *Degas, Sculpture: The Complete Works*, Abrams, New York, 1956

ROUART, DENIS, *Claude Monet: Historical and Critical Study* (tr. J. Emmons), Skira, Geneva, 1958

SANDBLAD, NILS G., *Manet: Three Studies in Artistic Conception* (tr. W. Nash), Gleerup, Lund, Sweden, 1954

SEITZ, WILLIAM C., *Claude Monet*, Abrams, New York, 1960

WEINTRAUB, STANLEY, *Whistler: A Biography*, Weybright & Talley, New York, 1974

5. POST-IMPRESSIONISM

GENERAL

CHASSÉ, CHARLES, *The Nabis and Their Period* (tr. M. Bullock), Praeger, New York, 1969

LÖVGREN, SVEN, *The Genesis of Modernism: Seurat, Gauguin, Van Gogh and French Symbolism in the 1880's*, 2d ed., Indiana University Press, Bloomington, 1971

LUCIE-SMITH, EDWARD, *Symbolist Art*, Praeger, New York, 1972

REWALD, JOHN, *Post-Impressionism from Van Gogh to Gauguin*, 2d ed., Museum of Modern Art, New York, 1962

ROOKMAAKER, H. R., *Synthetist Art Theories: Genesis and Nature of the Ideas on Art of Gauguin and His Circle*, Swets & Zeitlinger, Amsterdam, 1959

ROSKILL, MARK W., *Van Gogh, Gauguin, and the Impressionist Circle*, New York Graphic Society, Greenwich, Conn., 1970

SUTTER, JEAN, ed., *The Neo-impressionists* (tr. C. Deliss), New York Graphic Society, Greenwich, Conn., 1970

MONOGRAPHS

BADT, KURT, *The Art of Cézanne* (tr. S. Ogilvie), University of California Press, Berkeley, 1965

BERGER, KLAUS, *Odilon Redon: Fantasy and Color* (tr. M. Bullock), McGraw-Hill, New York, 1965

CHAPPUIS, ADRIEN, *The Drawings of Paul Cézanne*, 2 vols., Thames & Hudson, London, 1973

COURTHION, PIERRE, *Georges Seurat* (tr. N. Guterman), Abrams, New York, 1968

DE LA FAILLE, J.-B., *The Works of Vincent Van Gogh: His Paintings and Drawings*, 3d ed., Reynal, New York, 1970

FERMIGIER, ANDRÉ, *Toulouse-Lautrec* (tr. P. Stevenson), Praeger, New York, 1969

HODIN, JOSEF PAUL, *Edvard Munch*, Praeger, New York, 1972

JAWORSKA, WLADISLAWA, *Gauguin and the Pont-Aven School* (tr. P. Evans), New York Graphic Society, Greenwich, Conn., 1972

MACK, GERSTLE, *Toulouse-Lautrec*, 2d ed., Knopf, New York, 1953

MESSER, THOMAS W., *Edvard Munch*, Abrams, New York, 1971

PRESTON, STUART, *Edouard Vuillard*, Abrams, New York, 1972

READE, BRIAN, *Aubrey Beardsley*, Viking, New York, 1967

REWALD, JOHN, *Georges Seurat*, 2d ed., Wittenborn, Schultz, New York, 1946

——————, *Paul Cézanne: A Biography* (tr. M. H. Liebman), Schocken Books, New York, 1968

RUSSELL, JOHN, *Seurat*, Praeger, New York, 1965

——————, ed., *Vuillard*, New York Graphic Society, Greenwich, Conn., 1971

SCHAPIRO, MEYER, *Paul Cézanne*, 3d ed., Abrams, New York, 1965

——————, *Vincent van Gogh*, Abrams, New York, 1950

SUTTON, DENYS, *The Complete Paintings of Toulouse-Lautrec* (tr. G. M. Sugani), Weidenfeld & Nicolson, London, 1973

TRALBANT, MARK E., *Vincent van Gogh*, Viking, New York, 1969

VALLIER, DORA, *Henri Rousseau*, Abrams, New York, 1964

6. THE FAUVES AND EXPRESSIONISM

GENERAL

CRESPELLE, JEAN PAUL, *The Fauves* (tr. A. Brookner), New York Graphic Society, Greenwich, Conn., 1962

DUBE, WOLF D., *Expressionism* (tr. M. Whittall), Praeger, New York, 1973

DUTHUIT, GEORGES, *The Fauvist Painters*, Wittenborn, Schultz, New York, 1950

KUHN, CHARLES L., *German Expressionism and Abstract Art: The Harvard Collections*, Harvard University Press, Cambridge, Mass., 1957

LEYMARIE, JEAN, *Fauvism: Biographical and Critical Study* (tr. J. Emmons), Skira, New York, 1959

MULLER, JOSEPH-ÉMILE, *Fauvism* (tr. S. E. Jones), Praeger, New York, 1967

MYERS, BERNARD S., *The German Expressionists: A Generation in Revolt*, Praeger, New York, 1957

SELZ, PETER, *German Expressionist Painting*, University of California Press, Berkeley, 1957

ZIGROSSER, CARL, *The Expressionists: A Survey of Their Graphic Art*, Braziller, New York, 1957

MONOGRAPHS

BARR, ALFRED H., JR., *Matisse, His Art and His Public*, Arno Press, New York, 1951

CARLSON, VICTOR I., ed., *Matisse as a Draughtsman*, New York Graphic Society, Greenwich, Conn., 1971

COURTHION, PIERRE, *Georges Rouault*, Abrams, New York, 1962

ELSEN, ALBERT S., *The Sculpture of Henri Matisse*, Abrams, New York, 1972

GEELHAAR, CHRISTIAN, *Paul Klee and the Bauhaus*, New York Graphic Society, Greenwich, Conn., 1973

GROHMANN, WILL, *Wassily Kandinsky: Life and Work* (tr. N. Guterman), Abrams, New York, 1958

HODIN, JOSEF PAUL, *Oskar Kokoschka: The Artist and His Time*, New York Graphic Society, Greenwich, Conn., 1966

JACOBUS, JOHN, *Henri Matisse*, Abrams, New York, 1973

LIEBERMAN, WILLIAM S., *Matisse: Fifty Years of His Graphic Art*, Braziller, New York, 1954

7. THE SEARCH FOR FORM—CUBISM AND ABSTRACT ART

GENERAL

APOLLINAIRE, GUILLAUME, *The Cubist Painters* (tr. L. Abel), Wittenborn, Schultz, New York, 1949

BAROOSHIAN, VAHAN D., *Russian Cubo-Futurism 1910–1931: A Study in Avant-Gardism*, Mouton, The Hague, 1974

CARRIERI, ROBERTO, *Futurism* (tr. L. van R. White), Edizione del Milione, Milan, 1963

CASSOU, JEAN, et al., *Gateway to the Twentieth Century*, McGraw-Hill, New York, 1962

COOPER, DOUGLASS, *The Cubist Epoch*, Phaidon, New York, 1971

DOESBURG, THEO VAN, *Principles of Neo-Plastic Art*, New York Graphic Society, Greenwich, Conn., 1968

FRY, EDWARD F., *Cubism*, Thames & Hudson, London, 1966

GOLDING, JOHN, *Cubism: A History and an Analysis, 1907–1914*, 2d ed., Harper & Row, New York, 1968

GRAY, CAMILLA, *The Great Experiment: Russian Art 1863–1922*, Abrams, New York, 1962

HABASQUE, GUY, *Cubism: Biographical and Critical Study* (tr. S. Gilbert), Skira, New York, 1959

JAFFÉ, HANS L. C., *De Stijl, 1917–1931: The Dutch Contribution to Modern Art*, Meulenhoff, Amsterdam, 1956

——————, comp., *De Stijl*, Abrams, New York, 1971

KAHNWEILER, DANIEL-HENRY, *The Rise of Cubism*, Wittenborn, Schultz, New York, 1949

MARTIN, J. L., et al., eds., *Circle*, Praeger, New York, 1971

MARTIN, MARIANNE W., *Futurist Art and Theory 1908–1915*, Clarendon Press, Oxford, 1968

RICKEY, GEORGE, *Constructivism: Origins and Evolution*, Braziller, New York, 1967

ROSENBLUM, ROBERT, *Cubism and Twentieth-Century Art*, Abrams, New York, 1961

SEUPHOR, MICHEL, *Dictionary of Abstract Painting* (tr. L. Izod et al.), Tudor, New York, 1957

VALLIER, DORA, *Abstract Art* (tr. J. Griffin), Orion Press, New York, 1970

MONOGRAPHS

BLUNT, SIR ANTHONY, and POOL, P., *Picasso, The Formative Years: A Study of His Sources*, New York Graphic Society, Greenwich, Conn., 1958

BOECK, WILHELM, and SABARTÉS, J., *Picasso*, Abrams, New York, 1955

BORK, BERT VAN, *Jacques Lipchitz: The Artist at Work*, Crown, New York, 1966

DAIX, PIERRE, and BOUDAILLE, G., *Picasso: The Blue and Rose Periods* (tr. P. Pool), New York Graphic Society, Greenwich, Conn., 1967

DELEVOY, ROBERT L., *Léger: Biographical and Critical Study*, Skira, Lausanne, 1962

GEIST, SIDNEY, *Brancusi*, Grossman, New York, 1968

GRAY, CAMILLA, *Kasimir Malevich, 1878-1935*, Whitechapel Art Gallery, London, 1959

HAMMACHER, ABRAHAM M., *Jacques Lipchitz: His Sculpture*, Abrams, New York, 1960

HOFMANN, WERNER, *Georges Braque: His Graphic Work*, Abrams, New York, 1961

KUH, KATHERINE, *Léger*, Art Institute of Chicago, Urbana, Ill., 1953

MULLINS, EDWIN B., *The Art of Georges Braque*, Abrams, New York, 1968

PENROSE, SIR ROLAND, *Picasso: His Life and Work*, Harper & Row, New York, 1973

——————, and GOLDING, J., eds., *Picasso: In Retrospect*, Praeger, New York, 1973

SELZ, JEAN, *Vlaminck* (tr. G. Snell), Crown, New York, 1963

SEUPHOR, MICHEL, *Piet Mondrian: Life and Work*, Abrams, New York, 1957

SPIES, WERNER, *Sculpture by Picasso* (tr. J. M. Brownjohn), Abrams, New York, 1971

WALDEMAR-GEORGE, pseud., *Aristide Maillol* (tr. D. Imber), New York Graphic Society, Greenwich, Conn., 1965

8. FANTASTIC ART, DADA, SURREALISM

GENERAL

BRETON, ANDRÉ, *Surrealism and Painting* (tr. S. W. Taylor), Harper & Row, New York, 1972

FOWLIE, WALLACE, *Age of Surrealism*, Indiana University Press, Bloomington, 1960

GAUNT, WILLIAM, *The Surrealists*, Putnam, New York, 1972

JEAN, MARCEL, *The History of Surrealist Painting* (tr. S. W. Taylor), Grove Press, New York, 1960

MOTHERWELL, ROBERT, ed., *The Dada Painters and Poets: An Anthology*, Wittenborn, Schultz, New York, 1951

RICHTER, HANS, *Dada: Art and Anti-Art*, McGraw-Hill, New York, 1965

RUBIN, WILLIAM S., *Dada and Surrealist Art*, Abrams, New York, 1968

MONOGRAPHS

BROWDER, CLIFFORD H., *André Breton: Arbiter of Surrealism*, Droz, Geneva, 1967

DESCHARNES, ROBERT, *The World of Salvador Dali* (tr. A. Field), Harper & Row, New York, 1962

D'HARNONCOURT, ANNE, and McSHINE, K., *Marcel Duchamp*, New York Graphic Society, Greenwich, Conn., 1973

DUPIN, JACQUES, *Miró* (tr. N. Guterman), Abrams, New York, 1962

GABLILIA, SUZIE, *Magritte*, New York Graphic Society, Greenwich, Conn., 1970

GROHMANN, WILL, *Paul Klee*, Abrams, New York, 1954

HAFTMANN, WERNER, *The Mind and Work of Paul Klee*, Praeger, New York, 1954

MEYER, FRANZ, *Marc Chagall*, Abrams, New York, 1963

READ, SIR HERBERT, *The Art of Jean Arp*, Abrams, New York, 1968

RUSSELL, JOHN, *Max Ernst: Life and Work*, Abrams, New York, 1967

SCHMALENBACH, WERNER, *Kurt Schwitters*, Abrams, New York, 1967

SOBY, JAMES THRALL, *Giorgio de Chirico*, Museum of Modern Art, New York, 1955

TAILLANDIER, YVON, *Indelible Miró*, Tudor, New York, 1972

9. MODERN ARCHITECTURE

GENERAL

BANHAM, REYNER, *The New Brutalism*, Reinhold, New York, 1966

——————, *Theory and Design in the First Machine Age*, Praeger, New York, 1960

BLAKE, PETER, *The Master Builders*, Knopf, New York, 1960

COLLINS, PETER, *Changing Ideals in Modern Architecture 1750-1950*, Faber & Faber, London, 1965

CONRADS, ULRICH, and SPERLICH, H. G., *The Architecture of Fantasy* (tr. C. C. and G. Collins), Praeger, New York, 1962

EATON, LEONARD K., *American Architecture Comes of Age*, MIT Press, Cambridge, Mass., 1972

FLETCHER, BANISTER F., *A History of Architecture on the Comparative Method*, 17th ed., Scribners, New York, 1961

GIEDION, SIGFRIED, *Space, Time and Architecture*, 5th ed., Harvard University Press, Cambridge, Mass., 1967

HAMLIN, TALBOT F., *Forms and Functions of Twentieth Century Architecture*, 4 vols., Columbia University Press, New York, 1952

HATJE, GERD, ed., *Encyclopedia of Modern Architecture*, Praeger, New York, 1964

HITCHCOCK, HENRY-RUSSELL, *Architecture: Nineteenth and Twentieth Centuries*, 3d ed., Penguin, Baltimore, 1971

——————, and JOHNSON, P. C., *The International Style*, Norton, New York, 1966

NEUTRA, RICHARD, *Survival Through Design*, Oxford University Press, New York, 1954

PEHNTE, WOLFGANG, *Expressionist Architecture*, Praeger, New York, 1973

PETER, JOHN, *Masters of Modern Architecture*, Braziller, New York, 1968

PEVSNER, NIKOLAUS, *Pioneers of Modern Design*, Penguin, Baltimore, 1965

SCULLY, VINCENT, *The Shingle Style*, Yale University Press, New Haven, Conn., 1955

SHARP, DENNIS, *Modern Architecture and Expressionism*, Longmans, London, 1966

SMITH, GEORGE E. K., *The New Architecture of Europe*, World Publishers, Cleveland, 1961

ZEVI, BRUNO, *Towards an Organic Architecture*, Faber & Faber, London, 1950

MONOGRAPHS

BAYER, HERBERT, et al., *Bauhaus, 1919-1928*, 3d ed., Branford, Boston, 1959

BLASER, WERNER, *Mies van der Rohe: The Art of Structure* (tr. D. Q. Stephenson), Praeger, New York, 1965

BOESINGER, W., and GIRSBERGER, H., *Le Corbusier, 1910-65*, Thames & Hudson, London, 1967

BROOKS, HAROLD A., *The Prairie School: Frank Lloyd Wright and His Midwest Contemporaries*, University of Toronto Press, 1972

CARTER, PETER, *Mies van der Rohe at Work*, Praeger, New York, 1974

CHOAY, FRANÇOISE, *Le Corbusier*, Braziller, New York, 1960

COLLINS, GEORGE R., *Antoni Gaudi*, Braziller, New York, 1960

CONNELLY, WILLARD, *Louis Sullivan As He Lived*, Horizon, New York, 1960

DREXLER, ARTHUR L., *Ludwig Mies van der Rohe*, Braziller, New York, 1960

FITCH, JAMES MARSDEN, *Walter Gropius*, Braziller, New York, 1960

FRANCISCONO, MARCEL, *Walter Gropius and the Creation of the Bauhaus in Weimar*, University of Illinois Press, Urbana, 1971

HITCHCOCK, HENRY-RUSSELL, *The Architecture of H. H. Richardson and His Times*, 2d ed., MIT Press, Cambridge, Mass., 1966

——————, *In the Nature of Materials: The Buildings of Frank Lloyd Wright, 1887-1941*, 2d ed., Da Capo Press, New York, 1973

JENCKS, CHARLES, *Le Corbusier and the Tragic View of Architecture*, Harvard University Press, Cambridge, Mass., 1973

JORDAN, ROBERT F., *Le Corbusier*, L. Hill, New York, 1972

MORRISON, HUGH, *Louis Sullivan*, 2d ed., Peter Smith, New York, 1958

SAARINEN, ALINE B., ed., *Eero Saarinen on His Work*, 2d ed., Yale University Press, New Haven, Conn., 1968

SWEENEY, JAMES J., and SERT, J. L., *Antoni Gaudi*, 2d ed., Praeger, New York, 1970

TWOMBLY, ROBERT C., *Frank Lloyd Wright: An Interpretive Biography*, Harper & Row, New York, 1973

10. AMERICAN ART OF THE TWENTIETH CENTURY AND RECENT MOVEMENTS ELSEWHERE

GENERAL

BATTCOCK, GREGORY, ed., *Minimal Art: A Critical Anthology*, Dutton, New York, 1968

——————, ed., *The New Art*, 2d ed., Dutton, New York, 1973

BRION, MARCEL, et al., *Art Since 1945*, Abrams, New York, 1958

FINCH, CHRISTOPHER, *Pop Art: The Object and the Image*, Dutton, New York, 1968

GORDON, STEPHEN P., *The Contemporary Face: New Techniques and Media*, Van Nostrand Reinhold, New York, 1972

HUNTER, SAM, et al., *New Art Around the World (Painting and Sculpture)*, Abrams, New York, 1966

KAPROW, ALLAN, *Assemblage, Environments & Happenings*, Abrams, New York, 1966

KULTERMANN, UDO, *New Realism*, New York Graphic Society, Greenwich, Conn., 1972

LIPPARD, LUCY R., *Pop Art*, Praeger, New York, 1966

LUCIE-SMITH, EDWARD, *Late Modern: The Visual Arts Since 1945*, Praeger, New York, 1969

PELLEGRINI, ALDO, *New Tendencies in Art* (tr. R. Carson), Crown, New York, 1966

PONENTE, NELLO, *Modern Painting: Contemporary Trends*, Skira, New York, 1960

SANDLER, IRVING, *The Triumph of American Painting: A History of Abstract Expressionism*, Praeger, New York, 1970

WOODS, GERALD, et al., eds., *Art Without Boundaries 1950-70*, Thames & Hudson, London, 1972

MONOGRAPHS

ALLOWAY, LAWRENCE, *Jean Dubuffet: A Retrospective*, Solomon R. Guggenheim Museum, New York, 1973

FORGE, ANDREW, *Rauschenberg*, Abrams, New York, 1969

FRIED, MICHAEL, *Three American Painters: Kenneth Noland, Jules Olitski, Frank Stella*, Fogg Art Museum, Cambridge, Mass., 1965

FRIEDMAN, BERNARD H., *Jackson Pollock: Energy Made Visible*, McGraw-Hill, New York, 1972

FRY, EDWARD F., *David Smith*, Solomon R. Guggenheim Museum, New York, 1969

GLIMCHER, ARNOLD B., *Louise Nevelson*, Praeger, New York, 1972

HESS, THOMAS B., *Barnett Newman*, New York Graphic Society, Greenwich, Conn., 1971

HUNTER, SAM, ed., *Hans Hofmann*, 2d ed., Abrams, New York, 1964

JORAY, MARCEL, ed., *Vasarely* (tr. H. Chevalier), Éditions du Griffon, Neuchâtel, 1965

KOZLOFF, MAX, *Jasper Johns*, Abrams, New York, 1972

LEVY, JULIAN, *Arshile Gorky*, Abrams, New York, 1966

READ, SIR HERBERT, *Henry Moore: A Study of His Life and Work*, Praeger, New York, 1966

REICH, SHELDON, *John Marin: A Stylistic Analysis and Catalogue Raisonné*, 2 vols., University of Arizona Press, Tucson, 1970

ROSENBERG, HAROLD, *De Kooning*, Abrams, New York, 1974

SELDIS, HENRY J., *Henry Moore in America*, Praeger, New York, 1973

SELZ, PETER, *Rothko*, Museum of Modern Art, New York, 1961

Index

Page numbers are in roman type. Figure numbers of black-and-white illustrations are in *italic* type.
Colorplates are specifically so designated. Names of artists and architects are in CAPITALS. Titles of works are in *italics*.

Photographic Credits

The author and publisher wish to thank the libraries, museums, and private collectors for permitting the reproduction of works of art in their collections and for supplying the necessary photographs. Photographs from other sources are gratefully acknowledged below.

A.C.L., Brussels, 96, 97, 98, 99, 104, 107, 284, 367, 445; Adant, Hélène, Paris, 450; Agraci, Paris, 424, 434; Alinari, Florence, 1, 2, 3, 4, 5, 6, 7, 8, 9, 10, 14, 16, 17, 19, 20, 21, 22, 23, 27, 28, 30, 31, 36, 37, 39, 40, 41, 42, 44, 45, 46, 47, 48, 49, 51, 52, 53, 55, 58, 59, 63, 65, 67, 68, 73, 75, 76, 78, 79, 80, 81, 82, 84, 106, 110, 112, 125, 128, 133, 134, 137, 138, 143, 146, 147, 148, 149, 150, 151, 152, 153, 154, 155, 156, 158, 159, 160, 163, 164, 165, 166, 170, 171, 172, 176, 177, 178, 181, 182, 190, 191, 193, 194, 207, 217, 226, 227, 228, 230, 231, 232, 233, 234, 235, 237, 239, 241, 244, 246, 249, 252, 255, 270, 278, 288, 290, 317, 318, 319, 320, 321, 374, 429, colorplates 2, 3, 4, 7, 23, 37; Andrews, Wayne, Grosse Pointe, Mich., 323, 358; Annan, T. R., Glasgow, 439; Aufsberg, Lala, Sonthofen im Allgau, Switz., 343; Austin, James, Cambridge, Eng., 326; Bibliothèque Nationale, Paris, 91, 118, 124, colorplate 15; Bildarchiv Foto Marburg, Marburg/Lahn, Ger., 248, 277, 337; Bohm, Osvaldo, Venice, 162, 322; Bruckmann, F., Munich, 180; Bulloz, Paris, 212, 213, 214, 215, 216, 266, 331, 389, 399; Burckhardt, Rudolph, New York, 571; Caisse Nationale des Monuments Historiques, Paris, 85, 86, 87, 267, 268, 271, 276, 327, 382, 385, 387, 390, 408, 409, 414; Calzolari, Mantua, 35; Cameraphoto,

Venice, colorplate 28; Camponogara, J., Lyons, 384; Canadian Consulate General, New York, 547; Canali, Ludovico, Rome, 43, colorplates 6, 9, 10, 11, 12, 24, 25, 27, 30; Leo Castelli Gallery, New York, 562; Chicago Historical Society, 508; Clements, Geoffrey, New York, colorplates 82, 85; Copyright Country Life, London, 265, 350, 351; De Menil, Adelaide, New York, 507; Department of the Environment, London, 347; Deutsche Fotothek, Dresden, 407; Deutscher Kunstverlag, Munich, 364; Dingjan, A., The Hague, 293, 301, 304, 305, 313; Edelmann, U., Frankfort, 94, 292; André Emmerich Gallery, New York, 570; Esser, Lotte, Darmstadt, colorplate 33; Fondazione Giorgio Cini, Venice, 175; Foto Rosso, Turin, 256; Foto Schönwetter, Glarus, 462; Fototeca Unione, Rome, 184; French Government Tourist Office, New York, 363, 397; French Tourist Service, Paris, 273; Gabinetto Fotografico, Galleria degli Uffizi, Florence, 50, 54, 57, 60, 66, 74, 77, 126; Gabinetto Fotografico Nazionale, Rome, 186, 188, 236, 247, 251, 262; Geist, Sidney, New York, 476; Gendreau, Philip, New York, 529; Gerlach, Vienna, 338; Giraudon, Paris, 90, 119, 121, 127, 129, 130, 208, 209, 258, 333, 383, 423, colorplates 21, 58; Gundermann, Würzburg, colorplate 48; Hammarskiold/Tio, Stockholm, 487; Hedrich-Blessing, Chicago, 517, 519, 532; Henrot, Paris, 272; Hervé, Lucien, Paris, 525, 526, 536; Hinz, Hans, Basel, colorplate 67; Istituto Centrale del Restauro, Rome, 13, 15; Johnson Wax Co., Racine, Wisc., 520, 521; Josse, H., Paris, colorplate 57; Juley, Peter A., New York, 551; Kersting, A. F., London, 279, 282, 324, 339, 344, 348, 349, 352, 365; Klein, Walter, Düsseldorf, 457; Kleinhempel, Hamburg, 453; Lichtbildwerkstaette Alpenland, Vienna, 120; McKenna, Rollie, Stonington, Vt., 25, 33, 174; Marlborough Gallery,

Inc., New York, 558, 574; MAS, Barcelona, 111, 161, 223, 314, 315, 316, 376, 377, 380, 511, 512, colorplates 18, 20, 35, 44, 51; Meyer, Erwin, Vienna, colorplate 43; Mills, Charles, Philadelphia, 421; Muller, Erich, Kassel, 340; Museum of Modern Art, New York, 479, 514, 522, 524, 527; National Monuments Record, London, 283, 396; Philadelphia Museum of Art, 412; Rémy, Dijon, colorplate 16; Renger-Patzsch, A., Wamel-Dorf Uber Soest, Ger., 342; Roubier, Jean, Paris, 274; Royal Pavilion, Brighton, 395; Sansoni, R., Rome, 132; Scala Fine Art Publishers, New York, colorplates 13, 36; Schaeffer, J. H., Baltimore, 360; Schmidt-Glassner, Helga, Stuttgart, 336, 341; Schneider-Lengyel, Paris, 432; Service de Documentation Photographique de la Réunion des Musées Nationaux, Paris, 70, 100, 259, 263, 289, 306, 308, 329, 366, 368, 369, 370, 371, 381, 386, 388, 416, 422, 449, 452, 582, colorplates 17, 41, 47, 55; Shulman, Julius, Los Angeles, 528; Shunk-Kender, New York, 567; Smith, G. E. Kidder, New York, 253, 537; Smith, Malcolm, New York, 538; Stedelijk Museum, Amsterdam, 440; Steinkopf, Walter, Berlin, 205, 218, colorplate 46; Stoedtner, Dr. Franz, Düsseldorf, 375; Stoller, Ezra, New York, 533, 539, 540, 541, 542; Tass, from Sovfoto, New York, 372; Thomas Photos, Oxford, Eng., 346; United Nations, New York, 531; University of Virginia Department of Graphics, Charlottesville, 359; Victoria and Albert Museum, London, 410; von Matt, Leonard, Buochs, Switz., 238, 242, 243; Webb, John, London, 280, colorplates 40, 54; John Weber Gallery, New York, 580; Weill, E., Paris, colorplate 52; Whitaker, W. C., Richmond, Va., 373; Wildenstein et Cie., Paris, 413; Wyatt, A. J., Philadelphia, 473, 474, 500, 579, colorplate 73; Yale University Art Gallery, New Haven, 488.

527